A
Body of
Practical Divinity

JOHN GILL, D.D.
1697-1771

A Body of Practical Divinity;

OR
A SYSTEM OF PRACTICAL TRUTHS,

DEDUCED FROM THE
𝔖ACRED 𝔖CRIPTURES.

WHICH COMPLETES THE SCHEME OF
DOCTRINAL AND PRACTICAL DIVINITY.

BY JOHN GILL, D.D.

A NEW EDITION

he Baptist Standard Bearer, Inc.
NUMBER ONE IRON OAKS DRIVE • PARIS, ARKANSAS 72855

Thou hast given a *standard* to them that fear thee;
that it may be displayed because of the truth.
-- Psalm 60:4

ADVERTISEMENT.

SHOULD the Public require any pledge in order to create a confidence in, or *preference* for, *this* Edition of Dr. GILL'S BODY OF DIVINITY; they are respectfully assured that it is a *verbatim* reprint of the *original, in 3 vols. quarto,* (which was published under the inspection of the Author's own eye,) without any abridgment, or the *least* alteration, excepting in a few instances, where *typographical* errors may have been discovered. The work has undergone a very careful revisal; and is therefore presented as the most correct Edition which has ever yet appeared.

The Publishers also flatter themselves, that the *excellent* Portrait of the venerable Doctor, together with the interesting Memoir of his Life and Writings, which accompany the book, will be found greatly to enhance its value, and raise it far above the level of *all* preceding editions.

London, June 1839.

*Reprinted
by*

THE BAPTIST STANDARD BEARER, INC.
No. 1 Iron Oaks Drive
Paris, Arkansas 72855
(501) 963-3831

THE WALDENSIAN EMBLEM
lux lucet in tenebris
"The Light Shineth in the Darkness"

ISBN #1-57978-888-2

CONTENTS.

A BODY OF PRACTICAL DIVINITY.

BOOK I.
ON THE WORSHIP OF GOD.

CHAP.	PAGE.
1 Of the Object of Worship	697
2 Of Internal Worship, or Godliness	700
3 Of the Knowledge of God	705
4 Of Repentance towards God	713
5 Of the Fear of God	722
6 Of Faith in God	730
7 Of Trust and Confidence in God	746
8 Of the Grace of Hope	753
9 Of the Grace of Love	762
10 Of Spiritual Joy	774
11 Of Peace and Tranquillity of Mind	782
12 Of Contentment of Mind	786
13 Of Thankfulness to God	794
14 Of Humility	801
15 Of Self-denial	805
16 Of Resignation to the Will of God	810
17 Of Patience	815
18 Of Christian Fortitude	819
19 Of Zeal	824
20 Of Wisdom and Prudence	829
21 Of Godly Sincerity	833
22 Of Spiritual Mindedness	838
23 Of a good Conscience	842
24 Of Communion with God	846

BOOK II.
OF EXTERNAL WORSHIP, AS PUBLIC.

1 Of a Gospel Church, the Seat of Public Worship	852
2 Of the Duties of Church-members to each other	859
3 Of Church-officers, particularly Pastors	862
4 Of the Duties of Members to their Pastors	876

CHAP.	PAGE.
5 Of the Office of Deacons	881
6 Of Church Discipline	886

BOOK III.
OF THE PUBLIC ORDINANCES OF DIVINE WORSHIP.

1 Of Baptism	896
2 Of the Lord's Supper	915
3 Of the Public Ministry of the Word	924
4 Of Public Hearing of the Word	932
5 Of Public Prayer	939
6 Of the Lord's Prayer	948
7 Of Singing Psalms	957
8 Of the Place and Time of Public Worship	964

BOOK IV.
OF PRIVATE WORSHIP, OR OF VARIOUS DUTIES, DOMESTIC, CIVIL, AND MORAL.

1 Of the Duties of Husband and Wife	973
2 Of the Duties of Parents and Children	977
3 Of the Duties of Masters and Servants	980
4 Of the Duties of Magistrates and Subjects	983
5 Of Good Works in General	988
6 A Compendium of the Ten Commands	991

A DISSERTATION CONCERNING THE BAPTISM OF JEWISH PROSELYTES.

1 Of the Various Sorts of Proselytes	995
2 The Occasion of the Dissertation	999
3 The Proof of the Baptism of Jewish Proselytes inquired into	1001
4 The Proof of this custom only from the Talmuds	1009
5 Christian Baptism not founded on Proselyte Baptism	1014

Appendix 1 ....Memoir of John Gill
Appendix 2 ...Publisher's Foreward to our 1984 Edition

A BODY OF
PRACTICAL DIVINITY.

BOOK I.

OF THE WORSHIP OF GOD, OR PRACTICAL RELIGION.

CHAP. I.

OF THE OBJECT OF WORSHIP.

I HAVE in the former part of this work, proved there is a God, from the light of nature and reason, from the works of creation, &c. and now my business is to shew that this God is to be worshipped. I have treated of the nature, perfections, and attributes of God, which are the foundation of the worship of him; and now I shall treat of worship itself. I have considered the various works of God, the works of creation, providence, and grace; and these may be used as so many arguments to engage us to divine worship, or as so many reasons why we should glorify God with our bodies and spirits, which are his; or, in other words, worship him both internally and externally; and I shall begin with the object of worship, for which we have a plain direction, *Thou shalt worship the Lord thy God, and him only shalt thou serve*, Matt. iv. 10. Two things are to be observed and considered,——1. That the Lord God is the object of worship.—— 2. That he alone is the object of worship, to the exclusion of all others.

I. The object of worship is the Lord God, God essentially and personally considered.

First, God essentially considered, or as considered in his nature and essence, which is the foundation of worship. Many are the directions and instructions given to *worship God*, without specifying any of the persons in the Deity particularly to be worshipped; see Rev. xiv. 7. and xix. 10. and xxii. 9.

The *Lord* is to be worshipped; the Lord, who is the one Jehovah, and whose name alone is Jehovah, Deut. vi. 4. Psalm lxxxiii. 18. The word *Lord* in the New Testament answers to *Jehovah* in the Old, a name expressive of the existence or being of God, and of him as the fountain of being, and the author of being to all others; who is the everlasting *I am, which is, and which was, and which is to come;* these words of John are a proper deciphering of the word *Jehovah*, or the *I am that I am* in Exod. iii. 14. Now he whose essence is simple, uncompounded, immutable, infinite, eternal, &c. is to be worshipped, even the Lord *thy God,* thy Creator, thy Benefactor, thy Supporter, and Preserver. Thus the apostle describes the proper object of worship unknown to the Athenians, as he who made the world, and all things in it; and gives life, and breath, and all things to his creatures; and in whom they live, move, and have their being, Acts xvii. 23, 25, 28. Thus Jacob invoked God, which to do is a part of religious worship, who had *fed* him *all his life long to* that *day,* Gen. xlviii. 15. David says, his prayer, which is a part of worship, should be to the *God of* his *life,* who had given him life and upheld him in it, Psalm xlii. 8. he who is the *true God,* the *living God,* and the *everlasting King,* is the object of worship; the true God, in distinction from nominal gods, from such who are falsely so called; the living God, in distinction from idols of gold and silver, the work of men's hands, lifeless statues, in whom there is no breath; but the true God, and who is to be worshipped, has life in and of himself, originally and underivatively, and is the fountain and giver of life to others, and from everlasting to everlasting he is God. He is *by nature* God; there are some who are not so, and therefore not to be served and worshipped, Gal. iv. 8. but God is a Spirit, is of a spiritual nature, and to be worshipped in spirit and in truth; his nature is most perfect, has all perfections in it, though there is no finding him out unto perfection; his nature is infinite and incomprehensible, beyond all conception and thought, beyond all words and expressions, exalted above all blessing and praise. The name of God, the very first name by which he is called in scripture, *Elohim*, Gen. i. 1. implies worship, and that he is to be worshipped who created the heavens and the earth; for it comes from a word[1] which signifies to worship. And to this the apostle seems to allude, when he says that antichrist exalts himself *above that is called God*, or *that is worshipped*, intimating that the name of God signifies σιϐασμα, the object of worship, 2 Thess. ii. 4.

Secondly, God personally considered, or God considered in the three Persons, is the object of worship. *The Father, the Word, and the Holy Ghost, and these three are one*, are one God, and so equally the object of divine worship.

1st, The Father, of whom Christ expressly says, that men shall *worship the Father*, John iv. 21, 23. and of the propriety of this there can be no doubt, since his Deity is not denied by any, and was it, they would easily be confronted; he is expressly called *God the Father*, Phil. ii. 11. and sometimes *God even the Father*, 1 Cor. xv. 24. 2 Cor. i. 3. all the perfections of Deity are attributed to him, as immutability, eternity, &c. and the works of creation, providence, and grace; and he has undoubtedly a proper claim of worship from his creatures, and accordingly worship is given to him, and acts of it are exercised on him. Baptism, which is a solemn act of religious worship under the New Testament dispensation, is administered in his name; and his name stands first in the form of it, *baptizing in the name of the Father*, &c. which signifies not only its being done by his authority and command, but the persons, by submission to it, devote themselves to him, profess to be his, and lay themselves hereby under an obligation to serve him; and because to do this in the name of a creature would be idolatry and irreligion, the apostle Paul was thankful that he had baptized no more of the Corinthians than he had, when he found they were for setting him up as the head of a party among them, lest they should think they were baptized in his name. Prayer is another part of divine and religious worship, which is made to the Father, and indeed is generally made to him; the access and address are most frequently to him, not but that they may be equally made to the other two persons, as will be presently seen; but the reason why they are usually made to him is because he bears no office, whereas the others do, and an office which is concerned in the business of prayer. Christ is the mediator through whom the access is, and in whose name the petition is put up; and the Spirit is the spirit of supplication, by whose aid and assistance prayer is made; the whole of this may be observed in one passage; for *through him*, through Christ the mediator, *we both*, Jews and Gentiles, *have an access at the throne of grace by one Spirit*, who helps and assists us in our supplications *unto the Father*, the Father of Christ and of us, Eph. ii. 18. see an instance of a large prayer of the apostles to the Father of our Lord Jesus Christ in Eph. iii. 14—21. and it is easy to observe, that at the beginning of many of the epistles, such a prayer or wish is made, as *Grace be to you, and peace from God our Father*, as distinguished from the Lord Jesus Christ; which is a petition for grace, an increase of grace, and all necessary supplies of it, and for all spiritual prosperity and happiness. Thanksgiving, another act of religious worship, which is sometimes included in prayer, and sometimes performed as a distinct part of worship, is made to the Father. *Giving thanks always for all things* for all temporal and spiritual blessings, *unto God and the Father*, the Father of Christ and of us in him, *in the name of our Lord Jesus Christ*, Eph. v. 20. Acts of faith, hope, and love, which are acts of worship, are exercised on him; *ye believe in God*, that is, in God the Father, John xiv. 1. who raised Christ from the dead; that *the faith and hope* of saints *might be*

---

[1] See the Body of Doctrinal Divinity, book i. chap. 3. page 26.

in God the Father, who raised him from thence, 1 Pet. i. 21. and where those graces are, love is, and is exercised on the same object; and as the Father was the object of Christ's love as man and mediator, so he is the object of the love of those that believe in him, John xiv. 31.

2dly, The Word, or Son of God, is also the object of worship; *he is thy Lord, and worship thou him*, Psalm xlv. 11. yea, he is to be worshipped with the same sort of worship, and to be honoured with the same degree of honour the Father is, John v. 23. for he is the Lord, the Jehovah, thy God, as Thomas said, *My Lord, and my God;* the mighty God, the great God, God over all, the true God and eternal life; who has the same perfections his Father has; and the same works his Father does are done by him, Col. ii. 9. John v. 19. and therefore to be worshipped with the same worship, and so he is. Baptism is administered in his name, equally as in the Father's, *baptizing them in the name of the Father, and of the Son*, &c. and sometimes his name only is mentioned, Acts x. 48. and xix. 5. Prayer, which is an act of worship, is made to him; it is said, *prayer shall be made for him continually;* it may as well be rendered, as some think, *prayer shall be made to him continually*, Psalm lxxii. 15. Invocation of his name, which is a part of religious worship, is spoken of him; his disciples and followers are sometimes described by those that *called upon* his *name*, Acts ix. 14. 1 Cor. i. 2. and it may be observed, that in the beginning of many epistles before referred to, the same prayer or wish for grace and peace to the saints, is made to Christ as to God the Father. Stephen, the protomartyr, when expiring, called upon God, saying, *Lord Jesus, receive my spirit*, Acts vii. 59. to which may be added the doxologies or ascriptions of Glory, which are high acts of worship, are sometimes made to Christ separately, 2 Pet. iii. 18. Jude ver. 25. Rev. i. 5, 6. Also the acts of faith, hope, and love, are exercised on him as on God the Father; *Ye believe in God* the Father, says Christ, *believe also in me*, John xiv. 1. Trust and confidence are not to be put in a creature, *for cursed be the man that trusteth in man*, Jer. xvii. 5. Christ is the object of the hope and love of his people, and as such is often represented, 1 Tim. i. 1. 1 Pet. i. 8. in whom they hope for happiness, and who have an affectionate devotion for him. And it is easy to give instances of adoration which have been made unto him; thus he was worshipped by Jacob, when he invoked him to bless the sons of Joseph, saying, *The angel which redeemed me from all evil, bless the lads*, Gen. xlviii. 16. By the angel cannot be meant God the Father, for he is never called an angel; nor any created angel, whom Jacob would never have invoked; but the uncreated angel, Christ, the Angel of the covenant, his redeemer from all evil. He was also worshipped by Joshua, who appeared to him, and made himself known to him as *the captain of the host of the Lord*, who is *the leader and commander of the people, the captain of our salvation;* upon which notice, *Joshua fell on his face to the earth, and did worship*, for which he was not reproved, nay, encouraged, yea was further ordered to *loose* his *shoe from off* his *foot*, for it is said *the place whereon thou standest is holy, and Joshua did so;* which was never ordered to be done, but where God himself was, whose presence gave a relative holiness to the place where he appeared, Josh. v. 13—15. Christ was also worshipped by the wise men who came from the east to seek him and see him; and so by others in the days of his flesh, and by his disciples when he parted from them and went up into heaven; yea he has been worshipped not only by men, but by angels, and that by a divine order, *Let all the angels of God worship him*, Heb. i. 6. the first begotten; the same with the only begotten Son of God, who is God; or otherwise it would be a piece of idolatry to worship him; and we have an instance of many angels with others paying their adoration to him, Rev. v. 12, 13.

3dly, The holy Spirit is also the object of worship, equally with the Father and the Son. He is with them the one God. He is possessed of all divine perfections, such as eternity, omniscience, omnipresence, &c. he was concerned in creation, and is in the government of the world, and in the operations of grace, Psalm xxxiii. 6. Isa. xl. 13, 14. 1 Cor. xii. 4—11. and so worthy of worship, and it is given unto him. Baptism is administered in his name, equally as in the name of the Father and of the Son, Matt. xxviii. 19. Prayer is made unto him; not only is he the Spirit of grace and of supplication, and who helps the saints under their infirmities in prayer, but he is prayed unto; *the Lord*, that is, the Lord the Spirit, *direct your hearts*, &c. where all the three Persons are mentioned as distinct, 2 Thess. iii. 5. so grace and peace, as they are wished and prayed for from God and Christ, so *from the Seven Spirits which are before the throne;* by which are meant the one Spirit of God so called, because of the fulness of divine perfections in him, and because of the perfection of his gifts and graces, Rev. i. 4, 5. Moreover his graces wrought in the saints, as they come from him, they are exercised on him, as faith, trust, and a holy confidence in him, that he who has begun the good work in them will finish it; and there is also the love of the Spirit, a cordial love of him, and a carefulness not to grieve him by whom they are sealed unto the day of redemption.

II. God only is the object of worship, to the exclusion of all others.

1*st*, All idols of whatsoever kind are excluded, not only images of things in heaven or in earth, or in the sea, and the idols of gold and silver, the work of men's hands, forbidden by the second command; but also the idols set up in a man's heart, to which such respect is paid as is due to God only; of such may be read in Ezek. xiv. 4. and which God promises to cleanse his people from, by his Spirit and grace, Ezek. xxxvi. 25. and which when converted, they declare they will have no more to do with, in the manner they have, who before conversion *served divers lusts and pleasures,* Hos. xiv. 8. Tit. iii. 3. and these perhaps are the idols the apostle John warns the children of God to keep themselves from, 1 John v. 21. The idol the worldling is enamoured with, and in which he places his trust and confidence, is gold and silver; hence covetousness is called idolatry, and such a man is said to be an idolater, Eph. v. 5. Col. iii. 5. nor can the true God and this idol mammon be served and worshipped by the same, Matt. vi. 24. The epicure, or voluptuous person, his God is his belly, which he serves, and in which he places all his happiness, and cannot be said to serve the Lord and worship him, Phil. iii. 19. Rom. xvi. 18. The self-righteous man makes an idol of his righteousness, he sets it up and endeavours to make it stand, and to establish it, and then falls down to it and worships it, putting his trust and confidence in it, Luke xviii. 9.

2*dly*, Every creature in the heavens, or on the earth, are excluded from divine worship. As the sun, moon, and stars; these seem to be the first objects of worship among the idolatrous heathens; and indeed when men departed from the true God, what could they think of to place in his room, but those glorious creatures so visible to them, from whom they received light and heat, and many blessings? hence the Israelites were cautioned against lifting up their eyes unto them, and gazing on them, lest they should be ensnared into the worship of them, Deut. iv. 19. The next objects of idolatrous worship, were men, heroes and mighty kings, famous for their exploits; these are the gods many and the lords many, the Baalim often spoken of in scripture, as Baal-Peor, Baal-Berith, &c. Neither good nor bad men are to be worshipped; when an attempt was made to sacrifice to the apostles, they rejected it with the greatest vehemence and abhorrence, Acts xiv. and it is the height of iniquity and blasphemy in antichrist to suffer himself to be worshipped, yea, to command it; and a damnable sin in his followers to do it, Rev. xiii. 4, 8, 15. and xiv. 9—11. Yea, angels are excluded from divine worship; this sort of idolatry was introduced in the times of the apostles, but condemned, Col. ii. 18. and rejected by angels themselves, Rev. xix. 10. and xxii. 9. And much less are devils to be worshipped; and yet the worship of such has obtained among the blind and ignorant heathens, as in the East and West Indies; and even the sacrifices of the Jews to new gods their fathers knew not, and the sacrifices of the heathens are said to be offered to devils, and not to God; yea the worship of saints departed, by the Papists, as the doctrine of it is called the doctrine of devils, so the practice is represented as if it was no other than worshipping of devils; it being contrary to the worship of the true God, who only is to be worshipped, Deut. xxxii. 17. 1 Cor. x. 20. 1 Tim. iv. 1. Rev. ix. 20.

CHAP. II.

OF INTERNAL WORSHIP; AND OF GODLINESS THE GROUND-WORK OF IT.

HAVING considered the object of worship, worship itself is next to be treated of; and which is either internal or external. Internal worship requires our first attention, it being of the greatest moment and importance; external worship profits little in comparison of that; if the heart is not engaged in worship, bodily exercise is of little advantage, that being only the form without the power of godliness; yea vain is such worship where the heart is far removed from God. God is a Spirit, and must be worshipped with our spirits, the better and more noble part of man; if we serve his law, it should be with our mind, the inward man delighting in it; obedience to it should flow from a principle of love to God in the heart, and with a view to his glory; and if we serve him in the gospel of his Son, it should be with our spirits, with a fervent affection for it; if we pray to him it should be with the spirit and the understanding also; if we sing his praise, it should be with melody in our hearts to the Lord; herein lies powerful godliness; and godliness is the ground-work of internal worship, and without which there can be no worshipping God aright,[1] and therefore it deserves our first consideration. Godliness is sometimes used for evangelic doctrine, the doctrine that is according to godliness, and productive of it; the whole mystery of godliness, respecting the person, office, and grace of Christ, and salvation by him, which the apostle exhorts Timothy to exercise himself in, in opposition to fables, and vain and trifling things, of no moment, 1 Tim. iv. 7. Sometimes it signifies a holy life and conversation, under the influence and power of the grace of God, as in 2 Pet. iii. 11. *What manner of persons ought ye to be in all holy conversation and godliness?* Sometimes it intends some particular duty of religion, or rather some particular grace, *Add—to patience, godliness, to godliness brotherly love*, that is, exercise these, 2 Pet. i. 5—7. But in the subject I am upon, I consider it as an assemblage of graces, as containing the whole of grace in the heart, the exercise of which is necessary to serve and worship God with reverence and godly fear, Heb. xii. 28. and without this there can be no internal worship of God. This is no other than the inward devotion of the mind, a fervency of spirit in serving the Lord; it is a holy disposition of the soul towards God. This is θεοσέβεια, the true worship of God, 1 Tim. ii. 10. the ground and foundation of it, without which there can be none. This is *life and godliness*, or vital powerful godliness, 2 Pet. i. 3. and *the things pertaining* to it are faith, hope, love, and every other grace, of which it consists, and in the exercise of which it lies, and in this is all internal religion and worship.

First, Such a gracious disposition, God-ward, is not to be found in unregenerate men, only in such who are truly partakers of the grace of God. It is godliness which distinguishes between one who truly serves and worships God, and one that serves and worships him not. The one as he is denominated from it a godly man, so likewise θεοσέβης, a true worshipper of God, John ix. 31. the other, as from the want of it, he is called an ungodly man, so ασεβής, one that is without the worship of God, 1 Pet. iv. 18.

1st, Such a gracious disposition of the mind towards God, which is requisite to the service and worship of him, is not to be found in unregenerate men; their character is this, that they are *after the flesh*, or are carnal men; and only *mind the things of the flesh*, carnal things, fleshly lusts, &c. Rom. viii. 5. there is no disposition in their minds towards God and his worship; they savour not the things of God, but the things which be of men; and therefore having no inward disposition God-ward, they are truly reckoned ungodly men, and destitute of the worship of him.

2dly, Such a gracious disposition towards God and his service, which is rightly called *godliness*, is only to be found in such who are partakers of the grace of God in truth; for,———1. Their character is, that they are *after the Spirit*, or are spiritual men; they are born of the Spirit and his grace, and so are spirit or spiritual, in whom the Spirit of God dwells, and in whom grace is the governing principle; though they are not without flesh, and have much carnality in them, yet being renewed in their minds, their conversations are spiritual; they walk after and live in the Spirit. Hence,———2. They mind *the things of the Spirit*, they love spiritual doctrines, desire spiritual gifts, especially an increase of spiritual grace, and a clearer view of interest in all spiritual blessings; they savour the things of God, and of the Spirit of God; they have a gust for them, a relish of them, they are sweet unto them, their taste being changed. Wherefore,———3. The disposition of their souls is God-ward, and to his service; they have an understanding of him, and desire to know more of him, and follow on to know him in the use of means; their thoughts are employed about him, they think on his name, his nature, and perfections, and loving-kindness,

---

[1] Οσιοτης και ευσεβεια (θεραπεια) θεων, Platonis Euthyphro, p. 9.

as displayed in Christ; their affections are set upon him, and they love him cordially and sincerely; their desires are after him, and to the remembrance of his name; they pant after more communion with him, and the manifestations of his love unto them; they have their spiritual senses exercised upon him; they see him with the eyes of their understandings opened, his beauty, his power, and his glory, in the sanctuary; they hear his gospel with pleasure, it is a joyful sound unto them, and they can distinguish his voice from that of a stranger; they taste that the Lord is gracious; his word and the doctrines of it, his fruit and the blessings of his grace are sweet to their taste, these are savoury things which their souls love; they handle Christ the word of life, and feel the power of his gospel on them; that effectually working in them through the demonstration of the Spirit. Now, ——4. These are truly godly persons, ευσιβεις, 2 Pet. ii. 9. persons well-disposed to the worship of God, and who rightly perform it; these have their minds powerfully impressed with the doctrine that is according to godliness, under the influence of which they live soberly, righteously, and godly; these have all things given them pertaining to life and godliness, every grace, and every needful supply and increase of it; in the exercise of which lies internal worship, or inward, spiritual, experimental, and practical religion; which is called ευσιβεια, or *godliness*, and stands opposed to bodily exercise, or external worship, 1 Tim. iv. 8.

Secondly, Godliness not in name and profession only, but godliness in the life and power of it, an inward fervent devotion of the mind, a gracious disposition of the heart towards God, as has been explained, is the ground-work of true religion; and without this there can be no internal worship, nor indeed any external worship rightly performed; for,——1. Without the knowledge of God there can be no true worship of him; the Samaritans worshipped they knew not what, and so their worship[2] was not right. Whom the Athenians ignorantly worshipped, him the apostle declared unto them; nor is a natural knowledge of God by the creatures, sufficient to teach men the worship of God and engage them in it; the wise philosophers, who, by the light of nature, by the works of creation, knew there was a God, yet they glorified him not as God. True spiritual, experimental, and evangelical knowledge of God, is the knowledge of God in Christ; and as our worship of him is in and by Christ, there can be no true worship of him without such knowledge of him, even of him as our covenant-God in Christ; and as this will direct us to the right object of worship, and the true manner of worship, so it will influence and engage unto it; *whose I am, and whom I serve*, Acts xxvii. 23.——2. Without faith in God, which is another branch of powerful godliness, there can be no true worship of God; for whatsoever is not of faith is sin; and without it it is impossible to please God in any part of worship and service; all worship performed to God under the Old Testament dispensation which was agreeable to him, was by faith, as the instances of Abel and Jacob, of Moses and the children of Israel shew, Heb. xi. 4, 5, 21, 28. And under the gospel dispensation, whenever we draw nigh to God in any part of worship, it must be in faith; whoever comes to God, and is a worshipper of him, must believe that he is, and that he is a rewarder of those that diligently seek him; and if we come to the throne of grace and there ask any thing of God, it must be asked in faith; and if we attend upon him in the ministry of the word, it must be in the exercise of faith, for the word only profits as it is mixed with faith by them that hear it, Heb. x. 22. and iv. 12. Now faith is one of the things pertaining to life and godliness, and is a part of it; and therefore without godliness, or a gracious disposition of the soul towards God, there can be no true worship of him.——3. Without the fear of God, another branch of vital godliness, there can be no worship of him. The fear of God is sometimes put for the whole of worship, both internal and external, *God is greatly to be feared in the assembly of his saints*, where his solemn worship is performed, *and to be had in reverence of all them that are about him;* and fear and reverence are so necessary to the service and worship of God, that the Psalmist exhorts men to *serve the Lord with fear, and rejoice with trembling;* and as for himself, he says, *in thy fear will I worship toward thy holy temple;* see Psalm lxxxix. 7. and ii. 11. and v. 7. where there is no fear of God before the

---

[2] Ευσιβης δε ο την θειαν επιστημην εχων, Hierocles in Carmin. Pythag. p. 26. Ειναι τε την ευσιβειαν επιστημην θεων θεραπειας, Laert. l. 7. in Vita Zenonis.

eyes, and upon the hearts of men, there is no worship of him; grace in the heart, and that in the exercise, or inward powerful godliness, which is the same thing, is absolutely necessary to worship, God in an acceptable manner, Heb. xii. 28.——
4. Spiritual internal worship, cannot be performed without love to God, another branch of real godliness. Charity, or love, is the internal principle from whence obedience to God, and the worship of him, should spring; hence love to God with all the heart and soul, as well as fear, is premised unto it, Deut. x. 12. for such affectionate, cordial, and hearty service, is only acceptable to him, and can never be where the heart is destitute of godliness.——
5. And as they are spiritual worshippers that God seeks, and spiritual worship that is only acceptable to him, it being suitable to his nature who is a Spirit; none but a spiritual man can perform it, or that is possessed of true grace, or vital godliness; they that are in the flesh, in a state of nature, carnal men, who have no disposition Godward, cannot please God, or do that which is acceptable in his sight, Rom. viii. 8.——
6. Nor can a man worship God sincerely, if he has only the form and not the power of godliness; if he only draws nigh to God with his mouth, and honours him with his lips, and his heart is removed far from him, and his fear towards him taught by the precept of men, his worship will be in vain and unacceptable to him, Isa. xxix. 13. From all which it appears how necessary godliness is to the worship of God, and that it may well be reckoned the groundwork and foundation of it.

Now this gracious disposition of the mind God-ward, which may therefore be truly called godliness, and which is so necessary to the worship of God, that it cannot be performed without it, is not of a man's self, it is not naturally in man; yea, as has been seen, the bias and disposition of the minds of men are naturally the reverse; wherefore this disposition must be owing to the grace of God, and must be a gift of his; it is he that gives godliness itself, and all things appertaining to it; and indeed as it is an assemblage of all the graces of the Spirit, and every grace is a gift, that must be such. Knowledge of God is a gift of his; faith is not of ourselves, it is the gift of God. Hope that is good, is a good hope through grace; love cannot be purchased at any rate; the fear of God is what is implanted in the heart by the grace of God, and so all others; and even all supplies of grace to maintain, encourage, increase, and support such a disposition, are freely given of God; and all grace, as it comes from God, it points to God again, and disposes the heart God-ward.

Thirdly, Great is the profit, and many the advantages, that accrue from godliness to the possessors of it.

1st, That itself is said to be gain to the persons that have it; *Godliness with contentment is great gain,* 1 Tim. vi. 6. there were some indeed who *supposed that gain is godliness,* ver. 5. either who thought that godliness was to be gained with money, as Simon Magus thought the gifts of the Holy Ghost were; but as not they, so neither the graces of the Spirit are to be obtained in such a way: or they were such who took up a profession of godliness, and made an outward shew of it, for the sake of present or future gain; to gain a name in a church of Christ, to get a reputation among godly neighbours and acquaintance, and for the sake of worldly interest in godly wealthy relations, or to obtain the favour of God now, and heaven hereafter; but after all, what will be the hope and gain of such a person when *God takes away his soul?* Job xxvii. 8. or they are such who think, or at least act as if they thought, that all religion lay in gain, in getting money; since their serving God and Christ, and all they do in a religious way, is for filthy lucre's sake, every one looking for his gain from his quarter. But real godliness is itself true gain; it may be said of it as it is of wisdom, *the merchandise of it is better than the merchandise of silver, and the gain thereof, than fine gold,* Prov. iii. 14. Such who, whilst in a state of ungodliness, were *wretched, and miserable, and poor, and blind, and naked,* being possessed of godliness, come into good circumstances; who before were in debt, owed ten thousand talents, and had nothing to pay, and were liable to a prison, all their debts are freely forgiven them, and the whole score of them cleared; who before were in rags, and had nothing to cover their naked souls before God, are now clothed with change of raiment, with a robe of righteousness and garments of salvation; who before were starving, and would have been glad of husks which swine do eat, are now fed with the finest of the wheat, with angels' food, at Christ's table, as with marrow and fatness; these are come into very affluent circumstances, to great riches, durable and unsearchable; and to great honour also, being raised as beggars from the dunghill, to sit among princes, and to inherit the throne of glory; yea are made kings and priests unto God, have a kingdom of grace now, and are heirs of the kingdom of glory; they who lived without God in the world, and were aliens from the commonwealth of Israel, are now in a good family, fellow-citizens with the saints and of the household of God; and being children of God, are heirs of God and joint-heirs with Christ, possessed of the riches of grace, and entitled to the riches of glory; their gain is great indeed, and sufficient to give them full contentment.

2dly, Godliness is said to be *profitable unto all things*, 1 Tim. iv. 8. whereas *bodily exercise*, or a presentation of the body only, in an attendance on public worship, *profiteth little*, or *for a little time;*[3] for sometimes such sort of religion and worship lasts but for a little while, as in temporary believers, and in the stony-ground hearers, and where it continues, it profits not in matters of the greatest importance; it may be profitable to others, by way of example, as to children and servants in a man's family, and to a community with whom he attends for the secular support of it; and it may be profitable to himself, to keep him from being elsewhere, in bad company, which might lead into many snares and temptations, and hurtful lusts; but is of no profit to obtain eternal life, since a man may constantly hear the word, and attend on and submit unto all ordinances, and yet Christ may say to him at the last day, *Depart from me, I know you not;* for there may be such bodily exercise or external worship, where there is no true grace nor vital religion: but *godliness*, powerful vital godliness, internal religion, is *profitable unto all things;* it is even profitable to the health of a man's body, for the fear of the Lord, which is the same thing, is *health to the navel*, and *marrow to the bones;* whereas by an ungodly course of life, men bring upon themselves diseases painful and incurable. But more especially godliness is profitable to promote the welfare of the soul; for by means of that, and in the exercise of it, the soul of a good man, as of Gaius, prospers and is in good health; he finds it always good for him to draw nigh unto God, where he has much communion with him, and receives much from him: and such a man is profitable to others, for godly men are made a blessing to all about them, they are the light of the world, and the salt of the earth; though indeed no man can be profitable to God, by all his external and internal religion, as he that is wise and good may be profitable to himself and others; for when he has done all he can, or by the grace of God is assisted to do, he is but an unprofitable servant.

3dly, Godliness has *the promise of the life that now is, and of that which is to come*, 1 Tim. iv. 8.——1. Of the present life, both temporal and spiritual. A godly man has the promise of temporal life, of the blessings of it, of good things in it, yea that he shall want no good thing that is needful for him; and of a continuance of this life, when an ungodly man does not live out half his days; God satisfies the godly man with long life, and shews him his salvation, Psalm xxxiv. 9, 10. and xxxvii. 3. and lxxxiv. 11. and xci. 16. And of the present spiritual life, of all things pertaining to it, of all needful supplies of grace to maintain and to support it, and of the continuance of it, and of its springing up into and issuing in everlasting life.—— 2. Of the future life of happiness and glory. It is most certain that there is a future life, and that there is a promise of eternal life in it, made by God who cannot lie; this promise is made to the godly man, James i. 12. not to be enjoyed by him through any merit of his, for that is the gift of God through Christ; and a promise being made of it, and its being by promise, shew that it is not of the works of men but of the grace of God; and when godliness is said to have the promise of it, it is a promise God has made to his own grace, and not to the merits of men. However, it is a plain case, that real godliness is of great avail to men, both with respect to time and eternity.

Now as inward powerful godliness is, as has been seen, a disposition of the soul God-ward, from whom all grace comes and to whom it tends, and as it is an assemblage of every grace,[4] in the exercise of which all internal worship and experimental religion lies, I therefore begin with it, and shall in

---

[3] προς το ολιγον.

[4] Ευσεβεια, frequently used in scripture, and rendered godliness, is in heathen writers said to be ηγεμων αρχη και μητηρ, the leader the beginning and mother of all virtues; και σπερμα των αγαθων απαντων ημιν, and the seed of all good things in us, Hierocles in Carmin. Pythagor. p. 10. 69. 126.

the following chapters consider the branches of it in which it opens; as the knowledge of God, repentance towards God, fear of him, faith, and trust in him, the hope of good things from him, love to him, joy in him, humility, self-denial, patience, submission, and resignation to the will of God, thankfulness for every mercy, with every other grace necessary to the worship of God, and which belongs to experimental religion and godliness.

CHAP. III.

OF THE KNOWLEDGE OF GOD.

SINCE the knowledge of God and of divine things is a part and branch of true godliness, or of experimental religion, and a very essential one too, it is first to be considered; for without it there can be no good disposition in the mind towards God; for *ignoti nulla cupido*, there are no affections for, nor desires after an unknown object. And as we have seen there can be no true worship of God where there is no knowledge of God, as the cases of the Samaritans among the Jews, the Athenians among the Gentiles, and their wise philosophers shew; there can be no cordial obedience to him by those who are ignorant of him; the language of such persons will be like that of Pharoah, Exod. v. 2. It is a false maxim of the Papists, that "ignorance is the mother of devotion;" it is so far from being true, that it is the parent of irreligion, will-worship, superstition, and idolatry. Godliness, as has been observed, is an assemblage of the graces of the Spirit of God in the hearts of his people, in the exercise of which experimental religion or internal worship lies; now there can be no grace without knowledge, no faith without it; the object must be known, or it cannot be rightly believed in. The blind man's answer to Christ's question is a wise one, John ix. 35, 36. The Gentiles, who are described as such who *know not God*, are also said to be *without hope*, without hope and without God in the world; without hope in God and of good things from him now, and without hope of the resurrection of the dead, a future state, and enjoyment of happiness in it, 1 Thess. iv. 5, 13. an unknown object cannot be the object of love; an unseen person may, *Whom having not seen, we love*; but an unknown person cannot be truly and cordially loved; God must be known, or he cannot be loved with all the heart and with all the soul. The wise man says, Prov. xix. 2. *That the soul be without knowledge is not good*, or rather it may be rendered, *without knowledge the soul is disposed to that which is not good*;[1] it cannot be well-disposed towards God, nor be fit for any good work, or for the right performance of any religious exercise, but is disposed to that which is evil; where ignorance reigns no good thing dwells. Now,

First, Let it be observed, that whilst men are in a natural, unregenerate, and unrenewed state, they are destitute of divine knowledge; the time before conversion is a time of ignorance; this was not only the case of the Gentile world in general, before the gospel came unto them, but is of every particular person, Jew or Gentile, Acts xvii. 30. 1 Pet. i. 14. all the sons and daughters of Adam are in the same circumstances, for the illustration of which it may be noted,

1st, That Adam was created a very knowing creature, being made after the image and in the likeness of God, which greatly lay in his understanding and knowledge of things; and whilst he continued in a state of innocence, his knowledge was very great; it is not easy to say nor to conceive how great it was; as he knew much of things natural and civil, so of things moral and divine; as he knew much of the creatures and their nature, so as to give suitable names to them, he knew much of God, of his nature, perfections, and persons, and of his mind and will, and of all necessary truths and duties of religion; for what by the light of nature and the works of it, and by the exercise of his own rational powers, which were in their full force and vigour, and by that nearness to God and communion with him he had, and by those revelations which were made to him by God, his knowledge must be very great. But,

2dly, Our first parents not being content with the knowledge they had, but listening to the temptation of Satan, who suggested to them that if they eat of the forbidden fruit they should be wise and knowing as God, they sinned and fell in with it, and fell by it, and so lost in a great measure that knowledge they had; for *man being in honour*, as he was whilst in a state

---

[1] Vid. Vatablum in loc.

of innocence, and *understandeth not*, so he became by sinning, *is like the beasts that perish;* not only like to them, being through sin become mortal as they are, but because of want of understanding; yet *vain man would be wise,* would be thought to be a wise and a very knowing creature, *though man be born like a wild ass's colt,* which of all animals is the most dull and stupid; see Psalm xlix. 12, 20. Job xi. 12.

3dly, Adam being driven from the presence of God, and deprived of communion with him because of sin, by which his nature was corrupted, darkness seized his understanding and overspread it, and greatly dispelled that light which before shone so brightly in him; and this is the case of all his posterity, Eph. iv. 18. The darkness of sin has blinded the eyes of their understanding, that they cannot see and understand divine things; it has left an ignorance of God in them, to which are owing their want of a disposition to God, an alienation from him, and an aversion to a life agreeable to him; and this is the state and case of all men, even of God's elect before conversion, who are not only dark but *darkness* itself, till they are made light in the Lord; and when the true light of grace shines, the darkness passes away, Eph. v. 8. 1 John ii. 8.

4thly, This darkness and ignorance is increased by a course of sinning. Naturally man *is in darkness,* he is born in darkness and continues in it, *and walketh in darkness;* and by an habit and custom in sinning, increases the darkness of his mind; for notwithstanding the fall, there are some remains of the light of nature in man; some general notions of good and evil, according to which the natural conscience accuses or excuses; but sometimes through a course of sin, conscience is cauterized, seared as with a red-hot iron, so that it is become past feeling, and insensible to the distinction of good and evil, Isa. v. 20.

5thly, There is in many an affected ignorance, which is very criminal; they are *willingly ignorant,* as the apostle says of the scoffers who shall arise in the last time, or rather they are unwilling to understand what they might, *they know not, nor will they understand, they walk on in darkness;* they do not choose to make use of, but shun the means of knowledge, and shut their eyes against all light and conviction; they do not care to come to the light, and love darkness rather than light; they do not desire to know God and his ways, but rather that he would depart from them; with such as these, wisdom expostulates, saying, *How long, ye simple ones, will ye love simplicity?———and fools hate knowledge?* Prov. i. 21. see 2 Pet. iii. 5. Psalm lxxxii. 5. John iii. 19. Job xxi. 14.

6thly, Some, because of their sinful lusts they indulge themselves in, and their contempt of the means of light and knowledge, and the stubborn choice they make of error and falsehood, are given up to judicial blindness and hardness of heart; as many among the heathens, who because they liked not to retain God in their knowledge, were given up to a reprobate mind, or to a mind void of judgment, and so imbibed notions and performed actions not convenient, Rom. i. 28. and the Jews, who rejected Jesus the Messiah against all light and evidence, had a spirit of slumber given them, eyes that they should not see, and ears that they should not hear, nor understand with their hearts, John xii. 40. Rom. xi. 8. and the followers of Antichrist, who received not the love of the truth, had a strong delusion sent them to believe a lie, 2 Thess. ii. 10, 11. others have been left, under the power of Satan, the same with the power of darkness, who is the god of this world, and who is suffered to blind the eyes of them who believe not, lest the light of the glorious gospel of Christ should shine unto them, 2 Cor. iv. 4.

Now whilst men are in an unrenewed state, and in such a state of darkness and blindness, they are ignorant,———1. Of God, of his nature and perfections; for though they may by the light of nature, and from the works of creation, know that there is a God, and some of his perfections, as his wisdom, power, and goodness, which manifestly appear in them; yet not so as to glorify him as God, nor so as to preserve them from the worship of other gods besides him: indeed their knowledge of him is so dim and obscure, that after all, they are said by their wisdom not to know God, the true God, this was the case of the Gentiles; and as for the Jews who had a revelation, yet they were *ignorant of the righteousness of God,* which was the ground of their capital mistake in going about to establish their own righteousness, and reject the righteousness of Christ. And carnal men are very apt to think that God is such an one as themselves, and they measure him by themselves, and fancy that what is agreeable to the reasonings of their minds is approved of by him; or that he takes no notice of men and their actions, but leaves them to act as they please; that *the Lord hath forsaken the earth, and the Lord seeth not,* Ezek. ix. 9. and thus they live without God, or as atheists in the world; or they think that God is a God of mercy, and will have mercy on them at last, but never think of his justice and holiness.——2. They are ignorant of Christ, of his person and offices, and of the way of life and salvation by him; as they know neither the Father nor the Son, nor the distinction between them, so not the concern that each have in the salvation of men. *The way of peace they know not,* how God was in Christ reconciling the world to himself, forming the plan and scheme of reconciliation, and how Christ has made peace by the blood of his cross.——3. They are ignorant of the Spirit of God; *The world seeth him not, neither knoweth him,* John xiv. 17. neither his person nor his office, as a sanctifier and comforter; nor the operations of his grace on the souls of men. Nicodemus, a master in Israel, could not conceive how it should be that a man should be born again of water and of the Spirit, John iii. 8, 9. Nor can a natural man either receive or know the things of the Spirit of God, because they are spiritually discerned, and he has not a spiritual visive faculty to discern them, 1 Cor. ii. 14. ——4. They are ignorant of themselves, and of their state and condition by nature; they think themselves rich and increased with goods, when they are wretched, miserable, poor, and blind, and naked; they fancy themselves whole, sound and healthful, and need not a physician for their souls, when they are sadly diseased and distempered with sin; they reckon themselves alive without the law, in a good condition, and in a fair way for life, heaven, and happiness, till the law enters them, and cuts off all their hopes of salvation by the works of it. They are upon the brink of ruin, like a man on the top of the mast of a ship asleep, in the midst of the sea, insensible of their danger; they rush into sin like the horse into the battle, and hasten like a bird to the snare, which knows not it is for its life.——5. They are ignorant of sin and the sad effects of it; if they have any notion of the grosser sins of life, and the evil of them, they do not know that lust in the heart is sin; not the evil of indwelling sin and corrupt nature; nor consider that the wages of sin is death, eternal death; they are not sensible of their own insufficiency and inability to make atonement for their sins, nor to work out a righteousness that will justify them from their sins.——6. They are ignorant of the sacred scriptures, and the truths contained in them; though they are plain to them that understand, and right to them that find knowledge, Prov. viii. 9. yet they are like a sealed book to carnal men, whether learned or unlearned; the one cannot read them because sealed, and the other because he is not learned, Isa. xxix. 11, 12. The mysteries of the kingdom are delivered to them in parables, and they are riddles, enigmas, and dark sayings to them; the gospel, and the doctrines of it are hid from the wise and prudent; they cannot understand them, they are foolishness to them, and they pronounce them such. But,

Secondly, In every renewed person there is a knowledge of God and of divine things; the new creature or *new man is renewed in knowledge, after the image of him that created him,* Col. iii. 10. Spiritual and divine knowledge is a part of the new man, which is no other than an assemblage of grace consisting of various members, of which this is one; it is a part of the image of God and Christ enstamped upon the soul in regeneration, and which gives it a disposition god-ward; concerning which may be observed,

1st, The object of it, God; before conversion men know not God, but after that they know him, or rather are known of him, Gal. iv. 8, 9. there is a threefold knowledge of God, or a knowledge of God that is come at in a threefold way.

1. There is a knowledge of God by the light of nature through the works of creation, which shew his eternal power and godhead, declare his glory, and display his wisdom and goodness; and through the works of providence, by which he has not left himself without a witness of his Being and beneficence; and though these ways and works are past finding out, and a small portion of them is known by men, yet something of God is to be known by them, and that he is, as Jethro said, *greater than all gods;* but then such knowledge was always insufficient to teach men the true worship of God, and influence them to it; notwithstanding this, either they did not worship him at all, or ignorantly worshipped him; that is, not in a right way and manner. The wise philosophers of the heathens, though they in some sort knew

God, yet they did not glorify him as God, nor serve him only, but worshipped and served the creature more and beside the Creator; nor was such knowledge effectual to make the hearts of men better, nor to mend their lives; those to whom God left not himself without a witness, by the works of creation and providence, still walked on in their own ways, and those very bad ones, walking in lasciviousness, lusts, drunkenness, revellings, banquettings, and abominable idolatries, even committing abominable lewdness in their religious services. What a character does the apostle give of them, Rom. i. even of those who professed themselves to be wise, both as to their hearts and actions? their foolish heart was darkened and their imagination vain, and they were given up to the lusts of their hearts and to the uncleanness of them, to vile affections and a reprobate mind, being filled with all unrighteousness and wickedness; what a dreadful portrait does the apostle draw of them, ver. 29—31. Nor was this light and knowledge sufficient to point out to them the true way, how incensed Deity may be appeased, or sinners be reconciled to God; or by what means atonement for sin could be made, and therefore put such questions as in Mic. vi. 6, 7. not the least hint did it give of a sin-bearing and sin-atoning Saviour, and of the blood of Christ which makes peace with God, and cleanses from all sin; nor could it give men any good ground to hope for pardon of sin on any account whatever; though they might presume on the mercy of God, and conjecture that he would forgive their sins upon their repentance, this they could not be sure of; at most it was but an *who can tell* if God will repent and turn from his fierce anger, as said the Ninevites, Jonah, iii. 9. Nor was it sufficient to assure them of a future state of happiness, and describe what that is; as for the immortality of the soul, they had some faint views of it, and rather wished it to be true than believed it; of the resurrection of the dead they had no hope; and what that happiness of man hereafter they sometimes speak of, they had gross notions of, such as had any; and could not assure themselves by all their virtue that they should enjoy it. Life and immortality are only truly brought to light by the gospel.

2. There is a knowledge of God by the law, the law of Moses, the moral law; though this came by Moses, it was of God, and shews what is his good and perfect will; it is a transcript of his nature, his justice and holiness; but then it only gives knowledge of him as a lawgiver, who is able to save and to destroy, and as an incensed God, threatening wrath to the breakers of it, without any hope of mercy, not even on the foot of repentance; it accuses of sin, the breach of it; pronounces guilty for it, and is the ministration of condemnation and death; by it is the knowledge of sin, but not of a saviour from it. The ceremonial law was indeed a shadow of good things to come by Christ; its sacrifices prefigured the sacrifice of Christ; it was the Jews' schoolmaster that taught them Christ, and directed them to him.

3. There is a knowledge of God which comes by the gospel, the doctrine of grace and truth, that is by Christ, who lay in the bosom of his Father, and has declared him, his person, his nature, his grace, his mind and will to men; God has spoken by his Son, and made the largest discovery of himself by him; and makes use of the ministers of the gospel to give the light of the knowledge of the glory of God in the face or person of Christ, who is the brightness of his Father's glory and the express image of his person: and it is of this kind of knowledge of God in Christ, that souls are made partakers, when they are renewed in the spirit of their minds; this is not a mere notional and speculative knowledge, such as the carnal Jews had, who had a form of knowledge in the law, and by breaking it dishonoured God; and which some who call themselves Christians may have, who profess in words to know God, but in works deny him; who say, Lord, Lord, but do not do will of our Father in heaven: but this is a spiritual and experimental knowledge of God, such as a spiritual man has, and that from the Spirit of God as a spirit of wisdom and revelation in the knowledge of him; and which leads men to mind and savour spiritual things. This is a knowledge which is attended with faith in God as a covenant-God in Christ; it is a fiducial knowledge, such as know his name put their trust in him, in whom is everlasting strength, and from whom they expect all supplies of grace; and having knowledge of him as their portion and exceeding great reward, they hope in him for what they want in time, and for happiness with him hereafter; and such knowledge always includes in it love to God, and the most cordial affection for him; *he who loveth not, knoweth not God*, 1 John iv. 8.

for if he knew him he could not but love him, and say of him, *Whom have I in heaven but thee? and there is none upon earth that I desire besides thee.* Such knowledge is accompanied with a filial fear and reverence of God ; where there is no knowledge of God, there is no fear of God ; but where there is knowledge of God, of his grace and goodness, and of his pardoning mercy in Christ, men fear the Lord and his goodness ; for there is forgiveness with him that he may be feared; not with a slavish but a child-like fear; and where it is known he is so feared. And such a knowledge is practical, and it is known to be right by being so ; *hereby we know that we know him, if we keep his commandments,* 1 John ii. 3. for such only may be said to be *filled with the knowledge of his will in all wisdom and spiritual understanding,* in a true spiritual and evangelical manner, when the end for which they have it, and for which they desire it, is, to *walk worthy of the Lord unto all pleasing ;* that is, to do the will of God in the most acceptable manner, Col. i. 9, 10. and a knowledge attended with such graces and fruits of righteousness may be called saving knowledge; that is, salvation is annexed unto it and follows upon it; for *this is life eternal,* the beginning of it, and in which it issues, John xvii. 3.

Now this knowledge of God may be considered as respecting the three divine Persons in the godhead distinctly, Father, Son, and Spirit; and that acquaintance and fellowship with each which such knowledge leads into. For there is a fellowship and communion which believers have with each divine Person, which arises from their distinct knowledge of them, 1 John i. 3. 2 Cor. xiii. 14.

1. Every renewed soul has knowledge of God the Father. *I write unto you, little children,* says the apostle John, 1 Epist. ii. 13. *because ye have known the Father,* the Father of Christ and their Father in Christ; for he that is Christ's Father is their Father, though they are not in the same class of sonship with him; *I ascend to my Father and your Father,* John xx. 17. and this relation is made known to them, as children are taught to know their father; and this the saints know by the Spirit of adoption sent down into their hearts, crying, Abba, Father; and witnessing to their spirits that they are the children of God; and this leads into communion with him, and into the enjoyment of many privileges with pleasure. They have knowledge of the love of the Father which is bestowed on them, and is in them, and which appears in their election, in the gift of Christ to them, and in their adoption, and in other blessings of grace; and this is shed abroad in their hearts by the Spirit, and they are led by him into the heights and depths, and lengths and breadths of it ; they are warmed by it, and comforted with it ; it is a source of joy, peace and comfort to them ; and the knowledge of it is what they glory in and should do, and in that only, Jer. ix. 23, 24. They have also knowledge of God the Father as having chosen them in Christ, and blessed them with all spiritual blessings in him; for though their election is so early as before the foundation of the world, and so secret as it is in Christ, yet it may be known by them ; *Knowing, brethren beloved, your election of God ;* how and by what means ? by the powerful influence of the gospel upon their hearts, *for our gospel came not unto you in word only but also in power,* 1 Thess. i. 4, 5. they have knowledge of him as their covenant-God in Christ, who has blessed them with all covenant-blessings, with the sure mercies of David ; with justification by the righteousne. s of Christ, pardon of sin for his sake, reconciliation and atonement, adoption, and every other blessing ; the knowledge of all which draws out their hearts in thankfulness to the Father of Christ, in love to him, and praise of him, Eph. i. 3, 4. They have knowledge of him as *in Christ reconciling the world unto himself,* planning the scheme of their peace, reconciliation and atonement by Christ, *not imputing their trespasses* to them, but to their Surety and Saviour; which scheme he has executed by him, and has *by him reconciled* them *to himself,* of which they have knowledge, and hence reason in the strong and comfortable manner as the apostle does, Rom. v. 11. Moreover they have knowledge of God the Father, as having proclaimed his name in Christ, a God *gracious and merciful, pardoning iniquity, transgression and sin ;* as a God that does abundantly pardon, and which engages their souls to turn unto him, and fills them with wonder and amazement; so that they say, *Who is a God like unto thee, that pardoneth iniquity ?* and this raises in them the highest gratitude and thankfulness to God; they call upon their souls, and all within them, to *bless his holy name, and not*

forget his benefits, who forgiveth all their iniquities, Mic. vii. 18. Psalm ciii. 1—3. To observe no more; they know him as *the God of all grace, who has called* them *to his eternal glory by Christ Jesus* his Son; that is, that he is the author and giver of every grace unto them; that their faith is not of themselves, it is the gift of God; that their good hope through grace is of him, and therefore he is called the God of hope, because not only the object but the author and giver of it; for the same reason he is called the God of love, the God of patience, &c. and this knowledge of God the Father, leads to deal with him for reshf supplies of grace, and that he would make all grace to abound towards them; this draws them to the throne of grace to seek grace and mercy of him to help them in their time of need.

2. Every renewed soul has knowledge of Christ the Son of God, John xvii. 3. where the *only true God* designs God the Father, yet not to the exclusion of Christ the Son of God, for he is expressly called the *true God* also, 1 John v. 20. and *eternal life* is made to depend equally upon the knowledge of the one as upon the knowledge of the other; now would Christ ever have ranked himself in this manner with the only true God, if he was not equal with him? and such an interpretation of the passage as would exclude him from being the one only true God with the Father, would exclude the Father from being the one only Lord with the Son, 1 Cor. viii. 6. Now truly gracious souls have knowledge of the person of Christ, as being truly God and truly man; as being true God, and therefore they venture their souls on him, commit their all unto him, and look unto him for salvation, and trust in him for it, because he is God and there is none else; and as being truly man, partaker of the same flesh and blood with them, and in all things made like unto them, and so their near kinsman, and who cannot but have sympathy with them; and thus being both God and man, he is fit to be the mediator between both, and to take care of things belonging to God, and to make reconciliation for the sins of the people. They have knowledge of him in all his offices, and deal with him as such; with him as their prophet to teach and instruct them by his word, his ministers, and his Spirit; with him as their priest, who by his sacrifice has made atonement for their sins, and by his intercession pleads for every blessing for them; and with him as their king, to rule over them, protect and defend them; and they become willingly subject to his commands and ordinances, and esteem all his precepts concerning all things to be right; they know him as their living Redeemer, as Job did; and their souls rejoice in God their Saviour, as Mary the mother of our Lord did; they know him in the various relations he stands in to them, as their everlasting Father, who bears an everlasting love to them, takes an everlasting care of them, and makes everlasting provision for them; as their head of eminence over them, and influence to them; as their husband, who has betrothed them to himself in righteousness and loving-kindness; as their brother, and one that sticks closer than a brother; and as their friend that loves at all times, and of whom they say as the church did, *This is my beloved, and this is my friend.* And this knowledge which such souls have of Christ is,——
(1.) Not merely notional and speculative, such a knowledge the devils have: they know Christ to be the holy one of God, and that he is the Son of God, and the Messiah, Luke iv. 34, 41. and men destitute of the grace of God may know and give their assent to those truths, that Christ is truly God, and existed as the Son of God from all eternity; that he assumed human nature in the fulness of time, that he lived a life of sorrow and trouble, died the death of the cross, was buried and rose again from the dead, ascended to heaven, and is set down at the right hand of God, and will come a second time to judge the world in righteousness; but this spiritual special knowledge gracious souls have, is, ——(2.) An affectionate knowledge, or a knowledge joined with love and affection to Christ; he is in their esteem the chiefest among ten thousand, and altogether lovely; he is precious to them, and there is none in heaven nor in earth so desired by them as he is.——(3.) Their knowledge is a knowledge of approbation, they approve of him above all other lovers, and above all other saviours; they reject all others, and say, *Ashur shall not save us;* we will have no regard to our works, duties and services, as saviours; but they say of him, as Job did, *Though he slay me yet will I trust in him—he also shall be my salvation,* I will have no other, Job xiii. 15, 16.——(4.) Their knowledge of him is fiducial; they know his name, his nature, his abilities, his fulness, and suitableness, and therefore

they put their trust in him, give up themselves to him, rely and lean upon him, and trust him with all they have, and for all they want, for grace here and glory hereafter.
―――(5.) Their knowledge of him is experimental, they have their spiritual senses exercised on him; they *see* the Son and believe on him, see the glories of his person, the riches of his grace, the fulness of his righteousness, the efficacy of his blood, and the virtue of his atoning sacrifice; they *hear* his voice with pleasure and delight, the voice of his gospel, so as to understand it, approve of it, and distinguish it from the voice of a stranger; they *feel*, they handle him the word of life by faith, lay hold on him and retain him; they *taste* that the Lord is gracious, and *savour* the things which be of Christ and not of men.―――
(6.) Their knowledge of Christ is appropriating; it does not lie in generals but in particulars, they know him themselves and for themselves; they do not only say as the Samaritans did, *We know that this is indeed the Christ the Saviour of the world,* John iv. 42. but that he is their Saviour and Redeemer; and say with Thomas, *My Lord and my God;* and with the apostle Paul, *Who loved me, and gave himself for me;* and with the church, *My beloved is mine, and I am his,* John xx. 28. Gal. ii. 20. Cant. ii. 16.

3. Every renewed soul has knowledge of the Spirit of God, the world does not know him, but truly gracious souls do; our Lord speaking of him says, *Whom the world cannot receive, because it seeth him not, neither knoweth him,* neither his person, nor his office, nor his operations; *But ye know him,* meaning his apostles and followers; and gives a very good reason for it, *for he dwelleth with you, and shall be in you;* and therefore they must have a feeling and experimental knowledge of him, John xiv. 17. Such as are renewed in the spirit of their minds, have a knowledge of him as a Spirit of conviction and illumination, he having convinced them of sin, the evil nature and sad consequences of it; of righteousness, of the insufficiency of their own righteousness to justify them before God, and of the fulness and suitableness of Christ's righteousness for that purpose; and having had the eyes of their understandings enlightened by him as a Spirit of wisdom and revelation in the knowledge of Christ, as an able, willing, and complete Saviour; and having received him as the Spirit which is of God, whereby are made known to them the things that are freely given to them of God; the free-grace gifts of righteousness, peace, pardon, and eternal life. They have knowledge of him as the Comforter, who comforts them by shedding abroad in their hearts the love of the Father and of the Son; by opening and applying the exceeding great and precious promises of the gospel, and by taking the things of Christ and shewing them to them, and their interest in them; and these comforts they have a feeling experience of, for they delight their souls amidst the multitude of their thoughts within them; yea they walk in the comforts of the holy Ghost, and are edified by them. They have knowledge of him also as the Spirit of adoption, who manifests to them their interest in this blessing; and not only from his witnessing do they know their relation to God as children, but also from their being led by him out of themselves to Christ, and into the truth as it is in Jesus, for such *are the sons of God,* Rom. viii. 14―16. Moreover they have knowledge of the Spirit as a *Spirit of grace and of supplication,* who first works grace in the soul, and then draws it forth into act and exercise; and perhaps there is no season in the christian life in which this grace is more drawn forth into exercise than when in prayer, public and private, under the influence of the Spirit of supplication; who helps saints under all their infirmities in prayer, and makes intercession in them according to the will of God, impresses a sense of their wants upon them, puts strength into them, and fills their mouths with arguments to plead with God in the exercise of grace. Once more, such souls have knowledge of him as the Spirit of truth, that guides into all truth necessary to be known by them, and powerfully applies it to them; who teaches them all things they should know, and brings to their remembrance truths or promises, at proper seasons, for their relief and comfort; and who is the unction they have received from the holy one, the anointing which teacheth all things, and from which they are denominated Christians. To say no more, they have knowledge of him as an inhabitant in them, for he dwells in them as in his temple; of whose indwelling they are sensible by the operations of his grace upon them; they find he is in them as the earnest of their inheritance, and as the sealer of them unto the day of redemption. Now in this distinct, special, and peculiar knowledge of Father, Son, and Spirit, and in that

communion with them, which arises from hence, inward experimental religion greatly lies.

To this head of the object of knowledge, all divine things may be reduced that are knowable, that are to be known or should be known by the Christian; there are some things that are not to be known, and which will never be known, neither in this life nor in that to come; there are some things that angels know not, yea which the human soul of Christ knew not in his state of humiliation; this is not to be called ignorance, but nescience, or non-knowledge. *Secret things belong unto the Lord our God, but those things which are revealed belong unto us and to our children for ever*, Deut. xxix. 29. The former we should not curiously search into, as not belonging to us, nor should we exercise ourselves in things too high for us, and which are out of our reach, nor should we seek to be wise above what is written; the latter we should study the knowledge of, and to improve therein, even the knowledge of the several truths and doctrines of the gospel, so as to try and know the things that differ, and to approve the more excellent; and also of the will of God, or duties of religion, which are to be observed, that so we may walk worthy of God in all well-pleasing. The next thing to be considered is,

2*dly*, The causes of this knowledge, and from whence it springs. It is not to be attained to by the light of nature, or what light the works of nature give; for it may be said of this knowledge what Job says of wisdom and understanding, when he asks, *Where shall wisdom be found? and Where is the place of understanding?* to which he answers, it is not known by man, nor is it here nor there, nor can any estimation be made of it, only *God understandeth the way thereof, and he knoweth the place thereof;* what place it is to be found in, and in what way, and from whence it cometh, Job xxviii. 12, 23. Nor is it to be found in the law of Moses; by that God may be known to be holy, just and righteous, but not as a God gracious and merciful; by it is the knowledge of sin, but not the knowledge of Christ as a Saviour from sin; by it may be known what is the will of God with respect to what should be done and what should be avoided, but no knowledge does it give of the Spirit of God to help in the performance of duty, or in the exercise of grace. Nor is it to be acquired by carnal reason; the deep things of God, the mysteries of his grace, are what the carnal eye of man has not seen, nor his ear heard, nor has it entered into his heart to conceive of. When Peter made that excellent confession of the Deity, Sonship, and Messiahship of Christ, our Lord said unto him, *Blessed art thou, Simon Bar-jona, flesh and blood hath not revealed it unto thee;* not carnal reason, nor carnal men, *but my Father which is in heaven*, Matt. xvi. 17. This is not to be had from men; the knowledge the apostle Paul had of the mystery of God, and of the Father, and of Christ, and of the glorious doctrines of the gospel, he had them not at the feet of Gamaliel, nor from his mouth, but by the revelation of Jesus Christ, Gal. i. 11, 12.——1. The efficient cause of this knowledge is God; it is God that teacheth men knowledge, and none teaches like him; and this he teaches persons the most unlikely to learn, even such as *are weaned from the milk, and drawn from the breast;* that is, just weaned, who were but the other day babes and sucklings; this knowledge is from God, Father, Son and Spirit. Such as have *heard and learned of the Father, come to Christ;* that is believe on him, John vi. 45. It is the Father who knows the Son, and reveals him, as he did to Peter, and who reveals the things he hides from the wise and prudent, even unto babes; and *no man knows the Father save the Son, and he to whom the Son will reveal him*, Matt. xi. 27. he who lay in his bosom declares him, his mind and will, his love and grace; and he *gives an understanding* to *know* himself, who *is the true God and eternal life*, 1 John v. 20. and the Spirit, he is the Spirit of wisdom and revelation in the knowledge of God and Christ; he searches the deep things of God, and reveals them to men; and by him they know the things that are freely given them of God, Eph. i. 17. 1 Cor. ii. 10—12.——2. The impulsive cause is the sovereign will and pleasure of God. *Even so, Father, for so it seemed good in thy sight*, Matt. xi. 25, 26. it being solely owing to his good will and pleasure to make known to whom he would make known, the mysteries of his grace and gospel concerning himself, his Son and Spirit; see Col. i. 27.——3. The instrumental cause or means, is the word of God. *Faith*, which sometimes goes by the name of knowledge, *comes by hearing, and hearing by the word of God*, Rom. x. 17. that is, by the external ministration of the word, the Lord owning and blessing it. John the Baptist, the forerunner of Christ, was appointed, commissioned, and sent of God *to give knowledge of salvation to his people;* and the apostles and ministers of the gospel had the treasures of evangelical truths put into their earthen vessels, *to give the light of the knowledge of God in the face of Jesus Christ.* The ministry of the word is appointed as a standing ordinance in the church, *till we all come in the unity of the faith, and of the knowledge of the Son of God,* Luke i. 17. 2 Cor. iv. 6. Eph. iv. 13.

3dly, The nature and properties of this knowledge deserve notice. And,——1. This knowledge is practical; the mere theory of any science, unless reduced to practice, is of little avail; men may have all knowledge that is notional and speculative, and yet be nothing; a profession to know God and Christ, and in works to deny them, is far from being saving knowledge; such who walk as other Gentiles do, have not truly learned Christ; the gospel of the grace of God, when it comes with power, teaches men to deny ungodliness, and to live a sober, righteous, and godly conversation. ——2. It is of a soul-humbling nature; as the instances of Job, Isaiah, and the apostle Paul shew, Job xlii. 6. Isa. vi. 5. Eph. iii. 8. whereas other knowledge puffs up, makes men conceited, proud, haughty, and overbearing.——3. It is pleasant, savoury, and satisfying; *he that increaseth natural knowledge, increaseth sorrow,* Eccl. i. 18. for the more he knows, he finds he knows less than he thought he did; and this gives him pain, that his knowledge is so small; and his larger knowledge attracts the envy of others, and raises an opposition to him; but spiritual knowledge, and an increase of that, yields him joy, peace, and comfort: we read of the *savour of the knowledge* of Christ, and of the savour of his good ointment; and of his name being as ointment poured forth, which emits a most fragrant and delightful smell, 2 Cor. ii. 14. Cant. i. 3.——4. This knowledge is excellent, yea super-excellent; the apostle *Paul counted all things but loss for the excellency* of it, Phil. iii. 8. it is to be preferred to gold and silver, to jewels and precious stones, and all desirable things, Prov. iii. 13, 14. and viii. 10, 11. it far excels all other kind of knowledge. What if a man had knowledge of all the heavenly bodies, and of whatsoever is in the bowels of the earth, or dwells upon it, or grows out of it, so that he could with Solomon speak of trees and their nature, from the cedar in Lebanon to the hyssop that grows out of the wall; it would be nothing in comparison of the knowledge of Christ, and of God in Christ, since to know them is life eternal.——5. This knowledge indeed is but imperfect in this life; those that know most, only *know in part,* yet it is progressive; there is such a thing as growing in grace, and in the knowledge of Christ; the light of saints is an increasing one, the path of the just is as the shining light, which shines more and more unto the perfect day; they that know the Lord shall follow on to know him, and shall know more of him, for so the words in Hosea vi. 3. should be rendered; *and we shall know, we shall follow on to know the Lord,* the *if* ought to be left out, not being in the original.——6. There are various means which should be made use of for the increase of this knowledge, such as reading the scriptures, which are profitable for doctrine, and for instruction in righteousness; constantly and diligently searching into them, since they testify of Christ, of his person, and office, and grace; likewise attendance upon the ministry of the word, waiting at wisdom's gates, and watching at the posts of her door, which is the way to find wisdom and get understanding; also frequent and fervent prayer, *if thou criest after knowledge,* thou shalt *find the knowledge of God,* Prov. ii. 3, 5. great is the encouragement given to make use of such a method; see James i. 5. Matt. vii. 6. Conversation with wise and good men, and such as fear the Lord, who by conferring together find the advantage of it; they build up one another on their most holy faith, establish each other in it, and increase in knowledge; for *he that walked with wise men shall be wise,* grow wiser and wiser, Prov. xiii. 20.

CHAP. IV.

OF REPENTANCE TOWARDS GOD.

REPENTANCE is another part of internal worship; it is a branch of godliness which lies in the disposition of the soul Godwards; for in the exercise of this the sensible sinner has much to do with God; he has a special respect to him against whom he has sinned, and therefore it is with great propriety called *Repentance towards God,* Acts xx. 21. Concerning which may be observed,

I. Its name, and the words and phrases by which it is expressed, both in the Old and in the New Testament, and by Jews, Greeks, and Latins, which may give some light into the thing itself.

1st, The Jews commonly express it by תשובה a *turning*, or *returning*, and it is frequently signified in the Old Testament by a man's turning from his evil ways, and returning to the Lord; the term from which he turns is sin, the term to which he turns is the Lord, against whom he has sinned; and what most powerfully moves, encourages, and induces him to turn, is the pardoning grace and mercy of God through Christ, Isa. lv. 7. and so in the New Testament, repentance and turning are mentioned together, and the latter as explanative of the former; see Acts iii. 19. and xxvi. 20.

There is another word in Hebrew used for repentance, נחם Hosea xi. 8. and xiii. 14. which also signifies *comfort;* because such who sincerely repent of sin, and are truly humbled for it, should be comforted, lest, as the apostle says, they should be *swallowed up with overmuch sorrow,* 2 Cor. ii. 7. and it is God's usual way to bring his people *into the wilderness,* into a distressed state, to lead them into a sense of sin, and humiliation for it, and then to speak comfortably to them, Hos. ii. 14. and the Spirit of God is first a reprover for sin, and a convincer of it, and then a comforter; he first shews men the evil nature of sin, and the just desert of it, and gives them the grace of repentance for it, and then comforts them with the application of pardon through the blood of Jesus, John xvi. 7, 8, 14. and blessed are they that mourn for sin in an evangelical manner, for they shall be comforted, Matt. v. 4.

2dly, The Greek word more frequently used in the New Testament for repentance is μετανοια, which signifies an *after-understanding,* or *after-wit;* as when a man takes into serious consideration a fact after it is committed, and thinks otherwise of it, and wishes he had not done it, is sorry for it, and resolves, through the grace of God, to forsake such practices; this is a proof of a man's wisdom and understanding; now he begins to be wise, and to shew himself an understanding man; even an heathen[1] could say, "Repentance is the beginning of wisdom, and an avoiding of foolish works and words, and the first preparation to a life not to be repented of." It is a change of the mind for the better, and which produces change of action and conduct: this, as it is expressive of true repentance, flows from the understanding being enlightened by the Spirit of God, when the sinner beholds sin in another light it did, even as exceeding sinful; and loaths it, and abhors it and himself for it. There is another word the Greeks use for repentance, μεταμελεια, and though the noun is not used in the New Testament, the verb is, Matt. xxi. 29, 32. and signifies a care and anxiety of mind after a fact is committed, a concern with sorrow that it should be done, and a care for the future not to do it again; hence the apostle, among the genuine fruits of godly sorrow for sin, mentions this in the first place, *What carefulness it wrought in you,* not to offend more, 2 Cor. vii. 11. It also signifies a change of mind and conduct, as appears from Matt. xxi. 29. a penitent sinner has another notion of sin than he had; before it was a sweet morsel, now a bitter and evil thing; before his heart was bent upon it, now determined through divine grace to forsake it and cleave to the Lord with full purpose of heart.

3dly, The Latins generally express repentance by *pœnitentia,* from *pœna* punishment; hence our English word *penitence,* and the popish *penance,* which is a sort of corporal punishment for sin inflicted on the body by fastings, scourgings, pilgrimages, &c. but true penitence lies not in these things, but is rather an inward punishment of the mind, when a man is so displeased with himself for what he has done, and so severely reflects upon himself for it, that he takes as it were a kind of vengeance on himself within himself, which are the lashes of conscience;[2] so the apostle observes of godly sorrow, *What indignation, yea what revenge* it wrought in you, as in the above quoted place; and this inward revenge is sometimes expressed by outward gestures, as by smiting upon the thigh, and upon the breast, Jer. xxxi. 19. Luke xviii. 13.

There is another word which the Latins use for repentance, *resipiscentia,* which signifies a man's being wise again, a coming to his wits, to his senses again.[3] Lactantius[4] explains it of the recovery of a

---

[1] Η μετανοια αυτη φιλοσοφιας αρχη γινεται, &c. Hierocles in Carmin. Pythagor. p. 166.
[2] Ultrices Curæ, Virgil. Æneid. 6.
[3] Cæteri autem resipiscere, id est, ad priorem mentis statum. vel ad meliorem mentem redire solent, Vallæ Elegantiar. 1. 5. c, 3.
[4] Institut. 1. 6. c. 24.

man's mind from a state of insanity; a man, whilst he is in an unconverted and impenitent state, is not himself, he is not in his right mind; not only his foolish heart is darkened, and he is without understanding, and to do good has no knowledge, but *madness* is *in his heart while* he *lives* in such a state; every act of sin is not only folly but madness, as all acts of hostility committed against God, which sins are, must needs be; the man that dwelt among the tombs, Mark v. is a fit emblem of such persons: now when an impenitent sinner becomes penitent, he may be said to *come to himself*, as the prodigal did, Luke xv. 17. so the apostle Paul before conversion was exceeding mad against the saints, and thought he ought to do many things contrary to the name of Jesus; but when he was converted he was recovered from his insanity, and appeared sober and in his right mind, and said, *Lord, what wilt thou have me to do?* when a sinner is truly convinced of sin, and thoroughly humbled for it, and has repentance unto life given him, and a comfortable application of the blood and righteousness of Christ unto him for his pardon and justification, and his mind is become sedate, serene and quiet, the man who before was mad, is an emblem of him, when he was seen *sitting clothed and in his right mind*, Mark v. 15.

4*thly*, The word *contrition*, or brokenness of mind, is sometimes used for repentance, and there is some foundation for it in the word of God; we often read of a contrite heart and spirit; David says he was *feeble and sore broken*, Psalm xxxviii. 8. which seems to be under a sense of sin: a man's heart is naturally hard, as hard as the nether millstone, and therefore called a *stony heart*, and such an one is an impenitent one; hence *hardness*, and an *impenitent heart*, are put together, as designing the same thing, Rom. ii. 5. The word of God is made use of to break it in pieces, is *not my word—like a hammer to break the rock in pieces?* that is, to make the heart contrite, which is like to a rock, and whereby it becomes soft and tender, as Josiah's was, like an heart of flesh, susceptible of serious impressions, and of a true sense of things; and though this contrition of heart seems to be a work of the law, by which is the knowledge of sin, and which works wrath in the conscience on account of it, smites and cuts and wounds it; yet hereby it is prepared to receive the benefit of the gospel, by which the Lord *heals the broken in heart, and bindeth up their wounds*, Psalm cxlvii. 3. Isa. lxi. 1. However, great notice is taken of men of contrite hearts and spirits; the sacrifices of such hearts are acceptable to God; he looks unto, is nigh unto, and dwells with those who are of such a spirit and saves them, Psalm li. 17. and xxxiv. 18. Isa. lvii. 15. and lxvi. 2. besides the heart may be broken, made soft and melted down as much or more under a sense of pardoning grace displayed in the gospel, than under a sense of wrath through the threatenings and terrors of the law.

5*thly*, Repentance is expressed by sorrow for sin. *My sorrow is continually before me*, says David, *I will be sorry for my sin*, Psalm xxxviii. 17, 18. and which is signified not by outward gestures, not by rending garments, but by rending the heart, Joel ii. 13. it is a felt pain and inward sorrow of the heart for sin, and what the apostle calls a sorrow *after a godly sort*, κατα Θεον, *after God*, which is according to the mind and will of God; and because of sin committed against God; a God of love, grace, and mercy, and which springs from love to God and hatred of sin, and is attended with faith in God, as a God pardoning iniquity, transgression, and sin, for Christ's sake; but of this more hereafter.

II. The nature and kinds of repentance. Not to take notice of the penance of the Papists, which lies in punishing their bodies, as before observed; and in men making themselves, or in others making them, public examples in such a way; which though it may be called repentance before men, it is not repentance towards God, nor does it answer the end vainly intended by it, making satisfaction for sin; nor is an external reformation of life and manners, repentance in the sight of God. Men may be outwardly reformed, as the Pharisees were, and yet not repent of their sins, as they did not, Matt. xxi. 32. and xxiii. 28. and after such an external reformation, men may return to their former sinful course of life, and their last end be worse than the beginning; besides, there may be true repentance for sin where there is no time and opportunity for reformation, or shewing forth a reformation of life and manners, as in the thief upon the cross and others, who are brought to repentance on their death-beds; and reformation of life and manners, when it is best and most genuine, is the fruit and effect of repentance, and a bringing forth fruits meet for it, as evidences of it, and so distinct from that itself.

1st, There is a natural repentance, or what is directed to by the light of nature, and the dictates of a natural conscience; for as there was in the heathens, and so is in every natural man, a knowledge of good and evil, of the difference in some respects between moral good and evil, and a conscience which, when it does its office, approves of what is well done, and accuses for that which is ill; so when conscience charges a man with doing an ill thing, and he is convinced of it, the light of nature and conscience direct him to wish he had not done it, and to repent of it, and to endeavour for the future to avoid it; as may be seen in the case of the Ninevites, who being threatened with the destruction of their city for their sins, proclaimed a fast, and issued out an order that every one should turn from his evil ways, in hope that the wrath of God would be averted from them, though they could not be fully assured of it. The Gentiles laid great stress upon their repentance, to conciliate the favour of God unto them; for they thought this made complete satisfaction for their sins, and wiped them clean, so that they imagined they were almost if not altogether pure and innocent:[5] there is a repentance which the goodness of God in providence might or should lead men unto, which yet it does not, but after their hardness and impenitent heart, treasure up wrath against the day of wrath, and righteous judgment of God, Rom. ii. 4, 5.

2dly, There is a national repentance, such as the Jews in Babylon were called unto, to which temporal blessings were promised, and a deliverance from temporal calamities; as on the one hand, a living in their own land, and a comfortable enjoyment of good things in it; and on the other hand, captivity, and all the distresses of it threatened; *Repent, and turn yourselves from your transgressions, so iniquity shall not be your ruin*, Ezek. xviii. 30—32. and which has no connection with the special grace of God, and with spiritual and everlasting things. The same people were called to repent of their pharisaism, of their disbelief of the Messiah, and other evil works; and were told that the men of Nineveh would rise up in judgment and condemn them, who repented at the preaching of Jonah, and yet a greater than Jonah, even Christ himself, called them to repentance, Matt. xii. 41. The same people were called upon by the apostles of Christ to repent of their rejection of Jesus as the Messiah, and to turn unto him, and to save themselves from temporal ruin, which for their impenitence and unbelief came upon their nation, city, and temple, Acts iii. 19.

3dly, There is an external repentance, or an outward humiliation for sin, such as was in Ahab, which, though nothing more, it was taken notice of by the Lord, *Seest thou how Ahab humbleth himself before me?* and though it lay only in rending his clothes, and putting on sackcloth, and in fasting, and in a mournful way, yet the Lord was pleased to promise that the evil threatened should not come in his days, 1 Kings, xxi. 29. And such is the repentance Tyre and Sidon would have exercised, had they had the advantages and privileges that some cities had, where Christ taught his doctrines, and wrought miracles; and of this kind was the repentance of the Ninevites which was regarded of God, Matt. xi. 21. and xii. 41.

4thly, There is an hypocritical repentance, such as was in the people of Israel in the wilderness, who when the wrath of God broke out against them for their sins, *returned* unto him or repented, but *their heart was not right with him*, Psalm lxxviii. 34—37. so it is said of Judah, she *hath not turned unto me with her whole heart, but feignedly, saith the Lord;* and of Ephraim, or the ten tribes, *they return, but not to the Most High, they are like a deceitful bow,* Hos. vii. 16. who turned aside and dealt unfaithfully.

5thly, There is a legal and there is an evangelical repentance.——1. There is a legal one, which is a mere work of the law, and the effect of convictions of sin by it, which in time wear off and come to nothing; for,—(1) There may be a sense of sin and an acknowledgment of it, and yet no true repentance for it, as in the cases of Pharaoh and of Judas, who both said, *I have sinned,* Exod. ix. 27. Matt. xxvii. 4. yet they had no true sense of the exceeding sinfulness of sin, nor godly sorrow for it.—(2.) There may be a kind of sorrow for it, not for the evil of fault that is in sin, but on account of the evil of punishment for it, as appears in some cases, and in

---

[5] Quem pœnitet peccasse pene est innocens, Senecæ Agamemnon, act 2. v. 241. Another heathen calls repentance, Omnium fortunatissimum factum, the most happy deed of all, Terent. Heautont. act 4. sc. 7. v. 1.

Cain's, Gen. iv. 13.—(3.) There may be a great deal of terror of mind because of sin, a great outcry about it, a fearful looking for of judgment for it, abundance of tears shed on the account of it, as were by Esau for the blessing, without success; the devils believe and tremble, but do not repent;[6] there is weeping and wailing in hell, but no repentance.—(4.) Such a repentance, if no more than a mere legal one, issues in despair, as in Cain, whose words may be rendered, *My sin is greater than that it may be forgiven;* it is a repentance that may be repented of and is not unto life, but ends in death, as it did in Judas; it is *the sorrow of the world* which *worketh death*, 2 Cor. vii. 10.

2. There is an evangelical repentance, which lies,—(1.) In a true sight and sense of sin; in a sight of it, as in itself considered as exceeding sinful in its own nature, and not merely as in its effects and consequences ruinous and destructive; not only in a sight of it in the glass of the divine law, but as that is held in the hand, and seen in the light of the blessed Spirit; and in a sight of it as contrary to the pure and holy nature of God, as well as repugnant to his will, and a breach of his law; and in a view of it as it appears in the glass of pardoning love and grace.—(2.) In a hearty and unfeigned sorrow for it; this sorrow for it is the rather because it is against God, and that not only as a holy and righteous Being, but as good, and gracious, and merciful, of whose goodness, both in providence and grace, the sinner is sensible; the consideration of which increases his sorrow, and makes it the more intense and hearty.—(3.) It is attended with shame and confusion of face, as in Ezra, chap. ix. 6, 8, 10. Luke xviii. 13. this shame increases the more, the more a sinner is sensible that God is *pacified towards* him *for all that* he *has done*, Ezek. xvi. 63.—(4.) Such a repentance is accompanied with a loathing, detestation, and abhorrence of sin as the worst of evils; to truly penitent sinners, sin appears most odious and loathsome; nay they not only loathe their sins but themselves for them; and the rather when most sensible of the goodness of God in bestowing both temporal and spiritual blessings on them, and especially the latter, Ezek. xx. 40—44. and xxxvi. 25—31. yea they abhor it as of all things the most detestable, when they are in the exercise of this grace; so it was with holy Job, when favoured with a special sight of the greatness and goodness of God, Job xlii. 6. see also Isa. vi. 5.—(5.) Where this repentance is, there is an ingenuous acknowledgment of sin, as may be seen in David, Psalm xxxii. 5. and li. 3. in Daniel, chap. ix. 4, 5. and in the apostle Paul, 1 Tim. i. 13—15. so the prodigal, as soon as he came to himself, and was made sensible of his sin, and repented of it, went to his father, and said to him, *Father, I have sinned against heaven and in thy sight,* Luke xv. 21. and to encourage such a sincere repentance, ingenuous confession, the apostle John says, *If we confess our sins, he is faithful and just to forgive us our sins, and to cleanse us from all unrighteousness,* 1 John i. 9.—(6.) It is followed with a resolution, through the grace of God, to forsake sin; this the sinner is encouraged unto, as before observed, by the abundance of pardon through the mercy of God in Christ, Isa. lv. 7. and indeed it is only such who can expect to share in it; *Whoso confesseth* (sins) *and forsaketh them, shall have mercy,* Prov. xxviii. 13. Now such a repentance appears to be evangelical; inasmuch, as ——1. It is from the Spirit of God, who reproves for sin and convinces of it, enlightens the eyes of the understanding to see the exceeding sinfulness of sin; and as a Spirit of grace and supplication, works this grace in the heart, and draws it forth into exercise, to mourn over sin in a gospel manner at the throne of grace, Zech. xii. 10.——2. Such repentance, in the exercise of it, follows upon real conversion and divine instruction, *Surely after that I was turned I repented, and after that I was instructed, I smote upon my thigh,* Jer. xxxi. 19. upon such a turn as is made by powerful and efficacious grace, and upon such instruction as leads into the true nature of sin, the effect of which is blushing, shame, and confusion.——3. Is what is encouraged and influenced by gospel promises, such as those in Isa. lv. 7. Jer. iii. 12, 13. now when repentance proceeds not upon the terrors of the law, but upon such gracious promises as these, it may be called

---

[6] Clemens of Alexandria, Stromat. l. 1. p. 310, had a notion that the devil being possessed of free-will might be brought to repentance, which perhaps gave rise to the sentiment of Origen concerning the salvation of devils; but, according to Luther, free-will is the greatest enemy to righteousness, and to the salvation of men; and if so, then certainly to the salvation of devils, and can be no friend nor of any service to them. Luther de serv. Arbitr. c. 211.

evangelical.——4. It is that which is attended with faith and hope: repentance towards God, and faith in our Lord Jesus Christ, go together as doctrines, and so they do as graces; which is first in exercise is not easy to say; our Lord says of the Pharisees, that they *repented not, that they might believe*, which looks as if repentance was before and in order to believing, Matt. xxi. 32. and elsewhere faith is represented as first looking to Christ, and then repentance or mourning for sin; repentance, as some have expressed it, is a tear that drops from faith's eye, Zech. xii. 10. However, that is truly evangelical repentance which has with it faith in the blood of Christ for the remission of sins; for repentance and remission of sins, as they go together as doctrines, so also as blessings of grace, Luke xxiv. 47. Acts v. 31. for where true repentance for sin is, there must be faith in Christ for the remission of it, at least hope of pardon by his blood, or else such repentance would issue in despair, and appear to be no other than the sorrow of the world which worketh death.——5. It is such a repentance which flows not from dread of punishment, and from fear of the wrath of God, but from love to God, and of righteousness and holiness, and from an hatred of sin; they that love the Lord hate evil, and they love righteousness and hate evil because he does; and when tempted to sin, reason after this manner, *How can I do this great wickedness, and sin against God*, so holy just, and good, and who has shewn such love and kindness to me? Gen. xxxix. 9. It was love to Christ, flowing from a sense of pardoning grace and mercy, that fetched such a flood of tears from the eyes of the penitent woman at Christ's feet, with which she washed them, and wiped them with the hairs of her head; and which caused Peter, under a sense of sin, to go out and weep bitterly, Luke vii. 37, 38, 47. and xxii. 61, 62.

III. The object and subjects of repentance; the object is sin, the subjects are sinners.

First, The object of repentance is sin, hence called *repentance from dead works*, which sins be; and from which the blood of Christ purges the conscience of a penitent sinner, and speaks peace and pardon to it, Heb. vi. 2. and ix. 14. And,—— 1*st*, Not only grosser sins, but sins of a lesser size, are to be repented of; there is a difference in sins, some are greater, others lesser, John xix. 11. both are to be repented of; sins against the first and second tables of the law, sins more immediately against God, and sins against men; and some against men are more heinous and enormous than others, as well as those against God; as not only worshipping of devils, and idols of gold and silver, &c. but murders, sorceries, fornications, and thefts, which ought to be repented of, but by some were not, though they had deliverances from plagues, which was an aggravation of their impenitence, Rev. ix. 20, 21. and not only those, but also sins of a lesser kind are to be repented of; and even sinful thoughts, for the thought of foolishness is sin, and to be repented of; for the unrighteous man is to repent of, and forsake his thoughts, as well as the wicked man his ways, and turn to the Lord; and not only unclean, proud, malicious, envious, and revengeful thoughts are to be repented of, but even thoughts of seeking for justification before God by a man's own righteousness, which may be intended in the text referred to, Isaiah lv. 7.——2*dly*, Not only public but private sins are to be repented of. There are some sins which are committed in a very public manner, in the face of the sun, and are known to all; and there are others that are more secret; and a truly sensible sinner, as he desires to be *cleansed from secret faults*, or to have those forgiven him, so he heartily repents of them, even of sins known to none but God and his own soul; and this is a proof of the genuineness of his repentance.——3*dly*, There are sins both of omission and commission, which are to be repented of; when a man omits those duties of religion which ought to be done, or commits those sins which ought to be avoided by him; or omits the weightier matters of religion, and only attends to lesser ones, when he ought to have done the one, and not to have left the other undone; and as God forgives both, Isa. xliii. 22—25. so both sorts of sins are to be repented of; and a sense of pardoning grace will engage the sensible sinner to it. ——4*thly*, There are sins which are committed in the most solemn, serious, religious, and holy performances of God's people, which are to be repented of; for there is not a just man that does good and sinneth not in that good he does; there is not only an imperfection, but an impurity in the best righteousness of the saints of their own working out, and therefore called filthy rags; and as there was provision made under the law for the bearing and removing the sins of holy things, as by Aaron the high-priest, so there is a provision made for the atonement of these as well as all other sins, by Christ our high-priest; and therefore these are to be confessed and mourned over the head of him our antitypical scape-goat.——5*thly*, The daily sins of life, are to be repented of; no man lives without sin, it is daily committed by the best of men, in many things we all offend, and even in all things; and as we have need to pray, and are directed to pray daily for the forgiveness of sin, so we are to repent of it daily; repentance is not only to be exercised upon the first conviction and conversion of a sinner, nor only on account of some grievous sin, or great backsliding he may after fall into, but it is continually to be exercised by believers, since they are continually sinning against God in thought, word, and deed.——6*thly*, Not only actual sins and transgressions in thought, word, and deed, are to be repented of, but original and indwelling sin. Thus David, when he fell into some grievous sins, and was brought to a true sense of them, and a sincere repentance for them, he not only made a confession of them, in the penitential psalm he wrote on that occasion, but he was led to take notice of, and acknowledge and mourn over the original corruption of his nature, from whence all his sinful actions flowed, saying, *Behold I was shapen in iniquity*, Psalm li. 5. So the apostle Paul, though he lived a life unstained, and in all good conscience, free from any public, external, notorious sin, yet owned and lamented the sin that dwelt in him, and the force, power, and prevalence of it, as that it hindered him from doing the good he would, and put him on doing the evil he would not, Rom. vii. 18—24. Now when a sensible sinner confesses, laments, and mourns over the original corruption of his nature, and the sin that dwells in him, it is a clear case his repentance is genuine and sincere, since it is what he himself is only sensible of. Now all this is with respect to God; the sinner repents of sin with regard to God, and as it concerns him, and therefore is called *repentance towards God*, and a sorrow for it *after a godly sort*, Acts xx. 21. 2 Cor. vii. 11. and he repents of sin because sin is committed against him.——1. All sin is against God in a sense, as it is against his will, yet there is a distinction between sins against God and against men, 1 Sam. ii. 25. now sin committed against God, and considered as such, is a cutting consideration to a sensible sinner, sensible of the greatness and goodness of God, and causes his sorrow and repentance for sin to rise higher, as it was to David, *Against thee, thee only have I sinned, and done this evil in thy sight*, Psalm li. 4.——2. Because sin is a breach of the law of God, 1 John iii. 4. of that law, which is itself, holy, just, and good; of that law of which God is the giver, and who is that lawgiver that is able to save and to destroy, and on whose legislative power and authority a contempt is cast by sin, and which therefore gives pain and distress of mind to the penitent sinner.——3. Because sin is contrary to the nature of God, as well as to his law; he is of purer eyes than to behold it with approbation; he is not a God that takes pleasure in it, but is displeased with it; it is the abominable thing his righteous soul hates, and therefore they that love the Lord must hate it, and it cannot but give them a concern, and cause sorrow when they commit it.——4. And the rather as by sinning, a slight is cast on his goodness, grace, and love, and which occasions severe reflections on themselves, and much shame and blushing that they should sin against so much goodness, and against God, who has shewn them so much favour, loved them so greatly, and bestowed such blessings of grace upon them.——5. It appears that the sinner, in repentance, has to do with God, by confessing his sin and his sorrow for it; and also others glorify God for granting repentance to him, as the Christian Jews did on the behalf of the Gentiles, Acts xi. 18. and even there is joy in heaven, and God is glorified by the angels there, on account even of one sinner that repents, Luke xv. 7, 10.

Secondly, The subjects of repentance are sinners, and only such. Adam, in a state of innocence, was not a subject of repentance, for not having sinned, he had no sin to repent of; and such who fancy themselves to be perfectly righteous, and without sin in their own apprehensions, stand in no need of repentance, and therefore Christ says, *I am not come to call the righteous, but sinners to repentance*, Matt. ix. 13. see Luke xv. 7. Now,——1. All men are sinners, all descending from Adam by ordinary generation; all his posterity being seminally in him, and represented by him when he sinned, sinned in him, and they both have his sin imputed to them, and a corrupt nature derived from him; and so are transgressors from the womb, and are all guilty of actual sins and transgressions; and so all stand in need of repentance, even such who trust in themselves that they are righteous, and despise others as less holy than themselves, and think they need no repentance: yet they do; and not only they, but such who are in the best sense righteous, need daily repentance, since they are continually sinning in all they do.——2. Men of all nations, Jews and Gentiles, are the subjects of repentance; for all are under sin, under the power of it, involved in the guilt of it, and liable to punishment for it, and God has commanded *all men everywhere to repent*, Acts xvii. 30. During the time of John the Baptist, and of our Lord's being on earth, the doctrine of repentance was only preached to the Jews; but after the resurrection of Christ, he gave his apostles an instruction and order *that repentance and remission of sins should be preached in his name among all nations, beginning at Jerusalem*, Luke xxiv. 47. in consequence of which, the apostles first exhorted the Jews and then the Gentiles to repent, and particularly the apostle Paul *testified both to the Jews, and also to the Greeks, repentance towards God*, as well as *faith towards our Lord Jesus Christ*, Acts xx. 21.——3. Men are only subjects of repentance in the present life; when this life is ended, and the gospel-dispensation is over, and Christ is come a second time, the door of repentance as well as of faith will be shut, and there will be no place found for it; no opportunity nor means of it; nor any subjects capable of it; as for the saints in heaven, they need it not, being entirely without sin; and as for the wicked in hell, they are in utter despair, and not capable of repentance unto life, and unto salvation not to be repented of; and though there is weeping and wailing there, yet no repentance. Hence the rich man in hell was so solicitous to have Lazarus sent to his brethren living, hoping, that by means of one that came to them from the dead to warn them of the place of torment, they would repent, as well knowing they never would if not in the present life, and before they came into the place where he was; and therefore repentance is not to be procrastinated.

IV. The Author, and cause, and means of repentance.——1. The Author and efficient cause of it, is not man himself, but God; *then hath God also granted repentance to the Gentiles*, Acts xi. 18. it is not in the power of man to repent of himself, for he is by nature blind, and has no sight and sense of sin; his understanding is darkened with respect unto it, and he is darkness itself till made light in the Lord; and until he has a sight and sense of sin, he can never truly repent of it; his heart is hard and obdurate, his heart is an heart of stone, and he cannot really repent of sin until that stony heart is taken away, and an heart of flesh is given; and whenever he becomes sensible of his need of repentance, he prays to God for it, saying, *Turn thou me, and I shall be turned*. Nor do exhortations to repentance suppose it in the power of man to repent of himself; since these are only designed to bring him to a sense of his need of it, and of his obligation to it, and of his impotence to it of himself, through the hardness of his heart, and to direct him to seek it of God, who only can give it; for,——2. Though God may give men space to repent, yet if he does not give the grace of repentance, they never will repent. Thus he gave space to the old world, threatened with a flood, which some think is meant by the one hundred and twenty years allowed them, when the long-suffering of God waited in the times of Noah, while the ark was preparing, but without effect; so Jezebel, or Antichrist, is said to have *space* given her *to repent of her fornication, and she repented not*, Rev. ii. 21. and this, God sometimes gives to the children of men to shew his sovereignty, that he will have mercy on whom he will have mercy, and give repentance to whom he pleases; and for the sake of his elect, not willing that any of them should perish, but that they should all come to repentance, and therefore his long-suffering towards them is salvation; and this also he sometimes gives to shew his forbearance of the vessels of wrath, and to leave them inexcusable. Nay,——3. Though some men may have the means of repentance, yet grace not being given them of God they repent not; the word, unless attended with power, is ineffectual; the most severe judgments inflicted on men are insufficient, as the plagues on Pharaoh, whose heart was the worse and more hardened under them, Exod. xi. 10. and though the children of Israel were smitten with famine, with the pestilence, and with the sword, yet they repented not, nor returned unto the Lord, Amos iv. 6—11. so the fourth

and fifth vials poured forth on men, which will scorch and fill them with pains and sores, instead of repenting of their deeds they will blaspheme the God of heaven and his name, Rev. xvi. 8—11. And on the other hand, the greatest instances of mercy and goodness to men, and singular deliverances wrought for them, which should, and one would think would, lead men to repentance, and yet they do not, Rom. ii. 4, 5. Rev. ix. 20, 21. yea the most powerful and awakening ministry that a man can sit under, has no influence on the minds of men to bring them to repentance, without the power and grace of God, such as was the ministry of John the Baptist, who was the voice of one crying in the wilderness, preaching in a loud, vehement and powerful manner, the baptism of repentance; and yet though some publicans and harlots believed, the Pharisees repented not afterwards that they might believe, Matt. xxi. 32. our Lord spake as one having authority, yet few believed; and many cities where he preached, and mighty works were done by him, yet repented not; and if one was to rise from the dead, and describe all the happiness of the blissful state of the saints in heaven he was capable of, or paint all the horrors of the damned in hell, it would have no effect, neither to allure nor frighten to repentance, or bring men to it, without the exertion of powerful and efficacious grace, Luke xvi. 31.——4. The sole efficient cause and author of repentance is God, Father, Son, and Spirit. God the Father, *if God peradventure will give them repentance,* 2 Tim. ii. 25. Christ, the Son of God, as mediator, is exalted *to give repentance unto Israel, and forgiveness of sins,* Acts v. 31. and the Spirit of God reproves for sin, convinces of it, and works repentance for it, John xvi. 8.——5. The moving cause of it is the free grace of God; it is a grant and favour from him, a gift of Christ, which he, as a prince and a saviour bestows, Acts xi. 18. and v. 31. and an operation of the power and grace of the Spirit of God, and entirely flows from the sovereign will and mercy of God, *who hath mercy on whom he will have mercy, and whom he will he hardeneth,* Rom. ix. 18. not giving grace to repent.——
6. The usual means and instruments of repentance are the word, and the ministers of it; as faith, so repentance, comes by hearing the word; the three thousand were pricked in the heart, and were brought to repentance, through the ministry of the apostle Peter; and as all the apostles were ordered by Christ to preach repentance in his name among all nations, so they went forth everywhere, and God in and by their ministry, commanded all men everywhere to repent; and when and where the command was attended with power it produced the effect; and so the apostle Paul declared to Jews and Gentiles, that *they should repent and turn to God, and do works meet for repentance;* and the hand of the Lord being with him, great numbers everywhere believed and turned to the Lord, Luke xxiv. 47. Acts xvii. 30. and xxvi. 20.

V. The effects and consequences of repentance; such effects as are evidences of it, and shew it to be genuine; and such consequences which are salutary, and shew the blessings of grace are connected with it.

1st, The effects of it, which prove it to be genuine; such as the apostle mentions as fruits of godly sorrow, 2 Cor. vii. 11.——1. *Carefulness* to exercise repentance in a proper way, and to bring forth fruits meet for it; carefulness not to sin any more in a like manner, or to live a sinful course of live, but to abstain from all appearance of evil; and carefulness not to offend God again, who had been so good and gracious to them.——2. *Clearing of themselves;* not by denying the fact, as Gehazi, nor by extenuating and palliating it as Adam, but by an ingenuous confession of it, praying it might be forgiven, and that they might be cleansed from all sin by the blood of Jesus; so clearing themselves from the charges of hardness of heart, impenitence, and ingratitude, and of neglect of repentance when sin was discovered to them.——3. *Indignation;* against sin, expressing their abhorrence of it, and of themselves for it, as Job did, saying, what have we to do with it for the future? being filled with a loathing of it, and with shame and confusion for it; see Hosea xiv. 8.——4. *Fear;* not of the punishment of sin, of the wrath of God, and of hell and damnation, which is the fruit of legal and not evangelical repentance; but a fear of offending God, and of his grace and goodness in forgiving their sins, and of him for his goodness sake, Hosea iii. 5.——5. *Vehement desire;* to be kept from sin, that they may not dishonour God, grieve their own souls, offend and stumble God's people, and bring reproach on his ways, doctrines and ordinances; and that they might be indulged with nearness to God, communion with him, and fresh discoveries of his love to them.——6. *Zeal;* for God and his glory, for his doctrines and ordinances, for the discipline of his house, and for the performance of all good works.——7. *Revenge;* not on others but on themselves, and on their sinful lusts and corruptions, and on all disobedience, that their obedience might be fulfilled; striving against sin, acting the part of an antagonist to it, resisting even unto blood, not sparing but mortifying the deeds of the body, that they may live a holy life and conversation. But though these things are in a more peculiar manner applicable to the case of the Corinthians, yet they do more or less, and in a great measure appear in every repenting sinner.

2dly, The consequences of repentance, even blessings of grace, which follow upon it, and are connected with it, being promised unto it, and what it issues in; by which it appears to be salutary, and answers some valuable ends, and is of the greatest importance; as,——1. The pardon of sin; for though this is not procured by tears of repentance, by humiliation for sin, and confession of it, but by the blood of Christ only; yet to those who repent of sin sincerely, and are truly humbled for it, a manifestation and application of pardoning grace and mercy is made; and these two, repentance and remission of sins, are joined together in the ministry of the word, to encourage repenting sinners to hope in Christ for the forgiveness of their sin, who as he gives the one gives also the other, Luke xxiv. 47. Acts v. 31. none that ever truly repented of sin and confessed it, but had his sins pardoned; such as forsake their sinful ways and turn to the Lord, he pardons and abundantly pardons; his justice to the blood and sacrifice of his Son, and his truth and faithfulness to his word and promises, leave no room to doubt of it, Isa. lv. 7. 1 John i. 9.——2. True evangelical repentance, which is God's gift, and a grant of his grace, is *repentance unto life,* Acts xi. 18. It is not by repentance indeed by which men live spiritually, that is by faith in Christ; yet men begin to live spiritually when they are quickened by the Spirit of God, and have repentance from dead works given unto them; and though men by repentance do not procure eternal life, that is the free gift of God through Christ, yet true, special, spiritual, and evangelical repentance, issues in eternal life, and is inseparably connected with it; though all impenitent sinners shall certainly perish, who by their hardness and impenitent hearts treasure up wrath against the day of wrath and righteous judgment of God; yet all that come to true repentance, none of them shall ever perish, but shall have everlasting life.——3. Evangelical repentance, the work of godly sorrow, is *repentance to salvation not to be repented of,* 2 Cor. vii. 10. it is not the cause of salvation; Christ is the captain, cause, and author of salvation; but the means through and by which God saves his people; as they are saved *through faith,* so through repentance, and through both as *the gift of God,* flowing from his sovereign grace, Eph. ii. 8. as he *that believes* with the heart unto righteousness, so he that truly repents of sin *shall be saved,* Mark xvi. 16.

CHAP. V.

OF THE FEAR OF GOD.

The fear of God has so great a concern in divine worship, that it is sometimes put for the whole of it; and a worshipper of God is frequently described in scripture by one that fears him; and particularly internal worship, or experimental religion, as distinguished from an external observance of the divine commands, is expressed by it; for, according to the wise man, the whole of religion, experimental and practical religion, lies in these two things, to *fear God and keep his commandments,* Eccl. xii. 13. and as worship itself is expressed by the fear of God, so the manner in which it is to be performed is directed to be in it and with it, for God is to be served *with reverence and godly fear;* see Psalm ii. 11. and v. 7. and lxxxix. 7. Heb. xii. 28. concerning which may be observed,

I. The object of fear, not the creature, but God the Creator. There is a fear due to men, *fear to whom fear;* that is, it should be rendered to whom it is due, Rom. xiii. 7. there is a fear and reverence due to parents from their children, Lev. xix. 3. Heb. xii. 9. which is shewn by the honour and respect paid unto them, and the obedience yielded them, Eph. vi. 1, 2. and the argument from hence is strong to the fear and reverence of God the Father of spirits, Heb. xii. 9. 1 Pet. i. 14, 17. There is a fear and reverence in the conjugal state, due from wives to their husbands,

Eph. v. 33. 1 Pet. iii. 5, 6. and this relation affords a reason and argument why the church should fear and serve the Lord her God, because he is her husband, Psalm xlv. 11. there is a fear and reverence which servants should shew to their masters, Eph. vi. 5. and if such masters are to be obeyed with fear, much more our Master which is in heaven; and this is the argument the Lord himself uses, *If I be a Master, where is my fear?* Mal. i. 6. there is a fear and reverence which ministers of the word should be had in, by those to whom they minister, 1 Sam. xii. 18. this is one part of that double honour they are worthy of, to be esteemed very highly for their work sake. Herod, though a wicked man, *feared John*, that is, not dreaded him, but respected him, for *he heard him gladly*, Mark vi. 20. There is a fear and reverence to be rendered to magistrates, Rom. xiii. 7. and especially to the king, the chief magistrate, Prov. xxiv. 21. and if an earthly king is to be feared and reverenced, much more the King of kings and Lord of lords, *Who would not fear thee, O king of nations?* Jer. x. 7.

But then men are not so to be feared by the people of God, let them be in what character, relation, and station soever, as to be deterred by them from the service of God; *the fear of man* too often *brings a snare* in this respect. God is to be hearkened to, served, and obeyed, rather than men in the highest class and rank; they are not to be afraid of losing their favour and esteem, and of gaining their ill will thereby, as the Pharisees, who, though convinced that Jesus was the Christ, confessed him not, lest they should be put out of the synagogue, loving the praise of men more than the praise of God: nor should they be afraid of the revilings and reproaches of men, and be intimidated by them from serving the Lord their God, but with Moses should esteem reproach for the Lord's sake greater riches than the treasures of Egypt; nor should they be frightened from a profession of religion, and from an attention to it, by the threats and menaces of men, and by all the persecutions they may endure from them. They are not to be feared who can kill the body, but God is to be feared who can destroy both body and soul in hell; and such who fear men, so as to neglect the worship of God, are the *fearful* ones, who shall have their part in the lake of fire and brimstone, Matt. x. 28. Rev. xxi. 8. if God is on the side of his people, as he most certainly is, they have no reason to fear what man can do unto them.

God only is the object of fear, *Thou shalt fear the Lord thy God, and serve him;* that is, him only, Deut. vi. 13. and x. 20. this is the principal thing God requires of his people, and they are bound in duty to render to him; *Now, O Israel, what doth the Lord thy God require of thee, but to fear the Lord thy God?* this is the first thing, others follow, Deut. x. 12. hence because he is so much the object of the fear of good men, he is called *fear* itself; so the *fear of Isaac* is used for the God of Isaac, Gen. xxxi. 42. and by whom Jacob sware, ver. 53. who could be no other than the God of his father Isaac. In the Chaldee paraphrase[1] the word רחלא *fear*, is sometimes put for the true God, as well as used of idols; and with some Θεος, the Greek word for God, is by them derived from δεος, *fear*;[2] and by the Lacedemonians fear was worshipped as a deity, and had a temple for it;[3] as Pavor and Pallor, fearfulness and paleness, were by Tullus Hostilius among the Romans;[4] but none but the true God is the object of fear. And,

1st, He is to be feared because of his name and nature; *Holy and reverend is his name*, particularly his name Jehovah, expressive of his essence and nature; *that thou mayest fear this fearful and glorious name, The Lord thy God*, Psalm cxii. 9. Deut. xxviii. 58. a name peculiar to him; there is no name of God but is to be revered; and that by which he is commonly spoken of ought always to be used in a reverend manner, and not upon slight and trivial occasions, and with great irreverence, as it too often is, and when at every turn, men are apt to say, O Lord! O God! good God! &c. especially men professing the fear of God, should be careful of such language, for it is no other than taking the name of God in vain.

2dly, God not only essentially but personally considered is to be feared, God, Father, Son, and Spirit; it is said of the Jews in the latter day, that they shall *seek*

---

[1] Targum Jerus. in Deut. xxxii. 15. et Targ. Jon. in v. 18.
[2] Dictum volunt Θεον alii a nomine δεος, i. e. metus, Scapula.
[3] Plutarch in Cleomone, p. 808. vol. 1.
[4] Lactant. Institut. l. 1. c. 20.

the Lord their God, and David their king, and shall fear the Lord and his goodness in the latter days, Hos. iii. 5. where the Lord, who and his goodness will be feared by them, is Jehovah the Father, as distinguished from the Messiah the Son of God, and David their king, who will be sought for by them. So in Mal. iv. 2. *Unto you that fear my name*, whose name is Jehovah, the Lord of hosts, *shall the Sun of righteousness arise with healing in his wings;* even the Son of God, who is the brightness of his Father's glory, and the express image of his person, and so is distinguished from him whose name is feared. Jehovah the Son is also the object of divine fear and reverence, *Let him be your fear, and let him be your dread;* that is, the object of your fear and reverence; and what follows shews which of the divine Persons is meant; and *he shall be for a sanctuary* to worship in, and a place of refuge for his people in times of distress; *but for a stone of stumbling, and for a rock of offence*, Isa. viii. 13, 14. which phrases are applied to Christ, and can only be said of him, Rom. ix. 32, 33. 1 Pet. ii. 7, 8. Jehovah the Father, the lord of the vineyard, after sending many of his servants who had been ill used, says, *I will send my beloved Son*, meaning Christ, the only begotten Son of the Father, it *may be, they will reverence him when they see him*, Luke xx. 13. they ought to have done it; reverence should be given to him, the heir of the vineyard, his church, the son in his own house, whose house believers are, and therefore should reverence him. Jehovah the Spirit also is and should be the object of fear; the Israelites in the wilderness rebelled against him, and vexed him, and they smarted for it, for *he turned to be their enemy, and fought against them*, Isa. lxiii. 10. lying to the Holy Ghost, which was a most irreverent treatment of him, was punished with death in Ananias and Sapphira; and saints should be careful that they *grieve* not the holy Spirit by their unbecoming carriage to him, from whom they receive many blessings and favours.

3*dly*, God, in his perfections and because of them, is the object of fear; as his majesty and greatness in general; God is clothed with majesty, and majesty and honour are before him, and *with him is terrible majesty*, such as is sufficient to command an awe of him; particularly his omnipotence, for *he is excellent in power*, Job xxxvii. 22, 23. as also his omniscience, for nothing can be hid from his sight; the most enormous actions committed in the dark are seen by him, with whom the darkness and the light are alike; and his omnipresence, from whence there is no fleeing, for he fills heaven and earth with it; to which may be added, the justice and holiness of God, which make his majesty the more terrible and to be revered, since he is not only excellent in power, but also *in judgment, and in plenty of justice*, Job xxxvii. 23. see 2 Chron. xix. 7. and a fearful thing it is to fall into the hands of a just and sin-avenging God, the living God, the everlasting King, at whose wrath the nations tremble, and are not able to bear his indignation, Jer. x. 10.

4*thly*, The works of God make him appear to be a proper object of fear and reverence; his works of creation, the Psalmist on mention of them says, Psalm xxxiii. 5—8. *Let all the earth fear the Lord, let all the inhabitants of the world stand in awe of him;* who has made such a display of his greatness and goodness in them, as shew him worthy of fear and reverence. The prophet instances in what may seem small, yet a most wonderful thing, and enough of itself to command an awe of the divine Being; *Fear ye not me, saith the Lord? will ye not tremble at my presence? which hath placed the sand for the bound of the sea, by a perpetual decree that it cannot pass it;* and at the same time the stupidity of the people is observed, who, notwithstanding the goodness of God in his works of providence towards them, yet were wanting in their fear and reverence of him: *Neither say they in their hearts, Let us now fear the Lord our God that giveth rain, the former and latter rain in its season; he reserveth unto us the appointed weeks of the harvest*, Jer. v. 22, 24. which, though common providential blessings, yet are what should engage men to fear the Lord and his goodness; and especially God's works of grace should have such an effect upon the hearts of his people, as they have when they come with a divine power; particularly the pardoning grace and mercy of God; *There is forgiveness with thee that thou mayest be feared*, Psalm cxxx. 4. see Hosea iii. 5.

5*thly*, The judgments of God which he threatens, and sometimes inflicts, and the promises of grace he makes and always fulfils, render him an object of fear and reverence. The judgments of God on sinners, are awful to the saints themselves, and strike their minds with fear of God; says David, *My flesh trembleth for fear of thee, and I am afraid of thy judgments*, Psalm cxix. 120. not as coming upon himself, but as terrible to behold on others; and these are dreadful and formidable to sinners, when they see them near approaching, who go into the holes and clefts of rocks, and into the caves *for fear of the Lord, and the glory of his majesty, when he ariseth to shake terribly the earth*, Isa. ii. 19, 21. and nothing has a greater influence on a filial and godly fear in the saints, and to stir them up to the exercise of it, than the free, absolute, and unconditional promise of grace in the covenant; thus after the apostle had observed such promises, strongly urges to *perfecting holiness in the fear of God*, 2 Cor. vi. 16, 18. and vii. 1.

II. The nature and kind of fear. There is a fear which is not good nor commendable, and it is of different sorts; there is an idolatrous and superstitious fear, which is called δεισιδαιμονια, a fear of dæmons, which the city of Athens was greatly addicted to, observed to them by the apostle when there, to their disgrace; *I perceive that in all things ye are too superstitious*, or given to the fear and worship; of false deities; such is all will-worship, worship not founded in the word of God, which brings on a spirit of bondage unto fear; and all such false and vain imaginations which inject dread and terrors into the minds of men, and cause them to *fear where no fear is*, or where there is no reason for it; such as the pains of purgatory after death, invented by the Papists to extort money from men; and the beating of the body in the grave, a figment of the Jews. There is an external fear of God, an outward shew and profession of it, which is taught by the precept of men, as in the men of Samaria, who pretended to fear the Lord, as the priest instructed them, and yet served their own gods; and such an external fear of the true God, Job's friends supposed was all that he had, and that even he had cast off that, Job xv. 4. There is an hypocritical fear, when men draw nigh to God with their mouths and honour him with their lips, and their hearts are removed far from him; and when they fear and serve him for same sinister end and selfish view, which Satan insinuated was Job's case, *Doth Job fear God for nought?* and perhaps the same is suggested by Eliphaz, *Is not this thy fear?* Job i. 9. and iv. 6. And there is a servile fear, such as that of some servants, who serve their masters, not from love but from fear of punishment; and such a *spirit of bondage to fear*, the Jews were much subject to, under the legal dispensation; but now saints being *delivered out of the hands* of sin, Satan, and the law, they *serve* the Lord *without fear*, without slavish fear and with a filial one, Rom. viii. 15. Luke i. 74, 75. And this sort of fear arises ———1. From a sense of sin, and the guilt of it on the conscience, without a view of pardon; thus no sooner were Adam and Eve sensible of their sin and their nakedness by it, but they fled through fear from the presence of God, and hid themselves among the trees of the garden, as yet having no discovery of pardoning grace made to them; for said Adam to God, calling for him, *I heard thy voice in the garden, and I was afraid, because I was naked, and I hid myself*, Gen. iii. 10. Thus a wicked man, conscious of his guilt, flees when no man pursues, and is like Pashur, a Magor-missabib, fear round about, a terror to himself and others.———2. From the law entering the conscience of a sinner, having broken it and working wrath in it; for the law, when it comes with powerful convictions of sin, and with menaces of punishment for it, *it worketh* present *wrath*, or a sense of it in the conscience, and leaves a *fearful looking for of judgment* to come, and of *fiery indignation* which shall consume *the adversaries* of God; when persons in such a condition and circumstances would be glad of rocks and mountains to fall on them and hide them from the wrath of God, which appears to them intolerable. ———3. From the curse of the law, and the weight of it on the conscience. The voice of the law is terrible, it is a voice of words which they that heard intreated they might hear no more. It accuses of sin, pronounces guilty for it, is a ministration of condemnation and a killing letter; its language is, *Cursed is every one that continueth not in all things which are written in the book of the law to do them*, Gal. iii. 10. which to hear is dreadful, when the conscience of a sinner is awakened; but how much more terrible is it, when a sinner feels as it were in his own apprehension all the curses of the law upon him, as he does when *the anger of the Lord, and his jealousy smoke against* him, *and all the curses written* in the law *lie upon him*, Deut. xxix. 20. with what slavish fear must he be then filled?———4. From a view of death as the demerit of sin; *The wages of sin is* death, the just desert of it; sin is the sting of death, gives it its venom and fatal influence, and makes it that terrible thing it is; and some *through fear of death* are *all their life-time subject to bondage*, and are under a continual servile fear of it.———5. From a dread of hell and everlasting damnation. This fear is of the same kind with that of devils, who believe there is one God and tremble; tremble at present wrath and future torment. So wicked men, who have a fearful apprehension of everlasting punishment, it appears to them greater than they can bear, as it did to Cain.

But there is a fear of God different from this and opposite to it, and may be called a filial fear, such as that of a son to a father; the scriptures call it ευλαβεια, and which is rendered *godly fear*, Heb. xii. 28. and the same word is used of the fear and reverence of Christ to his divine Father, who was *heard in that he feared*, or *because of fear*, Heb. v. 7. his filial fear of his Father which lay in honouring him, in obedience to him, and in submission to his will, even when with supplications he deprecated death; and now a fear like this in the saints arises,———1. From the spirit of adoption, who delivers the people of God from a servile fear, and gives them a filial one, by witnessing their sonship to them; *Ye have not received*, says the apostle, *the spirit of bondage again to fear, but ye have received the spirit of adoption, whereby we cry, Abba, Father*, and so are freed from a spirit of bondage which induces a servile fear, Rom. viii. 17. They that fear the Lord are in the relation of children to him; wherefore their fear of him, which he takes notice of and regards, must be a child-like one, arising from their being put among the children, and their sense of it; and which seems to be implied in Psalm ciii. 13. *Like as a father pitieth his children, so the Lord pitieth them that fear him*, where they that fear the Lord, in the latter clause, answer to children in the former.———2. From the love of God shed abroad in the heart by the Spirit, which produces love to God again; *there is no fear*, no slavish fear, *in love, but perfect love*, a sense of the perfect, everlasting, and unchangeable love of God *casts out* such kind of fear; for the true fear of God is no other than a reverential affection for God flowing from a sense of his love; such do not dread his wrath, but desire his presence and communion with him, and say, *Whom have I in heaven but thee? and there is none on earth that I desire besides thee*, Psalm lxxiii. 25.———3. This filial fear is attended with faith and trust in God; it is a fiducial fear; hence they that fear the Lord and who trust in him, are characters put together, and which describe the same persons; and they that fear the Lord are exhorted and encouraged to trust in him, Psalm xxxi. 19. and cxv. 11. Job was a man that feared God, and yet such was his faith and confidence in him, that he could say, *Though he slay me, yet will I trust in him;* and what a strong expression of his faith in Christ as his living Redeemer have we in chap. xix. 25. see Job. i. 1. and xiii. 15.———4. It is a fear that is consistent with great joy in the Lord, *Serve the Lord with fear, and rejoice with trembling*, Psalm ii. 11. and with the utmost courage and magnanimity of mind; it is a fearless fear; a man that fears the Lord has no reason to fear anything, or what any man or devil can do unto him; he may say as David did, *The Lord is my light and my salvation, whom shall I fear, &c.* Psalm xxvii. 1, 3.———5. Such a fear is opposed to pride and self-confidence; it is an humble fear, a diffidence of a man's self, placing his trust and hope alone in God; *Be not high-minded, but fear*, Rom. xi. 20. this is that *fear* and *trembling*, or that modesty and humility, with which the saints are exhorted to *work* about or employ themselves in things that accompany *salvation;* as knowing that *both to will and to do*, the disposition and ability to perform any duty aright, are owing to the efficacious operation of the Spirit of God, and that it is by the grace of God they are what they are, and do what they do; they that fear the Lord are such who *rejoice in Christ Jesus, and have no confidence in the flesh*, declaring that when they have done all they can, they are but unprofitable servants, Phil. ii. 12, 13. and iii. 3.

III. Wherein the fear of God appears, and by what it is manifest.———1. In an hatred of sin. *The fear of the Lord is to hate evil*, Prov. viii. 13. as nothing is more opposite to good than evil, nothing is more to be abhorred; it is to be hated with a Stygian hatred, as hell itself, αποςυγυντες, *abhor that which is evil*, Rom. xii. 9. and a man that fears God, who has a reverential affection for him, will hate it as being contrary to him, *Ye that love the Lord, hate evil*, Psalm xcvii. 10. every thing that is evil is hated by such a man; as evil thoughts, which are only evil and that continually; the heart is full of evil thoughts, and out of it they daily proceed, and these are the object of a good man's hatred, *I hate vain thoughts*, says David, Psalm cxix. 113. and now as no one but a man himself is conscious of them and privy to them, to hate them shews that the fear of God is in his heart. Evil words are also hated by him; not only cursing, swearing, blasphemy, and all obscene and filthy language, but every vain and idle word, foolish and frothy expression, which comes out of his mouth when not on his guard, gives him uneasiness, as being displeasing to God, grieving to his Spirit, and what must be accounted for in the day of judgment; as *in many words* there are *divers vanities*, the wise man opposes the *fear of* God unto them, Eccl. v. 7. and if evil thougths and evil words are hated by such, then most certainly evil actions; and not only those of others, as the deeds of the Nicolaitanes, the garment, the outward conversation-garment spotted with the flesh, the filthy conversation of the wicked, but his own actions springing from corrupt nature, done by him contrary to the law of his mind; *What I would, that do I not, but what I hate, that I do*, Rom. vii. 15. Evil men and their company are abhorrent to those that fear the Lord, and are shunned and avoided by them; they choose not to have any fellowship with the unfruitful works of darkness, and the workers of them; society with them is a grief and burden to them, as it was to Lot, David, Isaiah, Jeremiah, and others, nay hateful to them: *Do not I hate them that hate thee? I hate them with perfect hatred*, Psalm cxxxix. 21, 22. see Prov. iv. 14, 15. All evil and false ways, not only of immorality, but of superstition and will worship, are rejected with abhorrence by men that fear the Lord, and make his word the rule of their faith and practice. Wisdom herself, or Christ, has set an example, proving the truth of the assertion in Prov. viii. 13. *Pride and arrogancy, and the evil way, and the froward mouth, do I hate;* and wisdom is justified of her children; says David, who was one of them, *I hate every false way*, Psalm cxix. 128. yea all evil doctrines, which reflect on the divine persons in the godhead, on the free grace of God in man's salvation, on the person and offices of Christ, and the operations of the Spirit, are the object of the hatred and aversion of one that fears God; he cannot bear them that are evil, neither receive them into his house, nor wish them God speed. In short, every thing that is evil in its nature, as sin is in every shape exceeding sinful, a breach of the law of God, contrary to his nature, that abominable thing his righteous soul hates, is also hateful to a good man, to a man that fears the Lord, and hereby the fear of the Lord is manifested by him.——2. It shews itself by departing from evil; *By the fear of the Lord men depart from evil*, Prov. xvi. 6. see chap. iii. 7. not only from open and public sins, but from private and secret ones; Job was a man that feared God and eschewed evil, avoided and departed from it, as every wise man does; yea to depart from evil is understanding, this shews a man both to be a wise man and one that fears the Lord, Job. i. 1. and xxviii. 28. Prov. xiv. 16. yea such an one will abstain from all appearance of evil, from every thing that looks like it or leads unto it; will shun every avenue, every by-path, that has a tendency to insnare into it, taking the wise man's advice, *Enter not into the path of the wicked, &c.* Prov. iv. 14, 15.——3. The fear of God appears in men in not allowing themselves to do what others do, and what they themselves formerly did; so Nehemiah, speaking of some ill things done by former governors, says, *So did not I, because of the fear of God*, Neh. v. 15. Not that such who fear God are without sin; Job feared God, but was not free from sin; he was sensible of it, acknowledged it, and implored the pardon of it; but they cannot give themselves that liberty to sin that others do, and walk as other Gentiles walk, in the vanity of their minds, and in a sinful course of life; they have not so learned Christ, and the grace of God teaches them other things.—— 4. The fear of God manifests itself by a carefulness not to offend God nor man; such study to exercise a conscience void of offence to both, and would willingly give no offence to Jew nor Gentile, nor to the church of God; and next to God they are careful that they offend not against the generation of his children, either by word or deed, and even to put no stumbling block before any, but fear the Lord their God, for to do otherwise would be contrary to it, Lev. xix. 14. Nay, such are not only on their guard to avoid sin and give no offence by it, but they are in an opposition to it; the spiritual part in them lusteth against the carnal part; there are as it were a company of two armies in them fighting one against another; they strive against sin, acting the part of an antagonist to it, take to themselves the whole armour of God, and make use of it against it.——5. The fear of God in men is seen by a constant attendance on the worship of God, and by a strict regard to his will and the observation of it; the fear of God has so great a share and concern in divine worship, as has been observed, that it is sometimes put for the whole of it, both internal and external; such who fear the Lord cannot be easy in the neglect of the worship of God, but as they desire to be filled with the knowledge of his will, so to be found in the practice of it; and, like Zacharias and Elizabeth, to walk in all the ordinances and commands of the Lord blameless; and to fear God, and keep his commandments, is the whole required of man; and such who make a custom of it to forsake the assembling of themselves together to worship God, do interpretatively cast off the fear of God.——6. The fear of God is seen and known in men by their withholding nothing from God, though ever so dear unto them, whenever he requires it of them; so Abraham, when he so readily offered up his son at the command of God, received this testimony from him, *Now know I*, saith the Lord, *that thou fearest God*, Gen. xxii. 12.; on the contrary, when men keep back a part from God of what he expects from them, as in the case of Ananias and Sapphira, it is a proof that the fear of God is not before their eyes and in their hearts.

IV. The springs and causes of the fear of God, or from whence it flows.——1. It is not from nature, nor is it in natural men; the want of it is a part of the description of corrupt nature, and of men in a natural state; *There is no fear of God before their eyes*, Rom. iii. 18. it may be said of the heart of every natural man, what Abraham said of Gerar, *Surely the fear of God is not in this place*, Gen. xx. 11. and which may be concluded from the wickedness that is in it, and that by what comes out of it; *The transgression of the wicked*, discovered by his words and works, his life and actions, *saith within my heart*, suggests this to my mind, speaks as plainly as well can be, it is an observation of David, *that there is no fear of God before his eyes*, Psalm xxxvi. 1.——2. It arises from the grace of God, it is a gift and grant of grace; *O that there were such an heart in them that they would fear me,* or *who will give such an heart?* Deut. v. 29. none but God can give it, and he has promised it in covenant; it is a blessing of his grace, which he has provided in it; *I will give them one heart and one way, that they may fear me for ever. I will put my fear in their hearts, that they shall not depart from me,* Jer. xxxii. 39, 40. In consequence of which promise and covenant,——3. It is implanted in the heart in regeneration; it is put there by the Spirit of God, where it was not before, and where it never could have been, had he not put it there, and it appears as soon in a regenerate man as any grace whatever; upon first conversion there is quickly found a tenderness of conscience with respect to sin, and a carefulness not to offend God; and indeed *the fear of the Lord is the beginning of wisdom,* Psalm cxi. 10. Prov. ix. 10. No man is truly wise until he fears God, and as soon as he fears the Lord he begins to be wise, and not before; yea the fear of the Lord is wisdom itself; it is that wisdom and truth which God desires and puts into the inward and hidden parts of the heart, Job xxviii. 28. Psalm li. 6.——4. The word and prayer are the means of attaining it; the fear of the Lord, as it is a duty, and expressive of worship, is to be learned; *Come ye children, hearken unto me,* says David, *I will teach you the fear of the Lord,* Psalm xxxiv. 11. The law of God, and especially the whole of doctrine both legal and evangelical, is the means of learning it, Deut. iv. 10. and xvii. 19. and therefore is called the fear of the Lord, Psalm xix. 7, 9. but as a grace, it is diligently sought after and earnestly importuned of God; the heart must not only be instructed but united to fear the Lord, and which is to be prayed for, Psalm lxxxvi. 11. Prov. ii. 3—5.——5. It is encouraged, promoted, and increased by fresh discoveries of the grace and goodness of God, *They shall fear the Lord and his goodness;* the goodness of God made known, bestowed, and applied, greatly influences the fear of him, Hos. iii. 5. especially an application of his pardoning grace and mercy, *There is forgiveness with thee that thou mayest be feared*, Psalm cxxx. 4.

V. The happiness of those that fear the Lord. There is scarce any one character by which the people of God are described, under which more promises of good things are made unto them, than this.

First, With respect to things temporal.

Godliness in general, and this part of it, the fear of the Lord, in particular, has the promise of this life, as well as of that which is to come.———1. It is promised they shall have no want, not of temporal good things, *O fear the Lord, ye his saints, for there is no want to them that fear him*, Psalm xxxiv. 9, 10. not of any good thing; that is, which is suitable and convenient for them, and God in his wisdom sees fit and proper for them; and rather than they shall want, he will do wonders for them, and open sources of relief they never thought of, Isa. xli. 17, 18. and xliii. 19, 20.———2. Though they may have but little of the good things of this world, yet *better is little with the fear of the Lord, than great treasures and troubles therewith*, Prov. xv. 16. this with the fear of God and with righteousness, is better than great revenues without right, and better than the riches of many wicked, Prov. xvi. 8. Psalm xxxvii. 16.———3. Yea wealth and riches are promised to be in the house of that man that fears the Lord, and that by humility and the fear of the Lord are riches, and honour, and life, Psalm cxii. 1, 3. Prov. xxii. 4. which can only be understood of some, not of all that fear the Lord; unless spiritual wealth, riches, honour, and life, are intended, since the fear of the Lord itself is the good man's treasure, Isa. xxxiii. 6. it is a treasure of itself.———4. It is said that the man that fears the Lord shall eat of the labour of his hands, and he shall not only be happy, and it shall be well with him in his person, but in his family; his wife shall be as a fruitful vine by the sides of his house, and his children shall be as olive plants round about his table, Psalm cxxviii. 1—4.——— 5. They that fear the Lord are in the utmost safety; in his fear is strong confidence, and they have no reason to be afraid of any thing; they shall not be visited with evil, yea the angel of the Lord encamps round about them and protects, defends, and delivers them from all dangers and from all enemies, Prov. xiv. 26. and xix. 23. Psalm xxxiv. 7.———6. The fear of the Lord prolongeth days, or adds unto them, Prov. x. 27. which was always reckoned a great temporal blessing; the wise man says of a sinner, *though his days be prolonged*, as they may be, and he not happy, *yet surely*, says he, *I know that it shall be well with them that fear God, which fear before him*, Eccl. viii. 12. be their days more or fewer.

Secondly, With respect to things spiritual, much is promised to them that fear the Lord, and they are spoken of as most happy persons.———1. The Lord is said to take pleasure in them that fear him, as having the utmost complacency and delight in them, being his special and peculiar people, his Hephzibah in whom he delights, his Beulah to whom he is married, Psalm cxlvii. 11.———2. They are accepted of him, and are acceptable to him; *Of a truth*, says Peter, *I perceive that God is no respecter of persons, but in every nation he that feareth him and worketh righteousness, is accepted with him*, Acts x. 34, 35. his person is accepted with him in Christ, the beloved, and his sacrifices of prayer and praise are acceptable to him through Jesus Christ.———3. The heart of God is towards them; he has a sympathy and fellow-feeling with them in all their distresses, trials, and exercises; in all their afflictions he is afflicted, and he comforts and supports them; *like as a father pitieth his children, so the Lord pitieth them that fear him*, Psalm ciii. 13. ———4. The eye of the Lord is upon them for good; *the eye of the Lord is upon them that fear him*, Psalm xxxiii. 18. not only his eye of providence, which runs to and fro throughout the earth to shew himself strong on their behalf, to protect and defend them, and to avenge himself on their enemies; but his eye of special love, grace, and mercy, is upon them, and is never withdrawn from them, but is ever delighting in them and caring for them, Psalm ciii. 11, 17. Luke i. 50.———5. His hand is open and ready to communicate to them; he *gives meat to them that fear him*, spiritual food, the blessings of his covenant, of which he is ever mindful; the comforts of his Spirit in which they walk, who walk in the fear of the Lord; he gives them grace, fresh and rich supplies of it, and at last gives them glory; and in the meanwhile withholds no good thing from them, to support their faith, encourage their hope, and engage their trust in him and dependance on him.———6. *The secret of the Lord is with them that fear him;* the secrets of his heart's love to them, and of his gracious designs towards them, are disclosed unto them, by which he uses them as his most intimate and bosom friends; and *he will shew them his covenant*, the blessings and promises of it, and their interest in them, Psalm xxv. 14. what is said of Christ the head of the covenant, is true of all the covenant ones in their measure, Mal. ii. 5. to which may be added, that the Lord grants the requests and fulfils the desires of them that fear him, hears their cries and saves them, Psalm cxlv. 19. ——7. They are remembered by him with the favour he bears to his own people, with his tender mercies and loving kindness, which have been ever of old; he remembers them when in a low estate, and brings them out of it; he remembers his promises to them, and fulfils them; *a book of remembrance is* said to be *written before him for them that feared the Lord*, Mal. iii. 16.—— 8. It is promised to them *that fear the name* of the Lord, that *unto them the Sun of righteousness shall arise with healing in his wings*, Mal. iv. 2. Christ the Saviour shall come and shew himself with a discovery and application of pardoning grace and mercy; nay, one that *fears the Lord*, though he *walks in darkness and hath no light*, yet he is encouraged to *trust in the name of the Lord, and stay upon his God*, Isa. l. 10.—— 9. *Salvation*, a fresh view of interest in it, a renewed application of it, as well as the full enjoyment of it, *is nigh them that fear the Lord*, Psalm lxxxv. 9. for that is nearer to them than when they first believed, and had the fear of God first implanted in them, and were set a seeking after it, and had first hope of interest in it.——10. Great and good things are laid up for such persons in the heart of God, in the covenant of grace, and in the hands of Christ, and in heaven; even a blessed hope, a crown of righteousness, and things which eye has not seen, nor ear heard of, nor has it entered into the heart of man to conceive of; *O how great is thy goodness, which thou hast laid up for them that fear thee!* Psalm xxxi. 19.

CHAP. VI.

OF FAITH IN GOD AND IN CHRIST.

FAITH is another branch of inward experimental religion and godliness, for *with the heart man believeth unto righteousness;* and of internal worship, and without which external worship cannot be performed in a manner acceptable to God, for *without faith it is impossible to please him:* there is no drawing nigh to God in any part of worship without it; if a man prays to God he must *ask in faith, nothing doubting;* for it is the *prayer of faith* that is availing and saving; if a man hears the gospel, unless the word is *mixed with faith* by them that hear it, it is not profitable; and both a profession of faith and the exercise of it, are necessary to a due subjection to the ordinances of the gospel. As to baptism, *if thou believest with all thy heart thou mayest,* said Philip to the eunuch desiring baptism; and so for the ordinance of the supper, a previous examination whether a man has faith, and the exercise of it, are requisite to eating of it; and without this, a man cannot discern the Lord's body, nor answer the ends and design of that ordinance; concerning which may be observed,

I. The kind of faith to be treated of; for faith is a word of different use and signification, and there are divers kinds of faith.——1. It sometimes signifies the veracity and faithfulness of God; as when the apostle says, *Shall their unbelief make the faith of God without effect?* Rom. iii. 3, 4. yea faith sometimes signifies veracity and fidelity among men, and is no other than a virtue belonging to the moral law, and is one of the weightier matters of it, Matt. xxiii. 23.——2. It is sometimes used for the doctrine of the gospel, the word of faith, which the apostle preached, though he once destroyed it as much as in him lay, Gal. i. 23. and is the faith once delivered to the saints, which they should earnestly contend for, and build up one another in Jude ver. 3, 20. so called, because it contains things to be believed, upon the credit and testimony of God; and because it directs to the great object of faith in salvation, the Lord Jesus Christ; and because it is the means of ingenerating and increasing faith in men, for *faith comes by hearing, and hearing by the word of God*, Rom. x. 8, 17.——3. There is a divine and an human faith; a divine faith proceeds upon a divine testimony, upon the authority and veracity of God the testifier; an human faith proceeds upon the testimony of man, and upon the authenticity and truth of the witness borne by him; concerning both which the apostle John says, *If we receive the witness of men, the witness of God is greater,* by how much the greater is his veracity and faithfulness; *for this is the witness of God, which he hath testified of his Son*, 1 John v. 9. namely, that life and salvation are in him and by him; and to believe this witness, and to receive it within a man's self, is what is commonly called saving faith.——4. There is a faith of miracles which proceeds upon a revelation some way or other made by God to a man, which he believes; either that a miracle should be wrought by him, or should be wrought for him, for his benefit and advantage; of the former sort, and which is called *faith in God*, Mark xi. 22, 23. the apostle is to be understood, when he says, *Though I have all faith, so that I could remove mountains*, 1 Cor. xiii. 2. see Matt. xvii. 20. Luke xvii. 6. of the latter sort was the faith of the centurion, of the woman having an issue, of Jairus, and of the Canaanitish woman, Matt. viii. 8, 10. and ix. 18, 20, 22. and xv. 28. and of the lame man at Lystra, Acts xiv. 9, 10. The one is called active, the other passive faith; and this faith of miracles, in the first times of the gospel, was common to good and bad men, to the true disciples of Christ, Matt. x. 1. Mark xvi. 17—20. and to Judas, and to false teachers, Matt. x. 1, 4. and vii. 22, 23.——5. There is what is called an historical faith, not because it is only giving credit to the historical part of the scripture, which is to be believed as well as other parts; nor because the scripture is read, and attention paid to it only as a common history or human testimony; for men, with this faith, believe it to be a divine testimony; and regard it as such; it may rather be called a *theoretic* faith, a speculative one, receiving all things in the theory, but reducing nothing to practice; or a bare naked assent to the truth of what is contained in the word concerning God and Christ, and divine things; it is a faith common to good men and bad men; it must be and is where true faith is, and there can be no true faith without it; but if a man stops here and goes no further, it falls short of spiritual, special faith, or the faith of God's elect, and is no other than the faith of devils, and of bad men.—— 6. There is also a temporary faith, which continues only for a time, in some persons, as in the stony ground-hearers, *Who for a while believe, and in time of temptation fall away*, Luke viii. 13. this sort of faith differs from the former, in that it is not a mere assent to truth, but is attended with affection, joy, and gladness, as in Herod, who heard John gladly, and did many outward things, Mark vi. 20. and in those the apostle speaks of, *who tasted the good word of God, and the powers of the world to come*, Heb. vi. 5. all of a natural and superficial kind, arising from a principle of self love, and from the novelty, harmony, and connection of truths, and from a false presumptuous hope of future happiness in consequence of their assent unto them; and so is different likewise from the faith of devils, who believe and tremble, but have no joy; and it differs also from true faith, because it is without the root of grace in the heart, and is loseable, is only for a time, for when trouble and persecution arise because of the word, such who have it, drop their profession of it; whereas where there is true faith, such do not *draw back*, but continue to *believe to the saving of the soul*, Heb. x. 39.——7. There is a special faith, which is peculiar to God's elect, and is by some called saving faith, though strictly speaking salvation is not in faith,[1] nor in any other grace, nor in any duty, only in Christ; there is no other name but his under heaven whereby we must be saved; he only is the author of eternal salvation; and yet there are some things in scripture which seem to countenance such a phrase; as when Christ said to the woman who repented of her sins, and had the forgiveness of them, loved Christ, and believed in him, *Thy faith hath saved thee, go in peace*, Luke vii. 50. unless the object of faith should be meant; and certain it is that salvation is promised to faith, and connected with it, *He that believes shall be saved*, and is what faith issues in; true believers receive *the end of their faith, even the salvation of their souls*, Mark xvi. 16. 1 Pet. i. 9. and this is the faith that is to be treated of; and will next be considered,

II. The objects of it, and acts of it on those objects. The objects of it are not bare axioms or propositions; for as Dr. Ames[2] observes, the act of the believer does not terminate at an axiom but at the thing; for axioms, are not formed, but that by them knowledge may be had of things; the principal term to which the act of a believer tends, is the thing itself, which is chiefly regarded in the axiom; and so promises are not to be considered as objects, unless in a tropical and metonymical sense, being put for the things promised; so the Old Testament-saints, *not having received the promises*, the things promised, *but having seen them afar off, that is, by faith, were persuaded of them, and embraced them*, Heb. xi. 12. nor even the benefits of Christ, or the blessings of his grace, no

---

[1] Salus nostra proprie non nititur fide nostra, sed eo uno potius quem apprehendimus per fidem nempe Jesu Christo, Bezæ Confessio Fidei, c. 4. art. 20. p. 51.
[2] Medulla Theolog. 1. 2. c. 5. s. 24.

otherwise than as they are the *end* faith has in view in receiving him; he is viewed and dealt with as the object of faith in order to enjoy the good things which come by him: or they may be considered as motives encouraging to acts of faith on him, and are the fruits and effects of it received thereby from him. The proper and formal object of faith is twofold, God and Christ; God as the first primary and ultimate object of faith, and Christ as mediator is the mediate object of it, *Ye believe in God, believe also in me*, John xiv. 1.

God is the principal object of faith, Mark xi. 22. Titus iii. 8. 1 Thess. i. 8. which act of faith on him is not barely to believe there is a God, and but one; which is *credere Deum*, and which the devils themselves believe; nor is it merely to believe whatever he delivers in his word, as prophecies, promises, doctrines, &c. this is *credere Deo*, to give credit to God, believe what he says; but *credere in Deum*,[3] by believing to cleave to God, lean upon him, and acquiesce in him as our all-sufficient life and salvation, Deut. xxx. 20. and so it is not merely to believe there are three Persons in the godhead, but to go forth in acts of faith and confidence on them, in things relative to our welfare and happiness here and hereafter. And,

1*st*, On God the Father, *Ye believe in God*, that is, in God the Father, the God of Israel, as distinct from Christ, for it follows, *in my Father's house are many mansions*, John xiv. 1, 2. and so our Lord further says, *He that believeth on me*, that is, not on him only, nor does his faith stop and terminate there, *but on him that sent me*, that is, on the Father of Christ, John xii. 44. and it is also observed, that Christ was raised from the dead and had glory given him, that the *faith and hope* of his people *might be in God*, in God his Father, who raised him, 1 Pet. i. 21.

1. On him as the Creator, though not only on him as such; so runs the first article in the creed commonly called the apostles' creed, "I believe in God the Father almighty, maker of heaven and earth;" to believe the creation of all things out of nothing by the word, even out of things which did not appear, is an act of that faith in God which is the substance of things hoped for, and the evidence of things not seen, Heb. xi. 1, 3. besides, a true believer in God, fetches arguments to strengthen his faith in God, for relief, help, support, and supply, from him with respect to things spiritual, as well as temporal, from his being the maker and creator of all things; *My help*, says David, *cometh from the Lord, who made heaven and earth*, Psalm cxxi. 1, 2. and it is a special act of faith believers are directed to under sufferings, to *commit the keeping of their souls* to God *in well-doing, as unto a faithful creator*, 1 Pet. iv. 19. and so likewise on him as the preserver and saviour of men, for he is *the Saviour of all men, especially of those that believe;* and therefore saints put their trust in him, the living God, as such, 1 Tim. iv. 10. But more especially,——2. Faith is exercised on God the Father as the object of it, as having loved his people in Christ before the foundation of the world; that the Father, as distinct from Christ, has loved his people with a free, sovereign, unchangeable, and everlasting love, is certain; *Now God, even our Father, which hath loved us and given us everlasting consolation*, 2 Thess. ii. 16. of which they may be most comfortably assured, and may most firmly believe, by his appearing to them as he did to his church of old, saying, *I have loved thee with an everlasting love*, Jer. xxxi. 3. by his Spirit witnessing it to their spirits, and by shedding it abroad in their hearts, and giving them some feeling sensations of it, so as to comprehend with other saints, the heighth and depth, the length and breadth of it; by remembering to them his former loving kindness, the favour he bears to his own people; and by acts of love done in eternity, as choosing them in Christ, &c. and by giving him for them in time, and by commending his love towards them through Christ's dying for them, while they were yet sinners; and by quickening them by his Spirit and grace when dead in trespasses and sins, and all because of the great love, wherewith he hath loved them; and by drawing them with loving kindness to himself, as well as by his word and oath, the two immutable things in which he cannot lie, Isa. liv. 9, 10. So that there is good and sufficient reason for the acting and exercise of faith, on the everlasting love of the Father; and what a strong act and expression of faith is that of the apostle with respect unto it; *I am persuaded*, I firmly believe it, that nothing, *nor any creature* whatever, *shall be able to separate us from the love of God,*

---

[3] Medulla Theolog. l. 1. c. 3. f. 15.

which is in Christ Jesus our Lord. Rom. viii. 38, 39. this is to be *rooted and grounded in love,* Eph. iii. 17.——3. Faith is exercised on God the Father, as having chosen his people in Christ to grace and glory from the beginning, from everlasting, before the world began, Eph. i. 3, 4. 2 Thess. ii. 13, 14. this is the act of the Father of Christ, *Elect, according to the foreknowledge of God the Father,* 1 Pet. i. 2. and this election of God is to be known by the gospel coming not in word only, but in power, by being effectually called, for *whom he did predestinate, them he also called;* and by their having the faith of God's elect, for *as many as were ordained to eternal life believed,* Rom. viii. 30. Acts xiii. 48. wherefore this may be most firmly believed, as it was by the apostle Paul, both with respect to himself and others, for which he blessed God, and gave thanks to him, Eph. i. 3, 4. 2 Thess. ii. 13. and our Lord exhorts and encourages his disciples to *rejoice because* their *names* were *written in heaven,* Luke x. 20. which supposes knowledge of it, and faith in it.——4. God, as the covenant-God of his people, is the object of their faith; the covenant runs thus, *I will be their God, and they shall be my people;* and this is made to appear in effectual calling, when they who were not the people of God, not known to be so, are openly such; then it is God makes good his promise, *I will say, It is my people; and they shall say, The Lord is my God,* Zech. xiii. 9. as David did, *I trusted in thee, O Lord; I said, Thou art my God,* Psalm xxxi. 14. and so may every believer say, and be assured, that this God is their God, and will be their God and guide unto death, for covenant-interest always continues; it was a noble act of faith in the sweet singer of Israel a little before his death, *Although my house be not so with God, yet he hath made with me an everlasting covenant, ordered in all things and sure,* 2 Sam. xxiii. 5.——5. God, as he is the Father of Christ, so he is the Father of all that believe in him; *I ascend,* says Christ, *to my father and your father,* John xx. 17. So God, in the covenant of his grace, has declared himself, *and will be a father unto you, and ye shall be my sons and daughters saith the Lord Almighty,* 2 Cor. vi. 18. and as such, faith is to be exercised on him with joy and wonder, saying, *Behold, what manner of love the Father hath bestowed upon us, that we should be called the sons of God,* 1 John iii. 1. of the truth of which the leadings and witnessings of the Spirit are an evident proof, from whence he is called the Spirit of adoption ; *for as many as are led by the Spirit of God,* off of themselves to Christ, and by him to the Father, *they are the sons of God;* and who also receive *the Spirit of adoption, whereby* they *cry, Abba, Father ; the Spirit itself beareth witness with* their *spirits, that* they *are the children of God,* Rom. viii. 14—16. so that their faith is grounded on good authority, on a divine testimony, true, sure, and firm ; this blessing of adoption is revealed to faith, the witness of it is received by it, and so believers become openly and manifestly *the children of God by faith in Christ Jesus;* for to *as many as receive him, to them* gives *he power,* authority, right, privilege, *to become the sons of God, even to them that believe in his name,* Gal. iii. 26. John i. 12. and henceforward it is enjoined them that in the exercise of faith they call God their father, and not *turn away from him,* by giving way to an evil heart of unbelief, but say to him, *Doubtless thou art our Father,* Isa. lxiii. 16. and they are directed in all their addresses to God at the throne of grace to say, *Our Father, which art in heaven,* Matt. vi. 9.——6. God is the object of faith as a God forgiving iniquity, transgression and sin for Christ's sake ; and in him he has proclaimed his name as such, and there is none like him on that account ; he has promised pardon in covenant, saying, *I will be merciful to their unrighteousness, and their sins, and their iniquities will I remember no more,* Heb. viii. 12. He has set forth Christ in his purposes to be a propitiation through faith in his blood for the remission of sin ; and he has sent him to shed his blood to obtain it, and has exalted him as a Saviour to give it, and to him give all the prophets witness, that whosoever believes in him shall receive it; and he applies it to them, saying, Son or *daughter, be of good cheer, thy sins be forgiven thee ; I, even I, am he that blotteth out thy transgressions for mine own sake, and will not remember thy sins,* Matt. ix. 2. Isa. xliii. 25. Hence upon such acts and declarations as these, the believer has sufficient ground to make God, as a forgiving God, the object of his faith, and to call upon his soul and all within him to bless his holy name, Psalm ciii. 1—3. such an act of faith David put forth on God as a forgiving God, when, having acknowledged his sin, and confessed it before the Lord, added, *And thou forgavest*

the iniquity of my sin, Psalm xxxii. 5.——
7. Faith deals with God as a justifier; its language is, *Who shall lay anything to the charge of God's elect? it is God that justifieth*, Rom. viii. 33. and iii. 30. and faith is exercised on him as he that *justifieth the ungodly;* and therefore not by works, nor on account of any good dispositions and qualifications in men; and they come to him not as workers, but as ungodly and sinners, and believe on him as justifying them without works, and that by imputing the righteousness of his Son unto them; *even as David also, describeth the blessedness of the man unto whom God imputeth righteousness without works*, Rom. iv. 5, 6. Christ, of God, is made to them righteousness; and they are made the righteousness of God in him; that is, by his gracious imputation of Christ's righteousness to them; and thus God appears to be a just God and a Saviour: just, whilst he is *the justifier of him that believes in Jesus;* and as such he is the object of faith; what Christ the fœderal head of his people, in whom they are all justified, said, his believing members may say, *He is near that justifieth me, who will contend with me?* Isa. l. 8.——8. The God and Father of Christ is *the God of all grace;* it has pleased him, the Father, that all fulness of it should dwell in Christ as Mediator; he has made large provisions of it, and stored the covenant of grace with it; and is the author, giver, and implanter of all grace in the hearts of his people by his Spirit; and as he is able to make all grace to abound towards them, so he grants them a supply of it from time to time: now as such he is the object of faith; faith deals with him as such, and the believer applies to the throne of his grace, that he may obtain mercy, and find grace to help him in time of need.——Lastly, God, as a promising God, is the object of faith, he has made many exceeding great and precious promises, and these are all yea and amen in Christ, and God is faithful who has promised, and is able also to perform; and though promises themselves are not, strictly speaking, the object, rather the things promised, yet especially a promising God is the object faith is concerned with, Heb. x. 23.

2*dly*, God the Son is the object of faith; which faith lies not merely in believing that he is the Son of God, which is most certainly to be believed; it was not only the confession of the faith of Peter, *Thou art Christ the Son of the living God;* which faith, or rather the object of it, is the Rock on which the church of Christ is built, and against which the gates of hell shall never prevail; but it was the faith of all the disciples, and which they express with the strongest assurance; *We believe and are sure that thou art that Christ the Son of the living God*, Matt. xvi. 16, 18. John vi. 69. and it was with respect to this article that the eunuch expressed his faith in Christ, previous to his baptism; *I believe that Jesus Christ is the Son of God*, Acts viii. 37. and all things relating to Christ, his doctrines, and his miracles, were written by the evangelists, *that* men *might believe that Jesus is the Christ the Son of God; and that believing*, they *might have life through his name*, John xx. 31. but true faith is not barely a believing that Christ is the Son of God, but a believing in him as such; according to the question put by Christ to the blind man; *Dost thou believe on the Son of God?* John ix. 35. *And this is his commandment*, the commandment of God, *that we should believe on the name of his Son Jesus Christ.* And again, *He that believeth on the Son of God hath the witness in himself*, 1 John iii. 23. and v. 10. Believing in him is a going forth in acts of faith and confidence, and is called *faith towards our Lord Jesus Christ*, Acts xx. 28. Christ, as the Son of God, is the true God and eternal life; he is God equal with the Father, and as such is equally the primary object of faith; which is strongly expressed by Thomas; *My Lord and my God!* and therefore our Lord says, *Ye believe in God*, in God the Father, *believe also in me* equally as in him, he being equal with him in nature, perfections, power, and glory. But Christ, as Mediator, Redeemer, and Saviour, is the mediate object of faith, or in and through whom men believe in God; thus the apostle Peter, speaking of Christ as Mediator, being foreordained before the foundation of the world; but made manifest in human nature in these last times for the sake of his people, described by him as such, *Who by him do believe in God*, 1 Pet. i. 21. As Christ is the Mediator through whom all grace is communicated to his people, so it is through him that all grace is exercised on God, and particularly faith, *Such trust have we through Christ to Godward*, says the apostle, 2 Cor. iii. 4. So believers reckon themselves *alive unto God through Jesus Christ our Lord*, Rom. vi. 11. Now faith in Christ as the Redeemer and Saviour includes in it the following things, and is expressed by a variety of acts, which shews the nature of it.

1st, I shall consider the several parts of faith in Christ, or what is requisite to constitute it.——1. Knowledge of Christ is necessary to the exercise of faith on him, for *How shall they believe in him of whom they have not heard?* and if they have not so much as heard of him, they cannot know him, and consequently cannot exercise faith upon him; and *How shall they hear without a preacher* to make him known unto them? Rom. x. 14. When our Lord put the question to the man who had been blind, *Dost thou believe on the Son of God? he answered and said, Who is he, Lord, that I might believe on him?* upon which Christ made himself known unto him, *Jesus said unto him, thou hast seen him, and it is he that talketh with thee;* his eyes had been opened to see him, and his ears now heard him, and both being true in a spiritual sense, he immediately expressed his faith in him, saying, *Lord, I believe,* and as a proof and evidence of it, *worshipped him,* John ix. 35—38. Previous to faith in Christ, as a Saviour, there must be knowledge of the want of him; as such a man must be made sensible of the sinfulness of his nature, and of the exceeding sinfulness of sin, and of the just demerit of it, and of the miserable state and condition it has brought him into, out of which none but Christ the Saviour can deliver him; and therefore he then applies to him, as the apostles in distress did, saying, *Lord, save us, we perish!* Matt. viii. 25. he must be made acquainted with his impotency to save himself; that his own right-hand, his works and services, cannot save him; that if ever he is saved it must be by the grace of God, through the blood and righteousness of Christ, and not by them; he must have knowledge of the fulness and ability of Christ as a Saviour; he must have seen him full of grace and truth, as having all the fulness of the blessings of grace in him suitable to his wants, whose redemption is plenteous, his salvation complete, he being made every thing to his people they want, and able to save to the uttermost all that come unto God by him; and he being just such a Saviour they need, and his salvation so suitable to them, they that know his name, Jesus the Saviour, put their trust in him; and the more ready they are to do this, as they are fully convinced there is no other Saviour; that salvation is in him, and in none else; that it is in vain to expect it from any other quarter, from the works and services of the creature, and therefore determine upon it they shall not be their saviours; but say, with Job, *Though he slay me yet will I trust in him——he also shall be my salvation!* Psalm ix. 10. Job xiii. 15, 16. Hence knowledge being so requisite to faith, and included in it, faith is sometimes expressed by it, Isa. liii. 11. John xvii. 3. both in spiritual knowledge and special faith, eternal life is begun, and with which it is connected; and so knowledge and faith are joined together as inseparable companions, and as expressive of the same thing; *And we have known and believed the love that God hath to us,* are firmly persuaded of it, 1 John iv. 16. and some of the strongest acts of faith in the saints, have been expressed by words of knowledge; *I know that my Redeemer liveth, &c. I know in whom I have believed, &c.* Job xix. 25. 1 Tim. i. 12.——2. An assent unto Christ as a Saviour, enters into the true nature of faith; not a bare naked assent of the mind to the truth of the person and offices of Christ; that he is the Son of God, the Messiah, Prophet, Priest, and King, such as has been yielded to him by men destitute of true faith in him, as by Simon Magus and others, yea, by the devils themselves, Luke iv. 34, 41. "Of all the poison, says Dr. Owen,[4] which at this day is diffused in the minds of men, corrupting them from the mystery of the gospel, there is no part that is more pernicious than this one perverse imagination, that to *believe in Christ* is nothing at all but to *believe the doctrine of the gospel!* which yet we grant is included therein." Such a proposition, that Christ is the Saviour of the chief of sinners, or that salvation is alone by him, is not presented merely under the notion of its being *true*, and assented to as such, but under the notion of its being *good*, a suitable, acceptable, and preferable good, and to be chosen as the good part was by Mary; as being both a *faithful saying* to be believed as true, and as *worthy of all acceptation*, to be received and embraced as the chiefest good. Faith is an assent to Christ as a Saviour, not upon an human, but a divine testimony, upon the record which God has given of his Son, and of eternal life in him. Some of the Samaritans believed on Christ because of the saying of the woman; but others because of his own word, having

On the Person of Christ, chap. x. p. 79.

heard him themselves, and knew that he was indeed the Christ, the Saviour of the world. True faith, in sensible sinners, assents to Christ, and embraces him not merely as a Saviour of men in general; but as a special, suitable Saviour for them in particular: it proceeds upon Christ's being revealed *in* them, as well as *to* them, by the Spirit of wisdom and revelation, in the knowledge of him as a Saviour that becomes them; it comes not merely through external teachings, by the hearing of the word from men; but having *heard and learned of the Father*, such souls come to Christ, that is, believe in him, John vi. 45. not the doctrine of him only, but in him himself.——3. Knowledge of Christ as a Saviour, and an assent unto him as such, is attended with love and affection to him; faith works by love, love always accompanies faith, at least follows it. Christ is precious to them that believe; they love him, value him, prefer him, to all others as a Saviour; and every truth respecting Christ is not *barely assented to*, but as they receive Christ, they receive the *love of the truth*, with him.——
4. True, spiritual, special faith in Christ includes in it a dependance on him, trust and confidence in him alone for everlasting life and salvation; it is a soul's venturing on Christ, resolving if it perishes, it will perish at his feet; it is a resignation of itself to Christ, a committing its soul, and the important welfare and salvation of it, into Christ's hands, trusting him with all, looking to him, relying on him, and acquiescing in him as the alone Saviour. All which will more fully appear by considering,

2*dly*, The various acts of faith on Christ, as described in the sacred Scriptures.——
1. It is expressed by seeing the Son; this is one of the first and one of the lowest acts of faith, and yet eternal life is annexed unto it; *This is the will of him that sent me*, says Christ, *that every one which seeth the Son, and believeth on him, may have everlasting life,* John vi. 40. it is a sight of the glories and excellencies of Christ's person, of the fulness of his grace and righteousness, and of the completeness and suitableness of his salvation. It is a looking to Jesus, the author and finisher of faith, a view of him as altogether lovely, the chiefest among ten thousand. Faith is a light struck into the heart of a sinner, whose understanding was darkened, yea, darkness itself, till God commanded light to shine in darkness; by which, though first but glimmering, he sees himself a sinner, miserable and undone, without a Saviour, when Christ is held forth in the gospel to be looked at by him; that is a glass in which he is to be beheld, and where he is evidently set forth crucified and slain for sinners; and so is the hope set before them, both to be looked at, and to be laid hold on by them, who was typified by the brazen serpent set upon a pole by Moses, for the Israelites bitten by the serpents to look at and live, John iii. 14, 15. And not only sensible sinners are directed to behold the Lamb of God which taketh away the sin of the world, as John's hearers were by him; and are encouraged by the ministers of the word, who shew unto men the way of salvation, to look to and believe on the Lord Jesus Christ and be saved; but they are encouraged by Christ himself, who says, *Behold me, behold me*, to a nation not called by his name, *look unto me, and be ye saved, all the ends of the earth, for I am God, and there is none else!* Isa. lxv. 1. and xlv. 22. which sight of him fills their souls with love to him, as the most lovely and amiable one, with eager desires after him, and an interest in him, which is signified by hungering and thirsting after his righteousness, and panting after his salvation. And this sight of Christ by faith is nigh, and not afar off; now, and not hereafter; and for a man's self, and not another; he looks to him not merely as a Saviour of others, but to him as a Saviour and Redeemer suitable for him.——2. Faith is a motion of the soul unto Christ; having looked and gazed at him with wonder and pleasure, it moves towards him; this is expressed by coming unto him; *He that cometh to me*, says Christ, *shall never hunger; and he that believeth on me*, which explains what is meant by coming, *shall never thirst*, John vi. 35. which coming to Christ, is upon an invitation given, encouraging to it; not only by others, by the Spirit and the bride, who say *come*, Rev. xxii. 17. and by the ministers of the word; *Ho, every one that thirsteth, come ye to the waters, and he that hath no money, come!* and who, through the gospel trumpet being blown with power, and the sound of it attended with efficacious grace, they that are *ready to perish*, come, Isa. lv. 1. and xxvii. 13. but also by Christ himself, who says, *Come unto me all ye that labour and are heavy laden, and I will give you rest!* Matt. xi. 28. such souls come, being influenced and powerfully wrought upon by the grace of God; *All that the Father*

giveth me, says Christ, *shall come to me;* efficacious grace will cause them to come, will bring them to him, through all discouragements, difficulties, and objections, and which are all removed by what follows; *and him that cometh to me I will in no wise cast out,* John vi. 37. This coming to Christ as a Saviour, or believing in him, is owing to the Father's teachings, instructions, and drawing; *No man can come to me,* says Christ, that is, believe in him, *except the Father, which hath sent me, draw him,* draw him with his loving-kindness, and through the power of his grace, and of his divine teachings; *every man therefore that hath heard and learned of the Father cometh to me,* yea, this is a pure gift of his grace, therefore *said I unto you, that no man can come unto me except it were given unto him of my Father,* ver. 44, 45, 65. and such souls come to Christ in a view of the blessings of grace, of righteousness and strength, peace and pardon, salvation and eternal life; these are the goodness of the Lord, they flow unto him for, with great eagerness, swiftness, and cheerfulness. For,——3. This motion of faith towards Christ is expressed by fleeing to him; and such souls that believe in him are described as having *fled for refuge to lay hold on the hope set before them,* Heb. vi. 18. and by *turning to the strong hold as prisoners of hope,* that is, to Christ, whose name is a *strong tower,* whither the *righteous run and are safe,* Zech. vi. 12. Prov. xviii. 10. fleeing supposes danger, and a sense of it; Christ is the city of refuge, the strong hold and tower, they are directed to; whither coming, they find shelter and safety from avenging justice and every enemy, a supply of wants, and ground of hope of eternal life and happiness, and thus being come to Christ, various acts of faith are put forth upon him; such as the following,——(1.) A venturing act of their souls, and of their whole salvation on him, like Esther, who ventured into the presence of king Ahasuerus, saying, *If I perish, I perish!* faith at first is such a venture of the soul on Christ, not knowing as yet how it will fare with it; yea, a *peradventure,* perhaps there may be salvation in Christ for it; as Benhadad's servants said to him; *Peradventure he* (the king of Israel) *will save thy life;* reasoning in like manner as the four lepers did, when ready to perish with famine; *Let us fall into the host of the Syrians; if they save us alive, we shall live; and if they kill us, we shall but die:* so sensible sinners, seeing their perishing condition, resolve to venture themselves on Christ; if he saves them it is well, if not they can but die, as they must without him.——(2.) A casting or throwing themselves into the arms of Christ, to be borne and carried by him as a nursing father bears and carries in his bosom a sucking child; so Christ carries the lambs in his arms, Isa. xl. 11. weak believers, who cast themselves and all their burdens, the whole care of their souls upon him; this sense מאון has Numb. xi. 12. from whence comes a word which in many places signifies to believe; see Isa. lx. 4. compared with Isa. lxvi. 12.[5]——3. A laying hold on Christ, who is *a tree of life to them that lay hold upon him,* Prov. iii. 18. from which tree they may pluck and eat all the fruits of grace and life. Christ is the hope of Israel, and the Saviour of his people; and there is great encouragement for sensible sinners to hope in him, because there is mercy and plenteous redemption with him; and he is in the gospel set forth before them as the ground of hope *to lay hold upon* Heb. vi. 18. he is that Jew who sprung from the seed of David and from the tribe of Judah; and his righteousness *the skirt* ten men are said to *take hold of,* Zech. viii. 23. even the robe of his righteousness, which being revealed and brought near to faith, it lays hold upon and puts [it on, as its justifying righteousness, seeing the insufficiency of its own, and the excellency of this. Socinus[6] treats such an apprehension of Christ by faith for justification, as a mere human invention, and a most empty dream; but the true believer finds abundance of solid peace and comfort in it. As Adonijah and Joab fled and laid hold on the horns of the altar for safety, and under a consciousness of guilt; so a sinner, sensible of its sin and guilt, and of its own incapacity to make atonement for it, flees to Christ, and lays hold on his sacrifice, and brings this offering in the arms of his faith, and pleads with God that he would be propitious to him through it, and take away his sin from him. Faith lays hold on the covenant of grace, and upon Christ the Mediator of it, and upon the promises in it, which are yea and amen in Christ, and on the blessings of it, the sure mercies

---

[5] Vid. Coccei. Lexic. Col. 43. Witsii Oecon. Fœderam, l. 3. c. 7. s. 22.

[6] De Servatore par. 4. c. 11. p. 239.

of David, redemption, justification, pardon, peace, reconciliation, and salvation; and claims interest in them. It lays hold on Christ for strength as well as righteousness; *Let him take hold of my strength,* to enable him to exercise every grace, perform every duty, bear the cross of Christ, and persevere in faith and holiness to the end, Isa. xxvii. 5, 6.———(4.) Faith is a retaining Christ, and an holding him fast; the soul being come to Christ, and having laid hold upon him, keeps its hold of him: it is said of Wisdom, or Christ, *happy is every one that retaineth her,* Prov. iii. 18. so the church having lost her beloved, and upon search found him, she *held him, and would not let him go,* as Jacob the angel that wrestled with him until he blessed him, Cant. iii. 4. which denotes not only an holding fast the profession of the faith of Christ, but a continuance of the exercise of the grace of faith on him; an holding to him, the Head, and deriving nourishment from him, a walking on in him as he has been received; a being strong in the grace that is in him, firmly believing its interest in him. It is expressive of strength of faith in Christ, and of great affection to him; for it is sometimes with difficulty it keeps its hold of him when things go contrary, and Christ has withdrawn himself, and is out of sight.———(5.) Faith is sometimes expressed by leaning on the Lord, and *staying* upon him, *the holy One of Israel in truth;* and even those who walk in darkness, and have no light, are directed and encouraged to *trust in the name of the Lord, and stay upon their God,* Isa. x. 20. and l. 10. where trusting in the Lord, and staying on him, are manifestly the same; faith or trust in the Lord, is a staying or leaning on him for all supports and every supply; so the church is said to be *leaning on her beloved,* while coming up out of the wilderness, Cant. viii. 5. which shews consciousness of her own weakness, a dependance on his mighty arm, and an expectation of all supplies of grace and strength from him. But,———(6.) The grand and principal act of faith, or that by which it is more frequently expressed, is, receiving Christ; *as many as received him, even that believe on his name,* John i. 12. where receiving Christ is interpreted of believing on him. Christ is received, not into the head; for not all that say Lord, Lord, shall enter into the kingdom of heaven; but into the heart; for it is with the heart man believes in the Son of God unto righteousness; and in it Christ dwells by faith. A soul made sensible of its need of Christ and his righteousness, and of salvation by him, comes down from self-exaltation, and self-confidence, and *receives Christ joyfully,* as Zaccheus did. Faith receives a whole Christ, not in part only, but in whole, he is *altogether,* or *all of him lovely;*[7] the whole of him is amiable in the sight of a believer, and acceptable to him. As the passover Lamb was to be eaten wholly by the Israelites, no part of it to be left, so faith feeds upon a whole Christ, Christ in his person, offices, grace, and righteousness. *Is Christ divided?* He is not, not in his person; he is but one, God manifest in the flesh; nor in his doctrines; nor from his ministers; nor from his ordinances; where Christ is received, all are received.———1. Christ in all his offices. Christ is received as the great Prophet in the church, whom God promised to raise up, and has raised up, and sent to instruct his people; and by whom grace and truth, the doctrines of grace and truth, are come, and he is to be attended to; *hear ye him,* not Moses, nor Elias, but God's well-beloved Son, by whom he has spoken his whole mind and will in these last days; and who himself says, *Receive my instruction, and not silver; and knowledge rather than fine gold;* that is, his gospel published by him; and such who are spiritually enlightened in the knowledge of him by the Spirit of God, these receive the love of the truth; truth, with a cordial affection for it; receive the word gladly, with all readiness and meekness; they receive the ministers of Christ, and the doctrines preached and messages sent by them; which is interpretatively receiving Christ himself; *he that receiveth you, receiveth me; and he that receiveth me, receiveth him that sent me,* Matt. x. 40. And faith receives Christ also as a Priest, and the atonement which he has made; it views him as a merciful, faithful, and suitable one, who has made reconciliation for sin, put it away by the sacrifice of himself, and made full satisfaction for it, and by his one offering has perfected for ever them that are sanctified. Faith regards him and receives him as the advocate with the Father, as ever living to make intercession; as always at the golden altar, ready to offer

---

[7] כלו מחמדים. Cant. v. 16.

up the prayers of all saints with his much incense; and by whom, as their great high Priest, saints offer their spiritual sacrifices of prayer and praise, which become acceptable to God through him. And faith also receives him as King in Zion; *as ye have therefore received Christ Jesus the Lord*, Col. ii. 6. there seems to be an emphasis on that clause τον κυριον, *the Lord;* one that receives Christ, a true believer in him, acknowledges Christ as his Lord and Head, and gives homage to him as such, saying as the Church did, *the Lord is our Judge, the Lord is our Lawgiver, the Lord is our King, he will save us*, Isa. xxxiii. 22. Christ is received and owned by such, not only as a Priest, but as a Prince; not only as a Saviour, but as a Lawgiver; they take upon them his yoke, submit to his ordinances, and observe his commands; and walk as Zacharias and Elizabeth did, in all the commandments and ordinances of the Lord blameless.——2. Christ, and all the blessings of grace along with him, are received by faith; such as adoption; as Christ gives a power to them that believe in him to become the children of God, they by faith receive this power, right, and privilege from him; and hence we read of *receiving the adoption of children*, through the redemption that is by Christ, Gal. iv. 5. and because faith receives it, believers in Christ become manifestly the children of God. They likewise receive the blessing from the Lord, even a justifying righteousness from the God of their salvation. They receive abundance of grace, and the gift of righteousness, by and from Christ, by which they are justified from all things, and put it on as their robe of righteousness, and glory in it. By faith they receive the pardon of their sins; as Christ is exalted as a Prince and a Saviour, to *give* repentance to Israel, and *forgiveness of sins*, so whosoever believes in him shall *receive remission of sins*, Acts v. 31. and x. 43. and that upon the foot of the atonement made by him; hence they are said to *receive the atonement*, Rom. v. 11. by faith they *receive* out of the fulness of Christ *grace for grace*, all supplies of grace needful for them; as they want more grace, and God has promised it to them, and provided it for them in Christ; so they apply to him for it, and receive it at his hands; and as he gives both grace and glory, they receive both; grace as a meetness for, and as the earnest of glory: not only do they *receive* the forgiveness of their sins, but also *an inheritance among them which are sanctified by faith*, Acts xxvi. 18. they receive grace from God the Father, to make them meet for it; and as the Spirit is given as an earnest of it, they receive him as the earnest of the inheritance, until they are put into the full possession of it.——3. Christ is received as a free gift; he is the gift of God; *if thou knewest the gift of God*, John iv. 10. and an unspeakable gift of his love he is, a gift freely given and unmerited; *God so loved the world that he gave his only begotten Son*, John iii. 16. and he is received and owned as such; *to us a Son is given*, Isa. ix. 6. and all blessings of grace are given, and freely given, along with him, and received as such, Rom. viii. 32.—— 4. Faith receives Christ in preference to all others; it receives him, and him only, as the one Lord and Head, as the one Mediator between God and man, and as the one and only Saviour of sinners; it chooses Christ, the good part that shall never be taken away, above all others: faith works by love to Christ in a stronger manner than to any creature-object whatever; than to the dearest and nearest relation and friend whatever; than to father, mother, brethren and sisters, houses and lands; yea, he that loves any of these more than Christ, is not worthy of him. Nay, faith prefers the worst things belonging to Christ to the best in creatures; the believer is willing to do and suffer any thing and every thing for Christ; none of these things, as afflictions, bonds, and imprisonment for Christ's sake, move the believer from Christ, and its faith and hope in him; he esteems reproach for Christ's sake, greater riches than all the treasures in Egypt, and takes pleasure in persecutions and distresses endured on his account; and even reckons his own best things, his highest attainments in knowledge and righteousness, but loss and dung in comparison of the excellency of the knowledge of Christ Jesus his Lord, and of his righteousness, in which, and in which only, he desires to be found.

3dly, God the holy Spirit is also the object of faith; though we read and hear but little of faith in him, yet as he is God equal with the Father and the Son, he is equally the object of faith as they are: not only his being, perfections, deity, and personality, his offices as a sanctifier and comforter, and his operations of grace on the souls of men, are to be believed; but there are particular acts of faith, trust, and confidence, to be exercised upon him; as he is truly God, he is the object of religious worship, and this cannot be performed aright without faith. Baptism is administered in his name, as in the name of the other two Persons, and this is to be done and submitted to by faith in him; he is particularly to be prayed unto, and there is no praying to him nor in him without faith in him, yea, a true believer trusts in him for his help and assistance in prayer, as indeed he does in the exercise of every religious duty, and of every grace; and besides all this there is a special act of faith put forth upon him, with respect to salvation, as upon the other two persons; for as we are to trust in God the Father to keep us by his power through faith unto salvation, and to trust in Christ for the salvation of our souls, so we are to trust in the Holy Spirit for carrying on and finishing the work of grace in us, who is equal to it; we are to trust the whole of it with him, and be *confident of this very thing*, as we may, as of any one thing in the world, *that he*, the Spirit of God, *who hath begun a good work in us, will perform it until the day of Jesus Christ*, Phil. i. 6.

III. The subjects of the grace of faith, on whom this grace is bestowed, and in whom it is, in some more in others less, in all like precious faith.

First, The subjects of faith are not angels, neither good nor bad. Not the good angels; they live not by faith on God and Christ, as believing men do, but by sight; they are possessed of the beatific vision of God, and are always beholding the face of our Father in heaven, and are continually in his presence, waiting upon him and worshipping him, and enjoy complete and inexpressible happiness in their access unto him, and communion with him, and in the service of him. They are ministering spirits to Christ, always attend him, ever behold the glories of his person, and the fulness of his grace; one part of the great mystery of godliness respecting Christ is, that he is *seen of angels*, and being *received up into glory*, is the object of their vision continually, 1 Tim. iii. 16. much less are the evil angels the subjects of this grace. There is a kind of faith that is ascribed to them, the belief of a God, and that there is but one; *thou believest there is one God, thou dost well, the devils also believe and tremble*, James ii. 19. but then they have no faith on or towards God; no trust in him, and dependance on him; they have cast off allegiance to him, and have rebelled against him; and much less have they any faith in Christ; for though they know him, and cannot but assent to the truth of things concerning him, yet can have no faith in him as their Redeemer and Saviour: and therefore they themselves very justly observed, *What have we to do with thee, Jesus, thou Son of God?* they had nothing to do with him as Jesus a Saviour, and could wish they had nothing to do with him as the Son of God, to whom all judgment is committed, and theirs also, and therefore dread him; but faith in him as a Saviour they could not exercise, for he was not provided as such for them; he took not on him their nature; he was not sent, nor did he come, to seek and save them, nor to die for them; when they sinned God spared them not, made no provision of grace for them, nor promise of it to them, but cast them down from heaven to hell, and has reserved them in chains of darkness to the judgment of the great day, to everlasting wrath and damnation; so that there is not the least ground for faith and hope in Christ concerning their salvation.

Secondly, Men only are the subjects of the grace of faith; and not all men; *for all men have not faith*, 2 Thess. iii. 2. that is, special faith in God and Christ; there are but few[a] who have it; there are many who never heard of Christ, of his gospel, and of the way of life and salvation by him; *and how shall they believe in him of whom they have not heard?* And of those that have heard of him, and of the good news of salvation by him, *they have not all obeyed the gospel; for Esaias saith, Lord, who hath believed our report?* Rom. x. 14, 16. There are some who do not belong to Christ, are none of his; and which is a reason why they do not believe in him; and is a reason which Christ himself gives, and a better cannot be given; *Ye believe not, because ye are not of my sheep*; they that are the sheep of Christ hear his voice, by which faith comes; they know him spiritually and savingly; they follow him, and yield the obedience of faith unto him, John x. 26, 27. There are some of whom it is said, *they could not believe*, because they were left of God to the blindness and hardness of their hearts; and whose minds, by permission, the god of this world blinds,

---

[a] Quæ (fides) donum Dei est singulare et rarum, Luther de Servo Arbitrio, c. 92. p. 142.

lest the gospel should shine into them, and so they believe not, John xii. 39, 40. 2 Cor. iv. 4. In short, none but the elect of God, become true believers in Christ; and all these do, in God's due time, and through the efficacy of his grace; so it has been, and so it ever will be, until they are all brought to believe in Christ; *as many as were ordained unto eternal life believed*, Acts xiii. 48. for, *the belief of the truth*, of Christ, who is the truth, and of the gospel of truth, that comes by him, is the means through which God has chosen men to salvation; and which is as certain to them thereby as the thing itself; for faith is given in consequence of this choice, and is peculiar to the objects of it; hence called *the faith of God's elect*, 2 Thess. ii. 13. Tit. i. 1. such only are the partakers and subjects of this grace, who are regenerated, called, and sanctified. Such that receive Christ and believe in him are described as *born of God*; yea, it is asserted, that *whosoever believeth that Jesus is the Christ is born of God*, John i. 12, 13. 1 John v. 1. whomsoever God calls by his grace with an holy calling, he bestows faith upon them; whoever are converted and turned to the Lord, believe in him; *faith* is one of the *fruits* of the Spirit in sanctification, Gal. v. 22. none but such who are made spiritually alive, believe in Christ; whilst men are dead in trespasses and sins they are *in unbelief*, in a state of unbelief, as the apostle was before conversion, shut up in it, till mercy is displayed in quickening and relieving them; there must be first spiritual life, before there can be faith; hence says Christ, *whosoever liveth and believeth in me shall never die*, John xi. 26. As well may a dead carcass fly, as a dead sinner believe in Christ, or have any will and desire to it.[9] Such only who are alive, see and hear in a spiritual sense, and believe in Christ with a special faith, and shall never perish, but have everlasting life.

Thirdly, Those who are the subjects of this grace of faith, it is different in them as to the degree and exercise of it, though it is in all *alike precious faith* as to its nature, objects, and acts; and in such is the *common faith*, common to all true believers, of which they have a mutual experience; hence the apostle calls his faith, and the faith of the believing Romans, *the mutual faith both of you and me*; yet as to the measure and degree of it, it is in some more, in others less; see 2 Pet. i. 1. Tit. i. 4. Rom. i. 12.——1. In some it is *great faith*; instances of which we have in the centurion, and in the woman of Canaan, Matt. viii. 10. and xv. 28. and many great and heroic actions are ascribed unto it in Heb. xi. though all its greatness, power, and efficacy, are to be ascribed to the Object of it.——2. In some it is but small or *little faith*; in God, and in his providence for the supply of their temporal wants; in Christ, as to his presence with, and powerful preservation and salvation of them, Matt. vi. 30. and viii. 26. and xiv. 31.——3. In others it is very little, *least of all*; it is like a grain of mustard seed, which is the least of all seeds, Matt. xvii. 20. and xiii. 32. and as the apostle Paul calls himself less than the least of all saints, these are the least of all believers; *the little ones*, as Christ calls them, who believe in him; the lambs he carries in his arms; the smoking flax and bruised reed, the day of small things he does not despise. ——4. In these it seems to be next to none, and as if there was none at all; hence these words of Christ to his apostles, *How is it that you have no faith?* and again, *Where is your faith?* Mark iv. 40. Luke viii. 25. that is, in act and exercise; otherwise they had faith as a principle of grace in them, though so little exercised by them as scarcely to be discerned; yet little faith, even that which is the least, differs from no faith. Where there is no faith there is no desire after God, nor after Christ, nor after salvation by him, and communion with him; such neither desire him nor the knowledge of his ways; but where there is ever so small a degree of faith there is a panting after God, a desire to see Jesus, and to have fellowship with him, and a view of interest in him: where there is no faith there is no sense of the want of it, nor complaint of it, nor desire of it, and an increase; but where there is faith, though of the least degree, the soul is sensible of the deficiency of it, and complains of its unbelief, and prays for an increase of faith; as the poor man did, *Lord, I believe, help thou mine unbelief*, Mark ix. 24.——5. In some faith is weak; in others strong: of Abraham it is said, that he was *strong in faith*, and staggered not at the promise through unbelief; but *believed in hope*

---

[9] Nec minus difficile nobis fuerit velle credere, quam difficile fuerit, cadaveri volare, Bezæ Confessio Fidei, c. 4. p. 18.

against hope; these circumstances shewed the strength of his faith. But of others it is said, *him that is weak in the faith receive ye; but not to doubtful disputations,* Rom. iv. 18, 20. and xiv. 1. See an instance of strong faith in Hab. iii. 17, 18, 19.——6. Faith, as to its exercise, differs in the same individuals at different times; as in Abraham, the father of all them that believe, and who was so eminent for his faith; and yet what unbelief and distrust of the power and providence of God did he discover, as to the preservation of him in Egypt and in Gerar, which put him on undue methods for his security? and in David, who sometimes in the strongest manner expresses his faith of interest in God, and in his favour, and at other times was strangely disquieted in his soul, and ready to imagine that he was cut off from the sight of God: and in Peter, who not only strongly asserted his faith in Christ as the Son of God, but so confident was he, that though all men forsook him he would not; and yet, that night denied him thrice, intimidated by a servant-maid and others!——7. In some it arises to a plerophory, a full assurance of faith; as it is expressed in Heb. x. 22. which signifies going with a full sail, in allusion to ships when they sail with a prosperous gale; so souls, when they are full of faith, as Stephen was, move on towards God and Christ in the exercise of it with great spirit and vigour, bearing all before them that stand in the way; being fully persuaded of the love of God to them, and that nothing can separate them from it, and of their interest in Christ, as having loved them and given himself for them; and therefore can say with Thomas, *My Lord and my God!* and with the Church, *My beloved is mine and I am his;* but this is not to be found in all believers; and where it is, it is not always in the same plerophory, without any doubt, hesitation, and mixture of unbelief.

Fourthly, The seat of this grace, in the subjects of it, is the whole soul of man; it is *with the heart* man believes in Christ for righteousness, life, and salvation; says Philip to the eunuch, *If thou believest with all thine heart,* &c. It has been a dispute among divines, whether faith has its seat in the understanding, or in the will, or in the affections; it seems to possess the whole soul, or the whole soul is in the possession of it, and according to its various actings faith has a concern in each faculty. As it lies in the knowledge of divine things, and presents truth to the mind, and is the evidence of things unseen, it has to do with the understanding; and the apostle says of it as such, *by faith we understand,* &c. Heb. xi. 1, 3. and sometimes the strongest acts of faith, even assurance of interest in Christ as the Redeemer and Saviour, is expressed by knowledge of him; *I know that my Redeemer liveth,* Job xix. 25. as it is an act of choice, preferring Christ, as a Saviour, to all others; and of affiance, trust, and dependance on him, it is an act of the will; *though he slay me, yet will I trust in him:—he also shall be my salvation,* Job xiii. 15, 16. and neither of these acts can be without love to Christ, and a strong motion of the affections towards him, saying, *Whom have I in heaven but thee,* &c. Faith works by love.

IV. The causes of faith, from whence it springs, and how it comes to pass that any who are naturally in a state of unbelief, and shut up in it, should be possessed of this grace.

First, The efficient cause is God; hence it is called the *work of God,* John vi. 29. which he works by his power and grace in the hearts of men; it is expressly said to be of *the operation of God,* Col. ii. 12. it is a very considerable part of the *good work* of grace, which is begun, carried on, and performed, by the Spirit of Christ; and from it the whole is denominated the *work of faith,* which is wrought and finished with the *power* of God, 2 Thess. i. 11. and it is also called *the gift of God,* who deals forth to every man *the measure of faith* as he pleases, Eph. ii. 8. Rom. xii. 3. All the Three divine Persons, Father, Son, and Spirit, are concerned in it.——1. God the Father; as he is the *God of all grace,* so of this: *No man,* says Christ, *can come unto me,* that is, believe on him, as it is explained ver. 35. *except the Father, which hath sent me, draw him; and except it were given unto him of my Father,* John vi. 44, 45, 65. see Matt. xvi. 16, 17.——2. The Lord Jesus Christ the Son of God, has a concern in it; it is prayed and wished for, as from God the Father, so from the Lord Jesus Christ; and is obtained through the righteousness of God and our Saviour Jesus Christ; nay, Christ is expressly called, *the Author and Finisher of faith,* Eph. vi. 23. 2 Pet. i. 1. Heb. xii. 2.——3. The Holy Spirit is, with the Father and the Son, the co-efficient cause of faith; not only faith is given by the Spirit, as it intends the faith of miracles, but the special grace of faith is reckoned among the fruits of the Spirit; and from hence he is called *the Spirit of faith*, because it is his gift, and of his operation, 1 Cor. xii. 9. Gal. v. 22. 2 Cor. iv. 13.

Secondly, The moving cause of faith, is the free grace of God; it is not of men themselves, the produce of their free will and power; but it is *the gift of God*; a gift of his pure grace, unmerited, and unmoved to it by any thing in the creature; hence those that believe, are said to have *believed through grace*; it is a fruit of electing grace, and flows from that; the same grace that moved God to ordain any of the sons of men to eternal life, bestows the grace of faith upon them in consequence of it, Acts xviii. 27. and xiii. 48. and this is owing to sovereign and distinguishing grace, according to which it is bestowed on some and not on others, as it seems good in the sight of God, Matt. xi. 25, 26.

Thirdly, The word and ministers of it are the usual means and instruments of faith in the hand of God, and are used by him; the end of the word being written is, that men *might believe that Jesus is the Christ the Son of God*, John xx. 31. and the word preached is, *the word of faith*; and so called, with other reasons, because faith comes by it, Rom. x. 8, 17. this has often been the effect and consequence of hearing the word preached, Acts xvii. 4. and xviii. 8. and the ministers of it are the instruments by whom and through whose word, doctrine, and ministry, others believe, John i. 17, 20. 1 Cor. iii. 5. but this is only when it is attended with the power and Spirit of God, 1 Cor. ii. 4, 5.

V. The effects of it, or the various things which are ascribed unto it in some sense or another, which shew the usefulness and importance of this grace. As,

First, Several blessings of grace are attributed to it; and with which it is, on some account or another, connected; by it access is had unto them, and an enjoyment of them, and comfort from them.—— 1. Justification; hence we read of being *justified by faith*, Rom. iii. 30. and v. 1. Gal. ii. 16. and iii. 8. not by it, or through it, as a work of righteousness done by men, for then they would be justified and saved by works, contrary to the Scriptures, Rom. iv. 2, 6. Tit. iii. 5. Nor as a grace of the Spirit of God wrought in men; for that is a part and branch of sanctification; and would tend to confound justification and sanctification, which are two distinct things; the one an act of God's grace towards men, the other a work of his grace in them: nor as a cause of it; for it is *God*, and not faith that *justifies*, Rom. viii. 33. for though men are said to be justified by faith, yet faith is never said to justify them: nor as a condition of justification; for God *justifies the ungodly*, Rom. iv. 5. nor as a motive; for that is the free grace of God; *being justified freely by his grace*, Rom. iii. 24. nor as the matter of it; that is the righteousness of Christ: faith and righteousness are two different things, and are frequently distinguished; that by which men are justified are the obedience and blood of Christ, Rom. v. 9, 19. but faith is neither of them; faith is a man's own, but justifying righteousness is another's; *not having on mine own righteousness*, Phil. iii. 9. faith is imperfect; but the righteousness by which men are justified is perfect, or it cannot be reckoned righteousness, Deut. vi. 25. it is not the τὸ, *credere*, or act of faith, but the object who, or what, is believed in, that is imputed for righteousness, it is Christ and his righteousness, the object of faith, by which men are justified; faith objectively, or the object of faith, Christ, who is sometimes called faith, Gal. iii. 23. he is made righteousness unto them; faith only relatively considered, as it relates to Christ, receives the blessing of his justifying righteousness from him, being revealed from faith to faith, and given to it, and put into its hands; which faith puts on as a robe of righteousness, and rejoices and glories in it.——2. Adoption; faith, as before observed, receives the adoption of children from Christ, the power he gives to become the children of God; and they are said to be *the children of God by faith in Christ Jesus*, Gal. iii. 26. that is manifestly so; faith does not make them the children of God, but makes them appear to be such.——3. The remission of sins; *God has set forth Christ to be a propitiation, through faith in his blood, for the remission of sins*, Rom. iii. 25. not that faith has any virtue or merit in it to procure it; nor is it for the sake of faith that God forgives sins; but for his own name's sake, for Christ's sake, whose blood was shed for it; but faith receives the remission of sins, as flowing from the grace of God through the blood of Christ, Acts x. 43.—— 4. Sanctification and purification are ascribed to faith. So it is said of such that receive the forgiveness of sins, that they also receive *an inheritance among them which are sanctified by faith that is in me,* in Christ, Acts xxvi. 18. and again, *purifying their hearts by faith,* Acts xv. 9. not that faith has such virtue in it as to sanctify and purify from sin; but as it has to do with the blood of Christ which cleanses from all sin.———5. Eternal life and salvation are connected with faith; yea, it is life eternal to know Christ, that is, to believe in him; nay, he that believes in him *has everlasting life,* John xvii. 3. and vi. 47. not that faith is the procuring and meritorious cause of it; for *eternal life is the gift of God through Jesus Christ our Lord;* and faith looks unto the mercy of Christ for it, Rom. vi. 23. Jude ver. 21.

Secondly, By faith souls have communion with God, with Christ, and with his people, in his word and ordinances.——— 1. They have access to God at the throne of grace, and can use freedom, boldness, and confidence with him, in asking of him what they stand in need of; *in whom,* says the apostle, *we have boldness and access with confidence by the faith of him;* that is, by faith in Christ, Eph. iii. 12. Christ is the way of access to God; there is no coming to him but by Christ the Mediator, and by faith in him; faith gives freedom and boldness to speak to God; faith presents Christ's righteousness, pleads his blood, and brings his sacrifice in its arms, and boldly enters into the holiest of all thereby; and goes to God, even up to his seat, and lays hold on him, and claims interest in him, and will not go without a blessing.———2. The inhabitation of Christ in the hearts of his people is through faith; the apostle prayed for the Ephesians, that, says he, *Christ may dwell in your hearts by faith,* Eph. iii. 17. not in their heads by fancy and notion; but in their hearts by faith: there is a mutual indwelling of Christ, and believers in each other; he dwells in them by faith, and they dwell in him by faith; *he that eateth my flesh and drinketh my blood, dwelleth in me and I in him,* John vi. 56. that is, who feeds by faith upon him; Christ and believers are not only inmates in the same house, and dwell under the same roof, but they mutually dwell in each other by faith, which is expressive of great nearness, intimacy, and communion.——— 3. Believers feed and live upon Christ by faith; *he,* says Christ, *that eateth me,* his flesh and blood by faith, *even he shall live by me,* a life of grace, which will issue in eternal life; yea, such as thus feed on Christ *have eternal life,* John vi. 54, 57. and a most comfortable life this is, which a believer lives by faith on Christ, and so a very desirable one; *the life which I now live in the flesh,* says the apostle, *I live by the faith of the Son of God,* Gal. ii. 20. nor did he desire any other; a better and more comfortable life cannot be lived in this world; *the just shall live by faith;* not upon his faith; but by faith on Christ, Rom. i. 17.———4. It is by faith that believers stand, and walk, and go on comfortably in their Christian race; *thou standest by faith,* in a gospel-church-state, in a profession of Christ, and in the enjoyment of his word and ordinances: *by faith ye stand;* keep your ground; turn not back, nor are moved from the hope of the gospel, Rom. xi. 20. 2 Cor. i. 24. *We walk by faith, and not by sight;* so did the apostle, and so he directs others; *as ye have therefore received Christ Jesus the Lord, so walk ye in him,* 2 Cor. v. 7. Col. ii. 6. go on believing in him till ye receive the end of your faith, the salvation of your souls.———5. Faith makes Christ precious to souls; *to them that believe he is precious,* 1 Pet. ii. 7. Faith beholds the glories of Christ's person; the riches of his grace; the treasures and wonders of his love; which render him altogether lovely and the chiefest among ten thousand.———6. *Faith works by love,* Gal. v. 6. both by love to Christ and by love to his people; the clearer views a soul has of Christ by faith, the more it loves him; and the more closely it cleaves unto him, leans upon him, and embraces him by faith, the more its affections are drawn out to him; and the more it feeds on him by faith, and the more tastes it has of him that he is gracious, the more are its desires to him, and to the remembrance of him; and it cannot but love all that bear his image, and partake of his grace; these precious sons of Zion are precious to whom Christ is precious, and are the excellent in the earth, in whom is the delight of such, even such who are Christ's Hephzibah and his jewels.——— 7. It is faith which makes the word useful and the ordinances pleasant and delightful. Where faith is wanting, the word is of no use: *the word preached did not profit them, not being mixed with faith in them that heard it,* Heb. iv. 2. the word is compared to food, which though notionally received, yet if not heartily digested by faith, does not nourish; it is only when Christ is held forth, and seen in the galleries, and shews himself, through the lattices to faith, that the ordinances are amiable and lovely, or when he is fed upon by faith in them; as the Israelites by faith kept the passover, a type of Christ our passover, sacrificed for us; so believers keep the feast of the Lord's Supper in commemoration of that sacrifice, and when they do it in faith, it is with joy and comfort, and to great usefulness.

Thirdly, There are various other useful things ascribed to faith, as the effects of it: as,——1. It makes not ashamed. It is said, *he that believeth shall not make haste*, Isa. xxviii. 16. after another Saviour, or to lay another foundation, being satisfied with Christ. In some places in the New Testament the phrase is rendered, *shall not be ashamed*, and *shall not be confounded*, Rom. ix. 33. and x. 11. 1 Pet. ii. 6. such who believe, shall not be ashamed of their faith and hope in Christ; nor of their profession of him; nor of the reproaches, sufferings, and persecutions they endure for his sake; nor shall they be confounded by any of their enemies; nor meet with a disappointment in their expectations here or hereafter, Psalm xxii. 5.——2. It fills the soul with joy on hearing the word, the good news of salvation by Christ; so the gaoler, on hearing the word of salvation preached, *rejoiced, believing in God*, Acts xvi. 31—34. and indeed, a sight of Christ by faith will fill a soul *with joy unspeakable and full of glory*, 1 Pet. i. 8. hence we read of *the joy of faith*; for as faith increases, joy does, wherefore the apostle prays that the Romans might be filled *with all joy and peace in believing*, Phil. i. 25. Rom. xv. 13.——3. It is by faith that saints get the victory over Satan, and the world, and every enemy; faith holds up Christ, the shield, whereby it keeps off every fiery dart of Satan, yea, quenches them; though he, like a roaring lion, goes about seeking whom he may devour; yet the true believer so resists him, being stedfast in faith, that he cannot get an advantage over him, but is obliged to flee from him, Eph. vi. 16. 1 Pet. v. 9. and though the world is a very powerful enemy, yet *this is the victory that overcometh the world, even our faith; who is he that overcometh the world, but he that believeth that Jesus is the Son of God?* 1 John v. 4, 5.——4. It is by faith that saints are kept unto salvation, and are saved by grace through it. *Salvation* is the *end* of their *faith*, and what it issues in; and they *are kept by the power of God through faith*; the power of God supporting their faith that it fail not, until they are brought *unto salvation*, to the full enjoyment of it, 1 Pet. i. 5, 9. nor does this at all detract from the grace of God; since faith itself is a gift of grace, and gives all the glory to it, Eph. ii. 8, 9.

VI. The properties or adjuncts of faith, which may lead more into the nature and excellency of it, and serve to comfirm what has been said concerning it.——1. It is the first and principal grace, it stands first in order, and takes the precedence of other graces; *now abideth faith, hope, charity*, which last, though the greatest, yet not as to quality and use, but as to quantity or duration; faith is not only of the greatest importance in duty, service, and worship, without which it is impossible to please God; but it has the greatest influence on other graces, it sets them all at work, and as that is in exercise so are they more or less.——2. It is a grace exceeding precious, even the least degree of it; as it is in the least believer, it is *like precious faith*, as to its object, nature, and acts, with that in the greatest; it is more precious than gold that perisheth, for richness, brightness, splendour and glory; it makes poor men rich, and is more bright and glorious than pearls and rubies, and all desirable things; it is more valuable than gold because that perishes, but this does not; and it makes Christ precious, or shews him to be so, to them that believe, 2 Pet. i. 1. 1 Pet. i. 7. and ii. 7.——3. It is but *one*; as there is but one Lord to be believed in, and to be subject to, so but *one faith*; as but one doctrine of faith, that faith once delivered to the saints, so but one grace of faith; though there are divers sorts of faith, there is but one that is special, spiritual, and saving, the faith of God's elect; though there are many subjects of it in whom it is, and many are the acts of it, and there are different degrees, as to the exercise of it, yet the grace itself is but one and alike in all, Eph. iv. 5. 2 Pet. i. 1.——4. Though faith is called *common* faith, common to all God's elect, yet every man has his own faith; *the just shall live by his faith*, and not another's, Hab. ii. 4. The faith of one man is of no service to another in the business of salvation; and no further useful to another than for imitation and encouragement to believe also; hence we read of *thy faith*, and *my faith*, as distinct from one another, James ii. 18. Christ said to Peter, *I have prayed for thee that thy faith fail not*, Luke xxii. 32.

meaning his particular, personal faith; not but that Christ has the same regard to all his people, and equally intercedes for them on the same account.——5. It is true, real, and unfeigned, 1 Tim. i. 5. 2 Tim. i. 5. There is an hypocritical faith, which lies only in profession, in saying that a man believes, when he does not, as Simon Magus; and there is a believing with the heart, even with all the heart, as the eunuch did, Acts viii. 13, 37. see Rom. x. 9, 10.——6. It is a grace that cannot be lost; it flows from, and is secured by, the firm and immutable decree and purpose of election; it is given in consequence of that, and remains sure by it; it is a gift of God, and one of those gifts of his which are without repentance, is irreversible and irrevocable; it is confirmed by the prevalent intercession of Christ, and which he himself is the Author and Finisher of.——7. It is indeed but imperfect; yet may be increased; as knowledge is imperfect; *We know but in part*; so faith is imperfect; it has its τα υςιρηματα, *its deficiencies*, or something *lacking* in it, to be perfected by prayer to God, saying, *Lord, increase our faith;* by the ministry of the word, and by a constant attendance on ordinances; and sometimes *faith grows exceedingly;* 1 Thess. iii. 10. 2 Thess. i. 3.——8. According to the apostle's account of it, *it is the substance of things hoped for, the evidence of things not seen,* Heb. xi. 1. it realizes things, and gives them a subsistence, and makes them appear solid and substantial; it brings distant things near, and future things present; it makes difficult things plain and easy, and unseen things visible, and gives a certainty to them all.

CHAP. VII.

OF TRUST AND CONFIDENCE IN GOD.

TRUST and confidence signify the same thing, whether with respect to God or men; to trust in men, is to confide or put confidence in them; and so to trust in God is to place confidence in him; and generally in all places where to trust in God is mentioned, the Latin versions are to confide in him; and this being so near akin to faith, if not a part, yet at least a fruit of it, deserves next to be considered. And,

I. What confidence signifies, and the sense in which it is sometimes taken, and to be treated of here.

First, It is sometimes used for a profession of religion, taken up in the name and strength of Christ, and with an holy resolution to continue it, and an holding it fast with courage and intrepidity; which, if supported and maintained, will issue well; hence it is advised not to *cast it away*, Heb. iii. 6, 14. and x. 35. a profession of religion is not to be taken up hastily, without due consideration of the nature and importance of it, and of the difficulties that attend it, and of the expense a man must be at to support it; to which reference may be had, Luke xiv. 27—33. and it is to be taken up, not in a man's own strength, but in the strength of Christ, on whom there ought to be a constant trust and dependence for supplies of grace to maintain it; and it should be made openly before many witnesses, without shame and fear; without being ashamed of Christ and his gospel; and without fear of men: and when it is taken up, should be held fast with an holy courage and confidence; to which many things induce; as the consideration of Christ, the great high Priest of our profession; and the faithfulness of God in his promises, Heb. iv. 14. and x. 23.

Secondly, It sometimes signifies that alacrity in which men engage in any branch of religious service, and continue in it with boldness and intrepidity, exercising faith and hope in God, that he will be with them in it, and carry them through it; as particularly in preaching the gospel of Christ boldly, as it ought to be spoken; thus says the apostle, *Many of the brethren in the Lord, waxing confident by my bonds, are much more bold to speak the word without fear*, Phil. i. 14.; boldness in the ministry of the word, is a necessary qualification for a preacher of it; this the apostle Paul was so sensible of, that he desires the Ephesians to pray for him that he might have *utterance given*, and that he might *open his mouth boldly to make known the mystery of the gospel*; and this he did wherever he went, at Thessalonica, and other places, Eph. vi. 19. 1 Thess. ii. 2. Peter and John, though unlearned men, were taken notice of for their boldness and courage; who, notwithstanding the threats of the rulers, spoke the words of life to the people; declaring, that they ought to obey God rather than men, Acts iv. 13, 18, 19, 20. and v. 20, 28, 29. and so private christians, in every branch of religious service, should exercise an humble boldness, and an holy confidence, and a stedfastness in all the duties of religion, knowing that though they can do nothing of themselves, yet, through Christ strengthening them they can do all things; trusting and placing their confidence in the Lord Jehovah, in whom is everlasting strength, and not fearing a lion in the way or in the streets; nor solicitous what will be the issue and consequence of their persisting in the way of their duty; of which trust and confidence, Daniel and his companions were examples.

Thirdly, Sometimes confidence with respect to God in prayer is designed. *In whom*, that is, in Christ, *we have boldness and access with confidence by the faith of him*, Eph. iii. 12. through Christ the Mediator, and faith in him, souls may come to God with great freedom and liberty, tell him all their mind, and pour out their souls before him; especially they can do that when they are under the influences, and have the assistance of his Spirit; *for where the Spirit of the Lord is, there is liberty;* otherwise there is a straitness of soul, and saints are shut up that they cannot come forth in the lively exercise of grace; but they may come with boldness and intrepidity to the throne of grace, and ask such things of God they stand in need of, may look up and lift up their face, and shew their countenance, as they are allowed, and indeed desired to do; nay, they may have *this confidence* in God, that *if they ask any thing according to his will he heareth them*, 1 John v. 14. all which arise from faith in the person, blood, and righteousness of Christ: it is through the blood of Christ saints have boldness to enter into the holiest of all, and in his righteousness to stand before God with acceptance, and wait in faith for success; and which holy boldness and confidence is consistent with reverence of God and submission to his will.

Fourthly, Trust or confidence in God may be considered, as it has a connection with the grace of faith; faith is sometimes expressed by it; *Such trust* or confidence *have we through Christ to God-ward*, 2 Cor. iii. 4. it is at least a fruit and effect of it, what follows upon it; for when the grace of faith is wrought in the soul, it shews itself in trust and confidence in God, even when it has not a full persuasion of interest in him; *Though he slay me, yet will I trust in him:* some make it to be the form of faith, and of the essence of it; and that faith in Christ consists of these three parts, knowledge of him as a Saviour, assent unto him as such, and trust in him, or a fiducial application and appropriation of him as a man's own Saviour; hence it is commonly said by some, *fides est fiducia;* faith is confidence; it seems to be faith greatly strengthened; a strong exercise of it; such as in 2 Tim. i. 12. *I know whom I have believed* or *trusted;* if not a plerophory, and full assurance of it; and such a trust or confidence, which is so near akin to faith, and as it should seem a strong act of it, is what is to be treated of; and since it is so much spoken of in scripture, and so much recommended, and such instances of it, and so many happy consequences and effects of it, it deserves a distinct consideration. Particularly,

II. The objects of it.

First, Negatively; what are not the objects of it, and are dehorted from in scripture.———1. Idols; trust in which, and in things belonging to them, may be called idolatrous and superstitious confidence; to have other gods besides the Lord, as idols, to worship them, and yield religious service to them, is contrary to the first and second commands; and to trust in them is the heighth of folly and vanity, Psalm cxv. 4—8. Isa. xlii. 17. Such pray unto, serve and worship, and trust in what can neither see them, nor hear them, nor help, nor save them. And as vain and superstitious is the trust and confidence of such, who place it in religious buildings, in temples made with hands; as the Jews, in the temple at Jerusalem; who, because it was called by the name of the Lord, trusted in it, it being the place where they met and worshipped, and in which they confided for present safety and future happiness, Jer. vii. 4, 14. So the Gentiles gloried in their temples; as in the temple of Diana, at Ephesus; and of other idols in other places. Likewise all superstitious rites and ceremonies, which, though they have been in use, now abrogated; yet, if exercised, and especially trusted in, are condemned, as trusting in the flesh; as circumcision, &c. among the Jews; as well as a multitude of carnal and worldly ordinances among the Gentiles, which had a shew of wisdom in will-worship.———2. Men; trust in whom may be called human confidence; and which is not to be placed, no, not in the greatest of men, Psalm cxviii. 8, 9. even not in whole nations, strong and mighty. This was the sin of the Israelites, that they *trusted in the shadow of Egypt* to shelter and skreen them from their enemies, and which was vain and unprofitable unto them; therefore, says the Lord, *Trust in the shadow of Egypt shall be your confusion,* Isa. xxx. 2, 3. all outward means for safety in times of trouble and danger are of no avail, and are false things to be trusted in; *Some trust in chariots, and some in horses: but we will remember the name of the Lord our God,* that is a strong tower, where is safety and security; horses and armies, castles and fortresses, are vain things for safety; nor are they to be trusted in, Psalm xx. 7. and xxxiii. 16, 17. Prov. xxi. 31. and in some cases the most intimate friends are not to be confided in for secrecy; *Trust ye not in a friend; put ye not confidence in a guide,* Micah. vii. 5. Neither are men to be trusted in for the health of the body, any more than for the protection of lives and properties; physicians may be made use of, but not confided in; Asa's sin was, *that he sought not to the Lord* for the cure of his bodily disease, *but to the physicians;* only in them he put his confidence, to the neglect of the great Physician of soul and body, 2 Chron. xvi. 12.——

3. Self is another object not to be trusted in, on more accounts than one; and trust in which may be called self-confidence; as when men trust in their wealth, and make gold their hope, and say to the fine gold, Thou art my confidence; trust in uncertain riches, and not in the living God; have no regard to divine providence, and a dependence on that; but foolishly fancy they have goods laid up for many years, and promise themselves great ease and pleasure; when that very night their souls may be required of them; and so very true is that of the wise man, *He that trusteth in his riches shall fall,* Prov. xi. 18. see Jer. ix. 23. Nor should a man trust in his wisdom; since the way of man is not in himself; not even in civil, as well as not in religious things: nor is it in man that walketh to direct his steps; good is the advice of Solomon, *Trust in the Lord with all thine heart, and lean not to thine own understanding,* Prov. iii. 5. Nor should a man trust in his strength; not in his natural strength, as Samson; nor in his moral strength, to perform that which is morally good, to do which he wants both knowledge and strength of himself; and even the good man should not trust in his spiritual strength; since without Christ he can do nothing: nor should a man trust in his own heart; since he that trusts in it *is a fool,* Prov. xxviii. 26. that being so deceitful and desperately wicked, and out of which so much wickedness comes. Nor should men trust in their own works of righteousness done in obedience to the law of Moses; this is trusting in Moses, and resting in the law, as the Jews did; by the deeds of which there is no justification and salvation; such trust in themselves that they are righteous; but such a man's trust is no other *than a spider's web,* Job viii. 14, 15.

Secondly, Positively, the true and proper objects of trust and confidence are Jehovah, Father, Son, and Spirit, the true God, the God of our salvation; who is, or ought to be, the *confidence,* that is, the object of the confidence of *all the ends of the earth,* Psalm lxv. 5.

1*st,* Jehovah the Father; both as the God of nature and providence, and as the God of all grace: as the former, men are to trust in him to uphold them in their beings, to give them all the necessaries of life, to preserve them in life, and to protect them from all enemies and dangers, and to enable them to do the work of their generation according to his will. And as the latter, to supply them with his grace, to give them more grace to help them in every time of need, to be their God and guide in life even unto death, and through it, and bring them safe to his everlasting kingdom and glory; and being satisfied of their interest in him as their covenant-God and Father in Christ, they may be confident,——1. Of his love to them, and of the continuance of it; as God has graciously appeared to them, and told them that he has loved them with an everlasting love, and assured them that his *loving-kindness shall not depart from them;* they may trust in a promising God, and be confident *that he will rest in his love towards* them; and be *persuaded,* as the apostle Paul was, or have a strong confidence, as he had, that nothing shall be able to *separate them from the love of God,* since he has given his word and oath for it, that though he afflicts and chastises them for their transgressions, *neverthless* his *loving-kindness he will not utterly take from* them, Isa. liv. 10. Zeph. iii. 17. Rom. viii. 38, 39. Psalm xxxix. 33.
——2. Of the faithfulness of God in the fulfilment of his promises; he is faithful that has promised, and will never suffer his faithfulness to fail; nor any of the good things to fail of performance which he has promised; and this they may be confident of, since they flow from his love and grace, are made in a covenant ordered in all things

and sure, and which he will never break; and since they are all yea and amen in Christ, most certainly performed in and by him, and for his sake; and since the performance of them does not depend on the faith of men, but on the faithfulness of God; the unbelief of men does not make the faith, that is, the faithfulness of God, of none effect; for though they believe not, he abides faithful.——3. Of the grace of God to supply all their wants; of which they may be confident, since he is the God of all grace, the author and giver of it, the fountain and source of it, and of every supply of it; and since he is able to cause all grace to abound towards them, and his grace is sufficient for them; and since he has promised more grace unto them as they need; and has set up a throne of grace to come unto for it; and since it has pleased him the Father of Christ, and our Father in him, that all fulness of grace should dwell in him, that from thence grace for grace might be received; and who is a sun and shield, and gives both grace and glory.——4. Of his power to keep and preserve them to eternal glory and happiness: and of this they may be confident, since he is able to keep them from falling; and his hand is not shortened that he cannot save; his strength is everlasting, and never is any decay of it; and since it is certain that regenerated persons are *kept by the power of God through faith unto salvation;* to which salvation, glory, and happiness, they are called, and therefore may be assured that they shall enjoy it; *faithful is he that calleth you, who also will do it,* 1 Pet. i. 5. 1 Thess. v. 23, 24.

2dly, Jehovah the Son is the object of the saints' trust and confidence: it is said, *Kiss the Son,* the Son of God, the begotten Son of God; to whom it is said in the context, *Thou art my Son, this day have I begotten thee;* to whom worship, honour, and homage are to be given by the kings and judges of the earth; and it is added, *Blessed are all they that put their trust in him,* the Son of God, the object of the worship and adoration of angels and men. He gives *grace and glory to his people, and no good thing will he withhold from them that walk uprightly;* and then it follows, as before, *Blessed is the man that trusteth in thee,* Psalm ii. 12. and lxxxiv. 11, 12. the Targums or Chaldee paraphrases of which places are, *Who trust in his Word,* or in *the Word of the Lord,* his essential Word; so of Psalm xxxiv. 8, 22. Jer. xvii. 7. see Eph. i. 12. Now trust and confidence are to be exercised on Christ, not merely as the second and instrumental cause of happiness, as says Socinus,[1] but as the first and sole cause of it, which he denies: being the Author, Cause, and Captain of eternal salvation; trust is to be put,——1. In the salvation of Christ, or in him for salvation: it is said of the Israelites, that they *believed not in God, and trusted not in his salvation,* Psalm lxxviii. 22. but true believers in Christ trust in him as a Saviour, and in his salvation, he being an able and willing Saviour, and his salvation suitable, complete, and perfect; nor is there salvation in any other; and therefore they say, as Job did, *Though he slay me yet will I trust in him:—he also shall be my salvation,* Job xiii. 15, 16.——2. In his righteousness: a strong act of trust and confidence in Christ and his righteousness is exercised by the church in these words; *Surely shall one say,* verily, or only, *in the Lord have I righteousness and strength,* Isa. xlv. 24, 25. Christ is with great confidence and strength of faith called, *The Lord our righteousness,* Jer. xxiii. 6. and the apostle Paul, disclaiming all confidence in the flesh, and trust in his own righteousness, desired to be found in Christ and in his righteousness; the *righteousness which is of God by faith;* that is the righteousness which Christ has wrought out, and which God imputes without works, and reveals from faith to faith, Phil. iii. 4—9. ——3. In the grace of Christ, and the fulness of it in him, for the supply of all wants; all grace and the fulness of it, dwell in him; out of which saints in all ages have received an abundance of grace; and yet there is an over-flowing fulness of it in him; and they may be confident that their God will supply all their need from thence; and to exercise such confidence is to *be strong in the grace that is in Christ Jesus,* 2 Tim. ii. 1. ——4. In the power, might, and strength of Christ. Believers in Christ are ready to acknowledge their own weakness; yea, even to glory in it, *That the power of Christ may rest upon* them, overshadow and protect them; for when they are *weak,* as they are in themselves, and are sensible of it, then are they *strong,* that is, *in the Lord, and in the power of his might;* and trust in him that he will enable them to stand their ground, and to get the victory

---

[1] Contr. Wujekum. c. 4. p. 559.

over all their enemies; they are encouraged, as they are directed, *to trust in the Lord for ever, for in the Lord Jehovah is everlasting strength;* to help them in the exercise of every grace, and in the performance of every duty; to bear the cross of Christ, to fight his *battles, and to persevere* in faith and holiness to the end 2 Cor. xii. 8, 10. Eph. vi. 10. Isa. xxvi. 4.

3*dly*, Jehovah the Spirit is also the object of the trust and confidence of believers; as he is the Spirit of grace and of supplication; as the Spirit of grace, they trust in him to communicate more grace to them, to increase what is in them, and to draw it forth into lively exercise; and as the Spirit of supplication, in whom they confide for his help and assistance in prayer, and for his prevalent intercession for them, according to the will of God; and as the Spirit of counsel and might, to direct and guide them, and to strengthen them with all might in the inward man; and faith and trust in the Spirit of God, for the carrying on and finishing his own work of grace in the hearts of his people, is expressed by confidence of it, Phil. i. 6.

III. The encouragement there is to trust in the Lord, and that for all things and at all times

First, There is encouragement to trust in God for all things.——1. All things are of him; that is, all good things in nature, providence, and grace: all good things in nature; *He gives to all, life, and breath, and all things,* Acts xvii. 25. and all things in providence are at his disposal; *for of him, and through him, and to him are all things,* Rom. xi. 36. And all things in grace; all the blessings of grace; as reconciliation, peace, pardon, righteousness, life and salvation; *All things are of God, who hath reconciled us to himself by Jesus Christ,* 2 Cor. v. 18. and all the gifts of grace, even *every good gift and every perfect gift is from above, and cometh down from the Father of lights;* as regeneration, which is instanced in, with all the graces of the Spirit included in it, and come with it; as faith, hope, love, &c. James i. 17, 18.——2. All good things are promised by God to his people; the covenant of grace is *ordered in all things,* and is full of exceeding great and precious promises, suited to the case and circumstances of good men; godliness and godly men have the *promise of the life that now is, and of that which is to come;* and not one of the good things which God has promised ever fail; they are always fulfilled; the promises are yea and amen in Christ; they, and the blessings in them, are the sure mercies of David.——3. God keeps back no good thing he has promised, and which his people need, and which he knows is for their welfare. *No good thing will he withhold from them that walk uprightly;* therefore it follows, *O Lord of hosts, blessed is the man that trusteth in thee!* that is, for all good things, Psalm lxxxiv. 11, 12. they are bid to ask, and it is promised it shall be given; God is *nigh* to all that *call* upon him, and will *fulfil the desire of them that fear him; he will hear their cry and save them,* Psalm cxlv. 16, 18, 19.——4. God gives all things freely to his people; they cannot merit any thing of him; *Who hath first given to him, and it shall be recompensed to him again?* No man can be beforehand with God; he has nothing but what he has received from him; nor are any *worthy of the least of all the mercies, and of all the truth shewn* unto them; whatever they have, God gives them liberally, without any regard to any merit or desert of theirs; whether temporal or spiritual, and especially the latter; since with Christ he *freely gives all things,* Rom. viii. 32.—— 5. God gives all things plenteously, even with a profusion of goodness; so that the saint, with Jacob, can say, *I have enough,* or I have all things; for God, the living God, *gives richly all things to enjoy;* that is, in a large and liberal manner; for he is *rich* or plenteous in his goodness, *unto all that call upon him,* 1 Tim. vi. 17. Rom. x. 12. So that there is abundant encouragement to trust in the Lord for all things.

1*st*, For things temporal, the outward mercies of life.——1. For food: the promise is, *Trust in the Lord, and do good—and verily thou shalt be fed,* Psal. xxxvii. 3. with food convenient, and sufficient; though not with delicacies, yet with necessaries; *Take no thought, therefore,* says our Lord, no anxious and perplexing thoughts, *for your life, what ye shall eat, or what ye shall drink— is not the life more than meat?* And he that has given life, the greater favour, will give meat to support that life, to them who trust in him, and wait for it in a dependance on him, Matt. vi. 25. see Psal. xxxvii. 25.——2. For raiment: and this and food are both from the Lord; and necessary for the support and comfort of life; Jacob vowed a vow, and promised that if God would *give him bread to eat, and raiment to put on*—then, says he, *shall the Lord be my God,* Gen. xxviii. 20, 21. and indeed, having these, a saint has enough, and should be therewith content, 1 Tim. vi. 8. and for this God should be confided in; for if he so *clothe the grass of the field,* in the manner he does, *shall he not much more clothe you, O ye of little faith?* Matt. vi. 30.——3. For the preservation of life; from every accident, as usually so called; from every danger; and from every enemy: and because God not only gives life, but preserves it, he is peculiarly the Saviour and Preserver of them that believe, and put their trust in him; he is their keeper night and day; with the utmost confidence they may commit themselves to God, and trust in his protection from every evil, Psalm cxxii. 5, 8. and iii. 5. and iv. 8.——4. For these things may believers pray to God with an holy confidence, believing they shall have the petitions they ask of him; who has promised, *when the poor and needy seek water, and there is none, and their tongue faileth for thirst, I the Lord will hear them,* their cries and prayers, and supply their wants; yea, if need be, will rather go out of the common course of nature and providence than that they shall want, Isa. xli. 17, 18. and xliii. 19, 20. and if earthly parents, *who are evil,* know how to *give good gifts* to their children, who ask them of them, our Lord has taught believers in him to reason after this manner, *how much more shall your heavenly Father give the Holy Spirit to them that ask him?* And if he will give to them the Spirit and spiritual things, then much more may they expect earthly and temporal things from him they stand in need of, Luke xi. 13.——5. To trust and confidence in God with respect to those things, they may be encouraged by the experience of themselves and others. Good old Jacob in his dying moments expressed, in very strong language, his experience of the divine goodness throughout the whole of his life; *The God which fed me all my life long unto this day—the angel which redeemed me from all evil, bless the lads,* Gen. xlviii. 15, 16. David frequently takes notice of the goodness of God to him, in providence, to encourage his own faith in him, and that of others; *Thou art my hope, O Lord God, thou art my trust from my youth!* and from what he had experienced in time past, even from the very dawn of life, he strongly thus concluded; *Surely goodness and mercy shall follow me all the days of my life,* Psalm lxxi. 5, 6. and xxiii. 6. and every believer may look back on the past goodness of God unto him, and encourage himself in the Lord his God, in expectation and confidence of future favours; for their heavenly Father knows they have need of these things, and therefore will bestow them on them, Matt. vi. 32, 33.

2*dly,* There is great encouragement to trust in the Lord for spiritual things; that is, for after-supplies of grace; for faith respects present blessings of grace enjoyed, but trust and confidence future ones; and which may be depended on; since God is the God of all grace, whose grace is sufficient for his people now and hereafter; who has promised to give more grace as they want it; and has set up a throne of grace, to which they are encouraged to come with boldness, that they may find grace and mercy to help them in time of need. The covenant of grace is filled with all spiritual blessings, and promises of them, which are sure to all the spiritual seed of Christ; Christ has them all in his hands for his people, and will give them all things pertaining to life and godliness.

3*dly,* There is encouragement to trust in the Lord for eternal things; for,——1. God has chosen his in Christ to the enjoyment of them; they are ordained unto eternal life; appointed unto salvation; chosen through sanctification of the Spirit and belief of the truth unto it; and the purpose of God, according to election, stands sure, not upon the foot of works, but upon the will of him that calls; his purposes can never be frustrated and disappointed; and therefore the chosen ones may be confident of eternal glory and happiness.——2. God has made promises of eternal things to his people; to whom the promise of the life that is to come is made, as well as of that which now is; God that cannot lie, has promised eternal life before the world began, which promise can never be made void by any thing that comes to pass in time; wherefore the heirs of promise have reason to trust in God for the performance of the eternal good he has promised.——3. God has prepared and provided everlasting happiness for his people; it is inconceivable what God has prepared for them that love him; it cannot be said how great is the goodness which he has laid up in covenant for them that fear him; a crown of glory, life, and immortality is laid up safe and secure in the hands of Christ, with whom their life is hid; an inheritance, eternal, incorruptible, undefiled, and that fades not away, is reserved in heaven for them, and therefore confidently to be depended on.——4. God has called them to his kingdom and glory, even to eternal glory by Jesus Christ; and his calling is without repentance, whom he calls he glorifies; them he preserves safe to the coming of Christ; for *faithful is he that calleth you, who also will do it*, 1 Thess. v. 24.——5. Eternal things are freely given of God; as grace is freely given, so is glory; eternal life is the free gift of God through Christ; and therefore there is encouragement to trust in him for it; since it is not owing to the merit of the saints, but it is their Father's good pleasure to give them the kingdom. Christ, as Mediator, has power to give eternal life, and he gives it to all his sheep; *This is the record, that God has given unto us eternal life; and this life is in his Son*, safe and secure, and may be depended on, 1 John v. 11.

Secondly, There is encouragement to trust in the Lord always; *Trust in him at all times, ye people*, Psalm lxii. 8.——1. In times of darkness and desertion; it is said to a saint walking in darkness, and has no light, *Let him trust in the name of the Lord, and stay upon his God*, Isa. l. 10. and wait upon the Lord, who hides his face from the house of Jacob; since light is sown for the righteous, in the purposes and decrees, counsel and covenant of God, and gladness for the upright in heart, in the gospel, and doctrines of it; and sooner or later it will arise; hence the trust and confidence of the church; *When I sit in darkness, the Lord shall be a light unto me*, Mic. vii. 8, 9.——2. In times of temptation, saints may trust in the Lord, and be confident that his grace will be sufficient for them; and that his strength will be made perfect in their weakness; that he will bear them up, and not suffer them to sink under the weight of them; but will in due time make a way for their escape out of them, and deliver them from them; and as Christ has suffered, being tempted, he is able to succour them that are tempted; and whereas he has a sympathy with them, being in all things tempted as they, so he prays for them that their faith fail not; and therefore they have great reason to trust in him.——3. In times of adversity and affliction; God leaves in the midst of his church *an afflicted and poor people;* and it is said of them, *And they shall trust in the name of the Lord*, Zeph. iii. 12. believing, that when they pass through the waters of adversity, and fiery trials, the Lord will be with them and preserve them, and carry them through them, and not suffer them to be overwhelmed by them; will make all things work together for their good, and deliver them out of all their afflictions.——4. In the hour of death, they are encouraged to trust in the Lord; and believe, that when strength and heart fail, the Lord will be the strength of their heart and their portion for ever; that he will be, not only their God and Guide unto death, but through it; and that even when they walk through the valley of the shadow of death, they shall fear no ill; God will be with them, and his rod and staff shall comfort them, Psalm lxxiii. 26. and xlviii. 14. and xxiii.

Thirdly, What that is in the Lord which gives encouragement to trust in him; and that is every thing in God, and belonging to him; his nature, and the excellencies of it; all his perfections and attributes; the several names by which he has made himself known; his covenant and promises; his word and oath; his gospel, and the doctrines of it; the methods of his grace; and the dispensations of his providence: in particular,——1. He is El-Shaddai, God all sufficient; and therefore to be trusted in for every thing that is wanted for soul and body, for time and eternity. Creatures are insufficient, and therefore not to be depended on; friends oftentimes would help, assist, and supply, but cannot; but God is an help in every time of need, and is a never-failing supply, an inexhaustible fountain of all goodness; he has a sufficiency in himself and for himself, and for all his creatures, who all wait on him, and whom he satisfies with his good things; and his grace is sufficient for his people at all times, in all places, and in all ages; and therefore they have always encouragement to trust in him.—— 2. He is Jehovah, the rock of ages, the everlasting strength of those that put their trust in him; *Trust ye in the Lord for ever, for in the Lord Jehovah* (in *Jah-Jehovah*) *is everlasting strength*, Isa. xxvi. 4. to support his people under all their trials and exercises; to carry them through all their difficulties and distresses; to bear them up under all their temptations and afflictions; to enable them to do and suffer what is his will and pleasure; to bring them on in their journey through the wilderness of this world, and out of it: he has promised, that as their day is, their strength shall be; and which is continually experienced by them; and therefore they have reason to trust in him.——3. The loving-kindness, grace, mercy, and pity of God, give great encouragement to trust in him; *How excellent is thy loving-kindness, O God!* therefore *the children of men put their trust under the shadow of thy wings*, Psalm xxxvi. 7. the proclamation the Lord has made of himself, as gracious and merciful, long-suffering, and abundant in goodness and truth; Exod xxxiv. 6. is sufficient to engage trust and confidence in him; says David, *I trust in the mercy of God for ever and ever*, Psalm lii. 8.——4. His truth and faithfulness in his covenant and promises, strongly induce to trust in him; he will *not suffer his faithfulness to fail, nor break his covenant, nor alter the thing that is gone out of his lips;* to which he has added his oath for the confirmation thereof, Psalm lxxxix. 33, 34, 35.——5. The experience of the saints in all ages, and a man's own, animate him to put his trust in God; *our fathers trusted in thee, they trusted, and thou didst deliver them; they cried unto thee, and were delivered; they trusted in thee, and were not confounded!* Psalm xxii. 4, 5. and having such a cloud of witnesses before them; and such gracious experiences of their own in times past of the goodness of God unto them, they encourage themselves in the Lord their God.

IV. The happiness of those that trust in the Lord: it is often said, *Blessed are they that trust in the Lord!* Psalm ii. 12. and xxxiv. 8. and lxxxiv. 12. and Jer. xvii. 7.

1. They are in great peace, and will be in greater still; *Thou wilt keep him in perfect peace, whose mind is stayed on thee; because he trusteth in thee*, Isa. xxvi. 3. they have peace with God through Christ; they have peace in him, when in the world they have tribulation; a peace which the world cannot take away; great peace have they which love the Lord and trust in him; even perfect peace, at least hereafter; for the *end* of such a man is *peace*, everlasting peace.——2. They are in great safety; *They that trust in the Lord shall be as mount Zion, which cannot be removed, but abideth for ever;* they are like mount Zion, well fortified with the towers, walls, and bulwarks of salvation; and are as immoveable as that, fixed in the love of God, settled in the covenant of grace and peace, and secured in the hands of Christ, and can never be removed from either; but will abide in the state of grace until they come into the unalterable state of glory; the Lord is round about them, as the mountains about Jerusalem; a wall of fire about them, and they are kept by the power of God through faith unto salvation. ——3. They need be in no fear of any enemy whatever; *Behold, God is my salvation*, says the church, *I will trust and not be afraid*, Isa. xii. 2. not of men, the greatest, most powerful and numerous; nor of devils; Satan and all other enemies are conquered ones by Christ; he has destroyed him that had the power of death, the devil, and spoiled his principalities and powers; he has abolished death, and made an end of sin; he has ransomed his people from death and hell, so that they shall not be hurt of the second death, and has saved them from wrath to come; and therefore they have nothing to fear now nor hereafter; happy men that trust in the Lord. ——4. They want no good thing, nor ever shall; *O taste, and see that the Lord is good*, says the Psalmist, *Blessed is the man that trusteth in him! they that seek the Lord shall not want any good thing*, Psalm xxxiv. 8, 9, 10. no good thing is withheld now from them that trust in the Lord; and great goodness, inconceivable and unspeakable, is laid up for them to be enjoyed hereafter, Psalm lxxxiv. 11, 12. and xxxi. 19.

CHAP. VIII.

OF THE GRACE OF HOPE.

HAVING treated of Faith in God, and of trust and confidence in him, the next in course to be considered is the Grace of Hope; for in this order they stand, *faith, hope:*——*Faith is the substance of things hoped for*, and therefore go together; and the same word is rendered sometimes *trust*, and sometimes *hope*, so near akin are these graces; thus in Eph. i. 12. what we translate, *Who first trusted in Christ*, is in the Greek text, and so in the margin, *Who first hoped in Christ*. Concerning which grace, the following things may be observed:

I. The object, ground, and foundation of it, Jehovah, God, Father, Son, and Spirit. Not any creature whatever, angel or man; not the Virgin Mary, the mother of our Lord, as the papists impiously and blasphemously address her, *Salve regina, spes nostra; Save us, O queen, our hope!* Nor any creature-enjoyment; *If I have made gold my hope*, the object of it, says Job, meaning, he had not; though some have, placing their hope of future good in it, in this life, to the neglect of a dependence on divine providence, Job xxxi. 24. and indeed, have carried it so far, as to hope and imagine, that they are the persons whom God will delight in to honour in the world to come with happiness and bliss, who have had so great a share of it in this; forgetting, or not knowing, that *not many noble are called.* Nor creature-merits; of which there are none: a creature cannot merit any thing at the hand of God; he is not deserving of the least temporal mercy from him, having sinned against him; nor can he give him any thing which may lay him under an obligation to him, or which God has not a prior right unto; much less can he merit eternal happiness of him, and so have any hope of it on that account; for that is *the free gift of God through Christ.* Nor any creature-righteousness, which is the hope of the moralist and legalist, who fancy they have kept all the precepts of the law from their youth, and that touching the righteousness of the law they are blameless, and are not as other men are; and therefore hope for eternal life and happiness; but such hope is like a *spider's web*, spun out of their own bowels, and which has no strength, solidity, and substance in it; which, if they lean upon, *it shall not stand ;* and if they attempt to hold it fast, *it shall not endure*, Job viii. 14, 15. nor any supposed privileges of birth and education, and of profession of religion; as being born of religious parents, educated in the christian religion, and having some notions of the principles of christianity; and going yet further, making a profession of faith in Christ, subjecting to the ordinances of Christ, baptism and the Lord's-supper, and continuing in a round of religious exercises, and yet destitute of the grace of God in truth. *What is the hope of the hypocrite, though he hath gained* a place and a name in the church of God, *when God taketh away his soul?* Job xxvii. 8. But Jehovah, the creator and Lord of all, and the covenant-God of his people, is the principal object of hope, and the only solid sufficient ground and foundation of it; as David said, *Thou art my hope, O Lord God ; thou art my trust from my youth !* Psalm lxxv. 5. *Blessed is the man that trusteth in the Lord, and whose hope the Lord is!* Jer. xvii. 7. Psalm cxlvi. 5.

First, God, essentially considered, is the object of hope; *Hope in God*, says the Psalmist, for I shall yet praise him, Psalm xlii. 11. So the church speaks of him; *O the hope of Israel, the Saviour thereof in time of trouble!* Jer. xiv. 8. The grounds of which hope in God, are his grace, and mercy, and goodness; he has proclaimed his name, *The Lord God, merciful, gracious, abundant in goodness;* and it is the abundance of his mercy, grace, and goodness, which lays a solid foundation for hope in him, and encourages to it; *Let Israel hope in the Lord, for with the Lord there is mercy !* he is plenteous in it, rich in mercy, there is a multitude of tender mercies with him; he takes *pleasure* in those that *hope in his mercy*, and his eye is upon them to do them good; and therefore there is great encouragement to make the Lord God the object of their hope, Psalm cxxx. 7, and cxlvii. 11. and xxxiii. 18.

Secondly, God personally considered is the object of hope, God, Father, Son, and Spirit: God the Father, who is called, *The God of hope;* not only because he is the author and giver of that grace; but because he is the object of it, Rom. xv. 13. by whom Christ is said to be raised from the dead, that *faith and hope might be in God;* that is, in God the Father, 1 Pet. i. 21. and Christ the Son of God is called, *our hope*, and *Christ in you the hope of glory;* that is, the object, and ground, and foundation of it; which are his blood, righteousness, and sacrifice, 1 Tim. i. 1. Col. i. 27. The Spirit of God also is equally the object of hope, as of faith and confidence; that he will assist in the exercise of every grace, and the performance of every duty; and particularly, that he will carry on and finish the work of grace upon the soul.

Thirdly, The less principal objects of hope, connected with the divine Persons, are the promises of God, and the things therein promised; hence the word of God, the word of promise, is represented as the object of hope; says the Psalmist, *In his word do I hope*, Psalm cxxx. 5. the ground and foundation of which hope, is in the faithfulness and power of God. The faithfulness of God, *for he is faithful that has promised;* nor will he *suffer his faithfulness to fail ;* and therefore the performance of his promises may be hoped for; besides, he is *able also to perform;* and upon this footing Abraham believed *in hope against hope.* The hand of the Lord is not shortened that it cannot save; he is able to do exceeding abundantly above all that we ask or think; and therefore may hope, yea, believe, there will be a performance of whatsoever is spoken and promised by him.

1*st*, In general; things to be hoped for are represented,——1. As things unseen of which faith is the evidence; and gives encouragement to the exercise of hope upon them; *Hope that is seen, is not hope; for what a man seeth, why doth he yet hope for?* Rom. viii. 24, 25. the glories of another world are things not seen, so as thoroughly to understand and comprehend, yet hope of enjoying them, upon the divine promise, is conversant with them, which enters into that within the vail, Heb. vi. 19.—— 2. They are things future, yet to come, and therefore hoped for; hence saints are exhorted, *to hope to the end, for the grace that is to be brought unto them, at the revelation of Jesus Christ*, when he shall be revealed from heaven, and appear a second time; and therefore are directed, *to look for that blessed hope*, the hope laid up in heaven, the hope of happiness to be enjoyed, *at the glorious appearing of the great God, and our Saviour Jesus Christ*, 1 Pet. i. 13. Tit. ii. 13.——3. Things hoped for are difficult to come at and possess; many tribulations lie in the way to the kingdom, through which men must enter into it; the righteous, by reason of many afflictions, trials, and temptations, are *scarcely saved*, though at last certainly saved; and since the *gate is strait and the way narrow*, which lead to eternal life; hence there must be a labouring and striving to enter in; of which there is hope: and therefore, ——4. Hope is of things possible, or otherwise it would turn to despair, as in Cain, and those who said, *there is no hope, but we will walk after our own devices*, Jer. xviii. 12. but *there is hope in Israel concerning this thing*, eternal life and happiness, as well as concerning all things leading on to it; and which will certainly issue in it; and therefore *it is good that a man should both hope and quietly wait for the salvation of the Lord*, Ezra x. 2. Lam. iii. 26. at least he has encouragement to *put his mouth in the dust, if so be there may be hope*, ver. 29. or seeing hope of salvation is to be entertained.

2*dly*, The things, the objects of hope, or which are to be hoped for, are more particularly salvation by Christ, pardon of sin through him, all blessings of grace, and the supplies of it for the present life; and things after death, as the resurrection of the body and eternal life.

1. Salvation by Christ: as soon as ever a soul is made sensible of its lost state and condition by nature, its inquiry is, *What must I do to be saved?* and being shewn the way of salvation by Christ, and directed to him for it, in whom it is complete, perfect, and every way suitable, it is encouraged to hope in him for it, and say, as David did, *Lord, I have hoped for thy salvation*, Psalm cxix. 116. Salvation, though wrought out, yet the full possession of it is to come; and the difficulties in the way of enjoying it many; and yet it is possible to be had, and therefore hope is conversant about it. ——(1.) It has been thought of, contrived, and fixed; the thoughts of God were employed about it in eternity; he resolved upon the salvation of some of the sons of men; he appointed them to salvation, and chose them to it through certain means; he contrived the scheme of it in the wisest manner, and settled and established it in the covenant of grace: all which serve to encourage hope of it.——(2.) And as God appointed some to salvation, he appointed one to be the Saviour of them, and a great one, even his own Son, his equal and his fellow, every way and on all accounts capable of such a work; he promised him, he sent him, and he came to seek and save lost sinners; and he is become the author of eternal salvation, and his name is called Jesus, because he saves his people from their sins, and therefore have they reason to hope in him.——(3.) Salvation is actually wrought out by Christ; it is entirely finished, the work is done, and completely done; it is a full salvation, nothing wanting to make it perfect: wherefore, *Let Israel hope in the Lord, for with him is plenteous redemption*, Psalm cxxx. 7. which includes in it, and secures all the blessings of grace; as justification, forgiveness of sin; adoption, and eternal life.——(4.) Salvation being wrought out by Christ, it is in him, and to be had by him, and by no other; so said the apostle Peter, *Neither is there salvation in any other*, Acts iv. 12. but inasmuch as there is salvation in him, it may be hoped for from him; though there is no hope of it elsewhere; *Truly in vain is salvation hoped for from the hills and from the multitude of mountains; truly in the Lord our God is the salvation of Israel*, Jer. iii. 23 and in him only; and therefore such who are acquainted herewith, hope in him only, and will have no other Saviour.——(5.) Great encouragement is given by Christ to sensible sinners to hope

for and expect salvation from him; *Look unto me*, says he, *and be ye saved, all the ends of the earth*, men in every quarter of it, and in the uttermost parts thereof, of whatsoever rank, quality, and character; *For I am God, and there is none else*; and so able to save to the uttermost, Isa. xlv. 22. all *labouring and heavy laden sinners*, burdened with a sense of sin, and the guilt of it, he invites to come to him, and promises them to give them *rest* for their souls, Matt. xi. 28, 29. and assures them, that he will, *in no wise*, upon any account, reject, and *cast them out*, but receive them in the most kind and tender manner; and for their encouragement to come to him, and exercise faith and hope on him, it may be observed, *This man receiveth sinners, and eateth with them*, Luke xv. 2.——(6.) Salvation in and by Christ is to be had freely; it is wholly of free grace, and not of works; God saves and calls men according to his grace, and they are saved by grace, and not of works; not by works of righteousness done by them: but according to the abundant mercy and rich grace of God in Christ: were any conditions required on the part of sinners, qualifying them for, and intitling them unto salvation, they might despair of it; but since it is all of free grace they may be encouraged to hope for it.——(7.) Salvation by Christ is for sinners, even for the chief of sinners; as Christ came to call sinners to repentance, so to die for them, and by dying to save them: in this lies the high commendation of the love of God to us; that *while we were yet sinners, Christ died for us*, Rom. v. 8. and this is no small encouragement to such who see themselves polluted, guilty sinners, to hope for salvation by a dying Saviour; and the rather, since he *came into the world to save sinners, even the chief*, 1 Tim. i. 15.——(8.) The gospel-declaration gives great encouragement to sinners to hope in Christ for salvation; that he that believes shall be saved; that he that seeth the Son, and believeth on him, shall not perish, but have everlasting life: to a soul inquiring after salvation the gospel thus directs, *Believe on the Lord Jesus Christ, and thou shalt be saved!* Mark xvi. 16. John vi. 40. Acts xvi. 31.

2. Pardon of sin through the blood of Christ; this is what is immediately sought after and prayed for by a soul convinced of sin, righteousness, and judgment; with David it says, *for thy name's sake, O Lord, pardon my iniquity; for it is great!* Psalm xxv. 11. so great that a sinner cannot bear the weight of its guilt; so great that none but God can forgive it; and if he should mark iniquity, and insist on satisfaction for it, there would be no standing before him; but *there is forgiveness with him*, pardoning grace and mercy with him; and therefore there is encouragement to hope in him, Psalm cxxx. 3, 4, 7. and to come before him, though in the manner the publican did; saying, *God, be merciful to me a sinner!* Luke xviii. 13. or propitious; and there is ground and reason to hope for pardoning mercy, through the propitiatory sacrifice of Christ.

(1.) Because God is a sin-forgiving God; he can forgive sin, and none can do it but him; and he does *abundantly pardon!* pardons both abundance of sins and abundance of sinners; and all freely; sins of omission and commission, gross and grievous ones, Isa. xliii. 25. and there is none like him on this account, Micah. vii. 18. Jehovah has in covenant promised the forgiveness of sins: *I will forgive their iniquity; and I will remember their sin no more!* Jer. xxxi. 34. and he has proclaimed his name, merciful and gracious, *forgiving iniquity, and transgression, and sin*, even sins of every sort and size, Exod. xxxiv. 7. wherefore the greatest sinners may hope in him for pardon.——(2.) The blood of Christ has been shed on account of sin, and the pardon of it. God *set* him *forth* in his purposes and decrees, in his council and covenant, to be the *propitiation, through faith in his blood, for the remission of sins*; to make reconciliation and atonement for sin by his blood, that men believing in it might have the pardon of it; and God has sent him forth in the fulness of time to shed his blood for this purpose; *And his blood is shed for many, for the remission of sins;* and hence satisfaction for sin being made by it, *God is faithful and just to forgive us our sins, and to cleanse us from all unrighteousness*, 1 John i. 9.——(3.) Christ's blood being shed, and forgiveness of sin through it obtained, Christ is exalted as a *Prince and a Saviour, to give repentance to Israel, and forgiveness of sins*, Acts v. 31. and to whomsoever he gives the one he gives the other; so that penitent sinners have great reason to hope in him for pardon, and which they may expect to have of him freely; he *gives*, and he gives it freely; pardon of sin is according to the riches of his grace, and is owing to the tender mercy of God, and the multitude of it.——— (4.) The declaration of it made in the gospel, gives great encouragement to hope for it. Christ gave orders to his apostles, before his ascension to heaven, *that repentance and remission of sins should be preached in his name, among all nations ;* to all sorts of men in them, *beginning at Jerusalem,* where some of the chief and greatest of sinners lived ; even such who had been lately concerned in the shedding of his blood, Luke xxiv. 47. and according to this commission given them, wherever they came they made it known to men, that *through Christ was preached unto them the forgiveness of sins:* and in this both they and the prophets agreed and bare witness, *That through his name,* the name of Christ, *whosoever believeth in him shall receive remission of sins,* Acts xiii. 38. and x. 43. ———(5.) The instances of pardon recorded in scripture, and of some notorious sinners, serve much to encourage hope of pardon likewise ; as a Manasseh, guilty of the grossest of crimes ; a Mary Magdalene, out of whom Christ cast seven devils ; the woman a sinner, who washed Christ's feet with her tears, and wiped them with the hairs of her head, and loved much because much was forgiven her ; Saul the blasphemer, persecutor, and injurious person, who obtained mercy ; and many of the Corinthians, described as the worst of sinners, and yet were pardoned and justified in the name of the Lord Jesus.

3. The blessings of grace, and supplies of it in the present life, and through it, are the objects of hope, and about which that is conversant, and in the exercise of which there is much encouragement ; for as long as there is a throne of grace standing, and the God of all grace sitting on it, inviting souls to come to it for grace and mercy to help them in every time of need ; bidding them ask, and it shall be given ; there is good and sufficient ground and reason to hope in him for it ; and so long as there is a fulness of grace in Christ, and the communication of it not cut off, as it never will be from his people, they may most comfortably hope, yea, be assured, that their God in Christ will *supply all their need according to his riches in glory by Jesus Christ,* Phil. iv. 19. And seeing there are such exceeding great and precious promises of grace and strength from the Lord, that their strength shall be renewed ; that they shall go from strength to strength ; and that as their day is, their strength shall be ; there is abundant reason to hope in his word for the fulfilment of it.

4. There are blessings to be enjoyed after death, which are the objects of hope, not only of the soul, of its being with Christ immediately, and in a state of happiness and bliss ; but of the resurrection of the body also ; and of eternal life in soul and body for evermore.

1. The resurrection of the body is an object of hope, and is often so represented ; *Of the hope and resurrection of the dead,* that is, of the hope of it, *I am called in question,* says the apostle ; and again, *And have hope towards God, which they themselves also allow, that there shall be a resurrection of the dead, both of the just and of the unjust:* once more, *And now I stand and am judged for the hope of the promise made of God unto our fathers :———for which hope's sake, king Agrippa, I am accused of the Jews ;* and then adds, *Why should it be thought a thing incredible with you that God should raise the dead ?* Acts xxiii. 6. and xxiv. 15. and xxvi. 6, 7, 8. and the description of the object of hope entirely agrees with it, it being future, yet to come, what is unseen to carnal sense and reason, and difficult how it should be ; and yet possible, considering the omniscience and omnipotence of God, and not to be reckoned incredible ; it may be hoped for, and there is good ground and reason for it from scripture-testimonies of it ; from the resurrection of Christ, and from the union of his people to him ; and they are represented as *waiting for the adoption, to wit, the redemption of the body,* Rom. viii. 23. which they have reason to expect, and is worth waiting for, and the happiness that will follow upon it.

2. Eternal life to be enjoyed both in soul and body, is a grand object of hope ; and which is therefore called, the hope of eternal life, and hope of glory, the blessed hope, and hope laid up in heaven ; all intending the happiness hoped for, Tit. i. 2. and ii. 13. Rom. v. 2. Col. i. 5. and for which there is good ground and reason, ———(1.) From its being a free gift ; not to be obtained by the merits of men, or the works of the creature ; but is entirely owing to the free grace of God ; *The gift of God is eternal life through Jesus Christ our Lord,* Rom. vi. 23. if it was to be acquired by doing, it might be despaired of ; but since it is the good pleasure of our heavenly Father to give us the kingdom, it may be hoped for.———(2.) It is in the hands of Christ to give it ; he has power

to give to as many as the Father has given him, and he does give it to all his sheep; he is a sun and shield, and gives both grace and glory; and therefore it may be hoped for from him; yea, he himself is the ground of it; and is therefore, called *our hope*, and *Christ in us the hope of glory*, 1 Tim. i. 1. Col. i. 27. whose righteousness entitles to it; and his grace makes meet for it.——(3.) From the promise of it in Christ, called, *The promise of life which is in Christ Jesus*, 2 Tim. i. 1. and which was put into his hands as soon as made, where it is safe and secure, firm and stable; and which was very early made; *In hope of eternal life; which God, that cannot lie, promised before the world began;* who is faithful that has promised, and therefore it may be hoped for, expected, and depended on; and this is the declared will of God, that *whosoever seeth the Son, and believeth on him, may have everlasting life*, John vi. 40. hence all such persons may steadily hope and wait for it.——(4.) From the preparations and prayers of Christ for it; he is gone to prepare heaven and happiness for his people, by his presence and mediation; and has promised to come again and take them to himself, that they may be with him, where he is; and for this he prays and makes intercession, and which is always prevalent, and he is always heard, John xiv. 2, 3. and xvii. 24.——(5.) From the Spirit's work in the hearts of men, who works in them for that self-same thing, eternal glory, whose grace is a well of living water, springing up unto eternal life; and between grace and glory is an inseparable connection, and to whom grace is given, glory is also; whom God calls, justifies, and sanctifies, he also glorifies; therefore those who are partakers of the one may hope for the other.

II. The subjects of the grace of hope, or who they are that are partakers of it.

1. Not angels, good or bad; not good angels, they are in the full enjoyment of God and of all felicity, they see God, and what is seen is not hope; they are in the present possession of happiness; and so that is not future; nor is there any thing about them, or attends them, to make their happiness difficult or doubtful: nor evil angels, the devils; there is a kind of faith ascribed to them, the belief of a God, of one God, at whom they tremble; but have no hope; there is not the least ground and reason for them to hope for a recovery out of their apostate state, or of their being ever restored to the favour of God; for as soon as they fell they were cast out of heaven, and cast down to hell, and laid up in chains of darkness, reserved for the great and last judgment, when they will receive their final sentence and full punishment, which they expect, and have no hope of escaping; hence they said to Christ in the days of his flesh, *Art thou come hither to torment us before the time?* Matt. viii. 29. they have no foundation of hope of salvation by Christ; he took not on him the nature of angels, nor obeyed nor suffered for them, nor redeemed any of them by his blood; these were only men, out of every kindred, tongue, people, and nation: nor was the gospel, the good tidings of salvation by Christ, nor any messages of grace sent to them; nor any repentance given them; and so no remission of sins to be hoped for by them.——2. Only men, and these not all men; some are described as, *those without hope*, and who live and die without it; and all men are *without hope* whilst in a state of nature and unregeneracy, 1 Thess. iv. 13. Eph. ii. 12. for however they may feed themselves with a vain hope, they have no solid, well-grounded hope; and dying in such a state they die without hope; and some, through the force of their own corruptions, and the power of Satan's temptations, give into despair, and abandon themselves to a vicious course of living, saying, *There is no hope*, Jer. xviii. 12. ——3. Only regenerate men are subjects of the grace of hope. In regeneration every grace is implanted in the soul, and this with the rest; yea, to this, and the exercise of it, they are particularly regenerated; for *according to the abundant mercy of God*, souls are by him, *begotten again unto a lively hope*, 1 Pet. i. 3. hence when first quickened by the Spirit and grace of God, and see themselves lost and undone, in a captive state, and as it were, prisoners to sin, Satan, and the law; they are yet *prisoners of hope*, and are enabled to hope for deliverance; and are directed to *turn to the strong-hold*, Christ, where they find salvation, safety, and comfort.——4. Believers in Christ are partakers of this grace, and they only; faith and hope always go together; they are implanted at the same time, and grow up and thrive together; though one may be in exercise before the other; and one may be more in exercise at one time than the other; yet they are always together, and assist each other; Abraham *believed in hope against hope;* and the *experience* of faith, works or exercises *hope;* hence we read of

CHAP. VIII.   OF THE GRACE OF HOPE.   759

them together+ *That your faith and hope might be in God:—now abideth faith, hope, charity,* or *love,* 1 Pet. i. 21. 1 Cor. xiii. 13. faith is the ground-work of hope, lies at the bottom of it, and is its support; *Faith is the substance of things hoped for,* Heb. xi. 1.——5. They are the Israel of the Lord, whose hope the Lord is; and who are encouraged to hope in him, and do, even the whole Israel of God; his spiritual Israel, Jews and Gentiles, sooner or later, hope in the Lord; the Israel whom God has chosen for his peculiar treasure, and whom he has redeemed from all iniquity, and effectually calls by his grace, and who appear in due time to be Israelites indeed; and even all sensible sinners, who are quickened and born again, come under this character, and are encouraged to hope in the Lord for mercy and salvation; *Let Israel hope in the Lord,* Psalm cxxx. 7. hence he is called, *The hope of Israel,* Jer. xiv. 8.——6. The separate souls of saints, after death, in heaven, seem to be possessed of, and to be in the exercise of, the grace of hope, particularly with respect to the resurrection of their bodies; as *the flesh* of Christ, by a figure, is said to rest in *hope* of its resurrection, that is, his soul rested or waited in hope of the resurrection of his body, whilst in the grave, being confident of it, Psalm xvi. 9. so the souls of the saints, whilst in a separate state in heaven, and during the abode of their bodies in the grave, rest, wait, and hope for the resurrection of them; and this may be what Job has a reference to, when he says, *If a man die shall he live again?* He shall, in the resurrection-morn; *All the days of my appointed time* of lying in the grave, *will I wait till my change come,* until Christ changes the vile bodies of his people, and makes them like his glorious one, Job xiv. 14. and something of this kind may be observed in the answer to the souls under the altar, crying *How long, O Lord, &c.* to whom it was said, that they should *rest yet for a little season,* be still and quiet, hope and wait, *until their fellow servants and brethren, that should be killed as they were, should be fulfilled,* Rev. vi. 9, 10, 11.

III. The causes of the grace of hope, or from whence it springs; and the rather this should be inquired into, because all men in a state of nature are without it.

1. The efficient cause of it is God; hence he is called, *the God of hope,* Rom. xv. 13. not only because he is the object of it, but because he is the author of it;

even God, Father, Son, and Spirit. It is the God and Father of our Lord Jesus Christ who begets men again to a lively hope of a glorious inheritance; and this is owing to the virtue of the resurrection of Christ from the dead, 1 Pet. i. 3. and indeed it is the gift both of the Father and of Christ; *now our Lord Jesus Christ himself, and God, even our Father, who hath given us good hope through grace,* 2 Thess. ii. 16. and as it is *through the power of the Holy Ghost* that saints *abound in hope,* in the exercise of the grace of hope; it may well be thought that it is by this same power that it is first produced in them, Rom. xv. 13.——2. The moving cause of it is the grace and mercy of God; hence it is called, *good hope through grace:* it is not of nature; for it is not naturally in men; but is owing to the grace of God; it is not through the merits of men, nor any motives in them; but entirely through the grace of God, it is *given;* it is a gift of free grace, and is sometimes ascribed to the *abundant mercy* of God, as the spring of it, 1 Pet. i. 3. it is owing to mercy, and to the aboundings of mercy.——3. The gospel is the means of it, by which it is wrought, encouraged, and confirmed, and therefore called, *the hope of the gospel,* Col. i. 23. the doctrines of it greatly animate to it, the good news and glad tidings the gospel brings of free and complete salvation by Christ, of full pardon of sin by his blood, of peace, reconciliation, and atonement by his sacrifice, and of the fulness of grace that is in him, give great encouragement to hope in the Lord, as do the many exceeding great and precious promises in it; by means of which the *heirs of promise have strong consolation,* Heb. vi. 18. these are that *on which God causes his people to hope,* what are the ground and foundation of it, support it, and encourage to the exercise of it, Psalm cxix. 49.——4. There are many things which serve to promote and increase it; the whole scripture has a tendency thereunto, which is written that men, *through patience and comfort of the scripture might have hope,* Rom. xv. 4. particularly the promises contained in it; and the goodness, power, and faithfulness of God displayed both in making and fulfilling them; and especially when opened and applied by the holy Spirit of promise, serve greatly to cherish the grace of hope; the things said concerning the person, offices, and grace of Christ, his resurrection from the dead, ascension to heaven, session at the right-hand of God, intercession for his people, and the glorification of him in heaven, are all subservient to this end, *that our faith and hope might be in God*, 1 Pet. i. 21. the experience of the saints in all ages, of the grace, goodness, &c. of God, and particularly the saints' own experience of the same in times past, greatly strengthen the grace of hope, and encourage to the exercise of it; *experience, hope;* that is, works it, exercises it, and tends to increase it, Rom. v. 4.

IV. The effects of hope; which are produced through it, and follow upon it.

1. It is said of it, that it *maketh not ashamed*, Rom. v. 5. the reason given of which is, because the love of God is shed abroad in the hearts of such who have it, which supports it and gives it life and vigour; so that a soul possessed of it is not ashamed to appear before God and men; is not ashamed in his present circumstances; nor will be ashamed at the coming of Christ; this grace makes not ashamed, because it does not disappoint those that have it, who will most certainly enjoy the things that are hoped for: and as this grace makes not ashamed, those who have it need not be ashamed of it; as David prays, *Let me not be ashamed of my hope*, Psalm cxix. 116. when hope is a good one, he that has it has no reason to be ashamed of it; nor will he.———2. It weans from the world, and the things of it, and makes a man sit loose unto them, when he knows that he has in heaven a better and a more enduring substance, and can rejoice in hope of the glory of God; when he seeks those things that are above, and has hope of enjoying them, his affections are drawn off of things on earth, and are set on things in heaven; and he longs to be unclothed, that he might be clothed upon with his house from heaven, and chooses rather to be absent from the body that he might be present with the Lord.———3. It carries cheerfully through all the difficulties of this life, and makes hard things sit easy; whereas, if *in this life only saints had hope*, they would be *of all men the most miserable;* but hope of a future state of happiness beyond the grave, bears them up under all the troubles of the present state, and carries them comfortably through them, so that they glory in tribulation, Rom. v. 3, 4, 5.———4. It yields support in death; for *the righteous hath hope in his death*, Prov. xiv. 32. not founded on his own righteousness, but on the righteousness of Christ; a hope of being with Christ for ever, and of enjoying eternal life and happiness with him; and which gives him peace and joy in his last moments, and causes him to exult in the view of death and the grave. There are many other fruits and effects of a good hope; some of which may be gathered from what follows under the next head.

V. The properties and epithets of the grace of hope; which will more fully shew the nature, excellency, and usefulness of it.

First, It is called a good hope; *and hath given us—good hope through grace*, 2 Thess. ii. 16.———1. In distinction from, and in opposition to, a bad one. A bad one is that which is the hope of the moralist and legalist, which is founded on their own works of righteousness and deeds, done in obedience to the law; and is but a sandy foundation to build an hope of eternal salvation upon; and such is the hope of a carnal and external professor of religion, which is laid on birth privileges, education principles, a bare profession of religion, subjection to external ordinances, and a performance of a round of duties; and the hope of a profane sinner, formed upon the absolute mercy of God, without any regard to the merits, blood, and righteousness of Christ.———2. A good hope is that which has God, his grace and promises, for its object, Christ and his righteousness for its foundation, the Spirit of grace for its author, and is a part of the good work of grace begun upon the soul, and is an hope of good things to come, of which Christ is the high-priest: in this, hope differs from expectation; hope is an expectation of good things; and he that fears expects, but he does not expect good things, for fear is an expectation of evil things; but hope is of good things; wicked men expect things which have no substance and solidity in them, and their hope perishes.[2]———3. A good hope is that which is of great use both in life and death; it is the Christian sailor's anchor, and the Christian soldier's helmet; it carries through all the troubles in life, as before observed, and supports in the hour of death; whilst the hope of the hypocrite is like the giving up of the ghost, and expires with him; this continues, and the man that has it is saved

---

[2] Suidas in voce, ἐλπίς.

eternally; for *we are saved by hope*, Rom. viii. 24.

Secondly, It is also a *lively* or *living* one, 1 Pet. i. 3. So called,——1. Because the subject of it is a living man, one spiritually alive: a man dead in trespasses and sins is without hope; but a man regenerated and quickened by the Spirit of God is begotten again to a lively hope.——2. Because it has for its object, eternal life: one that is justified by the grace of God, is made an *heir according to the hope of eternal life*, Tit. iii. 7.——3. Has for its ground and foundation a living Christ, and not dead works; as faith lives upon a crucified Christ, hope receives its virtue and vigour from the resurrection of Christ; Christ, as risen, and at the right-hand of God, greatly encourages to seek and hope for things above, where he is.——4. It is of a cheering and enlivening nature; *hope deferred maketh the heart sick; but when the desire cometh it is a tree of life*, Prov. xiii. 12. it causes gladness and joy; hence we read of the *rejoicing of the hope*, and of *rejoicing in hope*, Heb. iii. 6. Rom. v. 2. see Prov. x. 28.——5. It is an abiding, ever-living grace, and is always more or less in exercise; as water that is always flowing and running is called *living water;* this grace is lively or living when others seem to be ready to die; and though it is sometimes in a low state itself, and a man puts his mouth in the dust, *if so be there may be hope*, yet still there is hope; and when he is in the worst case, a saint cannot give up his hope; nor will he part with it for all the world; it is one of the abiding graces, 1 Cor. xiii. 13.

Thirdly, It is represented as of a purifying nature; *every man that hath this hope in him*, of appearing with Christ, and being like him, and seeing him as he is, *purifieth himself even as he is pure*, 1 John iii. 3. that is, as Christ is pure: all men are by nature and through sin, impure: no man can purify himself by any thing that he can do; it is peculiar to the blood of Jesus to cleanse from sin. Neither faith, nor hope, nor any other grace, have such virtue in them as to make a man pure from his sin; no otherwise can they purify from it, but as they deal with the blood of Christ; and he that has hope in the blood and righteousness of Christ for justification and salvation, and expresses it, does thereby declare that he is righteous, as Christ is righteous, ver. 7. being made the righteousness of God in him.

Fourthly, Hope is sometimes compared to an anchor, because of its great usefulness to the Christian in this life; *which hope we have as an anchor of the soul both sure and stedfast* Heb. vi. 19. This world is a sea; the church, and so every believer, is like a ship sailing on it; Christ is the pilot that guides it; hope is the anchor of it; and a good hope is like an anchor cast on a good foundation, where remaining fixed, it is sure and stedfast; and as the ground on which an anchor is cast is out of sight; so Christ, on which hope is fixed, is unseen; as are also the glories of a future state, it is concerned with; and as an anchor is of no service without a cable; so not hope without faith; which is the substance and support of it: a ship when at anchor is kept steady by it; so a soul by hope: none of the things it meets with, afflictions, troubles, and temptations, can move it from the hope of the gospel, from the service and cause of Christ; but it remains stedfast and unmoveable, always abounding in the work of the Lord. In some things hope and an anchor disagree; an anchor is not of so much use in storms and tempests at sea as when in a calm, or in danger near rocks and shores; but hope is of use when the soul is in a storm sadly ruffled, discomposed, disquieted, and tossed about with sin, temptation, and trouble; hence David, in such a spiritual storm, cast out the anchor of hope; *Why art thou cast down, O my soul? and why art thou disquieted within me? Hope thou in God!* Psalm xlii. 11. and says the prophet Jeremy, chap. xvii. 17. *Thou art my hope in the day of evil*. A cable may be cut or broke, and so the anchor useless; but faith, which is that to hope as the cable is to the anchor, will never fail, can never be destroyed; an anchor is cast on what is below, on ground underneath; but hope has for its objects things above where Jesus is; when a vessel is at anchor, it continues where it is, it moves not forward; but a soul, when it abounds in the exercise of the grace of hope, through the power of the Holy Ghost, it is moving upwards, rejoicing in hope of the glory of God, and enters into that within the vail; and what gives it the preference is, that it is *the anchor of the soul*, and its epithets, *sure* and *stedfast*, serve to recommend it; and which certainty and stedfastness of it arise from the author, object, ground, and foundation of it.

Fifthly, Hope of salvation by Christ is

compared to an helmet; *and for an helmet the hope of salvation*, 1 Thess. v. 8. this is a piece of armour that is a defence of the head, a cover of it in the day of battle, and an erecter of it: of such use is hope of salvation by Christ; it serves to defend the head from false doctrines; a man whose hope of salvation is fixed on Christ, cannot give into errors contrary to the proper Deity and eternal Sonship of Christ, to justification by his righteousness and atonement, and satisfaction by his sacrifice; for these take away the foundation of his hope; and therefore he whose hope is sure and stedfast cannot easily be carried away with divers and strange doctrines, nor with every wind of doctrine. Hope of salvation by Christ is like an helmet which covers the head in the day of battle; it makes a man courageous to fight the Lord's battles, and fear no enemy; to engage even with principalities and powers, having on the whole armour of God, the shield of faith, the helmet of salvation, and the sword of the Spirit, and particularly having such an helmet, an enemy cannot hurt his head, or give him a mortal wound on it. Hope, like an helmet, is an erecter or lifter up of the head; in the midst of difficulties hope keeps the head above water, above the fear of danger; so that the hoping, believing soul, can even glory in tribulation, Rom. v. 3.

CHAP. IX.

OF THE GRACE OF LOVE.

AFTER faith and hope follows love; for in this order they stand, *now abide faith, hope, charity, or love, these three*, 1 Cor. xiii. 13. *but the greatest of these is charity*, or *love;* not that it is of greater use than the other, faith is of more use to the believer himself, and such things are ascribed to it as cannot be ascribed to love; but love is more diffusive of its benefits to others, and is of a longer duration. Love, in order of nature, follows faith and hope, as the effect its own cause, as Dr. Ames observes; for because by faith and hope we taste how good the Lord is, therefore we love him. Faith receives and embraces the promises of eternal life; and hope, on that, is entertained of enjoying it, and waits for it; hence flows love to God, who has promised it, and gives hope of it; faith spies it in the promise, and hope rejoices in it; and both attract the affections to God the giver of it. Of which grace of love there are these three principal branches, and to be treated of, love to God, love to Christ, and love to the saints.

I. Love to God, Jehovah, our God, the one Lord; *Hear, O Israel, the Lord our God is one Lord; and thou shalt love the Lord thy God with all thine heart and with all thy soul, and with all thy might:* this is what God requires of his people, and enjoins as a command to be obeyed; and it is but reasonable service; *What doth the Lord thy God require of thee—but to love him?* and says Moses in his name, *I command thee this day, to love the Lord thy God*, Deut. vi. 4, 5. and x. 12. and xxx. 16. and this is the chief and principal, the first and greatest command, and entirely agreeable to the law and light of nature and reason. In answer to the lawyer's question; *Master, which is the great commandment in the law?* said our Lord, *Thou shalt love the Lord thy God with all thy heart, with all thy soul, and with all thy mind; this is the first and great commandment*, Matt. xxii. 36, 37, 38. hence the apostle says, *love is the fulfilling of the law*, Rom. xiii. 10. Concerning which love as a grace, for though it is a command to love, it is of grace to keep it, may be observed,

First, On what account God is to be loved, and is loved by his saints.

1. For himself; because of his own nature, and the perfections of it, which render him amiable and lovely, and worthy of our strongest love and affection; as these are displayed in the works of creation and providence, and especially of grace, redemption and salvation; to all which the Psalmist has respect when he says, *O Lord, our Lord, how excellent is thy name*, nature, and perfections, *in all the earth!* Psalm viii. 1. as God is great in himself, and greatly to be praised! great, and greatly to be feared! so great, and greatly to be loved, for what he is in himself; and this is the purest and most perfect love of a creature towards God; for if we love him only for his goodness to us, it is loving ourselves rather than him; at least, a loving him for ourselves; and so a loving ourselves more than him: indeed, such is our weakness and imperfection, that we cannot come at a view of the divine perfections, but by these means, through which they, and particularly his goodness and kindness, are made known unto us, and with which we are first and chiefly affected; yet

hereby we are led into a view of his nature and perfections, and to love him for the sake of himself; which love, though it is not first in order, it is chief and ultimate, and comes nearest to the love which the divine Persons bear to each other, and to that with which God loves his people; which arises, not from any goodness shown to him, or received by him.——2. God is to be loved by his saints as their *summum bonum*, their chief good; yea, their only good, their ALL in ALL; and so to be only loved: *there is none good but one, that is, God;* God, Father, Son, and Spirit, the one Lord God, the object of his people's love: concerning whom they say, *Whom have I in heaven but thee?* Psalm lxxiii. 25. and he may be loved by them as their portion now and hereafter, and as their shield and exceeding great reward; and yet their love to him not be mercenary.—— 3. God is to be loved by his people for the blessings of his goodness communicated to them; he is the fountain of goodness to them; he is good, and does good, and therefore to be praised and loved, even for the bounties of his providence; he follows with his goodness, and daily loads with his benefits; but especially for the blessings of his grace, with which he blesses his chosen in Christ Jesus; as electing grace in him; predestination to the adoption of children by him; acceptance with God, in him, the beloved; redemption through his blood; forgiveness of sins, according to the riches of his grace; regenerating, quickening, calling, and sanctifying grace, and all things pertaining to life and godliness. Which benefits bestowed, though they are not in quality the chief motives to love God, as before observed; yet they are in order first, and chiefly strike the affections, and stir them up towards the Lord.—— 4. The various relations God stands in to his people, do and should engage their affections to him; for he is not only their faithful Creator and kind Benefactor in nature and providence; but in grace their covenant God and Father; and the direction to love him is usually, *Thou shalt love the Lord* THY *God;* and David heaps up a variety of titles and characters, under which, and on account of which, he professed to love the Lord; *I will love thee, O Lord, my strength!* &c. Psalm xviii. 1, 2, 3.—— 5. What greatly influences the love of the Lord's people to him, and lays them under obligation to love him, is his great love to them, 1 John iv. 19. which love appeared in choosing them in Christ to eternal happiness, of his own free favour and goodwill; in the provision of Christ to be the propitiation for their sins; in the mission of him into the world for that purpose; in the free and full forgiveness of all their sins, for his sake; in drawing them to himself, in effectual calling, with his loving-kindness, having, for the great love wherewith he loved them, quickened them when dead in trespasses and sins; and in openly espousing them to himself in conversion, called the *love* of their *espousals;* with all after manifestations of his love unto them.—— 6. The examples of the saints in all ages might be urged as motives to love the Lord; as of Enoch, Noah, and others before the flood; of the patriarchs Abraham, Isaac, Jacob, and Joseph after it; with Joshua, Samuel, David, and others; but especially our Lord Jesus Christ, in human nature, who, in the exercise of this grace, as in others, is an example to us, John xiv. 31.

Secondly, The subjects of this grace of love, in whom it is, by whom the Lord is loved, and how they come by this grace.

1. It is not of men, nor is it in men naturally; it is not in any natural man, who is in a state of nature and unregeneracy; such are *lovers of pleasures*, sinful lusts and pleasures, *more than lovers of God;* yea, some of them are described as *haters of God;* and, indeed, the *carnal mind*, in every man, is *enmity against God*, not only an enemy to God, but enmity itself; which denotes how great and intense, and what a rooted and implacable enmity there is in a carnal man to God, and all that is good: nor is there any love in the people of God themselves, before conversion; they are *without God*, without any knowledge of God, and love to him; they are *alienated* from God, and from the life of God, and have no desire after him, nor of communion with him; but are *enemies in their minds*, in the temper and disposition of them; and which is shewn by their *wicked works;* and in this state they were, when Christ died and shed his blood for them, to make peace and reconciliation for them, Col. i. 20, 21. Rom. v. 10. which circumstance greatly illustrates the love of God, in the gift of his Son to them, 1 John iv. 10.——2. The grace of love is of God; he is the efficient cause and author of it, as he is of every grace; the apostle John expressly says, *love is of God*, of God, Father, Son, and Spirit; it is of God the Father, who is the God of all grace,

and so of this, 1 John iv. 7. and *love with faith*, are wished for *from God the Father, and the Lord Jesus Christ,* Eph. vi. 23. and it stands in the first place among the fruits of the Spirit, Gal. v. 22. it is wrought in the soul in regeneration, when other graces are, and is an evidence of it; for *every one that loveth is born of God,* 1 John iv. 7. and a man cannot love God until he is regenerated, and renewed in the spirit of his mind, and is made a partaker of the spiritual circumcision of the heart, which is necessary to it, and which is promised, Deut. xxx. 6. this grace only appears with other graces, and when they do; there can be no love to God where there is no knowledge of him; according to that known phrase, *ignoti nulla cupido;* where there is knowledge of him, especially of him in Christ, as gracious and merciful, there will be love to him, 1 John iv. 7, 8. where ignorance is, there is no love; but it appears where knowledge is, and it accompanies faith: both spring from the same abundant grace, 1 Tim. i. 14. faith, hope, and love go together, 1 Cor. xiii. 13. as the subject of love is a regenerate man, the seat of it is the heart, not the head; nor the tongue, but the heart, it lies not in word and in tongue, but in deed and in truth; and true love to God is a love of him with all the heart, soul, and strength.

Thirdly, How, in what way and manner, love to God manifests itself.

1. In a desire to be like him; one that loves another, endeavours to imitate him; and such that love the Lord are followers of him, as dear children, beloved ones, and walk in love, and are obedient ones, and desirous of being holy, as he is holy, in all manner of conversation; nor can they be thoroughly satisfied and contented until they awake in his likeness.——2. In making his glory the supreme end of all their actions; as this is God's end in all he does in providence, who makes all things for himself, his own glory; so in all things in grace, they are all directed to the glory of it; nor will he give, nor suffer to be given, his glory to another; wherefore, in imitation of him, they that love the Lord, do all they do, whether in a natural and civil sense, or of a religious and spiritual kind, whether praying, or reading, or hearing, or preaching, their end is, *that God in all things may be glorified through Jesus Christ,* 1 Cor. x. 31. 1 Pet. iv. 11.——3. In desiring of, and delighting in, communion with God; longing to appear before God, and enjoy his presence in his courts; thirst for him as in a dry and thirsty land, where no water is, that they may see his power and his glory in his sanctuary; this is the one thing uppermost in their minds, and which they seek most importunately for, that they may behold the beauty of the Lord in his temple; if God lifts but up the light of his countenance on them, this puts joy and gladness into their hearts, more than the affluence of all earthly things can; and if they are indulged with communion with him, they exult and glory, saying, *Truly, our fellowship is with the Father, and with his Son Jesus Christ,* 1 John i. 3.——4. In a carefulness not to offend him, by sinning against him; *ye that love the Lord, hate evil,* Psalm xcvii. 10. and they will shew their hatred of it, and endeavour to avoid it, and even to abstain from all appearance of it; and when opportunity offers, and they are solicited by temptations to sin, argue, as Joseph; *How can I do this great wickedness, and sin against God?* Gen. xxxix. 9. against God, who has loved me, and I am under such great obligations to love him again?——5. In grief, when he has withdrawn himself, and in a diligent seeking after him until he is found; when he hides his face, and withdraws his gracious presence, a soul that loves God is troubled at it, and complains of it, as the church did; *Zion said, The Lord hath forsaken me, and my Lord hath forgotten me!* and therefore such a soul, with Job, expresses its concern to know where it could find him, and takes for it a course like his, goes forward and backward, to the right and left, where he used to work, and was wont to be seen, Job xxiii. 2, 8, 9.——6. In parting with and bearing all for his sake, leaving their own people and father's house, country, and kindred, as Abraham did, to go where he directs; saying as Ruth said to Naomi, *Whither thou goest I will go, where thou lodgest I will lodge, thy people shall be my people, and thy God shall be my God:* and such that love God are willing to endure all hardships for his sake, to suffer reproach, persecution, and distress of every kind, rather than forego their profession and enjoyment of him.——7. In a regard to his house, worship, and ordinances; they that love the Lord love the habitation of his house, the place where his honour dwells; his tabernacles are amiable and lovely; a day in his house is better than a thousand elsewhere; it is no

other, in their esteem, than the gate of heaven, and, like the disciples on the mount, think it good for them to be here, and are for making tabernacles to abide in.—— 8. By a value for his word, his gospel, and the truths of it. They that love the Lord receive the love of the truth; not only the truth, but a love of it, an affection for it; it is more to be desired by them than gold, and is more to them than thousands of gold and silver; it is more esteemed of by them than their necessary food; they find it, and eat it, and it is the joy and rejoicing of their hearts; the feet of them that bring the good tidings of it are beautiful unto them.——9. In love and affection to the people of God; who are, with those that love the Lord, the excellent in the earth, in whom is all their delight; as they love him that begets, they love those who are begotten of him, and bear his image; and they are taught of him to do this in their regeneration, and which is an evidence that they have passed from death to life, and are born again.——10. By a disesteem of all things in comparison of God: to love the world, and the things of it, in an immoderate manner, is not consistent with the love of the Father, or with profession of love to him; for the friendship of the world is enmity with God; and a man cannot be a friend of the world and a lover of God; no man can serve two masters, God and mammon; for either he will hate the one and love the other, or hold to the one and despise the other.

Fourthly, The nature and properties of the love of God; what it is, or should be.

1. It is, or ought to be, universal; a love of all that is in God, and belongs unto him; of all his attributes and perfections, of one as another; not of his goodness, grace, and mercy, and of him for them only; but of his holiness, justice, and truth; and of all his commandments, which are all to be respected, attended unto, and obeyed, Psalm cxix. 127, 128. and it is a love of all the truths and doctrines of the gospel, of whatsoever is contained in the Scripture; every word of God is pure to them that love the Lord; and all the words of his mouth are plain and right, and nothing froward or perverse in them. And this love extends to all the people of God, of whatsoever class, rank, degree, or denomination, Eph. i. 15.——2. It is, or ought to be, superlative: what exceeds all other love, or love to all other persons and things; as there is none like the Lord for greatness and goodness, so there is none to be loved like him, none in heaven nor in earth, neither angels nor men; not the greatest personages, and those of the most amiable qualities and characters; nor those in the nearest relation, as father, mother, husband, wife, &c.—— 3. It is, or ought to be, hearty and sincere; a love without dissimulation; not in word, nor in tongue, but in deed and in truth; it is required to be with *all the heart,* in the most cordial manner; and *with all the soul,* the powers and faculties of it, the affections being wholly engrossed and swallowed up in love to God; and *with all the might,* or *strength;* with all the strength of grace, or spiritual strength a man is possessed of.—— 4. Should be constant; such is the love of God to his people, he *rests in his love* towards them; such is the love of Christ to them; who, *having loved his own which are in the world, he loves them to the end,* immutably and invariably: the love of God's people falls short of this; it is variable and inconstant in its acts and exercises, though its principle remains.——5. It is imperfect in the present state, as every grace is: knowledge is imperfect; *we know but in part;* and faith is imperfect, and hence an increase of it is desired; and so is love, it sometimes waxes cold, through the prevalence of corruption, the force of temptation, and the snares of the world; and lukewarmness and indifference takes place, until there is a reviving of it through a fresh stream of love from God.——6. It may be increased, and sometimes is, the apostle prays for an increase of it, and he thanks God for it that it did abound, 1 Thess. v. 12. 2 Thess. i. 3. which though it refers to love to the saints, is equally true of love to God, which increases the one as the other.——7. This grace of love, like others, can never be lost; though it may wax cold, it does not sink to nothing, and though it may be less, and abated, and grow weak, as to the ardency and fervency of it, it is not lost; yea, will abide when other graces have dropped their exercise, which is one reason why it is said to be the *greatest,* 1 Cor. xiii. 13. it never fails, ver. 8.

Fifthly, The happiness of such that love the Lord.

1. They are loved by him; *I love them that love me;* not that their love is the cause of the love of God to them; his love is prior to theirs, and is the cause of that; but such that love the Lord, greater manifestations of his love are made to them, and more instances of it shewn; the secrets of his heart's love are disclosed unto them,

that is shed abroad in their hearts by the Spirit, and they are directed into it, and led more largely into a view of interest in it; which to enjoy is a great blessing; for *his loving-kindness is better than life*, Psalm lxiii. 3.——2. They are known of God; *if any man love God, the same is known of him*, 1 Cor. viii. 3. is taken notice of by him, owned and acknowledged as his; and to whom he makes himself known, uses him familiarly, and favours him with communion with himself, and knows his soul in adversity, supports him in it, and delivers out of it; the knowledge he has of him is special, peculiar, and distinct, and is joined with love and affection to him; *the Lord knoweth them that are his*, 2 Tim. ii. 19. ——3. They are preserved by him; *the Lord preserveth all them that love him*, Psalm cxlv. 20. and the same is made use of as an argument to love him, Psalm xxxi. 23. since the Lord takes them under his special care, and preserves them from every enemy, from hurts and dangers, from sin, Satan, and the world, and from a final and total falling away from him, by means of any of them; he preserves them in Christ, and preserves them safe to the coming of Christ, and to his kingdom and glory.—— 4. They have many instances of mercy, kindness, and respect shewn them; for *the Lord is a God shewing mercy unto thousands of them that love him*, Exod. xx. 6. hence David thus prays for himself; *Look thou upon me, and be merciful unto me, as thou usest to do unto those that love thy name*, Psalm cxix. 132.——5. All things that occur unto them in the present life are for their good, and work together for it, Rom. viii. 28. even all afflictions and adverse dispensations of providence, as well as more prosperous ones; either for their temporal good, as in the case of Jacob, who thought all things were going against him, when they were all working for him; or for spiritual good; for the trial and increase of grace, of faith, patience, &c. Rom. v. 5. 1 Pet. i. 7. James i. 2. and always for their eternal good, 2 Cor. iv. 17.——6. Great things are laid up and reserved for them that love the Lord, to be enjoyed hereafter, even things inconceivable, and which are expressed by the highest enjoyments in this life, and which vastly exceed them; by a *crown* and *kingdom* they are now made *heirs* of, 1 Cor. ii. 9. James i. 12. and ii. 5.

II. Love to Christ is another eminent branch of the grace of love; for he is not only a distinct divine Person in the God-head, but stands in an office-capacity, as Mediator, Redeemer, and Saviour of his people; and has given various surprising proofs and instances of his love to them; and therefore it is not to be wondered at that he should be represented in the Scriptures in so distinguished a manner as the object of their love; and he being so well known to be the object of the love of saints, and so deserving of it, the church only describes him by this periphrasis, *him whom my soul loveth;* without naming his name; supposing that every one she conversed with, knew who she meant, Cant. iii. 1, 2, 3. and very frequently she calls him, *My beloved*, without any other description of him, chap. i. 13, 14. and ii. 16. So the apostle Peter, after having made mention of the appearing of Jesus Christ, adds, *Whom having not seen, ye love*, 1 Pet. i. 8. and for himself, he could appeal to Christ, as the omniscient God, and say, *Lord thou knowest all things, thou knowest that I love thee*, John xxi. 17. Concerning which love to Christ, the following things may be considered,

First, On what accounts Christ is to be loved, and is loved, by them that know him and believe in him: and there are many things in him, and belonging to him, which engage their love and affections to him. And he is to be loved,

1. Because of the excellencies of his Person: as the Son of God, his glory is the glory of the only begotten of the Father; he is the brightness of his glory, and the express image of his Person; is equal to God, and in the glorious and lovely form of God; the whole fulness of the Godhead dwells in him; every perfection in Deity is to be found in him; and therefore has every thing to attract the love of his people to him; hence one of the ancients said, *Est aliquid in Christo formosius salvatore;* there is something in Christ more amiable, more lovely, and more beautiful than the Saviour. ——2. Because he is the beloved of his Father, his dear Son, the Son of his love, the darling and delight of his soul, always by him, near to him, as one brought up with him, carried in his bosom, in which he lay, and was daily his delight, rejoicing always before him; all which is expressive of his tender affection for him, and the inexpressible pleasure he took in him before the world began; and which he further declared by putting all things into his hands, and shewing him all he did; which instances our Lord makes mention of himself, as proofs of his Father's love to him,

John iii. 35. and v. 20. and when he was here on earth, in human nature, both at his baptism and at his transfiguration on the mount, he declared by a voice from heaven, saying, *This is my beloved Son, in whom I am well pleased*, Matt. iii. 17. and xvii. 5. yea, he loved him because he laid down his life for his sheep, John x. 17. all which most strongly move and excite the saints to love him.———3. Because of the fulness of grace in him for the supply of their wants; it is a very considerable branch of the glory of Christ, as Mediator, and which recommends him as such, that he is *full of grace and truth;* as the fulness of Deity in him renders him an object worthy of the highest love, as a divine Person; so the fulness of grace it pleased the Father should dwell in him, as Man and Mediator, cannot fail of recommending him as suitable to indigent sinners, and of raising in them an high esteem of him, as a most lovely Person, and of attracting their affections to him, Psalm xlv. 2. Cant. v. 10.———4. Because of his precious names and titles; his *name* in general, *is as ointment poured forth*, which diffuses a most sweet savour, alluding to his name, Messiah, which signifies *anointed;* and from whom the saints receive the *anointing*, the graces of the Spirit, which are his *ointments*, good and savoury, *and therefore do the virgins love him*, Cant. i. 3. who receive all their grace and beauty from him, which makes them amiable and lovely to him. His name Jesus, a Saviour, so called because he saves his people from their sins, is a delightful sound in their ears; as is also, *the Lord our Righteousness*, by whose righteousness they are justified before God, and become perfectly comely in his sight, Matt. i. 21. Jer. xxiii. 6. and every other name and title of his in Isa. ix. 6.———5. Because of the offices he bears, so useful and beneficial to his people; he is the *Mediator* between God and men, the day's-man between them both, who has brought them together, and reconciled them; the *Surety* of the better Testament, who engaged to be a ransom for them, to pay their debts, to bear their sins, and make satisfaction for them, and to bring them to God, and set them before him; their *Prophet*, to teach and instruct them, and enlighten in the knowledge of saving truths; their *Priest*, to make atonement for their sins, and to intercede for their persons; and their *King* to rule over them, protect and defend them; and who would not fear and love one so great and respectable!———
6. Because of the relations he stands in to them: he is their everlasting *Father*, who has the most affectionate concern for their welfare; he is the most tender *Husband*, who nourishes the church as his own flesh, and for whom he gave himself a sacrifice; he is the most kind and loving *Brother*, was born for the adversity of his brethren, and to bring them out of it, and is not ashamed of his relation to them; he is a most faithful *Friend*, a friend that loves at all times, that sticks closer than a brother; no wonder that the church, after she had described him at large, should break forth in such an exulting and affectionate strain; *This is my Beloved, and this is my Friend, O daughters of Jerusalem!* Cant. v. 16.———7. Because he has all blessings in his hands for them; peace, pardon, righteousness and eternal life; and God has blessed his people in him with all spiritual blessings; has given them grace in him, even all the blessings of grace, before the world began; and has made him to them wisdom, righteousness, sanctification and redemption; so that he is their ALL in ALL, and therefore it is not to be wondered at, that he should be the object of their highest love.———
8. Particularly, because he is their Saviour and Redeemer, who assumed their nature, in order to die in their room and stead, and became the author of eternal salvation to them, and who saved them and gave himself for them to redeem them from all iniquity, and out of the hand of every enemy, and has by his blood obtained eternal redemption for them, and who has loved them, and washed them from their sins in his blood, and has procured the remission of them, as well as cleansing from them; and on all accounts they have reason to love him, and sing his new song of redeeming grace, *Worthy is the Lamb*, &c. Rev. i. 5. and v. 9.———9. Nor does his love cease here, nor the obligations on his people to love him; for he appears in the presence of God for them, and ever lives to make intercession for them, and is their advocate with the Father, in consequence of which, various blessings of grace descend upon them.———
10. He will appear a second time, without sin, to the salvation of them that look for him; and his appearance is to be looked for, it being a glorious one; and is itself to be loved: and much more the Person, who shall appear in so much glory, and so much to the advantage of those that love him; for a crown of righteousness is laid up, and will be given to them *that love his appearing*, 2 Tim. iv. 8.

Secondly, The springs and causes of love to Christ.

1. It does not arise from nature; men in a state of nature are *without Christ*, without any knowledge of him, and affection for him; they see no form, nor comeliness, nor beauty in him, wherefore he should be desired by them: and this is not only the case of openly profane and carnal sinners, but even of some who have some notion of religion and sacred things; and yet ask, *What is thy beloved more than another beloved?* what peculiar charms, excellencies, and beauty are there in him, which give him a preference to all others? But this betrays their ignorance of Christ, and want of true affection for him, Cant. v. 9.——2. But it is owing to the abundant grace of God in regeneration; an unregenerate man is destitute of it; *If God was your Father*, says Christ to the Jews, their Father by adoption, of which regeneration is the evidence, *ye would love me; for every one that loveth him that begat, loveth him also that is begotten of him*, John viii. 42. 1 John v. 1. Whoever loves God, who has, of his own good will and abundant mercy, begotten him again to a lively hope of a glorious inheritance, loves Christ also, who is begotten of him, though in an higher sense, and who is the first-born among many brethren. Faith in Christ, and love to him, commence together; and both flow from the same grace and favour, 1 Tim. i. 14. none but true believers in Christ sincerely love him; *faith works by love; to them that believe he is precious*, Gal. v. 6. 1 Pet. ii. 7. and none but such who by an eye of faith have seen his glory, fulness, and suitableness, truly love him; for,——3. Love to him is owing to a special revelation of him, in effectual vocation; when God calls a man by his grace, he reveals his Son in him, and to him, in the glories of his person, and the riches of his grace; when he sees the King in his beauty, and is enamoured with him, he appears to him white and ruddy, a perfection of beauty, the chiefest among a thousand thousand, none like him among all the men on earth, nor among all the angels in heaven; he is in his esteem, *altogether lovely*, beyond all compare, beyond all expression; all things are reckoned loss in comparison of the knowledge of him.——4. Love to Christ arises, not only from a view of his loveliness; but also from a sense of his love, which passes knowledge, from a feeling sensation of it, shed abroad in the heart, which causes love again. This was the case of the sinful woman mentioned in the gospel, who loved much because much love was shewn her, in the forgiveness of her sins, through the blood of Jesus; and this is the experience of all the saints; *we love him because he first loved us*, in taking the care and charge of us, in assuming our nature, and in dying in our room and stead. ——5. This love is more and more heightened and increased through knowledge of union to him, and through communion with him; the church, sitting under the shadow of Christ with great delight, and his fruit sweet to her taste, and being brought by him into his banquetting house, with his banner of love displayed over her, served much to draw forth her love to him, and make her even sick with it; and especially being brought *into his chamber* by him, filled her with joy and gladness, and caused her to remember his love more than wine; and she observed this as the effect of it, *the upright love thee*, Cant. i. 4. and ii. 3, 4, 5. Thus John, the beloved disciple, being indulged with leaning on the bosom of Jesus, not only had a greater manifestation of Christ's love, but more strongly expressed his love to Christ.

Thirdly, How, in what way and manner, or in what instances, love to Christ shews itself.

1. In a regard to all that are his, and belong to him; *His mouth is most sweet* to such, and he is *altogether*, or *all of him, lovely*, in his person, in his offices, and in his people; his promises are like apples of gold in pictures of silver; the words of his mouth, the doctrines of his grace, are sweeter than the honey or the honey-comb; the ministers of the gospel, who bring the glad tidings of salvation, are beautiful and lovely; his saints are the precious sons of Zion, and comparable to fine gold; his ways are ways of pleasantness, his tabernacles amiable, and his ordinances delightful.——2. In keeping his commandments; *If ye love me*, says Christ, *keep my commandments*; this is the strongest and clearest proof of love; he that from a principle of love, *keepeth them, he it is*, says Christ, *that loveth me*; others may talk of their love to Christ; but he is the man that truly loves him, John xiv. 15, 21. ——3. In a carefulness not to offend him, and cause him to depart from them; thus solicitous was the church, and therefore fearful lest any offence should be given, and occasion his removal from her, Cant. ii. 7.

---4. In a jealousy of his love, lest he should not love them at all; or should not love them so much as another, or another more than they; *Jealousy is cruel as the grave,* fearful,[3] distressing, and insatiable, Cant. viii. 6.-----5. In a desire of, and delight in, his company; this delight is very great; *I sat down under his shadow,* under the shadow of his ordinances, enjoying his presence in them, *with great delight,* Cant. ii. 3. and this desire is very vehement, strongly expressed with great ardour and fervency, and the presence of Christ is importunately sought after, Isa. xxvi. 9.-----6. In grief and concern, when he has withdrawn his presence. *In his favour,* in his gracious presence, and under the smiles of his countenance, *is life,* a soul is alive and comfortable; but if he withdraws himself, and the manifestations of his favour, it is death, it kills, it is intolerable; *My soul failed,* swooned away, *when he spake,* or at the parting word, Cant. v. 8. So Mary, at our Lord's sepulchre, not finding him there, with an heart full of grief, and ready to break, burst out in a passionate manner, with tears, *They have taken away my Lord!* John xx. 13.-----7. In a strict search and inquiry after him until found; so the church, when she had lost her beloved, sought him first on her *bed,* in her chamber, and private retirement; then in the *city,* the assembly of the saints, in the *streets* and *broad* places, in the public ministry of the word and ordinances; and then of the *watchmen,* the ministers of the gospel personally; and throughout the whole of the search the enquiry was, *Saw ye him whom my soul loveth?* and in an after similar case; when, through her sleepiness, slothfulness, and ingratitude, he withdrew from her; which when she perceived, she sought him, but could not find him; she called to him, but received no answer; she met with ill usuage from the watchmen, but this did not deter her from going in quest of him; she lighted upon the daughters of Jerusalem, in her search of him, whom she charged, that if they found her beloved, that they would tell him, that she was sick of love for him, Cant. iii. 1, 2, 3. and v. 6, 7, 8.-----8. In expressions of joy upon finding him; as the church in the above case; *It was but little,* says she, *that I passed from them, but I found him whom my soul loveth; I held him, and would not let him go:* and in the other case how does she exult in the close of her account, upon finding him; *This is my beloved, and this is my friend!* Cant. iii. 4. and v. 16. So, after our Lord's absence by death, from his disciples, when he rose again, and shewed himself to them, it is said, *Then were the disciples glad when they saw the Lord,* John xx. 20. and so it is when Christ has withdrawn himself from his people, and they see him again by faith, they are filled *with a joy unspeakable and full of glory!* and there is great reason for such joy on finding him; for he that finds him, *finds life, and shall obtain favour of the Lord,* Prov. viii. 35.-----9. In pushing through all difficulties to enjoy him, as the church did; who in search of Christ, exposed herself to the insults, blows, wounds, and depredations of the watchmen. So souls at first conversion, when their first love, the love of their espousals to Christ, is warm and ardent, like Israel of old, go after him *in a wilderness, in a land not sown,* in very discouraging circumstances, through much reproach, tribulation, and affliction, from the world and others.-----10. In parting with and bearing all for Christ's sake; in leaving relations, friends, and former companions, houses, lands, and every thing dear and valuable, standing in competition with him: in denying themselves in every view, sinful self, righteous self, and civil self; taking up the cross cheerfully, and following him; and even loving not their lives unto death for his sake; Christ is the pearl of great price in their esteem, and they are willing to part with all things, and suffer the loss of all, that they may enjoy him.

Fourthly, The nature of this love.

1. Universal; all of Christ, as before observed; for he is all lovely; his person, his people, his word and ordinances, his precepts, and his promises.-----2. Superlative; *He that loves father or mother more than me,* says Christ, *is not worthy of me,* &c. Matt. x. 37. and the same holds good of any other person or thing; there is none in heaven nor in earth to be loved like him; he is the chiefest among ten thousand.-----3. Hearty and sincere; such who truly love Christ, love him *in sincerity,* or *in incorruption,* Eph. vi. 24. with a love that cannot be corrupted, with a love unfeigned, and without dissimulation; such was Peter's love to Christ, who could appeal to him as omniscient, for the truth of it.

---

[3] Res est soliciti plena timoris amor. Ovid.

———4. Warm and fervent; such as *many waters* of sin, temptation, and affliction, *cannot quench;* floods of the same, more forcible, *cannot drown;* and from which, *tribulation, distress, persecution, famine, nakedness, peril and sword, cannot separate,* Cant. viii. 7. Rom. viii. 35.———5. It should be constant, as Christ's is to us, who loves at all times, and to the end: but, alas! other objects present, and other lovers are followed after for a time ; yet true love is not totally and finally lost; first love, though left for a while, is revived and restored; and the first husband is returned unto and abode by.———6. It is very grateful and well-pleasing to Christ ; *How fair is thy love,* says he, *my sister, my spouse; how much better is thy love than wine!* Cant. iv. 10. he remembers the first love of his people, the love of their espousals, the kindness of their youth, when forgotten by them: what made him put the question so often to Peter, *Lovest thou me?* One reason, among others, might be, because it was pleasing to him to hear him say, and so strongly aver it, that he loved him.

Fifthly, The happiness of those that love Christ.

1. They are loved by him: *I love them that love me,* says Wisdom, or Christ, Prov. viii. 17. that is, he continues to love them, and makes greater manifestations of himself, and of his love to them ; and so he himself explains it, when speaking of those that shew their love to him, by keeping his commandments; he says, *I will love him, and manifest myself unto him;* and this he shews by his frequent love-visits to them, and by his prayers and preparations for them, that they may be with him where he is, and behold his glory.———2. They are blessed who love Christ; as a curse, an *anathema, maranatha,* is wished to those who love him not; so *grace,* the best of blessings, is desired for those who love him in sincerity, 1 Cor. xvi. 22. Eph. vi. 24.

———3. It is expressed prayer-wise, that it might be, and it is a prayer of faith, that it shall be ; *Let them that love him, be as the sun when it goeth forth in his might,* Judg. v. 31. for light, splendour, and glory ; as they are when clothed with the sun, and when the Sun of righteousness arises upon them with healing in his wings, and as they will be when they shall shine as the sun in the kingdom of their Father.———4. Those that love Christ, he, as he has promised, *Will cause to inherit substance,* Prov. viii. 21. even a better and a more enduring substance than is to be enjoyed in this world ; riches of grace, and riches of glory, durable riches and righteousness.

III. Another branch of the grace of love is, love to men.

First, The objects of it; men.———1. Angels indeed are objects of love; not the evil angels, because of their wickedness and apostacy from God, and because of their mischievous nature, continually seeking to do hurt to the persons of men, their souls and bodies, their properties and estates, as much as in them lies, and as far as they have leave ; but good angels, who are very amiable, because of the excellencies of their nature, their holiness, wisdom, and strength, in which they excel; they belong to the family in heaven, and are of great use to saints on earth; are ministering spirits to the heirs of salvation; though they are not to be worshipped by good men, being their fellow servants ; yet they are to be loved, being friendly to them, and wish their welfare, and rejoice at it; they expressed their joy at the good will of God to men, shewn in the incarnation of Christ for them ; and there is joy among them whenever a sinner is converted and repents; besides, the saints will be like them in the resurrection, and will join them in the worship of God, and in communion with him for ever. But,———2. It is with men, the branch of love under consideration is concerned; and, indeed, all men are to be loved ; for this is the second great commandment, *Thou shalt love thy neighbour as thyself;* and all mankind are neighbours ; they are all the offspring of God, and near akin to one another, being all of one man's blood ; nay, not only those that are kind and neighbourly, are to be loved, but even our very enemies ; so Christ has taught us by his precept; *I say unto you, love your enemies;* and by his example, in praying to his Father, *Forgive them, for they know not what they do!* Matt. xxii. 39, 40. and v. 44. Luke xxiii. 34. nay, we are directed to shew kindness to them, and heap favours upon them, and thereby overcome their evil with good, Rom. xii. 19, 20, 21.———3. The peculiar objects of this branch of love now to be treated of, are good men, the saints and people of God; who are,———(1.) called Brethren ; not in a natural but spiritual relation, the brethren of Christ, and brethren one of another ; who are brethren and partakers of the same heavenly calling, or are in the same church-state, and are called the *brotherhood*, and therefore should love as brethren, 1 Pet. ii. 17. and iii. 8. Hence this love has the name of Philadelphia, or brotherly love, Rom. xii. 10. Heb. xiii. 1.——(2.) Disciples and followers of Christ; such who have learned Christ, and have learned to deny themselves, and to take up the cross and follow him; these, as they should love Christ, so likewise one another, John xiii. 35. and the least instance of love and kindness shewn to such on account of what they are, is exceeding pleasing to Christ, Matt. x. 42.——(3.) Believers in Christ, who are called the household of faith, partakers of the grace of faith, and embrace and profess the same doctrine of faith, these are to be loved, and special kindness shewn unto them, Gal. vi. 10. Tit. iii. 15. the little ones who believe in Christ he is so tender of, and has such a special regard unto, that he would have no offence given unto them; but signifies, it would fare ill with those who should give it, Matt. xviii. 6.——(4.) Children of God, who are such by adoption, to which they are predestinated, and which they receive through and from Christ, and of which regeneration is the evidence, and the Spirit of God the witness; and who become apparently so by faith in Christ Jesus, and being children of the same Father, ought to love one another, 1 John v. 1, 2.——(5.) They are described as Saints, who are the objects of this grace of love; who are called to be saints, and are called with an holy calling, or sanctified by the Spirit of God, and have principles of grace and holiness wrought in them, and live holy lives and conversations; and frequently does the apostle speak in commendation of the churches for their *love unto all the saints*, Eph. i. 15. Col. i. 4.

Secondly, The nature of this grace of love, as exercised towards the saints.

1. It is wrought in regeneration. Men in a state of unregeneracy are destitute of it; *the world hates* those that are *chosen out of* it, and called; and that because they are so; yea, one part of the character of God's elect before conversion is, *hateful, and hating one another;* in regeneration, and not before, men are *taught of God to love one another*; and this is an evidence of their regeneration, 1 Thess. iv. 9. 1 John iii. 14.——2. This grace is very largely described, 1 Cor. xiii. for though our translators have rendered the word *charity* throughout, for what reason it does not appear, it should be *love*; for it is manifestly distinguished from alms-deeds, or relieving the poor and distressed, which the apostle supposes may be, and yet this grace be wanting; by which he seems to understand love to the saints; without which, he suggests the greatest gifts of knowledge are nothing, and all pretensions to, and professions of religion, are in vain: those who are possessed of it, *suffer long,* bear and forbear much, are *kind* to their fellow creatures and fellow christians; *envy not* the superior gifts and graces of others; *vaunt not* over those supposed inferior to them; and are *not puffed up* with their own attainments; *do not behave unseemly*, in a haughty, supercilious, and contemptuous manner to those in connection with them; *seek* not their *own* things, pleasures, profits, honours, and to exalt themselves above others; are not *easily provoked* to wrath against those that offend them; *think no evil* of others, give not way to groundless jealousies and surmises; *rejoice not in iniquity*, in committing it themselves, nor in seeing it done by others; not in lies, nor in any false representations of things; but *rejoice in the truth*, in hearing and telling truth of others; *bear all things*, all reproaches, insults, and indignities, with patience and meekness; *believe all things* of good report in fellow-christians, not giving credit to evil spoken of them, without sufficient reason; *hope all things*, the best concerning them, and that what is of ill report is not true of them; *endure all things*, the ill treatment and ill manners of others, with much mildness and gentleness.——3. It should be universal; *Love to all saints;* for which some churches are commended, before observed; whether they be weak or strong believers, more or less knowing christians, they are to be cordially *received* into the love and affections of the saints; and be they of whatsoever name and denomination in religion they may, provided they appear to be Christ's, and bear his image; and let their worldly circumstances be what they will, no respect as to affection, is to be had to persons; one in a christian assembly with a gold ring, and in goodly apparel, is not to be preferred to a poor brother in mean raiment, as James directs, chap. ii. 1, 2, 3.——4. It should be fervent, 1 Pet. i. 22. and iv. 8. and every method should be taken and means used to blow up the flame of love, and to keep it alive; it is a sign of bad times, and of things going ill in religion, when *the love of many waxes cold*, Matt. xxiv. 12.——5. It should be, and where it

is right it will be, unfeigned and sincere; so the apostle calls that love which springs from an heart purified under the influence of divine truths, by the Spirit, *unfeigned love of the brethren*, 1 Pet. i. 22. it is love without dissimulation, real and cordial; not *in word* and *in tongue* only, but *in deed* and *in truth*, 1 John iii. 18.——6. It is an active and laborious grace, by which the saints *serve one another*, both in things temporal and spiritual, Gal. v. 13. hence we read of the *work and labour of love*, 1 Thess. i. 3. Heb. vi. 10. it not only works and is busy, and continually exercises itself in doing good, but it labours at it, and yet is not weary of well doing.—— 7. The manner in which, or the exemplar according to which, it is to be exercised is, as Christ has loved his people; this is what he himself has enjoined, that is the argument and motive inducing to an observance of it, John xiii. 34. and xv. 12. yea, the apostle John, carries this pattern of love to such a degree, that as Christ has shewn his love to his people in laying down his life for them; they are to shew theirs in laying down their lives for the brethren, 1 John iii. 16.——8. It is a very excellent grace; after the apostle had exhorted, to *covet earnestly the best gifts*, he adds, *yet shew I unto you a more excellent way*, 1 Cor. xii. 31. something more excellent than the best external gifts, both ordinary and extraordinary, he had before been speaking of; and by the connection of the words with the following chapter, it appears to be the grace of love, which, ——(1.) Is the greatest of all the graces, 1 Cor. xiii. 13. because it is more diffusive of goodness and kindness, and so more beneficial to others, though the other graces may be more useful to a man's self; and because of its long duration, even as to the exercise of it, which will be throughout an endless eternity; for *charity*, or *love*, *never faileth*, 1 Cor. xiii. 8.——(2.) It is an evidence of a man's being born again; *Every one that loveth is born of God*, 1 John iv. 7. and iii. 14. and this is the grand criterion of a true disciple of Christ, John xiii. 35. In Tertullian's time the heathens knew the christians by their loving carriage to one another in public, and would point unto them and say, " See how they love one another!"[4] such times are now to be wished for.——(3.) It is called the *bond of perfectness*, Col. iii. 14. which perfectly knits and unites the saints together, and keeps the unity of the spirit in the bond of peace; it is the perfect bond of the church and its members; of the saints to one another, and of their several graces.——(4.) Without this, a profession of religion is an empty and useless thing; and the strongest expressions of regard unto it, speculative notions about it, and boastings of it, are insignificant, 1 Cor. xiii. 1, 2, 3. How super-excellent therefore must this grace be! It is in vain to talk of love to God and love to Christ, where this is wanting, 1 John iv. 20.——(5.) It is the exercise of this grace which makes the communion of the saints with one another delightful; *Behold, how good and how pleasant it is, for brethren to dwell together in unity!* the Psalmist compares it, for its cheering and refreshing nature, to the precious ointment poured on Aaron's head, and to the dew of Hermon, and that which fell on the mountains of Zion, Psalm cxxxiii. and it also tends greatly to their edification in church-fellowship; *Charity*, or *love*, *edifieth*; the body, the church, being united to Christ the head, and the members of it fitly joined together, *maketh increase of the body, unto the edifying of itself in love*, 1 Cor. viii. 1. Eph. iv. 16.——(6.) It is one part of the saints' spiritual armour; *The breast-plate of faith and love* is a good defence against the enemy, who cannot easily get an advantage where this piece of armour is carefully and constantly made use of; it makes the church of Christ as terrible as an army with banners; the love and union of saints to one another, is their great security against the common adversary; like the bundle of sticks in the fable, which, whilst bound together, could not be broken, but when separated were easily snapped asunder.

Thirdly, How, in what manner, and wherein this grace of love to one another manifests itself.

1. By praying with and for one another; hence when our Lord taught his disciples to pray, he directed them to pray to God as their common Father; saying, *Our Father, which art in heaven;* thereby teaching them, that they were to pray for one another, even for all saints, and that constantly and fervently, Eph. vi. 18. which availeth much, and tends to godly edification.——2. By bearing one another's burdens, Gal. vi. 2. and this is done by assisting and relieving each other in distress,

---

[4] Apolog. c. 39.

as much as in us lies, by sympathizing with each other in trouble, as the members of a natural body do, rejoicing with them that rejoice, and weeping with them that weep.———3. By forbearing and forgiving one another; as God, for Christ's sake, and as Christ also has forgiven them, Col. iii. 13. see also Eph. iv. 31, 32. Luke xvii. 3, 4.———4. By rebuking and admonishing one another in love. Sin known, should not be suffered to lie upon a brother, without reproving for it; this is not kindness to him; *Open rebuke is better than secret love*, Prov. xxvii. 5, 6. but then such rebuke should be given in love, and with much tenderness; which is most likely to be kindly received and to succeed; *Let the righteous smite me, it shall be a kindness, &c.* Psalm cxli. 5. when such who are overtaken in a fault, are restored in the spirit of meekness, this shews tenderness and brotherly love.———5. By endeavouring to establish one another in the doctrines of the gospel, and of increasing light and knowledge; which is called, *building up themselves in their most holy faith;* which is done by praying and conversing together, often speaking one to another about divine things; not disdaining to receive instruction even from inferiors; thus Aquila and Priscilla expounded in a private manner the way of God more perfectly to Apollos, a public teacher; which he attended to.———6. By exhorting and stirring up one another to the several duties of religion, both public and private, Heb. x. 24, 25.

Fourthly, There are various arguments and motives, which may be made use of to excite to the exercise of this grace of love.

1. It is Christ's new commandment; so he says, *A new commandment I give unto you, That ye love one another;* which yet, as the apostle John says, it was both old and new, John xiii. 34. 1 John ii. 7, 8. an old commandment, being founded upon the original law of God; a new commandment, being not only an excellent one, especially as now delivered out, since excellent things in scripture are often called new ones, as a new song, &c. but because of the new edition of it under the gospel-dispensation, and being given forth anew by Christ the lawgiver, in his house, called therefore, *The law of Christ*, which is the law of love; and having a new pattern and exemplar of it, and a new motive and argument added to it, mentioned by Christ himself; *As I have loved you, that ye also love one another*, John xiii. 34. and xv. 12.
———2. The love of God and Christ should engage unto it; the love of God in the mission and gift of his Son to die for us, and become the propitiation for our sins; *Beloved*, says the apostle, *if God so loved us, we ought also to love one another*, 1 John iv. 11. and the love of Christ in giving himself for us, an offering and a sacrifice to God, to atone for our sins; *Walk in love, as Christ hath loved us, &c.* Eph. v. 2.
———3. The relation the saints stand in one to another, is a reason why they should love one another; they are members of the same body, and should have an affection and sympathy for one another; as the members in a natural, so they in a spiritual way; they are children of the same Father, and belong to the same family, and are all brethren; this is the argument Moses used with the Israelites at variance, Acts vii. 26.
———4. The comfort and joy of ministers, should be an argument with saints to mutual love; it is with the greater pleasure they pursue their studies and labour in their ministrations, for the good of souls, when peace and love are cultivated among them; but when it is otherwise, it is greatly discouraging and distressing to them, and they go on heavily in their work; for where envying and strife are, there is confusion, and every evil work; which is very disagreeable, and makes uncomfortable; yea, the comfort of the saints themselves, and their edification, are hereby greatly hurt; wherefore both with respect to ministers and people, the apostle exhorts to love and unity, Phil. ii. 1, 2. and 2 Cor. xiii. 11. and that *brotherly love continue;* for the love of God and Christ continues; nothing can separate from it; they love to the end: the relation of saints continues; being once the children of God, and brethren of Christ, and of one another, they always remain such, and in the family, in the house of God, where they abide, and from whence they are never removed. And if brotherly love continues not, churches cannot continue long; a house divided against itself cannot stand; the church at Ephesus was threatened with a removal of the candlestick, or church-state, unless they repented, because they had left their first love.

CHAP. X.

OF SPIRITUAL JOY.

Joy is a fruit of the Spirit, which follows love; *The fruit of the Spirit is love, joy,* Gal. v. 22. it attends faith and hope; and as these graces are in exercise, and increase, so does spiritual joy; hence we read of *the joy of faith,* and *the rejoicing of hope,* Phil. i. 25. Heb. iii. 6. it enters very much into the christian's character and experience, and is peculiar to saints and believers in Christ. Concerning which may be observed,

I. The objects of it.

First, Not a creature, nor creature-enjoyment, nor outward privilege, nor duty; but Jehovah himself, the Lord and God of all; therefore called by David, *God, his exceeding joy;* that is, the object of his great joy and gladness, Psalm xliii. 4. To glory in riches, wisdom, and strength, and to boast of them, is not right; and to rejoice in such boastings, *All such rejoicing is evil,* James iv. 16. to rejoice in any thing of this kind, is to *rejoice in a thing of nought,* in a nonentity, and in what is of no account, Amos vi. 13. and so to rejoice in youthful pleasures and vanities, and indulge to them in the highest degree; such joy is not spiritual, or the fruit of the Spirit; but is carnal and sensual, and but for a season; and to glory, and boast of, and trust in fleshly descent, in birth-privileges, and in the duties of religion, and in a man's own righteousness, and please himself with such things, is only the joy of an unregenerate man, and of an hypocrite, which is but for a moment, but the Lord himself is the proper object of joy; to rejoice in him is what is exhorted to, both in the Old and New Testaments, Psalm xxxiii. 1. Phil. iv. 4. So the prophet Habakkuk did, and resolved to do, in the worst of times, when all creature-mercies failed; *Yet I will rejoice in the Lord; I will joy in the God of my salvation!* Hab. iii. 17, 18. not in him merely as the Creator, from whom are had being, life, and breath, and all things, which yet is matter of joy, Psalm cxlix. 2. Job xxxv. 10. nor in him merely as the God of providence, and a kind benefactor, the preserver of men, and gives them all things richly to enjoy, so that they have reason to rejoice *in every good thing,* which the Lord in his providence gives unto them; but more especially saints rejoice in him as their covenant-God; *I will greatly rejoice in the Lord,* says the church; *My soul shall be joyful in my God!* Isa. lxi. 10. as her covenant-God, which is the sum and substance of the covenant, and includes and secures every blessing of it, and always continues; who, as such, is the God of all grace, and blesses with all spiritual blessings, and gives both grace and glory, supplies all the wants of his people out of his riches in glory, by Christ; and causes all grace to abound towards them, and will never suffer them to want any good thing; he is their portion now, and will be for ever; and as such they rejoice in him; and particularly,

1. In the attributes of God; which are all on the side of his people, and are exercised for their good, and they receive benefit and advantage from; and not only his power, wisdom, truth, and faithfulness, his goodness, grace, and mercy, are matter of joy; but even his justice and holiness, in which he is so glorious; *Rejoice in the Lord, ye righteous, and give thanks at the remembrance of his holiness,* Psalm xcvii. 12.——2. The everlasting love of God is matter of joy to the saints; as the Lord rests in his love, and rejoices over them with joy, so they rejoice in his love to them; it is that river the streams whereof, the blessings which flow from it, make glad their hearts; see Jer. xxxi. 3. a view of interest in it puts more joy and gladness into the hearts of the Lord's people than the largest increase of worldly things; it makes what they do enjoy, blessings indeed; for there is no curse in their blessings; a little, with the favour of God, is better than the riches of many wicked; mean fare, a dinner of herbs, where the love of God is enjoyed, is preferable to the most delicious dainties without it; and greater reason there is for a man to boast of, and rejoice in this, that he knows the Lord, as exercising loving-kindness in the earth, and delighting therein, than to rejoice and glory in the greatest outward attainments of body, mind, and estate; a sense of the love of God shed abroad in the heart by the Spirit, supports under all the trials and exercises of this life; and even causes to glory in tribulations, and to rejoice in hope of the glory of God; since neither tribulation, distress, persecution, famine, nakedness, peril, nor sword, can separate from it; yea, the loving-kindness of God is better than life itself, than which

nothing is dearer to a man; yea, when men are influenced by this love, they love not their lives unto the death; it is death to them when they are without a sense of this love; but, *in the favour of God*, and the enjoyment of it, is *life*, it revives and comforts, Psalm xxx. 5. and what makes the love of God greater cause of joy is, that it is everlasting and unchangeable; though God may be displeased with his people, and chastise them because of their sins; yet he never takes away his lovingkindness from them; and though he hides his face from them for a moment, yet with everlasting kindness he has mercy on them; nor shall it ever depart from them; it is more immoveable than hills and mountains, and is established both by the promise and oath of God; and there is nothing in heaven, earth, and hell, that shall ever separate from it; every thought concerning it, meditation upon it, and discovery of it, fills with joy unspeakable; a thought of it is with the greatest pleasure and delight; meditation on it is sweet; and whilst musing upon it, the fire of divine love is inflamed, and burns within, and breaks forth in expressions of joy and gladness; and nothing can yield greater satisfaction than to be remembered with the favour God bears to his own people; and the love of God is to be remembered more, and is more exhilarating to the soul, than wine is to the animal spirits, Cant. i. 2, 4. see Zech. x. 7.———3. The saints' election of God is matter of joy unto them; that *their names are written in heaven*, Luke x. 20. in the Lamb's book of life, in the book of divine predestination to the adoption of children, and to eternal life; and therefore it cannot be such a gloomy and melancholy thing, as some who are strangers to it, and ignorant of it, represent it; but is, as the XVIIth article of the church of England expresses it, "Full of sweet, pleasant, and unspeakable comfort to godly persons." So Calvin[1] observes, that "those who search into it rightly and in due order, as it is contained in the word, fetch choice consolation from it." And even Arminius himself says,[2] "It serves to comfort afflicted consciences." It is the foundation-blessing of grace, and the standard according to which all others are dispensed; God blesses his people with all spiritual blessings in Christ, according as he hath chosen them in him before the foundation of the world; this stands at the head of them, it is the first link in the chain of salvation, to which the rest are fastened, and by it secured; *Whom he did predestinate—them he also glorified;* it always *obtains;* or those who are chosen certainly enjoy every blessing of grace, life, righteousness, and salvation, Eph. i. 3, 4. Rom. viii. 30. and xi. 7. from hence springs all the grace of the Spirit dispensed by him in regeneration and sanctification; sanctification of the Spirit is fixed and established in the decree of election, as a mean, 'and is as certain as the end, salvation; holiness of heart and life is what men are chosen to, and what certainly follows upon their election of God; and so belief of the truth, or faith in Christ; and as many as are ordained unto eternal life, believe; hence true faith is called, *the faith of God's elect:* eternal glory and happiness is secured by it; they that are chosen, are chosen to the obtaining of the glory of Christ; and which, in consequence, they most assuredly enjoy; they cannot finally and totally be deceived and come short of that glory; no charge can be brought against them; and should any, it would not issue in their condemnation; they that are written in the Lamb's book of life enter into the new Jerusalem; and those who are predestinated are glorified. This is the foundation which stands sure; the seal of which is, *The Lord knows them that are his;* men are elect according to the foreknowledge of God, and that foreknowledge never fails; and therefore the purpose of God, according to election, stands sure; not upon the will and works of men, but upon the sovereign will, certain knowledge, and everlasting love of God; all which lay a solid foundation for joy and gladness.———4. The covenant of grace God has made with his chosen in Christ, is another thing which yields abundance of joy to the believer, both in life and in death; in a view of which, with what joy and exultation does the sweet singer of Israel express himself among the last words he uttered, 2 Sam. xxiii. 5. what makes this covenant so desirable, pleasant, and joyful is, that it is *everlasting;* from everlasting to everlasting; from everlasting, for so early was Christ set up as the Mediator of it; blessings of grace were given, and grants of grace made, to the elect in Christ, before the foundation of the world; and eternal life was promised before the world began; **nor**

---

[1] Institut. l. 3. c. 24. s. 4.

[2] Disput. Public. Thes. 15. s. 14.

will it ever be broken, made null and void; nor be antiquated, and succeeded by another covenant; but will always remain in full force; and so administer constant and perpetual joy to the covenant-ones. It is also *ordered in all things*, to secure the glory of the divine Persons; and for the display of the divine perfections; and for the good and happiness of those who are interested in it; it is full of blessings of grace, mercy, and goodness, called, *The sure mercies of David*, which are sure to all the seed; and of exceeding great and precious promises, which are all yea and amen in Christ, and suitable to the cases and circumstances of the Lord's people; which fitly spoken and applied, are as pleasant and delightful as apples of gold in pictures of silver, and give inexpressible joy and delight; *I rejoice at thy word*, says David, a word of promise, *as one that findeth great spoil*, Psalm cxix. 162. which suggests a great degree of joy. To which may be added, that this covenant is free, absolute and unconditional: its promises do not depend on conditions to be performed by men; but run thus, *I will*, and they *shall*; *I will be their God, and they shall be my people; I will put my fear into their hearts, and they shall not depart from me, &c*. This covenant is also said to be *sure*, its matter, its blessings, and its promises; it is *confirmed of God in Christ;* it is established by the oath of God, and ratified by the blood of Christ, the blood of the everlasting covenant; it is as immoveable as hills and mountains, and more so; they may be removed, but the covenant of peace shall never be removed; it is what God has commanded for ever; so that there is no fear of its ever failing; and affords an all-sufficient source of joy: all, or the whole of *salvation* is contained in it, and secured by it, salvation spiritual and eternal; in it Christ is appointed and settled as the author of it; the blessings of salvation are provided, and the persons for whom they are designed, given to Christ; in it the Israel that shall be saved by him with an everlasting salvation. So that David had great reason to say, *This is all my desire;* as containing in it all that was desirable by him, delightful to him, and that could afford him joy and pleasure.

Secondly, Christ, and things relating to him, are the objects of the spiritual joy of saints; this enters into the very character of true christians and believers in Christ, who are described as such who *rejoice in Christ Jesus, even with joy unspeakable and full of glory*, Phil. iii. 3. 1 Pet. i. 8. The things relating to him, which are matter and ground of joy, are such as relate both to his person and to his work.

1*st*, That relate to his person, as the Word and Son of God, equally a divine person with his Father, the *brightness of his glory, and the express image of his person*, Heb. i. 3. As,—1. The greatness of his person; the great God, God over all blessed for ever, who thought it no robbery to be equal with God, having all the perfections of deity, the consideration of which yields joy to believers in him; hence they know and may conclude that all he did and suffered in human nature united to his person, answered the ends for which they were done and suffered; his righteousness is the righteousness of God, and so unto and upon all them that believe; his blood the blood of the Son of God, and as such has a virtue to cleanse from all sin; his sacrifice the sacrifice of himself, and so of a sweet-smelling savour to God, and of efficacy to atone for sin; and his salvation a great salvation, plenteous and complete, he being the great God and our Saviour; hence also they are satisfied that they must be safe in his hands, out of which none can pluck them; that he is able to keep them from falling, and to save to the uttermost all that come unto God by him.——2. The fitness of his person; having taken the human nature into union with his divine person, he is very proper to be the mediator between God and man, to be a days-man to lay his hands on both, to take care of things pertaining to the law and justice of God, and the honour of them; and to make reconciliation for the sins of the people; a work which neither angels nor men were fit for and capable of; but God in his infinite wisdom found Christ to be a proper person to give himself a ransom for his people, and deliver them from destruction, which is great joy unto them.——3. The fulness of his person; both the fulness of the godhead, which dwells substantially in him, and the fulness of grace which it has pleased the Father should dwell in him, for the supply of the wants of his people; in which grace they are strong, and out of which they receive grace for grace, and *with joy draw water out of the wells of salvation* in him, Isa. xii. 3.——4. The beauty of his person; who is fairer than the children of men, white and ruddy, a complete beauty, the chiefest among ten thousand, and altogether lovely; to see him, the King, in his beauty, is a ravishing sight, and which fills with joy unspeakable and full of glory; *this*, says the church, after she had described him at large with an air of joy and pleasure, *this*, this amiable lovely person *is my beloved and my friend*, Cant. v. 10—16.

I take no notice of the offices of Christ, of prophet, and priest, and king; nor of the relations he stands in to his people, of father, husband, brother, friend, though they are a fund of joy to true believers.

2dly, There are other things which relate to the work of Christ, which are matter of joy to gracious souls; as salvation by him in general, everlasting righteousness wrought out by him in particular, and atonement of sin by his sacrifice.

1. Salvation in general; this is the work Christ was appointed to, which was given him, and which was with him when he came into the world, and which he came to do, and is become the author of; the church is called upon to rejoice in a view of his being about to come to effect it; and it is prophetically said of those who should be upon the spot when he came about this work, that they should say, *We will be glad and rejoice in his salvation*, Zech. ix. 9. Isa. xxv. 9. and both Old and New Testament-saints have rejoiced in it, in a view of its certain accomplishment, of its fulness and suitableness to them, and of the glory of God displayed in it; *We will rejoice in thy salvation*, says David, Psalm xx. 7. and in such a frame of soul was Mary, the mother of our Lord, when she said, *My spirit hath rejoiced in God my Saviour;* and great reason there is for the exercise of spiritual joy on this account, since,—(1.) It is a salvation of the souls of men, not of their bodies from temporal evils, but of their souls from everlasting destruction, 1 Pet. i. 8, 9. it is a salvation of the soul, the more noble part of man, which is of more worth than a world, the redemption of which is precious, requires a great price to ransom, and must have ceased for ever, without any hopes of attaining it, had not Christ undertook it.—(2.) It is for sinners, for the chief of sinners, which makes it a joyful sound; and he has the name of Jesus for this reason, because he *saves his people from their sins*, than which nothing can be matter of greater joy to sensible sinners, 1 Tim. i. 15. Matt. ix. 13. and i. 21.—(3.) It is a salvation of them from sin, even from all sin, original and actual; and from the guilt of it, and from punishment for it, and from all wrath to come it is deserving of; for Christ has delivered them from that, having sustained it in their room; and being justified by his blood, they shall be saved from wrath through him; and indeed they are saved by him from every enemy, and from whatsoever they may fear any hurt to come to them, sin, satan, law, hell, and death.—(4.) This salvation is entirely free; it is by grace and not of works; according to abundant mercy, and not by works of righteousness done by men. The blessings of salvation, signified by gold, fine linen, &c. are indeed to be bought, but without money and without price; that is, they are to be had freely; they are all of free grace; every part and branch of salvation is free; it is only looking to Christ and being saved; *Look unto me, and be ye saved, all the ends of the earth*, Isa. xlv. 22. and what joyful news is this!—(5.) It is a great salvation, plenteous and complete; it is great, *How shall we escape, if we neglect so great salvation?* wrought out by a great Saviour, for great sinners; obtained at a great expense, the blood of Christ; and expressive of the greatest love; it is large and plenteous, it includes all the blessings of grace and glory; it is complete, it is from all sin and sorrow, and from every enemy; those that are saved, are saved to the *uttermost*, and for ever; for,—(6.) It is eternal; the Israel of God, all the chosen, redeemed, and called ones, are saved in the Lord with an *everlasting salvation;* Christ is the author of *eternal salvation* to his people; and he has, by his blood, obtained for them, *eternal redemption;* wherefore, *the ransomed of the Lord shall come to Zion with songs, and with everlasting joy upon their heads*, Heb. v. 9. and ix. 12. Isa. xlv. 17. and xxxv. 10.—(7.) It is exceeding suitable to the case and circumstances of sinners, and makes for the glory of God; such a Saviour as Christ is, becomes men lost and undone in themselves; and such a salvation he has wrought out, exactly answers their necessities, and therefore cannot but be joyful to them; and the rather do they rejoice at it, because of the glory of God, of all the divine perfections which is great in it; if the angels rejoiced at the good will of God to men in it, and sung glory to God on account of it, how much more reason have men to do so, who have hope of interest in it?

2. A branch of Christ's work in particular, which he had to work, and has wrought out, is everlasting righteousness; this, as a surety of his people, he was under obligation to fulfil, even all righteousness; he was sent, and came into the world, and was made under the law, that the righteousness of it might be fulfilled by him; and he is become the fulfilling end of it to them that believe; and such who are made to see their need of his righteousness, and are enabled to look unto it, and lay hold on it, as their righteousness before God, rejoice in it as the church did, Isa. lxi. 10. and there are many things respecting this righteousness which are matter and ground of joy to a believing soul.—(1.) It is *the righteousness of God* which is *revealed from faith to faith* in the gospel; a righteousness wrought out by one that is God as well as man; which is approved by God, and well-pleasing to him; and which he imputes without works: and being the righteousness of God, and not a creature's, it is unto all and upon all them that believe; and has a sufficient virtue in it to justify all the Lord's people, *all the seed of Israel*, Isa. xlv. 25.—(2.) It is satisfactory to the law and justice of God; it is commensurate to all the demands of the law; that *commandment is* indeed *exceeding broad;* it is very extensive, and reaches to every duty, respecting God and man; but the righteousness of Christ is as large and as broad as that, and exactly answers to it; and so secures from all condemnation by it; and being so complete, justice is well pleased and fully satisfied with it, spying no fault nor blemish in it; wherefore the Lord's people are presented by Christ in it to his Father, *unblameable and unreprovable in his sight*, Col. i. 22.—(3.) It acquits and absolves from all sin; by it those who believe in Christ are *justified from all things*, from all sins; from which there is no justification by the law of Moses, there being some sins for which no sacrifice was provided by that law; but when a soul is clothed with this *change of raiment*, the robe of Christ's righteousness, all his *filthy garments* are taken from him, and all his iniquities caused to pass from him, and he stands *without fault before the throne*, before God, the Judge of all.—(4.) It renders acceptable in the sight of God; such as have on the righteousness of Christ, are *accepted in the beloved;* God is well pleased with him, and with them in him, and that for his righteousness-sake; they are perfectly comely through his comeliness put upon them; they are all fair, and no spot in them; a perfection of beauty.—(5.) This righteousness of Christ is entirely free; it was freely wrought out by Christ, and is freely imputed to men; it is a free gift bestowed upon them, and as such is received by them; yea, faith, which receives it, is the gift of God; and therefore the justified ones are said to be *justified freely by the grace of God*, Rom. iii. 24.—(6.) It affords much peace and comfort to those who see their interest in it; *This work of righteousness is peace:* the *kingdom of God*, or reigning grace in the hearts of his people, lies in *righteousness and peace;* in the righteousness of Christ revealed unto them, and received by faith; the consequence of which is, peace of soul, and tranquillity of mind, Isa. xxxii. 17. Rom. xiv. 17. and v. 1.—(7.) This righteousness is an *everlasting* one; it always continues to justify, and to be a constant ground of peace and joy; it can never be lost: the righteousness of Adam was lost, and so was that of the angels that sinned; but this will always remain, and be in sight before God, as the justifying righteousness of his people; *My righteousness*, says the Lord, *shall be for ever*, Dan. ix. 24. Isa. li. 6, 8.—(8.) It entitles to eternal life; without a righteousness none can *inherit the kingdom of God;* and it must be a better righteousness than a man's own, that can give a man entrance into the kingdom of heaven; but being justified by that, men are *made heirs according to the hope of eternal life;* hence justification by the righteousness of Christ is called, *The justification of life*, Tit. iii. 7. Rom. v. 18.

3. Another part of Christ's work, and a very principal one, was to make atonement for sin; this was the work appointed for him in council and covenant, and declared in prophecy; namely, *To make reconciliation for iniquity*, Dan. ix. 24. and for this purpose he became man, *To make reconciliation for the sins of the people;* and in the end of the world appeared in human nature, *To put away sin by the sacrifice of himself*, Heb. ii. 17. and ix. 26. and by that one sacrifice he has made perfect expiation of the sins of his people, and which is matter of exceeding great joy unto them; *We joy in God, through our Lord Jesus Christ, by whom we have now received the atonement*, being reconciled to God by the

death of his Son, Rom. v. 10, 11. and great reason there is for it, since full and complete pardon of sin proceeds upon it; God, for Christ's sake, and upon the foot of his atoning sacrifice, forgives all trespasses; an application of which forgiveness, causes joy and gladness, and makes the bones which were broken to rejoice; a sense of pardoning grace, fills the soul with thankfulness to God, and yields abundance of spiritual consolation; and in this way God would have his people comforted by his ministers, Isa. xl. 1, 2.

Thirdly, Besides the person and work of Christ, there are other things either antecedent to it, or consequent on it; which are matter of joy to believers in him. As,

1. His incarnation, in order to do his work; this is spoken of by the evangelic prophet, as if it was over in his days, it being so certain to him and other believers; *To us a child is born;* and this he represents as occasion of great joy, that men would rejoice on account of it *according to the joy in harvest, and as men rejoice when they divide the spoil,* Isa. ix. 3, 6. times of as great rejoicing as can be well named; and when it actually came to pass, the angel who brought the tidings of it to the shepherds, said, *Behold, I bring you good tidings of great joy!* Luke ii. 10, 11. and the disciples who first had knowledge of the incarnate Saviour, how did they exult and rejoice, saying, *We have found the Messiah!* they describe their joy as such who had found a great spoil; as the prophet Isaiah foretold, John i. 41, 45.——2. The sufferings and death of Christ, by which he accomplished the work of redemption and salvation; for though they were painful to Christ, and in some respects occasion mourning to saints, whose sins were the cause of them; yet they make up a great part of the gospel of salvation; a crucified Christ is indeed the sum and substance of it; which, though foolishness to some, and stumbling to others, is to them that are saved, the wisdom and power of God; this is the first and grand article of it, that Christ died for our sins, according to the scriptures; and makes it the good news it is, and the saying worthy of acceptation; it affords matter of exultation, and even of glorying and boasting, Gal. vi. 14.——3. The resurrection of Christ from the dead, after he had finished his work, is another source and spring of joy; as an angel brought the good news of the incarnation of Christ, so likewise of his resurrection from the dead; to the women who attended the sepulchre of Christ, the angel who rolled back the stone from it said, *He is not here, for he is risen;* the tidings of which they brought with joy to the disciples, Matt. xxviii. 6, 8. and what joy did the disciples express on this account; *The Lord is risen indeed,* say they, *and has appeared to Simon!* and still more when they saw him themselves; *Then were the disciples glad, when they saw the Lord,* Luke xxiv. 34. John xx. 20. and such and so many are the benefits arising from the resurrection of Christ, as well as from his sufferings and death, that believers can take courage and say, *Who shall lay any thing to the charge of God's elect?* not only because Christ has died, but *rather* because *he is risen again,* risen again for their justification, Rom. viii. 33, 34. and iv. 25.
——4. The ascension of Christ to heaven, and his exaltation there, give joy to his saints; it did to his disciples, who were present at his ascension; for when he was parted from them, and carried up into heaven; instead of sorrowing for it, *they worshipped him,* and *returned to Jerusalem with great joy,* Luke xxiv. 51, 52. and all true believers, by faith *see Jesus crowned with glory and honour,* sitting at the right-hand of God, highly exalted above every name, angels, authorities, principalities, and powers being subject to him; and he having received gifts for men, which he bestows upon them, even unworthy and rebellious ones; all which affords them the greatest joy and pleasure; *The Lord reigns; let the earth rejoice,* Psalm xcvii. 1.——
5. The intercession of Christ, his appearing in the presence of God for his people, his advocacy with the Father, his ever living to make intercession for them, is matter of great joy, and from which they receive much benefit; this brings up the rear of those things which lay the foundation of the triumph of faith; *Who shall lay any thing to the charge of God's elect?* this is supported not only by the death of Christ, and by his resurrection from the dead, and by his session at the right-hand of God; but by his intercession there; *Who also maketh intercession for us,* and answers to, and removes all charges brought against them. And whereas to them that look for him, he will appear a second time without sin unto salvation, the fore-thoughts and fore-views, and firm belief saints have of it, cause them to exult in their present state; *To look up, and lift up their heads, since their redemption draweth nigh,* Luke xxi. 28.

Fourthly, Some things under the gospel-dispensation, and respecting that, are the objects of the joy of gracious souls. As,

1. The ministration of the gospel; this is matter of joy to all sensible and awakened sinners; the three thousand pricked in the heart under Peter's sermon, *gladly* received the word, preaching pardon and salvation by Christ; when Christ was preached in Samaria, there was *great joy in that city*, in such who believed Philip preaching the things concerning the kingdom of God; when the jailor, who said to the apostles, *Sirs, What must I do to be saved?* had the word of the Lord spoken to him, and to them in his house, he *rejoiced, believing in God, with all his house:* and there is great reason for it; it is the gospel of salvation, which publishes the good tidings of it; and when accompanied with the Spirit of God, it is the power of God unto salvation; it is the voice of Christ, the bridegroom, and every one that hears and knows that voice, *rejoiceth* greatly because of it; it is a joyful sound of love, grace, and mercy, of peace, pardon, righteousness and salvation; it is food to hungry souls; the sincere milk of the word, by which new-born babes are nourished and grow; and by those of riper age it is esteemed more than their necessary food; they find the word, and eat it, and it is *the joy and rejoicing of their hearts.*——2. The administration of ordinances, baptism and the Lord's supper; which give such views of Christ in his sufferings and death, burial, and resurrection from the dead, and of the benefits arising from them, as yield delight to believing souls; the eunuch, upon his baptism, *went on his way rejoicing;* the supper of the Lord is a *feast of fat things*, a rich entertainment, where the flesh of Christ, as *meat indeed*, and the blood of Christ, as *drink indeed*, are presented to faith to feed upon; these ordinances are *breasts of consolation*, at which saints may *suck and be satisfied*, and *milk out*, and be *delighted* with the abundance of the glory in them; these are the *lattices* through which Christ shews himself, and these the *galleries* in which he is beheld, to the great joy and satisfaction of those who are favoured with a sight of him.——3. The prosperity of the interest of Christ; whether it be through the numerous conversions of men, and additions of them to the church, gives joy; as when Paul and Barnabas, as they passed through Phœnicia and Samaria, in their way from Antioch to Jerusalem, declared the conversion of the Gentiles, *it caused great joy to the brethren*, Acts xv. 3. or whether through peace, love, and unity, prevailing and subsisting among the saints, which give pleasure to all the well-wishers to Zion's prosperity; as it did to David, who prayed earnestly for it, Psalm cxxii. 6—9.——
4. The reign of Christ, both spiritual and personal, will cause great joy in the saints. His spiritual reign, and the more glorious appearances of that, when the kingdoms of this world shall become his; upon which the four and twenty elders, the representatives of gospel-churches, will, with the greatest solemnity and reverence, *give thanks* to him, because he has taken to himself his *great power and reigned*, Rev. xi. 15, 16, 17. and when antichrist, and the antichristian-states, shall be destroyed, the fulness of the Gentiles brought in, and the Jews converted, these voices shall be heard in heaven, the church, *Let us be glad and rejoice, and give honour to him, for the marriage of the Lamb is come*, Rev. xix. 1.
——7. And especially when Christ himself shall appear, and his tabernacle shall be with men: and an anticipation of all this by faith, gives to believers a joy and pleasure now; that things will not always be in the state they now are, but in a much more happy one, even on the earth.

Fifthly, The heavenly glory and happiness of a future state to all eternity, is the object of the saints' present joy; when they shall actually possess it, they will then *enter into the joy of their Lord;* into the place of the celestial feast,[3] to partake of it, where will be fulness of joy; see Matt. xxv. 10. and even now, they can *rejoice in hope of the glory of God;* believing, that whereas they *suffer with* Christ, they shall be *glorified together;* and that when Christ, who is their life, shall appear, they shall *appear with him in glory!* and in the faith and hope of this they rejoice and are glad.

II. The author and cause of this spiritual joy.

1. The efficient cause is God; he who is the object is the author of it, God, Father, Son, and Spirit; and which is therefore called, *The joy of the Lord*, Nehem. viii. 10. and xii. 43. It is *the God of hope*,

---

[3] Verba dominica vix aliter grammatice, quam de diæta seu coenaculo possunt intelligi, quod dominus χαραν, vel appellasset, vel inscripsisset. Pignorius de Servis, p. 489.

the object, author, and giver of that grace, who *fills with joy and peace in believing* in Christ, Rom. xv. 13. who is God the Father: Christ himself is the author of this joy; and he calls it, *my joy;* as it is both objectively and efficiently; it is he that gives *beauty for ashes, the oil of joy for mourning, and the garment of praise for the spirit of heaviness,* John xv. 11. Isa. lxi. 3. And the Spirit of God is concerned in it; it is one of the fruits of the Spirit, and is ranked with the first of them, Gal. v. 22. and is called, *joy in the Holy Ghost;* because produced by him, Rom. xiv. 17.——
2. The instruments or means of it are, the ministers of the gospel, through the ministration of the word, and the administration of ordinances; they are the bringers of good tidings of good, the publishers of peace and salvation, and the means of spreading much joy among the saints, Isa. lii. 7. they do not pretend to have *dominion over the faith* of believers, but to be *helpers of their joy,* 2 Cor. i. 24.

III. The nature and properties of this joy.

1. It should be constant; the exhortations to it are, *Rejoice evermore,* and *rejoice in the Lord always!* 1 Thess. v. 16. Phil. iv. 4. and there is great encouragement from the Lord always to rejoice in him; and the character of the saints and people of God in this present state of things is, *as sorrowful, yet always rejoicing,* 2 Cor. vi. 10. yea, the apostle James exhorts believers, to *count it all joy, when they fall into divers temptations,* or afflictions, since these all work for good; are for the trial, brightening, and increasing the graces of the saints, and for the glory of God, James i. 2, 3. Yet,——2. It is imperfect in the present state, and often interrupted; sometimes, through the prevalence of indwelling sin, and the breakings forth of the corruptions of the heart; so that saints have *no rest in their bones,* no joy in their hearts *because of their sin;* and cry out with the apostle, *O wretched* men that they are! this was sometimes the case of David, Isaiah, and the apostle Paul, Psalm xxxviii. 3. Isa. vi. 5. Rom. vii. 23, 24. sometimes through the temptations of Satan, who throws his fiery darts, which give pain, and sorely grieve; and when he has leave, sifts as wheat is sifted, which occasions great disquietude and distress; and beats and buffets, which causes great trouble and uneasiness; and he goes about like a roaring lion, to affright and terrify when he cannot devour. And also through divine desertions, for when God hides his face from his people, they are troubled; nay, left in such darkness and distress, as even to be distracted with terrors, and ready to die; as was the case with David, Heman, and others. Yet,——3. This joy may come again, be restored, and greatly increase: joy sometimes comes in the morning, after a night of darkness; and the joys of salvation have been restored after the bones have been broken, through backslidings and falls into sin; yea, there may be an increase and overflow of joy; and it is promised, *The meek shall increase their joy in the Lord,* Isa. xxix. 19. this is done by enlarged discoveries of the love of God, directions into it, and a fresh shedding abroad of it in the heart; by Christ, the Sun of righteousness, arising with healing in his wings; by some renewed sights of Christ, and appropriating views of him; and by an increase of faith in him; for as that grace grows, there is a furtherance of joy, called, *The furtherance and the joy of faith;* it is in a way of believing, souls are filled with joy and peace, and through a sight by faith of an unseen Jesus. Meditation on the love of God, and person of Christ, contributes much unto it; and prayer is often a means of it; God makes his people joyful in the house of prayer; the preaching of the gospel is frequently blessed to this purpose; it has a tendency to promote spiritual joy; and, indeed, the end and design of it is, *that joy might be full,* Phil. i. 25. Isa. lvi. 7. 1 John i. 4. ——4. It is a joy that is unknown to the men of the world; a *stranger,* one that is a stranger to God and godliness, to Christ and the things of Christ, to the Spirit and to the gospel, *intermeddles not* with it, has no experience of it, nor share in it, Prov. xiv. 10. it passes the understanding of a natural man; it is an enigma, not to be unriddled by him, that the saints should be *sorrowful,* and *yet always rejoicing!*—— 5. It is *unspeakable;* not to be fully expressed by those who experience it; it is better experienced than expressed; it is something like what the apostle Paul felt, when caught up to the third heaven; and it is *full of glory,* being concerned with eternal glory and happiness; it is a *rejoicing in hope of the glory of God,* 1 Pet. i. 8. Rom. v. 2.——6. It is a joy that cannot be utterly lost or taken away in the present life; the principle of it always remains, though it is not always in exercise;

the ground-work and foundation of it always continues, the unalterable love of God, and the person and grace of Christ; *your joy no man taketh from you;* and in the future state it will be full and complete, John xvi. 22, 24.

CHAP. XI.

OF PEACE AND TRANQUILLITY OF MIND.

Next to Love and Joy, in order, stands Peace; now to be treated of; *The fruit of the Spirit is love, joy, peace,* Gal. v. 22. *Charity,* or *love,* and *peace,* are sometimes mentioned together, 2 Tim. ii. 22. and where the one is, there is the other; especially if joy is in company with love, peace must be an attendant. Concerning which may be considered,

I. What peace is meant, and is designed to be treated of. Not an external peace; such as is sometimes enjoyed by whole bodies of men; as in nations, when free from wars and rumours of wars; and in churches, when at rest from persecution, and clear of animosities and contentions among themselves; and in good men, when at peace with their neighbours; which they are to follow after, and cultivate as much as in them lies; and when God sometimes makes their enemies to be at peace with them; and in individuals, when every man sits under his vine and fig-tree, none making him afraid; and enjoying much prosperity and happiness. But it is an internal spiritual peace of soul, which is to be enquired into; which is an ease of mind from distress through sin and a sense of wrath.

First, Sin, upon conviction, is made exceeding sinful, and is very distressing; this is usually through the law; *By the law is the knowledge of sin;* not only of external acts of sin in life, but of the inward lusts of it in the heart; *I had not known lust,* says the apostle; that is, that it was sin, *except the law had said, Thou shalt not covet;* and when such knowledge is had of sin, it appears *exceeding sinful,* very odious, and gives great uneasiness, Rom. iii. 20. and vii. 7, 13. when the guilt of sin lies heavy upon the conscience, it is a burden too heavy for a guilty sinner to bear; as it was to David, Psalm xxxviii. 3, 4. and especially where there is not a glimpse of pardoning grace and mercy; as in Cain. There is a conscience in every man; and when it does its office, it causes great anxiety, grief, and trouble, more or less; when the mind is open by conviction, under a work of the law, wrath is let into the conscience; *The law worketh wrath;* along with the knowledge of sin by the law, wrath from heaven is revealed in it against all unrighteousness and ungodliness; and it leaves a fearful looking for of judgment, and fiery indignation against it; which wrath sometimes lies so hard and heavy as to cause terror, and even distraction; as in Heman, Psalm lxxxviii. 7, 15, 16. So that sin convicted of, makes dreadful work in the heart of an awakened sinner; such are pricked and pained at their very hearts; and in their compunction cry out, *What shall we do to be saved?* they are wounded with a sense of sin, and the arrows of divine wrath stick fast in them; the hand of God presses them sore; their wounds are grievous and intolerable; for *a wounded spirit, who can bear?* This inward distress is sometimes expressed by outward gestures and words; as by smiting upon the breast, not daring to look up to heaven; as in the publican, crying out, *God, be merciful to me, a sinner!* and by smiting upon the thigh; as in Ephraim, saying, he was ashamed and confounded, because he bore the reproach of his youth, Luke xviii. 13 Jer. xxxi. 19. such usually express themselves as the three thousand did, convinced under Peter's sermon, inquiring the way of salvation; *What shall we do?* or more explicitly, with the jailor, *What shall we do to be saved?* lamenting their lost and undone state, in the words of Isaiah, *Woe is me, I am undone!* Now,

Secondly, Spiritual peace is a deliverance and freedom from this distress; which in general is wrought by the Spirit of God, being the comforter of convinced sinners; for that is his particular and peculiar work; he first convinces men of sin, righteousness, and judgment; and then he comforts them, by taking of the things of Christ, and shewing them to them: he does by them as God did with the people of Israel of old, allured them, and brought them into the wilderness, and then spake comfortably unto them; he causes them to see their sicknesses and their wounds, as he did Ephraim and Judah, and the inability of themselves and others to cure them, and then he heals and binds them up. And all this he does more particularly,

1. By leading them to the blood of Christ, by which their wounds are healed;

CHAP. XI. OF PEACE AND TRANQUILLITY OF MIND.   783

With his stripes we are healed; that is, with the blood flowing from them, Isa. liii. 6. the blood of Christ is the balm in Gilead, the *panacea* that cures every wound, and he is the physician there; he is the *Sun of righteousness* that arises on distressed souls in beams of light, and joy, and love, and with *healing in his wings*; which healing is no other than pardon of sin, and the application of it, Psalm ciii. 3. the consequence of which must be, joy, peace, and tranquillity of soul; *Son, be of good cheer, thy sins are forgiven thee!* Matt. ix. 2. for what can make a soul more cheerful, and give it more peace and pleasure, than a view of pardon by the blood of Jesus, and this given by Jesus himself? through an application of pardon, guilt is removed from the conscience, the burden is taken off. The blood of Christ applied, cleanses from all sin, takes away the guilt of every sin, and leaves none behind; the heart sprinkled by it from an evil conscience, is purged from dead works, which lay as an heavy incumbrance upon it; *Blessed therefore is he whose transgression is forgiven;* or is lifted up, as the word signifies; which is lifted up from the sinner, and taken off from his conscience, as a burden on it, and he is eased of it. It is in this way that peace is spoken to a guilty sinner; hence the blood of Jesus is said to *speak better things than that of Abel;* the blood of Abel called aloud for vengeance on the shedder of it; but the blood of Christ speaks pardon and peace to condemned criminals. Peace is made for enemies and rebels by the blood of Christ; and this blood, by the Spirit of God, applied to such consciences who have been awakened by him, produces peace and quietness there; let a soul be as it were in a storm and tempest, if pardon by the blood of Christ is pronounced, all is hush and quiet in a moment.——2. By leading to the righteousness of Christ; a man's own righteousness will not yield him any solid peace; for there is no justification nor salvation by it; and it must at best be very variable, unstable, and inconstant; since man's righteousness is very imperfect, he sins in all, and in the best he does; and it is at most but while he is doing, or thinks he is doing, something good, that he has any peace; but when there is any interruption in doing, or he ceases from it, his peace is broken. But the righteousness of Christ, which is perfect, pure, and spotless, by which a man is justified from all his sins, lays a solid foundation for peace. "Every religion, says Beza,[1] which opposes anything to the wrath of God, than the alone innocence, righteousness, and satisfaction of Jesus Christ, apprehended by faith, robs God both of his perfect justice and mercy; and therefore is false, and formed to deceive men." This being revealed and applied to a sinner, and faith wrought in him to receive it, as his justifying righteousness before God; and the sentence of justification by it pronounced in his conscience by the Spirit of God, produce peace in it; hence righteousness and peace are mentioned together, the one as the fruit of the other, Rom. v. 1. and xiv. 17. Isa. xxxii. 17.——3. By leading into the truths of the gospel; which is the Spirit's work, and in doing which he acts the part of a comforter; *When he, the Spirit of truth, is come,* before spoken of as a comforter, *he will guide you into all truth,* John xvi. 13. it is not by the law that peace is had, that was delivered in a storm, in the midst of blackness, darkness, and tempest; and they that heard it, were terrified with it, and intreated it might not be spoken to them any more; and surely they that desire to be under it, do not hear it, so as to understand the voice of it; for it pronounces the whole world guilty before God; it curses in case of a breach of any of its commands: it is the killing letter, the ministration of condemnation and death. But it is by the gospel, and the truths of it, which the Spirit of God enlightens the minds of men into, and makes application of, that peace is enjoyed; that is called, *The gospel of peace,* not only because it proclaims peace made by the blood of Christ, is the word preaching peace by Jesus Christ, and the ministers of it, the publishers of that peace; but because it speaks peace to the conscience of a sinner, when Christ comes by his Spirit, and preaches peace unto them, and makes the word effectual to such a purpose: the several truths of the gospel have a tendency to speak comfort to them, and to free them from that spirit of bondage, the law has brought them into, and holds them in, for that genders to bondage, encourages and increases it; but they that *know the truth,* the truth of the gospel, spiritually and experimentally, especially that great truth, free and full salvation by Christ for sinners,

---

[1] Confessio fidei, c. 3. art. 26. p. 16.

the truth shall make them free, set them at liberty, and fill them with joy and peace, John viii. 32.——4. By leading them into the covenant of grace, its blessings and promises; which, as it is a covenant of life, so of peace; and is a covenant of peace which cannot be removed; and is so called, not only in relation to the article in it, concerning peace to be made by Christ, the Mediator of it; but because it lays a lasting foundation for peace and comfort; its blessings are the sure mercies of David, spiritual, solid, and substantial ones, and which last for ever, which are founded in the free sovereign grace and will of God, and come to men through Christ being made a curse for them. The promises of it are exceeding great and precious; great in themselves, their origin, matter, and use; and precious to them that believe, and see their interest in them; these, fitly and seasonably spoken, are like apples of gold in pictures of silver; and being opened and applied by the holy Spirit of promise, afford strong consolation to the heirs of promise; what peace did a view of covenant-interest in its blessings and promises yield to David, amidst his sinful infirmities, and the troubles of his family! 2 Sam. xxiii. 5.——5. By leading them into the love of God; for this is the Spirit's work; by whom not only the love of God is shed abroad in the hearts of his people, which occasions peace and joy, and even glorying in the midst of tribulations; but they are directed and guided by him into it; *The Lord*, that is, the Lord the Spirit, as he stands distinguished from the other persons in the text, *direct your hearts into the love of God*, κατευθυναι, direct, as in and by a straight line, immediately into it, not in a round-about-way, in a long train and course of duties, and from thence to fetch the evidence of interest in the love of God; which at best, makes it very precarious, and leaves great disquietude and uneasiness: but when the Spirit leads directly into a view of interest in it, and bears witness to it, and grants a delightful sensation of it, the effect of this is solid, permanent peace; *There is no fear in love*; the love of God the Spirit leads into; *But perfect love casteth out fear*, slavish, distressing, tormenting fear; where that has a place, the other removes, and instead of it, or the effect of it, is tranquillity and peace of mind, 1 John iv. 18.

Now this peace is enjoyed through faith in Christ; the God of hope *fills with all joy and peace in believing;* in believing in the person, blood, and righteousness of Christ; they that trust in him are kept *in perfect peace;* as their faith is, so is their peace; if their faith is stedfast, their peace is permanent: and it is much enjoyed also in the use of gospel-ordinances; gospel-churches, under the power and influence of a gospel-spirit, are *peaceable habitations, and quiet resting places;* gospel-ordinances are ways of pleasantness, and *paths of peace;* these are the *still waters,* or *waters of quietness,* or rest,[4] beside which the saints are led; and the *green pastures,* where they are made to lie down and take their ease and rest. I go on to enquire,

II. Who are the subjects of this peace; or who are possessed of it.

1. Not sinful men, or unregenerate sinners; *There is no peace, saith my God, to the wicked,* Isa. lvii. 21. whatever outward peace and prosperity they may enjoy, they have no inward spiritual peace; though *they are not in trouble as other men,* in outward trouble, as to body or estate; nor in soul-trouble, or in a concern about their immortal souls, and the welfare of them; yet this ease is no other than stupidity, and a carnal dangerous security and indolence; and is owing to the ignorance of themselves, and of their state; *The way of peace they know not,* the way to true peace with God, and peace of conscience; for whilst they cry, *Peace and safety,* sudden *destruction cometh upon them,* Rom. iii. 17. 1 Thess. v. 3.——2. Nor self-righteous persons, who trust in themselves that they are righteous, and fetch their peace from thence; but their trust is a spider's web, and such webs shall not become garments; nor shall they cover themselves with their works; and so shall not have peace and comfort; and of them it is said, *the way of peace they know not,* Isa. lix. 6, 8. and to such self-righteous persons Jehovah says, *I will declare thy righteousness,* what a vain, useless thing it is in the business of justification before God, and with respect to peace to a man's self; *and thy works, for they shall not profit thee,* in the affair of salvation, and to give peace and comfort, Isa. lvii. 12, 13.——3. Only justified and pardoned sinners have true, solid peace in themselves; those who are justified by

---

[4] מי מנוחה Psalm xxiii. 2.

Christ's righteousness have peace with God through him, and whose sins are pardoned through his blood, they are blessed, and blessed with peace; for with such righteous and happy ones it will be well at death, and to all eternity; when they die they enter into peace, and rest in their beds; the end of the perfect and upright man is peace; he enjoys much now, and shall be perfectly possessed of it hereafter.——— 4. Believers in Christ, and who trust in the Lord, enjoy true peace of soul, Isa. xxvi. 3. such whose hearts are fixed, trusting in the Lord, are *not afraid of evil tidings;* these do not disturb their peace, let them come from what quarter they will; from the suggestions of their own hearts, from the temptations of Satan, or from the world and wicked men in it; the falsehood of which they are soon able to detect; and their faith and trust in God fortifies them against them.———5. Spiritually-minded persons have a large share of inward peace of soul; *To be spiritually-minded is life and peace,* Rom. viii. 6. they who mind carnal and earthly things, though they seek peace to themselves in this way, do not find it; for *a man's life,* the peace, comfort, and happiness of it, *consisteth not in the abundance of the things which he possesseth;* for though he promises himself much peace, and that lasting, in the goods he has accumulated and laid up; yet these may be soon taken away from him, or he from them.———6. They that love the law of God, his doctrines, ordinances, ways, and worship, usually enjoy much peace of soul; this the Psalmist attests by his own knowledge and experience; *Great peace have they which love thy law, and nothing shall offend them,* Psalm cxix. 165. or thy doctrine, especially the doctrine of peace, pardon, and salvation by Christ; such who have drank into this doctrine experimentally, find peace in their souls; nor are they easily offended with what they meet with in themselves or from others: they are sons of peace, who receive the gospel of peace; and they enjoy much who walk in wisdom's paths, which are *paths of peace;* and such who worship God according to the rule of his word, peace is upon them, and upon the Israel of God.———7. They are the people and children of God who are the subjects of this peace; *The Lord will bless his people with peace,* Psalm xxix. 11. his covenant-people, the people given to Christ, and saved by him, and who are effectually called by his Spirit and grace, and who are the children of God, the sons and daughters of the Lord Almighty; *Great shall be the peace of thy children,* Isa. liv. 13. the children of the church, the children of Christ, and the children of God; all to whom the Spirit of adoption is given, crying, *Abba Father.*

Now the seat of this grace in these subjects, is the heart and mind; for it is an internal frame of mind, it rules in the heart, and keeps and guards the heart and mind, Col. iii. 15. Phil. iv. 7. it lies in the breast of a saint; and what protects, preserves, and keeps it there is, *the breast-plate of faith and love,* of faith in Christ and love to him.

III. The author and causes of this peace. 1. The efficient cause is God; hence called *the peace of God,* because it comes from him; and he *the God of peace,* because he is the author of it, even God, Father, Son, and Spirit. Sometimes the Father is meant; *The God of peace, that brought again from the dead our Lord Jesus;* that is, the Father of Christ, who raised him from the dead, to whom his resurrection is often ascribed, Heb. xiii. 20. and peace is often wished from him as in most of the Epistles; and also from Christ the Son of God, who is not only the peace-maker, but the peace-giver, in whom and from whom the saints have peace, when in the world tribulation; *My peace I give unto you, &c.* John xvi. 33. and xiv. 27. and peace is expressly called a *fruit* or grace of the Spirit, Gal. v. 22. and is prayed for from all the three persons together, Rev. i. 4, 5.———2. The moving cause of it is the grace and good-will of God; grace is always wished for along with it, and is usually set before it, as being the spring of it; and the angels in their song, sung, *Peace on earth, and good-will towards men,* signifying that the peace men had on earth, was owing to the good-will of God towards them, Luke ii. 14.——— 3. The instruments of it are the word, and the ministers of it; the gospel is the word not only preaching peace by Christ, but the means of administering peace to distressed minds; and the ministers of it, by publishing peace, are the instruments by whom the Lord speaks peace to wounded consciences.

IV. The nature and properties of it. 1. It is a gift of God, and which none can give but himself, and an excellent one it is, worth praying for and worth having;

Now the Lord of peace himself give you peace always by all means, 2 Thess. iii. 16. it is a free gift, unmerited, and springs from grace, and is what the world cannot give, John xiv. 27.——2. It is a blessing; the Jews, when they wished happiness to any, it was usually in this form, *Peace be to you*, that including all prosperity in it; and when the Lord blesses his people it is with peace, Psalm xxix. 11. And,——3. This is called *great* peace, Psalm cxix. 165. it is great in quality, and sometimes great in quantity, abundance of it, peace like a flowing river.——4. It is said to be *perfect*, Isa. xxvi. 3. though sometimes saints *for peace* have *great bitterness*, as Hezekiah had, yet the ground and foundation of their peace is perfect, solid, and substantial; as the love of God, which is unchangeable, the covenant of peace which can never be removed, the person, blood, and righteousness of Christ, which have always the same virtue and efficacy.——5. It is a peace which *passeth all understanding*, Phil. iv. 7. of a natural and unregenerate man, who is a stranger to it, has no experience of it, intermeddles not with it, and can form no judgment about it.——6. It is what cannot be taken away; *When he* (God) *giveth quietness, who then can make trouble?* Job xxxiv. 29. not at that time at least; and though it may be interrupted, it cannot be destroyed; not by the world's tribulations, nor by Satan's temptations, nor by a man's own corruptions.

CHAP. XII.

OF CONTENTMENT OF MIND.

CONTENTMENT of mind naturally follows upon Joy and Peace; where joy abounds, and peace rules in the heart, contentment is; it is nowhere to be found but in a godly man; in christians of the first rank and class: the heathens talked much of it, but were not found in the practice of it; and, indeed, few men are; it is *rara avis in terris;* an ungodly man is an utter stranger to it; the ungodly are like a troubled sea, never at rest. Contentment is a branch of true godliness, or rather a super-addition to it; which makes it greatly ornamental and profitable; for *godliness, with contentment, is great gain*, 1 Tim. vi. 6. And it will be proper to enquire,

I. What it is; and it is no other than an entire acquiescence of a man's mind in his lot and portion, in his state and condition in the present life, be it what it may, prosperous or adverse. And,

First, As contraries serve to illustrate each other, this may be known by what is contrary to it, or by what it is contrary unto; as,——1. Contentment and envy are contrary to one another; *envying and strife* go together, and where there is strife and contention there is no contentment, but *confusion and every evil work;* a man that envies the superior or equal happiness of another, neither of which he can bear, inwardly pines[1] and frets at it. Envying and fretting meet in the same persons, and are equally dehorted from; and are evils to be found in good men, when they observe the prosperity of the wicked, and dwell upon their own afflictions, Psalm xxxvii. 1, 7. and lxxiii. 3. and are contrary to that *charity* which *envieth not;* to rest and acquiescence in the will of God, which becometh saints; and where the sin of envy is predominant, a man can have no true contentment of mind, *envy is rottenness of the bones*, it gnaws upon a man, torments him,[2] eats out his very vitals; *Wrath killeth the foolish man, and envy slayeth the silly one*, Prov. xiv. 30. Job v. 2. ——2. Contentment is opposite to avarice, and avarice to that; and therefore the one must be quitted in order to possess the other. *Let your conversation be without covetousness, and be content with such things as ye have*, Heb. xiii. 5. a covetous man cannot be a truly contented man; he cannot be content with what he has, he always wants more.[3] The Greek word for *covetousness* is πλεονεξια, *a having* or a desire to *have more;* not but that there may be a lawful desire of having more, in some cases and for some good ends and purposes, and in submission to the will of God; but it is an anxious, immoderate, and unbounded desire of more, which is criminal; and especially to have it in an unlawful way, and when a person has much already; it is often usual with men to fix upon the pitch of wealth and riches they are desirous of attaining to, and think if they could attain to that, they should be content; now such

---

[1] Invidus alterius rebus macrescit opimis, Horat. Epist. l. 1. ep. 2. v. 57.

[2] Invidiâ Siculi non invenere tyranni majus tormentum. Horat. ib. v. 58, 59.

[3] Semper avarus eget, ib. v. 56.

persons, until they arrive at such a pitch, must be all the while in a state of discontent; and should they arrive to it they are not sure of content; nay they seldom have it, but then enlarge their desires and extend their limits: in short they never have enough, but are like the horseleech, crying, *Give, give,* more and more; and in other things persons of this complexion are like that creature, of which naturalists [4] observe it has no passage through, it takes in all it can, but lets out nothing; as a covetous man grasps at all he can, but will part with nothing; and like the said creature, which breaks and bursts with its own fulness.

———3. Contentment is opposite to pride and ambition. A proud ambitious man cannot bear that any should be above him, or upon a footing with him; and when he observes this, it gives him uneasiness, and fills him with disquietude and discontent; yea let his pride and ambition be ever so much gratified, he is not content, he still wants more; for the proud man *enlarges his desires as hell,* or the grave, and like that *cannot be satisfied,* which, how full soever, never says, *It is enough,* Hab. ii. 5. Prov. xxx. 16. for though the world is set in their hearts, and they have all that is in it, *the lust of the flesh, the lust of the eyes, and the pride of life,* they are not content; as it is reported of Alexander, when he had conquered the whole world as he thought, sat down and cried because there was not another world to conquer; so boundless were his pride and ambition, and so little contentment had he in his acquisitions.[5]

———4. Anxiety of mind, or a distressing care about worldly things; as about food, drink, and raiment, is contrary to true contentment of mind; and therefore our Lord dissuades from it by a variety of arguments; which may be read in Matt. vi. 25—34. *Take no thought for your life, &c.* to do this is to act below the creatures; they might learn better things from them: besides, such anxious care is needless, and of no avail, nothing is to be got by it; God will take care of his people; the grand point is, to seek the kingdom of God, and his righteousness, and leave all other things with him; which is the best way to have contentment and happiness.

———5. Murmurings and repinings under adverse dispensations of providence, are the reverse of contentment of mind; such as are frequently to be observed in the Israelites in the wilderness, who were a discontented people, often murmuring against Moses and Aaron, and repining at afflictive providences; and from which christians are dehorted by their example; *Neither murmur ye, as some of them also murmured;* and murmurers and complainers are joined together, and both must be reckoned among discontented persons; for which murmurs and complaints there is no reason, not even under afflictive providences: not with the people of God; for their afflictions are fatherly chastisements; nor with wicked men, though they are punishments; for *wherefore doth a living man complain, a man for the punishment of his sins?* since it is less than he deserves, Lam. iii. 39.

Secondly, What contentment of mind is, may be learned from the several phrases by which it is expressed in scripture. As,

1st, By being contented with what a man has; *Be content with such things as ye have,* Heb. xiii. 5. τοις παρϐσιν, *with present things;* things future are not the object of contentment; a man is not to look to things to come for it; which he may never have; and if he should have them, cannot promise himself contentment in them, as before observed; but they are present things, things he is now in the possession of, he should be content with.———1. Be they more or less, whether a man has a larger or a lesser share of the things of this world, whether riches or poverty, a man should be content; it was a wise petition of Agur, *Give me neither riches nor poverty; feed me with food convenient for me,* or that which is sufficient and enough, Prov. xxx. 8. but be it either, a man should be satisfied with what God gives; if God gives him riches, he should be thankful, knowing that these come of God; and if they increase, he should not set his heart upon them, considering they are uncertain things, fleeting ones, make themselves wings and fly away; and therefore should be prepared for the loss of them, and be content when so it is; and the way to be content with what a man has at present, is rather to magnify it in his own mind than to lessen it; and to think, that God has *given him all things richly to enjoy;* so said the apostle when he had but little, 1 Tim. vi. 17. It may be said, a man may very well be content with present riches; but

---

[4] Plin. Nat. Hist. 1. 11. c. 34.
[5] Unus Pellæo juveni non sufficit orbis: æstuat infelix angusto limine mundi, Juvenal. Satyr. 10. v. 168, 169.

how can he be content with present poverty? He may; for poverty is no disgrace to a man, when it does not come through negligence and sloth; many a good man and an honourable christian have been poor; God hath *chosen the poor of this world, rich in faith, and heirs of the kingdom;* Lazarus, now in Abraham's bosom, was once a beggar; and our Lord himself became poor, that we through his poverty might be made rich. The advice of the apostle James is, *Let the brother of low degree rejoice in that he is exalted;* exalted in Christ, and made a partaker of the riches of grace, and has a right to the riches of glory through him.——2. Men should be content, as with present advantages and growing profit, so with present losses, which might have been greater; as Job was with the loss of his substance, his children, and his health, and perhaps all in one day; saying, *The Lord gave, and the Lord hath taken away, blessed be the name of the Lord!* Job i. 21.; for let the saint lose what he may, he cannot lose his God, his portion, and his all, his Redeemer and Saviour, his better and more enduring substance, his inheritance reserved in the heavens; and therefore takes joyfully the spoiling of his goods, and is content with the loss of earthly things.——3. With present reproaches, indignities, and ill usage from men, on account of religion; like Moses, esteeming reproach for Christ's sake, greater riches than all the treasures in Egypt; yea, our Lord pleased not himself, but was content to bear all the reproaches of the people on him; and who for the encouragement of his followers, pronounces them blessed when reviled and reproached, Heb. xi. 25. 2 Sam. xvi. 10—12. Rom. xv. 1, 2, 3. Matt. v. 11. ——4. With present afflictions of whatsoever kind, whether from God or men; for in whatsoever way, they rise not out of the dust, nor come by chance; but according to the will and appointment of God; and though not joyous, but grievous, yet sanctified, yield good fruit, and work together for good; and are the means of making men more partakers of divine holiness; and those light present afflictions, which are but for a moment, work a far more exceeding and eternal weight of glory. Particularly,——5. *Having food and raiment;* food for the present day, and raiment for present use, σκιπασματα, coverings from the inclemencies of weather, among which houses to dwell in are included;

Let us, says the apostle, *therewith be content;* this was all that Jacob desired to have; and which sometimes good men have been without, and yet contented, 1 Tim. vi. 8. Gen. xxviii. 20. 1 Cor. iv. 11. But are saints to be content with present grace, present knowledge, present experience? &c. They may desire more grace, an increase of faith, and every other grace, as the apostles did; they may earnestly covet the best gifts, and yet not envy nor repine at the superior gifts and graces of others; they may forget things behind, and press towards those before, and yet be thankful for past experiences, and for present ones; and bless God for the measure of spiritual light and knowledge they have, and yet humbly desire an increase, and make use of proper means for that purpose; though the apostle, in the text referred to, seems to have respect only to temporal things.

2*dly,* This contentment of mind is expressed by the apostle from his own experience; *I have learned in whatsoever state I am, therewith to be content,* Phil. iv. 11.

1. The apostle means not his state of unregeneracy; he says not, *in whatsoever state I have been;* but, *in whatsoever state I am;* an unregenerate man is content to be in such a state, like Moab of old, at ease from his youth, and settled on his lees, and has not been emptied from vessel to vessel, but remains quiet and undisturbed; repents not of his wickedness, saying, What have I done? is in no apprehension of any danger, but like a man asleep and secure in the midst of the sea, and on the top of a mast; and, indeed, it is the business and policy of Satan, the strong man armed, to keep the goods in peace: a state of unregeneracy is a state of ignorance of God, and of his righteous law, and a state of unbelief, in which state the apostle had been, 1 Tim. i. 13. and while in it, he thought he ought to do many things, contrary to the name of Christ; and imagined himself to be in a good state and condition, and alive without the law: it was not only a sinful state, but a state of self-righteousness; when the apostle thought himself, touching the righteousness of the law, blameless, and so safe and secure, and greatly contented with it; but this is not here meant. But,——2. His state after conversion, his spiritual state; it may be believing his covenant-interest in God; *My God shall supply all your need, &c.* and being persuaded of his interest in the

CHAP. XII. OF CONTENTMENT OF MIND.

love of God, and that nothing should separate him from it; knowing Christ in whom he had believed, and being satisfied of his ability and faithfulness to keep what he had committed to him, and of his being found in him, not having on his own righteousness, but his; and in this the apostle was content; yea, with the worst part of his spiritual state, even when in temptation, when buffeted by Satan; since he was assured, that *the grace of Christ was sufficient for him;* and since Christ is able to succour them that are tempted, and prays for his tempted ones, that their faith fail not, knows how to deliver them that are tempted, and that in the best manner, and in the most seasonable time; therefore they are contented: as they are also even in times of desertion and darkness, when they are directed and encouraged to trust in the Lord, and stay themselves on the mighty God of Jacob, and to wait for him that hides his face from them, as the church was determined to do, Mic. vii. 7, 8, 9. and there is great reason for this contentment, faith, and expectation; since light is sown for the righteous, and to the upright it arises in darkness, Psalm xcvii. 11. and xcii. 4. But,——3. The apostle chiefly means his outward state after conversion; with which he was content: and which lay,—(1.) In his afflictions, reproaches, and persecutions; these attended him wherever he came, and he expected them, and not only bore them patiently, but endured them with pleasure; *I take pleasure,* says he, *in reproaches, in necessities, &c.* yea, he gloried in them, 2 Cor. xii. 9, 10. —(2.) In his bonds and imprisonment; in such a state he was when he expressed his contentment in whatsoever state he was, and so in that; for he was in bonds, a prisoner at Rome, when he wrote his epistle to the Philippians; see chap. i. 13, 14. and he seems to shew a sort of pride in his title and character as the Lord's prisoner, and a prisoner of Jesus Christ, Eph. iii. 1. and iv. 1. and reckoned himself so happy a man on all other accounts, that he wished king Agrippa, and all in court, were altogether as he was, excepting his bonds; and though he did not wish them to others, he was content with them himself.—(3.) The phrase, *in whatsoever state,* includes both prosperity and adversity; an abundance and a scarcity of the necessaries of life; a fulness, and want of them, as explained in the next verse; the wise man says, Eccles. vii. 14.

In the day of prosperity be joyful; that is no hard lesson to learn; *but in the day of adversity consider* from whence it comes, and for what end, and be content with your portion; this is not so easily learnt; the apostle had learned it: as also,— (4.) To be content both to live and to die; since he was persuaded Christ would be *magnified in his body, whether by life or death;* and though he knew it would be much better for him to depart and be with Christ, which was desirable by him; yet it would be more to the advantage of the interest of Christ, and the good of the churches, to continue longer on earth; this put him into a strait; however, he left it with God, and was content to depart or stay, as he thought fit: some good men, in a fit of discontent, have wished to die, and have expressed an uneasiness at life, by reason of their troubles and afflictions; as Job, and the prophets Elijah and Jonah, which was their infirmity; but one that has learned the lesson of divine contentment, and is under the influence of that grace, he is content to live whilst God has anything to do by him, and he is content to die, when he thinks fit to dismiss him from service. Now such a disposition of mind, as to be content in every state of life, appears in a man's thankfulness for all he enjoys; when, as advised, *in every thing,* in every state, and for every thing, be it what it may, he *gives thanks;* when he makes known his requests to God with thanksgivings, for what he has had, and asks for what he wants in submission to his will; thus Job blessed God for what he gave him; and when he took it away from him. This grace shews itself much in a quiet resignation of the will to the will of God, in what condition soever a man is, especially in adverse dispensations of providence; instances of which we have in Aaron, in Eli, in David, and others; as also in bearing cheerfully all things which are disagreeable to flesh and blood; as in the apostles, who departed from the council rejoicing that they were counted worthy to suffer shame for Christ; and in the believing Hebrews, who took joyfully the spoiling of their goods; and in the apostle Paul, who took pleasure in reproaches and distresses for Christ's sake.——4. The word used by the apostle in the place under consideration for *content,* αυταρκης, properly signifies *self-sufficient,* or being sufficient of one's self; which, strictly speaking, and in the highest sense, is only

true of God, who is *El Shaddai*, God all-sufficient, who stands in need of nothing; nor does the goodness of any extend to him, nor is it of any avail unto him; he is blessed in himself, and can have no addition to his happiness from a creature; but in a lower sense is true of some men; who, though they have not an inderivative sufficiency of themselves, yet receive a sufficiency in themselves from God; a sufficiency of spiritual things; his *grace is sufficient for them*, and they have a sufficiency of it to bear them up under temptations, trials, and exercises of life, and to carry them through them; the God of all grace, as he is able to make, so he does make all grace to abound towards them, that they always having all-sufficiency of grace thus received from him, may abound in the performance of every good work; a sufficiency of strength is given, so that they can do all things required of them through Christ strengthening them; and which is the reason the apostle gives of his being able to conduct in every state of life as he did, ver. 13. and a sufficiency of temporal things is given to the Lord's people, at least so as to answer to their exigencies, and even to give them content; and especially when they have Agur's wish, neither riches nor poverty, but food convenient for them; or *which is sufficient*, as some versions have it, Prov. xxx. 8.——
5. This lesson of contentment is explained by what the apostle says in the following verse; *I know both how to be abased, and I know how to abound; both to be full and to be hungry;* that is, he knew by experience what these things meant, and how to behave in such circumstances. As,—(1.) To be *abased*, or humbled, treated with contempt by men, and to be in low and mean circumstances; as when he was obliged to work with his own hands, and these ministered to his own and to the necessities of others; and when in very distressed circumstances, in voyages and journies, shipwrecked, and in perils on various accounts, in pain and weariness, hunger and thirst, cold and nakedness; and he had learned to bear all these things patiently, and with submission to the will of God, and to be content with them. Also, —(2.) He knew how to *abound*, or what it was to be high in the esteem of men, and to have an affluence of the things of life, an abundance, a fulness of them, at least,

as he judged it; and he knew how to behave in the midst of plenty, as not to be elated with it, and carry it haughtily to others; he learned not to abuse it, but to make a good use of it, for the relief of the necessitous, and for the interest of religion. —(3.) He knew what it was both to be *full* and to be *hungry*, to have a full meal and want one; to be at a good table, and to be almost starved and famished; and he was *instructed* of God, how to conduct in such different circumstances, as neither to abuse his fulness, nor repine at his wants; and for confirmation, and to shew how deeply his mind was impressed with these things, he repeats them, *both to abound and to suffer need*, to have an overflow of things, and to be entirely deprived of them; and yet in all to be content. To be stripped of every thing, to have nothing, and yet be content, is wonderful! if a man has something, though but little, there is a reason for contentment; but for a man to have nothing and be content, this is extraordinary; and yet this was the case of the apostle and his brethren, who were sometimes hungry, and had nothing to eat; thirsty, and nothing to drink; naked, and no clothes to put on; and had no dwelling-place to shelter them from inclemencies; and yet content: the truth of these words, and the riddle in them, the apostles knew, and knew how to solve; *as having nothing, and yet possessing all things;* and this made them contented.

3*dly*, This contentment of mind is expressed by a man's having enough. Esau, who was a worldly man, and Jacob, who was a spiritual, upright, and plain-hearted man, both said they had enough, Gen. xxxiii. 9, 11. but in a different sense; and, indeed, they use different phrases; for though they are the same in our version, yet not in the original; Esau at first refused the present of his brother Jacob, saying, *I have enough;* יש לי רב which may be rendered, *I have much;* now a man may have much, and yet not have enough in his own account; he may have much, and yet may want more, and so not be content:[6] but Jacob urged his brother to take his present, saying also, *I have enough;* or rather, as it should be rendered יש לי כל *I have all things*, or *every thing;* and a man that has every thing, has enough indeed, and has reason to be content; and this is the case of every gracious man, and these

---

[6] Nunquam parum est; quod satis est, nunquam multum est, quod satis non est. Seneca. Ep. 119.

the circumstances of every true believer in Christ, as will be seen hereafter; and therefore ought to be content.

4thly, This contentment is expressed by a man's being satisfied with what he has: earthly riches are not satisfying things, especially to such who are greedy of them, or have an immoderate love for them; one that knew human nature full well says, *He that loveth silver shall not be satisfied with silver*, Eccles. v. 10. but riches of grace are satisfying; the unsearchable riches of Christ, all spiritual things, are of a satisfying nature to spiritual men; the Lord *satisfies their mouth with good things;* with the provisions, the goodness, and fatness of his house; the poor of Zion he satisfies with spiritual bread; he satiates the weary soul, and replenishes every sorrowful soul, Psalm ciii. 5. and cxxxii. 14. Jer. xxxi. 25. especially the love of God is exceeding satisfying to a gracious soul; *O Napthali, satisfied with favour*, with the love of God, *and full with the blessing of the Lord*, even to contentment; such as are favoured after this manner, *are satisfied as with marrow and fatness*, Deut. xxxii. 23. Psalm lxiii. 5. and, indeed, a little of the good things of this life, and the love of God with them, are more satisfying, and give more contentment, than all the riches of the world can without it, Prov. xv. 17. I proceed to inquire,

II. How any come by true contentment of mind.

1. It is not natural to man; man is naturally a discontented creature, especially since the fall; nay, it was discontent which was the cause of that; our first parents not being content with the state of happiness in which they were, abode not in it, but fell from it; such was their ambition, prompted to it by the tempter, that they affected to be as God; or however, perceiving there was a class of creatures superior to them, more wise and knowing, they could not be content with their present case and circumstances; but wanted to be upon an equality with them; and being told, that by eating the forbidden fruit they would attain to it, took and eat of it, and thus by coveting an evil covetousness, lost the happiness which they had; hence it is most truly said of man, that he is, *at his best estate, altogether vanity*, Psalm xxxix. 5.——2. It is not to be found in a natural or unregenerate man; such a man is always uneasy and disquieted; as restless as the troubled sea, and the waves thereof; let him be in pursuit of what he may, he never arrives to it to satisfaction; is it wisdom and knowledge he seeks after, as his first parents did? he gets no content; but finds, that in much wisdom is much grief and vexation of spirit; and that, by an increase of knowledge sorrow is increased. Is it pleasure in the gratification of the senses? these are soon palled with it, and new pleasures are wanting; and these, when had, like the former, issue in bitter reflections and remorse of conscience. Is it worldly honour, fame, and applause of men? these are fickle, transitory things, not to be depended on, and seldom last long; and amidst them there is something that mars the pride and ambition of men; as Mordecai's not bowing to Haman made the latter uneasy and discontented, notwithstanding the profusion of honours conferred upon him. Or is it wealth and riches? these are very uncertain and unsatisfying things, as has been observed. There is nothing can satisfy the mind of man but God himself; and if a man lives without God in the world, let him have what he will, he lives a discontented life; none but a godly man is a contented man; there may be content with godliness, but without it there is none.——3. Contentment is a thing that is to be learned; but not in the school of nature, and by the help of carnal reason; the philosophers among the heathens talked of it, but did not enjoy it; they neither learnt it themselves, nor could they teach it to others; by all their wisdom and knowledge they knew not God truly, and therefore could have no solid satisfaction in what they did know; and even by what they knew of God, they glorified him not as God, *neither were thankful;* and if not thankful, then not contented. The apostle Paul says, he *learnt* it; but he learnt this not at the feet of Gamaliel, where he was brought up; nor among the traditions of the elders, where it is not to be found; for though he was taught after the perfect manner of the fathers of tradition, he was left ignorant of God, and of his law, and of Christ and his righteousness, and of salvation by him; without which there can be no true contentment: but he learnt it, being taught it of God; he had it as he had the gospel; and, indeed, he learnt it by that; which he says, he *neither received of men; neither was taught it, but by the revelation of Jesus Christ ;* he was instructed in it *by the Spirit of wisdom and revelation, in the*

knowledge of Christ; so that he learnt it of God, Father, Son, and Spirit.——
4. This is learnt, not as a theory; but practically and experimentally; and by a train of experiences, and generally through a series of afflictive providences; so that it is learned in quite a different way than a carnal man can conceive of; for these very things which breed discontent in others, are the means of producing true contentment in gracious souls. The apostle Paul learned to be content, not only *in,* but *by,* the adverse providences which attended him; by his dangers at sea and by land; by his distresses, afflictions, and persecutions for Christ's sake; and so other saints have been instructed in some measure, in the same way, and have found it true, what the apostle says, Rom. v. 4. *Tribulation works patience,* &c. in such afflicted and experienced souls; and from all this flows contentment.

III. The arguments moving to such a disposition of mind, and exciting, under a divine influence, to the exercise of this grace, are,

1*st,* The consideration of what we had when we came into the world; and what we shall have when we go out of it; which is just nothing at all; this is the argument the apostle uses to promote contentment in himself and others; *for we brought nothing into this world, and it is certain, we can carry nothing out;* and therefore upon it reasons thus; *and having food and raiment, let us be therewith content,* 1 Tim. vi. 7, 8. and that is enough for the present state, and is more than we shall carry with us, or shall hereafter have any need of; and this was what made Job contented with the loss of all he had; *Naked came I out of my mother's womb, and naked shall I return thither;* and now, as if he should say, I am stripped of all, I am but as I was when I was born, and shall be again when I die;[7] and therefore I am content; *the Lord gave* all that I have had from my birth, *and the Lord has taken away,* and he has taken only what he gave, and to which he had a right; *blessed be the name of the Lord,* Job i. 21. and the like argument the Wise Man makes use of to shew how fruitless and unprofitable it is for a man to be anxious to get perishing riches, and which his son, begotten by him, may not enjoy; but come into the world naked, and go out in like manner, Eccles. v. 14,

15, 16. and this is a reason urged by the Psalmist, why it should give no pain and uneasiness to persons at the increase of the riches of others; since, *when he dies he shall carry nothing away;* so that as it will be no longer his, it will remain to be enjoyed by others, Psalm xlix. 16, 17.

2*dly,* The unalterable will of God is an argument exciting contentment; who does according to his will, as in the armies of the heavens, so among the inhabitants of the earth; he gives to every one their portion in this life as he thinks fit. What they have, is not to be attributed to their wisdom and sagacity, and to their diligence and industry, however commendable these may be; but is to be ascribed to the sovereign will and pleasure of God, who does all things *after the counsel of his will,* in the wisest and best manner; and therefore men should be content; and after all, they cannot make things otherwise than they are; for *who can make that straight which he hath made crooked?* Eccles. ix. 11. and vii. 13. nor can any man, with all his care and thought, *add one cubit to his stature,* or make any change in his condition and circumstances, than what is according to the will of God.

3*dly,* Unworthiness to enjoy the least favour and mercy at the hand of God, should engage us to be content with what we have: we have reason to say, as Jacob did, *I am not worthy of the least of all thy mercies,* Gen. xxxii. 10. not of the bread we eat, nor of the clothes we wear; yea, if God was to deal with us according to our deserts, we should be stripped of all; and, indeed, it is of the Lord's mercies we are not consumed; and therefore have great reason to be content; since we merit nothing, have forfeited all, and cannot claim any thing as our due; what is enjoyed is pure favour, Psalm cxlv. 9.

4*thly,* A consideration of the great things which God has done for us; a dwelling in our thoughts, and meditation on what may excite thankfulness in us; a recollection of the benefits of every kind which God has conferred upon us, may tend very much to make us contented with what we have, giving thanks unto his name; where there is a proper sense of favours there will be thankfulness; and where there is thankfulness there will be content.

5*thly,* The great promises God has made to his people of good things, here and

---

[7] Nemo tam pauper vivit quam natus est. Seneca de Providentia, c. 6.

hereafter, on the fulfilment of which they may depend, are sufficient to make them easy and contented; this is an argument used by the apostle to engage to contentment, Heb. xiii. 5. where he says, *I will never leave thee nor forsake thee!* which promise itself, containing every favour and blessing, and securing every thing that can be needful for comfort and happiness, is of itself enough to excite to contentment. But besides this, there are many other exceeding great and precious promises; as, they that fear the Lord shall lack no good thing; that God will supply all their need; that his grace will be sufficient for them; that as their day is, their strength shall be; yea, godliness has the promise of this life, and of that which is to come: and therefore that, with contentment, is great gain.

6*thly*, Eternal glory and happiness; which is promised, prepared, and laid up for the saints, and which they will most certainly enjoy, may serve to make them content with present things, and even with some things that are not agreeable to the flesh; thus Moses having respect unto the recompence of reward, and a view of invisible things, cheerfully suffered affliction with the people of God, and esteemed reproach for Christ's sake greater riches than the treasures in Egypt; the sufferings of this present life are not to be compared with the glory of another; and though the saints now may have their evil things, they will hereafter have their good things, and shall be fully satisfied when they awake in the divine likeness; and therefore for the present should be content with their lot and portion.

7*thly*, The saints and people of God have all things in hand, or in promise, or in sure and certain hope; *all things are yours;* and therefore they may say, as Jacob did, *I have enough,* or *I have all things;* I am content: God has given us all things richly to enjoy; all things pertaining to life and godliness, both grace and glory; and what more can be desired?

1. God is theirs, Father, Son, and Spirit; all the perfections of God are on their side, and exercised for their good; and all the divine Persons are theirs, and they have an interest in them; and what can they have more?—(1.) God the Father is theirs; he is their covenant-God; he says, *I will be their God, and they shall be my people!* and he not only avouches them to be his peculiar people; but they say, *The Lord is my God!* and avouch him, profess him, and claim their interest in him as such: he is their Father, and has declared himself in covenant to be so; has predestinated them to the adoption of children; sent his Son to redeem them, that they might receive it; and his Spirit to witness it unto them. He is their shield and exceeding great reward, as he promised to Abraham; he is their portion now and for ever; and what, not content!—(2.) Christ the Son of God is theirs; the gift of his Father's love, an unspeakable one he is; given as an head unto them; as an head of government, to rule over them and protect them; and an head of influence, to supply them; he is their husband, to love, nourish, and cherish them, as his own flesh, and to all whose goods they have a common right; he is their Saviour and Redeemer from sin, Satan, the curse of the law, and wrath to come; he is their Mediator and Peacemaker, their Prophet, Priest, and King. All that belong to him are theirs; his righteousness is theirs, for justification; his blood is theirs, to cleanse and pardon them; his flesh is theirs, to feed upon by faith; his fulness theirs, to supply their wants; he is ALL in ALL unto them; and what, not content!—(3.) The Spirit of God is theirs; a gift which their heavenly Father has given them; and is given them to make known unto them the things which are freely given to them of God; he is the convincer of them of sin, righteousness, and judgment; the illuminator of them in the knowledge of divine things; their quickener and sanctifier, their comforter, and the spirit of adoption to them; the earnest and seal of their future glory; theirs to begin, to carry on, and perfect the work of grace in them; and what, not content!——2. The covenant of grace is theirs; made with them, and made for them; all the stores of it theirs; the blessings of it, the sure mercies of David; the blessings of grace and of glory, provided and laid up in it; the promises of it, both respecting this life and that which is to come; and what, not content!——3. The gospel, and the ordinances of it, and the ministers of it, are theirs! *all things are yours, whether Paul, or Apollos, or Cephas,* 1 Cor. iii. 21, 22. the whole Scripture is written for their use, for their learning and instruction, for their comfort and edification; the gospel is ordained for their glory; and is sent into and published in the world for their good; and the ministers of it are their servants for Jesus's sake; they are gifts to

the churches, to be their pastors and teachers; and have gifts given them to feed and instruct them; they are stewards of the mysteries of grace, and are appointed in the house of God, to give to every one their portion of meat in due season; and which surely must add to divine contentment.——4. Temporal things are theirs; *or the world, or life, or death, or things present, or things to come, all are yours*, 1 Cor. iii. 22.; the *world*, and the fulness of it, belongs to Christ, who is heir of all things; and saints being joint-heirs with him, are as Abraham was, *heirs of the world;* and all things in it are theirs, and work together, and contribute to their good; and they at last shall inhabit the new earth. *Life* is theirs in every sense, corporal, spiritual, and eternal. And *death* is theirs, a blessing to them whenever it comes; which will deliver them from the troubles of this life, and enter them into the glories of another. *Things present* are theirs; present mercies, no good thing is withheld from them needful for them, food to eat, and raiment to put on: and *things to come;* the unseen glories of a future state; an inheritance incorruptible, reserved in *heaven*, a kingdom prepared from the foundation of the world. And surely all this is enough to give contentment!

CHAP. XIII.

OF THANKFULNESS TO GOD.

Thankfulness follows contentment: a discontented man is not thankful for any thing; but a contented man is thankful for every thing. Thankfulness is a branch of godliness; none but a godly man is truly a thankful man: there are some things not to be named among saints, and are not becoming them; but this is; and rather becoming them than many other things, Eph. v. 3, 4. an unthankful saint is a very odd sound, if not a contradiction; *unthankful, unholy*, are characters joined together, and agree, 2 Tim. iii. 2. and so *unthankful* and *evil*, Luke vi. 36. and particularly none but an holy man can give thanks *at the remembrance of the holiness of God*, Psalm xcvii. 12. Concerning this gracious disposition of mind, thankfulness, may be observed,

I. The things for which thanks are to be given; and they are all things; the rule, and which is, according to the will of God, is *giving thanks always for all things;* and again, *In every thing*, or for every thing, *give thanks*, Eph. v. 20. 1 Thess. v. 18. to which agrees what the apostle says, Phil. iv. 6. And,

First, For temporal mercies; for God is the *Father of mercies*, even of all such mercies; the author and giver of them, and therefore thanks should be returned to him for them. As,

1. For our beings; to be, is better than not to be; and none could give us existence but God, the fountain of being; *In him we live, and move, and have our being:* that is, we have it from him, as well as are supported in it by him; *It is he that hath made us, and not we ourselves:—be thankful unto him, and bless his name*, Acts xvii. 28. Psalm c. 3, 4. the wonderful formation of man, the structure of his body, the symmetry and perfection of its parts, as well as soundness of limbs, are matter of praise and thankfulness; as they were to the Psalmist David, Psalm cxxxix. 14, 15, 16.——2. For our life, which is from God; he *giveth to all life, and breath, and all things*, Acts. xvii. 25. some creatures have a being, and yet not life, as inanimate ones; some have life, yet only a vegetative one, as plants; and others only an animal one, as brutes; but God has given to man a soul, both living and rational; Adam's body was made out of the dust of the earth, and then God breathed into him *the breath of life, and man became a living soul;* and such a life every man has, which is a grant and favour from God, Job x. 12. and therefore thanks should be given to him for it, and for all the mercies of life, and for that more than for them; since *the life is more than meat*, or drink, or raiment, and every thing by which life is nourished, supported, and made comfortable; and indeed, is preferable to all a man has besides, Matt. vi. 25. Job. ii. 4.——3. For the preservation of our being and life by God; his visitation, which is every day, every morning, preserves our spirits; he upholds our souls in life; he is therefore truly called the *preserver of men*, and is worthy of praise and thanksgiving on that account; the reason given is, not only because he has made the heaven, earth, and seas, and all therein; but because he *preserveth them all*, Nehem. ix. 5, 6.——4. For our health, and for the continuance of it, and for restoration to it when it has been interrupted; health is a very valuable mercy, and without which the outward blessings of life cannot be comfortably enjoyed; and therefore is

CHAP. XIII.   OF THANKFULNESS TO GOD.   795

greatly to be desired, both by ourselves and for our friends; thus the apostle John wished for Gaius, that he might *prosper and be in health, even as his soul prospered,* 3 John ver. 2. and persons favoured with such a mercy have reason to be thankful; as also when it has been lost and restored again; thus Hezekiah, when recovered from his sickness, said, *The living, the living, he shall praise thee, as I do this day,* Isa. xxxviii. 9, 19. and a contrary behaviour, as it is very unbecoming, is justly resented; as in the case of the ten lepers, Luke xvii. 15—18.——5. For every mercy enjoyed, be it what it may; not only for life and health, for food and raiment, which are the principal mercies; but for every other, the least that can be thought of, Gen. xxxii. 10. *Every creature of God is good, and nothing to be refused, if it be received with thanksgiving;* so that it seems the goodness of any creature-mercy to a man depends upon his thankfulness for it; and this is the difference between a thankful and unthankful man: an unthankful man thinks nothing good; and a thankful man thinks every thing good, and blesses God for it,   Tim. iv. 4. and this he does every day; mercies are returned every day, and are new every morning; and therefore men sensible of them will say, *Blessed be the Lord, who daily loadeth us with benefits!* Psalm lxviii. 19.

Secondly, For spiritual mercies, whether of a lower or of an higher kind. As,

1st, For the means of grace, the gospel, and the ministry of it; and a great mercy it is to be under the sound of it; *Blessed is the man that heareth me,* the voice of wisdom, the gospel of Christ, though only externally, Prov. viii. 34. It is an happiness to be born in a land where the gospel is preached, and not among Pagans, Mahometans, and Papists, where there is a *famine;* not a famine of bread, nor a thirst for water, but of *hearing the word of the Lord,* Amos viii. 11. and a dreadful judgment it is on a people when the Lord commands *the clouds,* the ministers of the word, *that they rain no rain upon them,* that is, preach not the gospel to them. The gospel was first restrained to the Jewish people, and forbid to be preached to the Gentiles; but afterwards the apostles had a commission to preach it to all nations; the Gentiles embraced it gladly, glorified it, or were greatly thankful for it; and when this is blessed to the conversion of sinners, it is matter of thankfulness; not only to them, but to all true believers, and to the ministers of the word: when the Jewish Christians perceived that God had given repentance to the Gentiles also, they glorified God, or were thankful to him, and blessed his name; and when the apostles declared the conversion of the Gentiles by the ministry of the word, it caused great joy among the brethren; and when they were successful in all parts, in making conquest of souls to Christ, they could not but express their thankfulness to God, saying, *Now thanks be unto God, which always causeth us to triumph in Christ,* 2 Cor. ii. 14. and when it is food to believers, and is sweet to their taste, as the honey and the honeycomb, and they esteem it more than their necessary food, then are they truly thankful for it. It is in itself glad tidings, and a joyful sound; and when it is experimentally heard and known, it causes praise and thankfulness, even among personages of the highest class; *all the kings of the earth shall praise thee, O Lord, when they hear the words of thy mouth;* the doctrines of the gospel, so as to understand them, as they will in the latter-day glory, Psalm cxxxviii. 4. when the gospel ministry will be the means of enlarging the interest of Christ, the earth shall be filled with the knowledge of the Lord as the waters cover the sea; and when the kingdoms of this world shall become the Lord's and his Christ's, then the four-and-twenty elders, the representatives of gospel-churches, will *worship God saying, We give thee thanks, O Lord God Almighty, because thou hast taken to thee thy great power, and hast reigned;* by making the gospel-ministry effectual to the enlargement of his kingdom and interest, Rev. xi. 15, 16, 17. To which may be added, as means of grace, the ordinances of the gospel, called the goodness and fatness of the house of God, the provisions of Zion; which, when saints are blessed with, and especially when blessed unto them, and made useful and beneficial, they *shout aloud for joy,* or are exceeding thankful for them: and with these may be mentioned, the ministers of the gospel, who are the gifts of God to his churches; *And he gave some pastors and teachers;* gifts to qualify them for such offices; and he gives them themselves to his churches, to officiate as such among them; *And I will give you pastors,* Eph. iv. 11. Jer. iii. 15. these are reckoned among the blessings and privileges of churches, and of all true believers; *All things are yours, whether Paul or Apollos, or Cephas;* and therefore they have reason to be thankful for them; and especially when, though their *teachers* have been *removed into a corner,* yet not so *any more,* but their *eyes see* their *teachers,* and their ears hear the joyful sound from them.

2dly, Thanks are to be given particularly for the blessings of grace themselves, the things which are freely given of God. And in order to thankfulness for these, in men there must be knowledge of them; which is had by the Spirit of wisdom and revelation; and there must be an application of them, a view of special interest in them; the Spirit of God must witness to their spirits that they belong unto them; he must take of the things of Christ, and shew them unto them; which will cause exultation and thankfulness. As particularly,

1. For electing grace; this may be known without any special and extraordinary revelation; even from the grace in effectual vocation; *For whom he did predestinate, them he also called;* and the *vessels of mercy afore prepared unto glory,* are explained of those *whom God has called,* Rom. viii. 30. and ix. 23, 24. so that those who are called by grace may comfortably conclude, that they are predestinated unto life, or are in the Lamb's book of life, and are fore-ordained unto eternal glory; and this may be known, as the apostle observes, from the efficacy of the gospel on the hearts of men, 1 Thess. i. 4, 5. and such therefore will call upon themselves and others to praise and thankfulness, saying, *Praise the Lord, for the Lord hath chosen Jacob unto himself, and Israel for his peculiar treasure,* Psalm cxxxv. 3, 4. And the rather this is matter of great thankfulness, because—(1.) The choice God has made of men to everlasting life is of grace, and not of works; even of free, unmerited grace, and without any motive to it from them; hence called, *The election of grace,* Rom. xi. 5, 6. and ix. 11—13. Something similar to this was the national election of the people of Israel, which was not because of their quality or quantity; but because of the Lord's pure love unto them, Deut. vii. 6—8.—(2.) This choice is an act of distinguishing grace; it is not a choice of all, only of some; or it would be no choice; *I speak not of you all; I know whom I have chosen,* John xiii. 18. all Christ's disciples were chosen to office, but not all to grace and glory; such so chosen are *vessels of mercy,* in distinction from others, called *vessels of wrath;* it is a choice of *us,* and not others: of us, who are in no wise better than others, as undeserving of the favour of God as others, being *children of wrath,* even as others.—(3.) It is a choice, which is the source, foundation, and security both of grace and glory. Sanctification of the Spirit, and belief of the truth, which include all grace, are fixed and secured in eternal election, and flow from it; men are chosen to faith and holiness before the foundation of the world, and these are in time bestowed upon them; *As many as were ordained unto eternal life believed;* hence true faith is called, *The faith of God's elect,* being peculiar to them, in consequence of their election, and with which their eternal happiness is connected; *For whom he did predestinate—them he also glorified.* Now if the apostle thought himself bound to give thanks for the election of others, then much more for his own, and so is every chosen vessel of salvation; see 2 Thess. ii. 13.

2. Thanks are to be given for redeeming grace. This was one of the benefits and blessings of grace, which lay uppermost on the mind of the Psalmist, when he called upon his soul, and all within him, to bless the name of the Lord, and not forget his benefits; *Who,* says he, *redeemeth thy life from destruction,* Psalm ciii. 1, 2, 4. having in view, no doubt, the redemption of it by Christ, from everlasting ruin; thus Zechariah, the Father of John the Baptist, began his prophecy, *Blessed be the Lord God of Israel, for he hath visited and redeemed his people,* and raised up a mighty Saviour and Redeemer from David's family; this he said, when *the day-spring from on high* had *visited them;* the Saviour was conceived, and become incarnate, though as yet not born, who was to be the Redeemer of his people, Luke i. 68, 69, 78. and great reason there is for praise and thankfulness on this account.—(1.) Because this redemption is special and particular. They are a *peculiar people* whom Christ has redeemed from all iniquity; they are *redeemed from among men,* and so not all men; they are *redeemed out of every kindred, and tongue, and people, and nation;* and not every kindred, every tongue, all people, and each nation; and therefore have the greater reason to be thankful that they are redeemed.—(2.) It is altogether free on their parts; though they are bought with a price, are redeemed from a vain conversation, with the precious

blood of Christ, to which redemption is frequently ascribed; yet they are *redeemed without money*, without any price or money of their own paid by them for it; it is wholly of free cost to them; they are *let go, not for price nor reward*, which they have given; their redemption is indeed through the blood of Christ, and yet it is *according to the riches of the grace of God*, who of his infinite wisdom and grace has found a ransom.—(3.) It is a plenteous one; *With the Lord is plenteous redemption*, Psalm cxxx. 7. a redemption from all iniquity, original and actual; from all sins of every kind, of heart, lip, and life, before and after conversion; from Satan, stronger than they, who held them captive; from all the curses of the law, to which they were subject by sin; and from hell and wrath, and from every enemy of their souls.—(4.) It is an eternal one; *Having obtained eternal redemption for us*, Heb. ix. 12. which will always continue; the redeemed will never more return to a captive state, or be brought into subjection to what they are redeemed from; but will always enjoy the benefits arising from this grace; and if therefore Moses and the children of Israel had reason to sing unto the Lord, who *in his mercy had redeemed them out of Egypt*, which was but a temporal redemption; much more reason have we to praise the Lord, and give thanks to him for eternal redemption by Christ.

3. Thanks are to be given for pardoning grace and mercy. This is the first thing the Psalmist mentions, after stirring up himself to bless and praise the Lord for all his benefits; *who forgiveth all thine iniquities*, Psalm ciii. 1, 2, 3. and indeed pardon of sin is a great blessing; and he is an happy man whose transgression is forgiven, and his sin covered, and to whom the Lord imputeth not iniquity! and therefore should express his thankfulness for it. And,—(1.) Because it is entirely free with respect to the persons who partake of it. It proceeds, indeed, upon a satisfaction made by another; for God, though he forgives sin, will by no means clear the guilty, without a full satisfaction to his justice; *Without shedding of blood there is no remission;* but though Christ's blood has been shed for the remission of sins, yet that is according to the riches of divine grace; it is free to men, though it cost Christ dear, his blood and life, Isa. xliii. 25. some, their debts are more, and others less numerous; one owes five hundred pence, and another fifty; but whereas neither the one nor the other *have any thing to pay*, God, the creditor, *frankly forgives them both*, Luke vii. 41, 42.—(2.) Pardon of sin, is not only free, but full and complete; and therefore sinful men should be thankful for it; God not only forgives all manner of sin, signified by iniquity, transgression, and sin; greater or lesser sins, such as are more or less aggravated; but all acts of sin committed by his people; God, for Christ's sake, forgives all; *Having forgiven all trespasses*. Col. ii. 13. no one sin is left unforgiven; the Lord's name be praised!

4. Thanks are to be given for adopting grace; this is one of the spiritual blessings with which the Lord's people are blessed in Christ, *according to the good pleasure of his will*, Eph. i. 3, 5. There is such a display of grace in the blessing of adoption as ravished the apostle John, and caused him to break forth in a rapture, and say, *Behold, what manner of love the Father hath bestowed upon us, that we should be called the sons of God!* 1 John iii. 1. Two things serve to excite thankfulness for this grace: —(1.) That it is bestowed on persons very unworthy; such who are by nature children of wrath, as others; and yet by this grace, children of God; such of whom God himself says, *How shall I put them among the children?* and yet of his grace puts them there; such who are like the wretched infant, cast out into the open field, in the day it was born, to the loathing of its person, and yet taken into the family of God; who have nothing lovely in them to recommend them, as Moses to Pharaoh's daughter, and Esther to Mordecai had; but all the reverse.—(2.) The various blessings annexed to this grace; such have the glorious liberty of the children of God; liberty of access to God, as children to a father; and a right to all privileges and immunities, which fellow-citizens with the saints, and those of the household of God have; these are never more servants, but heirs, and have a right to the heavenly inheritance.

5. Thanks are to be given to God for regenerating grace, 1 Pet. i. 3, 4. This is wholly owing to the free grace and rich mercy of God; it is denied to be of blood, or of the will of men, or of the will of the flesh; but of God, of his sovereign grace and favour; who, *of his own will, begat us with the word of truth;* and the rather should we be thankful for this grace, since without it there can be no enjoyment of eternal life; *Except a man be born again,*

he cannot see the kingdom of God, James i. 18. John i. 13. and iii. 3.

6. Thanks are to be given as for a right to eternal life; which lies not in the righteousness of men, but in the righteousness of Christ; so for a meetness for it, which is all of grace, Col. i. 12.

7. Thanks are to be given for victory over all spiritual enemies; and so for persevering grace in faith and holiness to glory, notwithstanding them all; nothing more distressing than a body of sin and death, and nothing more desirable than a deliverance from it; and yet no hope of it but through Christ; and having hope of it in this way, such a soul may say with the apostle, *I thank God through Jesus Christ our Lord!* that is, that there will be a deliverance from it; and not from that only, but from every enemy, sin, law, and death; and therefore can say, *Thanks be to God, which giveth us the victory;* over death and the grave; over sin, the sting of death; and over the law, the strength of sin; so that nothing shall hinder an abundant entrance into the kingdom and glory of God, Rom. vii. 23, 24. 1 Cor. xv. 57.

Thirdly, For Christ, the great blessing of grace and gift of God: *Thanks be unto God for his unspeakable gift,* 2 Cor. ix. 15. the donor of this gift is God, of whom are all things; hence Christ is called the *gift of God,* by way of eminence, John iv. 10. who is a sovereign Being, and disposes of all his gifts, and so this, to whomsoever he pleases; it is his own he gives, and he may do with that what he will; and this is a gift like himself, suitable to the greatness of his Majesty, as King of kings; it is a royal gift, like that *Araunah, as a king, gave unto the king,* 2 Sam. xxiv. 23. the gift is the Son of God; *To us a Son is given;* the only begotten Son of God, his own Son, the dear Son of his love, his Son and Heir; him he has given to be for a covenant of the people, the Mediator and Surety of it, and with whom he has entrusted all the blessings and promises of it; and to be an head over all things to the church; and to be the Saviour of the body, the church; even to be God's salvation unto the ends of the earth; for which purpose he has not spared him, but has delivered him up into the hands of men, justice, and death; and for which those to and for whom he has given, have reason to be thankful; when, besides these things, the nature of the gift is observed. As, ——1. It is entirely a free gift; it is one of those things, and the chief of them, which are *freely given unto us of God,* 1 Cor. ii. 12. unmerited and undeserved; wholly of free grace, and flowing from the pure love of God, to persons of all the most unworthy, John iii. 16. ——2. It is a suitable one; nothing could have been given us more suitable to our case and circumstances; *Such an Highpriest became us;* such a Prophet, such a King, such a Mediator between God and men, such a Redeemer and Saviour, such an Advocate and Intercessor, one so full of grace and truth, who is made unto us wisdom, righteousness, sanctification, and redemption, who is indeed ALL in ALL; all that we want, all that we can desire; for, ——3. It is a very large and comprehensive gift; *God, with Christ, freely gives us all things;* and blesses, *with all spiritual blessings in him,* the blessings of grace and of glory, Rom. viii. 32. Eph. i. 3. Christ being ours, all things are ours; and therefore we have reason to be thankful, 1 Cor. iii. 22, 23.——4. It is an unchangeable and irreversible gift; it comes from the *Father of lights, with whom is no variableness, neither shadow of turning;* and not only the giver, but the gift itself is unchangeable; who is *Jesus, the same yesterday, to-day, and for ever;* and is one of the gifts of God which are *without repentance;* to which may be added, that it is *unspeakable;* none can say how great it is, what is contained in it, and what the benefits arising from it in time and to eternity.

Fourthly, For the Spirit of God, and his gifts and graces. The Spirit himself is the gift of God, Luke xi. 13. and a great and glorious gift he is, for which we have reason to be thankful; especially when we consider to what ends and purposes he is given, as to be a Comforter of his people, *He shall give you another Comforter,* John xiv. 16. and to be a Spirit of wisdom and revelation in the knowledge of Christ, and to strengthen the saints with all might in the inward man, and to be the earnest and pledge of their future glory and happiness, 2 Cor. v. 5. Eph. i. 14, 17. and iii. 16. The several graces of the Spirit are gifts and free-grace gifts, and very valuable ones; faith, which is of the operation of the Spirit, is *not of ourselves, it is the gift of God,* which no man has nor can exercise unless it be given him of God; and all men have it or not, and therefore it is distinguishing grace to those who have it, and should be thankful for it; a good hope is through grace, and is given both by God the Father and our Lord Jesus Christ, 2 Thess. ii. 16. and so love is from grace, 1 Tim. i. 14. These are now the all things for which we should be thankful.

II. When, in what cases and circumstances, and for whom thanks are to be given.———1. When; always, this is the rule, *giving thanks always for all things;* every day, night and day, constantly, continually, all the days of a man's life; for there are ever new mercies, they are returning every day and every morning: hence says the Psalmist, *Every day will I bless thee,* Psalm cxlv. 2. and cxlvi. 2.———2. In what cases and circumstances, in what state and condition, are we to be thankful? in every one, *in every thing*, that is, in every state, *give thanks*, 1 Thess. v. 18.—(1.) Not in prosperity only, when we are to be joyful, cheerful, and thankful; and when we are not to attribute our prosperity to ourselves, nor to second causes, but to God, and be thankful; otherwise we shall only *sacrifice to* our own *net*, and *burn incense* to our own *drag*, Hab. i. 16.—(2.) But in adversity also; as Job blessed God, or was thankful, when he was stripped of all; and the people of God have reason to be thankful under afflictions, when the Lord puts underneath his everlasting arms, and supports them under them; when he strengthens them on a bed of languishing, and makes their bed in their sickness; when he chooses them in the furnace of affliction, and knows their souls in adversity; when he manifests his love and favour; when he is with them passing through the fire and water, so that the one shall not kindle upon them, nor the other overflow them; in short, since he makes all things work together for their good here and hereafter, they should be thankful. And also,—(3.) In times of temptation; since the temptation might have been suffered to have been greater and heavier than it is; and since the grace of God is sufficient to support under it, and carry through it, and the faithfulness of God will not suffer his people to be tempted above what they are able to bear; and since Christ is able to succour them that are tempted, and sympathizes with them, and prays for them that their faith fail not.—(4.) When in very uncomfortable frames; at least better might be wished for, since these might have been worse and have issued in despair, or bordering on it; and in the midst of all it should be considered, that though frames are changeable things, Jehovah changes not, Christ is the same always, the covenant of grace is sure, and the gifts and calling of God without repentance; and the Lord knows them that are his, and they shall never perish.—(5.) Amidst all the reproaches and persecutions of men; so the apostles were thankful that they were counted worthy to suffer shame for the name of Christ; the apostle Peter says such are happy, 1 Pet. iv. 14. and such who are persecuted for righteousness-sake are pronounced blessed by Christ, and are exhorted to rejoice, and be exceeding glad, Matt. v. 10—12.———3. For whom; for all men, for kings and all in authority, 1 Tim. ii. 1, 2. since these are powers ordained of God, and are ministers for the good of men, are terrors to evil doers, and a praise to them that do well; if they are good kings and worthy magistrates, such are to be honoured and obeyed, and thanks to be given for them, which is good and acceptable in the sight of God. We are to be thankful for our relations and friends, and for the continuance of them; children are the gifts of God to parents, and as such to be owned with gratitude, as they were by Jacob and Joseph, Gen. xxxiii. 5. and xlviii. 9. see Psalm cxxvii. 3—5. and likewise for the churches of Christ, and all the saints in them; for their prosperity, for their grace and the increase of it; for their faith, both as a doctrine and a grace, and for their love to one another; these are what the apostle expresses his thankfulness for, in almost all his epistles; and so for the ministers of the gospel saints should be thankful, who are the gifts of God to the churches, and are promised as such, Jer. iii. 15. These are the servants of the most high God which shew unto men the way of salvation, and who are the churches' servants for Jesus' sake, faithful stewards in the house of God, to give to every one their portion of meat in due season; and being thus useful, thanks should be given for them; and which likewise should be done for an increase of converts through the ministry of the word, when there are additions made to churches of such as shall be saved; when the gospel is succeeded for the gathering in of others to Christ and into his churches, besides those who are already gathered, 2 Cor. ii. 14.

III. To whom are thanks to be given on the above account? to God, of whom are all things, and to whom the glory of all belongs; he is the proper and primary object of thanksgiving; *I thank my God,*

through Jesus Christ, for you all, Rom. i. 8. God, Father, Son, and Spirit.——
1. Thanks are to be given to the Father, *Giving thanks always for all things unto God and the Father,* Eph. v. 20. and hence the same apostle blesses or gives thanks unto him as the God and Father of our Lord Jesus Christ, for blessing the saints in him with all spiritual blessings, Eph. i. 3. and the apostle Peter blesses or gives thanks to him as such for regenerating grace particularly, 1 Pet. i. 3. and he is to be considered in such an act of thanksgiving as Christ's God and our God, and as Christ's Father and our Father; for as we are directed to pray to him, saying, *Our Father, which art in heaven,* so we should give thanks to him as such, saying, *Blessed be God, even the Father of our Lord Jesus Christ,* 2 Cor. i. 3.——
2. Thanks are to be given to the Son of God, our Lord Jesus Christ; and these are sometimes given to him particularly and alone, *I thank Christ Jesus the Lord,* says the apostle, 1 Tim. i. 12. and if thanks are to be given him on such an account as there, then certainly for other favours received from him; as for his suretiship engagements, for his assumption of human nature, for suffering and dying in the room and stead of his people, and for many other acts of grace done by him, and blessings of grace received from him. Besides, it is in the name of Christ, and through him, we are directed to give thanks to God, Eph. v. 20. Rom. i. 8. as it is proper we should, since all our mercies come to us through him; it is in him we are blessed with all spiritual blessings, and it is out of his fulness we receive, and grace for grace; and all the grace that is wrought in us in regeneration, and in carrying on the work of sanctification, is all *through Christ;* nor can we come to God in any other way with our thanksgivings but by him; he is the only way to the Father, the way of access to him with boldness and confidence; and therefore *by him* we are to *offer the sacrifice of praise to God continually, that is, the fruit of our lips, giving thanks unto his name,* Heb. xiii. 15. Nor are our spiritual sacrifices, either of prayer or praise, acceptable to God, but through Christ Jesus our Lord, in whom our persons are accepted, even in him the beloved.——
3. Thanks are to be given to the blessed Spirit; for, as he is the object of prayer with the Father, and the Son, so the object of praise and thanksgiving; and great reason there is, that as we should be careful not to vex and grieve the good Spirit of God with our ingratitude; so that we should be thankful to him for all that he has done for us; in quickening and regenerating us; in beginning and carrying on the good work of grace in us, and in sealing us up to the day of redemption. Besides many other acts of grace which might be mentioned.

Now this work of thanksgiving, is to be performed towards God with a celebration of the divine perfections, which are displayed in his acts of kindness to us; as we are to give thanks at the remembrance of his holiness, so at the remembrance of every other attribute of his; it is in this way the living creatures are said to give glory, and honour, and thanks unto God, Rev. iv. 8, 9. This is also to be done by a recollection of the benefits of God, bestowed upon us; which, though so many that we are not able to reckon them up in order before him; yet, as much as in us lies, we are to call upon our souls to call to mind, and not forget, if possible, any of his benefits; and to enquire, what shall we render to him for them; see Isa. lxiii. 7. and this is to be performed with all our hearts, with all that is within us, with all the powers and faculties of our souls, and to the utmost of our abilities; as we are to love the Lord our God with all our heart, and with all our strength; we are to give thanks to him in like manner, in the most intense way we are capable of; as we are to serve him with grace in our hearts in every branch of duty; so in this, even in the exercise of every grace.

IV. The reasons or arguments for giving thanks.

1. It is the will of God; and that is reason sufficient why it should be attended to, 1 Thess. v. 18. it is that good, perfect, and acceptable will of God made known in his word, which he has commanded and directed to; *Offer unto God thanksgiving,* Psalm l. 14. this is a sacrifice acceptable to him, and well-pleasing in his sight, Psalm lxix. 30, 31. and the contrary is resented by him.——2. This is the will of God *in Christ Jesus,* which is made known by him; who, lying in the bosom of the Father, has declared his whole mind and will to the sons of men; and this among the rest; and it is also to be given unto God in and through Christ, as before observed.——
3. It is enforced by the example of Christ, who himself gave thanks to God, and that

for the distinguishing blessings of his grace bestowed upon his people, according to his sovereign will and pleasure; *I thank thee, O Father, &c.* Matt. xi. 25, 26. To which may be added,———4. The examples of saints in all ages, patriarchs, prophets, and apostles; the book of Psalms is full of instances.

CHAP. XIV.

OF HUMILITY.

AFTER *love, joy, peace,* mentioned as fruits of the Spirit, *long-suffering, gentleness,* and *meekness,* in which *humility* is included, are observed as fruits of the same Spirit also, Gal. v. 22, 23. and this naturally follows or accompanies *thankfulness,* last treated of; an humble man is always a thankful man; whereas *proud boasters,* are joined with the *unthankful, unholy,* 2 Tim. iii. 2. The proud philosophers would not allow of thankfulness to God for virtue and goodness: "That we live, is the gift of God, says Seneca;[1] but that we live well, is owing to philosophy; and, adds he, by so much we owe the more to this than to God, by how much the greater a good life is than life itself." And says Cicero,[2] "No man refers virtue to God; if it was a gift of his, we should have no praise nor glorying: did ever any man give thanks to God that he was a good man!" How contrary to this is that of the humble apostle, 1 Cor. iv. 7. Humility, or a *meek and quiet spirit,* is a branch of internal worship, or of experimental religion and godliness; it is called, *The hidden man of the heart,* 1 Pet. iii. 4. and is very necessary in the performance of every part of external worship and service; *Serving the Lord with all humility of mind,* Acts xx. 19. In considering which I shall,

First, Shew wherein it lies, and in what it appears and manifests itself.

1. In a man's thinking meanly and the worst of himself, and well and the best of others; observing that rule of the apostle's, *In lowliness of mind let each esteem other better than themselves,* Phil. ii. 3. such an humble saint was the apostle himself, who reckoned himself, *less than the least of all saints, and the chief of sinners;* such an humble soul thinks no good man has such a sinful corrupt heart as he has; or has so much sin dwelling in it: one reason is, because his own sins and corruptions are more known to himself; whilst those of others lie more out of sight; he thinks every saint has more grace and holiness, more spiritual knowledge and experience than he has, and says with Agur, *that he has not the understanding of a man,* that is, of a good man, Prov. xxx. 2. whereas, on the contrary, a proud Pharisee thanks God he is not as other men are, *such a great sinner* as others, and says, *Stand by thyself, I am holier than thou,* Luke xviii. 11. Isa. lxv. 5.———2. In not envying, but rejoicing at the gifts and graces of others. Humility is like charity, *it envieth not.* Moses was a very meek man, above all men which were upon the face of the earth, and he said to Joshua, *Enviest thou for my sake?* that is, the gifts bestowed on Eldad and Medad; *would God, that all the Lord's people were prophets,* Numb. xi. 29. and xii. 3. When David related his experiences of divine grace, his triumph of faith, and glorying in the Lord, he observes; *The humble shall hear thereof, and be glad,* Psalm xxxiv. 2. so John the Baptist, when he takes notice of the vastly superior gifts, grace, usefulness, and success of Christ, says he, in a very humble and modest manner, *He must increase, but I must decrease,* John iii. 30, 31.———3. In ascribing all he is and has to the grace of God; confessing that he has nothing but what he has received; and therefore would not glory, as though he had received it not; but says, with the apostle, *By the grace of God I am what I am,* 1 Cor. iv. 7. and xv. 10. he frankly acknowledges, that it is of the free grace of God alone, that he is elected, redeemed, justified, pardoned, regenerated, and shall be saved; and not through any works of righteousness done by him; and therefore gives all the glory to it.———4. In disclaiming his own righteousness, and submitting to the righteousness of Christ; the Spirit of God having convinced him of his want of righteousness, of the insufficiency of his own to justify him before God, and that after having done all he can, he is but an unprofitable servant; and that through pride in himself, and ignorance of God's righteousness, he heretofore submitted not to the righteousness of Christ, yet now he desires to be found in it, Phil. iii. 9.———5. In a willingness to receive instruction from the meanest saint; *Give instruction to a wise*

---

[1] Ep. 90.

[2] De Natura Deorum, l. 3. prope finem.

man, if he is an humble man, and not a scorner, he will be thankful for it, *and will be wiser: teach a just man*, not one that is righteous in his own eyes, and despises others, *and he will increase in learning*, Prov. ix. 9. so Apollos, though an eloquent man, and mighty in the scriptures, did not disdain to receive instruction from Aquila and Priscilla, tent-makers, who took him and taught him the way of God more perfectly.——6. In kindly receiving admonitions given; and indeed it is only to such that they are of any advantage, and meet with success; a proud, haughty scorner rejects them with contempt, Prov. ix. 8. an humble man will take the reproof well, and consider it as an instance of love to him, and will love the reprover more and better for it, as David says he should, Psalm cxli. 5.——7. In bearing patiently all injuries done to him, and putting up all affronts offered to him. Humility, like charity, is *not easily provoked*, and *beareth all things:* humble saints will bear, *with all lowliness and meekness, with long-suffering, forbearing one another in love;* such who *put on kindness, humbleness of mind, meekness, long-suffering*, will not only bear with and forbear one another, but will *forgive one another, even as Christ forgave them,* 1 Cor. xiii. 5, 7. Eph. iv. 2. Col. iii. 12, 13. When Miriam and Aaron spoke against Moses, who is observed to be the meekest man on earth; as an instance of it, he was so far from resenting the affront, that he prayed for Miriam that she might be healed of the leprosy with which she was stricken for it, Numb. xii. 1, 2, 3, 13.——8. In submitting quietly to the afflicting hand of God; humble souls are still under the rod, hearken to the voice of it, are obedient to it, patiently bear it without murmuring, humble themselves under the mighty hand of God, and resign their wills to his; as Aaron, Eli, David, and others have done, Lev. x. 3. 1 Sam. iii. 18. Psalm xxxix. 9.——9. In not seeking great things for a man's self, and after things too high for him. It is good advice given to Baruch; *Seekest thou great things for thyself? seek them not,* Jer. xlv. 5. an humble man will not: it is a sign of a proud, ambitious man so to do; to aspire after things out of a man's reach, and beyond his capacity; *Lord, says David, my heart is not haughty, nor mine eyes lofty; neither do I exercise myself in great matters, or in things too high for me,* Psalm cxxxi. 1. especially it argues great pride and vanity, when a man seeks to be wise above what is written; an humble man will not pry into things secret, but will be content with what is revealed, Deut. xxix. 29. And therefore,——10. Humility appears in subjecting a man's reason to divine revelation; then is a man humble when every imagination, reasoning, and all high thoughts are cast down, and brought to the obedience of Christ in his word; when men have recourse to the law and to the testimony, to the sacred scriptures, and make them the standard of their faith; and, like the noble, diligent, and humble Bereans, search into them, whether things be so or no; for *if any man teach otherwise, and consent not to wholesome words,* the doctrines of Christ contained in the scriptures, *he is proud, knowing nothing,* 1 Tim. vi. 3. This pride in men is the chief cause of all controversies and quarrels about religious things.

Secondly, Let us next consider from whence this grace of humility, or such a disposition of mind arises.

1. Not from nature; but from the grace of God: man is naturally a proud creature, though he has nothing really to be proud of; not of his wisdom, which is but folly; nor of his wealth, which is uncertain and transitory; nor of his beauty, which is vain, and may be made to consume away like a moth; nor of his outward goodness and righteousness, which pass away like a morning cloud and early dew. Pride is one of those things which are within a man, in his heart, and proceeds from thence, and defiles him; but true humility is from God, from his Spirit and grace; and therefore *meekness*, or humility, is reckoned among the fruits of the Spirit, Gal. v. 22,23. ——2. From a true sight and sense of sin, and the evil nature of it, under the illumination and conviction of the Spirit of God; when sin appears to be *exceeding sinful,* and such a sight is humbling. Whilst a man is insensible of the inward corruption of his nature, and of the sin that dwells in his heart, and is so inattentive to the sins of life that he thinks himself in a manner blameless; he will, like the proud and haughty Pharisee, thank God he is not as other men are: but when a man comes to see the vileness of his nature, the swarms of sin within him, as well as the iniquity of his life, like the humble publican, not daring to lift up his eyes to heaven, will smite upon his breast and say, *God be merciful to me, a sinner!* and very often so it is

that a sin which a man has been guilty of, though the guilt of it is removed from him, yet he retains such a sense of it, as that it keeps him humble all his days; this was the case of the apostle Paul, who, having been a persecutor of the church of God, though he obtained mercy, and knew his sin was pardoned, yet a sense of that sin always abode with him, and was an humbling consideration to him, 1 Cor. xv. 9. and if a man has not any particular sin that thus affects him, yet the consideration of indwelling sin, and the daily infirmities of life, a sense of them will keep him humble continually.——3. From a view of the insufficiency of a man's own righteousness to justify him before God; while a man trusts in himself that he is righteous, he will be proud of himself, and despise others; whilst he fancies that, *touching the righteousness of the law, he is blameless*, he will be stout-hearted, and not submit to the righteousness of Christ; whilst a Pharisee has a few husks to fill his belly, and some rags of outward righteousness to his back, he will be as proud as Lucifer: nor will any man be truly humble until he finds himself *wretched, and miserable, and poor, and blind, and naked;* which, when it was the case of the apostle Paul, and not before, then he desired to be *found in Christ, and in his righteousness;* Phil. iii. 9.——4. From a sight of the loveliness and glory of Christ; a sight of which will put a man out of conceit with himself, and make him look little and mean in his own eyes; as it did Isaiah, when he saw the glory of Christ in a very exalted and resplendent manner, Isa. vi. 5. Christ is the Sun of righteousness; and, as with respect to the natural sun, it is in its own light we see it, and in a ray or beam of it behold innumerable motes, otherwise not discerned by us; so when Christ, the Sun of righteousness, shines forth in his light, we see his glories and excellencies in their lustre and splendour; and our own sins, failings, and infirmities; all which tend to humiliation. When that supernatural light shone about Saul the Pharisee, he became at once as humble and submissive as may be, and said, Lord, *what wilt thou have me to do?* a sight of Christ, and of the glory of his person, though seen but through a glass, is transforming, and changes *into the same image;* one part of which image lies in meekness, or humility of mind. ——5. From a view of the greatness and majesty of God, and of the frailty and vileness of man compared together: this was what humbled Job, and brought him to a right sense of things, and to a suitable behaviour under the providence of God towards him; when having contended with God, he is called upon by him out of the whirlwind to answer; and, being confounded with a sense of God's greatness and his own vileness, replied, *Behold, I am vile; what shall I answer thee?* and still more plainly and fully, having observed the omnipotence and omniscience of God, thus humbly expresses himself, *I have heard of thee, by the hearing of the ear, but now mine eye seeth thee; wherefore I abhor myself, and repent in dust and ashes!* Job xl. 4, 5. and xlii. 5, 6.——6. From a spiritual knowledge of divine things; natural knowledge *puffeth up;* the wise philosophers among the heathens, with all their boasted morality, were as full of pride as men could well be; their characters are, *proud boasters,* Rom. i. 21, 30. a Pharisee, with all his knowledge of the law and of righteousness, is a vain empty man, and is proud of what he does not truly understand; and so he will remain, till he comes to know Christ and him crucified, and then he will *count all things but loss for the excellency of the knowledge of Christ Jesus* his *Lord*, whom he only then will determine to know, and in whom he will glory; no man is truly humble till he learns that mortifying lesson, *If any among you seemeth to be wise in this world, let him become a fool, that he may be wise,* 1 Cor. iii. 18. ——7. From an experimental knowledge of the gospel scheme; the tendency of which is, to stain the pride of man, to abase the creature, and exalt the riches of divine grace; to prevent men from glorying in anything of themselves, and to exclude all boasting in them: it places salvation entirely on the grace of God, to the exclusion of works, as the cause of it; the Spirit of God, in the Gospel, blows a blast upon all the goodliness of men; and such who are evangelized by it, or cast into a gospel-mould, that form of doctrine into which they are experimentally delivered, are always humble, meek, and lowly-minded. I say experimentally, because men may have notions of evangelical doctrine, and be proud of these notions, not having a true experience of them.

Thirdly, The excellency and usefulness of this grace.

1. It is well-pleasing to God; *A meek and quiet spirit is in the sight of God of*

great price, highly valued, 1. Pet. iii. 4. the Lord takes pleasure in such, and therefore beautifies them, and puts an honour upon them; he looks at him that is poor, of a contrite and humble spirit, with delight and complacency; and to such modest souls he says, *Let me see thy countenance—for thy countenance is comely;* when a proud look, and one proud in heart, are an abomination to him, Cant. ii. 14. Prov. vi. 16, 17. and xvi. 5.——2. It makes a man most like to Christ, who was prophesied of as *lowly*, meek, and humble; and who says of himself, and proposes himself for imitation, *Learn of me for I am meek and lowly;* and the apostle beseeches the saints, *by the meekness of Christ;* and which appeared throughout his whole state of humiliation on earth; see Zech. ix. 9. Matt. xi. 29. 2 Cor. x. 1.——3. It is the saint's clothing and ornament; pride is the devil's livery; but humility is the clothing of the servants of Christ, the badge by which they are known; so some observe the word signifies a servant's garment in 1 Pet. v. 5. *Be ye clothed with humility;* not that it is the saint's robe of righteousness, and garment of salvation, or his justifying righteousness before God; rather his inward garment of sanctification, at least a part of it, which makes all *glorious within;* and it makes a great shew in a man's outward conversation; both in his walk before God, with whom he is required to *walk humbly;* and in his conversation before men, humility makes him to shine, and greatly recommends him; it is very ornamental to him; the word translated, clothed, in the above text, has the signification of ornamental knots, as some think; and a meek spirit is called an *ornament;* it is thought there is an allusion to the ornaments of women, and to knots of ribbons worn by them in one part or another, as on their breasts; and it is as if the apostle should say, Let others adorn themselves with knots as they will, but let your breast-knot be humility. ——4. It is of great use in various duties and exercises of religion; it is of use in prayer, to behave before God with a proper awe and reverence of him; considering, that he is in heaven and they on earth; that he is the great God and an holy Being, and they *dust and ashes*, sinful dust and ashes, who take upon them to speak unto him; and such humble souls God regards; *he forgetteth not the cry of the humble*, Psalm ix. 12. the prayer of the humble publican was heard, and he preferred to the proud Pharisee, Luke xviii. 14. It is of use in preaching the word; which should be done, not in an ostentatious way, to shew a man's parts and abilities, and with great swelling words of vanity; but the Lord is to be served in the gospel of his Son, *with all humility of mind*, and with a subjection to the word of God, as the rule. And it is of use in hearing and receiving the word; *Receive with meekness the engrafted word, which is able to save your souls*, Acts xx. 19. James i. 21. And it is of use in giving a reason of hope, and making a confession of faith before men; *Be ready always to give an answer to every man that asketh you a reason of the hope that is in you, with meekness and fear*, 1 Pet. iii. 15. which may have respect both to him that asks the reason, which should be asked, not in a haughty, insolent, and imperious manner, and with an intention to expose and deride, such deserve no answer; for pearls are not to be cast before swine, nor what is holy to be given to dogs; and with respect to him that gives the reason, which should be done with the fear of God, and with a view to his glory, and not to display a man's own gifts and knowledge. Likewise it is of use in restoring backsliders, who are to be used in a spirit of meekness, gently and tenderly, Gal. vi. 1. and so in instructing such who oppose the gospel and contradict themselves, 2 Tim. ii. 24, 25. Also it may be made use of in a man's conversation to great advantage, and recommend him, and the religion he professes, unto others, James iii. 13. not in a way of pride and boasting, but with humility and lowliness of mind; see 1 Pet. iii. 1—4.

Fourthly, The arguments, reasons, and motives, encouraging to such a disposition of mind.

1. The displeasure of God at a contrary behaviour and conduct; *Be clothed with humility; for God resisteth the proud*, 1 Pet. v. 5. he sets himself against them, and it is a dreadful thing to have God an opponent; there is no standing against him and contending with him; of all men the proud are an abomination to him, these are a smoke in his nose; those who exalt themselves and despise others are sure to be abased; he scatters the proud in the imagination of their hearts, confounds their schemes, and brings them themselves to destruction.——2. God gives more grace to the humble; for that is the meaning

of the phrase, *He giveth grace unto the lowly,* Prov. iii. 34. which is referred to in 1 Pet. v. 5. and so explained in James iv. 6. that is, more grace; for a man must first have grace ere he can be humble, or to make him humble; and then more grace is promised and given to him as such.—— 3. The Lord dwells with humble persons; they are a fit and proper habitation for God, Isa. lvii. 15. see chap lxvi. 1, 2. ——4. When such are disconsolate and sorrowful, the Lord comforts them, and fills them with joy and gladness; for this end the gospel is preached, and was preached by Christ himself, to be *good tidings to the meek;* and when these are cast down, through the prevalence of sin, the force of temptation, and divine desertions, whereby they are humbled, the Lord raises them up again; *the Lord lifteth up the meek,* Psalm cxlvii. 6. and there is a gracious promise, that *the meek shall increase their joy in the Lord,* Isa. xxix. 19.——5. When they are hungry and in want of food, the Lord feeds them to satisfaction; *the meek shall eat and be satisfied,* Psalm xxii. 26. yea, when they are in distress, God will work miracles for them, rather than they shall want, Isa. xli. 17, 18, 19.—— 6. When they want direction and instruction, he will guide and teach them; *the meek will he guide in judgment; the meek will he teach his way,* Psalm xxv. 9. guide them into all truth as it is in Jesus; and teach them the ways and methods of his grace towards them; and the ways of duty in which he would have them to walk.——7. Humility is the way to preferment, to honour, grandeur, and happiness; *before honour is humility; yea, by humility and the fear of the Lord are riches, and honour, and life,* Prov. xvi. 18. and xviii. 12. and xxii. 4. and this is God's usual way, to abase those that exalt themselves, and to exalt them that are humble, Luke xviii. 14.——8. An inheritance is promised to the meek and humble; *the meek shall inherit the earth,* Psa. xxxvii. 11. the same is promised by Christ, Matt. v. 5. not the present earth, and the things of it, though good men have the promise of the life that now is, and are heirs of the world, and the world is theirs; but the new earth, in which none but righteous men will dwell with Christ a thousand years, 2 Pet. iii. 13.——9. Such are and shall be saved; *and he* (God) *shall save the humble person,* both temporally and eternally, Job xxii. 29. he saves such in time; in a time of temporal judgments on the earth, God then arises to save all the meek of the earth; and when Christ comes to judgment with righteousness, he will judge the poor, and reprove with equity, for the meek of the earth, Psalm lxxvi. 9. Isa xi. 4. and he will save them eternally; for they are the same with *the poor in spirit,* whose is the kingdom of heaven, Matt. v. 3.

CHAP. XV.

OF SELF-DENIAL.

SELF-DENIAL accompanies humility; where the one is, the other is; a self-denying man is an humble man, and an humble man is a self-denying man. *Proud, boasters, are lovers of their own selves,* and cannot by any means deny themselves; but the meek and humble, the followers of the lowly Jesus, *deny themselves,* and go after him; *If any man will come after me,* says Christ, that is, be a disciple of his, *let him deny himself, and take up his cross, and follow me,* Matt. xvi. 24. this is one of the hardest lessons to be learnt in the school of Christ, by his disciples; and no man can be a disciple of Christ without learning it.

I. It will be proper to inquire what self-denial is, or what it is for a man to deny himself.

1. It is not to deny what a man is or has; what he truly is, and what he really has; for that would be a falsehood; in this sense *God cannot deny himself,* 2 Tim. ii. 13. not his nature, and the perfections of it; or do, or affirm anything contrary thereunto. So a man ought not to deny himself as a man, nor the rational powers which he is possessed of; one may indeed, speaking in the language of another, and as expressing the meanness and contempt in which he is held by such, say, *I am a worm, and no man,* as David the type, and Christ his antitype, did; a man may also, in a comparative sense, with respect to others, and as exaggerating his own folly, ignorance, and stupidity, say, as Asaph did, *So foolish was I and ignorant, I was as a beast;* or was a very beast, *before thee,* in thy sight, or could not be otherwise reckoned of by thee: and so Agur; *Surely, I am more brutish than any man, and have not the understanding of a man,* in comparison of others, and having a very low share of it, in his own opinion, Psalm lxxiii. 22. Prov. xxx. 2. in these senses such phrases may be admitted; otherwise it would not

be true of a man, nor doing justice to himself, to say that he was no other than *a horse and a mule, which have no understanding.* Nor should a man deny what he has, of the external benefits and blessings of providence; if God bestows riches and honour upon a man, as he did on David, he should own them as coming to him from God, as David did, and bless God for such benefits, and make use of them for the glory of God, and the good of his interest; and if God has bestowed internal endowments on men, gifts and talents, qualifying for public service and usefulness, some way or another, they are to own them, and use them, and not wrap them up in a napkin, or hide them in the earth, which is interpretatively to deny that they have them. Nor should a truly good and gracious man deny what he is and has; but acknowledge it, and how by grace he came by it; and say with the apostle, *By the grace of God I am what I am;* if a man is a believer in Christ he should confess his faith in him, Rom. x. 10. there were some among the Jews, in the times of Christ, who believed he was the Messiah, and yet confessed him not; because they *loved the praise of men,* were lovers of themselves, and could not deny themselves of praise from men; yet such non-confession of Christ is tacitly a denial of him, and is so interpreted by Christ, Matt. x. 31, 32. but especially when a man has true faith in Christ, has spiritual knowledge of him, and is a real disciple of his, to deny this is very criminal; this was the sin of Peter, when challenged with being acquainted with Jesus, and being a disciple of his, denied that he knew him, and that he was one of them that belonged to him. And so if a man has faith in Christ, and good hope through grace, and the grace of God has been exceeding abundant, with faith and love, which is in Christ, he ought to be very careful that he does not deny these things. There is in some weaker Christians, I do not know well what name to call it by, it is an over-modesty, a thinking and speaking over-meanly of themselves; and which they affect to do, and carry things to too great a length very much this way, as if they had no faith, nor love, and scarce any hope; and are ready to express themselves in such sort as seems to border, at least, upon a denial of the work of grace upon their souls; and is like a tearing up by the roots, as much as in them lies, the very principles of grace in them; which should never be encouraged, but discountenanced; the least measure of grace should be owned, and men should be thankful for it, and pray for an increase of it.

2. To deny a man's self is not to refuse favours conferred on him in a course of providence; nor to neglect a lawful use of them; nor to take no care of himself and of his affairs.—(1.) Self-denial does not require that a man should refuse temporal honours and riches bestowed on him in a providential way; so Joseph, though a self-denying man, did not refuse the honours, and the tokens of them, Pharaoh gave him, when he made him ruler over the land of Egypt; nor David, when the tribes made him king over all Israel; nor Daniel, when he was advanced in Nebuchadnezzar's court, and was honoured by Belshazzar, and prospered in the reigns of Darius and Cyrus; but these good men improved them all to the glory of God and the good of others.—(2.) Nor are the creatures of God, and the use of them, to be rejected; *Every creature of God is good, and nothing to be refused,* 1 Tim. iv. 4. nor ought a man to debar himself of the free and lawful use of them; we are told there is nothing better for a man than to enjoy the fruit of his labour, and that is his portion, and the gift of God; and that to withhold it from himself is a sore evil under the sun, vanity, and an evil disease, Eccles. ii. 24. and v. 19. and vi. 1, 2. only care should be taken in using the world, and worldly things, that they are not abused, 1 Cor. vii. 31. this is all with respect to worldly things that self-denial requires; even a non-gratification of the carnal and sensual appetite to excess; which branch of self-denial the wise man expresses by *putting a knife to the throat;* see Prov. xxiii. 2.—(3.) Nor should a man be careless of his life, and health, and family, though he should not be anxiously careful for life, for food, and raiment to support and secure it; yet he may be lawfully careful for life, which is better than them; and so likewise for his health, to preserve it by proper means; as the apostle Paul advised the mariners with him, to take meat for their health's sake; and Timothy to the use of wine for his often infirmities, Acts xxvii. 33, 34. 1 Tim. v. 23. and in like manner a man should be careful for his family; which should he not, it would be so far from being reckoned self-denial, in a good sense, that it might be justly treated as a denial of the faith, 1 Tim. v. 8.—

(4.) There is a self-love which is not criminal, nor contrary to the grace of self-denial; *For no man ever yet hated his own flesh*, Eph. v. 29. himself, which he is not obliged to by, yea, would be contrary to, the law of nature, and the law of God; to take care of a man's self, and to preserve his life, is the first principle and law of nature;[1] and it is commanded by the law of God, that a man should love himself; for according to that, he is to *love his neighbour as himself*, and therefore must first love himself to love his neighbour as himself; there is a φιλαυτια, an inordinate love of a man's self, which is the source of all sin, of covetousness, pride, blasphemy, disobedience to parents, ingratitude, &c. which is carefully to be avoided, 2 Tim. iii. 2, 3, 4.— (5.) Nor is it self-denial, or any part of it, to abuse the body in any respect, and even on religious accounts, by cutting it with knives and lancets, as Baal's priests; or by lashing it with whips and scourges, as the *papists* for penance; or by severe fastings and abstinence, by *neglecting it, not in any honour to the satisfying of the flesh*, as some ancient heretics in the apostle's days, Col. ii. 23. nor should anything be done that endangers life, and much less should any, under whatsoever pretence, lay violent hands on themselves, to which sometimes the temptations of Satan lead, Matt. iv. 6. But,

3. Self-denial lies in a man's renouncing, foregoing, and postponing all his pleasures, profits, relations, interest, and whatever he enjoys, which may be in competition with Christ from love to him, and to be given up at his command; a self-denying man seeks first the kingdom of God and his righteousness, and leaves all other things with God, to bestow upon him as he thinks fit; and what he has given him he is ready to give back again when called for, preferring Christ to all things in heaven and earth; he is ready at command to bring all he has, and lay it at his feet; as the first Christians brought all they had and laid at the feet of the apostles. This is self-denial. The common distribution of it is not amiss, into natural or civil self, sinful self, and righteous self; all which a self-denying Christian is made willing to part with.

First, With natural and civil self, with things relative both to soul and body, of which a man's self consists.

1. The soul, with its powers and faculties of understanding, will, and affections; and there are self-denying acts, which respect each of these.—(1.) The understanding; and it is a self-denying act in a man, *to lean not to his own understanding*, which is natural to him; but give it up to God, to be instructed, guided, and directed by him in all religious matters, according to his word, and the influences of his grace and Spirit; thus Saul, when called by grace, *conferred not with flesh and blood*, with the carnal reasonings of his mind, whether he should profess and preach Christ the Son of God, or no; but immediately set about it, following the divine light and supernatural instructions given him: and this is the case of all self-denying Christians, when their reason is brought to stoop to divine revelation; and their carnal reasonings, and vain imaginations, and their high towering and exalted thoughts of themselves, and of their own understandings, are cast down, and brought into the obedience of Christ.—(2.) The will; and then does a man deny himself, when his will becomes subject to the will of God; when, with good old Eli, he says, *It is the Lord, let him do what seemeth him good*, though ever so disagreeable to himself, and the interests of his family; and so the friends of the apostle Paul, when they were so desirous of his continuance, and found that all entreaties prevailed not, said, *The will of the Lord be done!* and when in all cases, the will of a man is brought to this, then may he be said to deny himself, of which Christ is a pattern to him; *Not my will, but thine be done!* see 1 Sam. iii. 18. Acts xxi. 14. Luke xxii. 42.—(3.) The affections; these are sometimes called *inordinate affections*, Col. iii. 5. as when they are out of due course and order, when the world, and the things of it, are loved with an immoderate love, in a manner inconsistent with the love of God, and when friends or relations are loved more than Christ; now self-denial checks and restrains the affections, and reduces them to proper order, and forbids such a love of the world, and the things of it; and will not suffer a man to love father or mother, son or daughter, more than Christ; but will declare such unworthy of him, 1 John ii. 15. Matt. x. 37.

2. The body, and its members, and things relative to that, and all external

---

[1] Principio, generi animantium omni est a natura tributum, ut se, vitam corpusque tueatur, declinetque ea quæ nocitura videantur. Cicero de Officiis, l. 1. c. 4.

things: about these self-denial is exercised; as,—(1.) When the members of the body are restrained from the service of sin; when *sin is not suffered to reign in the mortal body*, and the *members* thereof are not *yielded as instruments of unrighteousness unto sin*, but *the deeds of* it are *mortified, and no provision is made for the flesh to fulfil the lusts thereof*, Rom. vi. 12, 13. and viii. 13. and xiii. 14.—(2.) When external honours from men are not sought for, only the honour which comes from God; when a man is content to suffer the loss of fame, name, and credit among men for Christ's sake; to be defamed, made the filth of the world, and the off-scouring of all things; to pass through honour and dishonour, good report and bad report, and suffer all indignities for the sake of religion. This is self-denial. An instance of this we have in Moses, who for forty years lived in the court of Pharaoh, and enjoyed the honours, pleasures, and riches of that court; yet denied himself of them all, chose to visit and rank himself among his brethren the Israelites, then in a low and despicable condition, and refused to be called the son of Pharaoh's daughter; choosing rather to suffer affliction with the people of God, and reproach for Christ's sake, than to enjoy the pleasures of sin and the riches of Egypt, Acts vii. 23. Heb. xi. 25, 26.—(3.) When worldly profits and emoluments are left for the sake of Christ, and the interest of religion; this is self-denial. As when the disciples, one and another of them, left their fishing-nets and boats, and worldly employments, and followed Christ; yea, Peter, in the name of them all, could say, *Behold, we have forsaken all, and followed thee*, Matt. iv. 20, 22. and xix. 27. So Matthew, at the receipt of custom, which, perhaps, was a lucrative and profitable employment; yet called by Christ, left it and followed him; Matt. ix. 9. And so many a gospel-minister has given up himself to the ministry of the word, when worldly offers and views have directed him another way; and many private Christians have joyfully suffered the confiscation of goods, and even imprisonment of the body, for the sake of religion and a good conscience; this is self-denial. An instance of the contrary of all this we have in a young man, who could not part with his worldly substance and follow Christ, of whom he asked, what good thing he must do to have eternal life? and was answered, *Keep the commandments;* these he thought an easy task, and what he had been always used to, and seemed highly delighted with it; *All these things I have kept from my youth; what lack I yet?* a hard lesson is then set him to learn; *Sell that thou hast, and give to the poor;* and though he was promised treasure in heaven, it did not countervail; *He went away sorrowful, for he had great possessions*, which he could not part with, and deny himself of, Matt. xix.16—22.—(4.) The nearest and dearest friends and relations, which are a part of a man's self, these are to be left, when God calls for it; so Abraham was commanded to come out from his country and kindred, and his father's house, which, though a self-denying order, he was obedient to; and so the people of God, when called by grace, are directed to forsake their own people, and their father's house, and when these attempt to obstruct them in the ways of God, they are not to be obeyed, but resisted; yea, even to be *hated*, comparatively, that is, less love and respect are to be shewn them than to Christ, Luke xiv. 26. a great instance of self-denial of this kind we have in Abraham, who was called to part with his son, his only son, his beloved son, the son of the promise, from whom the Messiah was to spring, to offer him upon a mount he should be shewn; this was a great trial of faith, an hard lesson of self-denial to learn, and yet he withheld not his son from God; by which he gave evidence of a self-denying spirit, of his love to God, his fear of him, and obedience to his command.—(5.) Health and hazard of life; as when men risk their health in the service of God and Christ, and true religion; so Epaphroditus, for the work of Christ was nigh unto death; and many, like the apostle Paul, have spent and been spent in the cause of God, by hard studies and frequent ministrations; so Paul and Barnabas hazarded their lives, through the rage of men, for the name of our Lord Jesus, preaching the gospel; and Aquila and Priscilla were ready to lay down their own necks for the apostle, that is, to risk their lives for his sake.—(6.) Life itself is to be laid down when called for; the apostle Paul did not count his life dear to himself, but ready to part with it for the sake of the gospel: and of others we read, that they loved not their lives unto death; and this is the great instance of self-denial Christ gives, Matt. xvi. 24, 25.

Secondly, Another branch of self-denial

lies in denying sinful self; this lesson, not nature, but grace, teaches, even to deny *ungodliness and worldly lusts,* which include all kinds of sin; internal lusts and external actions of sin; sins of heart, lip, and life; every thing that is contrary to God and his righteous law. This is a hard lesson to learn; to part with sinful self is not an easy task, sin is so natural to men, they are conceived and born in it, are transgressors from the womb, and have lived in sin from their youth upward; sin and the soul have been long companions, and are loth to part; sin is as natural to the sinner as blackness to the Ethiopian, and spots to the leopard; it is as grateful to him as cold water to a thirsty soul; and is like a sweet morsel in his mouth, and he hides and spares it, and cares not to forsake it; it promises him much pleasure, though short-lived, vain, and fallacious; some sins are right hand and right eye sins, as dear as the right hand and right eye be; and to cut off and pluck out such and cast them away, is a great piece of self-denial; and is hard work, until the Spirit of God thoroughly convinces a man of the exceeding sinfulness of sin, what an evil and bitter thing it is, and how pernicious in its effects and consequences; and then being called and required to forsake it, does, and says with Ephraim, *What have I to do any more with idols?* and this self-denial appears by loathing it and themselves for it; by detesting and abhorring it, and themselves on account of it; and by repenting of it in deep humiliation for it, by lamenting the indwelling and prevalence of it, and by praying against it; by abstaining from fleshly lusts which war against the soul, and from all appearances of sin; by making no provision for the flesh to fulfil the lusts of it; by opposing them, resisting unto blood, striving against sin; and by declaring to have no fellowship with the unfruitful works of darkness: so persons and things are said to be denied, when there is an aversion to them, a rejection of them, a disowning them as belonging to them, and as having any connection with them; so Moses was denied by the Israelites, and Christ by the Jews, Acts. iii. 14. and vii. 35. A branch of this part of self-denial lies in parting with sinful companions, which are a sort of second self; and especially sinful relations, whom to part with is difficult work, as to withstand their solicitations, earnest entreaties, enticing language, and fair promises of pleasure and profit; as also to bear their reproaches, revilings, and censures, on refusing to associate with them; for *he that departs from evil maketh himself a prey,* Isa. lix. 15. but being called by divine grace to come out from among them, and to be separate from them; and being convinced of the folly and danger of keeping company with them, and having better companions, and more preferable communion and fellowship, they are called into; and having had too long an abode with them to their great grief and loss, determine through the grace of God to leave them, and to have nothing more to do with them; which is self-denial.

Thirdly, Another branch of self-denial is to deny righteous self, which is not to refuse to do works of righteousness for necessary uses, to glorify God, to adorn the doctrine of God our Saviour, and a profession of it; to shew the genuineness and truth of faith, and to do good to others; this the grace of God teaches and obliges unto: but, to deny righteous self, is to renounce all trust in and dependance on a man's own righteousness for justification before God, and acceptance with him; and to submit to the righteousness of Christ, and depend upon that for such purposes. Now this is a hard lesson to learn, for a man to quit all trust in himself that he is righteous, and to depend upon the righteousness of another; to live out of himself upon another; to be beholden entirely to the free grace of God, and to the righteousness of Christ, disclaiming all works done by himself for his justification and whole salvation, is disagreeable to self; it is against the grain; a man's righteousness is his own, and he does not care to part with it, he would fain hold it fast; it is the effect of great toil and labour, and which he has endeavoured to establish and settle fast, and to have it all pulled down at once he cannot bear it; it is matter of glorying and boasting, and to have this excluded, and to be stript of all his feathers, is not pleasing to flesh and blood; it is his idol he has bowed unto, and to take this away from him is as cutting as it was to Micah, when his images were stolen from him, and he said, *Ye have taken away my gods, and what have I more?* but when the Spirit of God convinces a man of the insufficiency of his own righteousness to justify him before God, and of the excellency of the righteousness of Christ for such a purpose, then he quits his own, and lays hold on that; an instance of this kind of self-denial we have in the apostle Paul, who was at first a self-righteous man, who thought that touching the righteousness of the law he was blameless; he counted it gain unto him, and trusted in it, and expected to be justified and saved by it; but when he came to see the imperfection of it, and was convinced of its unprofitableness to God, he counted it loss and dung, and rejected it as such, desiring to be *found in Christ*, and in his righteousness, and not his own, Phil. iii. 6—9.

II. There are various arguments or motives, which may be made use of to excite truly gracious souls to the exercise of this grace of self-denial in the several branches of it.

1. It is required of them; it is an injunction of Christ on his disciples, even all of them, and therefore to be strictly regarded, complied with, and exercised; *If any man will come after me*, is desirous of being a disciple and follower of Christ, *let him deny himself*, Matt. xvi. 24. nay, this is necessary to a man's being a disciple of Christ, he cannot be one without it; see Luke xiv. 26, 27.——2. Christ has not only commanded it, but he has set an example of it himself; he denied himself for our sakes; came forth from his Father, and came down from heaven to serve us; though he was rich, for our sakes he became poor, that we through his poverty, might be made rich; though he was in the form of God, and thought it no robbery to be equal with God, yet he so far humbled and denied himself, as to be found in fashion as a man, and in the form of a servant, and became obedient unto death, the death of the cross; he pleased not himself, but patiently bore the reproaches of men, which could not but be very disagreeable to him; and he endured the contradiction of sinners against himself; and in all which and more, he was an example of self-denial, Phil. ii. 5—8.——3. The examples of saints in all ages may serve to excite and encourage to it; as of Abraham, in leaving his country and father's house, and especially in offering up his son at the command of God; in Moses, refusing to be called the son of Pharaoh's daughter; in the Old Testament-saints and martyrs, who suffered bonds, imprisonment, trial of cruel mockings, and death itself, in various shapes; and so in others since: in the apostles of Christ, who left all and followed him; an instance of denial of sinful self may be observed in Zaccheus and others; and of righteous self in the apostle Paul.——4. If a man does not deny himself, as required of God, he sets up himself for god, makes a god of himself, and is guilty of idolatry; such live to themselves, and not unto God and Christ, which the love of Christ constrains unto, namely, that they who live, should not live to themselves, but to him who died for them and rose again; yea, that they should none of them neither live to themselves, nor die to themselves, but to the Lord; that both living and dying they may appear to be his, and not their own, 2 Cor. v. 14, 15. Rom. xiv. 7, 8.——5. The loss and gain of not denying and of denying self, should be considered. Such who think to save themselves by not denying themselves, lose themselves and their own souls; lose Christ and his righteousness, heaven and eternal life; when those who deny themselves for Christ's sake, find the life of their souls, gain Christ and his righteousness, have treasure in heaven, the recompense of reward, the more enduring substance, Matt. xvi. 25, 26. Phil. iii. 7, 8. Heb. xi. 26, 27. and x. 34.

CHAP. XVI.

OF RESIGNATION TO THE WILL OF GOD.

SUBMISSION, or resignation of the will of man to the will of God, is a part of self-denial, as has been observed in the preceding chapter, and therefore properly next requires a distinct consideration. It is no other than an entire acquiescence in the will of God in all things, and especially in adverse dispensations of providence, which is a trial of it; as in Eli, when he was told of the distresses that should come upon his family, said, *It is the Lord, let him do what seemeth him good!* 1 Sam. iii. 18. and in much the same temper and disposition of mind was David, when he ordered the ark to be carried back to Jerusalem, which he was obliged to leave, 2 Sam. xv. 25, 26. This is no other than for a man to have his will swallowed up in the will of God, and to have no will of his own, but what is the Lord's; or only to will what he wills, and is pleasing to him; this, in its highest perfection, was in Christ in the midst of his agonies; *Not my will, but thine be done!* Something of this kind may be expected from a follower of Christ; but that anything similar to it should drop from the lips of an heathen, is somewhat extraordinary; and yet Epictetus gives this advice, *Will nothing but what God wills ;*[1] there is indeed a difference between giving advice and acting up to it, and between theory and practice; and yet this same heathen says,[2] "I yield my appetite to God; does he will that I should have a fever? I will it also. Does he will that I should attempt anything? I likewise will it. Would he have me desire anything? I also will it. Would he have me enjoy anything? the same is my will. Does he nill? I also nill. Would he have me die? I am willing to die." How far he said this with truth, and acted according to it, I will not say; but to have the will so resigned to the will of God, highly becomes a christian. But,

First, There must be much done to the will of man, and much management of it, under the power of divine grace, to bring the will of man to be subject to the will of God. For,

1. The will of man is very stubborn and inflexible; we often read of the hardness of the heart, and of its being hardened through the deceitfulness of sin; and of the stony heart, a heart as hard as a stone, yea, as an adamant stone, on which no impressions can be made, nor becomes pliable and flexible by any methods made use of; and such is the obstinacy of the will of man.——2. It is averse to all that is good; it hates the good and loves the evil; it hates the good law of God and is not subject to it; nor can it be, without the power of divine grace; it hates good men and all their good instructions; as men to do good have no knowledge, so neither will they *understand;* they have no will nor desire to understand what is good, and still less to practice it.——3. The will of men is biassed to, and bent upon that which is evil; their hearts are *fully set in them to do evil*, Eccles. viii. 11. their language is, *we will walk after our own devices, &c.* Jer. xviii. 12. and xliv. 16, 17. ——4. The will of man is opposite to the will of God in all things: yea, in things that are most for his good; even for his everlasting welfare and happiness. The will of God is, that men should be saved, or have everlasting life and salvation only by Christ; but the will of men is averse to this way of salvation; *Ye will not come to me, that ye might have life*, John v. 40.

the will of God is, that men should be justified in his sight, not by the works of the law, but by the righteousness of Christ; but, on the contrary, so stout-hearted, and far from this way of righteousness, are men, that they seek justification, not by faith, but, as it were, by the works of the law, and go about to establish their own righteousness, and will not submit to the righteousness of Christ. God has set up Christ as king over Zion, and requires obedience to his word and ordinances; but such is the perverseness of men's wills, that they declare, saying, *We will not have this Man to reign over us;* and therefore break the bands, and cast away the cords of his laws and ordinances from them: and if they are so averse to the methods of his grace and kingdom, then much more so to the dispensation of his providence.——

5. The carnal mind and will of man is *enmity* itself *against God*, his law and gospel, his purposes and providences; it is full of rebellion to him; it rebels against the light of nature, and against the law of God; the Israelites were always a rebellious people, though favoured with the knowledge of the will of God above all people; and so the elect of God, whilst in a state of nature, are styled *rebellious*, Psalm lxviii. 18.——6. It is one of the characters of sinful men, that they are *self-willed*, 2 Pet. ii. 10. men naturally desire to have their own wills and ways; they do not care to be contradicted and gainsayed; even God's elect, before conversion, are studiously *fulfilling the desires of the flesh*, or the wills of the flesh, their carnal wills, and choose to live to the lusts of the flesh, and not to the will of God. In such a bad and depraved state is the will of man naturally; so that much must be done with it to bring it into subjection to the will of God.

Now the various steps which God takes, and the various things he does to the will of man, in order to work it up, and bring it to a submission to his will, are these: ——1. He *breaks* the wills of men, he crosses them, by one afflictive providence after another; and brings them by degrees to give up their wills to his; he will not let them have their own wills and ways; but thwarts them, and denies them those things their wills are set upon; until at length they are content that his will should be done; as creatures not used to a yoke,

[1] Μηδεν αλλο θελε, η α ο θεος θελε, Arrian. Epictet. l. 2. c. 17.

[2] Ib. l. 3. c. 26.

at first are very reluctant, and wriggle and toss about, and will not easily submit, until some rough methods are taken to break them. Graceless men are sons of Belial, children without a yoke; such are the people of God before conversion; but then they are called to take a yoke upon them, not only of Christ's commands and ordinances, but of afflictions and reproaches for Christ's sake; when they are, at first, like *a bullock unaccustomed to the yoke*, and it sits uneasy upon them; but afterwards, when they are more used to it, they become more patient and quiet under it; hence it is said to be *good for a man that he bear the yoke in his youth;* for thereby he is inured to it, and bears it more quietly and patiently, Lam. iii. 27. it not being perceived so heavy as at first.[3]——2. The Lord exerts his mighty power upon the wills of men, and of unwilling, makes them willing; when the power of God is put forth upon them, then they are made willing, as to serve the Lord, and to be saved by him in his own way; so to part with every thing he calls for, and to bear and suffer whatever is his will and pleasure; but such a willing disposition is not *by might* and *power* of men; a man cannot make himself willing, or work himself to such a submissive frame; but it is effected by the Spirit of God, and the power of his efficacious grace; and this is not done by force and compulsion; God does not force the will, but allures and attracts it; works upon it, as Austin says, with an omnipotent sweetness, and a sweet omnipotence.——3. The Lord takes away the obduracy and hardness, the stubbornness and stiffness of the will, and makes it flexible to his will; he takes away the stony heart, and gives an heart of flesh, a soft heart, susceptible of impressions, by which it may be wrought upon to a compliance to the will of God; this he sometimes does by his word, which is as an hammer to break the rock in pieces; and sometimes by afflictive providences, by which God sometimes makes *the heart soft*, as he did Job's; though perhaps he may mean it in a somewhat different sense, Job xxiii. 16. men, in a state of nature, their *neck is an iron sinew*, or the sinew of their neck is like a bar of iron, which will not bend; but such a bar, when put into the fire, and made soft, it may be bent at pleasure; so men, called by grace, and put into the furnace of affliction, they become soft and pliable to the will of God.——
4. The will of man is made free by the power of divine grace in conversion, which before was a slave[4] to sin and Satan, and brought into bondage; and whilst it so continues it is not, and cannot be obedient to the will of God; whilst it is a servant to divers lusts and pleasures, it cannot willingly submit to adverse dispensations of providence; but if *the Son makes* it *free*, it is *free indeed*, to take up the cross and follow him; when men are *made free from sin*, from the dominion, bondage, and slavery of it, they become *the servants of righteousness, and servants to God*, and submissive to his will, both to do and suffer whatever is his pleasure to call them to. ——5. God effectually works in his people, *both to will and to do of his good pleasure;* he does not create a new faculty of the will, but he frees it from what hinders its operations in a right way, and influences it by his grace to act according to his own will and pleasure; when to *will is present* with them, though sometimes they find want of power to perform as they would; *the spirit is willing*, both to do and suffer what is the will of God; *but the flesh is weak*, and has no strength to act, but throws clogs and difficulties in the way; however the will is so powerfully wrought upon as to say, *Lord what wilt thou have me to do?* I am willing to do anything, and bear anything thou art pleased to call me to, Acts ix. 6. So submissive is the will under a divine influence. I proceed to consider,

Secondly, The various phrases by which submission to the will of God, especially under adverse dispensations of providence, is expressed.

1. To be *still*, and quiet and easy; *Be still, and know that I am God*, Psalm xlvi. 10. which is directed to, amidst the commotions, stirs, and tumults, in the world, and the desolations made in the earth, as the context shews; and is to be understood.—(1.) Not of insensibility and stupidity; that men should be as *still as a stone*, or be like stocks and stones, senseless and unconcerned; they should

---

[3] Magis urgent sæva inexpertos, grave est teneræ cervici jugum, Seneca de Providentia, c. 4.

[4] Luther wrote a book, "De servo arbitrio," of man's will a slave; in which he represents it as a beast of Satan, a captive to his will, which he rides on and guides as he pleases. c. 45. p. 65. c. 200. p. 305.

be sensible of the hand of God in his providences, and own it as directed to in the exhortation, *Know that I am God;* own and acknowledge my hand in all these things; so Eli said, *It is the Lord, let him do what seemeth him good!* and so Job; *The Lord hath given, and the Lord hath taken away!* they should be sensible of the cause of these things; for, as David said, *Is there not a cause?* There is; and that is sin; *If his children forsake my law, &c. then will I visit their transgressions with a rod:* and they should be sensible of the affliction itself; not only feel the rod, but bear it, take notice of it, and learn by it; indeed, sometimes so stupid are men, that *God speaketh once, yea twice,* by an afflictive providence, one after another, *yet man perceiveth it not,* takes no notice of it; it has no effect upon him; though he is *stricken* and *beaten,* he *feels* it not: there are two extremes often in men under the afflicting hand of God; either they are apt to faint, and sink under an affliction, or to neglect it, overlook it, ολιγωρει, make little or nothing of it; both which are guarded against in the exhortation in Heb. xii. 5. Nor,—(2.) Of a stoical apathy is the phrase to be understood; as if a man should be quite unaffected with an afflictive providence; though the affections are to be checked, when they become inordinate, yet there may be a due use of them; they are not indeed to be set on earth, and earthly things, but upon things in heaven; and such a disposition of them will make a man more quiet and easy under the loss of things temporal; yet he is not wholly divested of his affections under such losses; when Job lost all his substance, as well as his children, and was all submission to the will of God, yet he gave manifest tokens of his affections being moved by the providence; as by rending his mantle, shaving his head, and falling down upon the ground: and though christians are not to sorrow for the loss of relations and friends, as the heathens, without hope, and in that immoderate and barbarous manner they did, yet may with moderation; Abraham went to Hebron to mourn for Sarah, and to weep for her, when dead; and Joseph made a mourning for his father seven days; devout men carried Stephen to his grave, and made great lamentation over him; and Christ himself wept over the grave of Lazarus.—(3.) Nor is the phrase expressive of inactivity. The strength of men in such cases is not to *sit still* and do nothing; there is much to be done under afflictive providences; as various graces to be exercised; when men are chastened by the Lord, they are called upon to be *zealous,* and *repent;* and they have need of faith and confidence in the divine promises to support them, which should not be cast away, but exercised; and of patience, that when they have done the will of God, by suffering afflictions, they may receive the promises. And there are duties to be performed, as both prayer and praise; *If any be afflicted let him pray,* for support under affliction, and that it may be sanctified to him, and he may be delivered from it in due time: and praise too, so Job blessed the Lord when he was stripped of all he had; the cross is to be taken up, in which saints are active, and bear it patiently, and through many tribulations follow Christ, and enter into the kingdom. But,—(4.) It is opposed to the fretting of the mind at the prosperity of others, and at their own adversity; which is dehorted from, *fret not thyself,* Psalm xxxvii. 1, 7, 8. and to all impatience, restlessness, and disquietude, under the hand of God; a good man should not act like a bullock unaccustomed to the yoke, and much less like a wild bull in a net; but the phrase signifies, composure of mind, sedateness, a quiet submission to the will of God, and patience under his mighty hand.

2. Submission to the will of God, is expressed by a man's holding his peace, and being dumb and silent; thus Aaron, when he lost his two sons in an awful manner, by fire from heaven; it is said, *And Aaron held his peace,* Lev. x. 2. said not one word against what was done, or as complaining of the providence: so David was dumb when under a sore affliction, Psalm xxxix. 9. and of a good man under the yoke of affliction it is said, *He sitteth alone, and keepeth silence,* Lam. iii. 28. Now,—(1.) All this is to be understood, not as though there was nothing to be said under an afflictive providence; for it should be owned that it is of God, that it is of his appointing, in his secret purposes and decrees; *He performeth the thing that is appointed for me,* Job xxiii. 14. Job is there speaking chiefly of his afflictions, and has respect to them; and as they are appointed in God's purposes, they are brought on by his over-ruling providence; there is *no evil,* of such a kind, in a city, but the Lord has done it; he makes peace,

and *creates evil;* adversity and prosperity are from him, and he sets the one against the other. It should also be acknowledged by the saints, that they are deserving of such afflictions; *Shall we receive good at the hand of God, and shall we not receive evil?* it may be expected. Nor should the people of God be silent in prayer under such providences; God expects to hear from them then; *In their affliction they will seek me early,* for help, support, and deliverance. Nor should they be silent in praise to God, but bless his name; since it might have been worse with them than it is; especially when they are taught of God under their afflictions, and by them, and when they evidently see that they work together for their good; and they should not fail to speak to others of the goodness of God to them; of their gracious experiences in their afflictions, how that everlasting arms are underneath them, their bed is made in their sickness, God is with them when they pass through the fire and through the waters, and he chooses them in the furnace of affliction. But,—(2.) Such silence is opposed to murmuring against God, and complaining of his providence, as the Israelites in the wilderness did; and to charging his ways with inequality, as the Jews in the times of Ezekiel; but it denotes such behaviour as Job's under such providences, who sinned not, nor charged God foolishly, Job i. 22.

3. Submission to the will of God is expressed by *hearing the rod, and him who has appointed it,* Mic. vi. 9. by the *rod* is meant the rod of correction, with which God, as a father, scourges and chastizes his children, called *the rod of God,* because of his appointing, and which he makes use of in a fatherly way; and *the rod of man,* because it is no other than what is common to men, and is used in a kind and tender way, after the manner of men. In which rod there is the voice of the Lord, which cries unto men in a way of reproof for sin, and by commanding them to return from iniquity; which calls for humiliation, and instructs in the way of duty; and then it is heard and hearkened to, when men are obedient and submit to the will of God, signified by it; when their ears are opened to discipline, and they attend to it, and instruction is sealed unto them, and they are impressed by it.

4. The same is signified by men *humbling themselves under the mighty hand of God,* according to the exhortation in 1 Pet. v. 6. by the hand of God is meant his correcting and chastizing hand, which sometimes is heavy, and presses sore; and which Job felt, and therefore cried to his friends to have pity on him, because the hand of the Lord was upon him; and *strong is his hand, and high is his right hand;* and which, though it is laid on in mercy, yet sometimes is very heavy and distressing: and the end and use of it is to humble men; as all the Lord's dealings with the Israelites in the wilderness were to humble them, and to prove them; so are all the Lord's dispensations of providence towards his people, to hide pride from them, and to bring them to his feet, and to own his sovereignty over them; and this is the way to be exalted. In short, all these phrases are expressive of submission to the will of God; the language of them is, *The will of the Lord be done!* Acts xxi. 14. and indeed this should be submitted to in all things; and it should be the constant language of the saints, with respect to every thing in which they are concerned; *If the Lord will, we shall live and do this and that,* James iv. 15. see 1 Cor. iv. 19. It is a phrase often used by Socrates, as may be seen in the writings of Plato, ιαν θεος εθελη, *If God will;* [5] and which well becomes the mouth of a Christian at all times, who ought to be all submission to God, and be wholly absorbed in the will of God; for which,

Thirdly, The following reasons may be given among many.

1st, Whatever is done in providence is done by the Lord; his will and his hand are in it; and this should reconcile the will of man to it, be it what it may; so said Eli, *It is the Lord,* who has said it and will do it, *let him do what seemeth him good!* it was the consideration of this, that the Lord was concerned in all Job's losses, that it was he who gave and took away, which made them sit so easy on his mind; and even to say, *Blessed be the name of the Lord!* and this is what makes and keeps quiet and still, under the most afflictive

---

[5] Indeed this is often to be observed in the mouths of the vulgar; "What God wills must be: If it please God we shall do so and so." Every thing is what pleases God should be. Hence Luther observes, there remains in vulgar minds no less knowledge of God's predestination and prescience than of Deity. De Servo Arbitrio, c. 20. p. 32.

providences, to know that it is the Lord who wills them. As,

1. That he is a sovereign Being, who does according to his will in heaven and in earth, who has the disposal of the whole world, and of all creatures and things in it; he has a sovereign right to all, and may do what he will with his own; give and take away at pleasure; and therefore to be submitted to.——2. That he is immutable, and his will is irresistible; his mind is invariable, and his purpose unalterable; *Who shall disannul it?* make it void and of none effect: *And his hand is stretched out* in providence, to execute his purpose, *and who shall turn it back?* as it would be impious, so in vain to attempt it; for *who hath resisted his will?* his counsel shall stand, and he will do all his pleasure; and therefore his will is to be submitted to, Job xxiii. 13. Isa. xiv. 27.——3. He is not accountable to his creatures; nor is it fitting and reasonable that he should; they are accountable to him, but not he to them; therefore *he giveth no account of any of his matters*, Job xxxiii. 13. as none can *stay his hand*, or stop the course of his providence; so none ought to *say to him, What doest thou?* but a silent submission should be yielded to him.——4. That he is the wise, and the only wise God, and does all his works in wisdom; though he does all things according to his will, in a sovereign way, yet, *after the counsel of his own will;* in the best and wisest manner, as such things are usually done, when done with consultation; as all his works in nature and in grace are made in wisdom, so his works of providence, in which there is a *bathos*, a *depth of the riches both of the wisdom and knowledge of God.* What is said of Christ with respect to his miracles, *He hath done all things well*, is true of God in the dispensations of his providence, and therefore to be submitted to.——5. That he is holy and righteous in all his ways and works, and there is no unrighteousness in him; he cannot be charged with an unjust action, and with any inequality in his ways, and therefore not to be complained of in any respect.——6. That he is a faithful God, and it is in faithfulness he afflicts his people; and while they are under the affliction he will not suffer them to be tempted, or afflicted, above what they are able to bear; nor will he take away his kindness from them, nor break his covenant with them; all which displays his faithfulness, Psalm cxix. 75. and lxxxix. 33, 34. 1 Cor. x. 13.——7. That all his ways are mercy and love to his people; when he hides his face he loves, when he chides he loves, and when he chastizes he loves; the rod is in a Father's hand, and should be submissively attended to.

2dly, What is done by the Lord seems good to him; and what seems good to him must be good; *Let him do what seemeth him good:* he is good originally and underivatively, the fountain of all goodness; there is nothing but goodness in him, and nothing else comes from him, or is done by him; *Thou art good, and doest good*, says David, Psalm cxix. 68. all he did in creation was *very good*, and all he does in providence is very good, even in the adverse dispensations of it: when Isaiah, from the Lord, told Hezekiah what evil things should befal his posterity, he replied, *Good is the word of the Lord, which thou hast spoken*, Isa. xxxix. 6, 7, 8. What God does, it is his pleasure to do, and he will do all his pleasure; he sits in the heavens, and does whatsoever he pleases; and what pleases him should please us.[6] It is said of David, *Whatsoever the king did, pleased all the people*, 2 Sam. iii. 36. What the King of kings does, should please all his people, all his saints, of whom he is King. It was a flattering speech of a courtier to king Astyages, "All is pleasing that the king does,"[7] even when he had treated him in a shocking and barbarous manner: but without any flattery, and with a laudible submission of will to the will of God, every saint may say, whatever the Lord does is pleasing, is all well done; being for his own glory and the good of his people.

CHAP. XVII.

OF PATIENCE.

WITHOUT patience there can be no real self-denial, nor true submission to the will of God in adversity; nor contentment in every state; nor thankfulness for every mercy; it is what accompanies every grace, as faith, hope, and love; hence we read of *the work of faith, and labour of love,*

---

[6] Placeat homini, quidquid Deo placuit, Senecæ Epist. 74.

[7] Αριϛον ειναι παν το αν ϐασιλευϛ ιρδη, Herodot. Clio, Sive. l. 1. c. 119.

and patience of hope, as together in the same persons, remembered by the apostle, 1 Thess. i. 3. and to the exercise of every grace, this of patience is to be added, 2 Pet. i. 5, 6. and this, with other graces, is to be eagerly pursued, closely followed after, and constantly exercised, 1 Tim. vi. 11. it is so necessary in the things of God, that one, a stranger to this grace, as Tertullian[1] observes, cannot undertake to perform any command, nor do any work that is acceptable to the Lord. Concerning which may be enquired,

First, In what it lies, or wherein is the exercise of it.

1. In patiently bearing afflictions, of whatsoever kind it pleases God to exercise with; hence the exhortation to *be patient in tribulation,* Rom. xii. 12. afflictions are the lot of the children of God, who are described as a poor and afflicted people; these are what they are appointed unto, what Christ has given them reason to expect in this world, and of which all the children of God are partakers; for if without them, they are bastards, and not sons; and therefore should be patiently borne: every follower of Christ has a cross, his own peculiar cross; which he is to take up willingly and bear cheerfully; *Christianus est crucianus;* a Christian is a cross-bearer, as Luther used to say; nor should we be impatient under it. Afflictions lie in the way to the heavenly glory, which is a *narrow way,* τεθλιμμένη οδος, an afflicted way, strewed with afflictions; and through this rough way all Christian pilgrims and travellers pass, and enter the kingdom; so did Christ himself; and ere long they will come to the end of it, and out of great tribulations, and therefore should patiently endure them. They are no other than fatherly chastisements, given in love, and for good; and sooner or later apparently issue in good, either here or hereafter, and therefore to be yielded to with filial reverence and subjection; and though in themselves not joyous, but grievous; yet since peaceable fruits of righteousness follow them, those who are exercised with them, should be content to bear them. Now to the exercise of patience under afflictions, murmurings, and repinings at them, and complainings of them are opposite. Nor should saints be in haste to be rid of them, but wait the Lord's time; nor make use of any unlawful methods to get out of them; but should be willing they should take their course, and should let patience have its perfect work.

2. The exercise of patience lies in bearing reproach and persecution for the sake of Christ and his gospel; they that will live godly in Christ must expect these things; they are not to be thought new and strange, as if they were never before known or heard of; nor should saints be impatient under them. Moses esteemed reproach for Christ's sake, greater riches than the treasures of Egypt; and the apostles rejoiced that they were counted worthy to suffer shame for the name of Christ; yea, more than this, the followers of Christ have been called unto in all ages, especially in the first ages of christianity, under Rome pagan, and since under Rome papal, even to endure the most cruel persecutions and severe deaths; after an account of which this observation is made, *Here is the patience and faith of the saints;* that is, the trial of their patience and faith; and we are not yet out of antichristian times; the reign of antichrist is not yet at an end: and whatsoever saints are called to suffer for the sake of Christ, is cheerfully to be submitted to, and patiently endured; nor should they desert their station, nor withdraw themselves from their duty, nor drop their profession, nor forsake the fellowship of the saints, and be like the stony-ground-hearer, who *by and by is offended,* withdraws himself and is gone.

3. Patience is tried and exercised, in and by the temptations of Satan; our Lord suffered much himself, being tempted; and with what patience did he endure his sufferings by them, repelling every temptation only by saying, *It is written* so and so; though at the last temptation, and which was the most insolent and audacious, he added, *Get thee hence, Satan.* Saints have reason to bear them all patiently; since Christ their high Priest not only sympathizes with them, but succours them when tempted, and prays for them, that their faith fail not; and still the more, since he assures them his grace is sufficient for them, to bear them up under temptations, and carry through them, and that his strength shall be made perfect in their weakness, to deliver out of them.

4. Patience is exercised by divine desertions, and lies in quietly waiting for the Lord's gracious manifestations of himself

---

[1] De Patienta, c. 1.

unto his people again. Sometimes they are impatient on this account, and inquire the reason of it, and say, *Why hidest thou thyself?* and complain of the length of time, and ask, *How long wilt thou hide thy face from me?* Psalm x. 1. and xiii. 1. thinking the time of desertion so long as to be a sort of eternity; and, indeed, unbelief sometimes suggests, that God has cast off for ever, and will be favourable no more; but at other times we find the saints more patient, and in more quiet and waiting postures; as the prophet Isaiah, chap. viii. 17. and more especially the church, under the hidings of God's face, Mic. vii. 7—10.

5. Patience is exercised when answers of prayer are deferred, and it lies in a quiet waiting for them. Sometimes the Lord's people are very uneasy and impatient because they are not immediately answered, and imagine that God has covered himself with a cloud, that their prayer cannot pass through; or that he has turned a deaf ear to them, and will never regard them; though the vision is for an appointed time, and therefore should be waited for till that time comes, when it will not tarry; and so it has been found by experience; as by David, Psalm xl. 1, 2.

6. This grace appears and shews itself in a patient waiting for the heavenly glory; sometimes the saints are impatient, and want to depart, and be in the enjoyment of it before God's time, because of the afflictions, trials, and exercises they meet with in life; which does not become them; instances of which were Elijah, Job, Jonah, and others: but afflictions are to be endured patiently, in expectation of glory; since it is but a short time they will last; a little while and he that shall come will come, and will not tarry; and therefore they have need of, and should exercise patience in doing the will of God, that they may receive the promises; and should consider that their afflictions are but for a moment, as well as light, when compared with the eternal weight of glory that will shortly follow; and therefore should hope and quietly wait for it, Rom. viii. 25. I shall next consider,

Secondly, The causes of this grace, and from whence it comes.

1. The efficient cause is God, from whom every good and perfect gift comes; and as this is a gift, as every grace is, and a good one in its nature, use, and consequences; and is a perfect one, when it has its perfect work and effect, it must come from God; and hence he is called, *The God of patience,* because he is the author of it, as well as requires it, and it is exercised towards him, by whom seems to be meant God, even the Father of our Lord Jesus Christ, Rom. xv. 5, 6. We read also of the *patience of Christ,* and of being directed into it, as well as into the love of God, 2 Thess. iii. 5. and which may signify, not only the patience exercised by Christ in his human nature, amidst all his afflictions and sufferings; but what he works in the hearts of his people, and encourages them to exercise; for as he is the author and finisher of faith, so of patience; and the saints are companions of one another in the kingdom and patience of Jesus Christ: and even his patience as man is the exemplar and pattern of theirs; for he has left an example of it, that they may tread in his steps; and certain it is, that long-suffering, or patience, which is the same, is a fruit of the Spirit, Gal. v. 22. so that all the three Persons are concerned in it.——

2. The instrumental causes of it are the scriptures, and word of God and Christ; which are written, *that we through patience and comfort of the scriptures might have hope;* which, as they are the means of instruction and consolation, so of patience. The word of God encourages to it, furnishes with arguments for the exercise of it, and gives instances and examples of it, exciting thereunto; hence Christ calls it, the word of his patience; *Because thou hast kept the word of my patience,* Rev. iii. 10. and this word, accompanied with a divine power, and received into a good heart, made so by the Spirit of God, *brings forth fruit with patience,* and patience is one of its fruits, Luke viii. 13.——3. Afflictions themselves are a means of increasing it, for afflictions try faith; and *the trying of faith works patience,* and brings that into exercise, and inures unto it; yea, it is expressly said, that *tribulation works patience,* that is, when sanctified; otherwise it produces impatience and murmurings, James i. 3. Rom. v. 3. I proceed to observe,

Thirdly, The usefulness of this grace, and the exercise of it. As,

1. It makes a man comfortable and happy in himself; without this a man cannot enjoy himself, his mercies and his friends; hence the advice of Christ to his disciples, *In your patience possess ye your souls,* Luke xxi. 19. an impatient man can

have no enjoyment of himself, nor of any thing he has; he is always restless and uneasy, and has no peace in himself; whereas a man possessed of patience, and in the exercise of it, has a peace which the world can neither give nor take away, a peace in the midst of tribulation.——
2. It is of great use in running the christian race; *Let us run with patience the race that is set before us*, Heb. xii. 1. by the *race* is meant the christian's course of life in this world, and what still remains of it to be run out; the prize run for is the prize of the high calling, the heavenly glory, the crown of life, glory, and righteousness, laid up in heaven; this race is *set before us*, the way is marked out in which we are to run; the rubs, the troubles the impediments to be met with in the way are appointed; the mark to direct and steer the course by, and which is always to be had in view, is Christ, who is the hope set before us in the gospel; the length of the course to be run is fixed, the whole time of life, every year, month, day, and moment: and it requires patience to run it; partly through the length of the race, which sometimes appears tedious: and partly because of the troubles, difficulties, and discouragements in the way; and likewise because of the prize saints long to be in the enjoyment of.——3. There is need of it, and of its exercise, in *doing the will of God*, in order to receive the promise, Heb. x. 36. by doing the will of God is not so much meant obeying the preceptive will of God, as to submit to the will of God respecting afflictions and sufferings for his sake; for it is given, and it is the will of God, not only that men should believe in Christ, and follow him, but that they should *suffer for his sake;* and to do this requires patience, and a quiet submission to the will of God; which is the way to be quiet, patient, and humble under his mighty hand, whilst suffering according to his will, 1 Pet. iv. 19, and so patience is necessary to receive the promise, the promised glory, after the will of God is done in a way of suffering; for the promise is made to him that endures patiently; *Blessed is the man that endureth temptation*, afflictions with patience; *he shall receive the crown of life; obtain the promise*, as Abraham did, *and through faith and patience inherit it,* James i. 12. Heb. vi. 12, 15.——4. Another use of the grace of patience is, that when it has its *perfect work*, saints become *perfect* also, James i. 4. this grace is imperfect, as all others are, faith, hope, love, knowledge, &c. and even in the best, and in such who have been most eminent for it, as Job particularly: and yet what impatience was he guilty of at times? though it may be increased, as every other grace; for as there is such a thing as growing in grace in general, so in any grace in particular, and in this also: when it is said, that *tribulation works patience*, the meaning is, that it is the means and occasion[2] of increasing it. And it may be said to be perfect, when it appears to be sincere and genuine, as it does by its being tried by afflictions; and it has its *perfect work* when it is constant in its exercise, and continues to the end; and then will the saints be perfect, which they are not now in themselves, only in Christ their head; but when this grace, and every other, shall be perfect, then will they be perfect in holiness and happiness, as they will be at the resurrection in soul and body, and be entire, complete, and want nothing.

Fourthly, The motives or arguments exciting to the exercise of this grace, may next be considered,

1. It is what God calls his people to; as to suffer for well-doing, so to take suffering for well-doing patiently; *For even hereunto were ye called*, that is, to take it patiently, 1 Pet. ii. 21. hence these frequent exhortations to it; *Be patient in tribulation; be patient towards all men; be patient, brethren;* and again, *be ye also patient;* and which is enforced and exemplified in the case of the husbandman, patiently waiting for the fruits of the earth, after much trouble, toil, and labour; see Rom. xii. 12. 1 Thess. v. 14. James v. 7, 8.——2. The exercise of this grace is taken notice of, approved of, and commended by God, 1 Pet. ii. 20. hence Christ, in his epistles to the churches, frequently observes, with commendation, their patience among other things; *I know thy patience*, Rev. ii. 2, 3, 19. and iii. 10.——3. It is commendable in the sight of good men; Solomon extols it, Eccles. vii. 8. and the apostle Paul glories in the Thessalonians for it, 1 Thess. i. 3. 2 Thess. i. 4. a meek and patient christian is not only in the sight of God of great price, but is very amiable in the sight of good men.——4. The patience of God exercised towards his people may

---

[2] Calamitas virtutis occasio est, Seneca de Providentia, c. 4.

be improved into an argument exciting to it. The Lord is patient and long-suffering towards his people before conversion, whilst they are doing those things which might justly provoke the eyes of his glory; fulfilling the desires of the flesh and of the mind, being by nature children of wrath, as others; yet he is patient, and bears long with them, waiting to be gracious to them, and to have mercy on them, Isa. xxx. 18. and after conversion, he bears with their many provocations, backslidings, and revoltings from him; and, indeed, his patience with a wicked world, in not destroying it sooner, is for the sake of his chosen ones, waiting until they are called and brought to repentance; the long-suffering of the Lord is salvation to them, 2 Pet. iii. 9, 15.——5. The example of Christ, and of his patience, is very strong and forcible, and engaging to it; *Christ also suffered for us, leaving us an example*, not of sufferings only, but of patience in them, that we should *follow his steps* in the exercise of this grace, and learn patience of him, as well as meekness and lowliness of mind, 1 Pet. ii. 22, 23. we should consider him who *endured the cross* with so much patience, and the *contradiction of sinners against himself* with so much mildness and meekness; lest we be *wearied, and faint in our minds*, and grow impatient; this may animate to patience and long-suffering.——6. The examples of the saints in all ages may serve to encourage to the exercise of patience; of the prophets of the Old Testament; of the apostles of Christ; and of the martyrs of Jesus; and of other saints; and particularly Job; *Ye have heard of the patience of Job*, who was remarkable for it, when his afflictions came so thick, and fast, and heavy upon him; *and have seen the end of the Lord*, in his afflictions, and how they issued, James v. 10, 11. and those examples are on record to encourage the saints to be *followers of them*, Heb. vi. 12. ——7. The near coming of Christ is made use of to stir up to patience; it is but a little while and he will come that shall come; and then there will be an end of all afflictions and sufferings; *Be patient therefore, brethren, unto the coming of the Lord:* —again, *Be ye also patient, for the coming of the Lord draweth nigh*, James v. 7, 8. redemption draws near, suffering times will soon be over; the summer is at hand, halcyon days will come; peace will be like a river, and the glory of the church like a flowing stream!

CHAP. XVIII.

OF CHRISTIAN FORTITUDE.

Though saints are to be humble, self-denying, submissive to the will of God, and patient towards all men, and in all things; yet they are not to indulge to pusillanimity and to a meanness of spirit; but to shew firmness of mind, resolution, an undaunted courage, and fortitude of soul, a manly spirit, which is not at all unbecoming the christian; *For God hath not given us the spirit of fear, but of power, of love, and of a sound mind*, 2 Tim. i. 7. they should play the man, act the manly part, shew themselves to be men, as of wisdom, so of courage; *Quit you like men, and be strong;* which respects not strength of body, but fortitude of mind, 1 Cor. xvi. 13. and is the subject to be treated of. Concerning which may be observed,

I. The nature and necessity of it. It is not a natural fortitude which is meant, and which may be in brutes as well as in men; as in the lion, *which is the strongest among beasts, and turneth not away from any*, Prov. xxx. 30. its courage is equal to its strength; but such natural animosity, or greatness of mind, found among men, is not properly virtue, much less grace, as christian fortitude is; and which also does not lie in bold and daring enterprises, as when a man attempts things arduous and difficult, and encounters dangers; either of which he has no call unto, but rushes into them unnecessarily and unwarily, without any consultation and deliberation, and without having any good end in view to be answered. This is no other than audaciousness, or rather *temerity*,[1] or rashness; and not true fortitude. Also true christian fortitude is to be distinguished from civil fortitude, or what is exercised in war, in a military way; though the one may bear some resemblance to the other: and even civil fortitude is often but a false appearance; men will make a shew of courage, through fear of disgrace, rebukes of their superiors, and military discipline, or of being taken prisoners, and becoming captives; or it may arise from their confidence

---

[1] Fortitudo, non est inconsulta temeritas, nec periculorum amor, nec formidabilium appetitio, Seneca, Ep. 85.

in their bodily strength, and in the strength and safety of their armour, and in their military skill, and through ignorance of the strength of the enemy; and it is usually through hope of honour and the applause of men, and sometimes of the spoil;[a] and at most and best, it is exercised for their own good, and the good of their country, which is commendable: but Christian fortitude is concerned about things which are apparently the will of God, and is exercised in obedience to it; for the sake of a man's doing his duty, and with a pure view to the honour and glory of God; trusting in and depending upon his power, strenght and grace, to carry him through whatever he is called to do or suffer in the performance of it; and from which he is not to be deterred by any difficulties that occur, or dangers he may be exposed unto therein: this is fortitude becoming Christians.

Now of such fortitude there is a necessity in the Christian life. When we consider the many duties of religion to be performed by us, and that with constancy and perseverance, both public and private, relative, social and personal, in which we are to be steadfast and immoveable; and when our own weakness is considered, that without Christ we can do nothing, but all things, through Christ strengthening us, it requires great boldness of faith, and confidence in Christ for grace and strength: and since the Christian has so many difficulties and dangers to encounter with; so many discouragements in the way; so many trials, temptations, tribulations, and afflictions, from various quarters, he must be a man of fortitude not to be moved with these things; bearing all with an invincible courage and constancy. To which may be added, the numerous enemies he has to grapple with; enemies mightier than he, who are lively and strong; some not flesh and blood, as he is, but above his match; even principalities and powers, and spiritual wickednesses in high places. Good men dwell in a sinful world, called, *This present evil world;* and to live soberly, righteously, and godly in it; to bear the vexation arising from the filthy conversation of the wicked, as was the case of Lot; and to bear a testimony against them, and to suffer their mockings, insults, and injuries, who are for war when they are for peace, requires great fortitude of mind; their souls are sometimes *among lions,* men comparable to them, as David's soul was; and they had need to be as *bold as lions,* as the righteous man is. Now this being the case, and these the circumstances of the christian, he has need of great fortitude of mind and of strength, and grace from above to support under them; he has need to be *strong in the Lord, and in the grace that is in Christ Jesus;* to be fortified with the love of God, with the promises of the gospel, and with fresh supplies of grace and strength from Christ. But these things will more largely appear in what will be farther suggested by considering,

II. Wherein this fortitude of mind consists, and whereby it shews itself. And,

First, It appears in the performance of religious exercises, and especially in some. As,

1. In family-worship; which undoubtedly is incumbent on the people of God: but now for a man to distinguish himself in a neighbourhood from all about him, and to say in his practice, with Joshua, *As for me, and my house, we will serve the Lord,* Josh. xxiv. 15. let others do what they will; this shews religious fortitude of mind: and in particular when a man first sets up family prayer in his house; suppose the master of a family is the only one in it called by grace, and at a time when he has an irreligious yoke-fellow, irreligious children and servants, he sees it his duty, at least once a day, to call them together, and to pray with them; now for this man to fall down on his knees, and pray to his God, and his wife, children, and servants sneering at him and laughing, at least secretly to one another, requires a fortitude of mind: and if this is not the case, yet it may be he lives alone among wicked neighbours, and so contiguous to them that he cannot pray, nor read the scriptures, nor sing the praises of God, which is the usage of some christians in their families, without being over-heard by them, and exposed to their ridicule and contempt; to bear which constantly is an instance and evidence of fortitude.——

2. In a man's giving up himself to a church of Christ, to walk with it in all the commandments and ordinances of the Lord. For a man to attend public worship on Lord's days is no great trial of his fortitude, because it is what his neighbours in common do; but let him separate himself

---

[a] Which are observed by Aristot. Ethic. l. 3. c. 11.

from the world, and stand out from among them, and give himself up to the Lord in a public manner, and to his people in a church-state; and this will try it and shew it; for this is practically saying, he is not of the world, and belongs to another company; and this will unavoidably draw the hatred of the world upon him; and he will be liable to be challenged in a reproachful way, *Thou art also one of them;* as Peter was by a man in the high priest's hall, and who had not then courage enough to own it, but denied it.———3. Especially if such a man comes into a church in a regular manner, by previously submitting to the ordinance of baptism, and to that as it was first delivered and practised; if he declares against the sprinkling of infants, as an innovation, and openly avows the true doctrine of baptism, as to be administered only to such who profess faith in Christ, and that by immersion; and if he will proceed accordingly, and follow Christ in this now despised ordinance of his, he must be content to be nick-named, and to have reproach plentifully poured upon him; not only by the profane world, but by the generality of the professors of religion.

But when a man is satisfied that what he is called to do is his duty; that it is a command of God, and ought to be obeyed, though attended with some things disagreeable to flesh and blood, he will take courage, and *be strong, and do it;* as David advised his son Solomon, with respect to building the temple: and when he is encouraged with the divine presence, as Zerubbabel, Joshua, and the Jews were to be *strong and work; for I am with you, saith the Lord of hosts;* and as the apostles were, when ordered by Christ to preach his gospel, administer his ordinances, and teach men to observe all that he commanded; and added, *Lo, I am with you always, even unto the end of the world!* this will inspire a good man with courage and resolution to do his duty; nor will he be deterred from it by the edicts of men, though urged with the severest menaces; as the three companions of Daniel bravely refused to worship Nebuchadnezzar's image, though threatened to be cast into a fiery furnace, as they were; and Daniel, when an edict was obtained from the king, that no man should pray to his God for such a time, under the penalty of being cast into the den of lions; he boldly went on in the performance of his duty; opened his windows, and prayed to the God of heaven,

as he had been wont to do in times past: and as the apostles, when strictly charged by the rulers to preach no more in the name of Jesus, and were severely threatened if they did, with great firmness of mind and intrepidity answered, *We ought to obey God rather than man.* Promises of grace and strength will animate saints to a cheerful obedience to the will of God, and to the discharge of their duty, amidst all discouragements and difficulties; if God says, as their day is their strength shall be; and that his strength shall be made perfect in their weakness, and his grace be sufficient for them; and bids them, *Fear not, I am with thee; I will strengthen thee!* &c. this will give them a fortitude of mind which will overcome all their fears; and they will say, with David, *The Lord is my light and my salvation, whom shall I fear? the Lord is the strength of my life, of whom shall I be afraid?* Isa. xli. 10. Psalm xxvii. 1, 3, 4. this is now active fortitude, and shews itself in doing the duties of religion.

Secondly, Christian fortitude shews itself in bearing afflictions with constancy, and enduring sufferings with a firmness of mind, whether from the hands of God or men; and which may be called passive fortitude.

1. From the hands of God, from whom Job was sensible he received his, even his loss of substance, children, and health, and bore it all with an invincible fortitude of mind: this appears when a man's spirits do not sink under the weight of an affliction; but has strength of mind, a fortitude of soul under adversity; *The spirit of a man,* of a saint, animated with christian courage, *will sustain his infirmity,* his bodily infirmity, a tedious consumption, or racking pains; or go through any severe operation he may be called unto, with a becoming resolution and manliness, Prov. xxiv. 10. and xviii. 14.———2. From the hands of men; and especially for the sake of the gospel, the truths and ordinances of it; as when saints are called to suffer shame and reproach for the sake of Christ, they, in imitation of him, despise the shame, and account it an honour to bear reproach for his sake; of suffering as a christian, they are not ashamed, but rather glorify God on that behalf, the Spirit of glory and of God resting upon them; and when they endure cruel mockings, as some of the Old Testament-saints, did, bear them patiently, and with an invincible firmness of mind; as Christ

did on the cross; and as the apostles, when made a spectacle to the world, to angels, and men; when made the filth of the world, and the off-scouring of all things; when reviled, and persecuted, and defamed, they bore all with a temper of mind which shewed them to be possessed of christian fortitude. Others have suffered confiscation of substance, and took joyfully *the spoiling of their goods*, as the believing Hebrews did; and as our forefathers in the last century: and others, *scourging, bonds, and imprisonment;* as did the apostles of Christ, as well as the Old Testament-saints; and particularly the apostle Paul, who received of the Jews five times the scourging of forty stripes save one, and was thrice beaten with rods; which perhaps left those marks on him which he calls, *the marks of the Lord Jesus* he bore *in his body:* and who was in prisons frequent; and who seems to take a pleasure, and even to glory, in his being a prisoner of Christ, and in chains for his sake; of such an heroic spirit, and with such fortitude was he endued, that none of these things moved him from the gospel of the grace of God. Death itself, in its most formidable shapes, has been endured by the saints with an invincible courage; as by the martyrs in the ten pagan persecutions, and by the witnesses of Jesus against the papal hierarchy; and particularly by our reformers in queen Mary's days, such as Latimer, Ridley, Bradford, and others; who, surrounded with faggots, and these in flames about them, expressed their undaunted courage, firmness, and fortitude of mind to the last. These, with multitudes of others, loved not their lives unto death.

Thirdly, Christian fortitude appears in the spiritual warfare of the saints. There is a warfare for men on earth, and especially for good men, who are soldiers, and must endure hardness, as good soldiers of Christ, and to which christian fortitude is necessary; and therefore should be, as Joshua was exhorted to be, *strong and of a good courage*, when he was called to fight the Lord's battles, and against the enemies of the people of Israel; and as Joab said to Abishai his brother; *Be of good courage, and let us play the man, for our people, and for the cities of our God,* 2 Sam. x. 12. And christian fortitude will shew itself,

1. In the defence of the cause of God and truth, in appearing for, and on the behalf of the church of God: *the bed which is Solomon's*, which seems to design the church of Christ, *threescore valiant men* are said to be *about it, of the valiant of Israel,* Cant. iii. 7. who are valiant for the truth on earth, who are concerned for the welfare of the church, and for the protection of it from errors and heresies; and will not give way, no not for an hour, that the truth of the gospel may continue with the church, and its ordinances remain pure and incorrupt; and these are not only the ministers of the word, who are set for the defence of the gospel, and who war a good warfare, and fight the good fight of faith, and speak with the enemy in the gate, and are bold in their God to preach the gospel of Christ, as it ought to be spoken; but all professors of religion, and members of the church of Christ, should *stand fast in one Spirit, striving together for the faith of the gospel,* and should *contend earnestly, even to an agony, for the faith once delivered to the saints;* and in so doing they shew a fortitude of mind.——2. This also appears in fighting against spiritual enemies; as sin, and the lusts of it, which war against the soul; the law in the members warring against the law of the mind; the flesh lusting against the spirit; which are, as it were, a company of two armies. Now one of christian fortitude will strive against sin, be an antagonist to it, and act the manly part against it; and will wrestle against Satan, and his principalities and powers, and give no place to the devil; but by faith resist him, who, when resisted, will flee, for he is an arrant coward, and does not care to be handled with the armour of christians; and those young men who are *strong*, possessed of christian fortitude, and in whom the word of God dwells, overcome the wicked one: the world also with all its flattering lusts and frowning fury, is overcome by the saints in the exercise of faith, 1 John v. 4, 5.——3. The saints have great reason, in their militant state, to be of good courage; since more are they that are for them, than they that are against them; and if God be for them, as he is, who can be against them? and through God they shall do valiantly: the christian has a good cause, in which he is engaged; he wars a good warfare, and fights the good fight of faith; he has a good Captain, under whose banner he fights, the great Captain of salvation: saints have good weapons, with which they are accoutred; the shield of faith, the helmet of salvation, and the sword of the Spirit; which weapons are not carnal, but spiritual and mighty,

through God, and are such as are proved, and may, with confidence, be made use of; and they are sure of victory beforehand; for all their enemies are conquered, sin is made an end of, Satan, who had the power of death, is destroyed, the world is overcome by Christ, the warfare is accomplished, and believers are made more than conquerors, through him that has loved them; and therefore may be sure of the crown of life, righteousness and glory, laid up for all that love the appearing of Christ. All which may serve to fill them with an holy fortitude in their spiritual warfare.

Fourthly, Christian fortitude manifests itself in the hour of death. Death is very terrible to nature, and to natural men; the philosopher[3] calls it "the most terrible of all terribles;" and no wonder he should call it so, since he adds, according to his opinion, it is "the end of all things, and that to one that is dead there is neither good nor evil;" such a notion of death, as being an extinction, must be terrible; and the wise man, when he suggests what is most grieving, distressing, and intolerable, says, it is *more bitter than death;* as if besides there was nothing more grievous than that, Eccl. vii. 26. To Christless sinners death is the *king of terrors*, and even some gracious persons have been all their lifetime through fear of death subject to bondage; but as formidable as it is, there are some things which fortify the christian against the fears of it. As,——1. That Christ has abolished death as a penal evil, so that it will never be inflicted on the believer by way of punishment. The sting of death is taken away by Christ, which is sin, and a very venomous sting it is, and death thus armed is to be feared; but when its sting is taken out of it, it is not to be dreaded. Any insect with a sting we are naturally afraid of, but if its sting is removed we have no fear of it, though it flies and buzzes about us; so in a view of death being unstung, the believer may sing and say, Death, *where is thy sting?* and be fearless of it.——2. Death to believers is a privilege and blessing; it has a place in their inventory of goods that belong unto them, *death is yours;* it is an happiness to them, *Blessed are the dead that die in the Lord;* since they are by it delivered from all evils, from all outward afflictions and inward troubles; from a body of sin and death, under which they now groan being burdened; from the world and its snares, and from Satan and his temptations; and therefore are more happy than living saints; besides they are with Christ, enjoying communion with him, and beholding his glory, which is much better than to be in the present state.——3. Death, though it separates soul and body, and one friend from another, it does not separate from the love of God, but lets in to the more glorious discoveries and enjoyment of it. It is precious in the sight of the Lord, and therefore saints should not shrink at it themselves.——4. It is but once, it is appointed for men once to die, and no more; and it will soon be over and issue in an happy endless eternity; and when the body dies the soul does not, but immediately enters into a state of glory; death is the inlet into it, and the beginning of it; the birth-day of an eternal world[4] of bliss: besides there will be a resurrection of the body, when it will be fashioned like to the glorious body of Christ, and will be raised in incorruption, in power, in glory, and a spiritual body; so the saints will be no losers but gainers by death, and therefore need not fear it: the resurrection of the body yields comfort in the view of death, and amidst present afflictions, as it did to Job, chap. xix. 25—27.——5. Be it that death is an enemy, as it is contrary to nature, it is the last enemy that shall be destroyed; and when that is conquered, the victory will be complete over every enemy, sin, Satan, the world, death, and the grave.——6. Besides these things which may serve to promote a fortitude of mind against the fear of death; it may be proper frequently to meditate upon it, to think of it as near at hand, and to make it familiar to us by saying as Job did, chap. xvii. 14. by considering it as going to our God and Father, to our home, to our Father's house; by going to bed and resting in it; and by sleeping, and that in the arms of Jesus.

IV. From whence this fortitude flows, and what the causes of it, may be next considered. It is not from nature but from grace, it is a gift of God; it is he that gives strength and power to his people, not bodily strength only, but spiritual strength; it is he that girds them with strength, with an holy fortitude, and fills them with

---

[3] Των Φοβερωτα τον ο θανατος, Aristot. Ethic. l. 3. c. 9.

[4] Dies iste, quem tanquam extremum reformidas, æterni natalis est, Seneca, Ep. 102.

spiritual courage, and strengthens their hearts, and fortifies them against their spiritual enemies.——1. The efficient cause of Christian fortitude of mind is God, Father, Son, and Spirit. God the Father is prayed unto for it, Eph. iii. 14, 16. Col. i. 11, 12. and he which *stablishes* saints *in Christ*, gives them stability and firmness of mind, *is God*, that is, God the Father: and it is Christ who bids them *be of good cheer*, to be strong and of good courage in the midst of tribulation, since he has overcome the world; and it is *through him* who *strengthens* them that they can do and suffer all things for his sake; and the Spirit of the Lord as he rests as a *Spirit of counsel and might* on Christ the head, so on his members likewise; and it is a grant of God, a free grace gift of his, that his people be *strengthened with might by his Spirit in the inner man*, Isa. xi. 2. Eph. iii. 16. ——2. The word of God is the means of producing and increasing Christian fortitude; it is not only a part of the spiritual armour, called *the sword of the Spirit*, but having a place and abiding in the heart, fortifies it against spiritual enemies, and by it victory is gained over them, 1 John ii. 14. Rev. xii. 11. the precious promises contained in it, before hinted at, serve greatly to animate the saints, and to inspire them with fortitude amidst all surrounding evils.——3. Such a temper and disposition of mind is attainable by faith, prayer, and waiting upon God. By faith men so eminent for fortitude of mind performed those heroic exploits we read of in Heb. xi. who by faith subdued kingdoms, stopped the mouths of lions, quenched the violence of fire, and endured with such greatness of mind the many evils they did; and through constant prayer saints obtain a spirit of boldness both with God and before men; and by waiting upon the Lord in religious exercises their spiritual strength or fortitude is renewed; hence the exhortation, *Wait on the Lord*, Psalm xxvii. 14.—— 4. The patterns of courage, the examples of fortitude in the saints who have gone before us, of the prophets, apostles, primitive Christians, and martyrs in all ages, may be a means of promoting a like disposition, particularly that cloud of heroes before referred to; and above all Christ himself, the pattern of courage set before us, whom we are directed to look unto and consider, lest we be weary and faint in our minds, Heb. xii. 1, 2, 3.——5. The love of God, and a sense of that, a persuasion of interest in it, and that nothing shall separate from it, casts out fear,[5] and inspires with fortitude against every enemy, Rom. viii. 35, 38, 39. 1 John iv. 18.

CHAP. XIX.

OF ZEAL.

ZEAL is an ardour of mind, a fervent affection for some person or thing; with an indignation against every thing supposed to be pernicious and hurtful to it. As it is a divine grace, it is a vehement affection for God and his glory, an earnest study, by all proper means, to promote it; with a resentment of every thing that tends to obscure, let, and hinder it; it is hot, burning, flaming love, which cannot be quenched by water, nor drowned by floods, nor abated, restrained and stopped, by any difficulties in the way, Cant. viii. 6, 7. It is sometimes used for that strong affection God bears to his people, expressed by his earnest care of them, and indignation against their enemies, called, *The zeal of the Lord of hosts*, and his *great jealousy*, Isa. ix. 7. Zech. i. 14. and viii. 2. And sometimes for a gracious disposition in man, which has God for its object, and is called *zeal towards God*, an eager desire after his glory; and of which God is the author, and is called, *A zeal of God*, or *a godly jealousy*, 2 Cor. xi. 2. In treating of which I shall consider,

I. The various sorts and kinds of zeal; that it may be the better known what is right and genuine. And,

First, There is a *zeal of God*, which is *not according to knowledge* which the Jews had, as the apostle testifies, Rom. x. 2. and which lay in a zealous concern for the performance of legal duties, and in a studious attempt to set them up, and establish them as a justifying righteousness before God; to the entire neglect and rejection of the righteousness of Christ. Which zeal of theirs, in this attempt, arose,

1. From ignorance of the perfection of God's righteousness, which is displayed in all his ways and works, who is the Judge of the whole earth, and will do right; and will not clear the guilty without full satisfaction to his justice, nor justify any without a perfect righteousness; and his

---

[5] Non potest amor cum timore misceri, Seneca, Ep. 47.

judgment of things *is according to truth;* and he cannot reckon an imperfect righteousness a perfect one; nor account that for righteousness which is none: to secure his honour and glory in this point, he has set forth Christ to be the propitiatory sacrifice for sin, thereby making satisfaction for it; *to declare his righteousness;* but of this the legal zealot is ignorant, and therefore takes a wrong course.——2. It arises from ignorance of the righteousness which God in the law requires; the law is holy, just, and good, and requires a perfect righteousness; both as to the matter of it, and the manner of its performance; all that the law has commanded must be done, and as it is commanded, or it is no righteousness, Deut. vi. 25. and the law is spiritual, and reaches to, and is concerned with the heart, the spirit, and the soul of man; it forbids sinful thoughts, inward lusts, and irregular affections, as well as the outward and grosser sins of life; it allows of no peccadillo's, or little sins, but condemns all; so extensive is the law, and such the spirituality of it; which the Pharisee being ignorant of, sets up his own righteousness as sufficient, and zealously endeavours to establish it; but it will be of no service, Matt. v. 19, 20.——3. This ignorant zeal arises from a want of knowledge of the righteousness of God revealed in the gospel; which is no other than the righteousness of Christ, who is God as well as man; being ignorant of this, its excellency, fulness, and suitableness, men submit not unto it, but reject it, stumbling at the stumbling stone and rock of offence, Rom. i. 17. and iii. 21, 22.——4. It arises from ignorance of their own righteousness; the Spirit of God not having convinced them of it, how imperfect and polluted it is; how it is not answerable to the law of God; and how short it comes of its demands and requirements; and how insufficient it is to justify them before God; and whilst this is the case they are warmly attached to it, and zealous to establish it; but when they come to be made sensible of the imperfection and unprofitableness of it, they desire to be *found in Christ,* and in his righteousness, and not their own, Phil. iii. 9.——5. It arises from want of faith in Christ; being destitute of that, the zealots follow eagerly after righteousness, but do not attain it; *Because they seek it not by faith, but as it were, by the works of the law;* now, what is not of faith is sin, and therefore zeal without faith cannot be right; zeal without faith in Christ must be without knowledge, must be without the knowledge of Christ, and without the knowledge of God in Christ; and therefore cannot be well-pleasing and acceptable to God; nor is such a righteousness they are following after and endeavouring to establish. Wherefore,——6. Such a zealot goes contrary to the will and way of God, in the justification of a sinner; and therefore his zeal must be a false one: the declared will of God is, that a man is not, and cannot be justified in the sight of God by the deeds of the law; but that a man is justified by faith in the righteousness of Christ without the deeds of the law; the way and method God takes to justify men is by grace, freely imputing righteousness, without works, unto them; by making and accounting them righteous, through the obedience and righteousness of his Son, Rom. iii. 20, 28, 24. and iv. 6. and v. 19. And therefore it must be a blind, ignorant zeal, which sets up a man's post by God's post, and advances his own righteousness above that of Christ's.

Secondly, There is a mistaken zeal of the glory of God; and for it.

1. When that is opposed which is right, under a false notion of its being contrary to the glory of God; as when Joshua requested of Moses to forbid the young men prophesying in the camp; as being neither, as he thought, for the glory of God, nor to the honour of Moses; and when the priests and scribes were sore displeased at the children in the temple, crying *hosanna,* to the Son of David; and when they exclaimed against the works of Christ done on the sabbath-day, as if contrary to the honour of the sabbath, and the sanctification of it, and so to the glory of God in it; and such was the indiscreet zeal of Peter, in chiding Christ for saying he must suffer many things, as if it was injurious to his honour and glory; when all these things were right.——2. When that which is not for the glory of God, is wrongly thought to be so, and is zealously pursued as such: this is a mistaken zeal; as was the zeal of the idolatrous Gentiles for their idols, and idol-worship; and of the Papists, for their worship of images, angels, and saints departed, and for many other things; and of the Jews, for the traditions of the elders, of which the apostle Paul was very zealous, before conversion; and of the believing Jews who were zealous for continuing the ceremonies of the law, though

abrogated, Gal. i. 14. Acts xxi. 20.——
3. When ways and methods improper are taken to defend and promote the glory of God; as when the disciples, in their zeal for the honour of Christ, were for having fire come down from heaven upon those who had shewn some disrespect to Christ; and when Peter in his preposterous zeal, drew his sword in defence of his Master, and cut off the ear of the high priest's servant; for which both the one and the other were rebuked by Christ, Luke ix. 55. Matt. xxvi. 51.

Thirdly, There is a superstitious zeal, such as was in Baal's worshippers, who cut themselves with knives and lancets, whilst calling upon him; and in all idolaters using a multitude of superstitious rites, of which they are extremely zealous; particularly, in the Athenians, who were wholly given to idolatry, and whose city was full of idols; of whom the apostle says, that he perceived that they where *in all things too superstitious;* and therefore, lest they should be at all defective in the objects of their worship, they erected an altar to an unknown God, that they might be sure to comprehend all; and in the Jews, who were zealous of the traditions of the fathers, and were superstitiously careful that they did not eat with unwashen hands, and of the washing of their cups and pots, &c.

Fourthly, There is a persecuting zeal, under a pretence of the glory of God; so Saul, before his conversion, says of himself; *Concerning zeal, persecuting the church;* that is, he shewed his zeal, as he thought, for the glory of God, when he persecuted the Church of Christ, and made havoc of it; and he seems to have respect to this, when he tells the Jews that he was *zealous towards God, as ye all are this day;* so the *devout and honourable women*, whom the Jews stirred up to persecute the apostles, were, no doubt, under the influence of such a false zeal; imagining, that what they did was for the glory of God, and the honour of religion, Phil. iii. 6. Acts xxii. 3, 4. and xxvi. 9, 10. and xiii. 50. see John xvi. 2.

Fifthly, There is an hypocritical zeal for God; as in Jehu, when he said, *Come with me, and see my zeal for the Lord;* when, at the same time, he took no heed to walk in the law of the Lord, nor did he depart from the sins of Jeroboam; for though he destroyed the images of Baal, he worshipped the calves at Dan and Bethel: and in the Scribes and Pharisees, who brought the woman taken in adultery to Christ, under a pretence of a great regard to the law; and yet were guilty of like sins and others: and in Judas, who pretended regard to the poor, when he only sought to gratify his covetousness: and in the Pharisees, who made a shew of great zeal for piety, by their long prayers, when they only sought to devour widow's houses by that means, 2 Kings x. 16, 29, 31. John viii. 3, 9. and xii. 5, 6. Matt. xxiii. 14.

Sixthly, There is a contentious zeal; which often gives great trouble to Christian communities: of men of such a spirit the apostle speaks when he says, *If any man seems to be contentious,* about trivial matters, things indifferent, and of no moment, *we have no such custom, nor the churches of God;* nor should such be indulged: this sort of zeal is oftentimes no other than a mere logomachy, *a striving about words to no profit;* it is a contention about *foolish and unlearned questions,* which *gender strifes;* and at best about things curious and useless; whereas true zeal is always employed about the more solid and substantial doctrines of the gospel, and the ordinances of Christ.

Seventhly, Sometimes it is only a temporary passion; a flash of zeal, and continues not; so Joash, whilst Jehoiada the priest lived, did what was right, and shewed zeal in repairing the house of God; but after his death, left the house of the Lord God of his fathers, and served groves and idols. John the Baptist was a burning and shining light, and his hearers and disciples burned with zeal for him, his ministry, and baptism, and envied, on his account, the increasing interest of Christ; but it was but for a season they *rejoiced in his light:* so the Galatians were zealously affected towards the apostle Paul, to such a degree, that they would have been willing to have *plucked out their eyes,* and given them to him; whom they first received as an angel of God, even as Jesus Christ, so acceptable was his ministry; and yet he became their enemy, because of his preaching the same truths.

Eighthly, True zeal is no other than a fervent ardent love to God and Christ, and a warm concern for their honour and glory; such who are truly zealous for the Lord of hosts, love him with all their heart, with all their soul, and with all their strength; they love the Lord Jesus Christ in sincerity, as well as one another fervently; it is accompanied with a saving knowledge of God and Christ; of God in Christ, and of

Christ and him crucified; and such prefer the excellency of the knowledge of Christ above all things else, and prefer him to all created beings, Phil. iii. 8. Psalm lxxiii. 25. they have faith in God, and also in Christ; a faith which works by love, and this love constrains them, inspires them with zeal to seek their honour and glory; whatever they do, whether in things civil or religious, they do all to the glory of God. To true zeal there must be spiritual knowledge, unfeigned faith, and undissembled love; and this stands opposed,——1. To a neutral spirit in religion, to a halting between two opinions, condemned by Elijah in the Jews, 1 Kings xviii. 21. There can be no true zeal to the truth of worship, doctrines, and ordinances, where there is no stability; but a continual wavering and inconstancy. ——2. To carelessness and indifference about religious matters; when men, like the Jews of old, regard their own ceiled houses, and not the house of God; when they mind their secular affairs more than the interest of religion; when, as to the church of God, the truths of the gospel, and the ordinances of Christ, Gallio like, they care for none of these things.—— 3. To lukewarmness, with respect to divine and spiritual things; which the Laodicean church is charged with, and resented by Christ, Rev. iii. 15, 16. I proceed to consider,

II. The objects of zeal.

First, The object of it is God; even a false zeal is called, *a zeal towards God;* and that which is not according to knowledge, is said to be a *zeal of God;* Jehu called his hypocritical zeal, a *zeal for the Lord;* true zeal most deservedly bears this name; so Phinehas had the covenant of an everlasting priesthood given him, because he was *zealous for his God*, Numb. xxv. 13. which springs from a principle of love to God, and its end is his glory; and it has for its objects the worship of God, the word of God, and the truths contained in it.

1. The worship of God; who must be known, or he cannot be worshipped aright; the Samaritans worshipped they knew not what; and the Athenians erected an altar to an unknown God; and therefore, though they were both zealous of worship, their zeal was not according to knowledge; but true believers worship God in *the Spirit*, whom they know in a spiritual way; through faith in Christ, and with a zealous concern for his glory: and they worship him *in truth*, and keep close to the pattern of worship shewn them; to which they are zealously attached, and will not depart from it. Wherefore,——2. The word of God is the object of their zeal; to the law and to the testimony they appeal for the truth of all they say and do; they make that the standard of their faith and practice, and the rule of their worship; they earnestly contend for the perfection and integrity of it; and endeavour, with all their might and main, to preserve it pure and incorrupt, 2 Cor. ii. 17.——3. The truths contained in the word; they who have a true zeal are valiant for the truth; and can do nothing against it, but every thing for it, in defence of it, and for the continuance of it; they will buy the truth, give a great price for it, and highly value it; but will not sell it, nor part with it at any rate.

Secondly, The cause of Christ, is another object of zeal; and which is a good one, and the apostle says, *It is good to be zealously affected always in a good thing*, Gal. iv. 18. and those who are possessed of this zealous affection, seek not their own things, but the things of Christ; they have a sort of a natural care, as Timothy had, for the state of the churches, and interest of Christ, and of true religion, and for the support of it; not only in that branch of it to which they more peculiarly belong, but in others; as the Corinthian Church, who was not only zealously concerned for their own welfare, but for that of others; and the apostle testifies, that their *zeal* in their liberal ministration to the saints, had *provoked very many*, 2 Cor. ix. 2. True zeal for the cause of Christ, is concerned about the gospel of Christ, the ordinances of Christ, and the discipline of his house.

1. The gospel of Christ: great reason there is to be zealous for that; since it is the *gospel of the grace of God*, which displays the free grace of God in every part of our salvation; and therefore the apostle was so zealously concerned for it, as not to count his life dear to himself, so that he might finish his course with joy, by bearing a testimony to it: and because it ·is, *the gospel of salvation*, which publishes salvation by Christ; and declares, that whosoever believes in him shall be saved: and because it is, *the gospel of peace*, preaching peace by Jesus Christ, and by the blood of his cross; and because in it forgiveness of sin is preached in the name of Christ, and justification by his righteousness.—— 2. The ordinances of Christ; which every true christian should be zealous for, that

they be kept as they were first delivered, without any innovation or corruption; that the mode of administration of both Baptism and the Lord's Supper should be strictly adhered to; and that none be admitted to them but believers in Christ, or such who profess faith in him.——3. The discipline of Christ's house should be the object of our zeal, as it was of his; who said, *the zeal of thine house hath eaten me up;* and this is shewn when the rules of discipline are strictly observed, both with respect to private and public offences; when churches, and the members of them, like the church at Ephesus, cannot *bear them which are evil*, to continue them in fellowship with them; whether men of immoral lives, or have imbibed false doctrines; but withdraw from them that walk disorderly, and reject such who are not sound in the faith. Hence,

Thirdly, Every thing that is evil is the object of zeal, or against which true zeal should be expressed. As,

1. Against all false worship, particularly idolatry, or the having more and other gods than one; whether found among the heathens, or any that bear the christian name; as was by Moses, when his anger, zeal and indignation, waxed hot against the Israelites for their idolatrous worship of the calf, and he broke the tables of the law which were in his hands, and ordered the Levites to put their swords by their side, and slay every man his brother, companion, and neighbour: and so Elijah, who was jealous for the Lord God of hosts, because Israel had forsaken the covenant of the Lord, had thrown down his altar, and slain his prophets; and where there is true love for God, and zeal for his worship, there will be an hatred of every false way, be it in what shape it may.——2. Against all errors in doctrine; especially such as affect the Persons in Deity, Father, Son, and Spirit; with all others, which are the fundamental doctrines of religion; such as deny them are to be rebuked *sharply*, warmly, vehemently, with a becoming zeal, that they may be sound in the faith; such who bring not the doctrines of Christ, respecting his person, office and grace, are not to be received into the houses of saints, nor to be bid God speed.——3. Against all immorality in practice; true zeal will be as much levelled against a man's own sins as against the sins of others; he will be concerned to remove the beam out of his own eye, as well as the mote out of his brother's; he will be severe against right-hand and right-eye sins, such as are dear to the flesh as these be; and real godly sorrow for sin, and true repentance unto salvation, is always productive of zeal; *What zeal* it wrought in you? against a man's own sins more especially, as against others; and that which is against the sins of others, is tempered with commiseration and pity to the sinner, 2 Cor. vii. 11. and xii. 21.

Fourthly, True zeal is concerned in all the duties of religion, and shews itself in them; in the service of God in general, we should be *fervent in spirit,* warm, hot, zealous; *serving the Lord,* in such a manner, and not in a cold, indifferent way, and in the ministration of the gospel; it is said of Apollos, that being *fervent in spirit he spake and taught diligently the things of the Lord,* the doctrines of the gospel, so far as he was then acquainted with them, Rom. xii. 11. Acts xviii. 25. It is also very requisite in prayer to God; it is said of Epaphras, that he was always *labouring fervently in prayers* for the church at Colosse; and it is the effectual *fervent prayer* of the righteous man that availeth much, Col. iv. 12. James v. 16. And it should be shewn in the love of the saints to one another, 1 Pet. i. 22. and iv. 8. In short, believers in Christ ought to be *zealous of good works,* careful to maintain them, diligent in the performance of them, especially of those which are the greater and weightier duties of religion; though they are not to neglect and omit the lesser ones. To say no more, good men are the objects of true zeal; the apostle Paul was informed of the *fervent mind* or zeal of the Corinthians towards him, of the warm love and ardent affection they had for him; and he advises them to covet earnestly, to desire the best gifts, spiritual ones, fitting for public service, even prophecy, or preaching, 2 Cor. vii. 7. 1 Cor. xii. 31. and xiv. 1, 12, 39.

III. Motives or arguments exciting to the exercise of true zeal.

1. The example of Christ, whom David in prophetic language personated, saying, *The zeal of thine house hath eaten me up,* consumed his spirits, his strength, and life; so much did he exert himself in his public ministrations; he shewed his zeal for the doctrines of the gospel, by his warm and constant preaching them, even with power and authority, as the Scribes and Pharisees did not; in the indefatigable pains he took,

travelling from place to place to do it; running the risk of his life, and exposing himself to frequent dangers on that account: and for the worship of the house of God, as appears by inveighing so severely against the traditions of men; by asserting the purity of worship in spirit and in truth; by expressing his resentment at the profanation of the house of God, driving out the buyers and sellers from it; which brought the above passage to the mind of the disciples, who clearly discerned the fulfilment of it: the zeal of Christ against immorality, was seen also in his sharp reproofs of the vices of the age, both in professors and profane; and in all he is a pattern worthy of our imitation.——2. True zeal answers a principal end of redemption by Christ, Tit. ii. 14. and where there is no zeal for God, and for that which he requires an observance of, the claim to redemption seems very precarious. The love of Christ in redeeming his people will constrain them to shew a zeal for his glory, both with respect to doctrine and practice.——3. It is good, the apostle says, *to be zealously affected in*, and for that which is good; and it is approved and commended by Christ; as the church at Ephesus was for it, because she could not bear them that were evil; and a contrary disposition, that of lukewarmness, is disapproved of and resented; as in the church of Laodicea, threatened to be unchurched for it; and therefore strongly exhorted to be *zealous and repent*, Rev. iii. 15, 16, 19, 20.——4. A lukewarm temper, which is the opposite to zeal, seems not consistent with true religion, which has always life and heat in it; to be neither *cold nor hot* is condemned as having no religion at all.——5. The zeal of persons shewn in a false way, should stimulate the professors of the true religion to shew at least an equal zeal; for that *all people will walk every one in the name of his god*, and appear zealous for his worship, *we will walk in the name of the Lord our God*, at least we ought to do so, and determine upon it. The Pharisees shewed great zeal, and took great pains, compassing sea and land to make one proselyte, though made worse than he was, and worse than themselves; and should not we christians exert ourselves to the uttermost for the interest of the Redeemer, Mic. iv. 5. Matt. xxiii. 15. this must be a becoming zeal. And in order to keep up and promote such zeal, it will be proper frequently to meditate on the love of God, and Christ, the blessings of the gospel of the grace of God, the excellency of the christian religion, the benefits and privileges of the house of God, to converse often with warm and lively christians, and to sit under a savoury and fervent ministry.

CHAP. XX.

OF WISDOM OR PRUDENCE.

ZEAL without wisdom or prudence, and unless tempered with it, will be either ignorant, and not according to knowledge, or be rash and precipitant. I say wisdom or prudence, because they are much the same thing, and go together; *I wisdom dwell with prudence;* hence wisdom and prudence, and the characters of wise and prudent, are often mentioned together. Prudence lies in wisely fixing upon a right end of all actions, and in wisely choosing the best means conducive to that end, and in using them at the best time, and in the properest manner; *The wisdom of the prudent is to understand his way*, Prov. xiv. 8. in divine and spiritual things, to understand the way of salvation, and the way of his duty, and how to glorify God. Concerning which may be enquired,

I. What spiritual wisdom is, as it is an internal grace, or inward disposition of the mind respecting divine things; a man's duty, the salvation of his soul, and the glory of God. And,

First, It is in general, grace in the heart; which is called *wisdom in the hidden part*, Psalm li. 6. in the hidden man of the heart, where it lies hid, and is only seen in an hearty and sincere profession of religion, and in outward actions becoming such a profession; hence those who are truly wise, are said to be *wise in heart;* and these are the prudent ones; *The wise in heart shall be called prudent*, Prov. xvi. 21. and such is a man, *when wisdom entereth into his heart;* for it is not originally there, it is not of himself, it comes elsewhere, from without, from above, from God, who gives it entrance, and puts it there. The heart of man is naturally foolish; as it is desperately wicked, it is extremely foolish; *Their foolish heart was darkened;* and yet this is said of some thought to be very wise; and man is such by nature, by birth; *Vain man would be wise*, would be thought to be so, *though man be born like a wild ass's colt*, as stupid as that creature is; *foolishness is bound in the heart of a child*, in the heart of every child of Adam, and it is only the power of divine grace that can drive it far from him: this is the case of every man; *There is none that understandeth* divine and spiritual things, or things pertaining to salvation; not even so as to know God, and to glorify him as God, and to be thankful for mercies received from him: and this is not only true of a few illiterate men, or of such who have not the advantage of a good education; but even of the wisest philosophers that ever were in this world; for of them these things are said, who, *professing themselves to be wise, became fools,* Rom. i. 21, 22. yea, this is the case, and this the character of God's elect, whilst unregenerate, and until the grace of God takes place in their hearts; *We ourselves also were sometimes foolish, &c.* There is enough of carnal wisdom, of that which is earthly, sensual, and devilish, of wicked subtlety, and too much, *men are wise to do evil; but to do good they have no knowledge;* but in that respect are foolish, sottish, and without understanding, Jer. iv. 22. they have a quick and fruitful invention as to evil things, and get the character of *inventors of evil things;* but cannot think a good thought: men have no true spiritual wisdom, but what God gives them, and puts into them; it is he that makes them to know wisdom in the heart experimentally; it is a gift of his; *For the Lord giveth wisdom,* Prov. ii. 6.

Secondly, Spiritual wisdom in particular, is a right knowledge of a man's self; *nosce teipsum,* know thyself, was a maxim much talked of among the philosophers, but attained unto by none of them; witness the pride, the vanity, the self-conceit, they were swelled with; no man that is wise in his own eyes, and prudent in his own sight, knows himself; for one that was wiser than any of them, says, there is *more hope of a fool* than of such; whoever in his own conceit is wise and good, holy and righteous in himself, does not know himself; or who fancies that *touching the righteousness of the law he is blameless,* as said the apostle before he knew himself: a man that rightly knows himself, and is possessed of true wisdom, has knowledge of the sinfulness of his nature; of internal lust, as sinful; of indwelling sin, and the exceeding sinfulness of it; of the plague of his own heart, and therefore will not *trust* in it, or to the goodness of it, which he that does *is a fool;* he knows his own inability to perform that which is good, and that without Christ and his grace he can do nothing, and therefore will not presume upon nor attempt anything in his own strength; he knows the imperfection of his own righteousness, and therefore will not depend upon it, nor plead it as his justifying righteousness before God; he knows his soul-sickness, his spiritual maladies and diseases, incurable by himself and others, excepting the great physician Christ, to whom he only applies for healing; he knows his own poverty, and therefore seeks for true riches in Christ; gold to make him rich, white raiment to be clothed with, and Christ himself, the Pearl of great price; for which he is willing to part with all; with sinful and righteous self; and, in a word, he knows his own folly, and is ready to acknowledge what a foolish and ignorant creature he is; and until a man has learned this lesson he does not know himself, 1 Cor. iii. 18.

Thirdly, True spiritual wisdom is no other than *the light of the knowledge of the glory of God in the face of Jesus Christ,* which God commands to shine in the hearts of men; whilst men are destitute of grace, or true spiritual wisdom, they are *without God,* without the knowledge of him, his nature and perfections; they conceive of him as altogether like themselves, and fancy that he is pleased with what they are pleased with, and that he judges of things as they do; they are unacquainted with the purity and holiness of his nature, who cannot take pleasure in sin; they are ignorant of his righteousness, and therefore go about to establish their own; and are even strangers to the grace and mercy of God, as channelled in Christ, and conveyed through him; and therefore depend upon the absolute mercy of God, without any consideration of the propitiatory sacrifice of Christ; whereas the true light of the saving knowledge of God is in Christ, and as he has displayed his mercy and grace in him, and proclaimed his name in him, Exod. xxxiv. 6, 7. all the divine perfections shine most illustriously in Christ, the brightness of his Father's glory, and the express image of his person; and in the great work of redemption and salvation by him; and true wisdom lies in the knowledge of this.

Fourthly, True spiritual wisdom is no other than the fear of the Lord; both David and Solomon say, that *the fear of the Lord is the beginning of wisdom,* Psalm cxi. 10. Prov. ix. 10. there is no wisdom in a man before the fear of the Lord is put into him, and then he begins to be wise, and not before: but Job, earlier than them both, says, *The fear of the Lord, that is wisdom; and to depart from evil is understanding,* Job xxviii. 28. this includes the whole worship of God, internal and external, flowing from a principle of grace; it takes in the whole duty of man, which it is his wisdom to practise, internally and externally.

Fifthly, It is being wise unto salvation, or in things respecting that. The scriptures are said to be able to make a man wise unto salvation, 2 Tim. iii. 15. and he is a wise man indeed who is thus made wise; and he is one who sees himself lost and undone, and enquires the way of salvation, and says, as the jailor did, *What shall I do to be saved?* and being made acquainted that the way of salvation is by Christ, that there is salvation in him and in no other, applies unto him, says, as the disciples did, *Lord save us, we perish!* and, as ready to perish, such come to Christ, and venture upon him, and commit themselves to him, and say, as the leper did, *Lord, if thou wilt, thou canst make me clean,* or save me; such build their souls, and the faith and hope of the salvation of them, on Christ, the good, the sure, and only foundation; and as he is a wise master-builder who lays this foundation, such are wise unto salvation who build upon this Rock, where their house stands safe against every storm, and against which the gates of hell can never prevail; they give up themselves to him, to be saved alone by him; they prize and value him, and love him above all others; they rejoice in him as God their Saviour, and give him the glory of their salvation! I proceed to observe,

II. Wherein this wisdom practically shews itself.

1. In doing good things in general; such who are wickedly wise, are wise to do evil; but such who are spiritually wise, are *wise unto that which is good,* and *simple concerning evil,* Rom. xvi. 19. and these are capable of doing things both for their own good and for the good of others. They may do good for themselves; *He that is wise may be profitable to himself,* Job xxii. 2. see Prov. ix. 12. he may be profitable, though not to God, yet to himself; for his present good, and the present peace and tranquillity of his mind; for though not *for,* yet *in* keeping the commandments of God there is great reward; and great peace of mind such have who love and observe the law of God, without trust in and dependance on the observation of it for eternal life: and such wise persons may, by what they do, be useful to others; and therefore believers in God are exhorted to maintain good works; because they are *good and profitable to men;* both because of example and because of real benefit to them. Besides, what a wise man does, and in doing which he shews his wisdom, may be for the honour of religion, to stop the mouths of gainsayers, and put such to the blush who speak ill of religion, and of the professors of it falsely; they may and do adorn the doctrine of God our Saviour, and recommend it to others, and by their works shining before men, be the means of glorifying God, and even of winning souls to God by their good conversation; and then do they shew their spiritual wisdom, when what they do, they do from right principles, and to a right end; when what they do is from love to God, in the faith and strength of Christ, and with a view to the glory of God. And being thus done they are to be shewn *in meekness of wisdom,* without trusting to them, or boasting of them; acknowledging, that when they have done all they can, they are but unprofitable servants; and that it is by the grace of God they are what they are, and do what they do.

2. This spiritual wisdom shews itself in particular in a profession of religion. The kingdom of heaven, or the outward gospel-church-state, is compared to ten virgins; *Five of them were wise, and five were foolish;* the foolish virgins, or professors of religion, took the lamp of an outward profession, as the rest did, and were careful to trim it, and keep it bright and shining; but were not concerned for the oil of grace, that it might be a burning lamp; but the wise virgins not only took the lamp of profession, but they were concerned to have the oil of grace in the vessels of their hearts, with their lamps, and so continued burning till the bridegroom's coming; and in this they shewed their wisdom; as also in holding fast their profession without wavering. Such are wise professors, who, as they take up their profession on principles of grace, and upon a mature consideration of the cost and charges, difficulties and discouragements, trials and tribulations, they must expect to meet

with, so continue steadfast in it; having put their hand to the plough, neither turn back nor look back, but go on believing to the saving of their souls; and yet do not depend upon their profession, do not make it an house to lean upon, nor a plea for eternal life; as some at the last day will plead, that they have professed the name of Christ, embraced his gospel, and subjected themselves to his ordinances; to whom he will say, *Depart from me; I know you not!* Matt. vii. 22, 23. Luke xiii. 25, 26.

3. This spiritual wisdom shews itself in a becoming walk and conversation; in a conversation that is ordered aright, according to the rule of the word of God, and is becoming and ornamental to the gospel of Christ; it appears when a man walks *circumspectly*, with his eyes about him, with his eyes in his head, as the wise man's are, looking well to his going, to his steps, as the prudent man does; his eyes looking right on, and his eye-lids right before him, pondering the path of his feet, and neither turning to the right hand nor to the left; when he walks in wisdom towards them that are without, as well as in peace and love towards them that are within; and is careful to give no offence to Jew nor Gentile, nor to the church of God. This wisdom is seen when professors walk not *as fools*, in a vain, careless, and sinful manner, but *as wise:* and this they do when they walk as the word of God directs them, and when they walk uprightly, according to the gospel; when they walk as they have Christ for an example, and when they walk not after the flesh, but after the spirit; and one special and particular instance of their walking wisely is, *redeeming the time, because the days are evil;* and which is done when they lose no opportunity of doing good to others, nor of receiving good for themselves. Considering the days they live in are evil, and subject them to many temptations; and the days of old age, called evil, are hasting on, when they will be incapable of doing or receiving good, Eph. v. 15, 16.

4. This wisdom shews itself in observing the providence of God in the world, and the dispensations of it; in making useful remarks upon it, and in learning useful lessons from it; *Whoso is wise, and will observe these things*, things in providence, before related, *even they shall understand the loving-kindness of the Lord,* Psalm cvii. 43. and it shews wisdom to understand both the ways of God in his providence, and the ways and methods of God in his grace, and the ways he has prescribed his people to walk in, Hos. xiv. 9.

5. This spiritual wisdom shews itself in a man's concern about his last end and future state,[1] how it will be with him at last, and how it will go with him in another world, Deut. xxxii. 29. how near it is —what that may issue in;—that they be ready for death come when it will, and for an eternal world! The thing to be enquired into is,

III. From whence this spiritual wisdom comes. It is a question put by Job; *Whence cometh wisdom? and where is the place of understanding?* the answer to it is, *God understandeth the way thereof, and he knoweth the place thereof,* Job xxviii. 20, 23. for it is with him originally, and in full perfection, yea, it is in him infinite and unsearchable; it is in his gift to bestow, and is to be asked of him, *that giveth to all men liberally,* freely, richly, and bountifully, as they need, *and upbraideth not* with former folly, ingratitude, and misimprovement of what they have received, James i. 5.

1. God is the efficient cause of it; God, Father, Son, and Spirit; it is a good and perfect gift, which is from above, and comes from the Father of lights, from the King eternal, immortal, invisible, the only wise God, the fountain of all wisdom, who makes men in common wiser than the fowls of the heaven, and his saints wiser in spiritual things than the rest of mankind. It comes from Christ, who is the only wise God and our Saviour; the wisdom of God, whose is counsel and sound wisdom, and who is made to us wisdom, on whom the spirit of wisdom rests, and in whom are all the treasures of wisdom and knowledge; and it is by the Spirit of wisdom and revelation in the knowledge of Christ.——

2. The means of this wisdom, and of promoting and increasing it, are, the word of God, the ministers of it, and good men conversed with; the scriptures read and explained, when under a divine influence, and accompanied with a divine power, are *able to make wise unto salvation;* they are written for our learning; and the ministers

---

[1] Isthuc est sapere, non, quod ante pedes modo est, videre; sed etiam illa quæ futura sunt prospicere. Terent. Adelp. act. 3. sc. 4.

of the gospel, who shew unto men the way of salvation, and *win* souls to Christ, are *wise*, and make wise; and conversation with wise and good men, is a means of increasing wisdom; *He that walketh with wise men shall be wise*, Prov. xi. 30. and xiii. 20.

IV. The nature and properties of this wisdom; a full account of which is given, James iii. 17.

1. It is *from above;* from God, Father, Son, and Spirit, as before observed; it is conversant about heavenly things; it is celestial wisdom, and stands opposed to earthly wisdom in a preceding verse, wisdom about earthly things, the wisdom of this world, and the princes of it, that come to nought.——2. It is *pure* in itself, and in its effects; it is productive of purity of heart, life, and conversation; the effect of it is pure and undefiled religion, and the observance of it; those who have it, hold the mystery of the faith in a pure conscience, and are obedient to the divine precepts, out of a pure heart and faith unfeigned; it is opposed to that wisdom which is sensual, and employed in sensual gratifications, and to carnal wisdom, *the wisdom of the flesh*, or carnal mind, said to be enmity against God, Rom. viii. 7.—— 3. It is *peaceable;* it influences the professors of it to be at peace among themselves, and with one another; and to live peaceably as much as possible, with all men; to cultivate peace in families, among neighbours, and even with enemies. ——4. It is said to be *gentle;* it makes those who have it to be gentle towards all men, moderate, and humane, to bear and forbear, to bear the infirmities of the weak, to forbear and forgive one another injuries done; and for the sake of peace and love to recede from their just right, and not bear hard on others for their failings, but cover them with the mantle of love.—— 5. It is *easy to be entreated*, or persuaded, to put up with affronts, to condescend to men of low estate, and not mind high things; for *with the lowly is wisdom;* to yield easily to the superior judgment and stronger reasonings of others; to be readily inclined and induced to hope and believe the best of all men; and to entertain a good opinion of good men and their conduct.——6. It is *full of mercy and good fruits;* it fills men with compassion on those in distress, and puts them upon acts of beneficence to the poor, according to their ability; to feed and clothe them, to visit the widow and fatherless in their affliction, and comfort them; and to do other duties and good works, as fruits of righteousness, of the grace of God, and of the Spirit.—— 7. It is *without partiality;* without partiality to themselves, esteeming each other better than themselves; and to others, shewing no respect of persons, making no difference in christian fellowship between rich and poor, and giving to the poor and needy without distinction, favour, or affection.——8. It is *without hypocrisy*, to God and man; not making a shew of what they have not, and intend not to do; as it is a grace, it has a close connection with faith unfeigned, with hope which is without hypocrisy, and with love which is without dissimulation. All which shews how useful and desirable such wisdom is, and how necessary throughout the conduct of a christian life to do his duty, to avoid the snares and temptations he is liable to, to seek his own good, and the good of others; and, above all, the glory of God.

CHAP. XXI.

OF GODLY SINCERITY.

SINCERITY stands opposed to hypocrisy; than which nothing is more detestable to God; and nothing is more agreeable to him than uprightness and integrity: this is called *godly sincerity*, ειλικρινεια Θευ, *sincerity of God*, 2 Cor. i. 12. which God requires, approves of, and is a grace he bestows upon his people. What is sincere is pure and unmixed,[1] and what retains its native colours especially white, as milk, pure and unmixed; hence we read of the *sincere milk of the word*, 1 Pet. ii. 2. and fine flour without any bran, or any leaven in it; hence the phrase of *unleavened bread of sincerity and truth*, 1 Cor. v. 8. the Latin word *sincerus*, from whence our English word *sincere*, is composed of *sine et cera;*[2] and signifies *without wax;* as pure honey, which is not mixed with any wax. The Greek word ειλικρινεια, signifies properly, a judgment made of things by the light and spendor of the sun; as in

---

[1] Το καθαρον και αμιγες ετερω, Suidas in voce Ειλικρινες.

[2] So Donatus apud Vallum; but Valla himself thinks it is rather of συν et cera; quasi cum cera, mel quod integrum est et solidum et nulla sui parte fraudatur. Elegant l. 6. c. 31.

traffic men hold up goods they are buying to the light of the sun, to see if they can discover any defect in them: some think there is an allusion in it to the eagle, who holds up her young as soon as fledged, to the sun, and if they can bear the light of it without winking, she retains as her own; but if not, she rejects them as a spurious brood. Light makes every thing manifest; and such who are truly gracious and sincere, their principles and practices will bear the test of light, for the day declares them what they are; nor do they shun it: but they whose doctrines and deeds are evil, do not care to come to it, lest they should be discovered: and herein lies a principal difference between sincerity and insincerity; see John iii. 19, 20, 21.

I. I shall consider this grace of sincerity as it is truth in the heart; as it regards the truth of particular graces there; as it is concerned in doctrine professed or preached; as it has to do with divine worship; and as it appears in the walk and conversation of the saints.

First, As it is truth in the heart; for that seems to be meant in Psalm li. 6. *Thou desirest truth in the inward part*, sincerity, integrity, and uprightness of soul; hence we read of a *true heart*, which is sincere and upright in all its concerns with God; which is the same with a *clean heart*, and *a right spirit* renewed in a man; which David prays for, Psalm li. 10. and such who are possessed of this grace of sincerity in their hearts, are described as such who,——1. Are *pure in heart*. The apostle Peter wrote his second epistle to the saints, *to stir up their pure minds by way of remembrance*, 2 Peter iii. 1. it is in the Greek text, their *sincere mind;*[3] a sincere mind and a pure heart are the same, not that any man's heart is so pure as to be free from sinful thoughts, inclinations, desires, and affections; yet, though not perfect, may be sincere; and none are more ready than they, ingenuously to confess and lament the impurity of their hearts; nor any that more *love pureness of heart*, and desire it, which shews their sincerity; and that there are such it is certain, since our Lord pronounces them blessed; *Blessed are the pure in heart:* who, though not perfect, are yet sincere, and their hearts are right with God.—— 2. They are said to be *sound in heart*, in doctrine and practice; *sound in the faith*, in the doctrine of faith; using *sound speech*, and embracing things which become *sound doctrine*, such are the *wholesome words* of our Lord Jesus Christ: and sound in practice, who have a sincere regard to the ways and worship, ordinances and commands of God; have a cordial affection for them, and observe them in reality, and truth, and heartily as to the Lord; for this David prays, *Let my heart be sound in thy statutes*, Psalm cxix. 80. that is, sincere in the observance of them; see Prov. xiv. 30.——3. The same are described as single-hearted, having a single eye to the glory of God in all they do; and stand opposed to *a double minded man*, who is *unstable in all his ways;* and to those who have *a double heart, a heart and a heart*, as it were two hearts; or at least, whose hearts, words, and actions, do not agree; they are not sincere in what they say or do; speak one thing and mean another; so do not sincere persons, James i. 8. Psalm xii. 2.——4. Sincere persons, who have truth in their hearts, are the same with *the upright in heart*, who are hated and persecuted by wicked men; but *loved* by the Lord, and to whom he is good, and does good to them, Psalm xi. 2. and cxxv. 4. who have right spirits renewed in them, new hearts and new spirits given them; whose intentions, desires, and views are upright.——5. Who like Jacob, are *plain men*, or *plain hearted;* such a man as Job was, chap. i. 1. where the same word[4] is used of him as of Jacob; and is the character of all true Israelites; as of Nathanael, said to be an *Israelite indeed*, one of Jacob's genuine sons, *in whom was no guile*, Gen. xxv. 27. John i. 47. ——6. Such may be said to have truth or sincerity in the heart, the desires and affections of whose hearts are after God; as the church's, Isa. xxvi. 9. and who, as David, *pant* after the Lord, after more communion with him, and conformity to him; and express their strong and hearty affections for God, as Asaph did, Psalm xlii. 1. and lxxiii. 25.——7. Who approve themselves unto God, and are desirous to be searched and tried by him, if sincere or not, as David did, Psalm cxxxix. 23, 24.

Secondly, Sincerity may be considered as it regards the truth of particular graces in the heart, which it is connected with, and concerned about. *Sincere* is an adjective, and must have something put to it to

---

[3] Την ειλικρινη διανοιαν.

[4] תם

explain it; there must be a sincere something, and that something may be bad as well as good, wrong as well as right. Saul was a sincere Pharisee, and really thought that touching the righteousness of the law he was blameless; yea, a sincere persecutor, for he thought verily he ought to do many things contrary to the name of Jesus; as many others, who thought they should do God good service in killing the disciples of Christ. So that sincerity is to be judged according to what it is applied: and it seems not to be a distinct grace of itself, but to go through, and be an ingredient in every grace; which proves the genuineness of it. As,

1. Repentance; for there is a feigned repentance; as in Judah, Jer. iii. 10. such was the external humiliation of Ahab, which was not in reality, only in outward shew and appearance; yea, many tears may be shed, and yet no true and sincere repentance; as in Esau, Heb. xii. 17. and in others who pretend to repentance; their tears may be only what are called crocodile tears. But when repentance is from the heart, and sorrow is after a godly sort and sincere, it produces such like effects the apostle mentions in 2 Cor. vii. 11.——
2. Faith is a grace also which is distinguished by its sincerity; for there is a faith that is feigned, as was that of Simon Magus, who professed to believe, but truly did not; that is a sincere faith which is *with the heart unto righteousness;* or is a believing *with all the heart,* as was required of the eunuch, previous to his baptism; and is called *faith unfeigned,* 1 Tim. i. 5. 2 Tim. i. 5.——3. Hope, by the sincerity of it, is distinguished from the hope of the hypocrite, which is as the spider's web, and is of no avail at death: but a hope that is sincere, is fixed on a good foundation; not on man's riches or righteousness; but upon the person, blood and righteousness of Christ; and is lively, and he that has it purifies himself as he is pure.——4. Love, both to God, if true and genuine, is *with all the heart, with all the soul, and with all the strength;* and love to Christ is from the heart, and *in sincerity,* Eph. vi. 24. The church always describes Christ her beloved, even when she was in a disagreeable frame and posture; *Him whom my soul loveth!* And love to the saints, when right, is not in *word and in tongue, but in deed and in truth,* that is hearty and sincere, 1 John iii. 18. and is called *unfeigned love of the brethren,* 1 Pet. i. 22.

Thirdly, Sincerity may be considered as it regards doctrine professed or preached. *The sincere milk of the word,* unmixed and unadulterated, as desired by truly new-born babes; and by all such who have *tasted that the Lord is gracious;* they desire, as it is promised them, to be fed *with the finest of the wheat,* with the pure bread of the gospel, without the bran of human mixture, without the chaff of man's inventions; for *what is the chaff to the wheat?* they cannot live on husks, which swine do eat, but upon the kernel of divine truths, and cannot be satisfied, but *with honey out of the rock,* pure and unmixed; hence the church's lips, expressive of her profession, are said to *drop as the honey-comb,* pure virgin-honey, sincere and without wax; and *honey and milk* are said to be *under her tongue,* pure and sincere doctrine, received, retained, and spoken by her, Cant. iv. 12. for with the same sincerity the mouth confesses as the heart believes: whereas, an insincere man will not openly profess Christ and his truth, loving the praise of men more than the praise of God; as the Pharisees did. So the faithful and sincere ministers of the word do not *corrupt the word of God,* adulterate it, mix it with the doctrines of men; as hucksters mix their wine with water, or other liquors, to which the allusion is, 2 Cor. ii. 17. *Renouncing the hidden things of dishonesty, not walking in craftiness, nor handling the word of God deceitfully; but by manifestation of the truth,* in the most upright manner, *commending* themselves *to every man's conscience in the sight of God:* and then do they appear to be sincere, when their word, their doctrine, is not *yea and nay,* contradictory, and inconstant, but uniform, and all of a piece; and when the gospel trumpet, as blown by them, does not give an *uncertain sound,* 2 Cor. iv. 2. and i. 19. 1 Cor. xiv. 8.

Fourthly, Sincerity may be considered with respect to worship; which ought always to be performed in a sincere and upright manner, as Joshua said to the people of Israel; *Now therefore fear the Lord, and serve him in sincerity and in truth,* Josh. xxiv. 14.

1. Worship in general is sincere, when it is performed *in spirit and in truth;* in a spiritual manner, with the whole heart and spirit, and under the direction and influence, and by the assistance of the Spirit of God, and according to the truth of the divine word, and with truth in the heart;

for *God is a Spirit*, and must be worshipped in such a manner; and such worshippers, and such only, are agreeable to him; but as for those who *draw* nigh to him *with their mouth, and have removed their heart far from him*, or are insincere worshippers of him, he despises and rejects, John iv. 23, 24. Isa. xxix. 13.——2. Prayer in particular is to be put up to God *with a true heart;* that is with a sincere one, with which men should draw nigh to God; for he is nigh to them that *call upon him in truth;* that is in sincerity; it is the prayer which comes *not out of feigned lips*, that God hears; it is *the prayer of the upright*, that is, the sincere man, that is *his delight:* when such who, as the hypocrites, pray in synagogues and in corners of the streets, to be seen of men, are treated with contempt and abhorrence.——3. And then sincerity appears in the observance of ordinances; when men, like Zacharias and Elizabeth, walk in all the commandments and ordinances of the Lord blameless; and keep the ordinances, as they were delivered, without any innovation and corruption; and when they keep the feast, particularly that of the Lord's Supper, not *with the leaven of malice and wickedness, but with the unleavened bread of sincerity and truth*, 1 Cor. v. 8.

Fifthly, Sincerity may be considered with respect to the walk and conversation of the saints; *Blessed are the undefiled*, or the perfect and sincere *in the way;* in the way of God's commandments, walking according to the rule of the divine word, and as becomes the gospel of Christ, Psalm cxix. 1. and it is with respect to such an external walk before men that the apostle says, that *in simplicity*, in the singleness of his heart, *and godly sincerity*, such as God requires and approves of, *we have had our conversation in the world*, 2 Cor. i. 12. and they act the sincere and upright part, who,——1. Desire not so much to be seen by men, as to be approved of God. The Pharisees, hypocrites, did all they did to be seen of men; they gave alms, they prayed, and zealously observed the traditions of the elders; and all to get applause of men; but the sincere believer labours, that *whether present or absent he may be accepted* of God, and approved by him; for not he that commends himself, and seeks the praise of men, *is approved*, but *whom the Lord commendeth*, 2 Cor. v. 9. and x. 18.——2. Who have *respect to all the commandments* of God, *and esteem all his precepts, concerning all things to be right*, Psalm cxix. 6, 28. and are careful not to break the least of his commandments; who omit not the weightier matters of the law, or the more important duties of religion, and yet neglect not lighter and lesser ones.——3. Who make conscience of not committing lesser as well as greater sins; but abstain from all appearance of evil; who desire to be cleansed, and to be preserved from secret sins, as well as to be kept back from presumptuous ones; who are as severe upon their own sins, as on those of others, and even spare not right-eye and right-hand sins, those they are the most inclined unto; and are as careful to remove the beam out of their own eyes, as to observe the mote in the eyes of others.——4. Who do not seek to cover, palliate, and extenuate their sins; as Job says, *If I cover my transgressions as Adam*, and seek excuses for them as he did, such do not act sincerely; *He that covereth his sins shall not prosper*, Job xxxi. 33. Prov. xxviii. 13.——5. The man who walks according to the rule of the word, makes that the standard of his practice, and walks uprightly according to the gospel; and walks as he has Christ for an example, as in the exercise of every grace, so in the performance of every duty; and walks, not after the flesh, but after the Spirit.——6. Who has the glory of God, and the good of others in his eye, in all that he is concerned; who does whatever he does in things civil and religious with a view to promote the glory of God, and the interest of true religion, and the good of immortal souls; who naturally cares for the spiritual and eternal state of men; and whose concern throughout the whole of his own conversation is, that others, beholding his good works, may receive some benefit to themselves by his example, and glorify his heavenly Father. I go on to observe,

II. From whence this grace of sincerity springs.

1. Not from nature; it is not from descent and by birth; indeed, our first parents, previous to their fall, were in a state of simplicity, not as that signifies folly, but singleness of heart, integrity, and uprightness; such was the case of Eve, before she was beguiled, and corrupted from her simplicity by the serpent. *God made man upright*, innocent, holy, and harmless; but he sinned, and lost his integrity, *and sought out many inventions*, and

OF GODLY SINCERITY.

excuses, to palliate and cover his sin; what an insincere and disingenuous part did Adam act, when he would have thrown off the blame of eating the forbidden fruit from himself, and cast it upon his wife? and of the same disposition are all his sons and daughters naturally; there is none upright among men; the most upright are sharper than a thorn-hedge; and this is true, not of some particular nation only, and of some particular persons in it, and in some certain age and period of time; but of all the descendants of Adam; who, be they good or bad in the event, are transgressors from the womb, and go astray from thence, speaking lies; there is no truth in their inward part; yea, *their inward part is very wickedness;* not only wicked, but wickedness; yea, very wickedness, extremely wicked; the same is meant when the heart is said to be *desperately wicked,* irrecoverably such, but by the grace of God; hence flow all that dissimulation, deceit, hypocrisy, and falsehood which are in the world.——2. But sincerity is from the grace of God; though it is not a distinct grace of itself, as before observed, yet belongs to, and is an ingredient in every grace; and is what distinguishes true grace from that which is counterfeit; it is *the grace of God in truth*, in sincerity; it is every grace with that; and it is by the grace of God alone that men become sincere and upright; without this men are double-hearted, double-tongued, and deceitful; there may be a shew, an appearance of sincerity and uprightness, where there is none in reality; as in the scribes and pharisees, hypocrites, who appeared outwardly righteous to men, but within were full of hypocrisy and iniquity.——3. Wherever true sincerity is, it is of God; and is therefore called, *Godly sincerity,* or *sincerity of God*, that which has God for its author, who is the God of all grace; he that is the maker of the heart; the searcher of it, and sees what is in it, can only make it sincere and upright; who made a prophane Esau, and a plain-hearted Jacob to differ, but God by his Spirit and grace? and these fruits of the Spirit, grace, uprightness, and sincerity, are only found in regenerate persons, new creatures, who have *put on the new man*, which is *created in righteousness and true holiness*, or *holiness of truth*,[5] that which is in sincerity, and reality, and not dissembled and feigned, Eph. v. 9. and iv. 24. Wherefore,——4. Since it is of God, and him only, it is to be asked of him; he desires truth in the inward parts; he requires it, saying, *Thou shalt be perfect*, or upright, or sincere *with the Lord thy God*, before him, in his sight, Deut. xviii. 13. see Gen. xvii. 1. It is he only that can give a new heart and a new spirit, and create it in the new man, therefore to be prayed to for it by all sensible of their need of it; hence these petitions of David; *Renew a right spirit within me, and let my heart be sound in thy statutes,* Psalm li. 10. and cxix. 80. And so the apostle prays for the Philippians, that they might *be sincere and without offence till the day of Christ*, Phil. i. 10. And the rather, ——5. This should be sought for, since it is so much approved of by God, who sees and searches the heart; *I know also my God*, says David, *that thou triest the heart, and hast pleasure in uprightness,* 1 Chron. xxix. 17. *His countenance doth behold the upright,* Psalm xi. 7. he smiles upon him, and takes delight in him. What an approbation of Job does he express? and what a testimony does he give to him, because of his sincerity and uprightness, and his perseverance therein? Job i. 1, 8. and ii. 3. Which will still more fully appear by considering,

III. The happiness of such who are possessed of this grace.

1. The light of spiritual joy and gladness is provided for such persons; and is in this life, at least at times, bestowed upon them, Psalm xcvii. 11. and cxii. 4.——2. All the blessings of grace and goodness are not only wished for, but given unto them: *Grace,* the blessings of grace, are described to be *with all them that love our Lord Jesus Christ in sincerity;* and both grace and glory are given to, and *no good thing* will be *withheld from them that walk uprightly*, that is fit and proper for them, Eph. vi. 24. Psalm lxxxiv. 11.——3. Such are protected and defended from all evil, and from every enemy: the Lord himself *is a buckler to them that walk uprightly;* yea, his *eyes run to and fro throughout the whole earth, to shew himself strong in the behalf of them whose heart is perfect*, or sincere, *towards him,* Isa. xxxiii. 15, 16. Prov. ii. 7. 2 Chron. xvi. 12. ——4. Such who *walk uprightly, walk surely*, on good ground, in a good path, and by a good rule, and *shall be saved;*

---

[5] Οσιοτητι της αληθειας.

the way of the Lord, in which they walk, *is strength unto the upright,* they grow stronger and stronger, Prov. x. 9, 29. and xxviii. 18.
—5. Those enjoy the presence of God now; *The upright shall dwell in thy presence,* Psalm cxl. 13. *The pure in heart shall see God,* and be with him for ever; *The upright shall have dominion* over the wicked, in the morning of the resurrection; and as for the sincere and perfect man, his *end is peace,* everlasting peace and happiness, Matt. v. 8. Psalm xlix. 14. and xxxvii. 37.

CHAP. XXII.

OF SPIRITUAL MINDEDNESS.

THE contrast between a carnal man and a spiritual man, and between carnal-mindedness and spiritual-mindedness, is very strongly expressed by the apostle in Rom. viii. 5, 6. *They that are after the flesh,* carnal men, sinful and corrupt, who are as they were born, having nothing but flesh, sin and corruption in them, without the Spirit and his grace, who walk after the flesh, and fulfil the desires of it; these *mind the things of the flesh,* their minds are *fleshly minds,* they seek nothing but the gratification of the lusts of the flesh, and employ themselves in doing the works of it, which are called, *The sins of the flesh,* the consequence of which is death: *For to be carnally-minded is death,* eternal death, the just wages of sin; as it must needs be since such carnality is sin and sinful, and enmity against God, as in the following verse: now the spiritual man, and spiritual-mindedness, and the consequence of that, are the reverse of all this. As will appear by considering,

I. Who are the men who mind spiritual things, and are spiritual men. They are described as *they that are after the Spirit.* Not all that think they are spiritual men, and would be thought such, are so; *If any man think himself to be a prophet or spiritual,* as a man may, and yet be neither; and therefore *every spirit,* or every one that professes himself to have the Spirit, and to be a spiritual man, is not to be believed; but *the spirits,* or such who call themselves spiritual men, are to be *tried,* by the word of God, whether they are such or not; they may seem so to others, and yet not be such; and if only outwardly righteous, or externally reformed in their lives, they may be at most but moral men, not spiritual men; yea, men may have a *form of godliness,* a shew of spirituality, yet not have the truth and power of it; they may look like virgins, and appear as spiritually wise, and yet be foolish. Nor are all truly spiritual men, who have *spiritual gifts,* as they may be called, distinct from special grace; for the apostle, after having discoursed of spiritual gifts, speaks of a *more excellent way;* and observes, that men may have various gifts, extraordinary and ordinary, and yet be destitute of true grace, 1 Cor. xii. 1, 31. and xiii. 1, 2, 3. Nor are such only intended who have a greater degree of spiritual knowledge, and of real grace than others; for though these are most certainly spiritual men, and of the highest class, 1 Cor. iii. 1. Gal. vi. 1. yet they are not the only ones; others, who have less knowledge, and a lesser degree of grace, are also entitled to this character. Much less such are meant who have no flesh or sin in them; for there are no such spiritual men on earth; none but the saints in heaven, the spirits of just men made perfect; and who at the resurrection will have spiritual bodies. But,

1. They are such who are regenerated, renewed, and quickened by the Spirit of God; they are such as our Lord describes, as *born of water and of the Spirit,* or of the Spirit of God compared to water; and who and whatsoever is so born, is *spirit,* or spiritual, John iii. 5, 6. such are born of God, and made partakers of the divine nature; *not of blood,* by carnal generation and descent, *not of corruptible, but of incorruptible seed;* begotten again of God to a lively hope of a glorious inheritance, according to his abundant mercy, and of his own sovereign will and pleasure; and are a *kind of first fruits of his creatures;* yea, they are new creatures; for the grace bestowed on them is, *the washing of regeneration, and the renewing of the Holy Ghost;* they are renewed in the spirit of their minds, and have new hearts and new spirits given them, and the Spirit of God put into them, by whom they are quickened, who before were dead in trespasses and sins; but now the Spirit of life from God enters into them; and like the slain witnesses, and Ezekiel's dry bones, stand on their feet and live: and being thus made alive, they breathe in a spiritual manner, after salvation, and the way of it, and the knowledge of it; and after Christ, when directed to him; after God, and communion with him; after a discovery and application of

pardoning grace and mercy: all which, and more things of a spiritual nature, they vehemently desire, with their whole souls and spirits; and may be truly said to be spiritually-minded.——2. They are such who have their spiritual senses, and that in exercise, to discern both good and evil, to choose and mind the one, and to refuse and shun the other; they have a spiritual *sight*, a discerning of things, even of spiritual things, which are only *spiritually discerned;* and which spiritual discernment the natural man has not; but the spiritual man has, and can make a judgment of them; try things that differ, approve the more excellent, and prefer them; they have the seeing eye given them, the eyes of their understandings are enlightened by the Spirit of wisdom and revelation, in the knowledge of themselves and of Christ: this one thing they can say, *whereas* they *were blind*, they *now see;* see themselves lost and undone, and Jesus as their only Saviour; and they behold his glory, fulness, excellency and suitableness as a Saviour: they now *hear* the gospel with pleasure; it is a *joyful sound* to them, good news and glad tidings of peace, pardon, righteousness, eternal life, and salvation by Christ; they hear the voice of Christ, and are charmed with it, and their affections are drawn out to him; they hear it so as to understand it, and be delighted with it, and to distinguish it from the voice of a stranger, and therefore follow him, and not a stranger: they *taste,* and have a gust for spiritual things; they taste that the Lord is gracious, and invite others to come and taste, and see how good he is; the words of Christ, the doctrines of the gospel, are sweeter to their *taste* than the honey or honeycomb; the fruits that drop from Christ, whilst sitting under his shadow, the blessings of grace, which are from him are also sweet and pleasant to their palate: they *savour* the things which be of God and Christ, and which are of a spiritual nature; because of the *savour of his good ointment*, his rich graces, their love is drawn forth to him; they *smell a sweet savour* in his person, righteousness, and sacrifice; all his garments, his garment of salvation and robe of righteousness smell of myrrh, aloes and cassia: they *handle* the word of life, lay hold on Christ, the tree of life, and pluck, and take, and eat of the fruit that grows upon it; and when they have lost sight of Christ, their beloved, and have found him again, they embrace him in their arms, hold him fast, and will not let him go. The gospel of Christ is the power of God unto them; they receive it cordially, and the love of it, and feel it powerfully working in them, and find themselves strongly influenced by it to love and serve him.—— 3. They are capable of spiritual acts and exercises, and do perform them; spiritual men, and they only, *worship God in the Spirit,* in a spiritual manner, with their spirits, and under the influence of his Spirit; and such worship, as it becomes their character, is only acceptable to God; when the worship of carnal and formal professors is very disagreeable to him; they can talk and converse with each other about spiritual things; the Lord turns unto them, or bestows upon them a pure language, the language of Canaan, which they speak, and in which they speak one to another, so as to understand and be understood by each other; as they are favoured with abundance of rich inward experience, out of the abundance of their hearts their mouths speak, in christian conference with one another; and their speech in common conversation bewrays them, and shews to what company they belong, and that they are not carnal, but spiritual men: and they are capable of walking, and they do walk, not after the flesh, but after the Spirit; which distinguishes them from carnal men, and entitles them to the character of spiritual men; yea, they walk in the Spirit, and live in the Spirit, and are led by him, out and off of themselves, to Christ, and the fulness of grace in him, and into all truth as it is in Jesus; and such who are under his leadings and teachings, as they are the sons of God, they must be spiritual men, and mind spiritual things.——4. They have much of the Spirit of God in them, the several graces of the Spirit of God; as faith, hope, love, and all other fruits of the Spirit. The good work of grace, of which he is the author, the work of faith, and labour of love, and patience of hope, is begun in them by him, and will be carried on, performed and perfected; he works in them both to will and to do of his good pleasure, and whatsoever is well-pleasing in the sight of God, and strengthens them to do the will and work of God; under his influence they exercise every grace, and grace is the governing principle in their souls; they are not under the law, but under grace, and therefore sin has not the dominion over them; but grace reigns, through righteousness, unto eternal life, by Jesus Christ our Lord; yea, the law of the Spirit of life in Christ, frees them from the law of sin and death, from the tyrannical power of it; so that they appear to be spiritual men, and to be spiritually alive. And even the Spirit of God himself dwells in them, and is the criterion which distinguishes them from carnal men; *Ye are not in the flesh*, that is, ye are not carnal men; *but in the spirit*, spiritual men, *if so be that the Spirit of God dwell in you;* and therefore called the temple of God, and of the Holy Ghost; the world, carnal men cannot receive him, nor know him; but the true disciples of Christ know him; for he dwells with them, and shall be in them, Rom. viii. 9. John xiv. 17. though even in these spiritual men there is much carnal-mindedness, carnal affections, and lusts, and desires; *The flesh lusteth against the spirit;* and they are ready to say, with the apostle, *I am carnal; with the flesh I serve the law of sin*, Rom. vii. 14, 24, 25.

II. What the spiritual things are, spiritual men mind; from which they are denominated spiritually-minded men.

1. They mind their own souls, and the spiritual and eternal welfare of them; not only when they were first awakened to a sense of their sinful state and danger, and cried out, What shall we do to be saved? and when they first asked the way to Zion, with their faces thitherwards, and first gave up themselves to the Lord, and to a church of Christ, by the will of God; but afterwards, by making use of all opportunities, public and private, for their profit and edification, to promote the prosperity of their souls, which spiritual men are more mindful of than of their bodies.
——2. The law of God is spiritual, Rom. vii. 14. and this is minded by a spiritual man. This has great things in it worthy of consideration, and to be minded, respecting the good of men and the glory of God; and yet many are unmindful of it, yea, cast it away and despise it, *and count it as a strange thing*, Hos. viii. 12. unworthy of any notice and regard; but the spiritual man, whose eyes are spiritually enlightened, and the vail taken off from them, beholds *wondrous things* out of it, especially as in the hand of Christ, and fulfilled by him; and they may be said to mind it, and to be spiritually-minded towards it, when they meditate upon it, the author, nature, and usefulness of it. It is the character of a good and happy man, that *in his law* (the law of God) *doth he meditate day and night;* not in it as a terrifying, cursing, and condemning law; but as instructing, and informing into the nature of sin and duty, and as magnified and made honourable by Christ, who has fulfilled both the preceptive and penal part of it; and of which David says, *O how love I thy law, it is my meditation all the day!* Psalm i. 2. and cxix. 97. yea, spiritual men not only love it, *and great peace have they that love thy law;* but they delight in it, as did that spiritual man the apostle Paul; *I delight in the law of God after the inner-man;* see Psalm i. 2. Rom. vii. 22. and they are willingly subject to it, and serve it with pleasure. The *carnal mind*, φρονημα της σαρκος, *the wisdom of the flesh;* or the man who is under the influence of it, and is carnally-minded, is *enmity against God; for it is not subject to the law of God, neither indeed can be;* but the wisdom of the Spirit, or he who is under the influence of that, and is spiritually-minded, is subject to it, and with *his mind* serves the law of God.——3. The gospel, and the truths of it, which are spiritual things; *If*, says the apostle, *we have sown unto you spiritual things*, the seed of the word, and the precious truths of the gospel, *is it a great thing, if we should reap your carnal things?* partake of somewhat of your worldly substance, 1 Cor. ix. 11. these are the things of the Spirit of God, or the spiritual things which the natural man receives not, because foolishness to him; as the doctrine of the cross, or the doctrine of salvation by a crucified Christ is; nor does he know it, value and esteem it, it being only spiritually discerned; which spiritual discernment he has not; but the spiritual man judges spiritual truths, and discerns the difference of them from others, and the true value of them; his taste discerns perverse things, and distinguishes good and bad; and he esteems the word of truth more than his necessary food, and counts them savoury food, such as his soul loves; he finds the word of salvation by Christ, and he eats it, and it is the joy and rejoicing of his heart; it is like Ezekiel's roll, which was in his mouth *as honey for sweetness;* it is the *sincere milk of the word* which new-born babes desire; and is meat for strong men, to which spiritual men have their minds well-inclined: and on divine and evangelical truths they dwell in their thoughts and meditations; as on

the doctrines of everlasting love, of the covenant of grace, and the transactions of it; *We have thought of thy loving-kindness, O God, in the midst of thy temple!* and on the doctrines relating to the person, offices, grace, and righteousness of Christ; to which may be applied the words of the Psalmist, *My meditation of him shall be sweet!* Psalm xlviii. 9. and civ. 34.——4. Spiritual blessings are minded by spiritual men; such as the elect of God are blessed with in heavenly places in Christ, Ephes. i. 3. as election in Christ, acceptance with God in him, redemption, pardon, justification, adoption, and eternal life; these are things spiritually-minded men have their hearts set upon, and are often revolving in their minds; these are blessings indeed, which they are importunately desirous of; they seek first the *kingdom of God and his righteousness*, and such-like spiritual and heavenly things; believing, that all other things of a worldly kind shall be given unto them, needful for them, about which they are not anxiously solicitous, not minding them in comparison of others.——5. Being built up a *spiritual house*, and being a holy spiritual priesthood; they are concerned to offer up *spiritual sacrifices, acceptable to God by Jesus Christ*, even the sacrifices of prayer and praise, which they offer up by their great High-priest, and which become sweet odours, being perfumed with the incense of his mediation; and they themselves are made joyful in the house of prayer, their offerings being accepted with God upon his altar; which draw their spiritual minds hither, and make them intent upon such sacrifices.——6. Spiritually-minded men employ themselves in spiritual services; they present their bodies a holy, living, and acceptable sacrifice, which is but their reasonable service; and concerned they are to serve the Lord in every religious duty acceptably, with reverence and godly fear, and in righteousness and holiness all the days of their lives. Moreover,——7. They exercise themselves in the several graces of the Spirit of God; their minds are very intent upon, and very desirous of a growth in every grace, that their faith may be increased and grow exceedingly; that they may abound in hope, through the power of the Holy Ghost; and that their love also might abound yet more and more. To all which may be added,——8. That spiritually-minded men have their hearts, affections, and conversations in heaven; their hearts are where their treasure is, and that is in heaven; their affections are set on things above, where Jesus is; and their conversation is in heaven, from whence they expect Jesus their Saviour.

III. It may next be inquired, how any of the sons of men come to be spiritually men, and to be spiritually-minded. They are not so naturally, or by their first-birth; they are born of the flesh, and are flesh, carnal, sinful, and corrupt; their *minds* are *fleshly*, or they are carnally-minded; their minds and consciences are defiled with sin, and from thence nothing proceeds but what is sinful; their minds are vain and empty, and they walk in the vanity of their minds; they are without God, any true knowledge of him, love to him, and fear of him; they have not learned Christ, and think nothing about him; they are sensual, not having the Spirit, nor any of his graces; they mind earth, and earthly things, these engross all their thoughts, affections, and desires; all that is in the world, the lust of the flesh, the lust of the eyes, and the pride of life, are the principal entertainments of their minds, and what they are chiefly conversant with; their natural bias is to that which is evil; the imagination of the thought of their heart is evil, and that continually; yea, their hearts are fully set in them to do evil; and such is the disposition of their minds, that they cannot think anything of themselves, especially that which is spiritually good. This being then the case of the minds of men naturally, there must be a renewing of the mind, or it must be cast into a different mould: ere a man can be spiritually-minded, he must have a new heart and a new spirit put within him; the Spirit of God must *work* in him *to will*, must give him an inclination and disposition to that which is spiritually good; he must enlighten his mind, and fill it with the knowledge of spiritual things; must put the laws of God into the minds of men, and write them in their hearts; he must influence and attract their affections to spiritual things, and make them in love with them, and thoroughly convince them of the evil of carnal mindedness, and the sad effect of it, death; and of the advantages of spiritual mindedness, next to be considered.

IV. The effects and consequences, and so the evidence of being spiritually-minded. *1st*, Life: *To be spiritually-minded is life;* they must be alive who are spiritually minded, and they must be alive in a spiritual sense; their spiritual-mindedness is an evidence of their spiritual life, and makes it plainly appear that they are in such sense alive. This is manifest,——1. From the exercise of their senses, before observed; they have their spiritual senses of seeing, hearing, tasting, smelling, and feeling; and therefore must have life, without which there can be no senses, and the exercise of them; as he who has his natural senses, must be naturally alive, so he that has his spiritual senses must be spiritually alive. ——2. From acts of spiritual life performed by them; they breathe after spiritual things; prayer is the breath of every spiritually-minded man; *Behold he prays!* and this shews life; he discourses of spiritual things, which discovers the temper and disposition of his mind; his walk and conversation is spiritual, he walks and lives by faith on Christ, and walks on in him as he has received him. ——3. From the lively exercise of grace in him, and fervent discharge of duty. His faith is a living, and not a dead faith; his hope is lively, and his love is as strong as death, and cannot be destroyed by it; all which evidence his spiritual life; and the exercise of these graces evidences his spiritual-mindedness; and hence follow a fervency of spirit in serving the Lord, and a running in his ways without weariness, and a walking without fainting.——4. Such who are spiritually-minded are not only alive themselves, but they are the means of enlivening others by their spiritual conversation; by their spiritual counsel and advice; by the spiritual consolation they administer, and by their spiritual exhortations stirring up to love and good works. ——5. Spiritual-mindedness issues in everlasting life; which is the gift of God, and flows from his grace; which all that are spiritually-minded partake of, and shall have it; this is certain from the promise, that whosoever seeth the Son, and believes in him should not perish, but have everlasting life; and from the grace of God in them, which is a well of living-water springing up unto everlasting life; and from the Spirit of God in them, the earnest of it, and who makes meet for eternal life, and introduces into it, because of the righteousness of Christ, which entitles to it.

2*dly,* Another effect and consequent of spiritual-mindedness is peace; *To be spiritually-minded is peace;* inward peace of soul, which is a fruit of the Spirit, and is had in a way of believing in Christ; it flows from the righteousness of Christ received by faith, and from his peace-speaking blood in the conscience; and the spiritual things their minds are conversant with, are productive of internal peace, and serve to maintain and increase it. Spiritually-minded persons are of peaceable dispositions; they are desirous to *lead a quiet and peaceable life,* under whatsoever government they be; and *as much as lieth in them,* they endeavour to *live peaceably with all men,* in the neighbourhoods in which they are; to promote peace in their families, and among their friends; and *study to keep the unity of the Spirit in the bond of peace,* among the saints in a church-state, in which they are; to do otherwise would be to act the carnal part, and walk as men, 1 Cor. iii. 3. And to close all, spiritual-mindedness issues in everlasting peace, the end of such a man is peace, he departs in peace, he enters into it; and this is his everlasting portion and happiness.

CHAP. XXIII.

OF A GOOD CONSCIENCE.

The exercise of a good conscience is a branch of internal religion, and is concerned with the worship of God; God is to be *served with a pure conscience,* 2 Tim. i. 3. And it has to do not only with things natural and legal, accusing or excusing, as the law of nature directs; and with things civil, with obedience to civil magistrates, to whom we are to be subject, *not only for wrath,* or fear of punishment, *but also for conscience-sake;* their office being of God, and an ordinance of his, Rom. ii. 14, 15. and xiii. 5. but likewise with things religious, spiritual, and evangelical; things respecting both doctrine and practice; *The mystery of the faith,* or the peculiar and sublime doctrines of the gospel, are to be held *in a pure conscience;* and the ministry of the word is to be exercised, *holding faith,* the doctrine of faith, and a *good conscience* with it, 1 Tim. iii. 9. and i. 19. see Heb. xiii. 18. yea, every good work, rightly performed, springs from hence, 1 Tim. i. 5. A good conscience has God for its object, it respects his word, will, and worship; and therefore is called, *conscience towards God,* 1 Pet. ii. 19. as repentance is repentance towards God, and faith is faith towards our Lord Jesus

Christ; or συνείδησις Θεȣ, *conscience of God*, which is of God, has God for its author, being implanted in the mind of man by him; it is God's vicegerent, which acts for him, and under him, and is accountable to him. I shall consider,

First, What conscience is, and its office.

1*st*, What it is. It is a power or faculty of the rational soul of man; by which it knows its own actions, and judges of them according to the light it has: some take it to be an habit of the mind; others an act of the practical judgment, flowing from the faculty of the understanding by the force of some certain habit.

1. It is a *science*, or knowledge, as its name shews; a knowledge of the will of God, and of a man's actions, as being agreeable or disagreeable to it; it is a *common* science or knowledge, and therefore called *con-science*, common with other men, and also with God; by which it knows what is true, just, and right with God, and so what is fit to be done or not done; it is that by which a man is conscious to himself of his secret thoughts, as well as of his actions; it is the spirit of a man, which only knows the things of a man within him, and knows those things which only God and himself knows.——

2. From this knowledge arises a judgment which conscience forms of itself and actions, and accordingly approves or disapproves of them, and excuses or accuses for them: to which judgment the apostle refers when he says, *If we would judge ourselves, we should not be judged*, 1 Cor. xi. 31. and this is made in the view of the judgment of God, and is submitted to that, and has that joined with it, it is a joint testimony; and even sometimes God himself appeals to the judgment of conscience, as well as conscience appeals to God; *Judge, I pray you, betwixt me and my vineyard*, Isa. v. 3. see Rom. ix. 1.——3. It is the will of God revealed, which is the rule of conscience, its knowledge and judgment; either revealed, by the law and light of nature, which was the rule to the Gentiles, who had not the written law, Rom. ii. 14, 15. or by the moral law written, which contains that good, perfect, and acceptable will of God, concerning things to be done or not done; or by the gospel, which instructs in the doctrines of grace, and enforces the duties of religion by them, and is a rule to walk by, Gal. vi. 16.——4. Hence nothing can bind the conscience but the law and will of God; it is God's vicegerent, acts for and under him, and receives its authority and instructions from him, and is accountable to him, and to no other; it is a debtor to him, and owes obedience to his will; it is constrained by it, laid under a necessity to observe it, and cannot do otherwise: let men say what they will to the contrary, or be clothed with what authority they may, parents, masters, magistrates, have no power over children, servants, and subjects to oblige them to what is contrary to the dictates of conscience, according to the will of God; no laws of men are binding on conscience, which are not according to, or are contrary to the law and will of God; *We ought to obey God, rather than men*, is the determination of the apostles of Christ, Acts iv. 19, 20. and v. 29.

2*dly*, The office of conscience, what it does and ought to perform, when it does its duty.

1. It is a light to enlighten men in the knowledge of the will of God; it is that light which lightens every man that comes into the world; which is had from Christ the Creator of men; and shews unto men what is their duty to God and man; it informs them both what they are to do, and what to avoid; *The spirit of man*, which is his natural conscience, is *the candle of the Lord*, which he lights up in the soul of man, *searching* the inmost recesses of the heart; especially if enlightened by the word and Spirit of God, John i. 9. Prov. xx. 27.——2. It takes cognizance of a man's actions; it keeps a good lookout, and watches over them; it has a sort of an omniscience belonging to it; it sees all his goings, yea, it sees his heart, and what passes through that, marks his ways and works, and numbers his steps.——3. It takes an account of them, and registers them; it is a book in which all are written; and though it may be shut up for the present, and little looked into, there is a judgment to come, when the books will be opened, and the book of conscience among the rest; according to which men will be judged.——4. It acts the part of a witness for or against men, as even in the heathens; *Their conscience bearing witness* to their actions, good or evil; and so their thoughts excused or accused one another. So the conscience of a good man bears witness for him, and is a co-witness with the Holy Ghost, to which he can appeal, as the apostle did, Rom. ix. 1. so the consciences of Joseph's

brethren witnessed against them, when they said, *We are verily guilty concerning our brother*, Gen. xlii. 21. hence the common saying, " Conscience is as a thousand witnesses;" it is so whether as good[1] or bad.——5. Conscience is a judge, acquitting or condemning. So the conscience of Samuel acquitted him of all charges that could be brought against him, as did God and his people also, 1 Sam. xii. 5. Such a clear conscience had Job; *My heart*, says he, that is, my conscience, *shall not reproach*, or condemn *me, so long as I live*, chap. xxvii. 6. In this sense the apostle uses the phrase, and points at the office of conscience, 1 John iii. 20, 21.——6. In wicked men it has the office of a punisher, or tormentor; and a greater punishment, and a more severe torment cannot well be endured than the stings and lashes of a man's own conscience;[2] this is what the scripture calls the worm that never dies; and the heathens meant by a vulture feeding on men's hearts or livers.

Secondly, The various sorts of conscience; which may be reduced to these two, an *evil conscience*, Heb. x. 22. and a *good conscience*, 1 Tim. i. 19.

1*st*, An evil conscience; the consequences of which are guilt, terror, distress, and sorrow, sooner or later, unless the heart is purged from it by the blood of Christ; of which there are different sorts. ——1. Which is blind and ignorant, arising from an understanding darkened and alienated from the life of God, through ignorance; when in some it comes to that pass, as to have lost the distinction between good and evil, and between darkness and light; and some do not care to come to the light, lest their deeds should be reproved; and others, like corrupt judges, are bribed with a gift, which blinds the eyes of the wise; and others are so sottishly superstitious, that they think they do God good service when they take away the lives of his people; and such a conscience was Saul's, when he thought he ought to do many things contrary to the name of Jesus, and therefore made havoc of the church.——2. A dull, heavy, stupid conscience, which is no more affected than a man that is asleep; and though in danger, as a man asleep in the midst of the sea, and on the top of the mast, yet careless, unconcerned, and secure; and though stricken and beaten feels it not, and is quite stupified; and like a man in a lethargy, unless a great noise is made, is not easily roused; as Pharaoh, whose conscience was alarmed with the thunder and lightnings, and then he owned he had sinned; but when these were over, he returned to his former hardness and stupidity: and even in good men conscience may be lulled asleep, and continue stupid for a considerable time; as in the case of David, till Nathan was sent to him, and charged his conscience, saying, *Thou art the man*.——3. A partial one, when it overlooks greater sins, and is very severe on lesser ones; as Saul bore hard on the Israelites for the breach of a ceremonial law, in eating flesh with the blood, when he made no scruple of slaying fourscore and five priests of the Lord at once: and as the chief priests, who pretended it was not lawful to put the money into the treasury wherewith Christ was betrayed, because it was the price of blood, and yet it was the same money these wicked men had given to Judas to betray him: and likewise it is partial, when it suffers a man to neglect duties and services of the greatest importance, and puts him upon lesser ones; as Saul in his conscience thought he did well when he killed the lean kine, and spared the best of the flock and herd: and so the Pharisees, who omitted the weightier matters of the law, and were strict to observe the traditions of the elders, which were no part of the law.——4. A bribed one; as Herod's conscience was bribed with his oath, and pleaded that, for the cutting off of the head of John the Baptist: and the Jews endeavoured to make their conscience easy, in pleading for the taking away the life of Christ, that they had a law, that he who made himself the Son of God should die.——5. An impure one, as the conscience of every unregenerate man is; *unto them that are defiled and unbelieving, is nothing pure; but even their mind and conscience is defiled*, Tit. i. 15. and so the conscience of a weak brother may be defiled through the imprudent use of a liberty, by a stronger one, 1 Cor. viii. 7.——6. A seared one, one cauterized, seared, as it were, with a red-hot iron, 1 Tim. iv. 2. and so becomes insensible of sin and danger, and past feeling any remorse for sin; it is

---

[1] Bona conscientia turbam advocat; male etiam in solitudine anxi a atque solicita est——O te miserum si contemnis hunc testem, Seneca, Ep. 13.

[2] Nihil est miserius quam animus hominis conscius, Plaut. Mostellar. act. 3. sc. 1. v. 13.

without any consciousness of it, and repentance for it, Jer. viii. 6.——7. A desperate one, or one filled with despair; as Cain's was, when he said, *My punishment is greater than I can bear*; and Judas's, who said, *I have sinned, in that I have betrayed innocent blood!* and went and destroyed himself: and especially such will be the consciences of the damned in hell, whose worm dieth not, but they will be ever in black despair.

2dly, A good conscience. There may be in unregenerate men, a conscience in its kind, good; it may be naturally good, when it is not morally, spiritually, and evangelically good. Conscience, when it does its office according to its light, is a natural good conscience; as in the heathens, though they were guilty of sins their conscience did not charge them with; so the apostle Paul, before his conversion, *lived in all good conscience*, Acts xxiii. 1. though a blasphemer and a persecutor. And there may be in good men a conscience not commendable, and which, in a sense, cannot be called good. As,

1. There may be in them a mistaken and erring conscience; *Some with conscience of the idol*, thinking it to be something, when it is nothing, *eat it as a thing offered to an idol, and their conscience being weak is defiled*, 1 Cor. viii. 7.——2. A doubting conscience. The apostle Paul had no doubt, but was firmly persuaded, *that there is nothing unclean of itself;* yet observes, *that he that doubteth* whether it is unclean or no, and to be eaten or not, *is damned*, that is, is condemned by himself, Rom. xiv. 14, 23.——3. A weak conscience; which arises from weakness of faith about things lawful and pure, Rom. xiv. 1, 14. 1 Cor. viii. 7. which is soon and easily disquieted, grieved, and troubled, at seeing others do that which it doth not approve of, Rom. xiv. 15. and which at once judges and condemns another man's liberty, Rom. xiv. 3. 1 Cor. x. 29. or which, by the example of others, is easily drawn to the doing of that by which it is defiled, wounded, and destroyed, as to its peace and comfort, 1 Cor. viii. 7, 9, 10, 11, 12.——4. A conscience smitten and wounded, which, though not sinful, may be said to be evil, and not good, because distressed; thus David's heart, or conscience, smote him when he had numbered the people, and made him very uneasy, disquieted and uncomfortable; and sometimes it is so smitten, pricked, and wounded, and so loaded with guilt, that it is intolerable; a *wounded spirit*, or conscience, *who can bear?* Prov. xviii. 14.——5. There is a conscience enlightened and awakened with a sense of sin and danger; which, though for the present distressing, issues well; as in the three thousand pricked in their hearts, who said to the apostles, *Men and brethren, what shall we do?* and in the jailor, who came trembling before Paul and Silas, and said, *Sirs, what must I do to be saved?* which, though attended with great agonies in both instances, issued well, in repentance unto life and salvation, not to be repented of; the immediate effects of a truly awakened conscience, are shame and confusion of face for sin; as in our first parents, who attempted to cover their nakedness, and hide themselves; see Rom. vi. 22. dread of the divine Being, fear of punishment, and wrath to come, Rom. iv. 15. an ingenuous confession of sin, and sorrow for it, 1 Tim. i. 13. 2 Cor. vii. 10. from which shame, fear, and sorrow, it is relieved by a discovery and application of pardon through the blood of Christ, which, and which only, makes the conscience a good one. The epithets of a good conscience are,—(1.) A tender one; as in Josiah, humbled under a sense of sin, affected with a godly sorrow for it, one that cannot easily comply with a temptation to commit sin; as in Joseph, who said to his mistress, tempting him, *How can I do this great wickedness, and sin against God?* and having the fear of God before its eyes, and on its heart, cannot do what others do; as Nehemiah, 2 Kings xxii. 19. Gen. xxxix. 9. Neh. v. 15.—(2.) A conscience void of offence; such as the apostle Paul was studiously concerned to exercise, Acts xxiv. 16. careful not to offend, by sinning against God, and to give no offence to Jew nor Gentile, nor to the church of God; and this he studied to have *always*; not at one time only, but continually; and not in some things only, but in *all things*, Heb. xiii. 18.—(3.) A pure conscience, 1 Tim. iii. 9. 2 Tim. i. 3. Conscience is defiled with sin, as all the powers and faculties of the soul are: a pure or purified conscience, is a conscience purged from the dead works of sin by the blood of Christ; an heart sprinkled from an evil conscience by the same; that is the fountain to wash in for sin and for uncleanness, that only cleanses from all sin, Heb. ix. 14. and x. 22. such a conscience is only a good one.

Thirdly, The effects of a good and pure

conscience; which must make it very desirable and valuable.

1. Freedom from the guilt of sin. This the priests under the law could not remove with their sacrifices, and so could not *make the comers* to them *perfect;* could not make their consciences perfect, nor ease them of the burden of sin, and purge them from the guilt of it; then they would *have had no more conscience of sins*, whereas there was an annual remembrance of them, notwithstanding these sacrifices. From whence it appears, that such who have a truly purged and purified conscience, by the precious blood and better sacrifice of Christ, *have no more conscience of sins* they are purged from: not but that they make conscience, and are careful to avoid committing sin; but the guilt of sins being removed by the blood of Christ, their consciences do not condemn them for sins that have been committed by them, and from which they are purged, Heb. x. 1, 2.——2. Peace of soul and tranquillity of mind. The blood of Christ *speaks better things than that of Abel;* the blood of Abel, in the conscience of his brother, the murderer, spoke terror, wrath, and damnation; but the blood of Christ, in the conscience of a sinner, purified by it, speaks peace, pardon, and salvation; one that is justified by faith in the blood and righteousness of Christ, has peace with God, and peace in himself; the effect of this is, *quietness and assurance for ever.*——3. Joy, as well as peace, is another effect of a good and pure conscience; especially when atonement for sin by the sacrifice of Christ is applied and received into it, Rom. v. 11. yea, the testimony of conscience, with respect to integrity and uprightness in conversation, under the influence of divine grace, yields joy and pleasure to a good man, 2 Cor. i. 12. as an evil conscience troubles and distresses, and gives sorrow; a good conscience exhilarates, and makes joyful and cheerful;[3] the wise man says, *a merry heart*, which some interpret of a good conscience, *makes a cheerful countenance*, and *hath a continual feast*, Prov. xv. 13, 15. ——4. Boldness, confidence, and glorying in the midst of calumnies, reproaches, and persecutions from the world, is another effect of it; a man of a good conscience can defy all his enemies, and put them on proof of making good their calumnies, and can easily refute them; as Samuel said, 1 Sam. xii. 3. and such a man, for *conscience towards God, can endure grief, suffering wrongfully;* not as an evil-doer, but as a Christian; and therefore is not ashamed, but *glorifies God on this behalf*, 1 Pet. ii. 19. and iv. 15, 16. yea, if a man's heart and conscience does not condemn him, then has he *confidence towards God*, 1 John iii. 21. as well as towards men.[4] ——5. The effect of a good conscience, purified by the blood of Jesus, is a deliverance from the fears of death and judgment to come; such a man is not *afraid of evil tidings* now, of evil times approaching, and of judgments coming upon the earth; nor is he terrified at the alarms of death, but meets it with a composed mind, and has confidence that he shall not be ashamed before the Judge of all at his coming. And these are so many arguments why,

Such a conscience is to be *held*, and held fast; a good man should exercise himself to have it, and to exercise it, and himself in it, and be careful to do nothing contrary to it; but make use of all means to preserve it, by frequently communing with his own heart, by taking heed to his ways, and by having respect to all the commandments of God: and especially should deal with the blood of Christ continually for the purifying of his heart by faith in it, and for cleansing him from all sin.

CHAP. XXIV.

OF COMMUNION WITH GOD.

Communion with God is the top of the saints' experience in this life, it is the height of experimental religion and powerful godliness. This, of all the enjoyments of God's people on earth, is the nearest to the heavenly bliss; and could entire *perfection* and *endless duration* be added to it, it would be that. I shall consider,

First, Communion with God in general, which appears chiefly in a large communication of grace, and the blessings of it from him conveyed through Christ, and applied by the blessed Spirit; and in a free exercise of grace upon him, under a divine influence: in all which is enjoyed much of the divine presence.

---

[3] Gaudium hoc non nascitur nisi ex virtutum conscientia; non potest gaudere nisi fortis, nisi justus, nisi temperans.—Seneca Ep. 59.

[4] ——hic murus aheneus esto,
Nil conscire sibi, nulla pallescere culpa.—Hor. Ep. l. 1. ep. l. 1. 60.

1st, Communion is founded in union and arises from it. There is an union between God and his people; for the more open manifestation and evidence of which our Lord prays, John xvii. 21. *That they all may be one, as thou, Father, art in me, and I in thee; that they also may be one in us!* This original union is a federal union between God and them, taking them into a covenant relation to himself; by virtue of which he becomes their God, and they become his people; it is a conjugal union between them, as between husband and wife; *thy Maker is thine Husband*, Isa. liv. 5. The evidence of which union is the gift of the Spirit to them in regeneration and conversion; when there appears to be a vital union and a mutual inhabitation of God in them, and of them in God; *hereby we know that we dwell in him, and he in us, because he hath given us of his Spirit*, 1 John iv. 13. The bond of this union is the everlasting love of God to them. As it is the love of one friend to another which knits their souls together; as the soul of Jonathan was knit to the soul of David, and Jonathan loved him as his own soul; and as the saints in a spiritual relation are *knit together in love*, and by it; love is the cement which unites them: so it is the love of God in his heart towards his people which attracts them to him, and unites them with him; and which bond is indissoluble; for nothing shall be able to *separate from the love of God*, nor to separate from him, who are interested in his love; and in the manifestation of this love unto them lies much of their sensible communion with God; as an effect and evidence of this his everlasting love to them, he with loving-kindness draws them to himself in effectual calling, when large displays are made of it to them, and at times they have some plentiful effusions of it; the love of God is shed abroad in their hearts, by the Spirit that is given them, and their hearts are directed into the love of God; insomuch that they are *rooted* and *grounded* in it, and are persuaded of their interest in it; and comprehend, with all saints, what is the breadth, and length, and depth, and height of it; they are made to drink largely of this river of pleasure, the river, the streams whereof make glad the city of God; in the participation of which they have much solace and refreshment, and enjoy much communion with God.

2dly, The grand blessing of grace flowing from this union, is covenant-interest in God; than which there cannot be a greater blessing; *happy is that people whose God is the Lord!* and this covenant-interest always continues, it can never be destroyed; *This God is our God for ever and ever!* and this is the foundation-blessing, from whence all others take their rise; *he that is our God, is the God of salvation!* of all the blessings of it, Psalm cxliv. 15. and xlviii. 14. and lxviii. 20. of all the spiritual blessings saints are blessed with in Christ, and of all grace from him, and all the supplies of it; *My God, my covenant-God, shall supply all your need!* Eph. i. 3. Phil. iv. 19. Now in the perception and enjoyment of this grand blessing, covenant-interest in God, communion with him greatly lies; God sometimes says to his people, even when they are fearing and doubting, *Be not dismayed, for I am thy God!* and they in the exercise of faith, say, as David, *I trusted in thee, O Lord, I said unto thee, Thou art my God!* Isa. xli. 10. Psalm xxxi. 14. they avouch the Lord to be their God, and he avouches them to be his peculiar people; *I will say*, says the Lord, *It is my people; and they shall say, The Lord is my God!* Zech. xiii. 9. and when this is the case, sensible communion with God must be enjoyed: the Lord is the portion of his people; and when he says to them as he did to Abraham, *I am thy shield, and thy exceeding great reward;* and they in return say, *The Lord is my portion, saith my soul, therefore will I hope in him*, Gen. xv. 1. Lam. iii. 24. their portion now in the land of the living, and their portion for evermore; under such a discovery, and in such a view of things, there must be communion with God: they have a mutual interest in each other; the Lord's people is his portion, and he himself is the portion of Jacob; and therefore with great propriety may they be said to be *heirs of God;* an amazing phrase! expressive of property, interest, and fellowship. Hence,

3dly, There is a mutual intercourse between God and his people; which is variously expressed in scripture.——1. By their mutual indwelling in each other, and which follows upon covenant-interest, and is an evidence of it; as was the Lord's dwelling among the people of Israel; *I will dwell*, says Jehovah, *among the children of Israel, and will be their God*, make it manifest to them thereby, as follows, *and they shall know that I am the Lord their God*: hence he ordered a *sanctuary* to be made, that he might *dwell among them;* and in this sanctuary, or tabernacle, an ark was put, and over the ark a mercy-seat, and on that the cherubim, between which Jehovah dwelt; and from whence he promised to commune with Moses concerning all things relative to the people of Israel; an emblem this of saints' communion with God, through Christ, at the throne of grace, Exod. xxix. 45, 46. and xxv. 8, 22. And God not only dwells in particular congregated churches of Christ, who are built up an habitation for God, through the Spirit; such as were the churches at Corinth and at Ephesus, 2 Cor. vi. 16. Eph. ii. 22. but in particular persons, who love Christ, and keep his commandments; of whom he says, *We will come unto him, and make our abode with him!* a phrase expressive of constant and continued communion, at least for a while, John xiv. 23. and on the other hand, such dwell in God, who has been *the dwelling-place of his people in all generations*, and is their *strong habitation, whereunto they may continually resort,* Psalm xc. 1. and lxxi. 3. and such dwell in God, who live in the continual exercise of grace upon him; and particularly of the grace of love towards him, and towards his people; *He that dwelleth in love, dwelleth in God, and God in him,* 1 John iv. 16. this is communion.——2. By a mutual walking together; which shews agreement, and is expressive of fellowship; *Can two walk together, except they be agreed?* Amos iii. 3. God and his people are agreed; reconciliation to God is made for them by the death of Christ, and reconciliation is made in them by the Spirit of Christ; and both are signified in Rom. v. 10. and being thus agreed, they walk together; God walked with the children of Israel in a tent and in a tabernacle, which moved from place to place; and he walks in the midst of his golden candlesticks, particular churches, as he has promised; *I will dwell in them and walk in them*, and so in individual believers, 2 Cor. vi. 16. and they walk with him; thus *Enoch walked with God;* as did Noah and others, Gen. v. 24. and vi. 9. as do all believers, they walk by faith on God as their covenant-God, and walk humbly before him, and in all his commandments and ordinances blameless; in which they have much communion with him.—— 3. By a mutual converse together; they talk together, God speaks to them, and they speak to him; such familiar fellowship had Abraham with God, about the affair of Sodom; which, when over, it is said, *he left communing with him,* Gen. xviii. 33. and such had Moses also, with whom God is said to *commune,* to *talk* with him, and to *speak* to him *face to face,* Exod. xxv. 22. and xxxi. 18. and xxxiii. 9, 11. and something similar to this, is the experience of all the saints, when the Lord appears unto them, and talks with them, and tells them that he has loved them with an everlasting love, and has drawn them to himself with the cords of it; when he visits them, and discloses the secrets of his heart unto them, Psalm xxv. 14. and they talk with him, and speak to him in prayer; they have access to him through Christ, and that with freedom and boldness, through his blood and righteousness, and come up even to his seat, and tell him all their mind, make known their requests unto him, and pour out their souls before him; much of communion with God lies in prayer, private, family, and public.—— 4. By a mutual sitting down and feasting together; the table on which the shewbread, or bread of faces, was set, was typical of the saints' communion with God, and the enjoyment of his presence, through the mediation of Christ; so was the meat-offering, part of which was burnt for a savour, a memorial of it to the Lord, and the rest was eaten by Aaron and his sons. God has spread a table for his people, and made a feast of fat things for them on his holy mountain; where they feast with him, and he with them; more particularly in the ordinance of the Lord's Supper, in which much spiritual communion is enjoyed; of which more hereafter.

Secondly, Who the persons are who have communion with God.

1*st*, Not unregenerate men, such who are in a state of nature; for they are in a state of alienation from the life of God; they are at a distance from him, their sins separate between God and them. Adam, in his state of innocence, had nearness to and communion with God; God frequently conversed with him, made known his mind and will to him, and bestowed very special favours upon him; but that whisperer, sin, soon separated chief friends; and man falling into sin, was banished from the divine presence; *So he drove out the man* from the garden of Eden, as an emblem of the estrangement of him and his posterity from God; which is the case of them all.

2*dly*, Not any who are in the native

darkness and blindness of their understandings, and walk therein; which is the condition all men are in by nature; every one *walks in darkness:* and now *what communion hath light with darkness?* As persons enlightened by the Spirit and grace of God, can have no spiritual communion with such who are altogether in the dark about spiritual things; much less can there be any communion between God, who is light, and such who walk in darkness, 1 John ii. 11. and i. 5, 6.

3*dly,* Such who are dead in sin, as all men naturally are, can have no communion with God; for as *what agreement hath the temple of God* (the temple of the living God) *with idols?* lifeless creatures, so what agreement can there be between the living God and dead sinners? Such must be quite strangers to a life of communion with God, when it is *a time of life,* and so of open love; then, and not before, does God spread his skirt over such persons, as a token of their conjugal relation to him, and enters into covenant with them, or manifests to them their covenant-interest in him; and so they openly become his, and are admitted to fellowship with him, Ezek. xvi. 8.

4*thly,* No unholy and unrighteous persons have communion with God; for *what fellowship hath righteousness with unrighteousness?* as not righteous men with unrighteous men in a church-state; so not a pure, holy, and righteous God, with impure and unsanctified sinners; even with none but such who are created in righteousness and true holiness; who are washed, sanctified, and justified in the name of the Lord Jesus, and by the Spirit of our God.

5*thly,* Not any in whom sin is the governing principle; in whom it reigns, and who commit it with as much boldness and impudence as if they had a law for it, Psalm xciv. 20. but God is of such unspotted purity and holiness, that he cannot take pleasure in sin, neither shall evil men dwell with him, not now nor hereafter; but shall be bid to depart from him as workers of iniquity. But,——1. Such only have communion with God, or are admitted to fellowship with him, who are loved and chosen by him; such whom for the great love wherewith he has loved them, he has quickened them by his Spirit and grace, and with loving-kindness has drawn them to himself; those whom he has chosen to be holy, and without blame before him in love, he causes to approach to him now, and gives them nearness to him, and fellowship with him. ——2. Such who are redeemed and reconciled by Christ, through his sufferings and death; by which he has made satisfaction for sin, and so removed that which lay in the way of a sinner's communion with God: Christ suffered for sins, the just for the unjust, *that he might bring us to God,* into a state of open communion with him; and such *who are sometimes afar off,* with respect to communion, *are made nigh by the blood of Christ;* by which means obstructions in a way of fellowship are removed, and only such persons are admitted to it.——3. Such chosen and redeemed ones, who are regenerated and sanctified by the Spirit of God; for his work is necessary to communion with God; *Without holiness no man shall see the Lord,* enjoy him, and have fellowship with him, neither now nor hereafter. The gift of the Spirit, as a Spirit of sanctification, and the operations of his grace on the hearts of men, are the great evidence of union to God, from whence flows communion with him, 1 John iii. 24. and iv. 13. I go on to consider,

Thirdly, The special fellowship which such persons have with the Father, Son, and Spirit, distinctly; the apostle John says, it is *with the Father, and with his Son Jesus Christ,* 1 John i. 3. to which may be added, Phil. ii. 1. *If any fellowship of the Spirit:* and also 2 Cor. xiii. 14. *The communion of the Holy Ghost be with you all.* All which put together, shew that the saints have a communion with each person in the Godhead.

1*st,* With God the Father, as he is the Father of Christ; who, as such, has blessed them with all spiritual blessings in Christ, and as such, has chosen them in him to holiness and happiness, and as such, regenerates them, according to his abundant mercy; and is the Father of mercies, and the God of all grace and comfort to them; and as he is their covenant-God and Father in Christ, through whom they have access to him as their Father, and address him as their Father in heaven, and call upon him for what they want, and under the witnessings of the Spirit of adoption, cry Abba, Father; and say, *doubtless, thou art our Father:* and then may they be said to have communion with him as such, when their faith and hope are exercised on him; and they are affected with his wondrous love in taking them into his family, and putting them among the children, and encouraging them to call him their Father, and not turn away from him; which obliges them to say, *What manner of love the Father hath bestowed upon us, that we should be called the sons of God!* 1 John iii. 1. and when they are sensible of the feelings of his heart for them, his sympathy with them, pity and compassion on them, under all their afflictions, temptations, trials, and exercises, Isa. lxiii. 9. Psalm ciii. 13. then have they fellowship with the Father.

2dly, With Christ: fellowship with him is what the Lord's people in effectual vocation are particularly called unto, 1 Cor. i. 9. and what Christ himself invites them to, Cant. iv. 8. and which lies, ——1. On his part, in a communication of grace unto them, which they receive at his hands; he is full of grace, all fulness of it dwells in him, and out of his fulness they receive, and grace for grace, an abundance of it, especially at first conversion, when the grace of Christ is exceeding abundant, flows and overflows; and afterwards they have a sufficiency of it to help them in all their times of need, a constant supply of it as they want: Christ has been, in all ages, *the fountain of gardens, the well of living waters,* and as *streams from Lebanon* to all his churches and people; and with joy do they draw water out of the full wells of salvation in him, and become strong in the grace that is in him, to which they are allowed and encouraged to have recourse at all times.——2. On their part, this fellowship lies in the exercise of grace upon Christ; in the goings forth of their souls to him in acts of faith, hope, love, joy, &c.—(1,) Upon his Person, as the Son of God, beholding his glory as the glory of the only begotten of the Father, and the express image of his Person; when he appears to them altogether lovely, and the chiefest among ten thousand, and the only and all-sufficient Saviour, able to save to the uttermost all that come to God by him; and when they are encouraged to look to him and be saved, and live by faith on him, the Son of God, who hath loved them and given himself for them; and when their love is attracted to him, the unseen Saviour, and the desires of their souls are to his name, and to the remembrance of him; and they have hope of eternal life, and an expectation of it, as the free gift of God through him, and rejoice in him, having no confidence in the flesh, then have they fellowship with him.—(2.) Upon him as considered in his offices of Prophet, Priest, and King. They have communion with him as their Prophet, who teaches them by his Spirit, word, and ordinances; and from whom they receive that anointing which teacheth all things; to him they hearken as the great Prophet of the church, embrace the doctrines of his gospel, and pay a regard to all the instructions of his lips, and in whose hearts the word of Christ dwells richly, and works effectually: they deal with Christ, and have fellowship with him in his Priestly office; they have to do with his blood, for the remission of their sins, and the cleansing of their souls; and with his righteousness for their justification before God, and acceptance with him; and with his sacrifice, for the atonement and expiation of their iniquities; and on account of all this, have much peace, joy, and comfort in a way of believing. They consider him as the High-priest over the house of God, who transacts all affairs for them; they make use of him as their advocate and intercessor with the Father, and put their petitions into his hands, to be offered up by him, perfumed with the much incense of his mediation; they acknowledge him as their King, submit to his government, yield obedience to his commands, and esteem all his precepts concerning all things to be right. Saints have such communion and fellowship with Christ in his offices, that they have in some sense a share in them; that is, they are made by him prophets, priests, and kings; prophets to teach and instruct others, having received the anointing from him; and kings and priests unto God and his Father, 1 John i. 27. Rev. i. 6.—(3.) Much of fellowship with Christ is enjoyed in the use of, and by the means of the ordinances of his house, especially the ordinance of the Supper. The church is a banqueting-house, into which Christ brings his people, where they sit under his shadow, and in his presence, with delight, and his banner over them is his love displayed; here he has a table spread, and at it he himself sits, and welcomes his guests, saying, *Eat, O friends! drink abundantly, O beloved!* which encourages them, and causes their *spikenard to send forth the sweet smell* thereof, or their graces to go forth in exercise on him; so that the communion is mutual; he sups with them, and they with him.

Now this communion with Christ greatly arises from the saints' relation to him; he is the Husband of his church and people, and they are his spouse and bride; hence a communion both of name and goods; they have the same common name, *The Lord our Righteousness*, Jer. xxiii. 6. and xxxiii. 16. and all that Christ has is theirs, they being Christ's and he theirs; is made to them *wisdom, righteousness, sanctification*, and *redemption*, 1 Cor. i. 30. and iii. 21—23. Christ is the head, to which his body, the church, is joined, and the saints are members of him, and one Spirit with him; from whom they receive life and nourishment, and increase with the increase of God: he is the vine, they the branches; and by virtue of union to him, a communication of the fruits of grace, holiness, and perseverance therein, is made to them from him.

3dly, Saints have also a special and particular communion with the Holy Ghost, in the gifts of his grace unto them, and which they exercise under his influence; as the grace of faith, which is of his operation, and from whence he is called, *the Spirit of faith;* and a *good hope through grace*, in the exercise of which believers abound, *through the power of the Holy Ghost;* and love is a fruit of the Spirit, and which is under his cultivation. Moreover, this fellowship of the Spirit, appears in the offices of grace, which he performs towards them; as the guide, teacher, and comforter of them; as a Spirit of grace and supplication, making intercession in them; as a Spirit of adoption, witnessing to their spirits, that they are the children of God; and as the earnest of the heavenly inheritance to them, and the sealer of them up unto the day of redemption; in whom he dwells, as in his temple, enabling them to exercise every grace and perform every duty, working them up for the self-same thing, eternal glory and happiness.

IV. The properties of it; shewing the excellency of this communion and fellowship.

1. It is a wonderful instance of condescension in God; that he who is the high and lofty One, who dwells in heaven, the high and holy place, and yet with such also who are of a contrite and humble spirit; that he whose throne is the heaven, and the earth his footstool, yet condescends to dwell with men on earth; that Wisdom, or the Son of God, should build an house, furnish a table, and invite sinful unworthy creatures to partake of the entertainments of it; that Father, Son, and Spirit should come and make their abode with sinful men, and admit them to the greatest intimacy with them.——2. It is very honourable to the sons of men, to be favoured with such communion. If it was an honour to Mephibosheth to sit at the table of king David, as one of the king's sons; or for an Haman to be invited to a banquet with the king and queen; how infinitely more honourable is it to be admitted to sit with the King of kings at his table, and be entertained by him as royal guests!——3. This is a privilege very desirable, nothing more so; this is the one thing saints are desirous of in public worship, to behold the beauty of the Lord; to see his power and his glory in his sanctuary; to sit under his shadow, and taste his pleasant fruits. This is no other than the gate of heaven.——4. It is exceeding valuable; it is beyond all the enjoyments of life, preferable to every thing that can be had on earth; the light of God's countenance, his gracious presence, and communion with him, put more joy and gladness into the hearts of his people, than the greatest increase of worldly things; it is this which makes wisdom's ways, ways of pleasantness, and her paths paths of peace; it is this which makes the tabernacles of God amiable and lovely, and a day in his house better than a thousand elsewhere; and because so valuable, hence the apostle John, in an exulting manner, says, *Truly our fellowship is with the Father, and with his Son Jesus Christ!* 1 John i. 3.

A BODY OF PRACTICAL DIVINITY.

BOOK II.

OF EXTERNAL WORSHIP, AS PUBLIC.

CHAP. I.

OF THE NATURE OF A GOSPEL-CHURCH, THE SEAT OF PUBLIC WORSHIP.

HAVING treated of the object of worship, and distinguished worship into internal and external; and having considered internal worship as it lies in the exercise of various graces; I now proceed to consider external worship, both public and private: and first public worship; and as public worship is carried on socially in a church-state, I shall begin with considering the nature of a gospel-church, the seat of it. The word *church* has various significations, which it may be proper to take notice of, in order to settle the true sense of it, as now to be discoursed of.

First, Some take it for a place of worship, and call such a place by that name; but wrongly, at least very improperly. It is a remarkable saying of one of the ancients, even of the second century, "Not the place, but the congregation of the elect, I call the church."[1] Indeed, any place of worship was formerly called an house of God; so the place where Jacob and his family worshipped, having built an altar for God, was called Bethel, or the house of God, Gen. xxxv. 1. so the tabernacle of Moses is called, the house of God in Shiloh, Judg. xviii. 31. and the temple built by Solomon, the house of the Lord, 1 Kings vi. 1, 2, 39. but neither of them are ever called a church. The papists, indeed, call an edifice built for religious worship, a church; and so do some protestants; I might add, some dissenting protestants too; who call going to a place of public worship, going to church; though with great impropriety. It must be owned, that some of the ancient fathers used the word in this metonymical and improper sense, for the place where the church met for worship; and some passages of scripture are pleaded for this use of it; which yet do not seem to be plain and sufficient: not Acts xix. 37. for the word ιεροσυλυς, should not be rendered *robbers of churches*, but *robbers of temples*; and design not edifices built for christian worship; but the temples of the heathens, as that of Diana, at Ephesus: but what may seem more plausible and pertinent, are some passages in 1 Cor. xi. 18, 20, 22. *When ye come together in the church I hear*, &c. which is thought to be after explained; *When ye come together into one place:— have ye not houses to eat and drink in? or despise ye the church of God?* All this, indeed, supposes a place to meet in; though rather not the place, but the assembly that met in it, is called the church; and their coming together in the church, may intend no other than some of the members coming and meeting together with the rest of the church; and επι το αυτο, which we render *into one place*, may design, not the unity of the place, but the unanimity of the people in it: nor is the opposition between their own houses and the place of meeting; and

---

[1] μ του τοπου, αλλα το αθροισμα των εκλεκτων εκκλησιαν καλω, Clement. Alexandr. Stromat. 1. 7. p. 715.

CHAP. I.   OF THE NATURE OF A GOSPEL-CHURCH.   853

this is only mentioned to shew, that it would have been much more suitable and decent in them, to have ate and drank in their own houses, than in the presence of the assembly and church of God, which was to their scandal, reproach, and contempt; for not the place, but the people that met in it, were properly the object of contempt: however, it is certain, that there are numerous places of scripture which cannot be understood of any material edifice or building; whether of stone, brick, or wood;[2] as when it is said, *tidings of these things came unto the ears of the church*, Acts xi. 22. it would be absurd to understand it in such a sense; and so many others.

Secondly, The word εκκλησια, always used for *church*, signifies an *assembly* called and met together,[3] and sometimes it is used for an assembly, whether lawfully or unlawfully convened; so the people who got together, upon the uproar made by the craftsmen at Ephesus, is called, *a confused assembly*, and suggested to be an unlawful one; since the town-clerk told them the matter should be determined in *a lawful assembly*; and when he had thus spoken, *dismissed the assembly*, Acts xix. 32, 39, 41. in which passages the same word is used which commonly is for a *church;* and which may be considered either as a general, or as a particular assembly of persons.

1*st*, As a general assembly, called, *The general assembly and church of the firstborn, which are written in heaven,* Heb. xii. 23. and which include all the elect of God, that have been, are, or shall be in the world; and who will form the pure, holy, and undefiled Jerusalem-church-state, in which none will be but those who are written in the Lamb's book of life; and this consists of the redeemed of the Lamb, and is the *church* which Christ has *purchased* with his blood; and who make up his spouse, the *church* he has *loved*, and given himself for, to wash, and cleanse, and present to himself a glorious church, without spot or wrinkle; this is the *body*, the church, of which Christ is the *head;* and in which he is the sole officer, being Prophet, Priest, and King of it; it being, not the seat of human government, as a particular church is: and this church is but *one*, though particular churches are many: to this may be applied the words of Christ; *My dove, my undefiled, is but one*, Cant. vi. 9. and this is what sometimes is called by divines, the *invisible* church; not but that the whole number of God's elect is visible to him, and known by him; *The Lord knows them that are his;* and the election of particular persons may be known by themselves, by the grace bestowed upon them; and, in a judgment of charity, may be concluded of others, that they are the chosen of God, and written in the book of life. But all the particular persons, and the number of them, were never yet seen and known; John had a sight of them in a visionary way, and they will be all really and actually seen, when the new Jerusalem shall descend from God out of heaven, as a bride adorned for her husband; which will be at the second coming of Christ, and not before; till that time comes, this church will be invisible. It is sometimes distinguished into the church *triumphant* and *militant*, the whole family named of God in heaven and earth. The church triumphant consists of the saints in glory, whom Christ has taken to himself, to be with him where he is; and this is continually increasing. The church militant consists of persons in the present state, which is said to be, *as an army with banners*, Cant. vi. 4. this is made up of such who become volunteers in the day of Christ's power; who put on the whole armour of God, and fight the good fight of faith; and in this state it will continue to the end of the world.

There is another sense in which the church may be said to be *catholic*, or *general*, as it may consist of such in any age, and in the several parts of the world, who have true faith in Christ, and hold to him the head, and are baptized by one Spirit into one body; have one Spirit, one Lord, one faith, one baptism, and one God and Father of all, and are called in one hope of their calling: and this takes in, not only such who make a visible profession of Christ; but all such who are truly partakers of his grace; though they have not made an open profession of him in a formal

---

[2] Ecclesia est verum templum Dei, quod non in parietibus est, sed in corde et fide hominum qui credunt in eum et vocantur fideles, Lactant. de vera sap, l. 4. c. 13.

[3] Ecclesia, ut omnes norunt, Græca vox est, quæ apud nos cœtum, concionem, congregationemque significat hujusmodi erant particulares dictæ ecclesiæ, ut Laodicæa, &c. Aonii Palearii Testimonium, c. 10. p. 321.

manner; and this is the church which Polycarp called, *the whole catholic church throughout the world* :[4] and Irenæus,[5] *The church scattered throughout the whole world to the ends of the earth:* and Origen,[6] *The church of God under heaven:* and this is the church built on Christ the rock, against which the gates of hell shall never prevail; such a church Christ has always had, and will have; and which may be, when there is no visible particular congregated church, or a particular church gathered according to gospel-order; and of this the apostle seems to speak, when he says, *Unto him be glory in the church, by Christ Jesus, throughout all ages, world without end,* Eph. iii. 21. But,

2dly, The church may be considered as a particular assembly of saints meeting together in one place for religious worship. Such was the first church at Jerusalem, which is called, the *whole church*, that met together in one place at the same time, Acts i. 14, 15. and ii. 1. and iv. 46. and xv. 22, and the church at Antioch, convened by the apostles, to whom they rehearsed what God had done with them, Acts xiv. 27. and these churches, in after times, continued to meet in one place; the whole church of Jerusalem, at the destruction of the city, removed to Pella, a town beyond Jordan, which was sufficient to receive the christians that belonged to it;[7] and two hundred and fifty years after Christ, the church at Antioch met in one house.[8] And so the church at Corinth, 1 Cor. xiv. 23. and v. 4. and the church of the disciples at Troas, who came together on the first day of the week to break bread, Acts xx. 7. of these there were many in one province; as the churches of Judea, besides that at Jerusalem, and the churches of Galatia, Gal. i. 2, 23. and the seven churches of Asia, Rev. i. 4. and the churches of Macedonia, 2 Cor. viii. 1. the church at Cenchrea, a port of Corinth, and distinct from the church there, as were all these churches distinct from one another; so that he that was of one church, was not of another; as Epaphras is said to be *one of you*, of the church at Colosse, a peculiar member and minister of that church, and not of another, Col. iv. 12. And this is the church, the nature of which is to be treated of; and may be considered *essentially*, as to the matter and form of it; and *organically*, as to its order and power; or as a body corporate, having its proper officers.

I. *Essentially* considered, as to its matter and form of which it consists.

First, As to the *matter* of it, both as to quantity and quality. As to number, Tertullian[9] thought that three persons were sufficient to constitute a church; which may seem to be confirmed by Matt. xviii. 20. *Where two or three are gathered together in my name,* &c. who may be sufficient to meet and pray together, and edify one another; but a judicial process in a church way, in case of offence, as directed to in some preceding verses, seems to require more; seeing, if the offending and offended parties, cannot compromise things among themselves, one or two more are to be taken, which if two make four; if reconciliation cannot be made, the matter must be brought before the church, which must consist of a greater number than the parties before concerned; and which it should seem cannot be less than six more, and in all ten; which was the number of a congregation with the Jews[10]: and a church organically considered, or as having proper officers, seems to require more; the church at Ephesus was begun with twelve men, or thereabout, Acts xix. 7. yet a church should consist of no more than can meet together in one place, where all may hear, and all may be edified; and if it should be so increased that this cannot be, then it should be divided into lesser communities; as an hive of bees, when too many, swarms; and which seems to be the case of the church at Jerusalem; which, upon the departure of those who were converted at Pentecost, and on the scattering of the church by persecution, formed several churches in Judea, and accounts for the early mention of them. But not to dwell on this, the quality of the materials of a gospel-church more especially deserves attention. In general, it may be observed, that all such who are of immoral lives and conversations, and of unsound principles, as to the doctrines of the gospel, are not proper persons to be members of a gospel-church; no unclean persons, nor thieves,

---

[4] Apud Euseb. Eccl. Hist. l. 4. c. 15.
[5] Adv. Hæres. l. 1. c. 2, and 3.
[6] Apud Euseb. l. 6. c. 25.
[7] Euseb. Eccl. Hist. l. 3. c. 5.
[8] Ib. l. 7. c. 30.
[9] De Baptismo, c. 6.
[10] Misn. Sanhedrin, c. 1. s. 6.

nor covetous, nor drunkards, nor revilers, nor extortioners, have, or should have, any inheritance, part or portion in the kingdom of God, as that may signify, as it sometimes does, a gospel-church-state; and though there may be such secretly, who creep in unawares, yet when discovered are to be excluded; and such persons, therefore, who are to be put away from a church, as wicked men, and such as walk disorderly, are to be withdrawn from, and such as have imbibed false doctrines, are to be rejected; then most certainly such are not knowingly to be admitted into the original constitution of a church of Christ, or be at first received into the fellowship of one. The persons who are fit materials of a visible gospel-church, are described,

1. As regenerate persons; *Except a man be born again of water and of the Spirit,* of the grace of the Spirit of God, *he cannot enter,* of right he ought not to enter, and, if known, ought not to be allowed to enter, *into the kingdom of God*, into a gospel-church-state; none but such who are begotten again to a lively hope of the heavenly inheritance, and who, as new-born babes, desire the sincere milk of the word and ordinances, that they may grow thereby, having tasted that the Lord is gracious; or, in other words, of whom it is *meet to think*, and, in a judgment of charity and discretion, to hope and conclude that God hath begun a *good work* in them; such were the members of the church at Philippi, Phil. i. 6, 7.———2. As called ones; a church is a congregation of such who are called out from among others, by the grace of God; both the Hebrew and Greek words קהלה and εκκλησια, signify an assembly of persons called and convened together; so the members of the church at Rome are styled, *the called of Jesus Christ*, Rom. i. 6. such who are called out of the world, and from fellowship with the men of it, *into the fellowship of Jesus Christ:* such who are proper materials of a gospel-church, are such who are called out of a state of bondage to sin, satan, and the law, into the liberty of the gospel; and out of darkness into marvellous light; and are called with an holy calling, and called to be saints, not merely by the external ministry of the word, to outward holiness of life and conversation, who are never effectually called by the grace of God, nor have any appearance of it, and so unfit to be members of churches; for,———3. Such are not only called to be saints, but in and by effectual vocation become really saints, at least are judged to be so, by a charitable discretion of them; so the members of the churches at Rome, Corinth, Ephesus, Philippi, and Colosse, are described as *saints*, and *sanctified* persons, and as *holy temples*, built for habitations of an holy God; hence they are called *churches of the saints*, because they consist of such; and Christ, who is king and head of the church, is called *King of saints*, 1 Cor. xiv. 33. Rev. xv. 3.———4. They are described as *the faithful in Christ Jesus*, or believers in him: so in the article of the church of England, a church is defined, "A congregation of faithful men, in which the pure word of God is preached, and the sacraments duly administered." For only faithful men, or believers in Christ, can have fellowship with the saints in a church-state; and none but such can have communion with Christ; for he dwells in the hearts of men by faith, and they live by faith upon him: and only such have a right to the ordinances of Christ, and can receive benefit by them; unless they believe with all the heart, they have no right to baptism; and unless they have faith in Christ, they cannot discern the Lord's body in the supper; nor is the gospel preached of any profit to them, not being mixed with faith; so that they are on all accounts unfit for church-membership; and hence we read, that those who were joined to the first church at Jerusalem, were believers, Acts. v. 14. see chap. ii. 41, 47. Hence, ———5. Those that were added to the church at Jerusalem, are said to be *such as should be saved;* as all those who believe and are baptized, shall be saved; according to Mark xvi. 16. And besides, these were added by the Lord himself, as well as to him, and therefore should be saved by him with an everlasting salvation: and such who are admitted to church-fellowship, should be such, who, in a judgment of charity or in charitable discretion, may be hoped, that they are the chosen of God, the redeemed of Christ, are called, sanctified, and justified, and so shall be everlastingly saved.———6. They should be persons of some competent knowledge of divine and spiritual things, and of judging of them; who have not only knowledge of themselves, and of their lost estate by nature, and of the way of salvation by Christ; but who have some degree of knowledge of God, in his nature, perfections, and works; and of Christ, in his Person, as the Son of God; of his proper Deity;

of his incarnation; of his offices, as Prophet, Priest, and King; of justification by his righteousness; pardon by his blood, satisfaction by his sacrifice; and of his prevalent intercession: and also of the Spirit of God; his person, offices, and operations; and of the important truths of the gospel, and doctrines of grace; or how otherwise should the church be *the pillar and ground of truth?*——7. The materials of a gospel-church, should be men of holy lives and conversations; holiness both of heart and life becomes the house of God, and those who are of it; none should have a place in it but such; see Psalm xv. 1, 2. and xxiv. 3, 4.——8. Such who are admitted into fellowship with a particular church of Christ, should be truly baptized in water, that is, by immersion, upon a profession of their faith; so the three thousand penitents, after they had gladly received the word, were baptized; and then, and not before, were added to the church: so the first church at Samaria consisted of men and women baptized by Philip, they believing what he said concerning the kingdom of God: and Lydia, and her household, and the jailor and his, being baptized upon their faith, laid the foundation of the church at Philippi: and the church at Corinth was begun with persons who, hearing the word, believed, and were baptized; and the church at Ephesus was first formed by some disciples baptized in the name of the Lord Jesus, Acts ii. 41. and viii. 12. and xvi. 15, 33. and xviii. 8. and xix. 5. so the members of the churches at Rome, Galatia, and Colosse, were baptized persons, Rom. vi. 3, 4. Gal. iii. 27. Col. ii. 12. But,——9. Not their infants with them; who were neither baptized nor admitted to membership in the churches; no one instance of either can be produced in scripture: they are not members by birth;[11] for *that which is born of the flesh, is flesh*, carnal and corrupt, and unfit for church-fellowship: nor do they become such by the faith of their parents; for even their faith does not make them themselves church-members, without a profession of it, and giving up themselves to a church, and received by it into it: men must be believers before they are baptized; and they must be baptized before they become members; and they cannot be members till they make application to a church, and are admitted into it. Infants, as they are born, are not meet for membership, being unregenerate, unholy, and impure by their first birth, and must be born again ere they are fit for the kingdom of God, or a gospel-church-state; their federal holiness, talked of, is a mere chimera, and is unsupported by 1 Cor. vii. 14. they are not capable of understanding and of answering questions put unto them; nor of giving up themselves to a church; nor of consent and agreement to walk with it, the nature of which they are unacquainted with, and of what belongs to a member of it, either as to duty or privilege; nor are they capable of answering the ends of church-communion, the mutual edification of members and the glory of God: and such who plead for their membership, make a poor business of it; not treating them as members, neither by admitting them to the ordinance of the supper, nor by watching over them, reproving, admonishing, and laying them under censures, when grown up, and require them, were they members.

Secondly, A particular church may be considered as to the *form* of it; which lies in mutual consent and agreement, in their covenant and confederation with each other.

1. There must be an union, a coalition of a certain number of persons, to form a church-state, *one* cannot make a church; and these must be united, as the similies of a tabernacle, temple, house, body, and a flock of sheep, to which a church is sometimes compared, shew; the tabernacle was made with ten curtains, typical of the church of God; but one curtain did not make a tabernacle, nor all the ten singly and separately taken; but there were certain loops and taches, with which they were coupled together; and being thus joined, they composed the tabernacle. So the temple of Solomon, which was another type of the gospel-church; and which was made of great and costly stones; these stones, not as in the quarry, nor even when hewed and squared, lying singly by themselves, made the temple, until they were put and cemented together, and the headstone brought in and laid on: thus truly gracious souls, though they are by grace separated from the common quarry of mankind, and are hewn by the Spirit of God, and by the ministry of the word, and are fit materials for the church of God, yet do not constitute one, until *fitly framed together*, and so grow unto an holy temple

---

[11] Fiunt, non nascuntur christiani, Tertullian. Apologet. c. 18.

CHAP. I.   OF THE NATURE OF A GOSPEL-CHURCH.

of the Lord. A church is called the house of God, a spiritual house, built up of lively stones, living saints; but these be they ever so lively and living, they do not form a church, unless they are builded together, *for an habitation of God*. A church of Christ, is often compared to an human body; which is not one member, but many; and these not as separate, but members one of another; who are *fitly joined together, and compacted by that which every joint supplieth*: and sometimes it is called a flock, the flock of God; and though a little flock, yet one sheep does not make a flock, nor two or three straggling ones; but a number of them collected together, feeding in one pasture, under the care of a shepherd.

2. This union of saints in a church-state, is signified by their being *joined*, and as it were, glued together;[12] see Acts v. 13. and ix. 26. it is an union of spirits so close, as if they were but one spirit; so the members of the first christian church were *of one heart and one soul*, being *knit together in love*; and it becomes members to endeavour to *keep the unity of the Spirit in the bond of peace*, Acts iv. 32. Col. ii. 2. Eph. iv. 3.

3. This union between them is made by voluntary consent and agreement; a christian society, or a church of Christ, is like all civil societies, founded on agreement and by consent; thus it is with societies from the highest to the lowest; kingdoms and states were originally formed on this plan; every body corporate, as a city, is founded on the same plan; in which there are privileges to be enjoyed, and duties to be performed; and no man has a right to the one, without consenting to the other: and in lower societies, no man can be admitted into them, nor receive any benefit from them, unless he assents to the rules and articles on which the society is founded. All civil relations, except the natural relation of parents and children, which arises from the law of nature, are by consent and covenant; as that of magistrates and subjects, and of masters and servants, and of husband and wife; which latter, as it is by compact and agreement, may serve to illustrate the relation between a church and its members added to it, and the manner in which they be, by consent; see Isa. lxii. 5.

4. As the original constitution of churches is by consent and confederation, so the admission of new members to them, is upon the same footing: the primitive churches in the times of the apostles, *first gave their ownselves to the Lord*, as a body, agreeing and promising to walk in all his commandments and ordinances, and be obedient to his laws, as King of saints; *and to us*, the apostles, pastors, guides, and governors, to be taught, fed, guided, and directed by them, according to the word of God; and to one another also, *by the will of God*, engaging to do whatever in them lay, to promote each other's edification and the glory of God: and so all such who were added to them, it was done by mutual consent, as it always should be; as no man is to be forced into a church, or by any compulsory methods brought into it, so neither can he force himself into one; he has no right to come into a church, and depart from it when he pleases; both the one and the other, his coming into it and departure from it, must be with consent: a man may propose himself to be a member of a church, but it is at the option of the church whether they will receive him; so Saul assayed to join himself to the disciples, that is, he proposed to be a member with them, but they at first refused him, fearing he was not a true disciple, because of his former conduct; but when they had a testimony of him from Barnabas, and perceived that he was a partaker of the grace of God, and was sound in the faith of Christ, they admitted him, and he was with them, going out and coming in: and it is but reasonable a church should be satisfied in these points, as to the persons received into their communion, not only by a testimony of their becoming lives, but by giving an account of what God has done for their souls, and a reason of the hope that is in them; as well as by expressing their agreement with them in their articles of faith.

5. Something of this kind may be observed in all religious societies, from the beginning, that they were by agreement and confederation; so the first religious societies in families, and under the patriarchal dispensation, it was by the agreement of families, and the common consent of them, that they met and joined together

---

[12] Κολλᾶσθαι αυτοις, proprie notat glutine coadunare,&c. metaphorice designat arctiorem conjunctionem, &c. quia quæ glutine coadunata sunt, arcte conjuncta sunt, tenaciterque adhærent, ut non facile queant separari, Stockius in voce.

for public worship, to call on the name of the Lord, Gen. iv. 26. so the Jewish church, though national in some sense, yet was constituted by confederation; God prescribed to them laws in the wilderness, and they covenanted and consented to obey them, Exod. xxiv. 7. he avouched them to be his people, and they avouched him to be their God; and then, and not before, were they called a *church*, Acts vii. 38. and so the gospel-church was spoken of in prophecy, as what should be constituted and increased by agreement and covenant, Isa. xliv. 5. and lvi. 6, 7. Jer. l. 5. all which agrees with New Testament-language; from whence it appears to be a fact, that it was by consent and agreement that the first churches were formed, as before observed, and not otherwise; and nothing else but mutual consent, can make a man a church-member: not faith in the heart, for that cannot be known until a man declares and professes it; nor a bare profession of faith, which, though necessary to membership, does not declare a man a member of one church more than of another, nor entitle more to one than to another; unless he gives up himself to a church, and professes his desire to walk with it in a subjection to the gospel of Christ: nor baptism, though a pre-requisite to church-fellowship, does not make a man a member of a church, as it did not the eunuch: nor hearing the word; for men ignorant and unbelievers, may come into an assembly and hear the word, 1 Cor. xiv. 24. yea, persons may hear the word aright, have faith, and profess it, and be baptized, and yet not be church-members; it is only mutual consent that makes them such: persons must propose themselves to a church, and give up themselves to it, to walk in it, in an observance of the ordinances of Christ, and duties of religion; and the church must voluntarily receive them in the Lord. And,

6. Such a mutual agreement is but reasonable; for how should *two walk together except they be agreed?* Amos. iii. 3. and unless persons voluntarily give up themselves to a church and its pastor, they can exercise no power over them, in a church-way; they have nothing to do with them that are without, they have no concern with the watch and care of them; nor are they entitled thereunto, unless they *submit themselves to one another in the fear of God;* they have no power to reprove, admonish, and censure them in a church-way; nor can the pastor exercise any pastoral authority over them, except by agreement they consent to yield to it; nor can they expect he should watch over their souls as he that must give an account, having no charge of them by any act of theirs. Now,

7. It is this confederacy, consent, and agreement, that is the formal cause of a church; it is this which not only distinguishes a church from the world, and from all professors that walk at large, the one being within and the other without, but from all other particular churches; so the church at Cenchrea was not the same with the church at Corinth, though but at a little distance from it, because it consisted of persons who had given up themselves to it, and not to the church at Corinth; and so were members of the one and not of the other; *one of you,* as Onesimus and Epaphras were of the church at Colosse, and not of another, Col. iv. 9, 12. From all which it follows,

8. That a church of Christ is not parochial, or men do not become church-members by habitation in a parish; for Turks and Jews may dwell in the same parish: nor is it diocesan; for we never read of more churches under one bishop or pastor, though there may have been, where churches were large, more bishops or pastors in one church, Phil. i. 1. nor provincial, for we read of churches in one province; as of the churches of Judea, and of Galatia, and of Macedonia: nor national; nay, so far from it, that we not only read of more churches in a nation, but even of churches in houses, Rom. xvi. 5. 1 Cor. xvi. 19. Col. iv. 15. Philem. ver. 2. nor presbyterian; for we never read of a church of presbyters or elders, though of elders ordained in churches; by which it appears there were churches before there were any presbyters or elders in them, Acts xiv. 23. But a particular visible gospel-church is congregational; and even the church of England, which is national itself, defines a "visible church to be a congregation of faithful men;" and, indeed, the national church of the Jews was in some sense congregational; it is sometimes called the *congregation,* Lev. iv. 13, 14, 15. they were a people separated from other nations, and peculiarly holy to the Lord; they met in one place, called, *the tabernacle of the congregation,* and offered their sacrifices at one altar, Lev. i. 3, 4. and xvii. 4, 5. and three times in the year all

their males appeared together at Jerusalem; and besides, as Lightfoot[13] observes, there were *stationary men* at Jerusalem, who were representatives of the whole congregation, and were at the sacrifices for them: the synagogues also, though not of divine institution, were countenanced by the Lord, and bore a very great resemblance to congregational societies; and is the word which answers to *congregation* in the Septuagint version, and is used for a christian assembly in the New Testament, James ii. 2. to which may be added, that such congregations and assemblies as gospel-churches be, are prophesied of as what should be in gospel-times; see Eccles. xii. 11. Isa. iv. 5. A church of saints thus essentially constituted, as to matter and form, have a power in this state to admit and reject members, as all societies have; and also to choose their own officers; which, when done, they become a complete organized church, as to order and power; of which more hereafter.

CHAP. II.

OF THE DUTIES OF THE MEMBERS OF A CHURCH TO EACH OTHER.

A CHURCH thus confederated and united by consent and agreement, there are several duties incumbent on its members; which, both for their own comfort, credit, and edification, and for the glory of God, it is highly necessary to observe. As,

First, And which is a principal one, to love one another; *Owe no man anything, but to love one another*, is an apostolical advice, and good advice; this is a debt which every man owes to another, and should be always paying, especially christians and members of churches, Rom xiii. 8. and xii. 10.

1. This is the great law of Christ, as King in his church, his royal commandment, which he enjoins on all his subjects, and frequently repeats, John xiii. 34. and xv. 12, 17.——2. The example of Christ should influence and engage unto it, John xiii. 34. and xv. 12. 1 John iii. 16.——3. The relations that members of churches stand in to each other, oblige to love; being fellow-citizens of the same family, are brethren to each other, and make one fraternity, or *brotherhood*, which they should love, 1 Pet. ii. 17. and iii. 8. and are members one of another, 1 Cor. xii. 13, 25, 26, 27.——4. Mutual love is an evidence of being the disciples of Christ, John xiii. 35.——5. It is this which makes communion in a church-state delightful and comfortable, as well as honourable; *Behold, how good and how pleasant it is for brethren to dwell together in unity!* it is as pleasing and refreshing as the fragrant oil poured on Aaron's head, and as the dew that fell on mount Hermon, Psalm cxxxiii. when, on the contrary, nothing is more uncomfortable and dishonourable, as well as nothing is more pernicious and ruinous to a church-state, than want of love, Gal. v. 15.

This love of members one to another ought to be *fervent*, and it should be *unfeigned*, and without dissimulation, 1 Pet. iv. 8. and i. 22. and it should be universal, love to all the saints, weaker as well as stronger, poor as well as rich, Eph. i. 15.[1]

Secondly, It is incumbent on church-members, as much as in them lies, to endeavour to *keep the unity of the spirit in the bond of peace;* to press to which the apostle uses various arguments in Eph. iv. 3—6.

1. Care should be taken to promote and preserve unity of affection; so as to be of *one heart, and of one soul, having the same love*, as the apostle advises to, Phil. ii. 2. But this falls in much with the first duty, before inculcated.——2. There should be, as much as may be, an unity of mind and judgment in the doctrines of the gospel; being, as the apostle in the above place directs, *of one accord and of one mind;* or as he elsewhere says, that *all speak the same thing;* and that they *be perfectly joined together in the same mind and in the same judgment*, or otherwise there is danger of schism, divisions, and contentions, 1 Cor. i. 10, 11.——3. And which is much the same, an *unity of faith;* for there is but *one faith*, Eph. iv. 5, 13. one doctrine of faith, or scheme and system of divine truths to be believed; and church-members should *stand fast in one spirit, with one mind, striving together for the faith of the gospel*, Phil. i. 27.——4. There should be a zealous concern for unity of worship, and that nothing be introduced into it contrary to the pattern shewed and directed to in the word of God; and that they *serve the Lord with one consent, and with one mind, and with one mouth*

---

[13] Temple-service, ch. 7. s. 3.

[1] Of this see more in Book I. chap. 9.

glorify God, Zeph. iii. 9. Rom. xv. 6. and to prevent discord in affection, judgment, and worship, and to secure peace, all strife should be avoided, and even checked at the beginning of it; the advice of the wise man is good, Prov. xvii. 14. and equally good is the advice of the apostle, *Let nothing be done through strife or vain glory*, Phil. ii. 3. Proud and contentious men, who seek to promote strife and division, are not to be encouraged in christian communities, 1 Cor. xi. 16. the peace of a church is to be laboured after by its members, and by all means to be pursued; the comfort of saints in fellowship with each other, is a strong argument for peace and unity, Phil. ii. 1, 2. and above all, as saints would be desirous of having the presence of God with them, they should be concerned to *be of one mind*, and *live in peace;* and then may they expect and not otherwise, that *the God of love and peace shall be with them*, 2 Cor. xiii. 11.

Thirdly, It is the duty of members of churches to sympathize with each other in all conditions and circumstances they come into, Rom. xii. 15. and upon this their membership with one another cannot but have a considerable influence, 1 Cor. xii. 26. this sympathy should be with respect to things outward and temporal; any calamity, affliction, and distress, of whatsoever kind; they *that are in bonds*, especially for the sake of religion, should be remembered as *bound with them*, as if in the same circumstances, and should pity and relieve them as much as may be; and *them which suffer adversity* in body, family, or estate, *as being themselves in the body*, and liable to the same adversities, Heb. xii. 3. and therefore should visit, comfort, and assist them; so Job's three friends, when they heard of his afflictions in his person, family, and substance, though they lived at a distance from him, by appointment met together, *to come to mourn with him, and to comfort him*, Job ii. 11. and much more should members of churches act such a part to one another. Likewise when in inward trouble and distress of soul, through the hidings of God's face, the temptations of Satan, the weakness of grace, and the strength of corruptions; it becomes fellow-members to *comfort the feeble-minded, support the weak, and bear one another's burdens, and so fulfil the law of Christ*, which is the law of love and sympathy, 1 Thess. v. 14. Gal. vi. 2. and the sympathy of God with his people in their afflictions, and also of Christ, who is *touched with the feeling of the infirmities* of his people, should direct to such a temper and carriage, Isa. lxiii. 9. Heb. iv. 15.

Fourthly, It is the duty of church-members to communicate to each other in such circumstances.

1. In outward things, to such as are in want of them, Rom. xii. 13. Gal. vi. 10. hence in the times of the apostles, the churches had orders to make collections on the first day of the week, for the poor saints, that thereby they might be relieved who were in necessitous circumstances, 1 Cor. xvi. 1, 2. brotherly love demands such a conduct in church-members to their brethren in distress; for, *how dwelleth the love of God in* such, who, having a portion of worldly things, shut up their bowels of compassion from their brethren in need? 1 John iii. 17. besides, to communicate to such persons, is well pleasing in the sight of God, and will be taken notice of in the great day of account, when forgotten by the saints, Heb. xiii. 16. Matt. xxv. 40.

——2. It is their duty to communicate in spiritual things, to mutual comfort and edification; to speak often one to another about divine things; to impart spiritual experiences, and to declare to each other what God has done for their souls; to communicate spiritual light and knowledge in the mysteries of grace; and according to the gift one has received, be it more or less, to minister it to one another, and to build up one another in their most holy faith, by christian conference and praying together; and through the word dwelling richly in them, to teach and admonish one another in psalms, hymns, and spiritual songs; and care should be taken that no communication proceeds out of the mouth but what is for edification, and ministers grace to the hearers.

Fifthly, It is the duty of church-members to watch over one another; that they do not indulge to sinful lusts and pleasures, and make provision for the flesh, to fulfil the lusts thereof; and so bring a reproach on the good ways of God, and the doctrines of Christ; and to warn them that are unruly, or err from the rule of the word, and recover them from any evil way they seem to be going into; as also to watch over them, lest they receive any notion contrary to the gospel of Christ; for not only pastors of churches are to watch over them for this purpose, but members of churches are to look *diligently*, or act the part

CHAP. II.   OF THE DUTIES OF CHURCH MEMBERS.   861

of a bishop or overseer in some respect,[2] *lest any man fail of the grace of God*, or fall from the doctrine of grace, Heb. xii. 15. they should not suffer sin to lie upon a brother; but rebuke and admonish him for it, according to the gospel-rule, first alone, and then, if such rebuke succeeds not, to do it with, and before others; and such rebukes and admonitions should be in love, and with much tenderness, as well as faithfulness; for such only are like to be kindly received, and to be successful; such that are fallen, whether into immorality or error, should be endeavoured to be restored by those who are spiritual, in the spirit of meekness, Lev. xix. 17. Psalm cxli. 5. Gal. vi. 1.

Sixthly, It is incumbent on members of churches, to bear with one another; the strong to bear the infirmities of the weak; and to bear one another's burdens, and to forbear with each other, and not bear hard on one another, considering the patience, forbearance, and long-suffering of God to them; and it becomes them to forgive one another, as Christ, and God for Christ's sake, has forgiven them; and especially when repentance is declared and discovered, then forgiveness should be extended, not only to seven times, but to seventy times seven; for if we forgive not, neither will our heavenly Father forgive our trespasses, Rom. xv. 1. Gal. vi. 2. Col. iii. 12. Matt. xviii. 21, 22. Mark xi. 26.

Seventhly, It is the duty of members of churches to pray for one another; as they have all one common Father, who is attentive to their supplications, and is able and willing to help them in their times of need, they are directed to address him in this manner, saying, *Our Father, which art in heaven;* and are thereby instructed to pray for others as for themselves, to whom he stands in the same relation as to themselves, even for all saints, as the apostle intimates, Eph. vi. 18. and especially for such who are in the same church-state; and particularly when they are in any distress, inward or outward; and not for ministers of the gospel only; though members should never be forgetful of their own pastors, who are set over them in the Lord, that they may be fitted for their work, be assisted in it, and be made useful to their souls; but for the several members of the church, that they may have their several wants supplied; that they may grow in grace and spiritual knowledge; be kept faithful, and preserved blameless, to the coming of Christ; it becomes them in general to pray for the peace of Jerusalem, and in particular for the hill of Zion, to which they belong, that peace may be within its walls, and prosperity in its dwellings.

Eighthly, It becomes church-members to separate themselves from the men of the world, and not touch persons and things which are defiling; they are in a church-state, which is as a *garden enclosed;* they are a separate people, and should dwell alone, and not be reckoned among the nations or the people of a vain and carnal world; they are called out of the world, and therefore should not be unequally yoked with the men of it; with men unrighteous, ignorant, lawless, disobedient, dead, and profane sinners, with whom they can have no profitable communion; and, indeed, from all such in their own societies who walk disorderly, they are directed to withdraw themselves.——1. In conversation they are to abstain from sinful men; not that they are to have no commerce nor correspondence with them in civil things, for then, as the apostle says, they *must needs go out of the world;* but that they are not to join with them in their sinful practices, but bear a testimony against them; they are not to walk, as other Gentiles do, in the vanity of their minds; nor to walk with them in the same paths of sin and folly; nor to keep up any intimate and familiar converse with them; knowing, that *evil communications corrupt good manners*.——2. Nor should they keep company with erroneous persons, with men of unsound principles; for such, who cause divisions and offences, contrary to the gospel of Christ, are to be avoided, and their conversation shunned; and such who cavil at, and consent not unto the wholesome words of Christ, and the doctrine according to godliness, are to be withdrawn from; and such who have imbibed heretical notions, repugnant to the sacred Trinity, and to the person of Christ, and the grace of the Spirit, are to be rejected; and such who bring not the doctrine of Christ with them, are not to be bid God-speed, nor received into the houses of God's people, Rom. xvi. 17. 1 Tim. vi. 3, 4, 5. Tit. iii. 10. 2 John ver. 10, 11.

Ninthly, Church-members should be

---

[2] επισκοπουντες.

constant in assembling together for religious worship; it is remarked of the members of the first Christian church, to their honour, that they *continued stedfastly in the apostles' doctrine and fellowship, and in breaking of bread and in prayer*, Acts ii. 42. that is, they constantly attended on hearing the doctrines of the apostles, which they gladly received and persevered in; and kept up their communion with them and one another, and were not missing at the Lord's Supper, and at times of public prayer; though in after-times, an evil manner, a bad custom prevailed among some of those Christian Hebrews; as to *forsake the assembling of themselves together*, which the apostle takes notice of to their dishonour, Heb. x. 25. a custom of bad consequence, both to communities and particular persons; for what one may do, every one may do, and in course public worship cease, and churches break up; and such a practice is very prejudicial and hurtful to individuals; it is not known what may be lost by missing an opportunity or an ordinance; and what trouble and distress of soul may follow upon it, as the case of Thomas shews, who was not with the rest of the disciples when Christ first appeared to them. It is dangerous to indulge to an indifference to, and to any degree of neglect of the service of God in his house; the evil may grow, and at last issue in apostasy, as in the stony-ground hearers.

Tenthly, There should be no respect of persons among members of churches in their assemblies, and when met together on church-affairs, with regard to rich or poor, greater or lesser gifts; there should be no overbearing, no browbeating, nor any supercilious airs used; no affectation of superiority one over another, they being on an equal foot, in the same relation to one another, abating the difference of offices, Matt. xx. 26, 27. all the strife should be *in honour to prefer one another;* and such who are highest, with respect to spiritual gifts or worldly riches, should *condescend to men of low estates*, Rom. xii. 10, 16.

Eleventhly, It behoves them to strive together for the faith of the gospel, and earnestly to contend for it; and not part with any of the truths of Christ and doctrines of grace; and should be careful to keep the ordinances as they were delivered, and not suffer any innovation in them, neither as to the matter and substance of them, nor as the manner in which they are to be observed; and they should walk in them all with great unanimity and constancy, and should stand fast in the liberty wherewith Christ has made them free, and not be entangled with any yoke of bondage, nor suffer any human inventions and unwarranted practices to be imposed upon them.

Twelfthly, It becomes them to be examples to each other in a holy walk and conversation, and in an observance of all the duties of religion. Holiness becomes the house of God, and the members in it; their light should shine both in the church and in the world, that others beholding their good works, may imitate them, and glorify God: they that name the name of Christ, and profess to be his, should depart from all iniquity, doctrinal and practical; they should be concerned to walk circumspectly, not as fools, but as wise, and shew out of a good conversation their works with meekness of wisdom; they should endeavour to fill up in a becoming manner all stations and relations in life, civil or economical, in the world and family; as of magistrates and subjects, of husbands and wives, parents and children, masters and servants; as well as in the church, as pastors, deacons, and private members, and be careful to perform all duties relative to them; that so their fellow-members may not be grieved nor stumbled; nor the good ways of God be evil spoken of; nor the name of God, and his doctrine, be blasphemed; nor any occasion given to the adversary to speak reproachfully; and by a strict attention to these several duties of religion, they will shew that they behave themselves in the house of God as they ought to do.

CHAP. III.

OF THE OFFICERS OF A CHURCH, AND PARTICULARLY PASTORS.

HAVING treated of a church, as *essentially* considered, with respect to its matter and form, I shall now proceed to consider it,

II. *Organically*, or as an organized church, a corporate body, having its proper officers. In the first churches there were officers both extraordinary and ordinary; the extraordinary officers were apostles, prophets, and evangelists.

1. *Apostles*, 1 Cor. xii. 28. These had the *first* and chief place in the church, and the signs of the apostles were found with them: they had their call and mission from Christ, and were not of men, nor by

OF THE OFFICERS OF A CHURCH.

men, but by Jesus Christ; and as they had their mission and commission immediately from Christ, so their doctrine; they neither received it from men, nor were taught it, but had it by the revelation of Christ; they were infallibly guided into all truth by the inspiration of the Spirit, and had the power of working miracles, in confirmation of all this; they went out by authority everywhere, preaching the gospel, to the conversion of multitudes; and were the first planters of churches, which others watered; they were not limited to any particular church, but had the care of, and presided in all the churches wherever they came. This office is now ceased; the apostles have no successors in it: not such who are called lord bishops; for as the apostles had not their pompous titles, nor their grandeur, nor their wealth, so neither have these lordly bishops their gifts, power, and authority; they have neither mission nor commission, nor work similar to theirs. ——2. There were set in the churches, *secondarily, Prophets*, 1 Cor. xii. 28. Eph. iv. 11. who had extraordinary gifts for explaining the word of God; for instruction and confirmation in the truths of it; and had the gift of tongues, to preach in them to all nations; such were in the church at Antioch, and such were Silas and Judas, Acts xiii. 1. and xv. 22. and who also had the gift of foretelling future events; as Agabus and others, who were of great use to the churches in those times, Acts xi. 28. and xxi. 10. This office is also no more; only the ordinary gift of interpreting the scriptures is sometimes called *prophesying*, and those who have it *prophets*. ——3. *Evangelists*. This name is sometimes given to the writers of the four gospels; two of which were apostles, Matthew and John; the other two, evangelists, Mark and Luke: evangelists were companions of the apostles in their travels, assistants to them in their work, and who were sent by them here and there, with messages from them to the churches, where they had been, and to finish what they had begun; for which purpose they were sometimes left in certain places; but not to reside and continue there. This office is now extinct; only that every truly gospel-preacher may be called an evangelist, or evangelizer. The ordinary officers of the church are pastors and deacons, and these only; though antichrist has introduced a rabble of other officers, the scripture knows nothing of.

1. Pastors: these are shepherds under Christ, the great Shepherd and Bishop of souls; who take the care of the flock, and feed it, as their name signifies; such were promised to be given under the gospel-dispensation; and such Christ has given to his churches, Jer. iii. 15. Eph. iv. 11. and still gives; to whom he says, as he did to Peter, *Feed my lambs, feed my sheep*, John xxi. 15, 16. Who,——2. Are the same with *teachers*, according to Eph. iv. 11. *Some pastors and teachers;* not *some pastors* and *some teachers*, as if they were different; but *and teachers*, the καὶ or *and*, being exegetical, explaining what is meant by pastors, *even* such who are teachers, to instruct in the knowledge of divine things; which is the pastor's work, to feed men with knowledge and understanding: and it may be observed, that in 1 Cor. xii. 28. where the several officers of the church are enumerated, mention is made of *teachers*, but *pastors* omitted, because they are the same; for they are not to be distinguished with respect to the place where they perform their work, as if the office of pastors was in the church, the flock they are to feed; but teachers or doctors in the school; whereas, it is certain, that a teacher is an officer in the church, as well as pastor, 1 Cor. xii. 28. nor are they to be distinguished as two distinct officers in the church, because of the subject of their ministry; the one, the pastor attending to exhortation, to things practical; and the teacher to things doctrinal, asserting, explaining, and defending the doctrines of the gospel, and refuting errors; since both belong to one and the same: if these were distinct, it should seem rather that teachers design gifted brethren, called to minister the word, but not to office-power; and are only assistants to pastors in preaching, but not in the administration of the ordinances; yet it is pretty plain, that those who have a commission to teach, have also a commission to baptize, and to attend to whatsoever Christ has commanded; yea, it may be observed, that even extraordinary officers are called *teachers;* as apostles and prophets, Acts xiii. 1. 1 Tim. ii. 7.——3. These pastors and teachers are the same with *bishops*, or overseers, whose business it is to feed the flock, they have the episcopacy or oversight of, which is the work pastors are to do; which office of a bishop is a good work; and is the only office in the church distinct from that of deacon, 1 Tim. iii. 1, 8. Phil. i. 1.

―――4. And these bishops are the same with *elders*;[1] when the apostle Paul had called together at Miletus the elders of the church at Ephesus, he addressed them as overseers, επισκοπυς, *bishops*, Acts xx. 17, 28. and when he says, he left Titus in Crete, to ordain elders in every city, he proceeds to give the qualifications of an elder, under the name of a bishop; *A bishop must be blameless*, &c. plainly suggesting, that an elder and a bishop are the same, Tit. i. 5, 6, 7. and the apostle Peter exhorts the *elders*, to *feed the flock of God, taking the oversight*, επισκοπης, acting the part of a bishop, or performing the office of one, 1 Pet. v. 1, 2.―――5. These pastors, teachers, bishops, and elders, are called rulers, guides, and governors. A pastor, or shepherd, is the governor and guide of his flock; a teacher, and a ruling elder are the same, 1 Tim. v. 17. One qualification of a bishop is, that he know how to rule his own house; or how shall he take care of the church of God, to rule that well, which is a considerable branch of his office? 1 Tim. iii. 1, 4, 5. these, indeed, are not to lord it over God's heritage, or rule according to their own wills, in an arbitrary manner; but according to the laws of Christ, as King of saints; and then they are to be respected and obeyed; *Remember them that have the rule over you, and obey them;* for they are *over* the churches *in the Lord*, and under him as the great Lawgiver in his house; and though they are described as such who have the rule over churches, and are guides to them, Heb. xiii. 7, 17. yet they are the churches servants, for Jesus's sake, 2 Cor. iv. 5.―――6. These are sometimes called the angels of the churches; so the pastors, elders, bishops, or overseers of the seven churches of Asia, are called the angels of the seven churches; and the pastor, elder, bishop, or overseer of the church at Ephesus, the angel of the church at Ephesus, Rev. i. 20. and ii. 1. so called because of their office, being sent of God, and employed by him in carrying messages of grace to the churches, and publishing the good tidings of salvation. ―――7. They are said to be *ministers of Christ*, or his *under-rowers*, as the word υπηρετας signifies, 1 Cor. iv. 1. the church is the ship or boat, which they work; Christ is the pilot, who is at the helm, under whom, and by whose direction, they row; and the oars they row with, are the word, ordinances, and discipline they administer. And in the same place,―――8. They are called, *Stewards of the mysteries of God;* and sometimes, *Good stewards of the manifold grace of God;* that is, of the more sublime truths of the gospel, and the various doctrines of divine grace, 1 Peter iv. 10. so a bishop or elder is called a *steward of God*, Tit. i. 7. a steward in his house or family, to give to every one in it their portion of meat in due season: and which office requires wisdom and faithfulness, to execute it aright, Luke xii. 42. 1 Cor. iv. 2. Concerning these persons may be observed,

I. The qualifications of them for their office; which, as it is a *good office*, the necessary qualifications should be found in those who are put into it, and which the apostle directs to, 1 Tim. iii. 1, &c. Some of which,

1. Respect the internal and spiritual character and accomplishments of a bishop or elder. As,―(1.) He must not be a *novice;* which does not mean a young man; for such an one was Timothy himself, to whom the apostle writes, who was more than an ordinary officer, even an evangelist; hence he says, *Let no man despise thy youth*, 1 Tim. iv. 12. but the word νεοφυτος, translated *novice*, signifies, *one newly planted*,[2] that is, in the church of God; there must be time, after such a plant is planted, to observe whether it has taken good root, and how it grows and thrives, and whether a plant of Christ's heavenly Father's planting. A bishop or elder should be first of some standing in the church, before he is called to such an office, that his gifts, grace, and conduct may be known, *lest being lifted up with pride*, elated with the high station he is advanced to, and with the gifts he is supposed to have, *he fall into the condemnation of the devil;* fall by pride as he did, and under the same sentence, and be degraded from his office.―(2.) He must have a competency of knowledge and understanding in divine things; for a pastor is to feed men with knowledge and understanding; and therefore must have a good share of it himself, that so he may be *able to teach others also*, 2 Tim. ii. 2. this is a principal part of his work, to teach and instruct men in the knowledge of evangelical

---

[1] So Jerom, in his Comment. on 1 Tim. iii. 10' and on Tit. i. 5.

[2] Novam plantam, Grotius; Nuper baptizatum et ascriptum in numerum christianorum, Vatablus.

truths; in which he should be assiduous; *He that teacheth, on teaching,* Rom. xii. 7. and for this he must have a ministerial gift; which is not natural parts, nor human learning, nor grace in common with other christians; which, though all needful and useful, yet neither of them separately, nor all together, will qualify a man to be a public teacher of the word. He must have a special and peculiar gift from Christ; such as he received at his ascension, and gives to men, to ordinary ministers of the word; and it was according to the measure of such a gift, though a large one, the apostle Paul himself was made a minister of the gospel, and to such a gift he ascribes his being one, Eph. iii. 7, 8. and iv. 7, 8.—(3.) He must not only be able to teach, but he must be *apt to teach;* which aptitude lies in a good degree of elocution, and a free utterance of speech; for it is of little avail what is a man's capacity, what the furniture of his mind, and what stock of knowledge he has, unless he can clothe his ideas with proper words to convey the understanding of them to others; the royal preacher *sought to find out acceptable words;* such as were suitable to express his meaning, and to give delight and pleasure, as well as yield profit to them that heard him; and especially the taught words of the Holy Ghost are to be made use of. Apollos was an eloquent man, and mighty in the scriptures, well versed in them, and which greatly improved his gift of elocution; a good textuary makes a good preacher; a free and ready utterance is necessary; such an one is like the scribe and householder, Matt. xiii. 52. The apostle Paul himself desired the Ephesians to pray for him, *that utterance might be given him,* Eph. vi. 19.

2. There are other qualifications of a bishop or pastor, which respect his domestic character. He must be *the husband of one wife:* this does not oblige a bishop or elder to be a married man; nor restrain from a second marriage after the decease of his wife; only that he should have but one wife at a time. Polygamy having been much in use among Jews and Gentiles, the first christians were not easily brought off of that practice; however, the apostle thought fit to enjoin that a bishop or pastor should not practise it, that he might not set an example of it, which might serve to countenance and continue it; there are some peculiar laws, respecting the marriage of the high-priest among the Jews, and by which it seems he was to have but one wife, Lev. xxi. 13, 14. and much the same laws are directed to for priests or ministers of the word, under the gospel-dispensation, Ezek. xliv. 22. also a bishop or elder must be *one that ruleth well his own house, having his children in subjection with all gravity,* or reverence of him; obedient to his commands, and who behave respectably to him; and especially he should be careful to lay his commands upon them to keep the ways of the Lord, and to restrain them from vices, and severely reprove them for them; in which good old Eli was deficient, and therefore blamed and corrected for it: the apostle gives a good and strong reason why a bishop or elder should have this qualification; *For,* says he, *if a man know not how to rule his own house, or family, how shall he take care of the house of God?*

3. There are other qualifications, which respect his personal character, conduct, and behaviour. As,—(1.) That he must be *blameless* in his conversation. So the priests under the law were to have no blemish on them, nor any natural defect in them, Lev. xxi. 17—23. though they were men encompassed with moral infirmities. And this rule, respecting a bishop or pastor of a church, does not imply that he must be perfect and without sin, only that he should not be guilty of any scandalous sin, and especially should not live in any known sin; otherwise there is no man, not the best of men, without sin; no, not in the highest office; the prophets of the Old Testament, and the apostles of the New, were men of like passions with others.—(2.) Such an one must be *of good behaviour,* and *must have a good report with them that are without;* he should have a good report of all men, as Demetrius had; not only of the church and its members, of those that are within, to whom he is to be an *example in word, in conversation, in charity, in spirit,* in faith, *in purity,* 1 Tim. iv. 12. but of those without the church, the men of the world; that the ministry be not blamed and had in contempt, the ways of God, and doctrines of Christ, evil spoken of, and the ministers' usefulness to the souls of men hindered.— (3.) He must not be given to any vice; *Not given to wine,* that is, to excessive drinking of it; otherwise it is no more criminal to drink that, than to drink water; and Timothy is advised by the apostle to refrain from drinking water, and to make

use of wine for his health's sake, chap. v. 23. nor given to quarrels; he must be *no striker*, neither with his fist nor with his tongue; no calumniator, no *brawler*, not litigious and contentious; but *patient*, and bear all reproaches, indignities, and insults; *not greedy of*, nor *given to filthy lucre*, should not enter on his work and take upon him such an office, with a lucrative view; nor be *covetous*, but *given to hospitality*; not insatiably desirous of wealth and riches, and making use of any unlawful way to obtain them; but should, according to his abilities, be liberal in relieving the poor and necessitous; and in entertaining christian strangers and travellers, when well recommended; and by all this set a good example to others; and for which he should be supplied by the church to whom he ministers.—(4.) A bishop, elder, or pastor, should be *vigilant*; watch over himself and his flock, and take heed to both: to himself; to his doctrine, that it be sound, pure, and incorrupt, and according to the word of God; and to his conversation, that it be as becomes the gospel of Christ; to his flock, to feed them with wholesome food, to lead and direct them to good pastures, and to preserve them from wolves, from false teachers, that lie in wait to deceive; he is to watch for the souls of men, for their spiritual good and welfare, as one that must give an account with joy, and not with grief; and he should be *sober* and modest, wise and prudent, and *think soberly of himself*, Rom. xii. 3. I proceed to consider,

II. How any come into such an office, and are instated into it.

First, There must be a call to the ministry of the word, both inward and outward, previous to this office; *no man*, under the law, *took to himself the honour* of the priest's office, but he that was *called of God, as was Aaron*, Heb. v. 4, 5. nor ought any man to take upon him the office of a prophet, or minister of the word, without a call; there were some in the times of Jeremiah complained of by the Lord, who were not sent nor spoken to by him; and yet *prophesied*, Jer. xxiii. 21.

1. An internal call; which lies in gifts bestowed, and in the furniture of a man's mind, and in the disposition of it to make use of them in the service of God; for God never calls a man to any service, but he gives him abilities for it; which, when a man is sensible of, and is satisfied God has bestowed a gift upon him, he cannot be easy to wrap up his talent in a napkin, but is desirous of making use of it in a public manner; not by a mere impulse, through vanity of mind, and with ambitious views, and sordid ends; but from a principle of love to the souls of men, and to the glory of God; this is the internal call, of which a man's gifts are an evidence to himself and others.——2. The outward call is not immediately by Christ, as the twelve disciples were called, and sent forth by him to preach the gospel; and particularly, as the apostle Paul was called to be an apostle; not of men, neither by man, but by Jesus Christ and God the Father; but mediately by the church; it being by some means or another made known to the church, that such an one is thought to have a gift for public usefulness, the church calls him to exercise it before them, and submit it to their examination and trial; and having sufficiently tried it, and being satisfied of it, the church calls and sends him forth in the name of Christ, to preach the gospel, where he may be directed in providence to do it; and being thus called and sent forth, he is eligible to the office of a pastor of a church who shall think fit to choose him.

Secondly, The procedure of instating him into the office of a pastor, or the ordination of him, is in this manner.

1. He must be a member of a church to whom he is to be ordained as a pastor. So an extraordinary officer, an apostle, was chosen and ordained to be one, in the room of Judas, from among the disciples who had accompanied Christ and his apostles from the baptism of John; and so inferior officers, deacons, were selected out of the church, and appointed to that office, Acts i. 21, 22, 23. and vi. 3, 5. so Epaphras, a faithful minister of Christ for the church at Colosse, is said to be *one of you*, a member of that church, Col. i. 7. and iv. 12. one that is not a member of the church, cannot be a pastor of it.——2. His qualifications, such as before observed, must be known by the members of a church, and must be proved and approved of by them; yea, they must be satisfied that he has gifts for *their* edification; for a man may have gifts for the edification of one church, which are not for the edification of another; and this should be known, previous to their choice and call of him.——3. After sufficient trial and due consideration of his gifts, to satisfaction, and after seeking the Lord by prayer, for every thing is sanctified by the

word of God and prayer, the church proceeds to the choice and call of him to be their pastor; for every church has a right and power to choose its own officers, pastors, and deacons.——4. This choice and call being signified to him, he taking proper time, and seeking the Lord also, accepts thereof, and shews a readiness and willingness to take the *oversight* of them, 1 Pet. v. 2. for there must be a mutual consent and agreement in this affair.—— 5. To the public instating of him into his office, it is necessary there should be a recognition and repetition both of the church's choice and call of him, and of his acceptance of it, for the confirmation thereof, and for the satisfaction of ministers and churches in communion; who meet to see their order, and to assist, especially the former, by prayer for them, and by giving a word of exhortation to them, if desired. ——6. As every civil society has a right to choose, appoint, and ordain their own officers; as all cities and towns corporate, their mayors or provosts, aldermen, burgesses, &c. so churches, which are religious societies, have a right to choose and ordain their own officers, and which are ordained, αυτοις, *for them*, and for them *only:* that is, for each particular church, and not another, Acts xiv. 23.——7. The election and call of them, with their acceptance, is ordination. The essence of ordination lies in the voluntary choice and call of the people, and in the voluntary acceptance of that call by the person chosen and called; for this affair must be by mutual consent and agreement, which joins them together as pastor and people. And this is done among themselves; and public ordination, so called, is no other than a declaration of that. Election and ordination are spoken of as the same; the latter is expressed and explained by the former. It is said of Christ, that he *ordained twelve*, Mark iii. 14. that is, he chose them to the office of apostleship, as he himself explains it, John vi. 70. see Acts i. 2. Paul and Barnabas are said to *ordain elders in every church*, Acts xiv. 23. or to choose them;[3] that is, they gave orders and directions to every church, as to the choice of elders over them; for sometimes persons are said to do that which they give orders and directions for doing, as Moses and Solomon, with respect to building the tabernacle and temple, though done by others; and Moses particularly is said to choose the judges, Exod. xviii. 25. the choice being made under his direction and guidance. The word that is used in Acts xiv. 23. is translated *chosen*, 2 Cor. viii. 19. where the apostle speaks of a brother, χειροτονηθεις, *who was chosen of the churches to travel with us;* and is so rendered when ascribed to God, Acts x. 41.——8. This choice and ordination in primitive times, was made two ways;[4] by casting lots and by giving votes, signified by stretching out of hands. Matthias was chosen and ordained to be an apostle in the room of Judas, by casting lots; that being an extraordinary office, required an immediate interposition of the divine Being; a lot being nothing more nor less than an appeal to God for the decision of an affair. But ordinary officers, as elders and pastors of churches, were chosen and ordained by the votes of the people, expressed by stretching out their hands; thus it is said of the apostles, Acts xiv. 23. *When they had ordained them elders in every church*, χειροτονησαντες, by taking the suffrages and votes of the members of the churches, shewn by the stretching out of their hands, as the word signifies;[5] and which they directed them to, and upon it declared the elders duly elected and ordained. So Clemens Romanus, who lived at the latter end of the apostolic age, says,[6] the apostles appointed proper persons to the office of the ministry, *with the consent or choice of the whole church;* and this practice continued to the third century; in which century Cyprian[7] was chosen bishop of Carthage, by the suffrage of the people; and so he says[8] was Cornelius, bishop of Rome, in the same age; as was Fabianus, before him:[9] the council of Nice, in the beginning of the fourth century, in their synodical epistle,[10] to the churches in

---

[3] χειροτονειν, hic simpliciter vertamus per eligere, decernere, designare, ordinare per electionem, Vitringa de Synagog. vet. l. 3. par. 1. c. 14. p. 821.
[4] Of these two ways of choosing officers with the Jews, Philo speaks, de Judice, p. 718. in initio.
[5] χειροτονησαντες, per suffragia delegissent, creassent: so Beza, Erasmus, Vatablus, H. Stephanus. ortum est hoc verbum ex Græcorum consuetudine, qui porrectis manibus suffragia ferebant, Beza in Act. 14, 23.
[6] Ep. 1. ad Corinth. p. 100.
[7] Pontii vita Cyprian. p. 2. et Cyprian, ep. 40. p. 75. et ep. 55. p. 115, 116.
[8] Ib. ep. 52. p. 97. et ep. 67. p. 163.
[9] Euseb. Eccl. Hist. l. 6. c. 29.
[10] Apud Theodoret. Eccl. Hist. l. 1. c. 9.

Egypt, ordered, that when any were removed by death, their places should be filled up by others, provided they were worthy, and such as the people chose; the bishop of Alexandria agreeing to and confirming the choice: in the same century Martin was chosen bishop of Tours, by a vast concourse of the people:[11] indeed, the council at Laodicea, Can. XIII. in this century, ordered, that from thenceforward the people should not be allowed to choose their own ministers; which shews it had been practised before: yea, after, in the *fifth* century, Austin, in his old age, recommended to the people Eradius,[12] to be his successor; which they shewed their approbation of, by their loud and repeated acclamations.[13] But,——9. Though there was χειροτονια, *a stretching out of the hands;* yet there was no χειροθεσια, *imposition of hands*, used at the ordination; neither of extraordinary officers, as apostles; nor of ordinary pastors or elders of churches, in the times of Christ and his apostles.

1. Christ ordained the twelve apostles himself; but we read not a word of his laying his hands upon them, when he ordained them; nor on the seventy disciples, when he appointed them, and sent them forth into every city. Matthias was chosen and ordained an apostle in the room of Judas, upon a lot being cast by the church, which fell upon him; and upon counting the lots he was numbered, συγκατεψηφισθη, *chosen*, or by the number of lots declared to be chosen, and so took his place, and was reckoned with the apostles; but no mention is made of any hands being laid on him; see Acts i. 22—26. ——**2.** The apostles are said to *ordain elders in every church*, not by laying their hands upon them, but by taking the votes of the people, on the stretching out of their hands; when they declared the elders duly elected and ordained, as before observed. The apostle Paul directed Titus, chap. i. 5. to *ordain elders in every city;* that is, in such sort and manner as he and Barnabas had done in the above instance; but gave him no orders and instructions to lay hands upon them; which he would not have omitted, had it been material, and so essential to ordination, as some make it to be: and if he was to ordain elders by the laying on of his hands, then not by the hands of a presbytery, since he was a single person; and if this was to be done by him as a bishop, which some say he was, though the subscription of the epistle to him not being genuine, which asserts it, is no proof of it, it would justify ordination by a diocesan bishop.——**3.** No instance can be given of hands being laid on any ordinary minister, pastor or elder, at his ordination; nor, indeed, of hands being laid on any, upon whatsoever account, but by extraordinary persons; nor by them upon any ministers, but extraordinary ones; and even then not at and for the ordination of them. The instance in Acts xiii. 1, 2, 3. is no proof of laying on of hands at the ordination of a pastor or elder of a church; Paul and Barnabas were extraordinary persons, apostolical men, and were never ordained pastors or elders to any particular church; nor is there the least hint given of any such ordination of them at that time; nor was this the first time of the separation of them to the sacred office of the ministry: they had been in it, and had exercised it long before, and in as public a manner as afterwards; and what they were now separated to, was some peculiar and extraordinary work and service[14] the Holy Ghost had for them to do in foreign parts, whither they travelled; and the persons who were directed by him

---

[11] Vide Sulpicii Severi vit. Martin, p. 224.

[12] Inter opera ejus, tom. 2. ep. 110.

[13] Electionis formula de episcopis et præfectis ecclesiæ per suffragia populi constituendis, ea semper mihi visa est optima, quam legimus apud Augustinum de creatione Eradii. Aonii Palearii Testimonium, c. 16. p. 367. This learned Italian was a glorious confessor and martyr of Jesus; who, for the noble witness he bore against Popish innovations, and particularly against the popish inquisition; which he said was a sword drawn to cut the throats of learned men,* was taken up at Milan, bound, and sent to Rome, where he was adjudged to the flames, and was burnt alive, after he had made a bold confession of his faith, about the year 1566, some say 1570, under pope Pius V. The above Testimonium referred to, was written by him, and designed to be sent to the emperor, the Christian kings and princes, and the presidents of a general council then deliberating, to be held at Trent; which, when written, was very worthy of their regard, and now to be read by every Protestant.

[14] Imponuntur quidem manus etiam Paulo et Barnaba in ecclesia Antiochena, Spiritu sancto jubente; sed opus illud videtur plane extraordinarium, seu in ministerium illic singulare designatio; nec alterutrius eorum in presbyteratu facultatem ordinatio, Selden de Synedriis, l. 2. c. 7. s. 7.

* Vid. Lampe, Synops. Hist. Sacr. et Ecclesiastic. l. 2. c. 13. s. 29. p. 453.

to separate them to it, were extraordinary ones also; and their prayers for them, with the rite of imposition of hands, seem only to express their good wishes for a prosperous success in their work :[15] and it may be observed, that this rite was used, not *at*, but *after* the separation of them to the work and service unto which they were appointed, and after fasting and prayer for them: this was the last act done, just when upon their departure; for so it is said, *And when they had fasted and prayed*, καὶ ἐπιθέντες τας χειρας αυτοις, *then putting hands upon them, they sent them away*, or dismissed them with this token, or sign of their good wishes for them. The apostle Paul, indeed, speaks of the hands of the presbytery being laid upon Timothy, 1 Tim. iv. 14. but it should be observed, that Timothy was an extraordinary officer in the church, an evangelist, and was not chosen or ordained a pastor of any particular church; nor did he reside in any one place for any length of time; the subscription of the *second* epistle to him being not to be depended upon as genuine, no more than of that to Titus;[16] and therefore he can be no instance of imposition of hands at the ordination of any ordinary elder, or pastor of a church; and who the presbytery were, who laid hands on him, be it upon what account it may, they must be extraordinary persons through whose hands an extraordinary gift was conveyed: we are sure the apostle Paul was one, since he expressly speaks of a gift which Timothy had *by the putting on of his hands;* and it can scarcely be thought that any other should join with him herein, but an apostolical man; very probably Silas; see Acts xvi. 1, 19. However, upon the whole, it appears to be an extraordinary affair transacted by extraordinary persons, on an extraordinary one, and by it an extraordinary gift was conveyed; which no man of modesty will assume to himself a power of conveying. And let it be observed, it was not an *office*, but a *gift*, which was conveyed this way; see 1 Tim. iv. 14. 2 Tim. i. 6.———4. The hands of ministers being now empty, and they having no gifts to convey through the use of this rite, of course it ought to cease, and should; it not appearing to have been used but by extraordinary persons on any account; upon which, at least for the most part, if not always, extraordinary things followed. ———5. To say that this rite is now used at the ordination of a pastor, to point him out to the assembly, is exceeding trifling: the church needs it not, having before chosen and called him, and he having accepted their call in a more private way: and it is needless to others met together publicly to observe the order of the procedure; since usually the members of the church are desired to recognize their choice and call of their pastor, and he is desired to renew his acceptance, and frequently he makes a confession of his faith; and after all this, to use this rite to point him out to the people, is such a piece of weakness for which no excuse can be made.

Should it be urged, that imposition of hands was used at the ordination of deacons, and then why not at the ordination of elders or pastors of churches, which is an higher office? It may be answered, that the church, as directed, chose out from among them seven men, so and so qualified, Acts vi. in which choice the essence of ordination lay; whom they presented to the apostles, who, approving their choice, confirmed it, and *constituted* and settled them in their office, as they proposed, ver. 3. and the rite of imposition of hands was used after this, and even after prayer for them; for it is said, *When they had prayed*, not while they were praying, as the custom is now, *they laid their hands on them;* which, done for what end soever, was done by extraordinary persons, the apostles, and it may be for extraordinary service; and so no rule to ordinary ministers in the ordination of persons to an ordinary office; and it may be, it was done by way of benediction, wishing them happiness and success in their office, for which this rite was used among the Jews, and for the confirmation of this office, it not being the immediate institution of Christ, but of the apostles:[17] and the use of it seems to be temporary, since we have no other instance of it on such an account; nor any injunction of it, nor any direction for it; nor is it made mention of by the apostle, when he treats of the office of deacons, their

---

[15] Manus impositio; quid est enim aliud nisi oratio super hominem? Augustin. contra Donatist. l. 3. c. 16.

[16] See Lord Brook's Discourse of the Nature of Episcopacy, p. 76, 77.

[17] Meminisse autem diaconi debent, quoniam apostolos, id est, episcopos et præpositos dominus elegit: diaconos autem post ascensum domini in cœlos, apostoli sibi constituerunt episcopatus sui et ecclesiæ ministros, Cyprian, ep. 65. p. 158.

qualifications, the proving and instalment of them into their office, and their use of it, 1 Tim. iii. 10. nor does it appear that there was afterwards any ordination of deacons, by imposition of hands, until the fourth century, when church offices and church officers were both magnified and multiplied. Besides, if the seven persons spoken of in Acts vi. were *extraordinarily* and *pro tempore* appointed to take care of the poor, and of the widows of the first church at Jerusalem, and particularly of the Grecian widows in it, to answer their present exigency; and were different from the ordinary deacons of the churches, afterwards spoken of in Paul's epistles, which is the sense of Vitringa;[18] who observes, that these men are never called *deacons*, only described by their number, the *Seven*, as in Acts xxi. 8. that their work was not similar to that of ordinary deacons, their *ministration* being not monthly, nor weekly, but daily, and of an extraordinary kind; for they succeeded the apostles in the care of the secular affairs of the church; they had all the estates, and the whole substance of the community, which was made one common stock in their hands, to dispose of to them as they needed; which was a very extraordinary and uncommon piece of service; though their destination was more peculiar to the care of the Grecian widows; and these seven men appear by their names to be all of them Greeks, or Jewish proselytes from the Greeks, as one of them most certainly was; and had it not been for the murmuring of the Greeks, no such an appointment would have been made; nor does it appear that they continued in their office, but when this was over, it ceased; and some of them, at least, were afterwards employed in other ministerial services, and elsewhere: now if this was the case, which is not easy to be disproved, we have no scripture-instance of the imposition of hands at the ordination of ordinary deacons; nor any instruction and direction for it. I go on to consider,

III. The work of such persons, who are instated into the office of pastors of churches.

First, The chief and principal of their work is to feed the church of God committed to their care; they have the name of pastors, *a pascendo*, from feeding; Christ the chief Shepherd and Bishop of souls, feeds his flock like a shepherd; and so it is the business of all under-shepherds to feed their respective flocks, 1 Pet. v. 2.

1*st*, Whom they are to feed.———1. Not dogs that worry the flock; but the flock itself. The *children's bread*, that which is fit and suitable food for them, is not to be taken and *cast to dogs;* that which is holy is not to be given to them; the holy word of God, its precious truths and promises, do not belong to them; nor are the holy ordinances to be administered to them; *without are dogs*, they are without the church, out of the flock, and so do not belong to the care and feeding of the pastors or shepherds.———2. Nor swine; such who for the impurity of their hearts and lives, wallowing in the filth of sin, are comparable to these creatures; and which are creatures that never look upwards, but downwards to the earth, and so fit emblems of those who mind earth and earthly things, and feed on them. The prodigal was sent by the citizen of the country, the legal preacher, to whom he joined himself, into his fields to feed swine; but pastors of churches are not swineherds, but shepherds.———3. Nor the world's goats; the Lord judges and distinguishes between cattle and cattle, the sheep and the goats; though these are sometimes folded together, he threatens to punish the goats, which will be done at the second coming of Christ, when he will divide the sheep from the goats, and set the one on his right-hand and the other on his left; when the latter shall go into everlasting punishment, and the former into life eternal. ———4. They are Christ's sheep and lambs, that pastors of churches are to feed, according to the directions given by Christ to Peter; *Feed my sheep, feed my lambs*, John xxi. 15, 16, 17. such whom Christ has an interest and property in, through the Father's gift of them to him, and through his laying down his life for them, John x. 15, 29. and which is an argument why pastors should be careful and diligent to feed them, because they are Christ's; *My lambs, my sheep;* both are to be fed; the tender lambs, otherwise new-born babes, little children, as well as the grown sheep, otherwise young men and fathers. Christ, the great Shepherd, has set an example of diligence and tenderness, Isa. xl. 11. So that,———5. All the flock, the whole flock, is to be taken heed unto, and taken care

---

[18] De Synagog. vet. l. 3. par 2. c. 5.

of, by pastors and shepherds, *over which the Holy Ghost has made them overseers, or bishops;* and for which reason they should be careful of them; and another follows, *to feed the church of God, which he has purchased with his own blood;* and therefore of great value, and great care should be taken of it to feed it.

2dly, What they are to feed the church or flock of God with?

1. Not with chaff and husks, or what is comparable to them, Jer. xxiii. 28. chaff is light, has no substance in it, and yields no nourishment, and is not fit for food; as bread made of wheat is, and denotes the solid and substantial doctrines of the gospel, with which the souls of men are to be fed. Husks are food for swine, but not for sheep; the externals of religion satisfy some minds, but not truly gracious souls, they cannot live upon these.——2. Pastors of churches are to feed their flocks with such food as is suitable to lambs and sheep; milk is for tender lambs, for new-born babes, who desire the sincere milk of the word. Milk designs the more plain and easy truths of the gospel, which are suited to tender minds; strong meat, the more sublime doctrines of it, fitter for those of full age, more grown Christians, who have a better exercise of their spiritual senses, and can discern things that differ, 1 Pet. ii. 2. 1 Cor. iii. 2. Heb. v. 14. ——3. Sound doctrine, salutary truths, the wholesome words of our Lord Jesus, are what pastors are to teach and feed souls with; these are nourishing, when unsound doctrines, the unwholesome words of false teachers, eat as do a canker.——4. The word of God in general, and especially the gospel-part of it, is food for souls, and is esteemed by them more than their necessary food; being that to their souls, what the richest and choicest food is to their bodies; they find it and eat it, and it is the joy and rejoicing of their hearts; it is sweeter to their taste than the honey or the honey-comb.——5. Pastors are promised and given to the churches, to feed them *with knowledge and understanding,* Jer. iii. 15. which may denote both the matter they are to feed them with, and the manner in which they are to do it.

1. The matter or things they are to feed souls with, are things worthy to be known; not trifling things, matters of curiosity, and of no importance, which are vain and unprofitable, and serve to gender strife, and tend not to godly edification: not philosophy and vain deceit, or science falsely so called; nor mere human knowledge, or knowledge of natural things; but divine knowledge, knowledge of divine things; which, though a minister cannot give, he may teach and instruct; for it is the Lord that gives understanding in all things; it is the Spirit of wisdom and revelation who leads men into the knowledge of Christ; and it is the Son of God himself who gives men an understanding to know him that is true; yet ministers are instruments of bringing men into an acquaintance with divine things, and of their improvement in the knowledge of them; the light of divine truths shines in their hearts, that they may be able to communicate, in a ministerial way, *the light of the knowledge of the glory of God,* of the glory of his divine perfections, displayed *in the face* or *person,* and in the work and office *of Jesus Christ.* Their work is to preach Christ, and him crucified; and they determine to know, that is, to make known, none but him, as the Saviour of lost sinners; and they are the servants of the most high God, which shew unto men the way of salvation by Christ; and direct souls to him, who enquire, What shall we do to be saved? yea, they may be said *to give knowledge of salvation,* as John the Baptist is said to do, being instruments of conveying the knowledge of it to men; so likewise they feed men with the knowledge and understanding of gospel-truths; as they have knowledge of the mysteries of Christ themselves, they impart it to others; as they have freely received, they freely give, and keep back nothing that may be profitable, but declare the whole counsel of God; and such knowledge is food to the mind as bread is to the body. ——2. This phrase, *With knowledge and understanding,* may signify the manner in which pastors are to feed the souls of men, wisely and prudently; which they do, when, as wise and faithful stewards, they give to every one their portion of meat in due season, and feed them in proportion to their age and capacity; give milk to babes, and meat to strong men.

3dly, By what means they are to feed and do feed the churches of Christ, over which they are set.

1. By the ministry of the word, or by the preaching of the gospel; which is the means appointed of God for the gathering in his elect ones, for the perfecting the

number of them in conversion, and for the edification of the body, the church, and all its members; for their growth in grace, and in the knowledge of Christ, and of all divine things: an unpreaching pastor, bishop, or elder, is a contradiction in terms; and such are like those described by the prophet, as blind and ignorant watchmen, dumb dogs that cannot bark, shepherds that cannot understand; who every one look for their gain from their quarter, though they do not the duty of their office. But,—(1.) Such feed the flock, who do their work aright; give themselves up to the ministry of the word, neglect all other services, at least as much as may be, that they may not be entangled with them, and be diverted by them, from their grand employment; to which they have devoted themselves, for the glory of God and the good of souls. Such give attendance to reading, to exhortation, and to doctrine; and meditate on these things, and give themselves wholly to them, that their profiting may appear to all, and their usefulness to many.—(2.) They addict themselves to the study of the sacred scriptures more particularly; and endeavour to bring forth from thence things new and old, which may be for the use of edifying; they study to shew themselves approved of God, skilful workmen, who need not be ashamed of their ministrations, rightly dividing the word, which will not fail of feeding, more or less, the souls of men; as they have the word of God, the knowledge and experience of it, they are faithful to dispense it as stewards of the mysteries of God; of whom it is required that they be both faithful and wise.—(3.) They are assiduous and constant in this work; they as the apostles of Christ, give themselves continually to prayer, and to the ministry of the word; do not preach a sermon only now and then, but preach the word constantly, and are instant in season and out of season; and take every opportunity of feeding and of doing good to the souls of men; they are constant and immoveable, always abounding in the work of the Lord; knowing that their labour is not in vain in the Lord.—(4.) They not only give themselves up to this work, and are studious and constant in it, but labour therein; they are not loiterers, but labourers in the Lord's vineyard; and are labourers together with him, and are approved by him; and their labours are blessed and succeeded among men, and they receive honour from them, of which they are worthy, 1 Tim. v. 17.—(5.) They are careful to preach the pure and whole gospel of Christ; they study a consistence in their ministry, that it be not yea and nay, and contradict itself; they are not of them who corrupt the word with human doctrines and the inventions of men; but speak it with all sincerity, renouncing all arts of dishonesty, commending themselves to every man's conscience in the sight of God; keeping back no part of divine truths, but declaring the whole of what is revealed in the word of God, so far as they have knowledge of it; and such are more or less blessed for the feeding the flock and church of God.

2. Pastors of churches feed souls by the administration of ordinances; these are the goodness and fatness of the house of God, with which the saints are richly fed, and abundantly filled and satisfied; these are the provisions of Zion, which the Lord blesses; these are breasts of consolation, out of which gracious souls suck, and are delighted and refreshed; these are green pastures, into which the shepherds of Israel lead their flocks and feed them.

3. This act of feeding, includes the whole work, and every part of the work of a shepherd or pastor to his flock, doing all good offices to them, and all the service they can for them; such as seeking the lost sheep, bringing again that which was driven away, binding up that which was broken, and strengthening the sick, Ezek. xxxiv. 16. preserving them from the lion and the bear, and from grievous wolves, false teachers, who will not spare the flock; watching over them even in the night-seasons, when needful; watching for their souls, the good and welfare of them, as those who must give an account of them; being diligent to know the state of the flock, and ready to administer all relief to them in their power, by comforting the feeble-minded, and supporting the weak.

4. A concern for the spiritual good of the flock the pastor has the care of, appears by his constant, fervent, and earnest prayers for it; for this is one part of the work they give themselves up unto, along with the ministry of the word, namely, prayer; particularly for those to whom they minister, that the word preached by them might be blessed unto them, and be food for their souls; thus we find the apostle

Paul, in all his epistles, makes mention of his prayers for all the churches, and the members of them, he having the care of all the churches on him.

5. Pastors may feed the souls of men under their care, not only by their public ministrations, but by their private visits, counsels, instructions, and conversation; so the apostle Paul taught from house to house, as well as publicly, Acts xx. 20.

6. To all which, love to Christ and to his people, is requisite; such only who have a true affection for both, will naturally care for the good of immortal souls, will be willing to spend and be spent for them, and to bear the reproach, and go through the fatigue and trouble which attend such service; hence said Christ to Peter, once, twice, and thrice, *Lovest thou me?* and at each answer given to the question, enjoined him to feed his lambs and his sheep; suggesting, that only such who loved him, were proper persons to take the care of them.

Secondly, Another part of the work of pastors, is to rule the church they take the oversight of; the same word in the Greek language which signifies to feed, signifies to rule also; see Matt. ii. 6. and kings are sometimes called shepherds; as Cyrus and others; so Agamemnon, in Homer,[19] is called, ποιμὴν λαῶν, *the shepherd of the people*. The church of Christ is a kingdom; it is frequently called so in the New Testament; Christ is King of it, set as King of Zion by his divine Father, and is owned as King of saints by his church and people; and ministers of the word, and pastors of churches, are *over them in the Lord;* they are under Christ, and subject to him, but are over the churches by his appointment; hence they are represented as guides, governors, and rulers, as before observed; and obedience to them is required; *Obey them that have the rule over you,* Heb. xiii. 17. And their pre-eminence in the church appears,——1. In giving the lead in divine worship, they go before the congregation in acts of divine service, in public prayer and thanksgiving, and in the ministry of the word, Rev. iv. 9, 10. and v. 14. and this they do in an authoritative way; they are the mouth of the people to God, and present their prayers and thanksgivings as representing them; and they are the mouth of God to the people, and speak in his name, and are ambassadors in Christ's stead.——2. In presiding at church-meetings; where they have the conducting of all affairs with order and decency, directing in all acts of discipline, according to the word of God; putting up the votes of the church, giving admonitions, and passing censures, as they may be necessary, by the agreement and consent of the church.——3. In receiving and rejecting members; the keys of the kingdom of heaven, the gospel-church, as usually understood, are committed to them, to open and shut the doors of the church according to its direction; for though the power of admission and rejection of members is originally in the church, it is executively in the pastors, in the name of the church.——4. In taking care of the whole discipline of the church of God, that it is observed, and that the rules respecting it are put into execution; which they are to explain, enforce, and see that they are attended to; they are to shew to the house, the church of God, *the form of the house, and the fashion of it;* the nature of it, as to matter, form, power, and order; *and the goings out thereof, and the comings in thereof;* the rules respecting the reception of members, and the excommunication of them; *and all the ordinances, and all the laws thereof,* even every thing Christ has commanded and appointed to be observed, Ezek. xliii. 10, 11. Now the rule and government of pastors of churches is not to be exercised in an arbitrary way; they are not to rule with force and cruelty, as the shepherds of Israel are complained of; they are not to lord it over God's heritage; they have not dominion over their faith, nor the command of their practice at their wills; they cannot oblige them to receive a doctrine, nor to follow a practice, that is of their own or of human invention; but they are to govern according to the word of God, and the laws and rules which Christ, as King and Head of the church, has given: and when they rule according to these, they may be said to rule well, and should be respected and obeyed, and counted worthy of honour. And this ruling, as well as feeding, should be with knowledge and understanding, in a wise, prudent and discreet manner; as David, who fed the people of Israel according to the integrity of his heart, and guided them with the skilfulness of his hands. I proceed to answer,

---

[19] Iliad. 2. v. 243, 254.

IV. Some queries relative to the office of pastors.

First, Whether a pastor of one church, can officiate as such, in another church; or whether he can administer the Lord's Supper, which is a pastoral act, in and to a church of which he is no pastor. I answer, he cannot; that is, it is not lawful for him to do it. As well may it be asked, Whether the lord mayor of London, whose power as such may be thought to be as extensive as any other may or whatever, can exercise his power, in any branch of his office, in the jurisdiction of the mayor of York or of Bristol, or any other: no officer in a corporation can exercise his office in another corporation; this holds good of every officer in it, from the highest to the lowest. A church of Christ is a body corporate, in a spiritual sense; and its officers can only act as such within it, and within no other. For,

1. A man can never act as a pastor, where he is not so much as a member; a man must be a member of a church before he can be a pastor of it, as we have seen. Epaphras, the minister and pastor of the church at Colosse, the apostle Paul, writing to them says, *Who is one of you,* that is, one of their society, a member of theirs, Col. iv. 12. But where a man is not a member of such a society, he is not one of them; he cannot act as pastor among them, nay he cannot put forth any act or operation, or join in any act as a private member may, and much less act as a pastor; for membership is the foundation, not only of every office, but of every act and operation in a church. *All members,* the apostle says, *have not the same office,* Rom. xii. 4. but let the office be what it may, they must be members that have it, and they only; they have not all the same function or ministry; as they were not all apostles who were in the primitive churches, so not all pastors, and all deacons, who were in them, and in succeeding churches; yet all who are pastors or deacons, must or should be members; and members have not all the same act or action, and operation, as the word may be rendered,[20] in an office-way; though there are some acts indeed which are common to all members, yet there are such which only belong to members, and which pastors of other churches cannot act and exercise, as private members may and do: for instance, they have no vote or suffrage in other churches for the admission of a member, or for the exclusion of any; or in the choice and call of any officer, pastor or deacon: and if they cannot act, or cannot exercise an act, a private member can: then surely they can never act as a pastor, where they have not the power and privilege of a private member!——2. As one that is not a member of a church cannot be an officer in it, as a pastor of another church cannot be; then he has no office-relation to it, nor has he any office-power in it, and therefore cannot exercise in it any act of office-power; and, in consequence, cannot administer the Lord's Supper in it, which is an act of office-power. ——3. As well may he exercise other branches of his pastoral office as this; as well may he be a ruling elder in other churches, and preside at their church-meetings, and exercise every part of discipline, and the power of the keys, as by some called, and let in and shut out, receive and exclude members, give admonitions, lay on censures, and take them off, as a pastor, in the name of the church; and if he can act as a pastor in two churches, he may in ten, and twenty, and more, and so become a diocesan bishop; yea, an universal bishop or pastor, as the pope at Rome pretends to be; and popery stopped not until it came to that, to establish an universal pastor; and to which such an antichristian practice leads and paves the way; and it is an affectation in some to be thought of more moment and importance than they are; and to grasp at power and authority, and to appear in a character and figure which do not belong to them, if not something else; which tempts them to give into such an unwarrantable practice. For,——4. Should it be asked, as it may be reasonably asked, by what authority they do this thing? who or what gives them this authority? What answer can be returned? will they say they have their authority from Christ? this must be had, either immediately from him as the apostles had, for what they did; and then they must be called upon to work miracles in confirmation of it, as they did; or from the word of God and Christ; and then it lies upon them to give proof of it from thence. Neither can a pastor derive his authority from his own church, of which he is properly pastor; nor from the other, to whom, at their request, he administers the ordi-

---

[20] Την αυτην πραξιν, eundem actum, vel eandem actionem, Vatablus.

nance; neither the consent of the one, nor the desire of the other, can give him sufficient authority so to act: as for his own church, they invested him with office-power over themselves, and not over others; further they could not and cannot go: and as for the other church, that has no power to call in the elder or pastor of another church so to act; and if they have no power to call him, he can have no authority to act, as not from his own church, so neither from that: nor will the communion of churches warrant it; for communion of churches does not enlarge the office-power of a pastor, limited by the word of God to his own congregation only; this no more subjects the officers of one church to another, than it subjects the particular members of one church to another; in either of which cases there would be nothing but confusion and disorder; one church, by virtue of the communion of churches, might as well censure and cast out the members of another church; as the pastor of one church, by virtue of such communion, act as an officer in another church. Neither his grace nor his gifts can authorize him so to act; for then one that is no officer, only a private brother, might do it; nor will his being an ordained minister in one church, give him authority so to act in another church; for elders are only ordained to particular churches, and not to others; the elders ordained by the apostles in every church where such ordinations were, were αυτοις, *for them*, and not others, Acts xiv. 23. Epaphras was a faithful minister *for you*, for the church at Colosse; not for another church, Col. i. 7. the elders of Ephesus were ordered to feed all the flock over which the Holy Ghost made them overseers; but not all the flocks over which they were not overseers: so other elders are directed to feed *the flock* that was amongst them, not *flocks*, Acts xx. 28. 1 Pet. v. 2. the angel of the church at Ephesus was not angel of the church at Smyrna, and so *vice versa:* ordination fixes a man to a particular church or congregation; and does not make him an universal pastor, which he must be, if there was no boundary to his office. And therefore,——5. Such who take upon them to act in such a manner may be truly called, *busybodies in other men's matters*, 1 Pet. iv. 15.

the word there translated, *a busy-body*, is αλλοτριοιπισκοπος,[21] a bishop, in another parish or diocese, which were originally the same, or a pastor in a church which is not his own; and truly describes such a person we are speaking of, who meddles with a business he has nothing to do with. ——6. As well may a deacon of one church officiate as such in another, as a pastor of one church officiate in another, for they are both alike chosen by, and ordained to particular churches, and not to others.——7. No instance can be given of such a practice in the word of God, there may be instances of members of one church communicating with another church occasionally; so Phebe, a member of the church at Cenchrea, was to be admitted to communicate with the church at Rome; but then partaking of an ordinance is a privilege arising from the communion of churches; and is only a kind of spiritual hospitality, giving a meal to a traveller; and that by a pastor discharging his office in his own proper place, in his own church; but the administration of an ordinance is an act of office-power, which one church cannot give to another, nor a pastor exercise it in another church, Rom. xvi. 1, 2. see Acts xx. 4—7. The instance of the apostle Paul's breaking bread to the disciples at Troas, supposing it to be understood of the ordinance of the supper, is no proof and example of such a practice; since he was an apostle, and had the care of all the churches upon him, and could administer all ordinances unto them; but to urge and follow his example, is to usurp what is peculiar to apostles, and to confound ordinary and extraordinary ministers together as one; whereas, *Are all apostles?* They are not. Upon the whole, it may justly create a scruple in the minds of such who receive the ordinance in a church where the administrator is not a pastor: either such an one is not clear in it, or he is, that it is his duty to receive it from such hands: if he is not clear in it, but doubts, he is self-condemned; and be it he is clear in it, he is culpable, since hereby he approves and abets the pastor's unlawful power to administer it, and encourages him in it, and draws upon himself the guilt of his unlawful administration, and of a compliance with an authority assumed by him, but not legally given.[22]

---

[21] Qui fines alieni officii invadit, Gerhardus apud Stockium in voce.
[22] See more of this question in a little tract, called "A Discussion of the Lawfulness of a Pastor's acting as an Officer in other churches besides his own;" by Nathaniel Mather. London, printed

Secondly, Another question may be put upon the former, Whether a brother, or private member of a church, may be deputed by the church, to administer the ordinance of the Lord's Supper? This may seem to carry in it a better face than the former; since, though he is a non-officer, he is upon a par with the pastor of another church, who is no more an officer in such a church the brother belongs to, than he is; and besides, he is a member of the church, which the pastor of another church is not. But the ordinance of the supper cannot be administered authoritatively but by an officer, since it is an act of office-power, and must be administered in the name of Christ, by one as a substitute of him; and if the church may delegate and substitute others for the discharge of all ordinances whatsoever, without elders or pastors, then it may *perfect the saints*, and complete the *work of the ministry*, without them; which is contrary to Eph. iv. 11, 12. and, as Dr. Owen [23] further observes, it would render the ministry only *convenient*, and not absolutely *necessary* to the church, which is contrary to the institution of it; and such a practice would tend to make a church content without a pastor, and careless and negligent of seeking after one when without one.

Thirdly, Another question is, Whether a pastor may remove from one congregation to another? The answer is, if it is for worldly advantage, and he has a sufficient provision where he is, He ought not. There are some cases in which it may be lawful for him to remove; as when it appears to be for the good of the interest of religion, and of the church of Christ in general; but this should not be without the consent of the church of which he is pastor; nor without the advice of other churches and ministers; and when a church, of which he is pastor, indulges immoralities, or has imbibed erroneous doctrines, from which they cannot be reclaimed; and if there are such divisions in the church as are not to be cured; and especially if the pastor has such a concern in them, that there is no probability of their being healed but by his removal; also when a competent provision is not made for him and his family, but they are not only exposed to want, but the gospel also to the reproach and contempt of the world.

Fourthly, It may be asked, Whether on account of bodily weakness, or a decay of intellectual abilities, a pastor may resign his office, or be desired to desist from his work? the answer is, He may voluntarily lay down his office, with the consent of the church; or he may be desired to drop it, provided, if his case requires it, a provision is made for his temporal subsistence.

Fifthly, If it is a question, Whether a pastor of a church may be deposed from his office, and be cast out of the church for immorality or heresy, it may be answered in the affirmative; for he may be admonished and reproved for negligence in the discharge of his office, and be stirred up to it, Col. iv. 17. a charge of sin may be brought against him, under proper witnesses, according to the rule, 1 Tim. v. 19. an elder or pastor is a brother, and to be dealt with as such, according to Matt. xviii. 15. Indeed, if the sole power of excommunication lies in the pastor, he cannot be dealt with in such a manner; but that is not the case; it lies in the church, as will be seen hereafter; to which power a pastor of a church is equally subject as a private member.

CHAP. IV.

OF THE DUTIES OF MEMBERS OF CHURCHES TO THEIR PASTORS.

As pastors of churches have a work to do, which is both honourable and useful; so there are duties incumbent on those who are under their care, with respect to them, for their work's sake. Though they are *nothing*, with respect to God, to whom they owe all they have, 1 Cor. iii. 7. and with respect to the churches, they are theirs, for their use and service; yet they are not to be reckoned as nothing by them, and to be treated with contempt; *Let a man so account of us, as of the ministers of Christ;* made such and put into the ministry by him, being furnished from him with gifts and graces for it, and as such, to be highly accounted of; and though they are not lords and masters in the family of God, yet they are stewards in it, the highest officers in the house of God; and therefore are to be accounted of as *stewards of*

1698, which is sufficient to convince any of the unlawfulness of it, whose mind is open to conviction; and from whence I have borrowed many of the above hints.

[23] True nature of a Gospel Church, ch. 5. p. 94.

CHAP. IV. DUTIES OF MEMBERS TO THEIR PASTORS.

the mysteries of God, having the secret and hidden things of God entrusted with them; the mysteries of the kingdom of heaven, the sublime as well as plainer doctrines of the gospel, which they are to minister: and since it is given them of God to know them and make them known to others, they are worthy of respect on that account, 1 Cor. iv. 1. The several duties which members of churches are under obligation to perform to their respective ministers, pastors, and elders, will be considered farther as they lie in various passages of scripture.

First, In 1 Thess. v. 12, 13. *We beseech you brethren to know them*, &c.

1*st*, It is the duty of church-members to *know* their pastors; which is not to be understood of a bare knowledge of their persons; for it cannot be supposed, that there can be such a relation between pastors and members, and yet the members not know their pastors; the sheep know their shepherd and his voice.——1. To know them is to be acquainted with them; to make themselves and their cases known unto them; for sometimes to *know* signifies to make known; as in 1 Cor. ii. 2. Members of churches should freely converse with their pastors, and make known the state and condition of their souls; and especially when they have any matter of difficulty and cases of conscience to be resolved, or are in any soul-trouble and distress; they should open their minds to them, and declare their case, that they may speak a word in season to them; for though their cases may sometimes be hit upon and reached in the general ministry of the word, yet this is owing to an extraordinary direction of providence, and cannot in common be expected by all; at least it cannot be assured of, unless persons unbosom themselves to their ministers, and tell them their case.——2. To know them is to acknowledge them as their ministers and pastors. Not to know, is not to own and acknowledge; as in Luke xiii. 27. It is for membrs so to know their pastors, as to own them as such; as theirs in a peculiar sense, in which other ministers are not; as in a special relation to them, and under their particular care; and this acknowledgment of them, should be testified by their submission to them in their ministerial services and pastoral acts; of which more hereafter.——3. To know them is to take notice of them, to shew respect to them, to *hold such in reputation*, as the apostle advises, Phil. ii. 29. to give them the honour that is due unto them; not to know Christ, his ministers, and his people, is to despise them, and to treat them in a disrespectful manner, 1 John iii. 1. Luke x. 16.——4. To know them is to love them; for words of knowledge oftentimes connotate love and affection, 2 Tim. ii. 19. and so the apostle explains this of members knowing their pastors, by esteeming them *very highly in love*, ver. 13. such as the Galatians expressed to the apostle Paul, though they afterwards became cool and indifferent to him; yea, the reverse of their former love.——5. To know them is to shew a concern for their comfort and welfare, their safety and protection, Psalm cxlii. 4. people should be concerned for the safety of their minister in the discharge of his office; to protect him from the insolent attempts of wicked men, that he may be with them without fear, while he ministers to them; as the apostle exhorted the Corinthians, with respect to Timothy, 1 Cor. xvi. 10. and they should be careful to preserve his credit and reputation, and defend his character from the false aspersions of men, and not suffer, even among themselves, anything to be whispered to his discredit, and to the hurt of his usefulness; nor any accusation to be brought in public against him, without sufficient evidence, 1 Tim. v. 19.

Now the arguments and reasons made use of to enforce this duty are,—(1.) Because such persons *laboured among them;* they were not non-residents, but were upon the spot where the people were, they had the care of; as the flock was among them they were to feed, so they were among the flock, resided in the midst of them, or near them; for where should pastors be, but with their flocks, to feed them they have the oversight of? 1 Pet. v. 2. and faithful ministers are not only among their people, and continue with them, but they *labour* among them; they are not loiterers, slothful servants, who hide their talents in a napkin, and may be called idle shepherds, sleeping, lying down, loving to slumber, who serve not the Lord Jesus, nor the souls of men, but their own bellies: but faithful ministers are labourers, labour in the word and doctrine, and so are worthy of double honour.—(2.) Because they are *over* the churches to whom they minister; they are set in the first and most eminent place in the church, and have the rule over the members of it; and this superiority over them *is in the Lord,* in things pertaining to his interest and glory; not in civil, but spiritual things; and though they are *over* the churches, yet *under* Christ the Lord, as Head of the church and King of saints; and they are governors *in* and by his appointment, and therefore are to be regarded.—(3.) They *admonish* the saints, with whom they are concerned, or *put them in mind*, as the word signifies;[1] of their former experiences, which are delightful and refreshing to them; and of the doctrines of the gospel they have been instructed in, and have received, and are food to their souls; and of the duties of religion, which are incumbent upon them, the observance of which makes for their peace and good, and for the glory of God: and they admonish, warn, rebuke, and reprove; they warn of approaching danger from their spiritual enemies, sin, Satan, and the world; and rebuke and reprove for errors and immoralities they may fall into, for the recovery of them. On all which accounts they are deserving of respect.

2dly, It is the duty of church-members not only to know their pastors; but *to esteem them very highly in love for their work's sake*, or *superabundantly*,[2] as the word signifies; over and above common esteem and affection, and above common christians, in honour preferring them to others; they are to think highly of them, and entertain a high opinion of them, of their grace, gifts, and abilities for their work; for if they think meanly, and entertain a contemptible opinion of them, their ministry is not likely to be of much use unto them: and they should speak very highly and very honourably of them; for if members of churches do not speak well of their own pastors, it can hardly be thought they should have much respect and esteem from others; and they should speak respectfully to them, with a becoming decency, considering the character they bear, and the high office they are in, in the church; and this esteem must be cordial and affectionate, it must be *in love;* not through fear, nor in dissimulation and hypocrisy, but in sincerity and truth; and that, *for their work's sake*, which is laborious, attended with weariness of body; and sometimes, through it, are *nigh unto* death, as Epaphroditus was, Phil. ii. 30. and which also exposes to the reproach and contempt of the world.

To which may be added, that it is, notwithstanding, a good work and honourable, and very beneficial to the souls of men; and therefore those employed in it, should be esteemed for the sake of it; for the work that they have done, in which they have been useful to men for conversion, or for comfort and edification; and forasmuch as they have continued in it, and may be more useful in their day and generation, both for the good of souls and the glory of God.

Secondly, Other branches of the duty of members, to their pastors, are expressed in Heb. xiii. 7, 17, 18.

1st, In ver. 7. *Remember them*, &c.—— 1. They should remember them, be mindful of them at the throne of grace, as is after exhorted to; should remember the doctrines preached by them, and treasure them up in their minds; which may be of after use to them; these they should carefully retain in their memories, and not let them slip from them; they should remember to give them the honour and respect that is due unto them, and to make a suitable provision for the outward supply of life. The reasons enforcing this exhortation are, because they *have the rule over* them; being appointed by Christ, the Head and King of the church, to govern them under him; not in a lordly manner, according to their own wills; but according to the laws and rules which Christ has given; and when they rule according to these, they rule well, and are worthy of double honour: the words may be rendered, who are *your guides* or *leaders*.[3] Now such are the ministers of the gospel; they are the happy instruments of guiding men into the understanding of the scriptures; and of leading, under a divine direction and blessing, into the truths of the gospel; and of pointing out to them the way of life, peace, and salvation by Christ; and of directing them into the paths of faith and holiness, and are examples to them, and therefore deserve to be remembered by them. And moreover, they are said to have *spoken to* them *the word of God*, the scriptures, given by inspiration of God, which contain his mind and will, and the doctrines which declare his grace and favour to the sons of men; these they explain truly and faithfully, according to the best light and knowledge they have; and deliver

---

[1] Νουθετουντας.
[2] Υπερ εκ περισσου.
[3] Των ηγουμενων υμων.

out the doctrines of them with great freedom, boldness, and fidelity; and their memory, on these accounts, is and should be blessed, to truly gracious souls.——
2. Their *faith* is to be *followed*, or imitated; either their faithfulness in the several parts of their ministrations; or the grace of faith, their strong exercise of it, and the fruits and effects of it; or their profession of faith they hold fast without wavering; or the doctrine of faith they preach, by embracing it, abiding by it, standing fast in it, and persevering therein to the end: the motive to it is, *considering the end of their conversation;* either the drift and scope of it, which as in connection with the following verse, is Christ, his honour and glory, who is *the same yesterday, and to day, and for ever;* or the whole of their conduct in the discharge of the various duties of their office, and the manner of it; or else the issue of it in death; or the good end which, through the grace of God, they make; and which is to be considered for imitation and encouragement.

2dly, What is further observed in ver. 17. *Obey them that have the rule over you,* &c. This respects duties to be performed to the same persons, who are described as before, as their leaders, guides, and governors; to whom,——1. Obedience is to be yielded; *Obey them*, which obedience, in members of churches, to their pastors, lies,—(1.) In a due regard to the ministry of the word by them; which regard to it is seen in a diligent and constant attendance on it; for if their pastors are to be diligent and constant in their work, they are to be as diligent and constant in attending upon them in it; if ministers are to preach the word in season and out of season, or as often as they have opportunity for it, then members should as frequently assemble to hear it: they shew their obedience to the word, and to ministers in dispensing it, by their receiving it in faith and love; which they do when they receive it, not as the word of man, but as of God and Christ; when they mix it with faith as they hear it, and receive the love of it. Indeed, none are obliged to receive and obey their word or doctrine, than as it appears to be agreeable to the sacred scriptures, which are to be searched diligently, as our Lord directs, and as the noble Bereans did, to see whether these things be so or no; every spirit is not to be believed, but to be tried, whether of God or no; and, indeed, every thing delivered by pastors of churches is not binding on churches; nor are they obliged to receive it, but as it accords with the word of God.—(2.) Obedience of members to their pastors, lies in attendance on the ordinances of the gospel, as administered by them, and in joining with them constantly in the administration of them; not the ordinances of men; for they are not to be subject to ordinances of men's invention, or which are after the commandments and doctrines of men; for then they would be the servants of men, and not of Christ; but they are the ordinances of Christ, as they are faithfully administered by his servants, saints are to be subject to. The ministers of Christ are to teach all things Christ has commanded, and to urge the observance of them; and in this they are to be obeyed by those who are under their care, who, from a principle of love to Christ, should keep his commands, and constantly observe and attend his ordinances; but no farther are they obliged to follow their ministers, than as they are followers of Christ.—(3.) Obedience of members of churches to their guides and governors, lies in regarding their admonitions, reproofs, and rebukes, whether in case of error or immorality, and whether in private or in public; and as their business is to admonish when needful, their admonitions should be well taken; as they are to speak, exhort, and rebuke with all authority, their authority should not be despised, but be submitted to: likewise their counsels and advice should be observed, and taken, and acted up to; especially if it appears to be founded on the word of God, and is consonant to it.——2. Another branch of the duty of church-members to their pastors, is *to submit* themselves to them; that is, to the laws of Christ's house, as directed to and put into execution by them; and to their admonitions, reproofs, and censures, which are according to them; even though they may be not only public and before all, but sharp and severe as the case may require. The reason given for such obedience and submission to them, is because *they watch for their souls;* not for the preservation of their bodies, and outward affairs; though if such who watch over these, to preserve them from hurt and damage in the night-season, are to be regarded and valued, and obedience to be yielded to their alarms and directions, then much more those who watch for the good and welfare of immortal souls; which are of more worth than a world; their ministrations, in whatsoever way, are for comfort or edification, and are the instrumental means of saving souls: and what engages them to such watchfulness to preserve from error and heresy, from vice and immorality, is, that *they must give account;* to their own consciences, that they have discharged their work aright; to the church of God, to whom they are accountable if negligent; and especially to Christ, the Judge of all, to whom they must give an account of their ministry, and of the use of their talents, and of the souls put under their care, how they have discharged their duty towards them; and how such souls have behaved towards them under the ministry of the word and ordinances: and this they are desirous of doing *with joy, and not with grief;* either at the throne of grace, where they either rejoice or complain; or at the great day, when they will be witnesses either for or against those that have been committed to them; which latter would be *unprofitable* to them, and to the disadvantage of such who occasion grief and sorrow.

3*dly,* Another branch of duty in church-members to their pastors, is suggested in ver. 18. *Pray for us,* for us ministers; this is often inculcated in the sacred writings, as being of great moment and importance; see Eph. vi. 19. Col. iv. iii. 2 Thess. iii. 1. and members of churches should be solicitous at the throne of grace for their ministers.——1. With respect to their private studies and preparation for their work; that they may be led to suitable subjects, and be furnished with suitable matter; that their understanding may be opened to understand the word; that they may be led into the depths and mysteries of the gospel; that their gifts may be increased; and that they may be diligent, industrious, and laborious in their work.——2. With respect to their public ministrations; that they may come forth richly fraught with gospel-truths; that they may have freedom and utterance in the delivery of them; that they may speak them boldly, faithfully, and fully, as they ought to be spoken; and that their labours may be blessed to saints and sinners: and unless members of churches are observant of this their duty, they cannot expect the word will be blessed to them.——3. With respect to the world, and their conduct in it; that they may be kept from the evil of the world, that the ministry be not blamed; and from the temptations of Satan, who has a peculiar spite against them; and that they may be delivered from evil and unreasonable men, who, as much as can be, endeavour to discourage them, and hinder them in their work; and they should pray for them, that they may neither be intimidated by the frowns of the world, nor allured by the flatteries of it; and they should pray for their temporal good, for their bodily health, and for the sparing of their lives for farther usefulness, and for every thing needful for them. This part of duty is enforced with the following reason; *For we trust we have a good conscience,* exercised in an upright discharge of the ministerial work; *in all things, willing to live honestly;* not only as men, but as ministers, faithfully dispensing the word of truth; the temptations to the contrary being many, prayer is desired by them.

Thirdly, The duty of church-members to their pastors, is held forth in various passages, respecting their maintenance, or a provision for the subsistence of themselves and families; which is part of that double honour a ruling elder and a laborious minister is worthy of, since *the labourer is worthy of his reward,* 1 Tim. v. 17, 18. and he that is taught in the word, and instructed in it to his comfort and edification, should *communicate to him that teacheth in all good things,* temporal good things he stands in need of, Gal. vi. 6. This duty the apostle urges and presses with a variety of arguments, in 1 Cor. ix. 7-14. he argues from the law of nature and nations, exemplified in the cases of soldiers, planters of vineyards, and keepers of flocks, who, by virtue of their calling and service, have a right to a livelihood; between whom, and ministers of the gospel, there is a resemblance: also he argues from the law of Moses, particularly the law respecting the ox, not to be muzzled when it treads out the corn; which he interprets of ministers of the word, and applies it to them: he argues the right of the maintenance of the ministers of the gospel from the justice and equity of the thing; that since they minister spiritual things, it is but reasonable they should receive temporal ones: he makes this clear from the case of the priests and Levites under the legal dispensation, who ministering in holy things, had a provision made for them: and lastly, from the constitution and appointment of Christ himself, whose ordinance it is, that they that preach the gospel, should live of the gospel.

Fourthly, It is the duty of members of churches to adhere to their pastors, and abide by them in every condition and state, and in all cases and circumstances they come into; to support them under all their difficulties; to encourage them under all their discouragements; to sympathize with them in all their trials and troubles; to assist them all they can in their arduous work, against gainsayers, false-teachers, and such as may rise up among themselves, speaking perverse things, and doing evil ones; the apostle Paul complains, that all men forsook him in his troubles, and commends particularly Onesiphorus for his attachment to him and concern for him.

Now as there are duties belonging to the office of pastors, to be performed by them, and duties incumbent on members of churches towards them; on the performance of these mutual duties, the order, peace, good, and welfare of communities depend; and therefore should be strictly attended to and religiously observed.

CHAP. V.

OF THE OFFICE OF DEACONS.

The other officers in the gospel-church are deacons; and the things to be treated of respecting this office, are the nature and original of it; the work to be performed by those who are appointed to it; their qualifications for it, and the encouragement to the diligent performance of it; with the duties of a church respecting them.

First, The nature and original of it: It is not a political, but an ecclesiastic office; sometimes, indeed, the word is used in a political sense, for the civil magistrate; who is said to be Θευ διακονος the *deacon of God*; we render it, the *minister of God*, Rom. xiii. 4. one appointed by him, and who serves under him, for the public good: but it is commonly used in an ecclesiastic sense; sometimes for extraordinary ministers, as apostles, whose ministry is called διακονια, a *deaconship*, and is joined with apostleship, Acts i. 17, 25. and the apostle Paul calls himself and Apollos διακονοι, *deacons* or *ministers, by whom ye believed*, 1 Cor. iii. 6. and even our Lord Jesus Christ has this name and title, as the prophet of the church, and a preacher of the everlasting gospel; *Now I say that Jesus Christ was* διακονος, a deacon or *minister of the circumcision*, or to the circumcised Jews, Rom. xv. 8. not to take notice, that the ministry of angels is called διακονια, a *deaconship*, Heb. i. 14. To proceed, it is oftener given to ordinary preachers and ministers of the word; as to Tychicus, Epaphras, and others, Eph. vi. 21. Col. i, 7. and iv. 7. but elsewhere a deacon is spoken of as a distinct officer from either ministers extraordinary or ordinary; so the apostle speaks of the office of an elder, bishop, or overseer, and of the office of a deacon, as two distinct offices; and after he had given the qualifications of the one, he gives the qualifications of the other, 1 Tim. iii. and the officers of the church at Philippi are distinguished into bishops and deacons, Phil. i. 1.

Now the original of the institution of this office we have an account of, as is commonly thought, in Acts vi. 1—5. by which it seems to have been originally a branch of the ministerial office, as executed by the apostles; and, indeed, the whole of the ecclesiastic ministry was in their hands, the management of the secular, as well as of the spiritual affairs of the church: the first christians, the members of the church at Jerusalem, sold their possessions, and had all things common, and parted them to all, as every man had need; and the apostles had the disposal and distribution of them; for they were brought and laid at their feet for that purpose, Acts ii. 44, 45. and iv. 34—37. and v. 2. this church becoming very numerous, which at first consisted of about an hundred and twenty, increased to some thousands; and their poor likewise increased; for the poor from the first had the gospel preached to them, and received it; and these were chosen, called, and brought into the church, and this being the case, there was a murmuring of the Grecians, of the Hellenistic Jews, who were born and lived in Greece; but coming to Jerusalem at the time of Pentecost, were converted, and joined themselves to the church at Jerusalem: now a complaint was lodged by these against the Hebrews, who were natives of Judea, and particularly of Jerusalem, that their poor widows were neglected in the daily ministration, suggesting, there was some partiality used; that the widows of the natives of Jerusalem were more favoured than the widows of such who had lived in foreign parts; this greatly affected the apostles, and embarrassed them in the spiritual part of their ministry, in which they were hindered by their attention and application to the secular affairs of the church; and therefore called the church together, and thus argued with them; *It is not reason, that we should leave the word of God and serve tables;* as it is not proper that any ordinary minister of the word should be *entangled with the affairs of this life,* if possible; that he may *give attendance to reading, to exhortation, to doctrine,* and *meditate* upon them, and *give himself wholly* to them. Wherefore the apostles proposed to the church, thus called together, to look out and choose from among themselves seven men, of such qualifications they mentioned, to attend this service: and as for themselves, they would *give up themselves continually to prayer, and the ministry of the word;* and this proposal being acceptable to the people, they chose men so qualified, and presented them to the apostles for their approbation; and so they were installed into their office.[1] This seems to be the original of the institution of this office. By which it appears,

1. That those who are chosen to this office must be members of the church, or they are not eligible; and that they are to be chosen by the vote and suffrage of the church; and their destination is only to that church to which they belong; they cannot officiate in another; nor have they any concern with the poor of another church; the collections of that church to whose peculiar service they are appointed, are to be received by them, and to be distributed to the members of that church, and of that only. Extraordinary collections from other churches, we may observe, were sent to the elders, to be disposed of by them, Acts xi. 30. Wherefore,——
2. The apostles, though they gave up themselves more especially to prayer, and the ministry of the word, yet they did not divest themselves wholly of this service; see Acts xii. 25. and deacons now have a connection and concern with elders and pastors of churches in the discharge of their office; they are to acquaint them with the state of the church, and the cases of the poor, and to take their advice in any matters of moment and importance, and to be assisting to them in the outward affairs of the church, and may be what the apostle calls *helps,* in 1 Cor. xii. 28. being helpful to the minister, church, and poor.——
3. This office was instituted when the church was numerous; wherefore the number of seven in the first church, is not a rule and example binding on all future churches;[2] but such a number are to be chosen, and may be increased, as the exigency of churches requires; and some have thought, that where a church is very small, a pastor may perform the whole work, with a little assistance from the church; but I cannot but be of opinion, that one deacon at least, if not two, are necessary to form an organized church.
——4. The objects of this office, are the poor of the church, which were in all churches in all ages; *The poor ye have always with you,* John xii. 8. and to be taken care of; so that the reason of its first institution continues, namely, to ease the ministers of the gospel from too much concern in the secular affairs of the church, Acts vi. 2. and such officers were appointed not only in the first church at Jerusalem, though extraordinary ones, as some think, but in other churches of the Gentiles, at least ordinary ones; as at Philippi, Phil. i. 1. and the particular qualifications are given of these officers; which seem to be given as a direction to the churches in future ages for the choice of them, 1 Tim. iii. 8, &c.

Secondly, The work and business to be performed by them who are appointed to this office.

1. Not to preach the gospel, and administer ordinances, as baptism and the Lord's Supper; and therefore ministerial qualifications are not required of them; Philip, indeed, one of the seven, did both preach and baptize, Acts vi. 5. and viii. 5, 38. but then he did both by virtue of his office as an evangelist, Acts xxi. 8. In Tertullian's time deacons were allowed to baptize; he says, the first right belongs to the bishop, then to the presbyters, then to the deacons,[3] but not without the authority of the bishop; but this appears to be an entire innovation.——2. Nor is their work and business to rule in the church; we read of ruling elders, but never of ruling deacons; if they were, women might not be deaconesses, as Phebe was, for they are not to rule: deacons may and should be

---

[1] Of their ordination and instalment see chap. 3. book ii. p. 866.
[2] Though the council at Neocæsarea ordered, that there should be seven deacons, according to the rule in Acts, Can. XIV. apud Magdeburg. cent. 4. col. 349. And in the Roman church there were seven, and no more; but in other churches the number was indifferent, or indeterminate, as the historian says, Sozomen. Eccl. Hist. l. 7. c. 19.
[3] De Baptismo, c. 17.

assisting to pastors or elders in the care of the church; as to watch over the walk and conversation of the members of the church, and to observe that they keep their places in it; and to exhort, admonish, and reprove, as they may find it necessary; and to visit the sick, and such that are in distress of any kind; and to report the state of the church to the elder or pastor; and to reconcile differences between one member and another, and to prepare matters to be laid before the church at church-meetings, when needful.——3. But their principal business is to *serve tables*, which the apostles relinquished and gave up to the seven, at the first institution of them, Acts vi. 2. As,——1. The Lord's table, as it is called, 1 Cor. x. 21. that is, at the administration of the ordinance of the supper, their business is, to provide every thing necessary for it; as the bread and the wine, and all kind of furniture needful on that occasion; and when the elements are blessed, and the bread broken, and wine poured out, and these given into their hands by the pastor or elder, they are to deliver out to the members; so in Justin Martyr's time, they that were called *deacons*, he says, gave to every one that were present, that they might partake of the bread and the wine, for which thanks were given by the president.[4]——2. The minister's table; to take care that a proper provision is made for the subsistence of himself and family; that whereas Christ has ordained, that those who preach the gospel, should live of it, and that he that is taught in the word, should communicate to him that teacheth in all good things; the business of deacons is to see to it, that every member contributes according to his ability; and that there be an equality, that some are not eased and others burdened: and it lies upon them to collect what the members give, for it is not proper the minister should collect for himself; this would be to prevent the design of the institution, which was, that those who are employed in the sacred office of the ministry of the word, should not be hindered in it. Besides, such a practice would not comport with the case and character of a minister, who would be obliged to receive what the people gave him, without making any remonstrance against it, as failing in their duty to him; and he might also be exposed to the charge of avarice; to which may be added, that a church would not be able to judge whether their pastor was sufficiently provided for or not.——3. The poor's table; it was an apostolical order given to the churches, that they should make a collection for the poor saints, on the first day of the week; and it seems as if it was designed to be every first day; to which every one was to give, having laid by him a store for it, as God had prospered him, 1 Cor. xvi. 1, 2. which collections, and those made at the Lord's Supper, are to be received by the deacons, with whatsoever gifts may come into their hands, and be distributed to the necessities of the saints; and they are, both by their own example, and by their exhortations, to stir up the members of churches to contribute liberally to the relief of the poor: and what they receive they are to communicate,—(1.) Impartially, that is, as the apostle expresses it, *with simplicity*, without partiality, and without favour and affection; shewing no respect to persons, taking more notice of, and giving more liberally to one than to another, which was the original complaint in the first church, and made the office necessary; and therefore the deacon should be careful to avoid any cause of it: the principal rule he should go by is, to give as every one needeth; to some more, and others less, as their case requires.— (2.) This should be done with *cheerfulness*, Rom. xii. 8. without any frowns in the countenance, and without any hard and rough words, which the tender minds of the poor, broken with distress, cannot well bear; when what is given cheerfully and pleasantly does them double good; nor should they be upbraided with misconduct in former life, which may have brought them into low circumstances. God loves a cheerful giver, and he himself gives liberally, and upbraids not.—(3.) This should be done with compassion and tenderness. The work of a deacon is expressed by his *shewing mercy*, Rom. xii. 8. and he should exercise it in a pitiful and merciful manner, as sympathizing with them in their poor and low circumstances; in imitation of the great High Priest of our profession, who is touched with the feeling of the infirmities of his people.—(4.) This office should be executed with great faithfulness; deacons are the church's stewards, and are intrusted with the church's stock; and it is required of stewards, that they distribute with

---

[4] Apolog. 2. p. 97. vid. Cyprian. de Lapsis. p. 244.

fidelity what is put into their hands, and for the uses for which it is given. The next thing to be inquired into,

Thirdly, Are the qualifications of persons for such an office; some of which may be taken from Acts vi. 3. As,

1. That they are to be of *honest report;* of whom a testimony can be given of their honesty, integrity, and good conversation; who have a good report of them that are without, of all men, of the men of the world, and of them that are within; and who are well reported of by the brethren, by the members of other churches, especially by the members of the church to which they belong.——2. *Full of the Holy Ghost*, of his gifts and graces; though they may not be so eminently endowed with them as Stephen and Philip were, which is not to be expected; yet that they should appear to be partakers of the grace of the Spirit, and to have such gifts as to *comfort the feeble-minded, support the weak*, and speak a word in season to those who are in distress.——3. Men of *wisdom;* for as they are stewards, wisdom, as well as faithfulness, is required of them; to give to every one of the poor a portion of the church's monies, as they need; and to distinguish cases and circumstances requires wisdom; besides, persons in such an office are sometimes called upon to make up differences between member and member; which is often a difficult task, and calls for all the prudence a man is possessed of; and to these, or such as these, the apostle refers, when he says, *Is it so, that there is not a wise man among you? no, not one, that shall be able to judge between his brethren*, without going to law before unbelievers, 1 Cor. vi. 5, 6.

There are other qualifications of a deacon observed in 1 Tim. iii. 8—12.——1. As to his personal character; he must be *grave* in his speech and gesture, and not light, frothy, and vain; and not only modest, chaste, honest, and of good behaviour, but as the word may signify also one that has some weight and influence, who is venerable[5] and respectable, and has some degree of reverence and esteem with the people : *Not double-tongued;* so as to express pity to the poor, yet shew no concern to relieve them; and to say one thing to them, and another to the church and minister; or to say one thing to one member, and another to another, which may tend to alienate the affections of one from another. *Not given to much wine;* which, though lawful to be used, yet not to excess; which would both destroy his character in the church and in the world, and render him unfit for the business of his office. *Not greedy of filthy lucre*, or covetous; such may be tempted to make a wrong application of the church's money; and besides, persons in such an office should be liberal themselves, according to their abilities, and set a good example to others; or otherwise they cannot with a good grace, stir up others to liberality; which is one part of their office.——2. Others concern his domestic character; he should be *the husband of one wife;* it is not necessary that he should be a married man; but if married, he should have but one wife, that is, at the same time; polygamy had been much in use among the Jews and Gentiles; and the first christians were not soon and easily brought to the disuse of that practice; but the apostle, by divine inspiration, judged it necessary that no officer of a church, bishop or deacon, should have more wives than one; since it would serve to continue and encourage the practice, set an example of it, and expose to reproach and censure: the apostle adds, *Ruling their children and their own houses well;* both wife, children, and servants; such ought to keep a good decorum in their families; or how else can it be expected that the affairs of the house of God, so far as they are concerned therein, should be dispatched with honour, faithfulness, and diligence. The apostle has also thought fit to give the qualifications of their wives, who must be *grave* in their speech, gesture, and dress; as well as modest, chaste, and of good deportment: *not slanderers, or accusers;* false accusers, acting the part of the devil, as the word signifies;[6] for such may do a great deal of mischief in the church, through their influence on their husbands: they must be *sober*, temperate, not given to excessive drinking, which would be scandalous; *faithful in all things*, respecting their husbands and family; and this is the rather mentioned, since otherwise they might have opportunities of embezzling the church's money, and which in some cases, they might be entrusted with to dispose of to the poor, in the absence of their husbands. ——3. With respect to the spiritual and

---

[5] Σεμνος.   [6] Διαβολος.

evangelical character of deacons, they should be such who *hold the mystery of the faith in a pure conscience;* are sound in the gospel, and the doctrines of it; for by *faith* is meant the gospel, the faith once delivered to the saints; and by the *mystery* of it, the more sublime and mysterious doctrines of the gospel, especially the doctrine of the Trinity; which, with the Jews, was commonly called, *the mystery of the faith;* and is the same the apostle calls, *the mystery of God, and of the Father, and of Christ,* Col. ii. 2. such doctrines which relate to the distinction of Persons in the Godhead; the divine Sonship, proper Deity, and distinct personality of Christ; the Deity, personality and operations of the Spirit; the incarnation of Christ, and the union of the two natures in him; the resurrection of the dead; with others: these things deacons are to hold, with a conscience purified by the blood of Christ, and with a holy, becoming life and conversation: this qualification is necessary in them, that they may be able to instruct and establish others in the faith, and to confute the erroneous; for should their principles be bad, their influence on others might be pernicious and fatal. Now these must first be proved, and *then let them use the office of a deacon, being found blameless;* not that they are to exercise any part of this office first, that it might be known how capable they are of it; but that it should appear that they are men of the above characters and qualifications; are of some standing in the church, and are well known and approved of for their soundness in the faith and purity of conversation. There is but one sort of deacons of this kind mentioned in scripture; unless it can be thought there were women-deacons, or *deaconesses;* and, indeed, Phebe is called διακονος, a *deacon* or *deaconess,* of the church of Cenchrea; we render the word *servant,* Rom. xvi. 1. and some render the *wives* of deacons, *their women,* 1 Tim. iii. 11. and by them understand *deaconesses;* and if the same with the *widows,* as some think, their qualifications, as to age, character, and conduct, are described, 1 Tim. v. 9, 10. and it seems certain there were such in the second century, whether virgins or widows;

such seem to be the two servant maids Pliny [7] speaks of, whom he examined on the rack, concerning the christians, and by whom he says they were called *ministræ*, ministresses, or deaconesses; and Clemens of Alexandria, in the *second* century, makes mention expressly of women-deacons, as spoken of by the apostle in his epistle to Timothy; [8] so Jerom, [9] in the fourth century, speaks of them as in the eastern churches: and, indeed, something of this kind seems not at all unnecessary, but of service and usefulness; as to attend at the baptism of women, and to visit the sisters of the church, when sick, and to assist them. In the third century an officer was introduced, called a *sub-deacon,* an under-deacon, who seems to have been an assistant to the deacon, when the churches became large, and their poor numerous, and the deacons required assistance; though it would have been much more proper to have increased their number of deacons; but as for that *meteor,* as Dr. Owen [10] calls him, an *arch-deacon,* he was not heard of until the fourth or fifth centuries; and then not as the creature which now exists under that name.

Fourthly, The encouragement given to the diligent and faithful performance of the office of a deacon.

1. Such *purchase,* or get, *to themselves a good decree.* The conjecture of Dr. Owen's[11] is very trifling, which I should not have expected from so great a man, as that it signifies a place of some eminence, a seat more highly raised up to sit in, in church-assemblies; something like the chief seats in a Jewish-synagogue: nor by it is meant a higher degree in his own office; for there are no degrees of higher and lower in the office of a deacon; no sub-deacon nor arch-deacon, as before observed; nor is it preparatory to an higher order; as of presbytery or eldership; since the office of a deacon lies chiefly in the management of temporal things; and not in study and meditation of spiritual things. In after times, in the third century, such a practice began to take place, as to go through all ecclesiastical offices, to the office of a bishop, as Cyprian [12] says Cornelius bishop of Rome did; and it is said to be ordered by Caius, bishop of the same place, in

---

[7] Ep. 1. 10. ep. 97. vid. Pignorium de Servis, p. 109.
[8] Stromat 1. 3. p. 448.
[9] Comment. in 1 Tim. iii. 11.

[10] True Nature of a Gospel-Church, ch. 9. p. 184.
[11] Ibid. p. 187.
[12] Ep. 52. p. 96.

the same century, that the degrees to a bishopric, through which men should pass to it, were a door-keeper, a reader, an exorcist, an acolyte, a sub-deacon, a deacon, a presbyter, and then a bishop;[13] but this is all of mere human and antichristian appointment: nor is a greater degree in glory meant, which it is questionable whether there will be any; but rather an increase of gifts and graces is designed; which, under a divine blessing, may be attained, through a deacon's more intimate conversation with the pastor and the members of the church, and even the poor of it: though it seems chiefly to intend a good degree of honour in the faithful discharge of his office, from both minister, church, and poor.—— 2. Such obtain *boldness in the faith;* in the exercise of faith at the throne of grace; and in asserting the doctrine of faith; and in vindicating their own character before men, as faithful men; and in reproving for immorality or error.

Fifthly, The duties belonging to a church and its members, to persons in such an office.

1. To supply them with what is sufficient to relieve the wants of the poor; for they are not to supply them out of their own purses; but to distribute faithfully what is put into their hands by the church.—— 2. They should be applied unto for direction and counsel in any private matters, and especially which relate unto the church; since they are supposed to be men of wisdom, and capable of judging of things, with respect to particular persons, and between one member and another.—— 3. They are to be esteemed highly for their work's sake; their office being a very useful one to the church, when diligently and faithfully performed.—— 4. To be prayed for; for if we are to pray for all civil magistrates and officers, then certainly for all ecclesiastical officers; not only pastors of churches, but deacons also; that they may be supported under all discouragements and difficulties; and that they may be able to discharge their office with reputation and usefulness.

CHAP. VI.

OF THE DISCIPLINE OF A CHURCH OF CHRIST.

Though the light of nature, and the laws and rules of civil society, may be very assisting in the affair of church-discipline; and may in many things serve to illustrate and confirm it; yet it does not stand upon human, but divine authority. By the light of nature it may be known, man being a sociable creature, that men may form themselves into societies for mutual good; that they have a right to make laws and rules binding on each other, which are not contrary to justice and truth; to admit such into their societies who have a right to dispose of themselves, and assent to the rules of the society, and to keep out or expel such who refuse to be subject to them; and to choose and appoint whom they think fit to preside over them, to see that their laws and rules are put into execution; with other things of like nature. But Christ is sole head, king, and lawgiver in his house and kingdom; and no man, nor set of men, have a power to set up a church-society, but what is by direction and according to the rule of his word, and the pattern of his house; nor to make laws and rules, but what he has made; nor to appoint any other sort of officers in his house, but whom he has appointed and directed to, and described the qualifications of; to whom he gives gifts and abilities; office-power and authority to rule under him in his church: nor are any to be admitted into it, nor excluded from it, but according to his directions and orders; hence Ezekiel after he had described the gospel-church in its purity, as it will be in the latter-day, is ordered to *shew the house to the house of Israel;* the form, fashion, laws and ordinances of it, to be copied after, and observed by them, chap. xliii. 10, 11. Now whereas there are various passages of scripture, which are taken for rules of church-discipline, which are misunderstood and misapplied, it will be proper to mark them, that none may be misled by them. As,

First, The words of our Lord to Peter, after he had made such a noble confession of his faith in him, as the Son of God; and Christ had declared, that upon that rock he professed faith in, he would build his church, against which the gates of hell should not prevail; he adds, *And I will give thee the keys of the kingdom of heaven, &c.* Matt. xvi. 19. which are usually understood of the admission of members into a church, and the exclusion of them; and of laying on of censures, and of taking

---

[13] Platinæ vit. Pontif. p. 34.

them off. But they have respect, not at all to discipline, but to doctrine. The keys have made a great noise and rattling in the world, and many contests have been raised about them; what they are, and the power of them, in whose hands they are lodged, and who has the right to the use and exercise of them; when, after all, they relate not to church-discipline, but to gospel-doctrine. By *the kingdom of heaven* is not meant, neither the church in heaven, nor the gospel-church-state on earth; nor do the keys signify any lordly power and domination in it; which Christ never gave to Peter, nor to any of the apostles, and much less to ordinary ministers and elders of churches, who are not allowed to lord it over God's heritage; Christ keeps the key in his own hand, the key of the house of David: but the gospel itself is meant; hence we read of *the mysteries of the kingdom of heaven;* that is, of the doctrines of the gospel: this kingdom of heaven was *shut up against men*, in the Jewish world, through the wickedness, or ignorance of the scribes and Pharisees, who took away the *key of knowledge* from the people, Matt. xxiii. 13. Luke xi. 52. and in the Gentile world, through the blindness, and ignorance, and want of divine revelation, they were left unto, Acts xvii. 30. Now a mission and commission to preach the gospel, and gifts and abilities for the same, are the keys by which the treasures of grace are unlocked, the stores of it opened and displayed, the mysteries of the kingdom of heaven explained, and clearly held forth to the view of others; now though these were given, not to Peter alone, but to all the apostles at the same time, yet Peter was the first who had the use and exercise of them; and with these he opened the *door of faith*, that is, the gospel; first to the Jews, on the day of Pentecost, which was the first sermon after the commission was given, and proved the conversion of three thousand souls:[1] and he was the first who preached the gospel to the Gentiles, to Cornelius and his family, to which first ministration of his to them, both he and James have a respect in the synod at Jerusalem, Acts xv. 7, 14. and that these keys, and the use of them, belonged to all the apostles, as well as to Peter, appears from hence, that to whomsoever the keys, and the use of them, belonged, the same had the power of binding and loosing conferred upon them; and that all the apostles had the latter, is manifest from Matt. xviii. 18. which words are also misunderstood of, and misapplied to, binding men with censures laid upon them, till they repent, and of loosing them from them when they do; but the words are spoken, not of persons, but of things; it is not said, *whomsoever ye bind;* but, *whatsoever ye bind,* &c. and signify no other than declarations of what is unlawful or lawful; of what is forbidden or free of use; in which sense the words *binding* and *loosing* are used in thousands of instances in Jewish writings; and our Lord expresses himself in a manner which the Jews thoroughly understood, and his apostles must; and his meaning is, that whatsoever they bound, prohibited, declared as unlawful to be used, was so, though before lawful; and whatsoever they loosed, declared to be lawful, and free of use, was so; though before the death of Christ, and their commission, was unlawful: thus for instance, they *bound,* prohibited, circumcision, and declared it unlawful; though it was of the fathers, and was enjoined Abraham, Isaac, and Jacob, and their male-seed, to the coming of the Messiah; but since his death, and their commission to preach the gospel, they declared it to be nothing at all, no more to be used and practised; yea that it was pernicious and hurtful; that Christ profited them nothing who used it, and was of no effect to them, Gal. v. 1, 2, 3, 4, 6. and vi. 15. they *bound*, or forbid, the observance of days, and months, and times, and years, and declared them weak and beggarly elements, and that no man was to be judged or condemned for the disuse of them, though they had been for ages past, used in the Jewish church; as the first day of the year, and of every month, the feasts of pass-over, pentecost, and tabernacles, the jubilee-year, the sabbatical year, and the seventh-day-sabbath, Gal. iv. 9, 10, 11. Col. ii. 16, 17. On the other hand, they *loosed*, or declared lawful and free of use, civil correspondence between Jews and Gentiles; which before had been unlawful at least according to the traditions of the Jews; and Peter was the first who had light into it, by the vision of the four-footed beasts, which was given him; for before he thought it was an unlawful thing for a man that was a Jew to come into or

---

[1] Ipse clavem imbuit, Acts ii. 22. Tertullian. de Pudicitia, c. 21.

keep company with one of another nation; but by that vision God shewed him that he was not to call any man common or unclean; see Acts x, 28. and xi. 2, 3, 18. and so they all afterwards understood, that under the gospel-dispensation there was neither Jew nor Greek, neither bond nor free, nor male nor female; but they were all one in Christ Jesus, Gal. iii. 28. likewise they *loosed,* or declared lawful and free of use, the eating of any sort of food, of which there was a distinction under the old law, and was forbid; but now they saw, from the words of Christ, Matt. xv. 11. and Peter, by the above vision; and Paul, by Christ, that there was nothing common and unclean of itself; and that the kingdom of God did not lie in meat and drink, but that every creature of God was good, and nothing to be refused if received with thanksgiving, Rom. xiv. 14, 17. 1 Tim. iv. 4. And this power of binding and loosing reached not only to practices, but to doctrines; for as the apostles were infallibly guided into all truth; whatever they *bound* or forbid, and declared as false doctrine, was so; and whatever they *loosed,* or declared to be truth, was so to be accounted; hence the anathema of the apostle Paul, Gal. i. 8. They had the whole counsel of God, the whole system of gospel-truths made known to them; and which they have declared in their writings; and are to be observed as the rule of faith to the end of the world, being delivered under divine inspiration; of which our Lord's breathing upon them after his resurrection, and their commission from him, was an emblem, when the following words were delivered by him, *Whosoever sins ye remit, they are remitted to them; and whosoever sins ye retain, they are retained,* John xx. 23. which respect not any discipline of the apostles in laying on, binding, and retaining censures on persons; and of loosing, remitting, and taking them off, according to their behaviour; but of the doctrine of remission of sins, preached by them: for this cannot be meant of remission of sins by them in an absolute and authoritative way; for none can forgive sins but God, and Christ, who is God; and who yet never gave any such power to his apostles; nor did they ever assume this to themselves; this is the mark of antichrist, who sits in the temple of God, and shews himself to be god, or to assume such a character, by taking upon him to dispense pardons and indulgences: but this is to be understood of the apostles, as ministerially and doctrinally preaching the forgiveness of sins; declaring that such who repent of their sins, and believe in Christ, shall receive the remission of them; but that whoever do not repent of their sins, and do not believe in him, shall perish eternally, according to Mark xvi. 16. and by this doctrine of the apostles God and Christ will stand; and sooner or later will appear the validity, truth, and certainty of their declarations.

Secondly, There are various passages of scripture, which are thought to respect excommunication, or exclusion from church-communion; which seem to have nothing to do with it, and are not to be considered as rules to proceed by, with respect unto it. As,

1st, The words in Matt. xviii. 17. *Let him be unto thee as an heathen man, and a publican;* which was no form of excommunication, neither with Jews nor with Christians. Not with Jews, for that with them was expressed by casting out of the synagogue, especially in the times of Christ: nor with Christians, with whom it was after signified by putting away wicked men from among them; between an excommunicated person, and an heathen man and publican, there was no agreement; for an heathen man and a publican, however considered by the Jews, were very familiarly conversed with by Christ and his apostles; with whom they frequently eat and drank, and Christ is called a friend of such; whereas, with an excommunicate person it was not allowed to eat, nor indeed to have any familiar conversation with them, as little as possible. Moreover, the words are not a rule to the church, how that was to proceed towards a person who behaved in the manner described; for it is not said, *If he neglect to hear the church, let him be to the church as an heathen man and a publican;* but it is a rule to the offended person how he should behave to the offender, under such circumstances; *Let him be to thee,* &c. and the design of the whole is to justify the offended party, that when he has taken all the steps directed to; as to reprove the offending party privately, and then with two or more, who would be witnesses of his obstinacy, and then lay the whole affair before the church or congregation, which, with the Jews, never consisted of less than ten persons; so that he would be abundantly vindicated in behaving towards

CHAP. VI.   OF THE DISCIPLINE OF A CHURCH.   889

such a man as חבר פחות a worthless neighbour, as the Jews used to call such, and to look upon himself as freed from all brotherly and neighbourly offices towards him.

2dly, Nor is excommunication expressed by the *delivery* of a man *to Satan;* for though that sometimes accompanied excommunication, yet they are very different and distinct things; the delivery of the incestuous person to Satan was the apostle's own act and deed; *I verily*, says the apostle, *as absent in body, but present in spirit, have judged*, or determined within myself, *already, concerning him that hath done this deed*, committed the incest before mentioned, *to deliver such an one unto Satan*, 1 Cor. v. 3, 5. for the fourth verse is to be read in a parenthesis, and the third and fifth connected together; which shews it to be a pure act of the apostle; as the like is elsewhere asserted by him, concerning Hymeneus and Alexander; *Whom*, says he, *I have delivered unto Satan, that they may learn not to blaspheme*, 1 Tim. i. 20. whereas, excommunication is called a punishment or censure *inflicted by many*, on the incestuous person; whom the church at Corinth were directed to purge themselves from, and to put away from among them, that wicked person; by which the excommunication of him from them as a church is expressed, ver. 7, 13. see 2 Cor. ii. 6. as a distinct thing from the delivery of him to Satan; which was a miraculous action, as appears from ver. 4. included in a parenthesis; *in the name of our Lord Jesus;* a way of speaking when a miracle was performing; see Acts iii. 6. *when ye are gathered together*, not to perform this miraculous action, but to be witnesses of it, *and my spirit;* for though in body he was absent from them, yet his spirit would be with them, to perform the miraculous operation; as the heart or spirit of Elisha was with Gehazi in a wonderful manner, when the man turned again to him from his chariot to meet him, 2 Kings v. 26. the apostle adds, *with the power of our Lord Jesus Christ*, to which all miraculous operations are to be ascribed, and so this; for it never was used, nor never ought to be, as a form of excommunication; it was not in the primitive churches; nay, it was cautioned against by the ancients, in one of their synods; nor never was, until excommunication was used as an engine of the church's, or rather of the priest's power to terrify and distress

this was only used in the apostle's time, and then ceased; it was the apostolic rod, with which they sometimes smote wicked persons with death, as Ananias and Sapphira, were smitten by Peter; and Elymas the sorcerer with blindness, by the apostle Paul; and others with diseases of body, and with violent agitations of it, and with terrors of mind; and it is remarkable that the words of the Lord concerning Job; *Behold, he is in thine hand*, are rendered in the Septuagint version, *Behold, I deliver him unto thee;* that is, to smite him with boils, Job ii. 6. and such a corporal punishment, or temporal chastisement, cannot be reckoned a severity, as inflicted on the incestuous person; for excommunication was too mild a punishment for him, who had been guilty of a crime not to be named among the Gentiles; as to have his father's wife! which was death, or cutting off by the hand of heaven, according to the law of Moses, Lev. xviii. and so the blasphemy of Hymeneus and Alexander, by the same law, was deserving of death. It is commonly said, that this delivery of a man to Satan is only a re-delivery of him into the kingdom of Satan, the world, out of which he was taken; and so is only a putting him *in statu quo;* but this is to allow the world to be the kingdom of Satan; whereas he has no true and proper right to it; it is only his by usurpation; the world is the Lord's: nor is it fact, that when a man is received into a church, he is received out of the world; for it is supposed by the church, that he is previously called by the grace of God out of it; and is by faith a partaker of Christ, and of the blessings of his grace, and is a member of the invisible church; and very often so it is, that when a person is dealt with by a church for sin; which, for the honour of Christ and his gospel, they are obliged to do, yet at the same time they cannot but hope, that he is not a man of the world, but a partaker of the grace of God; and therefore do not account him as an enemy, but admonish him as a brother.

3dly, The passage in Tit. iii. 10. *A man that is an heretic, after the first and second admonition, reject;* is usually thought, and so has been by myself, to be a rule for the ejection or casting out of church-communion, a person so described; but not only the word used, is never used of excommunication, nor indeed any other word in the singular number; it is not said, *reject ye*, but *reject thou*;[2] and so is no direction to a church, but to a single person: now let Titus be who he may, an extraordinary person, an evangelist, as he seems to be, or a bishop of Crete, as the subscription of the epistle suggests, which is not to be depended upon, or an ordinary pastor and elder of a church, which is not probable; but be he what he may, an extraordinary or ordinary minister, he had no power nor right of himself to reject or eject any person from church-communion; this would be to act the part of Diotrephes, who cast out the brethren, condemned by the apostle John; and the apostle Paul would never have advised Titus to act a part so unjustifiable; besides, could such a sense of the text be established, it would prove what the papists, prelates, and presbyterians produce it for, namely, that the power of excommunication lies in the hands of a bishop, or prelate, or presbyter, elder or pastor of a church, and not in the church itself; and it would not be easy to rescue such a proof out of their hands; whereas, not single persons, but churches, are always addressed and exhorted to perform the act of excommunication on persons deserving of it; see Rom. xvi. 17. 1 Cor. v. 7, 13. 2 Thess. iii. 6, 14. Nor were admonitions ever directed to be given to persons deserving of excommunication; in cases of private offences, admonitions were to be given; and so long as an affair lies between a person and a church, respecting either doctrine or practice, and is not known to the world and other churches, admonitions may be given and repeated as long as there are any hopes of good being done by them; but in case of atrocious public crimes, and notorious heresies, subversive of the fundamental doctrines of Christianity, no time should be lost, or trifled away with admonitions; but for the honour of Christ, the credit of religion, and for the removal of the odium brought on Christianity, such a person should be removed from communion at once; nay, even as some think, though he may seem to have some sense of his evil, and repentance for it. We have but one instance of excommunication from a Christian church in the whole New Testament, and that is of the incestuous person; and we are sure he had no admonitions from the church before the apostle had heard of the affair; so far were they from it, that they were puffed up, when they should rather have mourned, that he that had done the deed might be taken away from them; and we are sure he had none afterwards, for the apostle immediately orders the excommunication of him. And though there are orders given to several of the churches, as before observed, for the excommunication of such and such persons, yet no directions given for the admonition of any of them, previous to their ejection: sometimes admonition is directed to be given after a person is withdrawn from, when it is not on account of any notorious crime, of a public and scandalous nature; but idleness, an unwillingness to work; and such an one cannot be looked upon as an enemy to Christ and his gospel, and may be admonished as one who had been a brother, and it may be hoped will be restored again, 2 Thess. iii. 14, 15. The case of Titus was a personal one, and respects a man he had been in connection with, or supposed to have been, and now fallen into heresy; when, having reproved him again and again, and endeavoured to convince him of his error, but to no purpose; he is then directed to have nothing more to say unto him or do with him, to have no society with him, nor admit him to a familiar conversation with him, lest he should be hardened in his error, and weak Christians should be stumbled. Much such advice is given by the apostle John to private Christians, not to receive such persons into their houses, nor wish them God speed, 2 John ver. 10.

But though the above passages are not proper and pertinent to church discipline; yet there are rules and directions which do belong to it, and are to be observed with respect unto it; and as I have considered the materials, the form and fashion of the house or church of God, both as essential and as organized; I shall now proceed to consider the rules of admission into it, or the comings in thereof, and the laws and ordinances to be observed by those who are in it, and the rules concerning the goings out of it, whether by dismission or excommunication.

First, The rules concerning the comings in, or admission of members into a gospel-church.

1. The doors of it are not to be set wide open for any one to come in at pleasure; porters were set at the gates of the house

[2] Παραιτη.

of the Lord, that no unclean person should enter in; and in Ezekiel's temple, a figure of the gospel-church in the latter-day, orders are given, that no stranger, uncircumcised in heart and flesh, should enter into the sanctuary of the Lord; no materials were admitted to be laid in Solomon's temple, but what were hewn and squared before brought thither.——2. Persons should voluntarily propose themselves to the church for communion with it; for this should be a free act of their own, and not by the force or persuasion of others; or they should be proposed by the minister or elder, with whom a previous conversation should be had, and an enquiry made of their experience and knowledge of divine things; so Saul, when converted, *essayed to join himself to the disciples;* that is, he tried, he attempted, he proposed himself to them, to become a member of them, and to have communion with them, as one of them, Acts ix. 26.——3. In order to admission to communion, satisfaction must be given as to a work of grace upon the soul; when Saul desired communion with the church, *they were all afraid of him, and believed not that he was a disciple;* a real converted person, a true believer in Christ, because he had been so lately a persecutor of the saints; until it was declared to them, how he had seen the Lord in the way, and that he had spoken to him, and how boldly he had preached in his name; and then he was admitted, and was with them coming in and going out: and it is but fit and proper that such should give a reason of the hope that is in them, to the satisfaction of those with whom they desire to walk in fellowship; it was an early practice of the saints, to tell one another what God had done for their souls; the poor man whom Christ had dispossessed of a legion of devils, was bid to go home to his friends, and tell them how great things the Lord had done for him, and had had compassion on him; and this is best done by a man himself, than by the report of others; and better by a verbal declaration than by writing; for though the former may be made in a broken manner, yet it may best discover the true affection of the heart, and the savouriness of a man's spirit, and tend more to knit and unite the hearts of the Lord's people to him.——4. The way of entrance into a church is by a profession of faith in Christ; for as with the heart man believes unto righteousness, so with the mouth confession is made unto salvation; the church is the sheepfold, and Christ is the door unto it; and whoever climbs up another way than by faith in him, and profession of it, is a thief and a robber. The three thousand converts first professed repentance of their sins, faith in Christ for the remission of them, and their joyful reception of the gospel, and then were baptized and added to the church.——5. It is necessary that such who enter into a church-state, should have knowledge of the truths of the gospel, and confess them, and not be ashamed of Christ, and his words, before men; their soundness in the doctrine of faith should be enquired into, and this be testified by their assent to the articles of faith held and maintained by the church; *Open ye the gates,* that the *righteous nation which keepeth the truth may enter in,* Isa. xxvi. 1.——6. Allowances should be made for weaknesses and infirmities of men, both in their gracious experiences, and in their gospel-light and knowledge; the day of small things is not to be despised; the bruised reed is not to be broken, nor the smoking flax to be quenched; the tender lambs are gathered into Christ's arms, and carried in his bosom; the weak in faith are to be received, and not to doubtful disputations.—— 7. Testimony should be given of their becoming life and conversation; when the disciples demurred upon receiving Saul, because of his former conduct and behaviour, Barnabas informed them of the change that was in him, and that of a violent persecutor, he was become a bold and zealous preacher of the gospel, they gladly received him.——8. The reception of a member into church-communion must be by mutual consent; the person received must give up him or herself to walk with the church in holy fellowship; and the church must readily receive such in the Lord; it must be a voluntary act on both sides; and if there is a pastor, the person must be received by him, in the name and with the consent of the church; and if not, by a brother appointed by the church for that purpose, the token of which is by giving the right-hand of fellowship, Gal. ii. 9. I proceed,

Secondly, To consider the ordinances, laws, and rules to be kept and observed by those who are admitted into the church.

1. There are *ordinances* they are directed to the observation of. Shew them *all the ordinances* of the house, that they may *do* them; so Christ ordered his disciples to

teach those they baptized to observe all things whatsoever he commanded them. Besides the ordinance of baptism, which is preparatory to church-communion, there are the ordinances of public prayer and praise, and the public ministry of the word, which are constantly to be attended on; and it is very unbecoming members of churches to forsake the assembling of themselves together for public worship: it is observed, to the honour of the primitive Christians, that *they continued steadfastly in the apostles doctrine*, in a constant attendance on the ministration of it; and in holy *fellowship* with one another; and *in prayer*, in public prayers put up to God by the minister, as the mouth of the church; and particularly in *breaking of bread*, or in the ordinance of the Lord's Supper, which is to be frequently administered; *As often as ye eat this bread*, &c. which shews it is to be often done; and as often as it is, it should be attended on. But of these ordinances more hereafter, in their proper course.——2. There are also *the laws of* the house, which are to be shewn to members of churches, and to be observed by them; Christ is Lawgiver in it, and his commands are to be kept from a principle of love to him, even all that he has commanded. There is the moral law, which is still in force, and binding upon Christians; for Christ came not to destroy it, but to fulfil it; and his people are *under the law to him*, and should be obedient to it: such who are regardless of morality are not fit to be members of churches, and are not to be continued in them. There is likewise the law of Christ, which is the law of love, the new commandment Christ has given to his disciples, by the observance of which it is known that they are his disciples. There are, moreover, various duties to be performed by members of churches, mutually towards each other; they are to submit themselves to one another in the fear of the Lord; to have the same love one for another, both with respect to things temporal and spiritual, and to watch over one another in the Lord; but these, with other incumbent duties, have been treated of in a preceding chapter.——3. There are certain rules respecting private admonitions of church-members, which deserve special regard; both such as are given by ministers and elders of churches, who have not only power of admonishing those they have the rule over, and of rebuking publicly and with authority; but also in a private manner, as they go from house to house, and as they see occasion for it; which private admonitions are not to be slighted; and also those given by members, who are to admonish and rebuke one another, in a private manner, as there may be a necessity for it. The rule in Matt. xviii. 15, 16, 17. *If thy brother shall trespass against thee*, &c. is an excellent good one, and may be accommodated to all cases in difference between two persons; whether between one neighbour and another, or between one member of a church and another; the former seems to be the original foundation of this rule, for neighbour and brother are synonymous; the passage which the rule seems to have respect unto, and is the rise of it, is in Lev. xix. 17. *Thou shalt not hate thy brother in thine heart; thou shalt in any wise rebuke thy neighbour;* where a brother is explained by a neighbour: and when there is a difference between one neighbour and another, this rule should be observed; the neighbour offended, against whom the trespass is committed, and to whom the injury is done, is to go privately to the offender, lay the evil before him, and reprove him for it, in a gentle manner; if he pays a proper regard to it, takes the reproof kindly, acknowledges the offence, and declares repentance for it, it is all very well; he is to be forgiven, no mention hereafter is to be made of the matter; but if not, if he denies the fact, or extenuates or defends it, and shews no repentance, then the offended party is to take *one or two* neighbours, and lay the case before him in their presence, who will be witnesses of the charge, and of the proof of it, and join in the admonition; but if he still remains incorrigible, then it must be told to the *church*, τη εκκλησια, the same with עדה *the congregation*, which consisted at least of ten persons;[3] and when such a number were made acquainted with the whole affair, and the offender would make no acknowledgment, the offended person would be justified by all men, in treating him for the future as a worthless friend or neighbour, as the Jews used to call such an one, and take no more notice of him than of an heathen man and a publican. The rule also may be accommodated to any difference between one member of a church and another; between a brother and a brother,

---

[3] Vid. Rhenferd. observ. select. ad loc. Heb. Nov. Test. inter ejus opera, p. 729, &c.

who are in the same spiritual relation : and this rule must be observed in case of a private trespass only known to them, a secret fault which they are only privy to; and not a public sin, known to the whole church and to the world; for then another method must be taken : and it must be a *trespass*, a sin, that the offender is guilty of; yet not a sin of infirmity, common to human nature, and which all are encompassed with ; a man is not to be made an offender for a word, a small trifling thing; and yet it must not be a very atrocious and public one, which requires more than admonition, even excommunication at once ; such as was the sin of the incestuous person ; but a sin of a lesser nature, yet a fault, and which gives just cause of offence; and in such a case the offended brother must give the offending one private reproof, tell him his fault between themselves alone ; and if he can bring him to an acknowledgment of his fault, and he declares his sorrow for it, then the brother is gained, is restored from the error he has been guilty of; and it is to be buried in oblivion, and no more said of it to any one ; but if not, he must take another brother or two with him, and admonish him again; and if he pays no regard to it, as strengthened by the conjunction of the brethren with him, then the direction is, *tell the church :* but what is meant by it is not easy to say, whether the Jewish sanhedrim or Jewish synagogue ; since at that time there was no congregational church in being, unless the twelve disciples may be so called ; wherefore this can only at most respect a church in future time, when such a rule should take place ; however, so far as it concerns a private admonition, it is clear and manifest, and deserves attention ; for which reason only it is produced.

Thirdly, The next thing to be inquired into is what concerns *the goings-out of* the house or church of God, and what may be meant by them. There are but two ways of going out of a church ; either by a dismission from it, or by an excommunication out of it. There are, indeed, letters of recommendation, which are wanting in some cases, though the apostle needed them not, 2 Cor. iii. 1. such as were given to Apollos, Acts xviii. 27. to Phebe, Rom. xvi. 1, 2. and to Marcus, Col. iv. 10. But these do not give membership; only transient communion; the person recommended still remains a member from whence he is recommended ; the design of such letters is only to certify, that the person whose name is mentioned in them, is a member in full communion with the church which recommends him, and may be safely admitted to transient communion with the church to which he is recommended : but such letters ought not to continue long ; for if a person takes up his residence in a place where he is in providence brought, he should send for his dismission, and be received upon it into full communion ; a letter of dismission, when approved of, and the person dismissed is received, he is in all respects a member, and then his membership ceases in the church by which he is dismissed, and not before : there are cases in which a man may desire his dismission to another church ; as distance of habitation, non-edification, and when a church is become corrupt in doctrine and practice, that he cannot conscientiously abide with them. The other way of going out of a church is excommunication, concerning which it will be necessary to consider various things.

1. What excommunication is.——1. It is not a being reckoned as an heathen man and a publican ; nor a delivery of one to Satan, as has been shewn.——2. Nor does it affect the temporal estate and civil affairs of a man ; it does not subject him to fines, imprisonment, or death ; it does not interfere with the business of the civil magistrate; nor does it break in upon the natural and civil relations between man and wife, parents and children, masters and servants ; nor forbid attendance on the external ministry of the word.——3. Nor does it admit of degrees; the Jews had three sorts of excommunication, which proceeded gradually ;[4] but there is but one among Christians. Some talk indeed of a lesser and a greater excommunication, but without any foundation from the word of God. Some think a suspension from the Lord's table is in some cases necessary ; when a case is dubious, and there is not time thoroughly to inquire into it, and yet offence and scandal arise upon it : a person, indeed, may be desired to abstain from the Lord's table, and a man that seeks the peace of the church will consent to it ; but he cannot be obliged to abstain ; if he is obstinate and refractory, there is no other way but to expel him ; for a man is either in communion with a church or he

[4] Eliæ Tisbi in voce נדוי

is not; there is no middle state; to withdraw from a disorderly person, or to withdraw and separate him from communion, are the same thing.——4. Excommunication is no other than a removal of a man from the communion of the church, and from all privileges dependent upon it; it is a disfranchizing him from all the immunities of a fellow-citizen with the saints, and taking from him a place and a name in the house of God; for a church can take no more from him than what it first gave him.——5. This act is expressed by various phrases; as by avoiding familiar conversation with such; by not keeping company with them; and by not eating with them at the Lord's table; by purging out from them the old leaven; and by putting away the wicked from among them; by withdrawing from disorderly persons, and cutting them off from fellowship with them.

2. Who they are that are to be excommunicated.——1. Such who are disturbers of the church's peace, who cause divisions and offences, who are litigious and quarrelsome, 1 Cor. xi. 16. Such who are troublers of God's Israel ought to be cut off from his people, Gal. v. 12.——2. Who do not keep their places in the church, do not attend when the church assembles together for religious worship, but forsake the assembling of themselves together, and in a sense forsake the church; whose places are empty, as David's was at supper-time, and who do in a sort cut off themselves from the communion of the church, Jude ver. 19.——3. All such who walk disorderly, as the above persons do, are irregular in their lives and conversations, guilty of immoralities, though it may be thought of a lesser kind, which they continue and indulge themselves in; as sloth and idleness, not working at all, busy-bodies, going from house to house, doing mischief, and living upon others; from such the apostle commands us to withdraw ourselves, 2 Thess. iii. 6, 11, 14.——4. All such who commit atrocious crimes, unrepented of, and continued in; as fornicators, covetous, idolaters, railers, drunkards, extortioners, &c. *with such* we are bid *not to eat*, especially at the Lord's table; for such ought to have no inheritance in the kingdom of Christ and of God, that is, in the church of God, 1 Cor. v. 11. Eph. v. 5.——5. All erroneous and heretical persons, who hold and propagate doctrines contrary to what has been learnt from the word of God, and in the churches of Christ; such are to be avoided and declined from, Rom. xvi. 17. all such who bring in *damnable heresies*, as the apostle calls them; denying the Trinity of Persons in the Godhead, the Deity of Christ, &c. 2 Pet. ii. 1. who bring not with them, but oppose the doctrine of Christ, concerning his person and grace: these, as they are not to have a place in the private houses of the saints, ought to have none in the church of God; which is commended for not bearing them that are evil, either unsound in principle, or immoral in life, 2 John ver. 9, 10, 11. Rev. ii. 2.

3. By whom excommunication is to be performed.

1. Not by a member himself; no man has a right to cut off himself; such a man is a *felo de se*; as a man cannot come into a church without the consent of it; so neither can he go out of it, without its consent; for a man to depart of himself, is not standing fast in one spirit, but is a cowardly running away from a church; and to go without giving a reason, without asking leave, or desiring a dismission, to say the least of it, is a rude and unmannerly way of departure; and such churches who receive such persons, do not as they would be done by: yea, such men are covenant-breakers with a church, which is a great evil, and breakers up of churches, as much as in them lies; for what one member may do, others may; yea, if a member may leave a church at pleasure, a pastor may do the same: in a word, notwithstanding such departure, such persons may be proceeded against by direct excommunication; or, which amounts to much the same, should be declared by a vote of the church, non-members, and no longer under its watch and care; which is by some called indirect excommunication.——2. Nor is it to be performed by any single person of himself, whether an ordinary or an extraordinary minister; it never was done by an apostle, an evangelist, or any other one man; for it is a punishment inflicted by many.——3. Nor is to be done by the elders of a church separately; much less by the elders of other churches; but by the elders of churches, with the consent of the members of them; for they have a right to do this previous to their having elders, and when they have none, as to receive members, so to expel them; the power of it originally lies in the church; the authority of executing it lies in the

elders, with the consent and by the order of the church; as the directions to the churches concerning this matter testify.

4. What are the ends of excommunication.

1. The glory of God, which is the ultimate end of it; for as his name is dishonoured by the evil practices or principles of church-members, so this is the most open and most effectual way of removing that dishonour that is brought upon it; this ought to be always the chief aim and the sincere view in the administration of it; though sometimes this is only pretence, and under the cover of it; churches gratify sinful passions and resentments; as the Jews of old, in a similar case, Isa. lxvi. 5.——2. Another end is to purge the church, and preserve it from infection; a little leaven leavens the whole lump, and therefore the old leaven must be purged out, that a church may become a new lump; evil communications corrupt good manners, and therefore evil men must be put away from among the saints, 1 Cor. v. 7, 13. lepers were to be put out of the camp, that they might not infect others; and erroneous persons, whose words do eat as a canker, must be removed from the communion of churches.

——3. A church of Christ is like a garden or vineyard, which, if not taken care of, and this ordinance of excommunication not made use of, will be like the vineyard of the slothful, over-run with thorns and nettles and other weeds; but by means of this it is cleared of the weeds of immoralities, and the bitter roots of false doctrines are plucked up and eradicated, and withered branches are gathered and cast out.

——4. The good of persons excommunicated is another end, and is sometimes effected by it, God blessing his own institution when rightly performed, which is for edification, and not destruction; for the saving of the souls of men; and who are hereby brought to shame and repentance for their sins, and an acknowledgment of them; when they are to be received again with all love and tenderness, and to be comforted, that they might not be swallowed up with over-much sorrow, Jude ver. 23. 2 Thess. iii. 14. 2 Cor. ii. 7.

A BODY OF
PRACTICAL DIVINITY.

BOOK III.

OF THE PUBLIC ORDINANCES OF DIVINE WORSHIP.

CHAP. I.

OF BAPTISM.

AS the first covenant or testament, had ordinances of divine service, which are shaken, removed, and abolished; so the New Testament, or gospel dispensation, has ordinances of divine worship, which cannot be shaken, but will remain until the second coming of Christ: these, as Austin says,[1] are few, and easy to be observed, and of a very expressive signification. Among which, baptism must be reckoned one, and is proper to be treated of in the first place; for though it is not a church-ordinance, it is an ordinance of God, and a part and branch of public worship. When I say it is not a church-ordinance, I mean it is not an ordinance administered in the church, but out of it, and in order to admission into it, and communion with it; it is preparatory to it, and a qualification for it, it does not make a person a member of a church, or admit him into a visible church; persons must first be baptized, and then added to the church, as the three thousand converts were; a church has nothing to do with the baptism of any, but to be satisfied they are baptized before they are admitted into communion with it. Admission to baptism lies solely in the breast of the administrator, who is the only judge of qualifications for it, and has the sole power of receiving to it, and of rejecting from it; if not satisfied, he may reject a person thought fit by a church, and admit a person to baptism not thought fit by a church; but a disagreement is not desirable nor adviseable: the orderly, regular, scriptural rule of proceeding seems to be this: a person inclined to submit to baptism, and to join in communion with a church, should first apply to an administrator; and, upon giving him satisfaction, be baptized by him; and then should propose to the church for communion; when he would be able to answer all proper questions: if asked, to give a reason of the hope that is in him, he is ready to do it; if a testimony of his life and conversation is required, if none present can give it, he can direct where it is to be had; and if the question is put to him, whether he is a baptized person or no, he can answer in the affirmative, and give proof of it, and so the way is clear for his admission into church-fellowship. So Saul, when converted, was immediately baptized by Ananias, without any previous knowledge and consent of the church; and it was many days after this that he proposed to join himself to the disciples, and was received, Acts ix. 18, 19, 23, 26, 27, 28. and as it is water-baptism which is meant, I shall,

First, Prove that this is peculiar to the gospel-dispensation, is a standing ordi-

---

[1] De Doctrina Christiana l. 3. c. 9.

nance in it, and will be continued to the second coming of Christ. This is opposed to the sentiments of such who say baptism was in use before the times of John, of Christ and his apostles; and of such who restrain water-baptism to the interval between the beginning of John's ministry and the death of Christ, when they supposed this, with other external rites, ceased; and of such, as the Socinians,[2] who think that only the first converts to christianity in a nation are to be baptized, and their children, but not their after-posterity. There were indeed divers washings, bathings, or baptisms, under the legal dispensation, for the purification of persons and things unclean, by the ceremonial law; which had a doctrine in them, called *the doctrine of baptisms*, which taught the cleansing of sin by the blood of Christ; but there was nothing similar in them to the ordinance of water-baptism, but immersion only. The Jews pretend, their ancestors were received into covenant by baptism, or dipping, as well as by circumcision and sacrifice; and that proselytes from heathenism were received the same way, and this is greedily catched at by the advocates for infant baptism; who fancy that John, Christ, and his apostles, took up this custom as they found it, and continued it; and which they imagine accounts for the silence about it in the New Testament, and why there is neither precept for it, nor example of it; but surely if it was in such common use as pretended, though no new precept had been given, there would have been precedents enough of it; but no proof is to be given of any such practice obtaining in those times, neither from the Old or New Testament; nor from the apocryphal books written by Jews between them; nor from Josephus and Philo the Jew, who wrote a little after the times of John and Christ; nor from the Jewish Misnah, or book of traditions; only from later writings of theirs, too late for the proof of it before those times.[3] John was the first administrator of the ordinance of baptism, and therefore is called *the Baptist*, Matt. iii. 1. by way of emphasis; whereas, had it been in common use, there must have been many baptizers before him, who had a like claim to this title; and why should the people be so alarmed with it, as to come from all parts to see it administered, and to hear it preached, when, had it been in frequent use, they must have often seen it? and why should the Jewish sanhedrim send priests and levites from Jerusalem to John, to know who he was, whether the Messiah, or his forerunner Elias, or that prophet spoken of and expected? and when he confessed, and denied that he was either of them, they say to him, *Why baptizest thou then?* by which it appears it was a new thing, and which they expected when the Messiah came, but not before; and that then it would be performed by some great personage, one or other of the before-mentioned; whereas, had it been performed by an ordinary teacher, common rabbi or doctor, priest or levite, in ages immemorial, there could have been no room for such a question; and had this been the case, there would have been no difficulty with the Jews to answer the question of our Lord; *The baptism of John, whence was it; from heaven or of men?* they could have answered, It was a tradition of theirs, a custom in use among them time out of mind, had this been the known case; nor would they have been subject to any dilemma: but John's baptism was not a device of men; but the *counsel of God*, according to his will and wise determination, Luke vii. 30. John had a mission and commission from God, he was a man sent of God, and sent to baptize, John i. 6, 33. and his baptism was water-baptism, this he affirms, and the places he made use of for that purpose shew it, and none will deny it.

Now his baptism, and that of Christ and his apostles, were the same. Christ was baptized by John, and his baptism was surely christian-baptism; of this no one can doubt, Matt. iii. 13—17. and his disciples also were baptized by him; for by whom else could they be baptized? not by Christ himself, for he baptized none, John iv. 2. And it is observable, that the baptism of John, and the baptism of Christ and his apostles, were at the same time; they were cotemporary, and did not the one succeed the other: now it is not reasonable to suppose that there should be two sorts of baptism administered at the same time; but one and the same by both, John iii. 22, 23, 26. and iv. 1, 2.

The baptism of John, and that which was practised by the apostles of Christ,

[2] Vid. Socin. Disp. de Baptismo, c. 15, 16 17.

[3] See the Dissertation concerning the Baptism of Jewish Proselytes, at the end of this work.

even after his death and resurrection from the dead, agreed,——1. In the subjects thereof. Those whom John baptized were sensible penitent sinners, who were convinced of their sins, and made an ingenuous confession of them; and of whom he required *fruits meet for repentance*, and which shewed it to be genuine; and hence his baptism is called, *the baptism of repentance*, because he required it previous to it, Matt. iii. 6, 7, 8. Mark i. 4. So the apostles of Christ exhorted men to repent, to profess their repentance, and give evidence of it, previous to their baptism, Acts ii. 38. John said to the people that came to his baptism, *That they should believe on him which should come after him, that is, on Christ Jesus*, upon which they were baptized in his name, Acts xix. 4, 5. and faith in Christ was made a pre-requisite to baptism by Christ and his apostles, Mark xvi. 16. Acts viii. 36, 37.——2. In the way and manner of the administration of both. John's baptism was by immersion, as the places chosen by him for it shew; and the baptism of Christ by him is a proof of it, Matt. iii. 6, 16. John iii. 23. and in like manner was baptism performed by the apostles, as of the eunuch by Philip, Acts viii. 38, 39.——3. In the form of their administration. John was sent of God to baptize; and in whose name should he baptize, but in the name of the one true God, who sent him, even in the name of God, Father, Son, and Spirit? The doctrine of the Trinity was known to John, as it was to the Jews in common; it is said of John's hearers and disciples that they were *baptized in the name of the Lord Jesus*, Acts xix. 5. The same form is used of the baptism of those baptized by the apostles of Christ, Acts viii. 16. and x. 48. which is only a part of the form put for the whole, and is sufficiently expressive of christian baptism, which is to be performed *in the name of the Father, and of the Son, and of the Holy Ghost*, Matt. xxviii. 19. ——4. In the end and use of baptism. John's baptism, and so the apostles' was, upon *repentance for the remission of sins*, Mark i. 4. Acts viii. 38. not that either repentance or baptism procure the pardon of sin; that is only obtained by the blood of Christ; but baptism is a means of leading to the blood of Christ; and repentance gives encouragement to hope for it, through it. Now since there is such an agreement between the baptism of John, as administered before the death of Christ; and between the baptism of the apostles, after the death, resurrection, and ascension of Christ; it is a plain case, it was not limited to the interval of time from the beginning of John's ministry to the death of Christ; but was afterwards continued; which farther appears from the commission of Christ, Matt. xxviii. 19. *Go ye therefore, and teach all nations, baptizing them;* and though water is not expressed, it is always implied, when the act of baptizing is ascribed to men; for it is peculiar to Christ to baptize with the Holy Spirit, Matt. iii. 11. Acts i. 5. nor did he give to his apostles, nor to any man, or set of men, a commission and power to baptize with the Spirit: besides, an increase of the graces of the Spirit, and a large donation of his gifts are promised to persons after baptism, and as distinct from it, Acts ii. 38. The apostles, doubtless, understood the commission of their Lord and Master to baptize in water, since they practised it upon it; such was the baptism administered by Philip, who having taught the eunuch the doctrine of it, when they came to a *certain water*, he said to him, *See, here is water, what doth hinder me to be baptized?* that is, in water; and when Philip had observed unto him the grand requisite of it, even faith in Christ, which he at once professed; and the chariot in which they rode being ordered to stand, *they went down both into the water, and he baptized him;* this was most certainly water-baptism; and so was that which Peter ordered to be administered to Cornelius and his friends, upon their receiving of the Holy Ghost, and so a baptism different from that; *Can any man forbid water, that these should not be baptized?* Acts viii. 36, 38, 39. and x. 47, 48. And this was designed to be continued unto the end of the world, to the second coming of Christ; as the ordinance of the supper is to be kept to that time, the ordinance of water-baptism is to be continued as long; hence says Christ, to encourage his ministers to preach his gospel, and to baptize in his name; *Lo, I am with you always*, in the ministry of the word, and in the administration of baptism, *even unto the end of the world*, Matt. xxviii. 19, 20.

Secondly, I shall next consider the author of it; and shew, that it is not a device of men, but an ordinance of God; it is a solemn part of divine worship, being performed in the name of the Three divine Persons in Deity, Father, Son, and Spirit, and by their authority; in which the name of God is invoked, faith in him expressed, and a man gives up himself to God, obliges himself to yield obedience to him, expecting all good things from him. Now for an act of religious worship there must be a command of God. God is a jealous God, and will not suffer any thing to be admitted into the worship of him, but what is according to his word and will; if not commanded by him, he may justly say, *Who hath required this at your hands?* and will resent it: a command from men is not sufficient; no man on earth is to be called master; one is our Master in heaven, and him only we are to obey: if the commandments of men are taught for doctrines, in vain is the Lord worshipped; what is done according to them is superstition and will-worship. Indeed, as it is now commonly practised, it is a mere invention of men, the whole of it corrupted and changed; instead of rational spiritual men the subjects of it, infants, who have neither the use of reason, nor the exercise of grace, are admitted to it; and instead of immersion in water, and emersion out of it, a very expressive emblem of the sufferings of Christ, his death, burial, and resurrection from the dead; sprinkling a few drops of water on the face is introduced; with a number of foolish rites and ceremonies used by the papists, and some of their usages are retained by some protestants; as sponsors, or sureties for infants, and the signing them with the sign of the cross. In short, the face of the ordinance is so altered, that if the apostles were to rise from the dead, and see it as now performed, they would neither know nor own it to be the ordinance commanded them by Christ, and practised by them. But as it is administered according to the pattern, and as first delivered, it appears to be of an heavenly original; the *counsel of God*, a wise appointment of his, and in which all the Three Persons have a concern; they all appeared at the baptism of Christ, and gave a sanction to the ordinance by their presence; the Father by a voice from heaven, saying, *This is my beloved Son, in whom I am well pleased!* as in his person, so in this act of his, in submitting to the ordinance of baptism; the Son in human nature, yielding obedience to it; and the Spirit descending on him as a dove; and it is ordered to be administered in the name of all Three, Father, Son, and Spirit. Which, among other things, is expressive of divine authority, under which it is performed. Christ received from God the Father honour and glory, as at his transfiguration, so at his baptism, by the voice from heaven, owning his relation to him, as his Son, and expressing his well-pleasedness in him, as obedient to his will; the Son of God, in human nature, not only left an example of it, that we should tread in his steps; though he himself baptized none, yet he countenanced it in his disciples, and gave them orders to do it; which orders were repeated, and a fresh commission given for the same, after his resurrection from the dead: and the Spirit of God shewed his approbation of it, by his descent on Christ at his baptism; and his authority for it is to be seen in the administration of it in his name, as in the name of the other Two Persons; so that it is to be regarded, not as an institution of men, but as an ordinance of God; as a part of righteousness to be fulfilled, a branch of the righteous will of God, to be observed in obedience to it.

Thirdly, The subjects of baptism are next to be inquired into; or who they are to whom it is to be administered, and according to the scripture-instances and examples, they are such who,

1. Are enlightened by the Spirit of God to see their lost state by nature, the exceeding sinfulness of sin, and Christ as the only Saviour of sinners; who look to him and are saved; and such only can see to the end of the ordinance, which is to represent the sufferings and death, burial and resurrection of Christ; hence baptism was by the ancients called φωτισμος, *illumination;* and baptized persons φωτιζομενοι, *enlightened* ones; and the Syriac and Ethiopic versions of Heb. vi. 4. translate the word *enlightened* by baptized; an emblem of this was the falling off from the eyes of Saul, as it had been scales; signifying his former blindness, and ignorance, and unbelief, now removed; upon which he arose and was baptized, Acts ix. 18.

———2. Penitent persons; such who having seen the evil nature of sin, repent of it, and acknowledge it; such were the first who were baptized by John that we read of; they were *baptized of him in Jordan, confessing their sins*, Matt. iii. 6. being made sensible of them, they ingenuously confessed them; and such were the first who were baptized after Christ had renewed the commission to his disciples, upon his resurrection, to teach and baptize; such as were pricked in the heart, were exhorted to profess repentance and give evidence of it, and then be baptized, as they were, Acts ii. 37, 38, 41. and it is pity that these first examples of baptism were not strictly followed.——3. Faith in Christ is pre-required to baptism, Mark xvi. 16. this, is clear from the case of the eunuch, desiring baptism, to whom Philip said, *If thou believest with all thine heart, thou mayest;* by which it seems, that if he did not believe, he had no right to the ordinance; but if he did, he had; upon which he professed his faith in Christ; and upon that profession was baptized, Acts viii. 36. and the various instances of baptism recorded in scripture, confirm the same; as of the inhabitants of Samaria, who, upon believing in Christ, *were baptized, both men and women;* so the Corinthians, *hearing* the word preached by the apostle Paul, *believed* in Christ, whom he preached, *and were baptized*, upon their faith in him, Acts viii. 12. and xviii. 8. and without faith it is impossible to please God in any ordinance or part of worship; and what is not of faith is sin; and without it no one can see to the end of the ordinance of baptism, as before observed.——4. Such who are taught and made disciples by teaching, are the proper subjects of baptism, agreeable both to the practice of Christ and his commission; it is said, *that Jesus made and baptized more disciples than John,* John iv. 1. he first made them disciples, and then baptized them, that is, ordered his apostles to baptize them; and so runs his commission to them, *Go teach all nations, baptizing them*, that is, those that are taught, and so made disciples; and they are the disciples of Christ, who have learnt to know him, and are taught to deny sinful, righteous, and civil self, for his sake, and to take up the cross and follow him.——5. Such who have received the Spirit of God, as a Spirit of illumination and conviction, of sanctification and faith, as the persons before described may well be thought to have, should be admitted to baptism, Acts x. 47. see Gal. iii. 2. from all which it appears, that such who are ignorant of divine things, impenitent, unbelievers, not disciples and followers of Christ, and who are destitute of the Spirit, are not proper subjects of baptism, let their pretences to birthright be what they may; and so not the infants of any, be they born of whom they may; and to whom the above characters, descriptive of the subjects of baptism, do by no means belong; with respect to their first birth, though born of believing parents, they are carnal and corrupt, and children of wrath, as others; *That which is born of the flesh is flesh;* and they must be born again, or they cannot see, possess, and enjoy the kingdom of God, or have a right to be admitted into the church of God now, nor will they enter into the kingdom of God, into heaven hereafter, unless born again; their first and carnal birth neither entitles them to the kingdom of God on earth, nor to the kingdom of God in heaven, be it taken in either sense; for the baptism of such there is neither precept nor precedent in the word of God.

1*st*, There is no precept for it; not the words of Christ in Matt. xix. 14. *But Jesus said, Suffer little children,* &c. For,

1. Let the words be said to or of whom they may, they are not in the form of a precept, but of a permission or grant, and signify not what was enjoined as necessary, but what was allowed of, or which might be; *Suffer little children,* &c.——2. These children do not appear to be new-born babes. The word used by the evangelists, neither παιδία nor βρέφη, do not always signify such; but are sometimes used of such who are capable of going alone, and of being instructed, and of understanding the scriptures, and even of one of twelve years of age, Matt. xviii. 2. 2 Tim. iii. 15. Mark v. 39, 42. Nor is it probable that children just born should be had abroad; besides, these were such as Christ called unto him, Luke xviii. 16. and were capable of coming to him of themselves; as is supposed in the words themselves; nor is their being brought unto him, nor his taking them in his arms, any objection to this, since the same are said of such who could walk of themselves, Matt. xii. 22. and xvii. 16. Mark ix. 36.——3. It cannot be said whose children these were; whether they belonged to those who brought them, or to others; and whether the children of believers, and of baptized persons, or not; and if of unbelievers, and of unbaptized persons, the Pædobaptists themselves will not allow such children to be baptized.——4. It is certain they were not brought to Christ to be baptized by him, but for other purposes; the evangelist Matthew, ver. 13, 15. says, they were brought to him that he *should put his hands upon them, and pray*, as he did, that is, for a blessing on them, as it was usual with

the Jews to do, Gen. xlviii. 14, 15. The evangelists Mark and Luke say, they were brought to him, *that he would touch them,* as he did when he healed persons of diseases; and probably these children were diseased, and were brought to him to be cured; however, they were not brought to be baptized by Christ; for Christ baptized none at all, adult or infants; had they that brought them this in view, they would have brought them to the disciples of Christ, and not to Christ, whom they might have seen administering the ordinance of baptism, but not Christ: however, it is certain they were not baptized by Christ, since he never baptized any.——5. This passage rather concludes against Pædo-baptism than for it, and shews that this practice had not obtained among the Jews, and had not been used by John, by Christ, and his disciples; for then the apostles would scarcely have forbad the bringing of these children, since they might readily suppose they were brought to be baptized; but knowing of no such usage in the nation, whether of them that did or did not believe in Christ, they forbad them; and Christ's silence about this matter, when he had such an opportunity of speaking of it to his disciples, and enjoining it, had it been his will, does not look very favourably upon this practice.——6. The reason given for suffering little children to come to Christ, *for of such is the kingdom of heaven,* is to be understood in a figurative and metaphorical sense; of such who are comparable to children for modesty, meekness, and humility, and for freedom from rancour, malice, ambition, and pride; see Matt. xviii. 2. and which sense is given into by Origen,[4] among the ancients, and by Calvin and Brugensis, among the moderns.

Nor does the commission in Matt. xxviii. 19. contain in it any precept for infant-baptism; *Go, teach all nations, baptizing them,* &c. For,

1. The baptism of all nations is not here commanded; but the baptism only of such who are taught; for the antecedent to the relative *them,* cannot be *all nations;* since the words παντα τα εθνη, *all nations,* are of the neuter gender; whereas αυτυς, *them,* is of the masculine; but μαθητας, *disciples,* is supposed and understood in the word μαθητευσατε, *teach,* or *make disciples;* now the command is, that such who are first taught or made disciples by teaching under the ministry of the word, by the Spirit of God succeeding it, should be baptized.——2. If infants, as a part of all nations, and because they are such, are to be baptized, then the infants of Heathens, Turks, and Jews, ought to be baptized, since they are a part, and a large part, of all nations; as well as the children of Christians, or believers, which are but a small part; yea, every individual person in the world ought to be baptized, all adult persons, heathens as well as Christians; even the most profligate and abandoned of mankind, since they are a part of all nations.——3. Disciples of Christ, and such who have learned to know Christ, and the way of salvation by him, and to know themselves, and their need of him, are characters that cannot agree with infants; and if disciples and learners are the same, as is said, they must be learners or they cannot be disciples; and they cannot be learners of Christ unless they have learnt something of him; and according to this notion of disciples and learners, they ought to learn something of him before they are baptized in his name; but what can an infant be taught to learn of Christ? To prove infants disciples that text is usually brought, Acts xv. 10. which falls greatly short of proving it; for infants are not designed in that place, nor included in the character; for though the Judaizing teachers would have had the Gentiles, and their infants too, circumcised; yet it was not circumcision, the thing itself, which is meant by the intolerable yoke; for that was what the Jewish fathers, and their children, were able to bear, and had borne in ages past; but it was the doctrine of the necessity of that, and other rites of Moses to salvation; and which obliged to the keeping of the whole law, and was intolerable; and which doctrine could not be imposed upon infants, but upon adult persons only.——4. These two acts, *teaching,* or making disciples, and *baptizing,* are not to be confounded, but are two distinct acts, and the one is previous and absolutely necessary to the other: Men must first be made disciples, and then baptized; so Jerom[5] long ago understood the commission; on which he observes, " First they teach all nations, then dip those that are taught in water; for it cannot be that the body should receive

---

[4] Comment. on Matt. p. 372, 375.

[5] Comment. on Matt. xxviii. 19.

the sacrament of baptism, unless the soul has before received the truth of faith." And so says Athanasius,[6] "Wherefore the Saviour does not simply command to *baptize*; but first says, teach, and then baptize thus, *In the name of the Father, and of the Son, and of the Holy Ghost;* that faith might come of teaching, and baptism be perfected."

2dly, There is no precedent for the baptism of infants in the word of God. Among the vast numbers who flocked to John's baptism from all parts, we read of no infants that were brought with them for that purpose, or that were baptized by him. And though more were baptized by Christ than by John, that is, by the apostles of Christ, at his order, yet no mention is made of any infant baptized by them; and though three thousand persons were baptized at once, yet not an infant among them: and in all the accounts of baptism in the Acts of the Apostles in different parts of the world, not a single instance of infant-baptism is given. There is, indeed, mention made of households, or families, baptized; and which the *pædobaptists* endeavour to avail themselves of; but they ought to be sure there were infants in these families, and that they were baptized, or else they must baptize them on a very precarious foundation; since there are families who have no infants in them, and how can they be sure there were any in these the scriptures speak of? and it lies upon them to prove there were infants in them, and that these infants were baptized; or the allegation of these instances is to no purpose. We are able to prove there are many things in the account of these families, which are inconsistent with infants, and which make it at least probable there were none in them, and which also make it certain that those who were baptized were adult persons and believers in Christ. There are but three families, if so many, who are usually instanced in, the first is that of Lydia and her household, Acts xvi. 14, 15. but in what state of life she was is not certain, whether single or married, whether maid, widow, or wife; and if married, whether she then had any children, or ever had any; and if she had, and they living, whether they were infants or adults; and if infants, it does not seem probable that she should bring them along with her from her native place, Thyatira to Philippi, where she seems to have been upon business, and so had hired a house during her stay there; wherefore her household seems to have consisted of menial servants she brought along with her, to assist her in her business: and certain it is, that those the apostles found in her house, when they entered into it, after they came out of prison, were such as are called, *brethren*, and were capable of being *comforted* by them; which supposes them to have been in some distress and trouble, and needed comfort. The second instance is of the jailor and his household, which consisted of adult persons, and of such only; for the apostle spoke the word of the Lord to *all* that were in his house, which they were capable of hearing, and it seems of understanding; for not only he *rejoiced* at the good news of salvation by Christ, but *all* in his house hearing it, rejoiced likewise; which joy of theirs was the joy of faith; for he and they were believers in God, Father, Son, and Spirit; for it is expressly said, that he *rejoiced, believing in God with all his house;* so that they were not only hearers of the word, but rejoiced at it, and believed in it, and in God the Saviour, revealed in it to them, ver. 32, 33, 34. all which shews them to be adult persons, and not infants. The third instance, if distinct from the household of the jailor, which some take to be the same, is that of Stephanus; but be it a different one, it is certain it consisted of adult persons, believers in Christ, and very useful in the service of religion; they were the first fruits of Achaia, the first converts in those parts, and who *addicted themselves to the ministry of the saints,* 1 Cor. xvi. 15. which, whether understood of the ministry of the word to the saints, which they gave themselves up unto; or of the ministration of their substance to the poor, which they cheerfully communicated, they must be adult persons, and not infants. There being then neither precept nor precedent in the word of God for infant-baptism, it may be justly condemned as unscriptural and unwarrantable.

3dly, Nor is infant-baptism to be concluded from any things or passages recorded either in the Old or in the New Testament. Baptism being an ordinance peculiar to the New Testament, it cannot be expected there should be any directions about the observance of it in the Old

---

[6] Contr. Arian. orat. 3. p. 209.

Testament; and whatever may be gathered relative to it, from typical and figurative baptisms, under the former dispensation, there is nothing from thence in favour of infant-baptism, and to countenance that; and yet we are often referred thereunto for the origin and foundation of it, but to no purpose.

1. It is not fact, as has been asserted,[7] that the *infants of believers* have, with their parents, been taken into covenant with God in the former ages of the church, if by it is meant the covenant of grace; the first covenant made with man, was that of works, made with Adam, and which indeed included all his posterity, to whom he stood as a federal head, as no one ever since did to his natural offspring; in whom they all sinned, were condemned, and died; which surely cannot be pleaded in favour of the infants of believers! After the fall, the covenant of grace, and the way of life and salvation by Christ, were revealed to Adam and Eve, personally, as interested therein; but not to their natural seed and posterity, and as interested therein; for then all mankind must be taken into the covenant of grace, and so nothing peculiar to the infants of believers; of which not the least syllable is mentioned throughout the whole age of the church, reaching from Adam to Noah. The next covenant we read of, is that made with Noah, which was not made with him and his immediate offspring only; nor were any taken into it as infants of believers, nor had they any sacrament or rite as a token of it, and of God being their God in a peculiar relation. Surely this will not be said of Ham, one of the immediate sons of Noah. That covenant was made with Noah, and with all mankind to the end of the world, and even with every living creature, the beasts of the field, promising security from an universal deluge, as long as the world should stand; and so had nothing in it peculiar to the infants of believers. The next covenant is that made with Abraham and his seed, on which great stress is laid, Gen. xvii. 10—14. and this is said[8] to be "the grand turning point on which the issue of the controversy very much depends; and that if Abraham's covenant, which included his infant-children, and gave them a right to circumcision, was not the covenant of grace, then it is confessed, that the *main ground* is taken away, on which *the right of infants to baptism* is asserted; and consequently the principal arguments in support of the doctrine are overturned." Now that this covenant was not the pure covenant of grace, in distinction from the covenant of works, but rather a covenant of works, will soon be proved; and if so, then the main ground of infant's baptism is taken away, and its principal arguments in support of it overturned: and that it is not the covenant of grace is clear,——1. From its being never so called, nor by any name which shews it to be such; but *the covenant of circumcision*, Acts vii. 8. Now nothing is more opposite to one another than circumcision and grace; circumcision is a work of the law, which they that sought to be justified by, fell from grace, Gal. v. 2, 3, 4. Nor can this covenant be the same we are now under, which is a *new* covenant, or a new administration of the covenant of grace, since it is abolished, and no more in being and force.——2. It appears to be a covenant of works, and not of grace, since it was to be kept by men, under a severe penalty. Abraham was to keep it, and his seed after him; something was to be done by them, their flesh to be circumcised, and a penalty was annexed, in case of disobedience or neglect; such a soul was to be cut off from his people: all which shews it to be, not a covenant of grace, but of works.——3. It is plain, it was a covenant that might be broken; of the uncircumcised it is said, *He hath broken my covenant*, Gen. xvii. 14. whereas the covenant of grace cannot be broken; God will not break it, and men cannot; it is ordered in all things, and sure, and is more immoveable than hills and mountains, Psal. lxxxix. 34.——4. It is certain it had things in it of a civil and temporal nature; as a multiplication of Abraham's natural seed, and a race of kings from him; a promise of his being the Father of many nations, and a possession of the land of Canaan by his seed: things that can have no place in the pure covenant of grace, and have nothing to do with that, any more than the change of his name from Abram to Abraham.——5. There were some persons included in it, who cannot be thought to belong to the covenant of grace; as Ishmael, not in the same covenant with Isaac, and a profane Esau: and on the other hand, there were some who

---

[7] Baptism of infants a reasonable service, p. 14, 15.

[8] Bostwick's Fair and Rational Vindication of Infant-baptism, p. 19.

were living when this covenant of circumcision was made, and yet were left out of it; who nevertheless, undoubtedly, were in the covenant of grace; as Shem, Arphaxad, Melchizedek, Lot, and others; wherefore this can never be the pure covenant of grace.——6. Nor is this covenant the same with what is referred to in Gal. iii. 17. said to be *confirmed of God in Christ*, which could not be disannulled by the law four hundred and thirty years after; the distance of time between them does not agree, but falls short of the apostle's date twenty-four years; and therefore must not refer to the covenant of circumcision, but to some other covenant and time of making it; even to an exhibition and manifestation of the covenant of grace to Abraham, about the time of his call out of Chaldea, Gen. xii. 3.——7. The covenant of grace was made with Christ, as the federal head of the elect in him, and that from everlasting, and who is the only head of that covenant, and of the covenant-ones: if the covenant of grace was made with Abraham, as the head of his natural and spiritual seed, Jews and Gentiles; there must be two heads of the covenant of grace, contrary to the nature of such a covenant, and the whole current of scripture; yea, the covenant of grace, as it concerns the spiritual seed of Abraham, and spiritual blessings for them; it, and the promises of it, were made to Christ, Gal. iii. 16. No mere man is capable of covenanting with God; the covenant of grace is not made with any single man; and much less with him on the behalf of others: whenever we read of it as made with a particular person or persons, it is always to be understood of the manifestation and application of it, and of its blessings and promises to them.——8. Allowing Abraham's covenant to be a peculiar one, and of a mixed kind, containing promises of temporal things to him, and his natural seed, and of spiritual things to his spiritual seed; or rather, that there was at the same time when the covenant of circumcision was given to Abraham and his natural seed, a fresh manifestation of the covenant of grace made with him and his spiritual seed in Christ. That the temporal blessings of it belonged to his natural seed, is no question; but that the spiritual blessings belong to all Abraham's seed, after the flesh, and to all the natural seed of believing Gentiles, must be denied: if the covenant of grace was made with all Abraham's seed according to the flesh, then it was made with his more immediate offspring, with a mocking, persecuting Ishmael, and with a profane Esau, and with all his remote posterity; with them who believed not, and whose carcases fell in the wilderness; with the ten tribes who revolted from the pure worship of God; with the Jews in Isaiah's time, a seed of evil-doers, whose rulers are called the rulers of Sodom, and the people the people of Gomorrah; with the scribes and pharisees, that wicked and adulterous generation in the times of Christ: but what serious thoughtful man, who knows any thing of the covenant of grace, can admit of this? see Rom. ix. 6, 7. It is only a remnant, according to the election of grace, who are in this covenant; and if all the natural seed of Abraham are not in this covenant, it can scarcely be thought that all the natural seed of believing Gentiles are; it is only some of the one and some of the other, who are in the covenant of grace; and this cannot be known until they believe, when they appear to be Abraham's spiritual seed; and it must be right to put off their claim to any supposed privilege arising from covenant-interest, until it is plain they have one; if all the natural seed of Abraham, as such, and all the natural seed of believing Gentiles, as such, are in the covenant of grace; since all they that are in it, and none but they are in it, who are the chosen of God, the redeemed of the Lamb, and will be called by grace, and sanctified, and persevere in faith and holiness, and be eternally glorified; then the natural seed of Abraham, and of believing Gentiles, must be all chosen to grace and glory, and be redeemed by the blood of Christ from sin, law, hell, and death; they must all have new hearts and spirits given them, and the fear of God put into their hearts; must be effectually called, their sins forgiven them, their persons justified by the righteousness of Christ, and they persevere in grace to the end, and be for ever glorified; see Jer. xxxi. 33, 34. and xxxii. 40. Ezek. xxxvi. 25, 26, 27. Rom. viii. 30. But who will venture to assert all this of the one, or of the other? And after all,——9. If their covenant-interest could be ascertained, that gives no right to an ordinance, without a positive order and direction from God. It gave no right to circumcision formerly, for on the one hand there were persons living when that ordinance was appointed, who had an undoubted interest in the covenant of grace; as Shem, Arphaxad, Lot, and others, on whom circumcision was not enjoined, and they had no right to use it: on the other hand, there have been many of whom it cannot be said they were in the covenant of grace, and yet were obliged to it. And so covenant-interest gives no right to baptism; could it be proved, as it cannot, that all the infant seed of believers, as such, are in the covenant of grace, it would give them no right to baptism, without a command for it; the reason is, because a person may be in covenant, and as yet not have the pre-requisite to an ordinance, even faith in Christ, and a profession of it, which are necessary both to Baptism and the Lord's Supper; and if covenant-interest gives a right to the one, it would to the other.——10. Notwithstanding all this pother made about Abraham's covenant, Gen. xvii. it was not made with him and his infant seed; but with him and his adult offspring; it was they in all after ages to the coming of Christ, whether believers or unbelievers, who were enjoined to circumcise their infant-seed, and not all of them, only their males: it was not made with Abraham's infant-seed, who could not circumcise themselves, but their parents were by this covenant obliged to circumcise them; yea, others, who were not Abraham's natural seed, were obliged to it; *He that is eight days old shall be circumcised among you, which is* NOT OF THY SEED, Gen. xvii. 12. Which leads on to observe,

2. That nothing can be concluded from the circumcision of Jewish infants, to the baptism of the infants of believing Gentiles: had there been a like command for the baptism of the infants of believing Gentiles, under the New Testament, as there was for the circumcision of Jewish infants under the Old, the thing would not have admitted of any dispute; but nothing of this kind appears. For,——1. It is not clear that even Jewish infants were admitted into covenant by the rite of circumcision; from whence it is pleaded, that the infants of believers are admitted into it by baptism; for Abraham's female seed were taken into the covenant made with him, as well as his male seed, but not by any *visible rite* or ceremony; nor were his male seed admitted by any such rite; not by circumcision, for they were not to be circumcised until the eighth day; to have circumcised them sooner would have been criminal; and that they were in covenant from their birth, I presume, will not be denied; as it was a national covenant, so early they were in it; the Israelites, with their infants at Horeb, had not been circumcised; nor were they when they entered into covenant with the Lord their God, Deut. xxix. 10—15.——2. Circumcision was no seal of the covenant of grace under the former dispensation; nor is baptism a seal of it under the present: had circumcision been a seal of it, the covenant of grace must have been without one from Adam to Abraham: it is called a *sign* or *token*, but not a seal; it was a sign or mark in the flesh of Abraham's natural seed, a typical sign of the pollution of human nature, and of the inward circumcision of the heart; but no seal, confirming any spiritual blessing of the covenant of grace to those who had this mark or sign; it is indeed called, *A seal of the righteousness of faith*, Rom. iv. 11. but not a seal to Abraham's natural seed of their interest in that righteousness, but only to Abraham himself; it was a seal to him, a confirming sign, assuring him, that the righteousness of faith, which he had before he was circumcised, should come upon the uncircumcised believing Gentiles; and therefore it was continued on his natural offspring, until that righteousness was preached unto, received by, and imputed to believing Gentiles.——3. Nor did baptism succeed circumcision; there is no agreement between the one and the other; not in the subjects, to whom they were administered; the use of the one and the other is not the same; and the manner of administering them different; baptism being administered to Jews and Gentiles, to male and female, and to adult persons only: not so circumcision; the use of circumcision was to distinguish the natural seed of Abraham from others; baptism is the badge of the spiritual seed of Christ, and the answer of a good conscience towards God; and represents the sufferings, burial, and resurrection of Christ; the one is by blood, the other by water; and ordinances so much differing in their subjects, use, and administration, the one can never be thought to come in the room and place of the other. Besides, baptism was in use and force before circumcision was abolished, which was not until the death of Christ; whereas, the doctrine of baptism was preached, and the ordinance itself administered, some years before that; now that which was in force before another is out of date,

can never with any propriety be said to succeed, or come in the room of that other. Besides, if this was the case, as circumcision gave a right to the passover, so would baptism to the Lord's Supper; which yet is not admitted.

Now as there is nothing to be gathered out of the Old Testament to countenance infant baptism, so neither are there any passages in the New, which can be supported in favour of it.

1. Not the text in Acts ii. 39. *The promise is unto you and to your children*, &c. It is pretended, that this refers to the covenant made with Abraham, and to a covenant-promise made to him, giving his infant children a right to the ordinance of circumcision; and is urged as a reason with the Jews, why they and their children ought to be baptized; and with the Gentiles, why they and theirs should be also, when called into a church state. But,——1. There is not the least mention made in the text, of Abraham's covenant, or of any promise made to him, giving his infant seed a right to circumcision, and still less to baptism; nor is there the least syllable of infant baptism; nor any hint of it, from whence it can be concluded; nor by *children* are infants designed, but the posterity of the Jews, who are frequently so called in scripture, though grown up; and unless it be so understood in many places, strange interpretations must be given of them; wherefore the argument from hence for *pædobaptism* is given up by some learned men, as Dr. Hammond and others, as inconclusive.——2. The promise here, be it what it may, is not observed as giving a right or claim to any ordinance; but as an encouraging motive to persons in distress, under a sense of sin, to repent of it, and declare their repentance, and yield a voluntary subjection to the ordinance of baptism; when they might hope that remission of sins would be applied to them, and they should receive a larger measure of the grace of the Spirit; wherefore repentance and baptism are urged in order to the enjoyment of the promise; and consequently must be understood of adult persons, who only are capable of repentance, and of a voluntary subjection to baptism.

——3. The promise is no other than the promise of life and salvation by Christ, and of remission of sins by his blood, and of an increase of grace from his Spirit; and whereas the persons addressed had imprecated the guilt of the blood of Christ, they had shed, upon their posterity, as well as on themselves, which distressed them; they are told, for their relief, that the same promise would be made good to their posterity also, provided they did as they were directed to do; and even to all the Jews afar off, in distant countries and future ages, who should look on Christ and mourn, repent and believe, and be baptized: and seeing the Gentiles are sometimes described as those *afar off*, the promise may be thought to reach to them who should be called by grace, repent, believe, and be baptized also; but no mention is made of their children; and had they been mentioned, the limiting clause, *Even as many as the Lord our God shall call*, plainly points at and describes the persons intended, whether Jews or Gentiles, effectually called by grace, who are encouraged by the motive in the promise to profess repentance, and submit to baptism; which can only be understood of adult persons, and not of infants.

2. Nor Rom. xi. 16, &c. *If the firstfruits be holy*, &c. For,——1. By the first fruits, and lump, and by the root and branches, are not meant Abraham and his posterity, or natural seed, as such; but the first among the Jews who believed in Christ, and laid the first foundation of a gospel church-state, and were first incorporated into it; who being holy, were a pledge of the future conversion and holiness of that people in the latter-day.——2. Nor by the good olive-tree, after-mentioned, is meant the Jewish church-state; which was abolished by Christ, with all the peculiar ordinances of it; and the believing Gentiles were never ingrafted into it; the axe has been laid to the root of that old Jewish stock, and it is entirely cut down, and no engrafture is made upon it. But, ——3. By it is meant the gospel-church-state, in its first foundation, consisting of Jews that believed, out of which were left the Jews who believed not in Christ, and who are the branches broken off; into which church-state the Gentiles were received and engrafted: which engrafture, or coalition, was first made at Antioch, when and hereafter the Gentiles partook of the root and fatness of the olive-tree, enjoyed the same privileges, communicated in the same ordinances, and were satisfied with the goodness and fatness of the house of God; and this gospel-church may be truly called, by the converted Jews in the latter-day, their *own olive-tree*, into which they will be

engrafted; since the first gospel-church was set up at Jerusalem, and gathered out of the Jews; and so in other places, the first gospel-churches consisted of Jews, the first-fruits of those converted ones. From the whole it appears, that there is not the least syllable about baptism, much less of infant baptism, in the passage; nor can any thing be concluded from hence in favour of it.

3. Nor from 1 Cor. vii. 14. *For the unbelieving husband is sanctified by the wife, and the unbelieving wife is sanctified by the husband; else were your children unclean, but now are they holy;* which is by some understood of a federal holiness, giving a claim to covenant-privileges, and so to baptism. But,——1. It should be told what these covenant-privileges are; since, as we have seen, covenant-interest gives no right to any ordinance, without divine direction; nor is baptism a seal of the covenant: it should be told what this covenant-holiness is, whether imaginary or real; by some it is called *reputed*, and is distinguished from internal holiness, which is rejected from being the sense of the text; but such holiness can never qualify persons for a New Testament-ordinance; nor has the covenant of grace any such holiness belonging to it; that provides, by way of promise, *real* holiness, signified by putting the laws of God in the heart, by giving new hearts and new spirits, and by cleansing from all impurity, and designs real, internal holiness, shewn in an holy conversation; and such who appear to have that, have an undoubted right to the ordinance of baptism, since they have received the Spirit as a Spirit of sanctification, Acts x. 47. But this cannot be meant in the text, seeing,——2. It is such a holiness as heathens may have; unbelieving husbands and wives are said to have it, in virtue of their relation to believing wives and husbands, and which is prior to the holiness of their children, and on which theirs depends; but surely such will not be allowed to have federal holiness, and yet it must be of the same kind with their children's; if the holiness of the children is a federal holiness, that of the unbelieving parent must be so too, from whence is the holiness of the children. ——3. If children, by virtue of this holiness, have a claim to baptism, then much more their unbelieving parents, since they are sanctified before them, by their believing yokefellows, and are as near to them as their children; and if the holiness of the one gives a right to baptism, why not the holiness of the other? and yet the one are baptized, and the other not, though sanctified, and whose holiness is the more near; for the holiness spoken of, be it what it may, is derived from both parents, believing and unbelieving; yea, the holiness of the children depends upon the sanctification of the unbelieving parent; for if the unbeliever is not sanctified, the children are unclean, and not holy. But,——4. These words are to be understood of matrimonial holiness, even of the very act of marriage, which, in the language of the Jews, is frequently expressed by being *sanctified;* the word קדש to *sanctify*, is used in innumerable places in the Jewish writings,[9] to *espouse;* and in the same sense the apostle uses the word αγιαζω here, and the words may be rendered, *the unbelieving husband is espoused*, or married, *to the wife*, or rather, *has been espoused*, for it relates to the act of marriage past, as valid; *and the unbelieving wife has been espoused to the husband;* the preposition εν, translated *by*, should be rendered *to*, as it is in the very next verse; *God hath called us* εν ειρηνη, *to peace;* the apostle's inference from it is, *else were your children unclean*, illegitimate, if their parents were not lawfully espoused and married to each other; *but now are they holy*, a holy and legitimate seed, as in Ezra ix. 2. see Mal. ii. 15. and no other sense can be put upon the words, than of a legitimate marriage and offspring; nothing else will suit with the case proposed to the apostle, and with his answer to it, and reasoning about it; and which sense has been allowed by many learned interpreters, ancient and modern; as Jerome, Ambrose, Erasmus, Camerarius, Musculus, and others.

There are some objections made to the practice of adult baptism, which are of little force, and to which an answer may easily be returned.

1. That though it may be allowed that adult persons, such as repent and believe, are the subjects of baptism, yet it is nowhere said, that they are the *only* ones: but if no others can be named as baptized, and the descriptive characters given in scripture of baptized persons are such as can *only* agree with adults, and not with

[9] See my Exposition of 1 Cor. vii. 14.

infants; then it may be reasonably concluded, that the former *only* are the proper subjects of baptism.——2. It is objected to our practice of baptizing the adult offspring of Christians, that no scriptural instance of such a practice can be given; and it is demanded of us to give an instance agreeable to our practice; since the first persons baptized were such as were converted either from Judaism or from heathenism, and about the baptism of such adults, they say, there is no controversy. But our practice is not at all concerned with the parents of the persons baptized by us, whether they be Christians, Jews, Turks, or Pagans; but with the persons themselves, whether they are believers in Christ or no; if they are the adult offspring of Christians, yet unbaptized, it is no objection to us; and if they are not, it is no bar in the way of admitting them to baptism, if they themselves are believers; many, and it may be the greater part of such baptized by us are the adult offspring of those who, without breach of charity, cannot be considered as Christians. As for the first persons that were baptized, they were neither proselytes from Judaism nor from Heathenism; but the offspring of Christians, of such that believed in the Messiah; the saints before the coming of Christ, and at his coming, were as good Christians as any that have lived since; so that those good men who lived before Abraham, as far back as to the first man, and those that lived after him, even to the coming of Christ, Eusebius[10] observes, that if any should affirm them to be Christians, though not in name, yet in reality, he would not say amiss. Judaism, at the time of Christ's coming, was the same with Christianity, and not in opposition to it; so that there was no such thing as conversion from Judaism to Christianity. Zachariah and Elizabeth, whose offspring John the first baptizer was, and Mary, the mother of our Lord, who was baptized by John, when adult, were as good Christians, and as strong believers in Jesus, as the Messiah, as soon as born, and even when in the womb of the Virgin, as have been since; and these surely must be allowed to be the adult offspring of Christians; such were the apostles of Christ, and the first followers of him, who were the adult offspring of such who believed in the Messiah, and embraced him upon the first notice of him, and cannot be said to be converted from Judaism to Christianity; Judaism not existing until the opposition to Jesus being the Messiah became general and national; after that, indeed, those of the Jewish nation who believed in Christ, may be said to be proselytes from Judaism to Christianity, as the apostle Paul and others: and so converts made by the preaching of the gospel among the Gentiles, were proselytes from Heathenism to Christianity; but then it is unreasonable to demand of us instances of the adult offspring of such being baptized, and added to the churches; since the scripture history of the first churches contained in the Acts of the Apostles, only gives an account of the first planting of these churches, and of the baptism of those of which they first consisted; but not of the additions of members to them in after-times; wherefore to give instances of those who were born of them, and brought up by them, as baptized in adult years, cannot reasonably be required of us: but on the other hand, if infant children were admitted to baptism in these times, upon the faith and baptism of their parents, and their becoming Christians; it is strange, exceeding strange, that among the many thousands baptized in Jerusalem, Samaria, Corinth, and other places, that there should be no one instance of any of them bringing their children with them to be baptized, and claiming the privilege of baptism for them upon their own faith; nor of their doing this in any short time after. This is a case that required no length of time, and yet not a single instance can be produced. ——3. It is objected, that no time can be assigned when infants were cast out of covenant, or cut off from the seal of it. If by the covenant is meant the covenant of grace, it should be first proved that they are in it, as the natural seed of believers, which cannot be done; and when that is, it is time enough to talk of their being cast out, when and how. If by it is meant Abraham's covenant, the covenant of circumcision, the answer is, the cutting off was when circumcision ceased to be an ordinance of God, which was at the death of Christ: if by it is meant the national covenant of the Jews, the ejection of Jewish parents, with their children, was when God wrote a *Lo-ammi* upon that people, as a body politic and ecclesiastic; when he

---

[10] Eccles. Hist. l. 1. c. 4.

broke his covenant with them, signified by breaking his two staves, beauty and bands.——4. A clamorous outcry is made against us, as abridging the privileges of infants, by denying baptism to them; making them to be lesser under the gospel dispensation than under the law, and the gospel dispensation less glorious. But as to the gospel dispensation, it is the more glorious for infants being left out of its church-state; that is, for its being not national and carnal, as before; but congregational and spiritual; consisting not of infants, without understanding, but of rational and spiritual men, believers in Christ; and these not of a single country, as Judea, but in all parts of the world: and as for infants, their privileges now are many and better, who are eased from the painful rite of circumcision; it is a rich mercy, and a glorious privilege of the gospel, that the believing Jews and their children are delivered from it; and that the Gentiles and theirs are not obliged to it; which would have bound them over to fulfil the whole law; to which may be added, that being born of Christian parents, and having a Christian education, and of having opportunities of hearing the gospel, as they grow up; and that not in one country only, but in many; are greater privileges than the Jewish children had under the former dispensation.——5. It is objected, that there are no more express commands in scripture for keeping the first day of the week as a sabbath; nor for women's partaking of the Lord's supper, and other things, than for the baptism of infants. As for the first, though there is no express precept for the observance of it, yet there are precedents of its being observed for religious services, Acts xx. 7. 1 Cor. xvi. 1, 2. and though we have no example of infant baptism, yet if there were scriptural precedents of it, we should think ourselves obliged to follow them. As for women's right to partake of the Lord's supper, we have sufficient proof of it; since these were baptized as well as men; and having a right to one ordinance, had to another, and were members of the first church, communicated with it, and women, as well as men, were added to it, Acts viii. 12. and i. 14. and v. 1, 14. we have a precept for it; *Let a man,* ανθρωπος, a word of the common gender, and signifies both man and woman, *examine him or herself, and so let him or her eat,* 1 Cor. xi. 29. see Gal. iii. 28. and we have also examples of it in Mary the mother of our Lord, and other women, who, with the disciples, constituted the gospel-church at Jerusalem: and as they continued with one accord in the apostles' doctrine and in prayer, so in fellowship and in breaking of bread; let the same proof be given of the baptism of infants, and it will be admitted.——6. Antiquity is urged in favour of infant baptism; it is pretended that this is a tradition of the church received from the apostles; though of this no other proof is given, but the testimony of Origen, none before that; and this is taken, not from any of his genuine Greek writings, only from some Latin translations, confessedly interpolated, and so corrupted, that it is owned, one is at a loss to find Origen in Origen. No mention is made of this practice in the first two centuries, no instance given of it until the third, when Tertullian is the first who spoke of it, and at the same time spoke against it.[11] And could it be carried up higher, it would be of no force, unless it could be proved from the sacred scriptures, to which only we appeal, and by which the thing in debate is to be judged and determined. We know that innovations and corruptions very early obtained, and even in the times of the apostles: and what is pretended to be near those times, is the more to be suspected as the traditions of the false apostles;[12] the antiquity of a custom, is no proof of the truth and genuineness of it;[13] *The customs of the people are vain,* Jer. x. 3. I proceed to consider,

Fourthly, The way and manner of baptizing; and to prove, that it is by immersion, plunging the body in water, and covering it with it. Custom, and the common use of writing in this controversy, have so far prevailed, that for the most part immersion is usually called the *mode* of baptism; whereas it is properly baptism itself; to say that immersion or dipping is the mode of baptism, is the same thing

---

[11] See my Treatises, "The Argument from apostolic Tradition, in favour of Infant Baptism, considered;" and "Antipædo-Baptism, or Infant Baptism, an Innovation," with others.

[12] Quod longinquitas temporis objicitur, eo major suspicio, inesse debet, emanasse illas traditiones a Pseudo apostolis; qui mirandum in modum conterbaverunt sanctos apostolos; quo magis cavendum est, viri Christiani. Aonii Palearii Testimonium, c. 2. p. 238.

[13] Consuetudo sine veritate vetustas erroris est, Cyprian. epist. 74. p. 195.

as to say, that dipping is the mode of dipping; for as Sir John Floyer[14] observes, "Immersion is no circumstance, but *the very act of baptism*, used by our Saviour and his disciples, in the institution of baptism." And Calvin [15] expressly says, "The word *baptizing* signifies to plunge; and it is certain, that the rite of plunging was used by the ancient churches." And as for sprinkling, that cannot, with any propriety, be called a mode of baptism; for it would be just such good sense as to say, sprinkling is the mode of dipping, since baptism and dipping are the same; hence the learned Selden,[16] who in the former part of his life, might have seen infants dipped in fonts, but lived to see immersion much disused, had reason to say, "In England, of late years, I ever thought the parson *baptized his own fingers* rather than *the child*," because he dipped the one, and sprinkled the other. That baptism is immersion, or the dipping of a person in water, and covering him with it is to be proved,

1. From the proper and primary signification of the word βαπτιζω, *baptize*, which in its first and primary sense, signifies to *dip* or *plunge into*; and so it is rendered by our best *lexicographers, mergo, immergo*, dip or plunge into. And in a secondary and consequential sense, *abluo, lavo, wash*, because what is dipped is washed, there being no proper washing but by dipping; but never *perfundo* or *aspergo, pour* or *sprinkle*; so the lexicon published by Constantine, Budæus, &c. and those of Hadrian Junius, Plantinus, Scapula, Stephens, Schrevelius, Stockius, and others; besides a great number of critics; as Beza, Casaubon, Witsius, &c. which might be produced. By whose united testimonies the thing is out of question. Had our translators, instead of adopting the Greek word *baptize* in all places where the ordinance of baptism is made mention of, truly translated it, and not have left it untranslated, as they have, the controversy about the manner of baptizing would have been at an end, or rather have been prevented; had they used the word *dip*, instead of *baptize*, as they should have done, there would have been no room for a question about it.——2. That baptism was performed by immersion, appears by the places chosen for the administration of it; as the river Jordan by John, where he baptized many, and where our Lord himself was baptized by him, Matt. iii. 6, 13, 16. but why should he choose the river to baptize in, and baptize in it, if he did not administer the ordinance by immersion? had it been done any other way, there was no occasion for any confluence of water, much less a river; [17] a bason of water would have sufficed. John also, it is said, *was baptizing in Ænon, near Salim, because there was much water*, John iii. 23. which was convenient for baptism, for which this reason is given; and not for conveniency for drink for men and their cattle, which is not expressed nor implied; from whence we may gather, as Calvin on the text does, "That baptism was performed by John and Christ, by plunging the whole body under water;" and so Piscator, Aretius, Grotius, and others on the same passage.
——3. That this was the way in which it was anciently administered, is clear from several instances of baptism recorded in scripture, and the circumstances attending them; as that of our Lord, of whom it is said, *That when he was baptized he went up straightway out of the water*, which supposes he had been in it; and so Piscator infers from his going up out of it, that therefore he went down into it, and was baptized in the river itself; of which going down there would have been no need, had the ordinance been administered to him in another way, as by sprinkling or pouring a little water on his head, he and John standing in the midst of the river, as the painter and engraver ridiculously describe it: and certain it is, he was then baptized in Jordan; the evangelist Mark says *into Jordan*, Mark i. 9. not at the banks of Jordan, but into the waters of it; for which reason he went into it, and when baptized, came up *out* of it, not *from* it, but *out* of it; απο and εξ, signifying the same, as in

---

[14] Essay to Restore the Dipping of Infants in Baptism, p. 44.
[15] Institut. 1. 4. c. 15. s. 19.
[16] Opera, vol. 6. col. 2008.
[17] Some represent the river Jordan, from Sandys's account of it, as if it was a shallow river, and insufficient for immersion; but what Sandys says of it, is only that it was not navigably deep, not above eight fathoms broad, nor, except by accident, heady. Travels, b. iii. p. 110. ed. 5. But Mr. Maundrel says, for its breadth, it might be about twenty yards over, and in depth it far exceeded his height. Journey from Aleppo, &c. p. 83. ed. 7. vid. Reland. de Palestina, l. 1. p. 278. and Adamnan. in ib. And therefore must be sufficient for immersion. And Strabo speaks of ships of burden sailing through Jordan, Geograph. l. 16. p. 519. And that it was a river to swim in, and navigable, according to the Jewish writers, see my Exposition of Matt. iii. 5.

Luke iv. 35, 41. So the preposition is used in the Septuagint version of Psalm xl. 2. ἐξ and ἀπο are *æquipollent*, as several lexicographers from Xenophon observe. The baptism of the eunuch is another instance of baptism by immersion; when he and Philip were *come unto a certain water*, to the water-side, which destroys a little piece of criticism, as if their going into the water, after expressed, was no other than going to the brink of the water, to the water-side, whereas they were come to that before; and baptism being agreed upon, *they went down both into the water*, both Philip and the eunuch, *and he baptized him; and when they were come up out of the water*, &c. Now we do not reason merely from the circumstance of *going down into, and coming up out of the water*; we know that persons may go down into water, and come up out of it, and never be immersed in it; but when it is expressly said, upon these persons going down into the water, that Philip baptized, or dipped, the eunuch; and when this was done, that both came up out of it, these circumstances strongly corroborate, without the explanation of the word *baptized*, that it was performed by immersion; for these circumstances cannot agree with any other way of administering it but that; for a man can hardly be thought to be in his senses who can imagine Philip went down with the eunuch into the water to sprinkle or pour a little water on him, and then gravely came out of it; hence, as the above learned commentator, Calvin, on the text says, "Here we plainly see what was the manner of baptizing with the ancients, for they plunged the whole body into the water; now custom obtaining, that the minister only sprinkles the body or the head." So Barnabas,[18] an apostolic writer of the first century, and who is mentioned in the Acts of the Apostles, as a companion of the Apostle Paul, describes baptism by going down into and by coming up out of the water; "We descend," says he, "into the water full of sin and filth; and we ascend, bringing forth fruit in the heart, having fear and hope in Jesus, through the Spirit."

4. The end of baptism, which is to represent the burial of Christ, cannot be answered in any other way than by immersion, or covering the body in water; that baptism is an emblem of the burial of Christ, is clear from Rom. vi. 4. Col. ii. 12. It would be endless to quote the great number, even of *pædobaptist* writers, who ingenuously acknowledge that the allusion in these passages, is to the ancient rite of baptism by immersion: as none but such who are dead are buried, so none but such who are dead to sin, and to the law, by the body of Christ, or who profess to be so, are to be buried in and by baptism, or to be baptized; and as none can be properly said to be buried, unless put under ground, and covered with earth; so none can be said to be baptized, but such who are put under water, and covered with it; and nothing short of this can be a representation of the burial of Christ, and of ours with him; not sprinkling, or pouring a little water on the face; for a corpse cannot be said to buried when only a little earth or dust is sprinkled or poured on it.

5. This may be concluded from the various figurative and typical baptisms spoken of in scripture. As,—(1.) From the waters of the flood, which Tertullian calls[19] the baptism of the world, and of which the apostle Peter makes baptism the antitype, 1 Pet. iii. 20, 21. The ark in which Noah and his family were saved by water, was God's ordinance; it was made according to the pattern he gave to Noah, as baptism is; and as that was the object of the scorn of men, so is the ordinance of baptism, rightly administered; and as it represented a burial, when Noah and his family were shut up in it, so baptism; and when the fountains of the great deep were broken up below, and the windows of heaven were opened above, the ark with those in it, were as it were covered with and immersed in water; and so was a figure of baptism by immersion: and as there were none but adult persons in the ark, who were saved by water in it, so none but adult persons are the proper subjects of water-baptism; and though there were few who were in the ark, it was attended with a salutary effect to them, they were saved by water; so such who truly believe in Christ, and are baptized, shall be saved, and that *by the resurrection of Jesus Christ*, which was typified by the coming of Noah and his family out of the ark; to which baptism, as the antitype, corresponds, being an emblem of the same, Rom. vi. 4, 5. Col. ii. 12. —(2.) From the passage of the Israelites

---

[18] Ep. c. 9. p. 235. ed. Voss.

[19] De baptismo, c. 8.

under the cloud and through the sea, when they *were said to be baptized unto Moses, in the cloud and in the sea,* 1 Cor. x. 1, 2. There are several things in this account which agree with baptism; this was following Moses, who directed them into the sea, and went before them; so baptism is a following Christ, who has set an example to tread in his steps; and as the Israelites were baptized into Moses, so believers are baptized into Christ, and put him on; and this passage of theirs was after their coming out of Egypt, and at the beginning of their journey through the wilderness to Canaan; so baptism is administered to believers, at their first coming out of darkness and bondage worse than Egyptian, and when they first enter on their Christian pilgrimage; and as joy followed upon the former, *Then sang Moses and the children of Israel,* &c. so it often follows upon the latter; the eunuch, after baptism, went on his way rejoicing: but chiefly this passage was a figure of baptism by immersion; as the Israelites were *under the cloud,* and so under water, and covered with it, as persons baptized by immersion are; *and passed through the sea,* that standing up as a wall on both sides them, with the cloud over them; thus surrounded they were as persons immersed in water, and so said to be baptized; and thus Grotius remarks upon the passage.—(3.) From the divers washings, bathings, or baptisms of the Jews; called *divers,* because of the different persons and things washed or dipped, as the same Grotius observes; and not because of different sorts of washing, for there is but one way of washing, and that is by dipping; what has a little water only sprinkled or poured on it, cannot be said to be washed; the Jews had their sprinklings, which were distinct from washings or bathings, which were always performed by immersion; it is a rule, with them, that "wherever in the law, washing of the flesh, or of the clothes is mentioned, it means nothing else than טבילת כל הגוף *the dipping of the whole body* in a laver—for if any man dips himself all over except the tip of his little finger, he is still in his uncleanness,"[20] according to them.—(4.) From the sufferings of Christ being called a baptism; *I have a baptism to be baptized with,* &c. Luke xii. 50. not water-baptism nor the baptism of the Spirit, with both which he had been baptized; but the baptism of his sufferings, yet to come, he was desirous of; these are called so in allusion to baptism, as it is an immersion; and is expressive of the abundance of them, sometimes signified by deep waters, and floods of waters; and Christ is represented as plunged into them, covered and overwhelmed with them, Psalm lxii. 7. and lxix. 1, 2.—(5.) From the extraordinary donation of the Holy Spirit, and his gifts unto, and his descent upon the apostles on the day of Pentecost, which is called *baptizing,* Acts i. 5. and ii. 1, 2. expressive of the very great abundance of them, in allusion to baptism or dipping, in a proper sense, as the learned Casaubon[21] observes; "Regard is had in this place to the proper signification of the word βαπτιζειν, to immerse or dip; and in this sense the apostles are truly said to be baptized, for the house in which this was done, was filled with the Holy Ghost; so that the apostles seemed to be plunged into it, as into some pool." All which typical and figurative baptisms, serve to strengthen the proper sense of the word, as it signifies an immersion and dipping the body into, and covering it in water, which only can support the figure used. Nor is this sense of the word to be set aside or weakened by the use of it in Mark vii. 4. and Luke xi. 38. in the former, it is said, *Except they wash,* βαπτιζωνται, *baptize,* or *dip themselves, they eat not;* and in it mention is made of βαπτισμων, *washings* or *dippings* of cups and pots, brazen vessels, and of tables or beds; and in the latter, the Pharisee is said to marvel at Christ, that he had not first εβαπτισθη, *washed,* or *dipped, before dinner;* all which agrees with the superstitious traditions of the elders, here referred to, which enjoined dipping in all the cases and instances spoken of, and so serve but the more to confirm the sense of the word contended for; for the Pharisees, upon touching the common people or their clothes, as they returned from market, or from any court of judicature, were obliged to immerse themselves in water before they eat; and so the Samaritan Jews,[22] "If the Pharisees," says Maimonides,[23] "touched but the garments of the common people, they were defiled all one as if they had touched a profluvious person, and needed immersion," or were obliged to it: and

---

[20] Maimon. Hilchot Mikvaot, c. 1. s. 2.
[21] In Act. i. 5.
[22] Epiph. contra Hæres. l. 1. Hæres. 9.
[23] In Misn. Chagigah, c. 2. s. 7.

Scaliger,[24] from the Jews observes, "That the more superstitious part of them, every day, before they sat down to meat, dipped the whole body;" hence the Pharisee's admiration at Christ, Luke xi. 38. And not only cups and pots, and brazen vessels were washed by dipping, or putting them into water, in which way unclean vessels were washed according to the law, Lev. xi. 32. but even beds, pillows, and bolsters, unclean in a ceremonial sense, were washed in this way, according to the traditions of the elders referred to; for they say,[25] "A bed that is wholly defiled, if a man *dips* it part by part, it is pure." Again,[26] "If he *dips the bed* in it (a pool of water) though its feet are plunged into the thick clay (at the bottom of the pool) it is clean." And as for pillows and bolsters, thus they say,[27] "A pillow or a bolster of skin, when a man lifts up the mouth of them out of the water, the water which is in them will be drawn; what must be done? He must *dip* them, and lift them up by their fringes." Thus, according to these traditions, the several things mentioned were washed by immersion; and instead of weakening, strengthen the sense of the word pleaded for.

The objections against baptism as immersion, taken from some instances of baptism recorded in scripture, are of no force; as that of the three thousand, in Acts ii. not with respect to their number; it may be observed, that though these were added to the church in one and the same day, it does not follow, that they were baptized in one day; but be it that they were, there were twelve apostles to administer the ordinance, and it was but two hundred and fifty persons apiece; and besides, there were seventy disciples, administrators of it; and supposing them employed, it will reduce the number to six or seven and thirty persons each: and the difference between dipping and sprinkling is very inconsiderable, since the same form of words is used in the one way as in the other; and therefore it might be done in one day, and in a small part of it too.[28] Nor with respect to convenience for the administration of it; as water and places of it sufficient to baptize in: here can be no objection, when it is observed, what number of private baths were in Jerusalem for ceremonial uncleanness; the many pools in the city, and the various apartments and things in the temple fit for such a use; as the dipping room for the high priest, the molten sea for the common priests, and the ten brazen lavers, each of which held forty baths of water sufficient for the immersion of the whole body; all which they might be allowed the use of, as they were of the temple; they *having favour with all the people:* nor with respect to clothes, and change of garments; it was only every one's providing and bringing change of raiment for himself. Another instance objected to is, that of the baptism of Saul, Acts ix. 18. supposed to be done in the house where he was: but that does not necessarily follow, but rather the contrary; since he *arose* from the place where he was, in order to be baptized; and admitting it was done in the house, it is highly probable there was a bath in the house, in which it might be performed; since it was the house of a Jew, with whom it was usual to have baths to wash their whole bodies in on certain occasions; and had it been performed by sprinkling or pouring a little water on him, he needed not to have rose for that purpose. Besides, he was not only bid to arise and be baptized, which would sound very oddly if rendered, *be sprinkled,* or *poured,* Acts xxii. 16. but he himself says, that he, with others, were *buried by* or *in baptism,* Rom. vi. 4. Another instance is that of the jailer and his household, Acts xvi. 33. in which account there is nothing that makes it improbable that it was done by immersion; for it seems to be a clear case, that the jailer, upon his conversion, took the apostles out of prison into his own house, where they preached to him and his family, ver. 32. and after this they went out of his house,

---

[24] De Emend. Temp. l. 6. p. 771.
[25] Maimon. Hilchot Celim. c. 26. s. 14.
[26] Misn. Mikvaot, c. 7. s. 7.
[27] Ibid. s. 6.
[28] Ten thousand were baptized in one day by Austin the monk, in the river Swale, if our historians are to be credited. Fox's Acts and Monuments, vol. i. p. 154. Ranulph Polychron. l. 5. c. 10. The twelve sons of Wolodomir, Grand Prince of Russia, with twenty thousand Russians, in cent. 10. were baptized in one day, by a missionary of Photius the patriarch; and the ancient Russians would allow no person to be a Christian, unless he had been dipped quite under water. Strahlenberg. Histor. Geograph. Descript. of the Northern and Eastern parts of Europe and Asia, ch. 8. p. 283, 286. Vid. Fabricii Lux Evangel. p. 475. No doubt assistance was had in both instances; but these shew what numbers may be baptized in a day.

and he and his were baptized, very probably in the river without the city, where the oratory was, ver. 13. for it is certain, that after the baptism of him and his family, he brought the apostles into his house again, and set meat before them, ver. 33, 34. Upon the whole, these instances produced, fail of shewing the improbability of baptism by immersion; which must appear clear and manifest to every attentive reader of his Bible, notwithstanding all that has been opposed unto it. The next thing to be considered is,

Fifthly, The form in which this ordinance is to be administered; which is *in the name of the Father, and of the Son and of the Holy Ghost*, Matt. xxviii. 19. which contains in it a proof of a Trinity of Persons in the unity of the divine essence, of the Deity of each Person, and of their equality to, and distinction from each other; and shews, that this ordinance is performed under the authority of all Three; in which a person submitting to it, expresses his faith in them, and invocation of them, and gives up himself to them; obliging himself to yield obedience to what they require of him, as well as putting himself under their care and protection. This form is sometimes a little varied and otherwise expressed; as sometimes only *in the name of the Lord Jesus*, Acts viii. 16. which is a part of the form for the whole; and includes in it the substance of it, and of christian baptism; and every thing relating to the person and offices of Christ, and his relation to and connection with the other Two persons. Cornelius and his family were ordered to be baptized, *in the name of the Lord*, Acts x. 48. that is, in the name of Jehovah, Father, Son, and Spirit; for κυριος, Lord, in the New Testament, answers to Jehovah in the Old. The form of baptism in Matt. xxviii. 19. is in the name of *the Father*, &c. which single name denotes the one Deity, power, and substance of Father, Son, and Spirit; the equal dignity, co-eternal kingdom, and government in the Three perfect Persons; as it is expressed in the synodical epistle of the general council at Constantinople.[29]

Sixthly, The ends and uses for which baptism is appointed, and which are answered by it.

1. One end of it, and a principal one, as has been frequently hinted, is, to represent the sufferings, burial, and resurrection of Christ; which is plainly and fully suggested in Rom. vi. 4, 5. Col. ii. 12. his sufferings are represented by going into the water, and being overwhelmed in it, his burial by a short continuance under it, and being covered with it, and his resurrection by an emersion out of it.——2. It was practised both by John and by the apostles of Christ, for the remission of sins, Mark i. 4. Acts ii. 38. not that that is the procuring and meritorious cause of it, which only is the blood of Christ; but they who submit unto it, may, by means of it, be led, directed, and encouraged to expect it from Christ. And so,——3. In like manner it is for the washing away of sin, and cleansing from it; *Arise, and be baptized, and wash away thy sins*, Acts xxii. 16. this only is really done by the blood of Christ, which cleanses from all sin; baptism neither washes away original nor actual sin, it has no such virtue in it;[30] but it is a means of directing to Christ the Lamb of God, who, by his atoning blood and sacrifice, has purged and continues to take away the sins of men.——4. A salutary or saving use and effect is ascribed unto it; *The like figure whereunto, baptism, doth also now save us;* should it be asked how, and by what means? the answer follows, *By the resurrection of Jesus Christ*, 1 Pet. iii. 21. that is, by leading the faith of the person baptized to Christ, as delivered for his offences, and as risen again for his justification.——5. In the same passage it is said to be of this use, and to serve this purpose, *The answer of a good conscience towards God;* a man who believes baptism to be an ordinance of God, and submits to it as such, discharges a good conscience, the consequence of which is joy and peace; for though *for* keeping the commands of God there is no reward, yet there is *in* keeping them; and this is their reward, the testimony of a good conscience: for great peace have they which love God and keep his command-

---

[29] Apud. Theodorit. Eccl. Hist. l. 5. c. 9. This form was first changed and corrupted by Mark the heretic, and his followers, in the second century; who baptized into the name of the unknown Father of all; into truth the mother of all; into him who descended on Jesus; into union and redemption, and communion of powers: the same also first changed and corrupted the mode; taking a mixture of oil and water, poured it on their head, and then anointed with balsam. Vid. Irenæum adv. Hæres. l. 1. c. 18.

[30] Non enim aqua lavat animam, sed ipsa prius lavatur a Spiritu, Aonii Palearii Testimonium, c. 2. p. 24.

ments.——6. Yielding obedience to this ordinance of Christ, is an evidence of love to God and Christ, 1 John v. 3. and such who from a principle of love to Christ, keep his commandments, may expect according to his promise, to have fresh manifestations of his and his Father's love, and to have communion with Father, Son, and Spirit, John xiv. 15, 21, 23. This is an end to be had in view, in obedience to it, and a very encouraging one.

CHAP. II.

OF THE LORD'S SUPPER.

AFTER the ordinance of baptism, follows the ordinance of the Lord's Supper; the one is preparatory to the other; and he that has a right to the one has a right to the other; and none but such who have submitted to the former, ought to be admitted to the latter. Baptism is to be administered but once, when we first make a profession of Christ, and of faith in him; but the ordinance of the supper is to be frequently administered, and continued throughout the stage of life, it being our spiritual food, for the support and maintenance of our spiritual life. It goes by various names in scripture; it is called, *the body and blood of Christ*, from the subject-matter of it; and that by Christ himself, *This is my body, and this is my blood*, Matt. xxvi. 26, 28. which in this ordinance are symbolically represented to the faith of the Lord's people; and sometimes it is called, *The communion of the body and blood of Christ*, 1 Cor. x. 16. because the saints have in it communion with Christ, he sups with them and they with him; and particularly enjoys the fellowship of his sufferings, or partake of the blessings of grace which flow from the sufferings of Christ, from the offering up of his body, and the shedding of his blood. Sometimes it is called, *This bread*, and *this cup of the Lord*, 1 Cor. xi. 27. because the bread represents Christ himself, the bread of life, and the cup signifies the New Testament in his blood. Sometimes it is expressed by *breaking of bread*, Acts ii. 42. and xx. 7. a part for the whole, so denominated from a particular action used in the administration of it. And it is called, *The Lord's table*, 1 Cor. x. 21. by a metonymy, for the food and entertainment upon it; a table which the Lord has prepared and furnished, at which he himself sits and welcomes his guests: and with great propriety may it be called a *feast*, because of the richness and plenty of the provision in it; as it seems to be in 1 Cor. v. 8. *Let us keep the feast;* not the feast of the passover, now abolished, but the feast of the Lord's Supper, which exhibits Christ, the true passover, sacrificed for us. But its most significant and expressive name, and which is commonly in use, is *The Lord's Supper*, 1 Cor. xi. 20. a *supper*, being instituted after the passover, which was killed between the two evenings, and eaten in the night; and was first performed by Christ the evening in which he was betrayed: nor does this detract from the grandeur of the entertainment, since not only with the Romans their principal meal was a supper, but with the Jews also, especially their nuptial feasts were kept in the evening. And it is called the Lord's Supper, because it is by his appointment; it is made by him and for him;. he is the sum and substance of it, and when rightly performed, it is according to his will; he is the maker and master of the feast, and is the feast itself. There are divers other names which are given to this ordinance by the ancients; to recite which is to little purpose; the chief and principal, and the most ancient is, that of the *eucharist*, by which name it was called in the times of Justin Martyr,[1] and by Ignatius,[2] and Irenæus[3] before him, from a part of it, *thanksgiving*, and because the whole of it gives just occasion for thanksgiving, for the many blessings of grace it exhibits to the view of faith. In treating of it I shall consider,

First, The author of it, and shew it to be an ordinance of Christ peculiar to the gospel-dispensation, a standing ordinance in it, and which is to continue until the second coming of Christ.

1*st*, It was instituted by Christ himself; who not only has given an example to do as he has done, which has great force and authority in it; he not only practised and celebrated it himself, which was giving a sufficient sanction to it; but he has, by precept, enjoined it on his apostles and disciples, and all succeeding ministers, and

---

[1] Apolog 2. p. 97.
[2] Epist. ad Smyrn. p. 6. ad Philadelph. p. 40. ed Voss.
[3] Adv. Hæres. 1. 5. c. 2.

on all his followers, to the end of the world; which is contained in these preceptive words of his, used by him at the first institution of the ordinance; *Take, eat, this is my body; drink ye all of this, for this is my blood; this do in remembrance of me,* Matt. xxvi. 26, 27. Luke xxii. 19. and particularly the apostle Paul expressly declares, that what he delivered concerning this ordinance, he *received from the Lord,* 1 Cor. xi. 23. so that it is not a device, and an invention of his, nor did he receive it of men, nor was taught it, but he had it by the revelation of Christ; and this being instituted by Christ, and celebrated by him, *the same night in which he was betrayed,* shews the very great love of Christ to his church and people, and his affectionate concern for them, and care of the ; that at a time his sufferings were coming upon him to an amazing degree, when his soul was exceeding sorrowful, even unto death, when he that was to betray him was at hand, when he was just about to be delivered into the hands of sinful men, who would put him to death, and when he was just ready to suffer and die for his people; that he should then, midst all his sorrows, and in the near approach of his most dreadful sufferings, think of his people, and provide for them a divine repast, spiritual food for their entertainment to the end of the world.

2*dly,* This ordinance is peculiar to the gospel-dispensation. It was indeed typified by what Melchizedek did, who was himself a type of Christ, as king of righteousness and peace, and as the priest of the most high God, who brought forth *bread and wine* to refresh Abraham and his weary troops, returning from the slaughter of the kings; so saints, who are in a warfare-state, and are good soldiers of Christ, and are engaged in a war with potent and spiritual enemies, are regaled by Christ with bread and wine, and with what is signified by them; and what is better than these. This ordinance was also pointed at in prophecy, respecting gospel-times, as what should be in use when those times came. So in Prov. ix. there is a prophetic representation of the church of Christ in gospel-times, and of the provisions in it, and of guests invited to partake of them by the ministers of the gospel, who in Christ's name are bid to say, *Come, eat of my bread, and drink of the wine which I have mingled.* And in Isa. xxv. 6. this feast is hinted at, which is a prophecy respecting gospel-times; which, among other things, may include and have respect unto the ordinance of the supper; but that itself was not instituted nor practised till the night in which Christ was betrayed. And,

3*dly,* This is a standing ordinance in the church of Christ. It was not only kept the first night it was instituted and observed; but in after times, after the death and resurrection of Christ; it was observed by the first church at Jerusalem, the members of which are commended for continuing in fellowship, and in *breaking of bread,* meaning, the ordinance of the supper; the disciples at Troas met together on the first day of the week *to break bread,* that is, to celebrate this ordinance of Christ; and though there were disorders in the church at Corinth, in the celebration of it, yet the thing itself was not denied nor neglected by them, though they were disorderly in their attendance on it. Justin Martyr gives us a very particular account of the celebration of it in his time, which was in the second century, and so it has been continued in the churches of Christ ever since to this day, Acts ii. 42. and xx. 7. 1 Cor. xi. 20, 21.

4*thly,* It is to continue to the end of the world; it is one of those ordinances that cannot be shaken and removed, but will remain; it is among those *all things,* and a principal one of them, Christ ordered his apostles, and succeeding ministers, to teach his followers to observe; promising to be with them, so doing, *to the end of the world,* Matt. xxviii. 20. and this is plainly suggested by the apostle Paul, when he says, *As often as ye eat this bread, and drink this cup, ye do shew the Lord's death till he come,* 1 Cor. xi. 26. which cannot be understood of his coming by the effusion of his Spirit, as on the day of Pentecost; for in this sense he was come when this instruction was given; nor is it an objection of any force, that types, figures, shadows, and ceremonies are now ceased; for though the shadows of the ceremonial law, which were figures of good things to come, are ceased, Christ, the body and substance, being come; yet there may be and are figures and representations of him as come, and commemorative of him, and of the good things come by him; baptism is said to be a *figure,* that is, of the burial and resurrection of Christ, 1 Pet. iii. 21. and so the Lord's Supper is a *figure,* of his broken body and bloodshed, as will be seen hereafter. I proceed to consider,

Secondly, The matter of the ordinance, or the outward elements of it, the bread and wine, which are symbols of the body and blood of Christ.

1st, Bread; whether the bread was leavened or unleavened bread, has been a matter of warm dispute between the Greek and Latin churches; the latter insisting on the use of unleavened bread, since that was what was used by our Lord at the first institution of this ordinance, it being at the time of the passover, the feast of unleavened bread, when no other was to be had; and the apostle directs to keep the feast, not with the *leaven* of malice, but with the *unleavened* bread of sincerity and truth. That the bread of Christ used in this ordinance was unleavened bread, is not to be doubted; but that it was designed as a rule in after administrations, is a question; since Christ seems to have taken it without respect to its being leavened or unleavened, but as being at hand, and at that time in common use; nor does it seem so agreeable to retain and continue a Jewish ceremony at the passover, in a gospel ordinance: and though the apostle, in the exhortation referred to, alludes to the bread of the passover, yet by this figurative expression, he cannot be thought to design the use of unleavened bread in the Lord's Supper; but that every ordinance of God, and so this, should be observed with a sincere affection to Christ and one another. It seems to be quite an indifferent thing what bread is used in the ordinance, be it what it may, which is used in any country for common food; such was the bread the disciples used at Troas, when they met to break bread, which was several days after the Jewish feast of unleavened bread was over, and so that sort of bread was not then in use, Acts xx. 6, 7. However, the round wafers of the papists cannot be allowed of, they being not properly bread, nor so made as to be broken and distributed in pieces, nor palatable, nor fit for nourishment; and so improper emblems of what is spiritually nutritive.

Now the bread in the ordinance of the supper is a symbol of the body and flesh of Christ; *The bread*, says Christ, *that I will give, is my flesh*, John vi. 51, 55. which words, though not spoken of the Lord's Supper, which was not then instituted, yet might be said with respect to it, by way of anticipation, and, however, serve to illustrate and explain what our Lord said in it; *This is my body*, that is a symbol and sign of it, when he took the bread, blessed it, and brake it; and so says the apostle, *The bread which we break, is it not the communion of the body of Christ?* 1 Cor. x. 16. not his mystical body, the church, but his natural body, which was formed in the womb of the Virgin by the Holy Spirit, and which Christ took into union with his divine Person, and which he offered up upon the cross. And the bread in the supper is a symbol of his body, not as living either on earth or in heaven, but as dead, the life of it being laid down by Christ, and given for the life of his people; though now raised and alive, and lives for evermore: nor as glorified, the form of which was marred by his sufferings and death, but raised, has a glory given it, and is become a glorious body; but as such the bread broken in the ordinance is not a symbol of it; but as crucified, suffering, slain, and dead; for in it Christ is *evidently set forth* before the eye of faith, as *crucified*; and to him as such believers are directed to look, whom they have pierced, and mourn; and as he is to be beheld in the midst of the throne, so particularly in this ordinance; *A Lamb as it had been slain!* Christ's body broken by sufferings and death, is signified by the bread broken in it; for these words, *This is my body*,

1. Are not to be understood in a proper sense, as if the bread was transubstantiated into the real body of Christ; this is contradicted by the testimony of the senses, of seeing, tasting, and smelling [4]; by all which the bread appears to be the same after its separation to the use of the ordinance it was before: it is contrary to reason, that accidents should be without a subject; that the qualities and properties of bread should remain, and not the bread itself; that a body should be in more places at one and the same time, and Christ have as many bodies as there are consecrated wafers; which is most absurd: it is contrary to the nature of Christ's body, which was like ours when on earth; and at the time of the institution; and after his resurrection was visible and palpable, and consisting of flesh and blood;

---

[4] Exterius quidem panis, quod ante fuerat, forma prædentitur, color ostenditur, sapor accipitur—— quid enim aliud in superficie quam substantia vini conspicitur? Gusta, vinum sapit: odora vinum redolet; inspice, vini color intuetur. Bertram. de Corp. Sang. Domini, in principio.

and is now ascended to heaven, where it will be retained until the time of the restitution of all things; and is not every where, as it must be, if its real presence is in the ordinance in all places, and at all times, where and when it is administered: it is contrary to scripture, which declares the bread to be bread when blessed and broken; *The bread which we break;* and *this bread that ye eat,* and *this cup that ye drink;* and as the bread is still called bread, so the wine in the cup, *the fruit of the vine;* no real change is made in the one nor in the other: it is contrary to the very nature and design of the ordinance; it confounds the sign and the thing signified: if the bread is no more bread, it ceases to be a sign, and the body of Christ cannot be signified by it; the analogy between both is taken away; to say no more, it is impious and blasphemous for a priest to take upon him, by muttering over a few words, to make the body and blood of Christ, and then eat them! The folly, or rather madness of such, is reproved by Cicero the heathen, who thought no man could be so mad to believe what he eat to be a God.[5]

2. The phrase, *This is my body,* is to be understood in a figurative sense; the bread is a figure, symbol, and representation of the body of Christ; many scriptural phrases are so to be understood; as when Joseph said to Pharaoh, *The seven good kine are seven years, and the seven good ears are seven years;* so seven kine and ears signified, or were symbols, of seven years of plenty; and the lean kine and thin ears, so many years of famine, Gen. xli. 26, 27. Again, in the parable of the sower, the seed and tares, signified such and such persons, and were emblems of them. Also, *That rock was Christ,* 1 Cor. x. 4. that is, was a figure and representation of him; so the bread is the body of Christ, a figure,[6] sign, and symbol of it. Christ compares himself to a corn of wheat falling into the ground and dying, and reviving and bringing forth fruit, expressive of his sufferings and death, and of the blessed consequences thereof, John xii. 24. Bread-corn is a figure of Christ, as prepared for food, which is beaten out, winnowed, ground, kneaded, and baked, ere it becomes proper food for men; so Christ, by his various sufferings, being bruised, broken, crucified, and sacrificed for us, becomes proper food for faith; and as such is he represented, viewed, and received in the ordinance of the supper. Bread is the main sustenance of men, and is called the staff of bread, being the staff of life; which is of a very strengthening and nourishing nature, and is the principal means of maintaining and preserving life; of all which use is a crucified Christ, as he is held forth to faith, both in the preaching of the gospel and in the administration of this ordinance.

2*dly,* The wine is another part of this ordinance, and of the matter of it, and one of the outward elements of it, a symbol of the blood of Christ. It is a question, whether the wine used at the first institution of the ordinance was red or white; at the passover that which was the best, whether red or white, was ordered to be used, the red was generally so accounted; see Prov. xxiii. 31. Isa. xxvii. 3. it is reckoned by some a matter of indifference; and therefore some, to shew their sense of it as such, and to assert their christian liberty, have sometimes used the one, and sometimes the other; though it may not be essentially necessary, I cannot but be of opinion, that the red, called the blood of the grape, is most expressive of, and bears a greater resemblance to the blood of Christ, it is a symbol of, Gen. xlix. 11. Isa. lxiii. 2. It is also a question, whether the wine used was mixed or pure; since it was usual with the Jews, whose wines were generous, to mix them, Prov. ix. 2. but there is no need to dilute them in our climates; and as the quantity is so small drank at the ordinance, there is no danger of intoxication in those who are least used to it; though it is certain, mixing wine and water very early obtained, even in Justin's time; but that there should be a mystery in it, signifying, the blood and water which sprung from the side of Christ when pierced, and the union of the two natures in him, seems too fanciful. However,——1. The wine is a symbol of the blood of Christ; for Christ says of it, *This is my blood,* that is, a figure and representation of it; not that it was really changed into the blood of Christ, for it is called, *the fruit of the vine,* as before

---

[5] Ecquam tam amentem esse putas, qui illud quo vescatur, deum credat esse? Cicero de Natura Deorum, 1, 3. c. 19.

[6] Acceptum panem et distributum discipulis, corpus illum suum fecit, hoc est corpus meum dicendo, id est, figura corporis mei, Tertull. adv. Marcion. l. 4. c. 40.

observed, after it was poured into the cup and blessed, Matt. xxvi. 28, 29. and the apostle Paul says, *The cup of blessing which we bless, is it not the communion of the blood of Christ?* 1 Cor. iv. 6. and it is a symbol of it, not as in his veins, but as *shed* from the various parts of his body, particularly his hands, feet, and side, when pierced; and as wine is squeezed out of the grape in the wine-press, so the blood of Christ was pressed from him, when it pleased the Lord to bruise him, and when he trod the wine-press of divine wrath; and as wine cheers the heart of man, so the blood of Christ, applied by the Spirit, speaks peace and pardon to guilty minds, and puts joy and gladness into broken hearts and wounded spirits. The wine in the supper is called, *The blood of the New Testament;* and the cup, *The New Testament in Christ's blood;* by which is meant, the covenant of grace, sometimes called a testament or will, which became of force by the death of Christ, the testator, and which was ratified, its blessings and promises, by the blood of Christ; which is therefore called, *The blood of the everlasting covenant,* Heb. xiii. 20.——2. The wine in the supper is a symbol of the love of Christ, shewn in the shedding of his blood to obtain the remission of the sins of his people; which *love is better than wine*, than the most ancient, the most generous, the most pure and refined; and therefore the church determines to remember it more than that; *We will remember thy love more than wine*, and which is particularly done in the ordinance of the supper, Cant. i. 2, 4.

Now the bread and the wine being two separate articles, may denote and shew forth the death of Christ; the body or flesh being separated from the blood, and the blood from that, in which the life is, death follows; and these being distinctly attended to, is expressive of that separation; and yet both together make a feast, and afford nourishment, refreshment, and delight: with food there must be drink, and when with bread, wine, both made a banquet; Christ's church is a banquetting-house, and the banquet in it, like Esther's, is a banquet of wine; such is the ordinance of the supper, a feast of fat things, of wine on the lees well refined.

Thirdly, The next to be considered are the significant and expressive actions used by the administrator and the receiver; both with respect to the bread and the wine.

1*st*, With respect to the bread.——
1. By the administrator; Christ, in his own person, at the first institution of the ordinance, and by his ministers, under his direction, and by his orders and example, in all succeeding ones.

1. Christ *took* the bread. An emblem of his body, which he took, being actually formed; and consisting of flesh and blood, he partook of it in the fulness of time; he took upon him, not the nature of angels, but the seed of Abraham; he took the human nature, consisting of soul and body, into union with his divine person; and he took this body which he assumed, and offered it without spot to God, an offering and a sacrifice of a sweet-smelling savour; and of this body, his taking the bread in the supper was an emblem, and of his voluntary oblation of it.

2. He *blessed* it. Or as another evangelist has it, he *gave thanks*, Matt. xxvi. 26. Luke xxii. 19. such an action was sometimes used by him at other meals, Matt. xiv. 19. and xv. 36. This designs a separation of the bread from a common to a sacred use, as every thing is sanctified by the word and prayer; by this action the bread was set apart from common use, and appropriated to this solemnity. This is what is sometimes called the consecration of it; but is no other than its destination to this peculiar service. Blessing it, was asking a blessing on it, as spiritual food, that it might be nourishing and refreshing to those who partook of it; and giving thanks, is expressing thankfulness for what is signified by it, for Christ, the true bread the Father gives; for him, the unspeakable gift of his love, and for all the blessings of grace that come by him.

3. He *brake* it. From this action the whole ordinance is denominated, *breaking of bread*, Acts ii. 42. and xx. 7. and it was not only used by Christ at first, as an example to be followed; but by ministers in the churches, in all succeeding ages; in the first church at Jerusalem, and by the disciples at Troas, as the passages referred to shew; and was practised by the apostle at Corinth, and in other places, *the bread which we break*, &c. 1 Cor. x. 16. So Clemens of Alexandria,[7] in the second century, says, "As some divide the eucharist, they suffer every one of the people to take

---

[7] Stromat, l. 1. p. 271.

a part." And Irenæus,[8] before him, calls it, *the broken bread;* and even Ignatius[9] speaks of the bishop and presbytery *breaking the one bread.* And nothing is more common with the ancients than to speak of the *parts* and broken pieces in the supper; yea, to call the supper itself by these names: and this is a very expressive and significant action, and by no means to be omitted; and was used by Christ, not purely for the sake of dividing and distributing the bread; but for the sake of representing his death; it is an emblem of his sufferings, how his *body* was *broken* for us, 1 Cor. xi. 24. how it was torn by the scourges and lashes of the Roman soldiers, at the order of Pilate; how his head and temples were torn by the crown of thorns platted about them; how his hands and feet were pierced with nails, and his side with a spear; and how body and soul by death were torn and parted asunder; and he was brought to the dust of death, and liable to be crumbled into innumerable particles; but that his body was preserved from seeing corruption. Moreover, it is an emblem of the communion of the many partakers of the one bread and of the one body of Christ; *For we, being many, are one bread, for we are all partakers of that one bread,* 1 Cor. x. 17.

4. He gave it to the disciples, Matt. xxvi. 26. So the minister now gives the bread to the deacons, and they distribute it to the people; and thus they did in the times of Justin Martyr;[10] that every one may have his part and portion. So at the extraordinary and miraculous meals of the loaves and fishes, Christ, after looking up to heaven, and having *blessed and broke, he gave the loaves* (broken) *to his disciples, and the disciples to the multitude; and they did all eat and were filled,* Matt. xiv. 19, 20. and xv. 36.

2. There are other significant and expressive actions respecting the bread used by the receiver, or communicant; as to *take* and *eat.*

(1.) He is to *take* the bread, or receive it, according to our Lord's direction to his disciples, *take:* at the Jewish passover every one had a piece of the bread broken set before him, by him that broke it, and he took it in his hand;[11] and, as before observed from Clemens, it was the usage of the church at Alexandria, for every one of the people to *take* his part of the eucharist when divided; and so Dionysius,[12] bishop of the same place, speaks of one at the Lord's table, *stretching out his hand to receive* the sacred food; and Cyril of Jerusalem[13] says, it was received in the hollow of the right hand, the left-hand being underneath it; for as yet it was not put into the mouth by the administrator, as now the wafer is, by a popish priest. This action of taking the bread, is an emblem of the saints receiving Christ by the hand of faith, and all the blessings of grace with him, John i. 12. see Col. ii. 6.

(2.) The receiver is to *eat* the bread, being taken; not as common bread, and as at a common meal; but in an ordinance-way, being separated from common to holy use, and as a symbol of the body of Christ; and he eats it in such a way worthily, when he discerns the Lord's body in it, as represented by it, and can distinguish that from it, and by faith feed on it; for this is not to be understood of an oral manducation, or a corporal eating of the flesh and body of Christ, which the Capernaite Jews stumbled at, saying, *How can this man give us his flesh to eat?* but of a spiritual eating it by faith; Socinus[14] says, that nothing but bread and wine are received in the Lord's Supper, either by believers or unbelievers, neither corporally nor spiritually. It is by faith believers eat the flesh and drink the blood of Christ; it is by faith Christ dwells in their hearts; and it is by faith they live upon him, and by him; *He that eateth me, even he shall live by me,* John vi. 57. it denotes a participation of Christ, and of the blessings of grace by him: to eat of this bread spiritually, is no other than *the communion of the body of Christ,* or an having fellowship with him, while feeding on it, and an appropriation and enjoyment of spiritual blessings in him: as bread taken into the mouth and chewed, is received into the stomach, and digested there, and becomes incorporated into the very substance of a man, and by which he is nourished and refreshed; so Christ being received and fed upon by faith, believers are one body and

---

[8] Adv. Hæres. 1. 5. c. 2.
[9] Epist. ad Ephes. p. 29.
[10] Apolog. 2. p. 97.
[11] See my Exposition of Matt. xxvi. 26.
[12] Apud Euseb. Eccl. Hist. 1. 7. c. 9. Vid. Theodorit. Hist. Eccl. 1. 5. c. 18.
[13] Catech. Mystagog. 1. 5. s. 18.
[14] De Cœna Domini Tract. Brev. p. 754. inter opera ejus. Tom. 1.

spirit with him, have union to him and communion with him, there is a mutual indwelling of Christ and them, they are one bread. And having spiritual appetites, hungering and thirsting after Christ, they feed upon him, and grow up in him: the encouragement to eat this bread, as a symbol of Christ's body; and the argument enforcing it is, *This is my body which is given for you*, Luke xxii. 19. a token of the body of Christ, given for them: as their daily bread is the gift of God, and prayed for as such, so Christ, the true bread from heaven, is the gift of his Father, a free-grace-gift; and may be freely fed upon; and his body, which is signified by the bread, is given by himself an offering and a sacrifice to God *for*, in the room and stead of, his people; the phrase denotes the voluntary substitution of Christ in their stead, to make atonement for their sins, being delivered for their offences into the hands of justice and death, on account of them; and therefore they may be encouraged to lay hold upon him by faith, and take him to themselves, as their Saviour and Redeemer; it is thus expressed by the apostle Paul, in 1 Cor. xi. 24. *This is my body which is broken for you;* a sign of Christ's broken body, and so fit food for faith to feed upon; and by it is signified, that the sufferings Christ endured in his body, were in the room and stead of his people, to make satisfaction to divine Justice for their sins; and since he, the passover-Lamb, is *sacrificed for them*, they have great encouragement to keep the feast, to eat the broken bread, and to *do this*, as they are directed, *in remembrance of* Christ's body being given a sacrifice for them; and of its being broken, by the hand of divine Justice, in their room and stead, Luke xxii. 19. 1 Cor. xi. 24.

2*dly*, There are also very significant and expressive actions to be performed, both by the administrator and receiver, with respect to the wine.

1. By the administrator; after the example of Christ, *who took the cup, and gave thanks, and gave it to them,* the disciples, Matt. xxvi. 27. He *took the cup*, wine being first poured into it, which, though not expressed, is implied, and the thing signified by it, is the shedding or pouring out of the blood of Christ, aftermentioned, ver. 28. or the pouring out his soul unto death. Christ's taking it, shews his readiness and willingness to drink of it himself, John xviii. 11. and then he *gave thanks*, for the blessings of grace, which came through his blood, of which this was the symbol; such as justification by his blood, remission of sins, for which it was shed, redemption through it, and peace by the blood of his cross: and having given thanks, *he gave it to them*, his disciples, to drink of it; his immediate disciples drank of the cup of sufferings, as well as partook of the blessings of his grace; here not the former, but the latter is meant.

2. Other actions were to be performed by the receiver; particularly one, every one was to drink of the cup; *Drink ye all of it*: this shews that the ordinance was to be administered under both species; as the bread was to be eaten, the wine was to be drank; which is confirmed by the apostle's account of it, 1 Cor. xi. 25—29. and all were to drink of it; the cup is not to be denied to the common people, and restrained to the minister, as by the papists; both clergy and laity partook of it, from the earliest ages, as appears by innumerable instances in the writings of the ancients, quite down to the council of Constance, in the fifteenth century, when it was ordered not to be given to the common people; *hoc non obstante*, the institution of Christ, and the practice of the primitive church as the edict of the council expresses it.[15] But according to the first institution of the ordinance, and the explanation of it by the apostle Paul, any and every man who examined himself aright, might drink of the cup, as well as eat of the bread: which drinking is to be understood in a spiritual sense, as eating before; and both are done by close meditation on the sufferings of Christ, and by a special application and appropriation of the blessings of grace by faith; the wine is not to be drank as common wine, but as a symbol of the blood of Christ; and the encouraging motive is, *This is my blood of the New Testament*, a token of it, by which the New Testament, or the dispensation of the covenant of grace, under the gospel, is ratified and confirmed; *which is shed* freely and abundantly; as it was in the garden, in the hall, and especially on the cross; *for many*, for as many as are ordained to eternal life; for as many as Christ has

---

[15] Quæ hæc est in verbis Pharisaicis audacia? quæ uno edicto anti-christi impietas et truculentia? Aonii Palearii Testimonium, c. 14. p. 344.

given himself a ransom for; for as many as are made righteous by Christ's obedience; and for the many sons the great Captain of salvation will bring to glory: and this is shed for them; it was shed for *the remission of sins;* by which it is procured in a way consistent with the holiness and justice of God; and in this ordinance the faith of the Lord's people is directed to the blood of Christ to look for it.

Fourthly, The subjects of this ordinance, or who are the proper persons to be admitted to it, as communicants.

1. Not infants. In a literal and natural sense, bread and wine are not food for them, but milk; and in a spiritual sense, they are not capable of eating the body and drinking the blood of Christ by faith; nor of examining themselves, previous to such eating and drinking; nor of recollecting, remembering, and shewing forth the death of Christ. In the third century, infant communion was admitted of, on a mistaken sense of John vi. 53. Indeed, infants have as good a right to this, as to the ordinance of baptism, which they were admitted to in the same century, on a like mistaken sense of John iii. 5. and which practice of infant communion continued in the Latin church six hundred years after, and still does in the Greek church.

2. Adult persons, who have the use of reason, and know what they do, are the proper subjects of this ordinance. Yet only regenerate persons, who are quickened by the Spirit of God; for such only have spiritual life in them, and are only capable of receiving spiritual food, for the maintenance of it; such only can discern spiritual things, and so the Lord's body, which they that discern not, eat unworthily; such only have their taste changed, and can relish divine things: such only hunger and thirst after Christ, and can be satisfied with feeding on him by faith, and be nourished thereby: to others it must be a dry breast, and of no use.

3. Ignorant persons, are unfit for this ordinance. Such who partake of it, ought to know themselves, the sinfulness of their state by nature, and the guilt of sin; that they may see their need of, and be affected with the grace of God in the remission of their sins, through the sufferings, death, and bloodshed of Christ; they ought to have knowledge of Christ, of his person and offices, and especially of him as crucified, and as being the propitiatory sacrifice for sin; they ought to have knowledge of God as their covenant-God, whose covenant, testament, and will, is ratified and confirmed by the blood of Christ; and they ought to be acquainted with the various doctrines of the gospel, which this ordinance has a connection with; as justification, pardon of sin, reconciliation, atonement, &c. so Justin, in his time says, [16] It is not lawful for any other to partake, but he that believes that what things are taught to them are true.

4. Persons scandalous in their lives and conversations, are by no means to be allowed subjects of this ordinance; *with such* we ought *not to eat,* described 1 Cor. v. 11. that is, at the Lord's table.

5. None but penitent sinners, and true believers, and those baptized, upon a profession of their repentance and faith, are to be allowed communicants at this ordinance; for such only can look to Christ whom they have pierced, and mourn, and exercise godly sorrow and evangelical repentance; such only can eat the flesh and drink the blood of Christ in a spiritual sense by faith; to such only Christ's flesh is meat indeed, and his blood drink indeed; such only can by faith discern the Lord's body, and please him in this ordinance; for without faith it is impossible to please God; wherefore a man, before he eats, should examine himself, whether he has true repentance towards God, and faith in our Lord Jesus Christ; whether he is truly sensible of sin, and humbled for it, and believes in Christ for the remission of it, 1 Cor. xi. 28. 2 Cor. xiii. 5.

Fifthly, The ends of this ordinance; which are to be answered by it.

1. To shew forth the death of Christ; to declare his death, that he did die for the sins of his people; to set forth the manner of his death, by crucifixion, by his being pierced, wounded, bruised, and broken; and to express the blessings and benefits of his death, and the faith of his people in them, and thankfulness for them; for in this ordinance Christ is evidently set forth as crucified and slain.——2. To commemorate the sacrifice of Christ; Christ was once offered, and needs not to be offered up again; he has by one offering made perfect atonement for sin; but because Christ the passover is sacrificed for us, we should keep this feast as a memorial of his

---

[16] Apolog. 2. p. 97, 98.

sacrifice, and through it look to Christ, the Lamb of God, who takes away the sins of men.———3. To remember the love of Christ in dying for us, and in becoming a sacrifice for sin; hence he directed his disciples both to eat the bread and drink the wine in remembrance of him, of his body being broken and of his blood being shed for them; that is, to remember his love to them, which he expressed thereby, 1 Cor. xi. 24, 25.———4. To shew our love to Christ, and thankfulness to him, for the blessings of his grace, by an attendance on this ordinance; we should call upon our souls, and all within us, to bless his name, and not forget his benefits, especially the great benefit of the redemption of our lives from destruction, by his blood, sufferings, and death.———5. Another end of it is to maintain love and unity with each other; for by joining together in holy fellowship in this ordinance, we keep the unity of the spirit in the bond of peace. But by no means is this ordinance to be used to qualify persons to bear any office under any government, and in any city or corporation. This is a vile and scandalous prostitution of it, which is only intended for sacred uses.

Sixthly, The adjuncts of this ordinance, the circumstances attending it, and the concomitants and consequences of it.

1. The time of administering it is to be considered; not the time of day, morning, noon, or evening, which latter was the time of the first celebration of it, and is most suitable to a supper; but what day of the week or year, which in ancient times, was variously observed; some were for keeping it every day in the week, and considered it as daily food; others were for observing it four times in the week; and others every Lord's day, which Dr. Goodwin[17] thinks is the stated fixed time for it in scripture; and so others. The disciples at Troas met together on the first day to break bread; but whether they did so for that purpose every first day, is not clear and certain. Some kept it once a month, as many churches do now; at length it came to be observed only three times in the year, at the three grand festivals; and even to once a year. But though the precise time seems not to be ascertained in scripture, yet it is plain that it ought to be often practised; as may be concluded from the apostle's words, *As oft as ye eat this bread and drink this cup*, &c. And from the nature of the ordinance, it being in memory of Christ, which ought to be frequent; and a spiritual repast for souls, which ought to be often repeated.———2. The gesture of the body to be used at it, whether kneeling, standing, or sitting; the former of these looks too much like the adoration of the host, the Papists plead for; standing is more eligible, being the gesture of servants, ready to do the will of their masters; but sitting is to be preferred, being a table-gesture, and conformable to the practice of Christ and his diciples, at the first institution of the ordinance.———3. The place where celebrated; not in private houses, unless when the churches were obliged to meet there in time of persecution; but in the public place of worship, where and when the church convened; so the disciples at Troas *came together* to break bread; and the church at Corinth came together in one place to eat the Lord's Supper, Acts xx. 7. 1 Cor. xi. 18, 20, 33. for this being a church ordinance, is not to be administered privately to single persons; but to the church in a body, assembled for that purpose.———4. When the supper was ended, an hymn was sung by Christ and his apostles, Matt. xxvi. 30. which fulfilled what was prophetically spoken of Christ, and by him, Psalm xxii. 22. and to this Pliny may be thought to have respect when he says, that Christians at their meetings sung an hymn together to Christ, as to a God; and by a sacrament, bound themselves not to commit such and such sins.[18]———5. A collection was made for the poor, and distributed to them; which, perhaps, the apostle may have some respect unto, 1 Cor. xvi. 1, 2. and so Justin says,[19] When prayer and thanksgiving were finished, the richer sort, and as many as would, freely contributed what they thought fit; and what was collected was deposited with the president, out of which were relieved the fatherless and widows, the sick, and those in bonds, and strangers; and a very fit season this to make a collection for the poor, when the hearts of believers are regaled with the love of Christ, and enlarged by it.———6. The continuance of this ordinance is to the second coming of Christ, 1 Cor. xi. 26.

---

[17] Government of Churches, b. 7. ch. 5. p. 328, &c.

[18] Epist. l. 10. ep. 97.

[19] Ut Supra.

and so as it shews forth the end of his first coming to die for his people, it assures them of his second coming; and it is not to be made a question of, that this ordinance, and all other public ordinances of the present dispensation, and the ministers of them, will continue to the end of the world, to the second coming of Christ, and then all will cease, Matt. xxviii. 20. Rev. xxi. 23. and xxi. 5.

CHAP. III.

OF THE PUBLIC MINISTRY OF THE WORD.

NEXT to the ordinances of Baptism and the Lord's Supper, is the Public Ministration of the Word; which is an ordinance of Christ, under the gospel-dispensation, to be continued in the church unto the end of the world. Christ, as the ascended Lord and King, having received gifts for men, gives them to men, qualifying them for the work of the ministry; which work is to be exercised by them until all the elect of God are gathered in, the members of Christ's body, the church, completed, and the number of the saints perfected, and all brought to a state of maturity in grace, and to everlasting glory and happiness; all which and more may be observed in Eph. iv. 11, 12, 13.

I. The public ministry of the word is an ordinance of Christ in the New Testament, and to be continued till his second coming; it is not, indeed, confined to the New Testament, nor peculiar to it, though most eminent in it.

First, There was something similar to it from the beginning, during the Old Testament dispensation.

1. In the patriarchal state; the gospel was first preached by the Son of God to Adam and Eve, in the garden of Eden; the great salvation first began to be spoken by him, who revealed himself as the *Seed of the woman,* that should *bruise* the *head* of the serpent, Gen. iii. 15. which was the grand text the patriarchs preached from; the truths and doctrines contained in which, as handed down to them, they opened and explained to their posterity, according to the revelation of the mind and will of God made to them. In the times of Enos, the grandson of Adam, social worship was set up, and men began to perform the public exercises of religion, Gen. iv. 26. Enoch, the seventh from Adam, prophesied or preached of the second coming of Christ to judge the world; and no doubt, as he prophesied or preached of that, so of the first coming of Christ, to save men. Noah was the *eighth preacher of righteousness;* for so the words in 2 Pet. ii. 5. may be rendered;[1] though they will admit of another sense, "Even a preacher of the righteousness of faith," of which he was an heir, Heb. xi. 7. and Christ, by his Spirit in him, preached to a disobedient multitude with much long-suffering and patience, 1 Pet. iii. 19, 20. Enoch, the seventh from Adam, was one; who the other six preachers were, is not said. The first Adam, no doubt, was one, whom God, as a learned divine[2] says, "made for this end, that he might be a witness, a *preacher,* and a praiser of his virtues and works, and, as the common master of mankind, might admonish and instruct his children and grand-children what they might hope for, or fear, in this life and after it." And righteous Abel was another, who not only preached while alive, *but being dead, yet speaketh:* and perhaps it may not be very difficult to find out the other four. The distinction of the sons of God, professors of religion, and the sons of men, profane persons, obtained in the times of Noah, and before, Gen. vi. 2. Maimonides[3] observes, that their wise men say of the prophets that went before them, of the house of the judgment of Eber, and the school of Methuselah, that they were all prophets, and taught men as preachers, doctors, and preceptors do. As Abraham had the gospel preached to him, so he preached it to others, as he had opportunity; the *three hundred and eighteen* servants born in his house, were *trained* up, or *instructed*[4] by him in religious things, as the word used signifies, Gen. xiv. 14. and a testimony of this is borne of him by the Lord himself, Gen. xviii. 19. In the times of Job, who seems to have lived before the giving of the law, the sons of God, professors of religion, met together on a certain stated day, to present themselves, soul and body to the Lord, in the performance of religious duties, which was but their reasonable service; and though then they had no

---

[1] Vid. Poli Synopsin in loc et alios criticos, Zegerum, Drusium, &c.
[2] Witsii Ægyptiac. l. 2. c. 15. s. 5. p. 179.
[3] Moreh Nevochim, par. 2. c. 39.
[4] הניכיו Catechumenos suos, Drusius.

written word to read or explain, yet they had a revelation of the mind and will of God to them, by one means or another; as in visions, by dreams, &c. which they kept not from, but made known to one another, Job. vi. 10. see chap. iv. 12—19.

2. Under the Mosaic dispensation there was a tabernacle pitched, called, the *tabernacle of the congregation;* and by Onkelos, *the tabernacle of the house of doctrine;* where the people resorted and sought doctrine. Priests and Levites were appointed, among other things, to instruct the people of Israel; they were interpreters and expounders of the law of Moses to them; the tribe of Levi in general, Deut. xxxiii. 10 and the priests, the sons of Aaron particularly, Lev. x. 11. hence we read of *a teaching priest,* and that *the priest's lips should keep knowledge,* and publish it, 2 Chron. xv. 3. Mal. ii. 7. And the Levites also, who were dispersed among the tribes, were employed in this way; in the times of Jehoshaphat they taught the people the law of the Lord throughout all the cities of Judah; and in the times of Josiah they are described as those who *taught all Israel what was holy to the Lord,* 2 Chron. xvii. 9. and xxxv. 3. and in the times of Ezra and Nehemiah, they *read in the book of the law distinctly,* in the hearing of all the people; *and gave the sense, and caused them to understand the reading,* Neh. viii. 8.

3. Under the first and second temples were prophets, who also were interpreters and expounders of the law and instructors of the people; some of which were trained up for that purpose; hence we read of companies, colleges or schools of the prophets, and of the sons or disciples of the prophets, at Naioth, Bethel, and Jericho: some were more immediately raised up and inspired by God. And these prophets had certain places and stated times, weekly and monthly, where and when the people resorted to them for counsel, direction, and instruction; as appears from 2 Kings iv. 23. the note of Gersom on the place is, " It seems, that in those days, they used to come before great men, to hear their words; and they taught them in the way in which they should walk, and the work they should do;" see 2 Kings iv. 38. and vi. 32. The prophesies of Isaiah, Jeremiah, Ezekiel, and others, were delivered as the word of the Lord, and published separately and singly, as sermons and discourses to the people; and particularly it is observed of Ezekiel, that the people came in a body and sat before him, and heard him, and seemingly with great attention and with much pleasure and delight; but it is complained of them, that they only heard his words, but did them not, Ezek. xxxiii. 31, 32.

4. Some time after the Babylonish captivity, synagogues were erected, and synagogue-worship set up; one part of which lay in public reading and preaching the law in them every Sabbath-day; and this was a practice which had obtained *of old time,* long before the times of Christ and his apostles; as appears from Acts xv. 21. In these synagogues our Lord himself taught, and it was a custom with him so to do, and which he was allowed; and we read of his going into the synagogue at Nazareth on a sabbath-day, where he stood up to read, and had the book of the prophet Isaiah delivered to him, which he opened, and out of it read his text, and then explained and applied it, Luke iv. 15—21. And so the apostles of Christ preached the word of God in the synagogues of the Jews; and which they were not only allowed, but were called upon by the rulers of the synagogue at a certain place, to give a word of exhortation to the people, if they had any; by which it appears, that it was not only usual to read the law, but to preach or deliver out a discourse to the people; and accordingly, we have an account of a sermon the apostle Paul preached in the synagogue, at their invitation, Acts xiii. 5, 15, 16, &c. and this custom of the synagogue is confirmed by Philo the Jew,[5] who says, that when " they come to the holy places, called synagogues, according to their age in order, the young men sit under the elders (at their feet,) and with a decent composure attend to hearing; when one taking the book, reads; and another one of the most skilful explains what is not known," or is more obscure.

Secondly, The public ministry of the word more clearly and generally obtained under the New Testament, or gospel-dispensation, according to the prophecy of it, Isa. ii. 3. The first public preacher of this kind, and under this dispensation, was John the Baptist; *The law and the prophets were until John,* Luke xvi. 16. he came first

---

[5] Quod Omnis Probus, p. 877.

preaching in the wilderness of Judea, in a very loud and clamorous way; he was *the voice of one crying*, ϐοωντος, *of one bellowing like an ox*, as the word signifies. The doctrine he preached was the baptism of repentance for the remission of sins; which though rejected by the Scribes and Pharisees, was received by publicans and harlots; and this was called, *his course*, the course of his ministry, which he fulfilled in a very public manner, to all the people of Israel, Acts xiii. 24, 25. Our Lord Jesus Christ, whose forerunner John was, was *the minister of the circumcision*, the minister of the word to the circumcised Jews; he was sent of God to preach the gospel to them, and was anointed with the gifts and graces of the Spirit of God, without measure, for that purpose; at whose doctrine his audience was astonished; he spoke such words of grace and wisdom as never man spake, to the amazement of those that heard him; and this he did in the most public manner, in the synagogues and in the temple. The apostles of Christ were called and sent forth by him to be public ministers of the word; they were called by him from their nets to be fishers of men; they were sent forth by him at first to preach the gospel to the lost sheep of the house of Israel; but after his resurrection he enlarged their commission, and sent them into all the world, to teach all nations, and preach the gospel to every creature; and since, there has been a succession of ordinary ministers of the word, more or less, in all ages, whom Christ, by bestowing gifts upon them, has made pastors and teachers, able ministers of the New Testament, and faithful dispensers of the mysteries of grace. For,

Thirdly, The public ministry of the word is an ordinance of Christ. There are private teachings, which are not only commendable, but are obligatory on men; as on the heads of families, parents, and masters; parents are to teach their children, and bring them up in the nurture and admonition of the Lord; and masters are to instruct their servants, and command their household to keep the way of the Lord; and even women, particularly aged women, are to be *teachers of good things*; and every man who has received a gift, though only for private use, should minister it to one another in private conference and conversation; but it is the public ministry of the word which is the special ordinance of Christ for public good and for general usefulness. This is not a device of men for sinister ends, and with selfish and lucrative views; but is by the appointment of Christ, who ordered his disciples, that what they heard in the ear, they should *preach upon the house-tops*; that is, in the most public manner; and therefore sent them into all the world, to preach the gospel to every creature under heaven; and accordingly the apostle Paul, that eminent minister of the word, preached it publicly, as well as from house to house, and even from Jerusalem round about to Illyricum. It is Christ that appears to men, and calls them, and makes them able and faithful ministers of the New Testament; hence such are called *ministers of God*, of his making, and not man's; and *good ministers of Jesus Christ*; educated, not at schools and academies, but *nourished up in the words of faith and of good doctrine*. The gifts qualifying them for such service are from Christ; the apostle Paul himself was made a minister of the gospel, *according to the gift of the grace of God given unto him*; and it is he who gives gifts to ordinary ministers of the word, and makes them pastors and teachers in his churches; the apostles had their mission and commission from him, John xx. 21. and so all ministers of the word in successive ages; for *how shall they preach, except they be sent?* Rom. x. 15. and they have their doctrines from him, which they are to preach; the words of the wise are from *one Shepherd*, who is Christ; and it is with words and doctrines from him, they, as under-shepherds, are to feed the flock, even the doctrines of the gospel; which are not of man, nor taught by man, but are by the revelation of Christ; particularly such as pardon by his blood, justification by his righteousness, and atonement by his sacrifice; which he has ordered to be published in his name, to all nations, and which accordingly has been, Luke xxiv. 47. Acts xiii. 38, 39.

Fourthly, The public ministry of the word is a standing ordinance, to be continued to the second coming of Christ; there will be ministers, and so a ministry unto the end of the world, Matt. xxviii. 20. and xxiv. 3, 14. and this will not be until all the elect of God are gathered in; the world, and the continuance of it, is for their sakes; the reason why the coming of Christ to destroy the world is seemingly deferred, is, because God is not willing that any of his beloved ones should perish, but that all should come to repentance;

and when they are all brought in, he will then come and burn the world: hence the work of the ministry, Christ has given gifts to men to qualify them for, will be continued,

1. Until all the elect of God *come to the unity of the faith*, until all and every one of them believe in Christ; for as many as are ordained unto eternal life, do and shall believe in him; and as faith comes by hearing the word, the ministration of it will be continued until they all believe.——2. Until they all and every one come to *the knowledge of the Son of God*, whom to know is life eternal; and this knowledge is by the Spirit of wisdom and revelation, and which Christ himself gives, and that by means of the word, called, the word of knowledge; which must be continued till all know him from the least to the greatest; and their knowledge, which is now in part, is perfect. ——3. Until they come *to a perfect man;* that is, until the church of Christ, which like a man, consists of various members, is complete, and all the members joined into one body, and set in their proper place, and become as one man; and till every individual is perfect; not only as to parts, but as to degrees, and that in faith, in knowledge, in holiness, and in every grace. And,——4. Until they come *unto the measure of the stature of the fulness of Christ;* that is, the mystical body of Christ, his church, which is his fulness, and will appear so; when all the elect are gathered in, and are filled with the graces of the Spirit, and these at their full growth, and they have arrived to their just proportion in the body, and to the measure of their stature in it they are appointed to; and till all this is accomplished, the gospel-ministry will continue; see Eph. iv. 12, 13. I proceed to shew,

II. That the ministry of the word is a work; it is called *the work of the ministry*, Eph. iv. 13. it is a ministering work, a service, and not a dominion; such who are employed in it have not the dominion, neither over the faith nor over the practice of men, no further than enjoined by the word of God: the ministry is a service, as the word imports, and not a *sinecure;* there is business to be done, and a great deal of it; enough to employ all the time and talents of ministers, and no room nor leisure to indulge to sleepiness, to laziness, and slothfulness: and it is a laborious work; the ministers of the gospel are not to be loiterers, but labourers in Christ's vineyard; they labour in the word and doctrine, which requires much reading of the scriptures, frequent prayer, and constant meditation and *study*, in preparing for their work, which is a great *weariness to the flesh;* and much zeal, fervour, and affection in the performance of it, which is attended with much fatigue, and an expense of the animal spirits; to which the apostle may have some respect, 2 Cor. xii. 15. and the ministers of the gospel are not only fellow-labourers with one another, but with the Lord himself in his church; the manuring, cultivation, planting, and watering his vineyard, and the building up of his people in a church-state, are laborious services; so that if the Lord did not go forth working with them, it would be to no purpose; *Neither is he that planteth any thing, neither he that watereth*, which are both parts of the gospel-ministry, but *God that giveth the increase*, success to their ministrations; *And except the Lord build the house, they labour in vain that build it*, 1 Cor. iii. 7, 9. Psalm cxxvii. 1. but the presence of the Lord with them, and the operation of his hands seen in their ministry, are an encouragement to them: and besides, their work is a good work, 1 Tim. iii. 1. A work pleasantly, profitably, and honourably good; pleasant to a minister, whose heart is in it; profitable to them that sit under it, when attended with a divine blessing; and honourable in itself; what more so than to be the servants of the most high God, and to be employed in such service, as to shew unto men the way of salvation? than to be the ambassadors of Christ, and to stand in his stead? than to be stewards of the mysteries of Christ, and of the manifold grace of God? than to be the lights of the world, stars in Christ's right-hand, the messengers or angels of the churches, and the glory of Christ? And it is a work worthy of honour from men; such who labour in it, are *worthy of double honour;* of an honourable maintenance, and of an honourable respect; they are to be received with gladness, to be had in reputation, to be known, owned, and acknowledged by those over whom they are, as their fathers, guides and governors; and to be highly esteemed for their work's sake: and it is the *work of the Lord and of Christ*, 1 Cor. xvi. 10. Phil. ii. 30. to which they are called by Christ, qualified for it by him, and assisted in it; of which he is the sum and substance, and when rightly done, makes for his glory. And in this they should be constant, steadfast, and immoveable, always abounding in it, since their labour is not in vain in the Lord; though no man is sufficient for it of himself; his ability is of God, and his dependance must be upon him both for assistance and success. I go on to inquire,

III. Who are fit and proper persons to be employed in this work.

1. They must be of a good moral character; an immoral man is not fit to be a member of a church, much less a minister of the word: among the qualifications of a bishop, overseer, or pastor of a church, several moral characters are observed; as, that such must be blameless, of good behaviour, and have a good report of them that are without; inoffensive in life and conversation, lest the ministry should be blamed, and lie under reproach: but then he must be more than a moral man, both in theory and practice; a mere moralist is not capable of doing the work of an evangelist or of a gospel-preacher.——2. They must be such who are partakers of the grace of God, in truth, or otherwise they will not be able to speak of divine things feelingly and experimentally, of which they cannot say they have heard and seen, and felt them, and therefore cannot speak of them; in some cases they must be dumb, and not able to speak to them; nor can they have a fellow-feeling with souls tempted and deserted; nor have compassion on the ignorant; nor speak a word in season to weary souls: but then, they must have more grace, have more than in common other christians have; or else, as Moses wished, all the Lord's people would be fit to be prophets and ministers of the word.——3. They must be endowed by Christ with ministerial gifts, such as Christ received for men, and gives unto them, whereby they are made and fitted by him to be pastors and teachers; it is not grace, nor human learning, nor natural parts, which qualify for the ministry of themselves, though they are all meet and useful; but a gift from Christ; the apostle Paul had all the above things, but he ascribes his being a minister of the gospel to neither of them, but to a *gift* he had received, fitting and qualifying him for this important work, Eph. iii. 7, 8. and this gift is in some greater, in others less; but in all where it is, it more or less qualifies for the work of the ministry, Rom. xii. 6.——4. They must be studious in the scriptures, and have a competent knowledge of things contained in them; whereby *the man of God*, the minister of Christ, *may be perfect, thoroughly furnished unto all good works*, and particularly unto the work of the ministry, 2 Tim. iii. 16, 17. They should make the Bible their chief study, and attend to the diligent and constant reading of it, and meditate upon the things in it; and give themselves up wholly to them, that their profiting in the knowledge of the mystery of Christ might be manifest; for as they are to feed the churches *with knowledge and understanding*, it is necessary they themselves should have a good share of such knowledge; and such who are like Apollos, mighty in the scriptures, are as scribes, well *instructed unto the kingdom of God*, Matt. xiii. 52.——5. They must have a call both from God and men to this work; *No man takes this honour to himself, but he that is called of God;* which is the inward call, and is known by the furniture of gifts bestowed upon a man, fitting for such service; and by the providence of God, inclining and directing the church to separate him to the work to which he has called him; and the outward call is by the church itself, upon trial of his gifts. And,——6. They must be sent forth, they must have a mission from Christ, and that by the church, Rom. x. 15. the apostles of Christ were sent forth by him, as he was by his Father, John xx. 21. there were some in Jeremy's time who ran, and were not sent; prophesied, though not spoken to; but these were not true prophets and ministers of God.——7. They must be such who are counted faithful, and *put into the ministry* by the Lord himself; as the apostle Paul was, 1 Tim. i. 12. not who thrust themselves, who intrude into this office, and take it to themselves, without the leave of God or men. ——8. They are the only proper persons to exercise this ministry, to whom it is given, and who have received it of the Lord, and have given themselves up to it: the apostle speaks of the ministry of the word, as what he had *received of the Lord Jesus;* as a gift bestowed on him, a trust committed to him, and therefore was concerned to fulfil it; and directs to it as an argument to be used with Archippus, *to fulfil it*, Acts xx. 24. Col. iv. 17. and therefore such should give themselves up wholly to it, and employ their time and talents in it; addict themselves to the ministration of the saints, as the house of Stephanas did;

and as little as possible entangle themselves with the affairs of life, but give themselves to the ministry of the word and prayer, as the apostles chose, Acts vi. 4.——
9. They should be both *able* and *apt* to teach, have abilities from Christ for this work, who only makes men *able ministers of the New Testament*; and also have utterance of speech, a gift of elocution, so as to be able to clothe their ideas with proper words, conveying in an easy manner the sense of them to the understanding of others; and should seek to find out acceptable and suitable words, as the royal preacher is said to do, Eccles. xii. 10. giving pleasure and profit to those that hear them, 2 Tim. ii. 2. 1 Tim. iii. 2.——
10. They must be such who *study* to shew themselves *workmen that need not be ashamed, rightly dividing the word of truth;* giving the true sense of it, searching into the deep things in it, and imparting to every one their portion, agreeable to their age, of children, young men, and fathers; to children, the sincere milk of the word; to those more grown, strong meat; also should distinguish between saints and sinners, the precious and the vile, giving the children their bread, and not holy things to dogs.

IV. The subject-matter of the work of the ministry, is next to be inquired into. This, in the whole compass of it, takes in the ministration of the word, the administration of ordinances, the exercise of church-discipline, and the whole care of the flock; but that branch of it under consideration is, the ministration of the gospel; and what that is may be learnt,

1*st,* From the names by which it is called.——1. The *ministry of the word*, in general, the apostles proposed to give themselves up to, Acts vi. 4. which is not the word of men, but of God; and which is spoken by the ministers of it as such, and received by the hearers of it, in whom it works effectually, Heb. xiii. 7. 1 Thess. ii. 13. and is called the word of faith, the word of truth, the word of reconciliation, and the word of life and of salvation, Rom. x. 8. Eph. i. 13. 2 Cor. v. 19. Phil. ii. 16. Acts xiii. 26.——
2. The ministration of the Spirit, 2 Cor. iii. 8. so called, because it is to be spoken in words which the Holy Ghost teacheth; and it makes known the things of the Spirit of God, spiritual truths and doctrines, which the natural man receiveth not; and by means of it the Spirit of God, and his grace, are communicated and received; hence a minister of the gospel is described as one that *ministers the Spirit* to men; that is, is the instrument of their receiving the grace and gifts of the Spirit, Gal. iii. 2, 5.——3. The ministration of righteousness, 2 Cor. iii. 9. which is the *word of righteousness;* so called, because therein is *revealed the righteousness of God from faith to faith,* Heb. v. 13. Rom. i. 17. the grand and principal doctrine of it, is justification by the righteousness of Christ, Acts xiii. 39.——4. The ministry of reconciliation, 2 Cor. v. 18. called, the *word of reconciliation,* ver. 19. which is no other than the gospel of peace; the word preaching peace by Jesus Christ, who is Lord of all, Eph. vi. 15. Acts x. 36. which does not propose to men to make their peace with God; but declares that peace is made by the blood of Christ, and that reconciliation, atonement, and satisfaction for sin, are made by the sufferings, death, and sacrifice of Christ.

2*dly,* What this ministry is, may be learnt from what the ministers of Christ are directed to preach, and which they make the subject of their ministrations. As,

1. The gospel. Of the gospel they are ministers; their commission is to preach the gospel; it is the gospel of the blessed God, which is committed to their trust; and there is a woe upon them if they preach not the gospel. Which is called,—(1.) The gospel of the grace of God, Acts xx. 24. it being a declaration of the grace and favour of God in Christ; that salvation is entirely of grace, and not of works, from first to last; that the first step to it, election, is the *election of grace;* that justification is, *freely by the grace of God;* that forgiveness of sins, is *according to the riches of grace;* that adoption is owing to the amazing love of God; and that eternal life is the *gift,* the free grace-gift of God through Christ: all which are the subjects of the gospel-ministry.—(2.) It is often called the gospel of Christ, the word of Christ, and the doctrine of Christ; which treats of his person, as the Son of God; of his offices, as Mediator, Prophet, Priest, and King; and of the grace that is in him; and of the blessings of grace that come by him; and whoever brings not this doctrine, is not to be received and encouraged, 2 John ver. 9, 10.—(3.) The gospel of salvation, the word of salvation, and salvation itself; it is a publication of salvation by Christ; it is the faithful

saying and worthy of all acceptation, that Christ came into the world to save the chief of sinners; it declares, that there is salvation in him, and in no other; and that whoever believes in him shall be saved: this is the gospel every faithful minister preaches, and every sensible sinner desires to hear.

2. Christ and him crucified is the subject-matter, the sum and substance of the gospel-ministry. *We preach Christ crucified;* this is the preaching or the doctrine of the cross; the doctrine of salvation by a crucified Christ; of peace by the blood of his cross; of the reconciliation of God's elect in one body, by the cross; of the atonement and expiation of their sins by his sufferings and death upon it; this the apostle Paul determined to make the subject, and the alone subject, of his ministrations, 1 Cor. i. 23. and ii. 2.

3*dly,* The ministry of the word takes in every thing respecting doctrine; and in general it is required, that it be sound; the words of faith and sound doctrine, the form of sound words, sound speech, which cannot be condemned; and things which become sound doctrine, which are healthful and salutary, the wholesome words of our Lord Jesus; and which are opposed to unsound, unhealthful doctrines, false doctrines, which eat as do a canker: and sound doctrine is such as is according to the scriptures, which are *profitable for doctrine;* from whence every doctrine is to be fetched, and thereby proved and confirmed, according to which every minister of the word is to preach, Isa. viii. 20. and it is by this rule every hearer is to judge of the soundness or unsoundness of it, as the Bereans did, Acts xvii. 11. the doctrine delivered in the ministry of the word should be the same that was preached by Christ and his apostles; the first christians continued stedfastly *in the apostles' doctrine;* and, indeed, if any other doctrine is preached, it is not to be received, Gal. i. 8, 9. and this is the doctrine which is *according to godliness;* which teaches it, encourages, promotes, and enforces it; such as the doctrines of election, of free justification by Christ's righteousness, of full pardon of sin by his blood, and of the final perseverance of the saints; which are no licentious doctrines, though slanderously so charged; but constrain men to live to Christ, who died for them and rose again; and to which every minister of the gospel should take heed: this is the apostle's advice to Timothy, *Take heed to thyself, and to thy doctrine,* 1 Tim. iv. 16. that it be pure and incorrupt, agreeable to the scriptures, the same with the doctrine of Christ and his apostles, and which promotes holiness of life and conversation.

4*thly*, The ministry of the word takes in the several duties of religion, which are to be insisted on in their course; and saints are to be exhorted to the exercise of them upon evangelical principles and motives; they are to be taught to observe whatsoever Christ has commanded, every ordinance of his, and every duty both with respect to God and men; they are to be put in mind to be ready to every good work, and to be careful to maintain them for necessary uses; every duty, public and private, personal, relative, and domestic, as well as every doctrine, are to be inculcated throughout the course of the gospel-ministry.

V. The manner in which the work of the ministry is to be performed may be next observed. And,

1. It should be done diligently and constantly, with great sedulity and perseverance, *in season and out of season,* 2 Tim. iv. 2. and the apostle having mentioned several important doctrines of the gospel, thus charges Titus, *These things I will, that thou affirm constantly,* publicly and privately, and from house to house, as he did, Tit. iii. 8. Acts xx. 20.——2. With great plainness and perspicuity, 2 Cor. iii. 12. and iv. 2. delivering out truth in a clear and open manner, without disguise; not using ambiguous expressions, phrases of a doubtful or double meaning, and an unintelligible jargon of words; but language plain and easy to be understood by those of the meanest capacity; yet not base and sordid, but above contempt; should speak, not in words which man's wisdom teacheth, but in the words of the Holy Ghost, in scripture-language, or what is agreeable to it.——3. Fully and completely; which is done when every truth is preached, and none concealed, and no duty omitted; when nothing that is profitable is kept back, and the whole counsel of God is declared; and when it is preached *fully,* as it was by the apostle Paul; and *full proof of the ministry* is made, which he directs to; and the ministry received of the Lord Jesus is fulfilled in the several parts and branches of it, Rom. xv. 19. 2 Tim. iv. 5. Col. iv. 17. ——4. Faithfully, Jer. xxiii. 28. ministers

are stewards of the mysteries of God, and of his grace; and *it is required of stewards, that a man be found faithful,* as well as wise, 1 Cor. iv. 1, 2. Luke xii. 42. a more honourable character cannot well be had, than what is given of Tychicus, that he was a *beloved brother, and faithful minister in the Lord;* and nothing can be more desirable, or confer a greater degree of honour, than at last to hear from Christ, *Well done, good and faithful servant!* Eph. vi. 21. Matt. xxv. 21, 23.———5. Sincerely; delivering out *the sincere milk of the word;* not corrupting it; not using any artful methods to colour things, and put a false gloss upon them; but exposing truth to public view in its native simplicity, without any sinister ends and selfish views; without any strife and contention, but of good will, to the glory of Christ, and the welfare of immortal souls, 2 Cor. ii. 17. and iv. 2. Phil. i. 15, 16.———6. Fervently; it is said of Apollos, that *being fervent in the Spirit, he spake and taught diligently the things of the Lord,* Acts xviii. 25. and the apostle Paul served God *with his Spirit in the gospel of his Son;* that is, his whole heart and soul were engaged in the ministration of it, Rom. i. 9.——— 7. The gospel, and the truths of it, should be ministered with certainty, and not with doubtfulness; there is such a thing as *the full assurance of understanding* in private christians, Col. ii. 2. and much more should be in ministers of the word; who should not be afraid of being reckoned dogmatical; they should be so; that is, they ought to be at a point about, and be *assured* of the truths they deliver to others; *We believe and are sure that thou art that Christ the Son of the living God,* said the apostles of Christ; and so with respect to every other truth; *We believe, and therefore speak,* with certainty and confidence, 2 Tim. iii. 4. John vi. 69. 2 Cor. iv. 13.——— 8. And so they may, as they should, *speak boldly as they ought to speak,* without the fear of men, which brings a snare; and not seeking to please them; for then they would not be the servants of Christ: thus the apostles, not intimidated with the threats and menaces of men, the persecutions of wicked men, and the opposition of false teachers, *were bold in their God to speak the gospel of God with much contention,* Eph. vi. 19, 20. 1 Thess. ii. 2, 4. ———9. The gospel should be preached consistently; it should be uniform, and all of a piece; no contradiction, no yea and nay in it; the *trumpet* should not give *an uncertain sound;* otherwise it will occasion great confusion in the minds of those that hear it, and throw them into the utmost perplexity, not knowing what to believe. ———10. The word should be dispensed wisely; the ministers of it should be wise, as well as faithful, to give to every one their portion, and that in due season; they should study to be skilful workmen, rightly dividing the word of truth; it requires that they should have the tongue of the learned, to speak a word in season to him that is weary; *he that winneth souls is wise;* and being *crafty,* the apostle says, he *caught the Corinthians with guile,* not with a sinful, but a laudable and commendable one.

VI. The utility of the public ministry of the word may be next considered. And,

1. In general; its use is for the enlargement of the interest of Christ in the world; and it is by means of the gospel being preached to all nations in all the world, that the kingdom of Christ has been spread every where; not only in Judea, where the gospel was first preached, but throughout the Gentile world, multitudes were converted, and churches were set up every where; christianity triumphed, and heathenism every where abolished. Julian the apostate, observing this, in imitation of the christians, and thinking thereby to increase and establish heathenism, appointed lectures and expositions of heathenish dogmas, respecting both morality and things more abstruse, and public prayers, and singing at stated hours, in pagan temples.[3]———2. The ministry of the word is for the conversion of sinners; without which churches would not be increased nor supported, and must in course fail, and come to nothing: but the hand of the Lord being with his ministers, many in every age believe and turn to the Lord, and are added to the churches; by which means they are kept up and preserved: and hence it is necessary in the ministers of the word, to set forth the lost and miserable estate and condition of men by nature, the danger they are in, the necessity of regeneration and repentance, and of a better righteousness than their own, and of faith in Christ; which things are blessed for the turning of men from darkness to

---

[3] Nazianzen orat. 3. adv. Julian. p. 101, 102. Sozomen. Eccl. Hist. l. 5. c. 16.

light, and from the power of Satan unto God.——3. Another use of it is, *For the perfecting of the saints;* for the completing of the number of the elect, in effectual vocation, even of those who are sanctified, or set apart by God the Father, by that eternal act of his, choosing them in Christ; or *for the jointing in of the saints,* as it may be rendered; who were disjointed and scattered abroad by the fall of Adam; these are gathered in by the ministry of the word; so that none shall perish, but all come to repentance; and be inserted into the body of the church, and presented perfect in Christ Jesus: hence after this, and previous to what follows, the phrase, *for the work of the ministry,* is placed; pointing out this two-fold use of it; as *for the perfecting the saints,* so,——4. *For the edifying the body of Christ,* Eph. iv. 12. that is, his church; for it is by means of the word it *maketh increase unto the edifying of itself in love,* ver. 16. and thus the churches in Judea, Samaria, and Galilee, having rest, and peace, and blessed with the ministration of the gospel, *were edified,* and built up in their most holy faith, as individuals are, Acts ix. 31. 1 Cor. xiv. 3. ——5. The principal end and use of it, to which all the others tend, is the glory of God, and which ought to be chiefly in view in the performance of it, 1 Pet. iv. 11.

CHAP. IV.

OF PUBLIC HEARING THE WORD.

THE public hearing of the word is another ordinance of divine service under the gospel-dispensation. Public reading of the scriptures was a part of synagogue-worship, Acts xiii. 15. and xv. 21. see Luke iv. 16, 17. and reading the scriptures publicly obtained in the primitive times of christianity; as appears from Justin Martyr[1] and Tertullian;[2] and in after-times there was a particular officer appointed to this service, called the *lector,* or reader. Public hearing is connected with the public ministry of the word; they go together, and support each other, and the one cannot be without the other: under the former dispensation there was a public hearing of the law, or word of the Lord, at certain stated times and seasons; at the end of every seven years, in the solemnity of the year of release, in the feast of tabernacles the law was to be read *before all Israel, in their hearing;* men, women, and children, were to be gathered together, that they might *hear and learn to fear* the Lord their God, Deut. xxxi. 10—13. at certain times, as at new moons and sabbaths, the people used to come and sit before the prophets, and hear the word of the Lord from their mouths; and even in the Babylonish captivity, it is said to Ezekiel, of the people of the Jews, *They come unto thee as the people cometh;* whence it appears it was a custom and usual so to do; see chap. viii. 1. and xiv. 1. Ezek. xxxiii. 31. when that people were returned from their captivity, in the times of Ezra and Nehemiah, the book of the law was brought forth publicly and read, in the open street, from morning till noon, *before men and women, and those that could understand; and the ears of all the people were attentive to it,* Neh. viii. 2, 3. In some periods of time, under the former dispensation, there was a great scarcity of hearing the word; in the times of Eli, and when Samuel was young, *the word of the Lord was precious;* that is, scarce and rare, as such usually be that are so; for *there was no open vision;* no public prophet, to whom the Lord spoke in vision, and to whom the people could have recourse, to hear and learn, and know the word and will of God. In the times of Asa, the people of Israel had been for a long season *without a teaching priest;* and so without hearing the law, or word of the Lord, from his mouth; they had, as it was sometimes threatened, a famine, *not a famine of bread, nor of thirst for water, but of hearing the words of the Lord,* 1 Sam. iii. 1. 2 Chron. xv. 3. Amos viii. 11. Under the gospel dispensation, opportunities of hearing the word have been more frequent, and of hearing it more clearly, plainly, and fully; of hearing what kings and prophets desired to hear, but heard not; and that by all sorts of people, and oftentimes in great numbers; *The law and the prophets were until John,* read, explained, and heard publicly; *Since that time the kingdom of God is preached,* the gospel of the kingdom, in a clearer manner, and *every man presseth into it,* to hear it, Luke xvi. 16. there were great flockings to hear John, when he came preaching in the wilderness of Judea; and multitudes attended the ministry of Christ and his apostles; in process of time the Jews indeed put away

---

[1] Apolog. 2. p. 98.

[2] De Anima, c. 9.

the word of God from them, and shewed themselves unworthy of it, and even of everlasting life; when the apostles, as they were ordered, turned to the Gentiles and they gladly received it, Acts xxviii. 28. and it is both the duty and privilege of all, who have the opportunity of hearing it, to hear it; *For faith comes by hearing, and hearing by the word of God,* Rom. x. 17. and this is what is to be treated of; concerning which may be observed the following things,

I. The object of hearing, or what is to be heard; this is a matter of moment, and about which men should be cautious; our Lord's advice is, *Take heed what you hear,* Mark iv. 24. not the cunningly-devised fables, and illusory dreams of men are to be attended to, and heard; but *the word of God;* between which there is as much difference as between chaff and wheat, Jer. xxiii. 28. that word, which comes from God, relates his mind and will, especially concerning salvation by Christ, is to be hearkened unto; and whatsoever is delivered by the ministers of the gospel, agreeable to the word of God, which is fetched out of it, and confirmed by it, is to be heard and received, not as the word of man, but as it is in truth, the word of God: not lies, spoken in hypocrisy, as all false doctrines are; for no lie is of the truth; not these, but *the word of truth,* is to be heard and embraced, Eph. i. 13. which comes from the God of truth; the substance of which is Christ, the truth, and which the Spirit of truth leads into the knowledge of, and contains in it nothing but truth: not the law, as in the hands of Moses; that voice of words, which they that heard, intreated they might hear no more, they were so terrible; but the gospel of salvation, which brings the good news and glad tidings of salvation by Christ. When Moses and Elias were with Christ on the mount, the voice there from the excellent glory directed to hear, not Moses and Elias, but the beloved Son of God, saying, *Hear ye him.* The sheep of Christ will not hear the voice of a stranger, which they know not, but the voice of Christ, the great and good Shepherd, in the gospel and in his ministers; which is a voice of love, grace, and mercy; a voice of peace, pardon, righteousness, life, and salvation by Christ; a soul-quickening voice, a very powerful one, a soul-charming, a soul-alluring voice; a comforting and rejoicing one, and therefore very desirable to be heard, and very useful and profitable to attend unto; blessed are the people that hear and know this joyful sound.

II. The act of hearing, which is twofold, internal and external; there may be one, the latter, without the other, the former; sometimes they go together; and then hearing is not only a duty, but grace, benefit, and blessing.

First, There is an internal hearing of the word; when it is so heard as to be understood, and when men know it to be the word of the Lord, as the flock of Christ do, even the poor of the flock, and can distinguish the voice of Christ from the voice of a stranger; when it is heard so as to approve of it, like it, love it, and receive the love of the truth, and that from love to it; when men feel the power of it, enlightening their minds in the knowledge of divine things, attracting their affections to Christ, bowing their wills to him; it coming not in word only, but in power, works effectually in them; when they taste the sweetness of it, and eat it, and it is the joy and rejoicing of their hearts; and they esteem the words of Christ's mouth more than their necessary food; when they hear it so as to believe it, not with a bare temporary faith, but with a spiritual saving faith in God and Christ revealed in it, John v. 24. and when they hear so as to receive the word into their hearts, and it becomes the ingrafted word, and springs up, and brings forth fruit in heart and life.

Should it be asked, how any come by such hearing of the word, since men are naturally and wilfully deaf unto it, are like the deaf adder, which stops her ear to the voice of the charmer, charming ever so wisely; they refuse to hearken, pull away the shoulder, stop their ears, that they should not hear? the answer is, that it is not of themselves, but of the Lord; as the seeing eye, so the hearing ear, both in a natural and in a spiritual sense, is from the Lord, Prov. xx. 12. it is he that gives them ears to hear, which he does not give to all, only to some; when he gives them new hearts and new spirits, then he gives them new ears to hear, what they never heard before, at least in such a manner; he opens their ears and hearts, as he did Lydia's, to attend to the things spoken in the ministry of the word; he circumcises their uncircumcised hearts and ears as to love him, so to hear his word with delight and pleasure; all which is done in regeneration; *He that is of God,* who is born of God, *heareth God's words,* internally and spiritually; *ye therefore*, says Christ to the Jews, *hear them not, because ye are not of God*, are unregenerate persons, John viii. 47.

Secondly, There is an external hearing of the word, which is both a duty and a privilege, since it is the word of God that is heard, and oftentimes much profit arises from it; and it is therefore to be heard, ——1. Constantly, and with great assiduity Prov. viii. 34. the public places of worship, meant by wisdom's gates and doors, where the word is to be heard, are daily or frequently to be attended; if the word is to be preached in season and out of season, it is to be heard as often; or otherwise preaching is to no purpose: much may be lost by a non-attendance on, and a neglect of public worship, as the case of Thomas shews; and much advantage may be got by a perseverant waiting on the means of grace, as the case of the man having an infirmity eight and thirty years, after long waiting at the pool, may encourage to hope for and expect.——2. The word of God should be heard early and eagerly. It is said of Christ's hearers, *that all the people came early in the morning to him in the temple, for to hear him*, Luke xxi. 38. these were such who were swift to hear, and their earliness to hear shewed eagerness to it: an instance of eagerness to hear, we have in Cornelius and his family, who having sent to Joppa for Simon Peter, who was to tell him what he ought to do, prepared to receive him, and therefore when he came, thus addressed him; *Here we are all present before God, to hear all things that are commanded thee of God*, Acts x. 33. they were ready waiting for the preacher, to hear what he had in commission to say unto them; and not the preacher for them, as the custom now is; so the Gentiles at Antioch, having heard the word of the Lord, desired that the same words might be spoken to them the next sabbath, when almost the whole city came together to hear the word of God, so eager and intent were they upon it, Acts xiii. 42, 44.——3. The word of God should be heard attentively; it is observed of Christ's auditory, *that all the people were very attentive to hear him*, Luke xix. 48. or *hung upon him*,[3] as they were *hearing;* they pressed to him, got close about him, and hung as it were upon his lips,[4] to catch every word that dropped from him; as Benhadad's servants, when they waited upon the king of Israel, on account of their master, *diligently observed whether any thing would come from him, and did hastily catch it*, to improve it in their master's favour, 1 Kings xx. 33. When our Lord entered into the synagogue at Nazareth, and had the book of Isaiah given him, out of which he read a passage, and explained it, *the eyes of all in the synagogue were fastened on him*, looked wistly at him, they attentively heard him, and wondered at the gracious words which proceeded out of his mouth, Luke iv. 20, 22. when *the eyes of a fool*, while hearing the word, *are in the ends of the earth*, roving and wandering here and there, and he inattentive to it.——4. The word of God should be heard with reverence; all irreverent looks and gestures should be avoided in hearing it; men should consider in whose presence they are, and whose word they are hearing; not the word of man, but the word of God; *Where the word of a king is, there is power*, and it commands awe and reverence; and much more the word of the King of kings; God is to be feared, and had in reverence, *in the assembly of the saints;* in every part of religious worship there performed, and particularly in hearing his word; we read of some that *tremble* at his word, which I understand not of a slavish fear, and legal terror at it, but of a reverential affection for it, and behaviour under it.——5. The word of God is to be heard with faith, since without it it is unprofitable, Heb. iv. 2. as food not being mixed with a liquid, an agreeable humour in the stomach, is not digested, and becomes unprofitable; so the word, not being mixed with faith, is not concocted, and yields no nourishment.——6. The word of God heard, should be carefully retained, and not let slip,[5] Heb. ii. 1. like leaking vessels, which let out the liquor put into them, or like strainers which immediately let through what is poured into them; such are the forgetful hearers of the word, which ought to be laid up in the mind and memory, as a jewel in a cabinet; and which, when heard, should be kept in an honest and good heart, not only for present use, but for future good, Psalm cxix. 11. I proceed to consider,

III. The various hearers of the word; for all men do not hear alike, and to like

---

[3] Εξεκρίματο, pendebat, Vatablus.
[4] Pendentque iterum narrantis ab ore, Virgil.

[5] Παραρρυῶμεν, perfluamus, Vatablus.

profit and advantage. Some writers[6] distribute hearers into four sorts, whom they compare to the following things; some are like *sponges*, which attract and suck in all, both good and bad; such are those hearers who receive and like all they hear; be it a sound evangelical discourse, they will express their approbation of it; and be it the very reverse, they will commend it as a good discourse, not being able to distinguish between truth and error, sound and unsound doctrine; the best in those hearers is, they are not difficult, but easily pleased. Others are compared to *hour-glasses*, in which the sand runs quick out of one glass into another; so some hearers, what they hear with one ear, they let out at the other, as is usually said. A third sort are compared to *strainers*, cloth-strainers, which let all the good liquor pass through, and retain the dregs and lees; so these let pass, and take no notice of what is valuable, which they hear; but if there is any thing in a discourse that is weak and impertinent, foolish and vain, that they are sure to observe. A fourth sort are compared to a sort of *sieves*, which let pass every thing that is good for nothing, and only retain the fine flour; these are the best of hearers, and who are fed with the finest of the wheat. But our Lord, with much greater propriety, has divided hearers of the word into four sorts also; one he compares to seed that falls on the way side, which the fowls of the air pick up and devour; another sort, to seed that falls on stony ground, or on a rock, which springing up hastily, soon withers and comes to nothing; a third sort, to seed that falls among thorns, which growing up with it, choke it, and it becomes unfruitful; and a fourth sort, to seed that falls on good ground, and brings forth fruit of various degrees, Matt. xiii.

First, One sort is comparable to seed that falls by the way side; by which seem to be meant casual and accidental hearers, who passing by a place of worship stop and step in; not with an intention to hear, but to gratify some curiosity or another; and therefore hear in a very careless and indifferent manner, and forget what they hear as soon as they hear it: these are compared to a way by the side of corn-fields, left for persons to walk on between them, and so a common path, a beaten road; to which their hearts are like, every sin, lust, and evil thought passing and re-passing in them, and become desperately wicked; and as a path thus frequently trodden becomes hard and unsusceptible of seed that falls upon it, so the hearts of men become hard through the deceitfulness of sin, and incapable of receiving any impressions upon them by the word they hear: and as such a way-side must be ploughed, broken up, and opened, ere seed can be received into it; so such hearts of men must be opened, as Lydia's was, to attend to the things spoken in the ministry of the word. These hearers are such who hear, but *understand* not what they hear, as a natural man does not, and so it is lost unto them. Our Lord interprets, *the fowls of the air*, catching away what was sown, and devouring it, of the wicked one, Satan, the devil; and it being in the plural number in the parable, *fowls of the air*, may denote the wicked one with the spiritual wickednesses in high places, satan and his principalities and powers, the devil and his angels, compared to fowls of the air, because of their habitation in it; satan being the prince of the power or posse of devils that dwell in the air; and because of their voraciousness, seeking whom and what they may devour; and as where seed is sowing, birds flock about to pick up what they can; so where there is a ministration and hearing of the word, satan is sure to be there, to hinder the benefit of it as much as in him lies; and who may be said to *catch away that which was sown in the heart;* not grace, which was not sown there, and which where it is, cannot be taken away, but remains; but as Mark and Luke have it, *the word,* that was sown in their hearts; not in their understandings, for such hearers understand it not; nor in their affections, these being distinguished from the stony-ground hearers, who receive the word with joy; but in their memories, and that very slightly, the heart being put for the memory, as in Luke ii. 51. out of which it is suddenly and secretly catched, being made to forget it immediately, by diverting the mind to other objects, and fixing the attention elsewhere, so that the word to such an hearer is entirely useless.

Secondly, Another sort is like to seed that falls on stony-ground, or on a rock, as Luke has it; by which such hearers are meant, who are constant and attentive, understand what they hear in some sort,

---

[6] Vid. Amesium de Casibus Conscientiæ, l. 4. c. 11. p. 187.

and assent to it, *believe* it, at least *for a while*, and make a profession of it, yea, receive it *with joy*, with a flash of natural affection, like Herod, and others of John's hearers, Mark vi. 20. John v. 35. yet but stony-ground still; their hearts are as hard as a rock, unbroken by the word, without any true sense of sin, and repentance for it, and destitute of any spiritual life and motion, stubborn, inflexible, stout-hearted, and far from righteousness. Now it is said of this seed, that it *withered away*, for want of depth of earth; and as Luke has it, because it lacked moisture, and through the scorching heat of the sun, and because it had no root; so hearers, comparable to such ground, and the seed on it, *wither* in their profession; the leaves of profession drop from them like leaves from trees in autumn, and leave them bare and naked; and because of the trouble they meet with in their profession, they are *offended and stumble, and in a time of temptation*, as a time of persecution is, they *fall away*; not from grace they never had, but from the doctrine of grace they professed: which is owing, partly to the word not being sown deeply in their hearts; for as the seed to which they are compared, soon sprung up, because it had but little depth of earth to get through, for the same reason it soon withered away; and so in these hearers, there being only some slight convictions, and superficial knowledge, and a temporary historical faith; but no solid substantial truth and wisdom in the inward parts, they soon decline in their profession: and partly to their not being watered continually with the rain of heavenly doctrine, and the dews of divine grace, and also to the sun of persecution beating upon them they cannot bear, and to their having no root, neither in the love of God, nor in Christ, nor in themselves; the root of the matter not being in them, in process of time they come to nothing.

Thirdly, A third sort is like to seed that falls among thorns, which choke it; these design such who having heard the word, *go forth*, as Luke says, not in acts of growth and fruitfulness, as in Mal. iv. 2. rather in the course of an external profession, as the virgins, wise and foolish, took their lamps of profession, and went forth to meet the bridegroom; or it may be, those hearers may be said to go forth, not to hear the word, but from it; neglecting and forsaking it, as Demas forsook the apostle Paul, having loved the world; of which complexion these hearers seem to be, and so went forth to their worldly business; like those invited to the wedding, who made light of it, and went their way, one to his farm, another to his merchandize. Our Lord interprets the thorns which choked the seed, of worldly cares, deceitful riches, the lusts of other things, and the pleasures of this life, which all are of a surfeiting and suffocating nature. By the *care of the world*, is not meant a laudable care of a man to provide for himself and family, and that he may have to give to them that need; but an anxious, immoderate one, which is, like thorns, distressing, afflictive, and perplexing; and which is vain and fruitless, since by all a man's care and thought, he cannot add a cubit to his stature; and yet so much engross his thoughts, as to hinder the usefulness of the word: riches are *deceitful* things, they do not give the satisfaction they promise, nor continue as long as may be expected; and are sometimes the means of leading out of the right way, and cause men to err from the faith, and drop the profession of it, or prevent their going into the right way, and following Christ, as the young man in the gospel: and like thorns, they are pricking, and pierce men through with many sorrows, who covet after them, 1 Tim. vi. 9, 10. and are injurious to others; the prince, the judge, and the great man, the best of them is as a brier, and the most upright is sharper than a thorn-hedge, who oppress and crush the poor; and they are unprofitable, as to another world, cannot profit in the day of wrath, nor give to God a ransom for the soul: and *other lusts*, worldly and fleshly ones, as they are contrary to the word, they war against the soul, and so are hurtful; and the *pleasures of life* are but for a season, and short-lived, and though they are sweet and pleasant for a while, they are bitterness in the end, and [are found to be vanity and vexation of spirit, and lead to destruction; such hearers, in whom these things prevail, are like the earth, described Heb. vi. 8. Now it is said of the thorns, that they *sprung up*, that is, of themselves, as thorns do, and are not sown and planted; and the lusts signified by them, are the works of the flesh, and spring from corrupt nature; and these *enter* into the heart, and overspread the powers and faculties of the soul, and so *choke* the word, as the thorns the seed, by overtopping it, and it becomes unfruitful, brings forth no fruit, at least none to perfection.

Fourthly, A fourth sort of hearers is like to seed that falls on good ground, and brings forth fruit of various degrees; by whom are meant such who hear, and *understand* what they hear; not merely notionally, but experimentally; into whose hearts the word enters, accompanied with a divine power; the entrance of which give light into the knowledge of divine things; by which such know the worth of it, and prize it above thousands of gold and silver, and can discern things that differ, and approve what is excellent; can distinguish between truth and error, and receive the one and reject the other; these are such hearers who hear the word, and *receive* it, as Mark has it; not into their heads only, but into their hearts, where it has a place, and dwells richly; who receive it not as the word of man, but as the word of God; as his witness and record which he bears of his Son, of his person and divine Sonship, and of eternal life and salvation by him; and receive it gladly, as did the three thousand pricked in the heart; and with all readiness, like the noble Bereans, having searched and examined what they heard; and also receive the ingrafted word with meekness, subjecting their reason to divine revelation; not exercising themselves in things too high for them, rejecting every vain imagination, carnal reasonings, and all high thoughts exalted against the knowledge of Christ: these are such hearers, as it is expressed in Luke, who, *in an honest and good heart, having heard the word, keep it;* where the good ground is explained of a good heart, made so by the Spirit and grace of God; otherwise the heart of man is wicked, yea, desperately wicked; nor is it in the power of man to make his heart good; it is God only that can create a clean and good heart in him; give him an heart of flesh, soft, and tender, susceptible of the word, on which, through divine grace it makes good impressions; and here it is laid up as a rich jewel in a cabinet, and kept and preserved for future use: here what is committed is kept and held fast, such will not part with it, nor depart from it, but keep it without wavering, being established in it, and with it; and stand fast in it, in the profession of it; and these *bring forth fruit with patience;* which fruit they have from Christ, the green fir-tree; and through an ingrafture into him, and abiding in him, as branches in the vine; and which is produced under the influence of the Spirit of God, and makes much for the glory of God; and which appears in the exercise of grace, and in the performance of good works: and this is brought forth *with patience* under sufferings and is increased thereby, and continues until it is brought to perfection; and is in some more, in others less, and in all good fruit, of the same quality, though not of the same quantity, Matt. xiii. 23. Mark iv. 20. Luke viii. 15. I go on to observe,

IV. What is requisite to the right hearing of the word, both before it, at it, and after it.

First, What is necessary previous to hearing the word, and in order to it.

1. Prayer should go before it. Such who are desirous of hearing the word to profit and advantage, should pray for the minister, that he may be directed to what may be suitable to their cases, be assisted in his work, and be greatly blessed to their souls' good: and for themselves, that they might have their minds disposed to hear the word, and be kept from wanderings under it, and that they may understand what they hear, and receive it in the love of it; otherwise how can a blessing on Zion's provisions be expected, when it has not been asked? and how unreasonable is it to blame the preacher, when reflecting on their own conduct, should take the blame to themselves.——2. There should be a previous consideration of the nature, use, and end of this service; that it is intended for the good and edification of the souls of men, and the glory of God; it should be considered of what importance it is to themselves, and how grateful to God when rightly performed, 1 Sam. xv. 22. men should consider into whose presence they are entering, whose word they are about to hear; what attention should be given to it, and what reverence of it! the advice of the wise man should be regarded, Eccles. v. 1. they should consider the advantages which may arise from hearing the word, which they should propose to themselves for their encouragement, and consider what need they stand in of instruction, and what to be instructed in; for if they are wise in their own conceits, and fancy themselves to be wiser than their teachers, there is no hope nor expectation of the word heard being of any advantage to them; it is the meek and humble, God will teach his way, and instruct by his word.——3. An appetite to the word is

necessary to hearing it. The word is food, hearing and receiving it in faith is feeding on it; this cannot be comfortably done without a spiritual appetite; there must be a desire after the sincere milk of the word; the church *desired and sat down*, as the words[7] may be rendered, Cant. ii. 3. desired to sit down under the shadow of Christ, his word and ordinances, and did sit down with delight; and it follows, *His fruit was sweet to her taste;* she had a gust for it, a relish of it; *Blessed are they which do hunger and thirst after righteousness*, the word of righteousness, *they shall be filled*, satisfied with it, as with marrow and fatness: to hear the word without an appetite, is like a man sitting down at a table well furnished with provision, with delicious food, and well dressed and served up, but has no appetite to feed upon it.

Secondly, There are some things necessary whilst hearing the word.

1. A man should try what he hears, and whilst hearing; for *the ear tries words;* not that persons should sit as critics upon the words, phrases, and expressions of the preacher, to judge of the justness of his style, the propriety of his diction, and the cadency of his words; hearing the word to profit, requires no such critical art: but men should try the things that are said, the doctrines that are delivered, by their own experience, whether agreeable to it; and by the word of God, whether according to it; and this they are to do whilst hearing it, so far as their judgment will reach, and they can recollect the sense of the sacred scriptures.——2. A man should take to himself what he hears, and whilst hearing it. Some hear not for themselves, but for others; when such and such expressions drop from the preacher, they presently conceive in their minds, that they are suitable to such a man, and hit such a man's case, and have no regard to themselves; whereas, in hearing, they should observe what is *for doctrine;* whether it is for the illumination of their minds in it, and for the establishment of them in the present truth; and if *for reproof* for sin, that it is for their own; and if *for correction* of conduct and conversation, that it is of their own; and if *for instruction in righteousness*, in any branch of duty, that it concerns them; so when they hear of Christ as a Saviour, and of the great salvation by him, and of the blessings and promises of grace, they are to take these to themselves by faith, as belonging to them; *To you is the word of this salvation sent*, Acts xiii. 26.——3. Faith is to be mixed with the word, whilst hearing it; men should make faith of what they hear, or believe it for themselves, digest it as food, and so will it be profitable unto them, Heb. iv. 2.

Thirdly, After hearing the word, some things are to be done, which may be of use and service.——1. There should be a recollection of what has been heard, as much as may be; persons should retire privately, and meditate upon what they have heard; the beasts that were accounted clean under the law, were such as chewed the cud; hearers of the word should endeavour to fetch back and call over again what they have heard, when their meditation on it is often as sweet or sweeter than at the first hearing it.——2. When two or more meet together after hearing the word, and converse together about what they have heard, this may tend to much profit and advantage, to refresh one another's memories; what one has forgotten, another may remember; or what has appeared difficult to one, may be explained by another; and thus by speaking to and conferring with one another, it is a means of building up each other in their most holy faith.——3. It is proper to consider how it has been with them whilst hearing the word; if they have been careless and inattentive, wandering, cold, and indifferent under it; they will see reason for humiliation and lamentation that so it should be with them, whilst hearing such evangelic truths, and such excellent doctrines delivered to them; or if their souls have been enlarged, their hearts warmed, their affections raised, their judgments informed, their knowledge increased, and their souls established in the present truth, they will be led to praise and thankfulness: and upon the whole, there should be a concern that what they hear is put in practice, that they are *doers of the word, and not hearers only, deceiving their own souls*, James i. 22.

V. The utility of hearing the word, or the advantages which under a divine blessing arise from it, are next to be considered; and which may be regarded as so many encouraging reasons and arguments to attend to this duty; and which will be only just enumerated; as,——1. Conviction

חמרתי וישבתי [7]

of sin, and of a lost and undone state and condition by nature, oftentimes comes by hearing the word; as the three thousand under Peter's sermon, Acts ii. 36. so sometimes an unbeliever comes into a congregation, where the word is preached, and he is *convinced of all*, of all his sins and iniquities, and he is *judged of all*, condemned for them in his own conscience, 1 Cor. xiv. 24, 25.——2. Conversion also is by means of it; the end of the word being preached and heard, is to turn men from the darkness of sin and error, to the light of grace and truth; from the power, dominion, and slavery of Satan, to serve the living God; from the ways of sin and folly, to the paths of righteousness and holiness; from a dependance on a man's own righteousness, to trust in the righteousness of Christ; see Acts xxvi. 18. hence one of the epithets of the law, or doctrine of the Lord, from its effect, is, *converting the soul*, Psalm xix. 7.——3. In this way, or by hearing the word, the Spirit of God, his gifts and graces, are conveyed into the hearts of men, Gal. iii. 2.——4. Particularly faith usually comes this way, Rom. x. 17.——5. The joy of faith, and an increase of that, and of every other grace, are by means of it, Phil. i. 25.—— 6. Comfort is had by it; he *that prophesieth*, or preacheth, *speaketh to comfort*, 1 Cor. xiv. 3. the end and use of the gospel-ministry is to comfort those that mourn; the commission given by Christ to his ministers, is to speak comfortably to his people, Isa. xl. 1, 2. and lxi. 2.—— 7. The knowledge of Christ, and an increase of it, are the fruits and effects of hearing the word, when blessed, 2 Cor. ii. 14. ——8. Love to Christ is drawn forth, and glowing affection to him raised by means of it, Cant. i. 3. Luke xxiv. 32.—— 9. Food and nourishment, in a spiritual sense, are by the word; it is found and eat, when heard, and souls are nourished with the words of faith and good doctrine, even with the wholesome words of our Lord Jesus Christ.——10. Hearing seasons are sometimes sealing ones, Eph. i. 13. Besides public hearing the word, there should be a private reading of the scriptures, which should be searched to see whether what is heard be true or not, John v. 39. Acts xvii. 11. and they should be read in families, for the instruction of them in righteousness; and hereby even children may come to know the scriptures betimes, 2 Tim. iii. 15, 16. Eph. vi. 4.

CHAP. V.

OF PUBLIC PRAYER.

PRAYER is one part of the saints' spiritual armour, and a principal one, though mentioned last, Eph. vi. 18. it has been often of use against temporal enemies, and for obtaining victory over them; as the prayers of Asa, Jehoshaphat, and others, shew, 2 Chron. xiv. 11, 12. and xx. 3, 4, 5, 22. It is reported of Mary, queen of Scots, that she dreaded the prayer of John Knox, an eminent minister, more than an army of twenty thousand men. And it is of use against the spiritual enemies of God's people, and for the vanquishing of them. Satan has often felt the force of this weapon; resist the devil, by faith in prayer, and he will flee from you. When the apostle Paul was buffeted and distressed by him, he had recourse to it; he besought the Lord thrice that the temptation might depart from him; and had for answer, *My grace is sufficient for thee!* and indeed, as this part of the christian-armour is managed, so it goes with the saint, for or against him. In the war between Israel and Amalek, when Moses held up his hands, an emblem of vigorous prayer, then Israel prevailed; but when he let down his hands, a token of remissness in prayer, Amalek prevailed. Prayer has great power and prevalence with God, for the removal or prevention of evil things, and for the obtaining of blessings. Jacob had the name of Israel given him, because, as a prince, he had power with God, and prevailed, that is, by prayer and supplication, Gen. xxxii. 26, 28. see Hos. xii. 3, 4. Elijah prayed earnestly, and his prayer was availing and effectual, James v. 16, 17, 18. Prayer is the breath of a regenerate soul; as soon as a child is born into the world it cries, as soon as a soul is born again it prays; it is observed of Saul upon his conversion, *Behold, he prayeth!* where there is life there is breath; where there is spiritual life, there are spiritual breathings; such souls breathe after God, pant after him, as the hart panteth after the water-brooks. Prayer is the speech of the soul to God;[1] a talking to him, a converse with him, in which much of its communion

---

[1] Ομιλια προς τον θεον η ευχη, Clem. Alex. Stromat. l. 7. p. 722, 742.

with God lies. Prayer is an address to God in the name of Christ, and through him as the Mediator, under the influence and by the assistance of the Spirit of God, in faith, and in the sincerity of our souls, for such things we stand in need of, and which are consistent with the will of God, and are for his glory to bestow, and therefore to be asked with submission. Now though it is public prayer, or prayer as a public ordinance in the church of God, I am in course to consider, yet I shall,

I. Take notice of the various sorts of prayer, which will lead on to that; for there is a praying with *all prayer*, which denotes many sorts and kinds of prayer.

1. There is mental prayer, or prayer in the heart; and, indeed, here prayer should first begin; so David found in his heart to pray, 2 Sam. vii. 27. and it is *the effectual fervent*, or ενεργουμενη, *the inwrought prayer of the righteous man that availeth much;* which is wrought and formed in the heart by the Spirit of God, James v. 16. Such sort of prayer was that of Moses, at the Red Sea, when the Lord said to him, *Wherefore criest thou unto me?* and yet we read not of a word that was spoken by him; and of this kind was the prayer of Hannah; *She spake in her heart*, 1 Sam. i. 13. and this may be performed even without the motion of the lips, and is what we call an ejaculatory prayer, from the suddenness and swiftness of its being put up to God, like a dart shot from a bow; and which may be done in the midst of business the most public, and in the midst of public company, and not discerned; as was the prayer of Nehemiah in the presence of the king, Neh. ii. 4, 5. and such prayer God takes notice of, and hears; and as an ancient writer [2] observes, "Though we whisper, not opening our lips, but pray in silence, cry inwardly, God incessantly hears that inward discourse," or prayer to him, conceived in the mind.——2. There is prayer which is audible and vocal. Some prayer is audible, yet not articulate and intelligible, or it is expressed by inarticulate sounds; as, *with groanings which cannot be uttered;* but God knows and understands perfectly the language of a groan, and hears and answers. But there is vocal prayer, expressed by articulate words, in language to be heard and understood by men, as well as by the Lord; *I cried unto the Lord with my voice*, &c.

Psalm iii. 4. and v. 2, 3. and to this kind of prayer the church is directed by the Lord himself, Hos. xiv. 2.——3. There is private prayer, in which a man is alone by himself; to which our Lord directs, Matt. vi. 6. an instance and example of this we have in Christ, Matt. xiv. 23. see also an instance of this in Peter, Acts x. 9. ——4. There is social prayer, in which few or more join together, concerning which, and to encourage it, our Lord says, *Where two or three are gathered together in my name, there am I in the midst of them*, Matt. xviii. 19, 20. an instance of this social prayer with men is in Acts xx. 36. and it is this social prayer with fewer or more, the apostle Jude has respect unto, ver. 20.——5. There is family-prayer, performed by the head and master of the family in it, and with it. Joshua set a noble example of family-worship, Josh. xxiv. 15. and an instance we have in David, 2 Sam. vi. 20. and even Cornelius, the Roman centurion, before he was acquainted with christianity, was in the practice of it, Acts x. 2, 30. and the contrary behaviour is resented, and the wrath and fury of God may be expected to fall upon the families that call not on his name, Jer. x. 25. and it is but reasonable service, since family-mercies are daily needed, and therefore should be prayed for, and family-mercies are daily received, and therefore thanks should be every day returned for them.——6. There is public prayer, which is performed in bodies and communities of men, who meet in public, unite and join together in divine worship, and particularly in this branch of it; for prayer always was made a part of public worship.

1*st*, This part of divine worship was set up in the days of Enos, for *then began men to call upon the name of the Lord;* that is, to pray in the name of the Lord, as it is paraphrased in the Targum,[3] of Gen. iv. 26. not but that good men before this time prayed personally, and in their families; but now families becoming more numerous and larger, they met and joined together, in carrying on public worship, and this part of it particularly; and so it continued during the patriarchal state.

2*dly*, Under the Mosaic dispensation, whilst the tabernacle was standing, this practice was used; for the tabernacle was called, the *tabernacle of the congregation;* because, as Munster observes, there the

---

[2] Clemens Alex. ut supra.

[3] In Reg. Hisp. Bibl.

congregation of Israel met to pray and to sacrifice, Exod. xxvii. 21. Moreover, there was another tabernacle which Moses pitched without the camp, which seems to be a temporary one, and which he called by the same name, Exod. xxxiii. 7. and which, according to the Targum of Jonathan, was not only a place for instruction in doctrine, but where every one who truly repented, went and confessed his sins, and asked pardon for them, and had it.

3*dly*, In the temple, both first and second, public prayer made a part of divine worship; here at the dedication of the first temple, Solomon prayed in public, all Israel present; and where the people in after times, were to pray and make supplication; and here Jehoshaphat stood and prayed, and all the congregation of Judah and Jerusalem with him: and hence the temple was called *the house of prayer*, Isa. lvi. 7. Likewise in the second temple, prayer was wont to be made in it; we read of two men going up to the temple to pray, and what they prayed, Luke xviii. 10. see Acts iii. 1. It was usual with the people to be employed in prayer at the time the incense was offered; so while Zechariah was burning incense in the temple, the people were praying without; see Luke i. 9, 10. hence prayer is compared to incense, and the prayers of the saints are called odours, and said to be offered with much incense, Psalm cxli. 2. Rev. viii. 3, 4. and Agatharcides,[4] an heathen writer, bears this testimony to the Jews, while the temple was standing, that they kept the seventh day as a rest from labour, and did no work in it, but continued in the temple, stretching out their hands in prayer unto the evening; and it should be observed, that there were a set of men at Jerusalem called *stationary-men*, who were the representatives of the people in the country, who, because they could not appear in the temple at the time of sacrifice, the reading of the law, and prayer, these attended for them and represented them.[5]

4*thly*, Public prayer was a part of synagogue-worship, and which may be learned from what our Lord says of the hypocrites, who loved to *pray standing in the synagogues*, where they might be seen and heard of men, Matt. vi. 5. the Jews in general have a great notion of public prayer, as being always heard, and that therefore men should always join with the congregation, and not pray alone; but should always attend morning and evening in the synagogue; since no prayer is heard but what is put up in the synagogue;[6] and they say, in whatsoever place are ten Israelites, they are obliged to fit up a house where they meet for prayer, at every time of prayer, and this place is called a synagogue;[7] and which some take to be the same with, though others think they differ from, the *proseucha*, oratory, or place, where prayer was wont to be made, into which Paul and Silas went near Philippi, and spoke to those who resorted thither; and in one of these it is thought our Lord continued a whole night praying, Acts xvi. 13. Luke vi. 12. in which the Jews met for instruction, as well as for prayer, especially on Sabbath-days; as is observed by Philo[8] and Josephus,[9] and was an ancient custom.

5*thly*, Under the New Testament dispensation, prayer was always a part of public worship in the several churches; as in that at Jerusalem, the first christian church. When the disciples returned thither after our Lord's ascension, they continued *in prayer and supplication*, with the women and others, who constituted that first church; and it is observed, in commendation of those that were added to it, that they continued stedfastly *in prayer*, in the public prayers of the church, whenever they met together; and where there was sometimes a remarkable appearance of the divine presence; and it was to this part of service, as well as to the ministry of the word, the apostles gave themselves continually, Acts i. 14. and ii. 42. and iv. 31. and vi. 4. Such was the prayer made by this church, without ceasing, for Peter, when in prison, and was remarkably heard, Acts xii. 5. so in the church at Corinth, public prayer was a part of divine worship; for it is with respect to that, the apostle gives directions to men and women praying, that is, attending that part of public service, the one with their heads uncovered, the other with their heads covered, 1 Cor. xi. 4, 5. and it is with respect to his own practice in public, that he says, *I will pray with the spirit*, &c. 1 Cor.

---

[4] Apud Joseph. contra Apion. l. 1. c. 22.
[5] Maimon. Cele Hamikdash, c. 6. s. 1, 5. See Lightfoot's Temple Service, c. 7. s. 3. p. 924, 925.
[6] Maimon. Hilchot Tephillah, c. 8. s. 1.
[7] Ib. c. 11. s. 1.
[8] De Vita Mosis, l. 3. p. 685. et de Leg. ad Caium, p. 1014.
[9] In Vita ejus, s. 54.

xiv. 15, 16, 19. The several directions and exhortations to the churches to attend to the duty of prayer, does not regard them merely as individuals, but as bodies and communities, joining together in that service, Eph. vi. 18. Phil. iv. 6. Col. iv. 2. 1 Thess. v. 17. and public prayer seems to be chiefly intended by the apostle, 1 Tim. ii. 1, 2, 8. and this was foretold of gospel-times, Mal. i. 11. Now this practice obtained in the earliest times of christianity, and is still continued in christian assemblies; so Justin Martyr[10] says, that after reading the scriptures, and preaching, we all *rise up* in common, and send up prayers; and after the administration of the supper, he observes, the president or pastor of the church, according to his ability, pours out prayers and thanksgivings, and all the people aloud cry *Amen;* and so Tertullian,[11] "We come together in the congregation to God, and as it were with our hands by prayer compass him about; this force is grateful to God: we also pray for emperors, for their ministers, &c." And from Justin, as well as from Origen, Cyprian, and others, we learn, that the gesture of the ancients in public prayer was *standing;* nay, Tertullian[12] says, "We reckon it unlawful to fast on the Lord's day, or to worship on the knees;" and it was ordered by the council of Nice, "that whereas there were some who bent their knees, it seemed right to the synod that they should perform their prayers standing."

Now though my subject is public prayer, yet as all prayer agrees in the object of it; and in the main as to the matter and manner of it; and in persons and things to be prayed for, I shall proceed to consider,

II. The object of prayer; which is not a mere creature, animate or inanimate; it is the grossest absurdity to set up the wood of a graven image, and pray unto it, which cannot save; to pray to idols of gold and silver, the work of men's hands, which cannot speak, see, nor hear; are unable to give any help, or bestow any favour upon their votaries: nor to saints departed; for the dead know not any thing of the affairs of men in this world; nor can they assist them in them; their sons come to honour, and they know it not; they are brought low, but not perceived by them; Abraham is ignorant of his sons, and Israel acknowledges them not; it is in vain to turn to any of the saints, or direct prayers unto them: nor to angels, who have always refused worship from men, of which prayer is a considerable part; the angel invoked by Jacob was not a created, but the increated one, Gen. xlviii. 16. God only is and ought to be the object of prayer; *My prayer*, says David, *shall be unto the God of my life,* who gives life and breath to all; he upholds their souls in life, and in him they live, move, and have their being; he is the Father of mercies, and the God of all grace, who only can supply with temporal mercies and spiritual blessings, and from whom every good and perfect gift comes; he only can hear the prayers of his people; he only knows men and their wants, and he only is able to help and relieve them; he is God all-sufficient, needs nothing for himself, and has enough for all his creatures; he is a God at hand and afar off, and is nigh to all that call upon him, and a present help in time of need; he is good to all, and his tender mercies are over all his works; he is gracious and merciful, abundant in goodness and truth. All which, as it makes him to be a proper object of prayer, and recommends him as such, so serves greatly to encourage men in their addresses to him.

God in his Three Persons is the proper object of prayer; Father, Son, and Spirit; who are the one true God; and it is lawful to address either of them in prayer, though not one to the exclusion of the others. Sometimes the Father is prayed unto singly, and as distinct from the Son and Spirit; *If ye call upon the Father,* 1 Pet. i. 17. as he may be called upon as a distinct divine Person in the Godhead, of which we have instances in Eph. i. 16, 17. and iii. 14, 15, 16. the second Person, the Son of God, is said to be invoked by all the saints in every place, Acts ix. 14. 1 Cor. i. 2. he is sometimes singly prayed unto; as by Stephen at his death; *Lord Jesus receive my Spirit!* and by the apostle John, for his second coming; *Even so, come, Lord Jesus!* Acts vii. 59. Rev. xxii. 20. and sometimes conjunctly with the Father; as when *grace and peace* are prayed for, as in almost all the epistles, *From God our Father, and from the Lord Jesus Christ,* Rom. i. 7, &c. and sometimes in prayer he is set before the Father; and

---

[10] Apolog. 2. p. 98.
[11] Apologet. c. 39.

[12] De Corona Mil. c. 3.

sometimes the Father before him, to shew their equality, 1 Thess. iii. 11. 2 Thess. ii. 16, the third Person, the Spirit of God, is also sometimes singly prayed to, and as distinct from the Father and Son, 2 Thess. iii. 5. and the blessings of grace are prayed for from all three together, 2 Cor. xiii. 14. Rev. i. 4, 5.

The first person in the Godhead is usually addressed in prayer, under the character of a Father; so Christ taught his disciples to pray; *Our Father, which art in heaven*, &c. as he is the Creator and the Father of spirits, and the author of their beings; so the church in the times of Isaiah, Isa. lxiv. 8. and also as he is the Father of Christ, and our Father in Christ; as such is he frequently addressed, 2 Cor. i. 3. Eph. i. 3. Now the reason why the address in prayer is generally made to him, though it may be made equally to either of the other two persons, is, because of the priority of order he has, though not of nature, in the deity, and because he bears no office; whereas the other two persons do bear an office, and an office which is concerned in the business of prayer.

Christ is the Mediator between God and men, by whom we approach to God, and offer up our prayers to him; there is no approaching to God in any other way; God is a consuming fire; the flaming sword of justice stands between God and sinners; there is no day's-man between them to lay his hands on both, but Christ; none can come to the Father but by him; he has opened a way to him through the vail of his flesh, and through his precious blood, which gives boldness to enter into the holiest of all; through him there is an access by one Spirit unto the Father; he is the way of acceptance with God, as well as of access unto him; it is by him we offer up the sacrifice of prayer and praise, which becomes acceptable to God through the incense of his mediation. The encouragement to prayer is taken chiefly from him; and the pleas at the throne of grace for blessings of grace, are founded on his person, blood, righteousness, sacrifice, and intercession; from his being an advocate with the Father for us, and the propitiation for our sins, and from our having such and so great an high Priest, that is passed into the heavens, and is over the house of God; we are encouraged to come boldly to the throne of grace, to draw near with true hearts, and even in full assurance of faith, 1 John ii. 1, 2. Heb. iv. 14, 16. and x. 21, 22. believing, that whatsoever we ask in his name, the Father will give it to us; yea, that Christ himself *will do it*; which shews his equality with his Father, and that he has the same power of doing what he does, John xiv. 13, 14, and xvi. 23, 24.

The Spirit of God has also a great concern in prayer; he is the author and enditer of it; he is the *Spirit of grace and of supplication*, who forms it in the heart; and therefore it is called *inwrought prayer*; he creates divine breathings, and holy desires after spiritual things in men; yea, puts words into their mouths, and bids them take them with them; he impresses their minds with a feeling sense of their wants; and fills their mouths with arguments, and puts strength into them to plead with God; he helps them under their infirmities, when they know not what to pray for, nor how; and makes intercession for them according to the will of God; he gives freedom to them when they are so shut up that they cannot come forth; where he is, there is liberty; he is the Spirit of adoption, witnessing to their spirits that they are the children of God; enables them to go to God as their Father, and to cry Abba, Father; and as the Spirit of faith, encourages them to pray in faith, and with fervency. Moses, when he prayed for Israel, when engaged in battle with Amalek, represented a praying saint in its conflict with spiritual enemies; a stone was put under him, on which he sat, whilst lifting up his hands, an emblem of Christ, the Eben-Ezer, the stone of help in time of need; Aaron and Hur, the one on one side, and the other on the other, held up his hands, and stayed them; Aaron, who could speak well, was a type of Christ the advocate and spokesman of his people, by whose mediation they are encouraged and supported in prayer; and Hur is a name which has the signification of liberty, and may point to the Spirit of God, who is a *free Spirit*, and as such upholds and supports the saints in the exercise of grace and discharge of duty. The next to be considered are,

III. The parts of prayer, of which it consists; the apostle, in Phil. iv. 6. uses four words to express it by; and which are commonly thought to design distinct species or parts of prayer; which are comprehended under the general name of *requests*, or petitions, as *prayer* and *supplication with thanksgiving*: and he also uses four words for it,[13] with some little difference, in 1 Tim. ii. 1. *Supplications, prayers, intercessions, and giving of thanks;* by which one and the same thing may be signified in different words, according to the different respects which it has;[14] but if these have different senses, and are different species or parts of prayer, Origen's[15] account of them seems as good as any; that *supplication* is for some good that we stand in need of; *prayer* for greater things, when in great danger, that is, deliverance from it; *intercession* is expressed with more freedom, familiarity, and faith, with greater confidence of having what is asked of God; and *thanksgiving* is an acknowledgment of good things obtained of God by prayer. But to proceed, and more particularly consider the parts of prayer, of what it consists; and I mean not to prescribe any form of prayer, but to direct to the matter and method. And,

1. In prayer there should be a celebration of the divine perfections; and it is proper to begin with this; we should declare the name of the Lord to whom we pray, and ascribe greatness to our God; we should begin with some one or other of his names and titles, expressive of his nature, and of the relation he stands in to us as creatures, and new creatures; and make mention of some one or more of his perfections, which may serve to command an awe and reverence of him; to engage our affections to him; to strengthen our faith and confidence in him, and raise our expectations of being heard and answered by him, as before observed; as of his purity, holiness, and righteousness; of his omniscience, omnipotence, and omnipresence; and of his immutability and faithfulness, love, grace, and mercy.——2. There should be an acknowledgment of our vileness and sinfulness, of our meanness and unworthiness in ourselves; we should come before a pure and holy God under a sense of the depravity and pollution of our nature, and of our unworthiness to be admitted into his presence, and to worship at his footstool; when we take upon us to speak unto the Lord, we should own, with Abraham, that we are but *dust and ashes;* not only frail and mortal creatures, but sinful and impure; and with Jacob, that we are not *worthy of the least of all the mercies* shewed us, nor of receiving any favour from God; and therefore do not present our supplications to him *for our righteousnesses, but for his great mercies.*——

3. There should be a confession of sin; of the sin of our nature, of original sin, of indwelling sin; of the sins of our lives and actions; of our daily transgressions of the law of God in thought, word, and deed; this has been the practice of saints in all ages; of David, Daniel, and others, Psalm xxxii. 5. and li. 3, 4, 5. and which is encouraged, 1 John i. 9.——4. There should be a deprecation of all evil things, which our sins deserve; so our Lord taught his disciples to pray; *Deliver us from all evil;* and this seems to be the meaning of the saints oftentimes, when they pray for the forgiveness of their own sins and those of others,[16] that God would deliver them out of present distress, of what kind soever, remove his afflicting hand, which lies heavy upon them, and avert those evils which seem to threaten them, and prevent their coming upon them; in which sense we are to understand many of the petitions of Moses, Job, Solomon, and others, Exod. xxxii. 32. Numb. xiv. 19, 20. Job vii. 21. 1 Kings viii. 30, 34, 36, 39, 50.——5. Another part or branch of prayer is, a petition for good things, which are needed; for temporal mercies, such as regard the sustenance of our bodies, the comfort, support, and preservation of life; so our Lord has taught us to pray; *Give us this day our daily bread;* which includes all the necessaries of life. Agur's prayer with respect to this, is a very wise one, and to be copied after, Prov. xxx. 7, 8, 9. Spiritual blessings are to be prayed for; which, though laid up in covenant, and are sure to all the covenant-ones, what God has promised, and will be performed; and we may have this confidence in him, that whatsoever we ask according to his will, we shall have; but then they must be asked for; seeing, for what he has promised, and will do, he will *yet for this be enquired of by the house of Israel, to do it for them,* Ezek. xxxvi. 37.——6. Prayer should always be accompanied with thanksgiving; this should always be a part of it; since, as we have always mercies to pray for, we

---

[13] They seem to answer to four words used by the Jews, of prayer, ברכה בקשה תפלה תחנה Vid. Vitringam de Synagog. vet. par. 2. 1. 3. c. 13. p. 1025. et c. 19. p. 1103.

[14] Witsius de Orat. Domin. Exercit. 1. s. 2, 4.
[15] Περι ευχης, c. 44. Ed. Oxon.
[16] Of praying for the Pardon of Sin; see the Body of Doctrinal Divinity, b. 6. c. 7. p. 500.

have always mercies to be thankful for, Eph. vi. 18. Phil. iv. 6.——7. At the close of this work it is proper to make use of doxologies, or ascriptions of glory to God; of which we have many instances, either of which may be made use of, Matt. vi. 13. Eph. iii. 21. 1 Tim. i. 17. Jude ver. 24, 25. Rev. i. 5, 6. which serve to shew forth the praises of God, to express our gratitude to him, and our dependance on him, and expectation of receiving from him what we have been praying for; and the whole may be concluded with the word Amen, as expressing our assent to what has been prayed for, our wishes and desires for the accomplishment of it, and our full and firm persuasion and belief of our having what we have been asking for, according to the will of God.

IV. The persons to be prayed for may be next considered. Not devils; for as God has not spared them, nor provided a Saviour for them, nor is any mercy promised to them, so none can be asked for them. But men; yet only the living, not the dead; for after death is the judgment, when the final state of men is inevitably fixed; and there is no passing out of one state into another: nor those who have sinned the sin unto death, the unpardonable sin, 1 John v. 16. yet those who are dead in sins, unconverted sinners, may be prayed for, Rom. x. 1. we may pray for unconverted friends and relations, for our children in a state of nature, as Abraham did for Ishmael; and especially we may pray in faith for the conversion of God's elect, as our Lord himself did, John xvii. 20. and it is an incumbent duty, to pray *for all saints;* of every country, of whatsoever denomination they may be, and in whatsoever circumstances; and therefore we are to pray to God as *our Father* and theirs, as the Father of us all; and for all that are his children, that love the Lord Jesus, bear his image, are called by his name, and call on his name; particularly for the ministers of the gospel, that they may speak the word boldly and faithfully, as they ought to speak it; that the word of the Lord, ministered by them, might have a free course, and be glorified, and be blessed for conversion, comfort, and edification; and that the Lord would raise up and send forth other labourers into his vineyard: yea, we are to pray *for all men;* for all sorts of men, *for kings, and all in authority,* for civil magistrates, that they may be terrors to evil doers, and a praise to them that do well; and that the time may hasten on, when kings shall be nursing fathers, and queens nursing mothers to the church and people of God: we are to pray for the peace and welfare of the inhabitants of any city or country in which we dwell, since in the peace thereof we have peace. Nay, we are to pray for our enemies, who despitefully use and persecute us; this is enjoined us by Christ, and of which he has set us an example, Matt. v. 44. Luke xxiii. 44. and so Stephen prayed for those that stoned him, Acts vii. 60.

V. The manner in which prayer is to be performed, is worthy of attention.

1. It must be done *with* or *in the Spirit; I will pray with the Spirit,* says the apostle, 1 Cor. xiv. 15.[17] by which he either means the extraordinary gift which he and other apostles had, of speaking with divers tongues, which he determined to make use of, yet only when he could be understood by others; or the ordinary gift of the Spirit, his grace, influence, and assistance, which are necessary in prayer; and is the same which the apostle Jude calls, *praying in the Holy Ghost;* and the apostle Paul, *supplication in the Spirit,* Jude ver. 20. Eph. vi. 18. The concern the Spirit of God has in prayer, and the need there is of his grace and assistance in it, and the use thereof, have been observed already; but it does not follow from hence that men ought not to pray but when they have the Spirit, and are under his influences; for prayer is a natural duty, and binding on all men, who are to pray as well as they can, though none but spiritual men can pray in a spiritual manner; and yet even such are not always under the gracious influences of the Spirit, and such, when destitute of them, should pray for them; for *our heavenly Father will give the holy Spirit to them that ask him;* and when men are in darkness and distress, without the light of God's countenance, the communications of his grace, and the influences of his Spirit, they stand in the more need of prayer, and should be more constant at it, Psalm cxxx. 1. Jonah ii. 2, 4, 7.——2. It should be performed *with the understanding also,* as in the fore-mentioned place; with an understanding of the object of prayer, God in Christ; or otherwise men will pray unto and worship they know not what, an

---

[17] See a Discourse of mine on this text.

unknown God; and with an understanding of the way of access unto him, Christ, the Mediator between God and man; and with a spiritual understanding of the things prayed for, having their understandings enlightened by the Spirit of God; by whom they are taught what to pray for, and how to pray as they ought, and know that what they ask according to the will of God, that they have the petitions they desire of him.——3. It must be done in faith, without which it impossible to please God in this or in any other duty; what we ask we should *ask in faith, nothing wavering*; it is the *prayer of faith* that is effectual; for our Lord assures us, *all things whatsoever ye shall ask in prayer, believing, ye shall receive*, Matt. xxi. 22.——4. Fervency in spirit is requisite to prayer; we should be fervent in spirit, *serving the Lord* in every branch of duty, and so in this of prayer; for it is *the effectual fervent prayer of the righteous man which availeth much*, James v. 16. Prayer, which is compared to incense, like that, burns sweetly, when kindled by the fire of the Spirit, and the flame of love; such earnest, fervent, and importunate prayer was made by the church for Peter incessantly; and we have an instance of earnest, intense, and fervent prayer in our Lord, whose prayers and supplications were with *strong crying* and tears; and being in an agony, prayed the more earnestly and fervently, Luke xxii. 44. Heb. v. 7.——5. Prayer should be put up to God in sincerity; it should go forth, *not out of feigned lips*, but from the heart; men should draw nigh to God with true hearts, and call upon him in truth; that is, in the sincerity of their souls; for when they cry not to him with their hearts, it is reckoned no other than howling on their beds, Hos. vii. 14.——6. It should always be made with submission to the will of God, as our Lord's was when he prayed so earnestly: so when we want to have a favour conferred, or an affliction removed, it becomes us to say, *the will of the Lord be done*, Luke xxii. 42. Acts xxi. 14.—— 7. It should be performed with assiduity and watchfulness; there should be a *watching thereunto with all perseverance*, Eph. vi. 18. for a fit opportunity of doing it, and for the proper suitable time of need, and when the Lord is nigh to be found: and there should be a watching in the same *with thanksgiving*, Col. iv. 2. for the aid and assistance of the Spirit; that the heart be lift up with the hands; that it does not wander in it, nor enter into temptation: and there should be a watching *after* it, for an answer to it, and a return of it; *In the morning*, says David, *will I direct my prayer unto thee, and look up* for the blessing of mercy prayed for; and again, *I will hear what God the Lord will speak*, Psalm v. 3. and lxxxv. 8.

VI. The time of prayer, with the continuance in it, and duration of it; it should be *always; Praying always with all prayer*, Eph. vi. 18. hence these exhortations, *Continue in prayer; Pray without ceasing*, Col. iv. 2. 1 Thess. v. 17. Not that men are always to be on their knees, and ever formally praying;[18] for there are many civil duties of a man's calling in life which are to be attended to; and other religious duties, besides prayer, which are not to be neglected; one duty is not to shut out another, whether on a civil or sacred account: but it is desirable to be always in praying frames, and the heart to be ready for it on all occasions; it should be daily, since there is daily need of it, daily cases call for it; we want daily bread for our bodies, and the inward man needs to be renewed day by day. Temptations are daily; our adversary, the devil, goes about continually like a roaring lion, seeking whom he may devour; and therefore we should pray daily that we enter not into temptation. The above exhortations are opposed unto, and strike at such who either pray not at all, judging it to be vain and fruitless, Job xxi. 15. or who have prayed, but have left off praying, which Job was charged with, though wrongly, Job xv. 4. or who discontinue it because they have not an immediate answer; our Lord spake a parable to this end, *That men ought always to pray, and not to faint;* to continue praying, and not be discouraged, because their prayers seem not to be heard at once; and gives an instance of the success of the importunate widow with the unjust judge, Luke xviii. 1, &c. or who pray only when in distress; it is right to pray at such a time, James v. 13. Psalm l. 15. but this is what graceless persons, who are in a state of

---

[18] There were a sort of heretics in the fourth century, called Euchetæ and Messalians; who, neglecting all business, pretended to pray continually, ascribing their whole salvation to it, Aug. de Hæres. c. 57. et Danæus in ib.

distance and alienation from God, and what carnal professors and careless souls will do, Isa. xxvi. 16. Hos. v. 15.

The Jews had stated times in the day for prayer. Daniel prayed three times a day; and what these times were we learn from David; *Evening, and morning, and at noon*, Psalm lv. 17. The prayer in the morning, according to Maimonides,[19] was from sun-rising to the end of the fourth hour (or ten o'clock) which is the third part of the day; see Acts ii. 15. The prayer at noon, was at the sixth hour (or twelve o'clock) at which time Peter went up to the house-top to pray, Acts x. 9. The evening-prayer was at the ninth hour (or three o'clock in the afternoon) about the time of the evening-sacrifice; at which time, which was the hour of prayer, Peter and John went up to the temple to pray; at this time we find Cornelius at prayer, Acts iii. 1. and x. 3. and this practice obtained among Christians in early times. Jerome[20] speaks of it as a tradition of the church, that the third, sixth, and ninth hours, are times for prayer; and it is a practice laudable enough, where there is leisure from other lawful exercises; and when no stress is laid on the punctual performance of it at these precise times; and is not made a term and condition of acceptance with God; which would bring us back to the covenant of works, ensnare our souls, and entangle us with a yoke of bondage. What Clemens of Alexandria[21] observes, is worthy of notice; some, says he, appoint stated hours for prayer, the third, sixth, and ninth hours; but "the Gnostic (who is endued with the true knowledge of God and divine things) prays throughout his whole life; his whole life is an holy convocation, a sacred festival:" yea, it is said of Socrates, the heathen philosopher, to the shame of Christians, "the life of Socrates was full of prayer." From the whole of this we learn, that at least a day should not pass over without prayer. I proceed to observe,

VII. The encouragement to prayer, and the advantages arising from it. Saints may be encouraged to it,

1. From the concern, which God, Father, Son, and Spirit have in it; which has been taken notice of already. God the Father, as the God of all grace, sits on the throne of grace, holding forth the sceptre of grace; inviting men to come thither, where they may find grace and mercy to help them in their time of need. Christ is the Mediator, through whom they have access to God, audience of him, and acceptance with him; Christ is their Advocate with the Father, who pleads their cause, and makes intercession for them; he introduces them into the presence of God, and as the Angel of his presence presents their prayers to God, perfumed with his much incense. And the Spirit of God is the Spirit of grace and of supplication, who supplies them with grace, and assists them in their supplications to God; and by whom, through Christ, they have access to God as their Father.——2. From the interest saints have in God, to whom they pray, they have encouragement to it; he is their Father by adopting grace, whose heart is full of love, pity, and compassion; his heart is towards them, his eyes are upon them, and his ears are open to their cries; he is their covenant-God and Father, who has provided blessings in covenant for them, and is ready to distribute them, upon their application to him by prayer, Phil. iv. 19.
——3. From the call of God in providence, and by his Spirit, to it, and his delight in it, saints may take encouragement to be found in the performance of it, Psalm xxvii. 8. he delights to see the face, and hear the prayers of his people, Prov. xv. 8. Psalm cii. 17.——4. Many promises are made to praying souls; as of deliverance from trouble, &c. Psalm l. 15. and xci. 15. For their encouragement it is said, *Ask, and it shall be given*, &c. Matt. vii. 7. yea, God has never *said to the seed of Jacob, Seek ye me in vain*, Isa. xlv. 19.——5. The experience the people of God in all ages have had of answers of prayers, either to themselves or others, serve greatly to animate them to this duty: this was the experience of David, and he observed it in others, Psal. xl. 1. and xxxiv. 6. and this was not the case only of a single, and of a private person, but of good men in times past, in all ages, Psalm xxii. 4, 5.——6. It is *good for* saints *to draw nigh to God*; it is not only good, because it is their duty, but it is a pleasant good, when they have the presence of God in it, and their souls are drawn out towards him; and it is a

---

[19] Hilchot Tephillah, c. 3. s. 1.
[20] Comment. in Dan. fol. 270. M.
[21] Stromat. l. 7. p. 722, 728. Maximus Tyrius apud Witsium in Orat. Domin. Exercitat. 2. s. 19. p. 43.

profitable good to them, when God owns it as an ordinance, for the quickening the graces of his Spirit, subduing the corruptions of their hearts, and bringing them into nearer communion and fellowship with himself. Praying souls are profitable in families, in churches, in neighbourhoods, and commonwealths; when prayerless ones are useless, and obtain nothing, neither for themselves nor others. Of all the fruits which faith produces in Christians, says Beza,[22] prayer, that is, calling on the name of God, through Christ, is the principal one.

CHAP. VI.

OF THE LORD'S PRAYER.

THE whole Scripture directs to and furnishes with matter for prayer; but more particularly the prayer which is commonly called *The Lord's Prayer*, may be considered as a directory to it; and so it seems to be designed by our Lord, when he says, *After this manner therefore pray ye*, in such a brief and concise manner, in a few comprehensive expressions, in words to this purpose, or to the sense following; which he directed to in opposition to the many words, much speaking, and vain repetitions of the Scribes and Pharisees; indeed, the evangelist Luke has it, *He said unto them, when ye pray, say*, the following words, that is, *after this manner*, or to this sense, as it is explained in Matthew, where both the introduction to the prayer, and the prayer itself, are more fully expressed; for that it was not intended as a prescribed set form, in so many words, is clear; since then it would not have been varied, as it is by the two evangelists, by whom it is recorded; for though they both agree in the main, as to the sense, yet not in the express words: the *fourth* petition is in Matthew, *Give us this day our daily bread*, which is a petition for present supply; in Luke it is, *Give us day by day our daily bread*, which is a prayer for a continued supply, for the future as it may be needed, as well as for the present: the *fifth* petition is expressed in Matthew, *Forgive us our debts*, and in Luke, *Forgive us our sins*; in Matthew it is, *as we forgive*; in Luke, *for we also forgive*: and the doxology, which Matthew gives at large, is wholly left out in Luke, *For thine is the kingdom*, &c. And that it was not understood by the disciples as a form of prayer to be used by them as such, seems evident; since we do not find that they ever so used it; but a most excellent summary of prayer it is, for its brevity, order, and matter, and a pattern of it worthy to be followed; and it is very lawful and laudable to make use of any single petition in it, either in the express words of it, or to the sense of it; and even the whole of it, provided a formal and superstitious observance of it is avoided, as used by the Papists. The matter of it is very full and comprehensive; by one of the ancients[1] it is said to be "a breviary of the whole gospel;" and by another,[2] "a compendium of heavenly doctrine." It may justly be preferred to all other prayers, because of the author, order, and matter of it; though not to the slight and neglect of other petitions the scriptures furnish us with: there were a set of men in the twelfth century, called Bogomiles, who among other odd notions, had this, that only the Lord's prayer was to be reckoned prayer; and that all other was to be rejected as vain clamour:[3] the Socinians say,[4] this prayer is an addition to the first command of the law; and which with other things, add to the perfection of the law, which they suppose to be imperfect until Christ came, and as if such prayer was unknown to the Old Testament-saints; but though this prayer is not formally, and in so many words, expressed in the Old Testament, yet it is materially, or the matter of it is to be found there; especially in the Psalms of David, of which this prayer may be said to be the *epitome*, as the Psalms may be considered and made use of as a *commentary* on that; it is indeed, the summary of the prayers and petitions used by good men in and before the times of Christ,[5] selected and put together, and inserted in this prayer by him in this manner, as a directory to his disciples; in which may be observed, a preface, petitions, and a conclusion, with a doxology.

I. A preface, *Our Father which art in heaven*; in which the object of prayer is

---

[22] Confessio Fidei, c. 4. art. 16. p. 34.
[1] Tertullian. de Oratione, c. 1.
[2] Cyprian. de Orat. Domin. p. 265.
[3] Harmenopulus apud Witsii Exercitat. 6. de rat. Domin. s. 28.
[4] Cateches. Racov. Qu. xix. and xx.

[5] Of the agreement between them, see my Exposition of Matt. vi. 9, &c. in which I have the happiness to agree with those celebrated writers, Witsius in Exercitat. 6. de Orat. Dominic. s. 32. et Vitringa de Synagog. vet. 1. 3. par. 2. c. 8. p. 962. et c. 18. p. 1099.

CHAP. VI.   OF THE LORD'S PRAYER.   949

described, by his relation to us, *Our Father*, and by the place of his habitation, *which art in heaven*.

First, By the relation he stands in to us, *Our Father;* which may be understood of God, essentially considered; of the Three Persons in the Godhead, who are the one God, the Creator, and so the Father of all; in which respect this term, *Father*, is not peculiar to any one person in the Deity, but common to all Three, being equally *Creators*, Eccles. xii. 1. as in the original; and so are addressed as the one God, Creator, and Father of all, Isa. lxiv. 8. Mal. ii. 10. and in this sense every man, good and bad, regenerate and unregenerate, may use this prayer, and say, *Our Father*. Or else this is to be understood of God personally, that is, of one person in the Godhead, even of God the Father, the first Person, who stands in the relation of a Father in a special sense, the Father of our Lord Jesus, who as such, is the object of prayer, Eph. iii. 14. and our Father in Christ; *I go to my Father and your Father*, says Christ, John xx. 17. my Father by nature, yours by grace; mine by natural filiation, yours by special adoption; our sonship is founded on our conjugal union and relation to Christ, the Son of God, and on our relation to him, as the first-born among many brethren. God, as the Father of Christ, has not only predestinated us to the adoption of children by him, and to be conformed to his image; but has actually put us among the children, and taken us into his family, by an act of special love and favour, 1 John iii. 1. of which adoption an evidence is given in regeneration; for such who have *power to become the sons of God*, are those who are *born of God;* whom he, as the God and Father of Christ, has *begotten again of abundant mercy*, of free grace and favour, of his own good will, John i. 12, 13. 1 Pet. i. 3. so that the Father of Christ is our Father, both by adoption and regeneration; and as such may be addressed by us, as here directed; which shews the true order and manner of prayer, which is to be made to the Father, the first Person; not because of priority of nature, but of order in the Deity; and through the Son, who is the mediator; and by the Spirit, the spirit of grace and adoption; and which are all laid together in one text, Eph. ii. 18. no man can come to the Father but by Christ; and as no man can call Jesus *Lord*, but by the Spirit, so no man can call God *Father*, in this special relation, but under the testimony of the Spirit of adoption.

Now the consideration of God as *our Father*, in our addresses to him, is of great use,

1. To command in us a reverence of God; a Son honours and reverences a Father, or ought to do; and if God is our Father, he expects honour and reverence; and when we approach him, it should be with *reverence and godly fear;* not with slavish fear, as a servant, but with filial fear, as a son.——2. It tends to encourage us to use freedom with him, as children with a Father; to pour out our souls before him, and tell him all our minds and all our wants; and *where the Spirit is*, as a Spirit of adoption, crying, *Abba*, Father, *there is liberty*.——3. It will serve to give us boldness at the throne of grace, and a fiducial confidence that we shall have what we ask of him, Luke xi. 13.——4. The idea of God as our Father, excites in us, and inspires us with sentiments of the tenderness of his heart, of his pity and compassion, and of the great love and affection he bears towards us, and therefore cannot deny us any good thing needful for us, Psalm ciii. 13. Isa. lxiii. 15, 16. Luke xv. 20, 22. 2 Thess. ii. 16.——5. It cannot but fill us with gratitude for the many favours which he, as a kind indulgent Father, has bestowed on us; having nourished and brought us up, fed us all our lives long, clothed us, and provided every thing for us, and protected us from all evils and enemies; and we may say, with David, *Blessed be the Lord God of Israel, our Father, for ever and ever!* 1 Chron. xxix. 10.——6. This may teach us subjection to him, the Father of Spirits, and submission to his will, in all things we ask of him, Luke xxii. 42.——7. Addressing him as *our Father*, instructs us to pray for others as well as for ourselves, even for all saints; for all the children of God, to whom he stands in the same relation, being the Father of us all, Eph. iv. 6.

Secondly, The object of prayer is described by the place of his habitation and residence; *which art in heaven;* see Psalm cxxiii. 1. Not that God is limited, included, and circumscribed in any place, for he is every where, and fills heaven and earth with his presence; but as such is the weakness of our minds that we cannot conceive of him but as somewhere, in condescension thereunto he is represented as in the highest place, in the height of heaven; for as he is the high and lofty One, he dwells in the high and lofty place; heaven is his throne, the habitation of his glory, where is his palace, where he keeps his court, and has his attendants; and so is expressive of the greatness of his Majesty, and therefore he ought to be approached with the highest reverence; and such a view of him will lead us to some of the divine perfections, which greatly encourage in the work of prayer; as the omniscience and omnipresence of God, Psalm xi. 4. and cxv. 3. and cxxxv. 5, 6. and since *God is in heaven*, and we *upon earth*, our *words should be few*, but full, and be expressed with great lowliness and humility, with great modesty and self-abasement, as being *but dust and ashes* who speak unto him, Eccles. v. 2. Gen. xviii. 27. and the consideration of his being in heaven, should draw off our minds from the earth, and all terrene things, and from asking them, and teach us to look upwards, to God in heaven, and seek those things which are above, from whence comes every good and perfect gift; and since our Father is in heaven we are directed to pray unto, we should look upon heaven, and not this world, as our native place; if we are born again, we are born from above, are partakers of an heavenly birth, and of an heavenly calling, and should seek the better country, the heavenly one; our conversation should be in heaven, and our hearts be where our treasure is; our Father is in heaven, and our Father's house and mansions of bliss in it are there; there is our portion, patrimony, and inheritance. From the preface I pass to consider,

II. The petitions in this prayer, which are six, some make them seven: the first three respect the glory of God; the other our good, temporal and spiritual.

The *First* petition is, *Hallowed be thy name;* which teaches to begin our prayers with the celebration of the name of God, and with a concern for his glory, and as the end for which he has made all things; nor will he give it, nor suffer it to be given to another; this we should have in view in all we do, and in whatsoever we ask of him; this should be uppermost in our minds, that his great name be glorified, Josh. vii. 9. By his *name* may be meant God himself, as when saints are said to trust in his name, to fear his name, and to love his name, and the like: or his nature and perfections; as when it is said, *What is his name?* that is, his nature, *if thou canst tell; and how excellent is thy name in all the earth!* that, is, what a glorious display is there of thy perfections in all the earth, Prov. xxx. 4. Psalm viii. 1. or any of the great names and titles of God, by which he has made himself known; as the Lord God Almighty, Jehovah, &c. Exod. vi. 3. and indeed, every thing by which he has manifested himself, particularly his word, his gospel, which is called his name, and which he has magnified above all and every of his names, and in which the greatest discovery is made of himself, his perfections and glory, John xvii. 6. Psalm cxxxviii. 2. Now when we pray that his name may be *hallowed*, or sanctified, for hallowed is an old English word, now in little use, and is the same as sanctified; the meaning is, not that God can be made holy, or be made more holy than he is; for he is originally, underivatively, immutably, and perfectly holy; there is none holy as the Lord; not the holy angels; *The heavens*, that is, the inhabitants of the heavens, *are not clean in his sight*, when compared with him: but the meaning is, that he be declared, owned, and acknowledged to be holy; as he is by the seraphs in Isaiah's vision, and by the four living creatures around the throne, who continually say, *Holy, holy, holy, Lord God Almighty!* and when the glory due to his holy name is given him, and particularly when thanks are given at the remembrance of his holiness: and he may be said to be hallowed, or sanctified, both by himself and by others, and both may be prayed for in this petition. He is sanctified by himself, when he makes a display of his perfections, as he does in all his works; in the works of creation, of providence, and redemption, and particularly of his holiness and justice, Psalm cxlv. 17. and when he shews his resentment against sin, takes vengeance on it, and inflicts punishment for it; thus he says of Zidon and of Gog, that he shall be known that he is the Lord when he *shall have executed his judgments on them, and shall be sanctified in them,* Ezek. xxviii. 22. and xxxviii. 16, 23. he may be said to sanctify his name, by giving his holy word and ordinances to men, which direct them in the paths of holiness and righteousness; and especially by making his people an holy people; he has not only chosen them to be holy, and called them with an holy calling, and unto holiness, but he implants principles of grace and holiness in them, and at last brings them to a state of perfect and unblemished holiness and purity. And his name may be sanctified by others; by civil magistrates, when they act for the punishment of evil doers, and for the praise of them that do well; and by ministers of the word, when they speak according to the oracles of God, that he in all things may be glorified; and by common saints, when they *sanctify the name of the Lord*, 1 Pet. ii. 14. and iv. 10. Isa. xxix. 23. and this they do when they exercise the grace of faith, fear and love; when they believe him, to sanctify his name, the not doing which was resented in Moses and Aaron; and they sanctify him when they make him their fear and dread, and love his name, Numb. xx. 12. Isa. viii. 13. Psalm v. 11. and when they shew a regard to his word, worship and ordinances; *which is but our reasonable service*, Rom. xii. 1. and when they study to promote holiness of life in themselves and others, 2 Cor. vii. 1. 1 Pet. i. 15, 16. Matt. v. 16. and are careful that the name of God may not be blasphemed through them, or on their account. And whereas nothing is more contrary to the sanctification of the name of God, than the profanation of it, by taking it in vain, by swearing falsely by it, and by the horrid oaths and cursings of wicked men; it is sanctified when magistrates punish for these things, ministers inveigh against them, and every good man discountenances and discourages them. And in the use of this petition we pray that the glory of God may be more and more displayed and advanced in the world, in the course of his providence, and the dispensations of it; that his word may run and be glorified, in the conversion and sanctification of 'sinners; and that there may be an increase of holiness in all his people; and that all profanation of the name of God among men, may be prevented and removed.

The *Second* petition is, *Thy kingdom come*. The Jews have a saying,[6] that prayer, in which is no mention of the kingdom, that is, of God, is no prayer. It may be enquired,

1*st*, Whose kingdom this is; by the connection of the petition with the preface, it seems to be the Father's kingdom; *Our Father—thy kingdom come;* but as the Father and the Son are one in nature and power, their kingdom is the same; and so it appears to be on one account or another in every sense of it. There is the kingdom of providence, in which both are jointly concerned; *My Father worketh hitherto*, in the government of the world, and the disposition of all things in it, and *I work* with him, says Christ, John v. 17. so that this *kingdom*, is also *his*: the mediatorial kingdom, which seems more peculiarly Christ's, is in some sense the Father's, since he is the Father's King, whom he has set over his church; and the kingdom he has is by his appointment, for which he is accountable to him, and at the end will deliver it up to the Father, Psalm ii. 6. Luke xxii. 29. The kingdom of grace, set up in the hearts of the Lord's people, is the kingdom of God, which lies in righteousness, and peace, and joy in the Holy Ghost; this also is the kingdom of God's dear Son, into which men at conversion are translated. Both the spiritual and personal reign of Christ, the Father has and will have a concern in. When the kingdoms of this world are converted to Christ, they will become the *kingdoms of our Lord*, of our Lord God the Father, *and of his Christ*, the Son of God. Christ speaks of drinking wine in his *Father's kingdom*, Matt. xxvi. 29. meaning either in the personal reign, or in the ultimate glory, which is a kingdom prepared by the Father, and is in his gift; and yet is called, *the everlasting kingdom of our Lord and Saviour Jesus Christ*, 2 Pet. i. 11.

2*dly*, It may be further enquired, which of these kingdoms it is, the coming of which is to be prayed for, as future. It seems not to be the kingdom of providence, since that took place from the beginning of the world; though it may be prayed for, that it might more fully appear, and that there may be a greater display of the power and providence of God in the government of the world; that men may know, as Nebuchadnezzar did, that the most High ruleth in it, to the terror of the wicked inhabitants of it, and to the joy of the righteous, Psalm xcvii. 1. and xcix. 1. But rather the gospel-dispensation, often called the kingdom of God, and of heaven, may be meant, which when this petition was directed to, was not yet come, though near. John and Christ began their ministry with saying, *The kingdom of heaven is at hand;* and which soon came, though not with observation, with pomp and splendour:

---

[6] T. Bab. Beracot. fol. 40. 2.

upon our Lord's resurrection, and especially at his ascension to heaven, it appeared more manifest, when he was made and declared Lord and Christ, and multitudes in the land of Judea became obedient to the faith of him; it had a further advance when the gospel was carried into the Gentile world, and the apostles were caused to triumph every where; and still there was a greater appearance of it when the Son of man came in his kingdom, and that came with power, seen in the destruction of the Jews for their unbelief and rejection of him, those enemies of his who would not have him to reign over them, Matt. xvi. 28. Mark ix. 1. and still more when paganism was abolished, and christianity established in the Roman empire; on occasion of which it is said, *Now is come the kingdom of our God, and the power of his Christ*, Rev. xii. 10. but this kingdom will come in greater glory, and which is yet to come, and so to be prayed for, at the destruction of antichrist, and when the spiritual reign of Christ will take place; and this voice will be heard in heaven, *The Lord God omnipotent reigneth!* Rev. xix. 1—6. and still more gloriously, when Christ shall appear a second time in person, and take to himself his great power and reign, called, *his appearing and his kingdom*, 2 Tim. iv. 1. when he will come in person, and the dead in him shall rise first; which happy dead will be made kings and priests, and shall reign with Christ a thousand years, during which time Satan shall be bound, as to give them no disturbance. This is yet to come; no such binding of Satan, and reign of Christ with his saints, as described Rev. xx. have as yet been;[7] the personal coming of Christ, and reign with his saints, are still future, and to be prayed for; as by John, Rev. xxii. 20. and seems to be chiefly intended in this petition, since it is so closely connected with,

The *Third* petition; *Thy will be done in earth as it is in heaven;* which as yet has never been done in the full sense of it, by any man on earth, excepting our Lord Jesus Christ; but will be done by all the saints in the personal reign of Christ. The will of God is either secret or revealed; the secret will of God is the rule of his own actions, in creation, providence, and grace, Eph. i. 11. see Rev. iv. 11. Dan. iv. 35. Rom. ix. 15. This is unknown to men, until it appears, either by prophecies of things future, or by facts and events that are come to pass; it is always fulfilled; *Who hath resisted his will?* it cannot be resisted, so as to be null and void. There is no counter-acting the will of God; whatever schemes contrary to it, formed by men, are of no avail; the *counsel of the Lord shall stand, and he will do all his pleasure*, Isa. xlvi. 10. The providential will of God, or what appears in the dispensation of his providence, are a guide to us in our actions; we should say, as James directs us, we will go here and there, do this or that, *if the Lord will,* James iv. 14, 15. and even as this will of God appears in adverse dispensations, it should be acquiesced in and submitted to, without murmuring and repining; with respect to every event it should be said, *The will of the Lord be done*, Acts xxi. 14. in imitation of Eli, Job, David, Hezekiah, and others, and even of our Lord himself, 1 Sam. iii. 18. Job i. 21. and ii. 10. 2 Sam. xv. 25, 26. Psalm xxxix. 9. Isa. xxxix. 8. Luke xxii. 42.

The revealed will of God is either what is made known in the gospel, and which expresses the good will of God, his grace and favour, declared in the way and method of saving sinners by Christ, or what is signified in the law, which is the *good, acceptable, and perfect will of God;* the matter of it is *good*, and when a right use is made of it, and when rightly and truly obeyed, is *acceptable to God*, through Christ, and is a *perfect* rule of life, and conversation to men. To the doing of which will, the knowledge of it is requisite, Col. i. 10. Faith in God; without which it is impossible to please him, Titus iii. 8. The grace and spirit of Christ; without which nothing can be done to any purpose; this may be expected, since it is promised, and may in faith be prayed for, Ezek. xxxvi. 27. and when it is done aright, it is done with a view to the glory of God, and without any dependance on it; acknowledging, that when we have done all we can, we are unprofitable servants.

The rule of doing the will of God, as expressed in this petition, is, *as it is done in heaven;* meaning not the starry airy heavens, though the inhabitants of them do the will of God, in their way, in a

---

[7] Quos mille annos ligati Satanæ in ecclesiæ historia non invenio; nunquam enim tamdiu ligatus fuisse videtur diabolus. Witsii Orat. Dominic. Exercitat. 9. s. 24. p. 151.

perfect manner; the sun knows, and punctually observes, its rising and setting, and the moon its appointed seasons of change and full, of increase and decrease; and the planetary orbs keep their stated courses; sun, and moon, and stars, praise the Lord, as they are called upon to do, and even the meteors in the air, Psalm cxlviii. 3, 8. But rather the third heavens are meant, the inhabitants of which are glorified saints, the spirits of just men made perfect, and are perfect in their obedience, and the holy angels, who may be chiefly designed; these readily, cheerfully, and voluntarily *do the commandments of God, hearkening to the voice of his word*, at once to fulfil it; so in this petition it is desired, that saints do the will of God, *not by constraint, but willingly;* at least not by any other constraint but that of love; angels are thought by some to be called *seraphim* from their flaming love and burning zeal for the glory of God; saints are desirous of being fervent in spirit, serving the Lord, and that in sincerity, in singleness of heart; angels do the will of God speedily, and without delay, hence wings are ascribed unto them, and Gabriel is said to fly with the Lord's message to Daniel; so saints desire, with David, *to make haste, and not delay* to keep the commandments of God; and not some of them only, but all; not a part, but the whole will of God, Psalm cxix. 60, 61, 128. Angels do the will of God constantly, they always behold the face of our Father in heaven, and serve him incessantly, day and night; and saints would, as they should, be *stedfast, immoveable, always abounding in the work of the Lord;* and though they cannot, in the present state, do it perfectly, as the angels do, yet they are desirous of it, and reach towards perfection; and when the kingdom of Christ comes on earth at his appearing, then will this petition be fulfilled.

The *Fourth* petition is, *Give us this day our daily bread;* by which is meant, either spiritual or corporal food. Some understand it of spiritual food; as the word read, preached, and heard, which is that to the soul as bread is to the body, refreshing, nourishing, and strengthening; and the ordinances, called the goodness and fatness of the Lord's house, particularly the Lord's Supper, the bread of the eucharist; but that was not instituted when this directory was given; and when it was, was not to be administered daily; rather Christ, the bread of life, with respect to which the disciples made a request to Christ, similar to this petition; *Lord, evermore give us this bread!* but it seems best of all to understand it of corporal food, which sense the order of the prayer directs to; and which, if not intended, would be imperfect; since then there would be no petition in it for temporal mercies, which yet is necessary. *Bread*, with the Hebrews, includes all the necessaries and conveniences of life; see Gen. iii. 19. and xxviii. 20. the epithets of it are, *our* bread and *daily* bread: ours not by desert, for we are not worthy of the least mercy; not what we have a natural right to, and a claim upon; Adam had a grant of all good things; sinning, all were forfeited; men in common now enjoy them, through the indulgence of providence; only believers in Christ have a real and proper right unto them; which they have through interest in him, and by being co-heirs with him: ours, what we have in a lawful way, by inheritance from our parents, by legacies from our friends, by our own labour and industry, and in a way of lawful trade and commerce: *ours*, and not another's; not what is got from others, neither by fraud, and is the bread of deceit; nor by force and rapine, and is the bread of violence and oppression; nor by theft, and is the bread of wickedness; nor enjoyed in sloth, and is the bread of idleness; such bread is not ours, but another's; and, indeed, to live upon alms, is to live on another's bread; and though lawful, is not desirable, but to be deprecated; *Give me neither poverty,* &c. and when we are directed to pray, give *us our* bread, we are taught to pray for others as well as for ourselves; that our fellow-creatures and fellow-christians might have bread as well as ourselves; even *the congregation of the Lord's poor,* Psalm lxxiv. 19. the other epithet, *daily* bread, the word used for it is only in this place, and differently rendered; in the Syriac version, *The bread of our necessity,* or indigence, what is *necessary for the day,* as the Persic version; and seems to be the same Job calls his *necessary food*, what is necessary for the support of life, and what our heavenly Father knows we have need of; food that is fit to eat, such as a father will give to a son; not a stone, nor a scorpion, but proper food; as every creature of God, designed for that purpose, is good; so ἐπιούσιος may signify, that which is fit for our nature, substance, and being, as a learned Lexicographer interprets[8] it; what is fit for the sustentation of our bodily substance, and the preservation of our life and being; and is what Agur calls food *convenient*, suitable to our nature, condition, and circumstances; and as much of it as is *sufficient*. The manna of the Israelites might with great propriety be called their daily bread; since it was rained about their tents every morning, and was gathered by them every day, and that by every one, *according to his eating;* that is, as much as he could eat, or was proper for him to eat, Exod. xvi. 16, 17, 18.

The petition is, *Give us* our daily bread; which shews it to be prayed for, and to be expected as the gift of God, from whom every good gift comes; and it may be expected, because promised; *Bread shall be given him:* and though it is our bread, gotten by our labour and industry, yet it is to be ascribed to the bounty and blessing of God, and acknowledged a gift of his; for it is *the blessing of the Lord* upon the *diligent hand that maketh rich*, Prov. x. 4, 22. and when we pray that this may be given, we pray for other things to be given with it, or it will be of no avail; as that God would give us health and appetite; for if our bones are chastened with strong pain, and our bodies filled with diseases, we shall be like the sick man, whose *life abhorreth bread, and his soul dainty meat;* and likewise that God would give nourishment with it; for this is not from food itself alone, nor at the option and will of men, but is of God; and therefore a blessing is to be asked upon our food, or otherwise how can we expect it should be nourishing unto us? see Deut. viii. 3. 1 Tim. iv. 5. yea, a *power to eat* of what we have is to be asked of God; for some are so unnatural and cruel to themselves, as to withhold from themselves what is meet, as well as from others; for, for a man to eat of the fruit of his labours in a sober way, is the *gift of God*, Eccles. v. 18, 19. and vi. 2. and what we ask, and God gives us, is for our use, and not to be abused by us; which is neither for true pleasure, nor profit, nor honour; and since what we have, is by gift, we should be content with such things as we have, and be thankful for them; and this petition teaches us, that we should be daily dependent on God, and his providence, and not trust in the gift, but in the Giver; and not think to set our *nest on high*, out of the reach of providence, and as if delivered *from the power of evil;* but remember, that he that gives can take away, 1 Tim. vi. 17. Hab. ii. 9. The time when food is to be prayed for is, *this day;* which may teach us the brevity and uncertainty of life, since we cannot boast, promise, and assure ourselves, of a to-morrow; and may instruct us to depress all anxious and immoderate care of what we shall eat, and drink, and wear on the morrow, since we know not what a day may bring forth; and sufficient for the day is both the evil and good of it: and we may learn by it, that our wants may be expected to return on us daily; the food of yesterday will not suffice for this day, nor the food of this day for the morrow; it must be asked for every day: and from hence it appears, that we should pray daily, always, and without ceasing; as the word of God directs.

The *Fifth* petition is, *And forgive us our debts, as we forgive our debtors.* By debts are meant *sins*, as appears from Luke xi. 4. where the same petition is, *Forgive us our sins;* these are called *debts*, not as owing to God; it is obedience we owe to God, and in case of sin, satisfaction to his law; and in failure of obedience, and not making satisfaction, we owe a debt of punishment, and become liable to the curse of the law, to eternal death, which is the wages and demerit of sin; and these debts are numerous, we owe ten thousand talents or more, and cannot answer to one debt of a thousand: men are incapable of paying their debts themselves, nor can any creature pay them for them; and so are liable to a prison. Christ only is the surety of his people, he has undertook to pay their debts, and has blotted out the hand-writing against them. And when we are directed to pray for the forgiveness of these debts, or sins, it supposes a sense of sin, and of the guilt of it, chargeable upon us; and likewise an acknowledgment of it, which God requires; and we are encouraged to give; since if we confess our sins, God is just and faithful to forgive them; also a sense of our inability to pay our debts, and of others paying them for us: and by application to God for the forgiveness of sins, it shews that we believe that God can forgive sin; and he only, as indeed none can but himself; and he forgives sin freely and fully; we not being able to pay,

---

[8] Ο επι τη υσια ημων αρμοζων, Suidas in voce, επιουσιος.

he frankly forgives, and even all trespasses, and that for Christ's sake, on account of his bloodshed, and satisfaction made: and therefore there is encouragement to pray for the forgiveness of sin, as David, Daniel, and other saints did, and as Christ's disciples and followers are directed to; that is, for the manifestation and application of pardoning grace; which is all that can be meant, and we want; it is not a request that Christ may be sent again to pay our debts for us, and his blood be shed again for the remission of sins, or a new act of pardon pass in the mind of God; but that we may have a fresh application of pardon, already procured and passed; and this we are to pray for daily, since we are daily sinning in thought, word, and deed; and therefore forgiveness is to be prayed for, as frequently as we pray for our daily bread, with which petition this is joined.

The reason or argument made use of to enforce this petition is, *as we forgive our debtors;* or, as Luke has it, *for we also forgive every one that is indebted to us.* Pecuniary debts are to be forgiven when the debtor is unable to pay; and criminal debts or sins, and injuries committed by one christian against another, are to be forgiven, as Christ has forgiven them: not that our forgiveness of others is the cause of God's forgiveness of us; for the moving cause of God's forgiveness is his free favour, grace, and mercy; it is according to the multitude of his tender mercies, and according to the riches of his grace; and not the deserts of men; the meritorious cause of it is the blood of Christ, shed for the remission of sins; and the satisfaction of Christ, for the sake of which they are forgiven. Nor is our forgiveness of fellow-creatures the model of God's forgiveness of us; there is no perfect comparison between them, much less an equality. God forgives as Lord of all, and who has an absolute power so to do; but men forgive those who are their equals, and sinners like themselves; God forgives for Christ's sake, and upon a satisfaction made; but men without, and at most upon repentance; God forgives great sins, and, indeed, all manner of sin; but what man forgives are trivial offences, injuries to their persons or properties; but not sins committed against God. But this is an argument taken from God's own grace, in the hearts of his people, and as an evidence of it; that if he has given them such grace, as to forgive their fellow-creatures and christians, then they may hope and expect, that he who is the God of all grace, and from whom they have received theirs, will forgive their sins, of his rich grace, and for Christ's sake; the reasoning is much the same with that in Luke xi. 13. Nor is it to be expected, that God should forgive us our sins without our forgiving the sins of others; nor can we put up such a petition without forgiving others; see Matt. vi. 14, 15. and xviii. 28—35. Mark xi. 25, 26.

The *Sixth* petition is, *Lead us not into temptation, but deliver us from evil,* which some make to be a *sixth* and *seventh;* but they seem to be two parts and branches of the same.

1*st, Lead us not into temptation.* There are various sorts of temptation.—— 1. Some are of God, as, by enjoining things hard, difficult, and trying; so God tempted Abraham, by ordering him to take and offer up his son, on one of the mountains he should shew him, whereby he tried his faith in him, his love and obedience to him, and his fear and reverence of him, Gen. xxii. 1, 2—12. and sometimes by laying afflictions upon his people; which, though they cause heaviness, should be accounted joy; because they try and prove faith and patience, whereby they become more illustrious and precious, 1 Pet. i. 6, 7. James i. 2, 3. but not by soliciting any to sin, James i. 13. yet there is a sense in which God may be said to lead into temptation, or there would be no occasion to deprecate it; and that either providentially, as Christ himself was led up by the Spirit into the wilderness, to be tempted of the devil, Matt. iv. 1. and as when things occur in providence, and objects are presented, which, though good and lawful in themselves, yet meeting with the corruptions of nature, are incentives to, and occasion of sin; as the Babylonish garment, the shekels of silver and wedge of gold spied and found by Achan, were to him; and as a train of circumstances, by meeting together in providence, which led on to David's sin with Bathsheba, Josh. vii. 21. 2 Sam. xi. 2. or however permissively; so Satan was suffered to tempt and beguile Eve, and to move and provoke David to number the people, and to sift Peter, and put him on denying his Lord and Master, for which he desired to have him; and God may be said to lead into temptation, when he withdraws the influence of his grace, which only can keep from it; leaves men to the corruptions of their own hearts, as he did

Hezekiah, 2 Chron. xxxii. 31.——2. Others are more immediately from Satan himself; hence he is called *the tempter*, Matt. iv. 3. 1 Thess. iii. 5. he solicits to sin, as he did our first parents, and does all men, both good and bad; he tempts by suggesting evil things into the mind, as he did into Judas, and Ananias and Sapphira; in the one to betray his Lord, and in the other to lie against the Holy Ghost; and by filling good men with doubts and fears, with unbelieving and desponding thoughts about their interest in the love, favour, and grace of God, and even with things blasphemous and atheistical, contrary to the dictates and sentiments of their own minds; all which are very distressing and afflictive, and therefore expressed by buffetings, siftings, and fiery darts; and his temptations with all sorts of persons are managed with great art and cunning, and are suited to the age, circumstances, conditions, constitutions, and tempers of men.——3. There are other temptations, which are from the world; some from the better things in it, as from riches, which are deceitful, and draw men to set their hearts upon them, and to trust in them, and to covet after them, and to seek to gain them in an illicit way; by which they fall into temptation and a snare, and into foolish and hurtful lusts, and pierce themselves through with many sorrows: and from the honours of it; seeking great things for themselves, honour from men, and not that honour which comes from God; and so are diverted from Christ, his gospel and interest, loving the praise of men more than the praise of God: and from the pleasures of it; the love of which detracts from the love of God; not only the pleasures of sin, to which few have the courage of Moses, to prefer afflictions with the people of God; but even lawful recreations men are tempted to carry to an excess; nay, the very necessaries of life, table-mercies, prove a snare; the good things of life are abused in their using. Some temptations arise from what may be called the evil things of the world; as poverty, which may be a temptation to steal, or to do things unwarrantable, either to prevent it, or to relieve under it. And afflictions of various sorts, under which even good men may be tempted either to neglect, overlook, and slight them; or to faint under them, and to murmur and repine at the hand of God upon them. The customs of the world, which are usually vain and sinful, are very ensnaring; and therefore the apostolical advice is, *Be not conformed to this world, but be transformed;* and it is no wonder that worldly and fleshly lusts, or that the sinful things in the world, the lust of the flesh, the lust of the eyes, and the pride of life, should be enticing and ensnaring, and which, by promising liberty, make men the servants of corruption. There are temptations to good men from the men of the world; by whom they are enticed to join them in things sinful, and whose conversation and evil communications corrupt good manners. Joseph, by being among Pharaoh's courtiers, learnt to swear by the life of Pharaoh. And the reproaches, menaces, and persecutions of the world, are temptations to men, either to make no profession of religion, or when made, to drop it; such a time is called, the *time of temptation,* Luke viii. 13. Rev. iii. 10. ——4. There are temptations from the flesh, from indwelling sin, from the corruption of nature, which of all are the worst and most powerful; *Every man is tempted when he is drawn away of his own lust, and enticed,* James i. 14. there is a deceitfulness in sin, in internal lust, which sadly entangles, ensnares, and captivates; *the flesh lusteth against the spirit.*

Now in this petition, *Lead us not into temptation,* we pray to be kept from every occasion of sinning, and inclination to it, and appearance of it, and from every object which may allure to it; and that we might be kept from the sin which most easily besets us, or we are most inclined to; and that God would not leave us to Satan and our own corruptions, but hold us up by his power, when only we shall be safe; and that he would not suffer us neither to enter into, nor to fall by a temptation; and especially that we may not sink under it, and be overcome by it; but that we may be able to resist every temptation, and be victorious over all.

2*dly,* The other branch of the petition is, *but deliver us from evil;* either from the evil of afflictions, called *evil things,* because the effects of sin, and disagreeable to men, Luke xvi. 25. from these God has promised to deliver, and does deliver, and therefore may be prayed for in faith; or from the evil of sin, from committing it; this was the prayer of Jabez, 1 Chron. iv. 10. and from the guilt of it on the conscience, by the blood of Christ, the same with the forgiveness of it; and from the dominion of it, that it might not reign in us; such a prayer see in Psalm xix. 13. and cxix. 133

and from the being of it, and the sad effects of it; see Rom. vii. 23, 24. or from evil men, unreasonable and cruel; from falling into their hands, and being ill-used by them 2 Thess. iii. 2. and especially from the *evil one*, Satan, and from his temptations; and agrees with the former part of the petition.

III. This prayer is concluded with a doxology, or ascription of glory to God; *For thine is the kingdom, and the power, and the glory, for ever;* see 1 Chron. xxix. 11. and these may be considered as so many reasons, pleas, and arguments, for obtaining the things requested, and to encourage faith therein; *For thine is the kingdom*, of nature, providence, grace, and glory; and so all things appertaining thereunto, are at the disposal of God: *and the power;* to give daily bread, to forgive sin, to preserve from temptation, to support under it, and deliver out of it: *and the glory;* arising from all this, to whom alone it is due; and to be for ever given: *Amen*, a note of asseveration of the truth herein contained; and used as an assent to the petitions made, and as a wish for the fulfilment of them; and as expressive of faith and confidence, that they would be answered.

CHAP. VII.

OF SINGING PSALMS, AS A PART OF PUBLIC WORSHIP.

NEXT to prayer may be considered, singing the praises of God, as a religious duty: this may be done in a private manner, by a person singly and alone, James v. 13. and between two or more; so Paul and Silas sang aloud praises to God in the prison, Acts xvi. 25. and in the family, between a man and his wife, with his children and servants: of this private singing of psalms in the family, Tertullian[1] speaks, and makes use of this as an argument with christians to marry among themselves, that this duty may be the better and more harmoniously performed; but I shall treat of it as an ordinance of divine and public service; and endeavour,

I. To shew what singing is, according to the common idea we have of it, as a natural act of the voice; and as a religious duty distinct from other acts of religion. Singing may be considered either in a proper or an improper sense. When used improperly, it is ascribed to inanimate creatures; the heavens, earth, mountains, hills, forests, trees of the wood, the pastures clothed with flocks, and the vallies covered with corn, are said to sing and shout for joy, or are exhorted to it, Isa. xliv. 23. and xlix. 13. Psalm lxv. 12, 13. Singing, taken in a strict and proper sense, and as a natural act, is an act of the tongue or voice; though not every action of the tongue, or sound of the voice, is to be called singing. Speech is an action of the tongue; but all kind of speaking is not singing; singing is speaking melodiously, musically, or with the modulation of the voice. These two sounds, speaking or saying, and singing, have not the same idea annexed to them; should we be told that such a man, as commonly expressed, said grace before and after meat, we should at once understand what is meant, that he asked of God a blessing upon his food, before eating, and returned thanks after it, according to the common use of speech, in prayer to God, and in conversation with men; but if it should be said, he sung grace before and after meat, we should not be able to form any other idea of it, but that he did it in a tonical, musical way, with a modulation of the voice. It is not any clamour of the tongue, or sound of the voice, that can be called singing; otherwise why should the tuneful voice and warbling notes of birds be called singing; Cant. ii. 12. any more than the sound of the voice of other animals; as the roaring of the lion, the bellowing of the ox, the bleating of the sheep, the neighing of the horse, the braying of the ass, the barking of the dog, or the grunting of the hog? The clamorous noisy shouts of conquerors, and the querulous notes, shrieks, and cries of the conquered, are very different from the voice of singing: when Moses and Joshua came down from the mount, says Joshua, *There is a noise of war in the camp; and he* (Moses) *said, It is not the voice of them that shout for mastery; neither is it the voice of them that cry for being overcome; but the noise of them that sing do I hear;* that sung and danced about the calf, Exod. xxxii. 6, 17, 18. And singing musically with the voice, as a religious action, is distinct from all other religious acts and exercises.

1. From prayer: James speaks of them as two distinct things in the place before

[1] Ad uxorem, 1. 2. c. 6. p. 190. c. 8. p. 191.

quoted; and so the apostle Paul, when he says, *I will pray with the Spirit, and I will sing with the Spirit also;* or if he means the same, he must be guilty of a very great tautology, 1 Cor. xiv. 15. Paul and Silas in prison, both prayed and sang praises, which are evidently two distinct exercises, Acts xvi. 25.——2. It is distinct from giving thanks; Christ, in the institution of the Supper, gave thanks, this he did as his own act and deed, singly and alone; but after supper he and his disciples sung an hymn or psalm together; and the apostle having directed the church at Ephesus to sing psalms, and hymns, and spiritual songs, makes mention afterwards of *giving thanks* to God in the name of Christ, as a distinct duty incumbent on them, Matt. xxvi. 26, 27, 30. Eph. v. 19, 20.——3. It is distinct from praising God; for though we do praise him in singing, yet all praising is not singing. Singing is only one way of praising God; there are others; as when we celebrate the adorable perfections of God, or speak well of them in preaching, or in common discourse; when we return thanks to him for temporal and spiritual mercies in prayer; when we shew forth his praise, and glorify him by our lives and conversations; in neither of which senses can we be said to sing; if praising is singing, what then is singing of praise!——4. It is different from inward spiritual joy, which is wrought in the soul by the spirit of God, and arises from views of interest in the love of God, in the covenant of grace, in the person, blood, righteousness, and sacrifice of Christ; and this indeeds fits a person for singing the praises of God, but is distinct from it; *Is any merry?* ευθυμει τις, is any of a good mind, or in a good frame of soul? *let him sing psalms:* but then the frame and the duty are different things; spiritual joy is not singing; but the cause and reason of it, and makes a man capable of performing it in the best manner.——5. Though there is such a thing as mental prayer, there is no such thing as mental singing, or singing in the heart, without the voice. Speaking or preaching, without the tongue or voice, are not greater contradictions, or rather impossibilities, than singing without a voice or tongue is. Such an hypothesis is suited for no scheme but *quakerism;* and we may as well have our silent meetings, dumb preachings, and mute prayer, as silent singing: *singing and making melody in the heart,* is no other than singing with or from the heart or heartily; or, as elsewhere expressed, *with grace in the heart,*[2] that is, in the exercise of it; it does not exclude the voice in singing, but hypocrisy in the heart, and requires sincerity in it, as a learned man[3] observes. I go on,

II. To prove, that singing the praises of God has always been a branch of natural or revealed religion, in all ages and periods of time, and ever will be.

1. It was a part of the worship of God with the heathens; as prayer is a natural and moral duty, so is singing the praises of God: as men by the light of nature are directed to pray to God, when in distress, or for mercies they want, Jonah i. 6. so they are directed by the same to sing the praises of God for mercies received. A modern learned writer[4] observes, that "though religions the most different have obtained in various nations and ages, yet in this they all agree, that they should be solemnized in hymns and songs:" according to Plato the most ancient kind of poetry lay in those devotions to God which were called hymns;[5] the credit and applause which Homer got,[6] was owing to the hymns he composed for the deities; and among his works is still extant an hymn to Apollo; as Orpheus before him, composed hymns to the several deities, which are yet in being under his name. The whole science of music was employed by the ancient Greeks in the worship of their gods, as Plutarch[7] attests. One part of the religious worship of the Egyptians, consisted of hymns to their deities, suitable to the honour of them, and which they sang morning and evening, at noon, and sun-setting, as Clemens of Alexandria and Porphyry relate; and the Indians also spent the greatest part of the day and night in prayers and hymns to the gods, as the last of these writers affirms.[8] Remarkable is the saying of Arrianus the Stoic philosopher;[9] "If," says he, "we are intelligent creatures, what else should we do,

---

[2] Necesse est hic in corde, ex corde intelligi, scilicet, ut non solum ore, sed etiam corde cantemus. Hieron. in Col. 3. 16.
[3] Zanchius in Eph. v. 19.
[4] Lowth de Sacr. Poesi Heb. Prælect. 1. p. 21.
[5] De Legibus, l. 3. p. 819. Ed. Ficin.
[6] Herodotus de vita Homeri, c. 9. p. 558. Ed. Gronov.
[7] De Musica, p. 1140.
[8] See my Discourse on Singing, p. 10, 11.
[9] Arrian. Epictetus, l. 1. c. 16. et l. 3. c. 26.

both in public and private, than to sing an hymn to the Deity?—If I was a nightingale, I would do as a nightingale, and if a swan, as a swan; but since I am a rational creature, I ought to praise God, and I exhort you to the self-same song:—this is my work whilst I live, to sing an hymn to God, both by myself and before one or many." From these, and other instances which might be produced, we may conclude, that the Gentiles were by the light of nature directed, and by the law of nature obliged, to this part of worship; and consequently that it is a part of natural religion——2. It was practised by the people of God before the giving of the law by Moses; the eighty-eighth and eighty-ninth psalms are thought by some[10] to be the oldest pieces of writing in the world; being composed long before the birth of Moses, composed by Heman and Ethan, two sons of Zerah, the son of Judah; the one in a mournful elegy deplores the miserable state of Israel in Egypt; the other joyfully sings prophetically their deliverance out of it. The ninetieth psalm was written by Moses himself, at what time it is not said; however, certain it is, that Moses and the children of Israel, sang a song at the Red sea, after their passage through it, and the destruction of the Egyptians in it; which is still on record, and it seems will be sung again when the antichristian Pharaoh, and the antichristian powers, are destroyed by the Christian conquerors, standing on a sea of glass, with the harps of God in their hands, Exod. xv. 1. Rev. xv. 2, 3. Now this being before the law of Moses, when first sung, it was not done by virtue of that law; nor was it of ceremonious institution, nor a part of worship peculiar to the Levitical dispensation; nor was it by any positive law of God to the sons of men that we know of; but was sung by the Israelites according to the dictates of their consciences, and the examples of others before them, by which they were influenced, as to cry to the Lord when in distress, so to sing his praises when they were delivered.——3. It was not a part of divine service peculiar to Israel under the law; but when psalmody was in the most flourishing condition, under the direction and influence of David their king, he in many of his psalms, calls upon and exhorts the nations of the earth, to sing the praises of God; *Make a joyful noise unto God, all ye lands,* or *all the earth; let the people, even all the people praise thee; let the nations be glad and sing for joy, sing unto the Lord all the earth!* &c. Psalm lxvi. 1, 2. and lxvii. 3, 5. and xcvi. 1. Now if singing was not a part of moral worship, but of a ceremonious kind, the nations of the earth would have had no concern in it, nor would it have been obligatory upon them.——4. When the ceremonial law was in its greatest glory, and legal sacrifices in highest esteem, singing of psalms and spiritual songs was preferred unto them, as more acceptable to God than the offering of an *ox or bullock,* Psalm lxix. 30, 31. Now no other reason of this preference can be given, but that the sacrifice of an ox was of ceremonial institution, whereas singing the praises of, God was a part of moral worship, which might be performed in a spiritual and evangelic manner. ——5. When the ceremonial law, with all its rites, was abolished, this duty of singing the praises of God remained in full force; at the same time the apostle tells the churches, that the law of the commandments was abolished, and they were no more to be judged with respect to meats, and drinks, and holy days, these shadows being gone; he exhorts them most strongly to sing psalms, hymns, and spiritual songs, Eph. ii. 14, 15. and v. 19. Col. ii. 16, 17. and iii. 16. Now it is not reasonable to suppose that the apostle, in the same epistles, written to the same persons, should declare them disengaged from the one, and under obligation to regard the other, if they equally belonged to the same ceremonial law.——6. That the churches of Christ under the gospel-dispensation were to sing, have sung, and ought to sing the praises of God vocally, appears—(1.) From the prophesies of the Old Testament concerning it. In many of the psalms respecting the times of the Messiah, the churches of God in them are invited to sing the praises of God; as in Psalms forty-seventh, sixty-eighth, and ninety-fifth, and in many of the prophesies of Isaiah it is declared, that not only the watchmen, the ministers of the word, *should lift up the voice, and with the voice together sing;* but that churches should *break forth into joy, and sing together,* Isa. lii. 7, 8, 9. see Isa. xxvi. 1. and xxxv. 1, 2. and liv. 1. blessed be God these predictions are in a great measure fulfilled; gospel-churches among the Gentiles, as

---

[10] Lightfoot, vol. 1. p. 699, 700.

well as in Judea, have lift up their voices and sung the praises of God according to these prophesies.—(2.) This also is evident from express precepts and directions given to gospel-churches concerning it; it is not only prophesied of in the Old Testament, but is commanded in the New; particularly the churches at Ephesus and Colosse, are expressly enjoined to sing *psalms, hymns, and spiritual songs*, Eph. v. 19. Col. iii. 16. and directions are given them in what manner they are to sing them, which will be observed hereafter.—(3.) This is clear from New Testament instances and examples. Christ and his disciples sang an hymn or psalm together, at the celebration of the Lord's Supper; which they did as a church, in the midst of which Christ sung an hymn, and they with him, Matt. xxvi. 30.[11] Heb. ii. 12. the church at Corinth sang psalms in the times of the apostles; there were indeed disorders among them in the performance of this ordinance as of others, which the apostle rectifies, and blames them, but not for that itself, provided they observed the rules he gave them, 1 Cor. xiv. 26.—(4.) This practice obtained in the earliest times of Christianity, and has continued to the present time. Pliny,[12] an heathen, in his letter to Trajan the emperor, written at the latter end of the first, or beginning of the second century, acquaints him, that the sum of the charge against the Christians was, that "they met together on a stated day, before it was light, and sung a song among themselves to Christ, as to God." And Tertullian,[13] in the beginning of the third century, speaks of reading the scriptures, singing psalms, preaching, and prayer, as parts of public worship. And Origen, a little later in the same century observes,[14] the need of the Spirit of God to assist in singing psalms and hymns to the Father in Christ, ευρυθμως, εμμελως, εμμερως, και συμφωνως, in good rhyme, melody, and metre, and in vocal concert. The proofs would be too numerous, and indeed endless to give, of its continuance and use in after-ages;[15] it will be sufficient to observe, the book of the Revelation is a representation of the service of the churches of Christ on earth, as well as of their state, condition, and sufferings, and their deliverance from them, in the several periods of time, until his second coming; in which we frequently have an account of their being concerned in this work of singing, chap. iv. 9, 10, 11. and v. 9—13. and vii. 10, 11, 12. particularly at the time of the reformation from popery, and at the fall of Babylon, or antichrist, chap. xiv. 1—8. and xv. 2, 3. and xix. 1—7. when the spiritual reign of Christ will take place; at which time, *from the uttermost parts of the earth* will be *heard songs, even glory to the righteous*, Isa. xxiv. 16. and in the millennium, upon the first resurrection, when the personal reign of Christ will begin, the raised ones will sing, as they will be exhorted, and will have reason so to do; *Awake and sing, ye that dwell in the dust*, Isa. xxvi. 19. in short, when all other ordinances will cease, this of singing the praises of God will be in its highest glory and perfection, Isa. xxxv. 10. I shall next enquire,

III. What that is which is to be sung, or the subject-matter of singing; and the direction is to these three, *psalms, hymns*, and *spiritual songs*, Eph. v. 19. Col. iii. 16.

1. By Psalms may be meant the Book of Psalms, composed by David, Asaph, and others; but chiefly by David; hence he is called *the sweet Psalmist of Israel*, 2 Sam. xxiii. 1. this is the only sense in which the word is used throughout the whole New Testament; nor is there any reason to believe the apostle Paul designs any other in the places referred to; nor the apostle James, in chap. v. 13. Those who are of a different mind ought to shew in what other sense the word is used, and where; and what those Psalms are we are to sing, if not the *Psalms* of *David*, &c. since it is certain there are psalms which are to be sung under the gospel-dispensation.——2. By *hymns* are intended, not any mere human compositions; since I can hardly think the apostle would place such between psalms and spiritual songs, made by men inspired by the Holy Ghost, and put them upon a level with them, to be sung; but rather this is only another name for the Book of Psalms; the running title of which may as well be the *Book of Hymns*, as it is rendered by Ainsworth.[16]

---

[11] See the old translation of this text exposed, which is pleaded for, and what was the hymn or psalm sung at this time, in a Discourse of mine on Singing, p. 34, 35, &c.
[12] Ep. l. 10. ep. 97. vid. Tert. Apol. c. 2. et Euseb. Ec. Hist. l. 3. c. 33.
[13] De Anima. c. 9.
[14] Περι ευχης, c. 6. p. 7. Ed. Oxon. 1686.
[15] See my discourse on Singing, p. 45, 46. &c.
[16] Vox υμνοι, cum Hebræo titulo תהלים multo melius congruit. Lowth. de Sacr. Poes. Heb. Prælect. 29. p. 376.

The hundred and forty-fifth psalm is called an hymn of David; and the psalm our Lord sung with his disciples after the Supper, is said to be an hymn; and so the psalms of David in general are called υμνοι, *hymns*, both by Josephus [17] and Philo the Jew [18]——3. By *spiritual songs* may also be meant the same psalms of David, Asaph, &c. the titles of some of which are songs; as sometimes *a psalm and song, a song and psalm, a song of degrees*, and the like; together with all other spiritual songs written by men inspired of God; called *spiritual*, because of the author of them, the Spirit of God; the penmen of them, such as were moved by the same Spirit; and the matter of them, spiritual, useful for spiritual edification; and are opposed to all loose, profane, and wanton songs. And as these three words, *psalms, hymns*, and *spiritual songs*, answer to תהלים מזמורים and שירים the titles of David's Psalms, and are by the *Septuagint* rendered by the Greek words used by the apostle, it may be reasonably concluded, that it was his intention that the churches he writes to, should sing them; but inasmuch as the *word of God* and Christ in general furnishes out matter for singing his praises, I deny not, but that such hymns and spiritual songs, composed by good men, uninspired, may be made use of; provided care is taken that they be agreeable to the sacred writings, and to the analogy of faith, and are expressed as much as may be in scripture language; of such sort were those Tertullian [19] speaks of, used in his time, as were either out of the holy scripture, or *de proprio ingenio*, of a man's own composure; and such seem to be the songs of the brethren, in praise of Christ, as the Word of God, ascribing divinity to him, condemned by some heretics.[20]

IV. The manner in which psalms, &c. are to be sung may be next considered.

1. Socially, and with united voices; so Moses and the children of Israel sung at the Red Sea; so Christ and his disciples sung after the Lord's Supper; so the watchmen will sing in the latter-day, even with their voice together; so did Paul and Silas in prison; and thus the churches are directed in Eph. v. 19. Col. iii. 16.——
2. With the heart along with the mouth, as heartily as well as vocally, which is making *melody in the heart*, Eph. v. 19. or performing the duty in sincerity and truth; and not as the Israelites, who flattered God with their lips, sung the praises of God, but soon forgot his works. ——3. *With grace in the heart*, Col. iii. 16. with the several graces; not one note, but a mixture of notes, makes melody; many voices, yet one sound make a chorus:[21] so singing must be with various graces; with faith in God, without which it is impossible to please him; and with strong love and affection for him; and also *with reverence and godly fear;* for God is *fearful in praises* נורא reverend in them, to be praised with great fear and reverence of his Majesty.——4. *With the Spirit*, as the apostle Paul determined to do, 1 Cor. xiv. 15. with the Spirit of God, whose assistance is necessary in this as in prayer; and with our spirits, sincerely, fervently, and affectionately, and in a spiritual manner, suitable to the nature of God, who is a Spirit.——5. *With the understanding also;* with the understanding of what is sung; and in such a manner, and in such language, as may be understood by others; for one end of the duty is, not only to speak to ourselves in it, but to *teach* and *admonish* others; and perhaps the apostle may have some regard to one of the titles of David's psalms משכיל *Maschil*, which signifies, a psalm giving instruction, and causing to understand. In a word, besides our mutual edification,——6. We should have in view the glory of God; for we are to *sing unto the Lord;* not to ourselves, merely to raise our natural affections, to gain applause from others, by the fineness of our voice, and by observing an exact conformity to the tune; but to the glory of Father, Son, and Spirit, the one God, who condescends to inhabit the praises of Israel. What remains now is only,

V. To answer some of the principal objections made to this duty; these are chiefly made against the matter and manner of singing, and the persons, at least some of them, who join in this service.

1*st*, The matter and manner of singing, particularly David's psalms; to which are objected,

1. That they were not written originally in metre; and therefore are not to be sung in such manner; nor to be translated into

---

[17] Antiq. l. 7. c. 12.
[18] L. de mutat. nom. et. l. de Somnis, et alibi.
[19] Apolog. c. 39.

[20] Euseb. Hist. Eccl. l. 5. c. 28. et. l. 7. c. 30.
[21] Seneca, Ep. 84.

metre for such a purpose. The contrary to this is universally allowed by the Jews, and appears from the different accentuation of them from that of other books, and is asserted by such who are best skilled in the Hebrew language, both ancients and moderns. Josephus[22] says, David, in a time of peace, composed divine songs and hymns, of various metre, some tri-metre, that is, of three feet; and others of penta-metre, that is, of five feet. And Jerom,[23] who, of all the fathers best understood the Hebrew tongue, takes the psalms to be of the Lyric kind, and therefore compares David, to Pindar, Horace, and others; and for the metre of them appeals to Philo, Josephus, Origen, Eusebius, and others. Gomarus[24] has given hundreds of verses out of the psalms, which agree with Pindar and Sophocles;[25] and the word commonly used throughout that Book, in the judgment of learned men, signifies metre;[26] and since then the Psalms were originally written in metre, it is lawful to translate them into it, in order to be sung in the churches of Christ.——2. It is doubted whether the Book of Psalms is suited to the gospel-dispensation, and proper to be sung in gospel-churches. Nothing more suitable to it, nor more proper to be sung in it; since it abounds with prophesies concerning the person and offices of the Messiah, his suffering and death, resurrection, ascension, and session at the right hand of God, now more clearly understood, and more capable of being sung in an evangelic manner; and also is full of precious promises; is a large fund of experience, a rich mine of gospel-grace and truth, and so is greatly suited to every case and condition the church of Christ, or a particular believer may be in at any time; a little care and prudence in the choice of proper psalms on particular occasions, would fully discover the truth of this.——3. It is objected, that cases are often met with in this book, we cannot make our own; and to sing them, it is suggested, would be lying to God; and that some are quite shocking, as curses and imprecations on wicked men; and seem to shew a want of that charity which is recommended in the gospel. To which it may be replied, that singing cases not our own, are no more lying to God than reading them is, singing being but a slower way of pronunciation, in a musical manner. Besides, when we sing the cases of others, we sing them as such, and not our own; which yet may be useful by way of example, advice, comfort, or instruction; and being sung in public, may be suitable to some in the community, though not to others; and so the end of singing be answered: and the same objection will lie equally against public prayer, and joining in that, since it cannot be thought that every petition is suitable to all: and as for curses and imprecations on wicked men, these may be avoided; we are not obliged to sing all that are in the psalms; besides, these may be considered only as prophetic hints of what may be expected will befal such persons, and may be sung to the glory of God, and with instruction to ourselves; since herein may be observed the justice and holiness of God, the vile nature of sin, the indignation of God against it, and abhorrence of it, and in which it is to be had with all good men.——4. It is urged, that to sing David's Psalms, and others, is to sing by a form, and then why not pray by one? I answer, the case is different; the one may be done without a form, the other not; the Spirit is promised as a Spirit of supplication, but not as a Spirit of poetry; and if a man had an extraordinary gift of delivering out an extempore psalm or hymn, that would be a form to others who joined him; add to this, that we have a Book of Psalms, but not a book of prayers. David's Psalms were composed to be sung by form, and in the express words of them, and were so sung; see 1 Chron. xvi. 7. 2 Chron. xxix. 30. hence the people of God are bid, not to *make* a psalm, but to *take* a psalm, ready made to their hands, Psalm lxxxi. 1, 2.——5. It is observed, that David's psalms were sung formerly with musical instruments, as the harp, timbrel, and cymbal, and organs; and why not with these now? if these are to be disused, why not singing itself? I answer, these are not essential to singing, and so may be laid aside, and that continue; it was usual to burn incense at the time of prayer, typical of Christ's mediation, and of the acceptance of prayer

---

[22] Antiq. l. 7. c. 12.
[23] Ep. ad Paulin. tom, 3. fol. 3. 2. præfat. in lib. Job fol. 8. 2.
[24] Davidis Lyra inter opera ejus, t. 2. p. 317. &c.
[25] See my Discourse on Singing, p. 23, 24.
[26] מזמור metrum, vel numeros, sive quam Græci ῥυθμον, vocant, significat, Lowth. de Sacr. Poesi Heb. Prælect. 3. p. 40. in marg. et Prælect. 4. p. 44. vid. Gejerum, et Michaelem, in Psalm iii. 1.

through it; that is now disused; but prayer being a moral duty, still remains: the above instruments were used only when the church was in its infant-state, and what is showy, gaudy, and pompous, are pleasing to children; and as an ancient writer[27] observes, "these were fit for babes, but in the churches (under the gospel-dispensation, which is more manly) the use of these, fit for babes, is taken away, and bare or plain singing is left." As for organs, of which mention is made in Psalm cl. the word there used signifies another kind of instruments than those now in use, which are of a later device and use; and were first introduced by a pope of Rome, Vitalianus, and that in the seventh century, and not before.[28]

2*dly*, There are other objections, which lie against some persons singing; as,——
1. Women, because they are ordered to keep *silence in the churches;* and are not *permitted to speak,* 1 Cor. xiv. 34, 35. but this is to be understood only of speaking and teaching in public, in an authoritative way, 1 Tim. ii. 11, 12. otherwise it would not be lawful for them to give an account of the work of grace upon their hearts; nor to give evidence in any case, and the like: as for singing the praises of God, it is a moral duty, and equally binding as prayer on both sexes; and the God of nature and grace has given women faculties capable of performing it; and having a voice suited for it, to join in harmonious concert, ought to be exhorted to it, and encouraged, and not discouraged and discountenanced. Miriam, and the women with her, sung at the Red Sea; and Deborah sung with Barak; and it is a prophesy of gospel-times, that *women* should come and *sing in the height of Zion,* Jer. xxxi. 8—12. and indeed, what else is the *woman's prophesying,* but singing, allowed by the apostle, with her *head covered;* as is well-judged by a learned writer;[29] since prophesying is explained by singing, as well as by praying and preaching, 1 Cor. xi. 5. and xiv. 15, 24, 26. see 1 Chron. xxv. 1, 2, 3. where prophesying is used in the same sense.——2. The singing of unbelievers, and singing with them, are objected to by some; but then this supposes that it is the duty of believers, and is allowed of; or otherwise the objection is impertinent. Now let it be observed, that singing the praises of God, as well as prayer, is a moral duty, and so binding on all men, believers and unbelievers; and though none but the former can sing in a spiritual and evangelical manner; yet the latter are obliged to do it, in the best way they can; and it may be as well objected to their admission to public prayer, as to public singing; and it will be difficult, if not impossible, to know who are such in public assemblies; and supposing they ought not to sing, how can this affect believers? it is not their sin; nor should they neglect their duty on this account; but rather blush to see such so forward to it, to whom it is thought it does not belong, and they so backward to it. Besides, it has been the practice of the saints in all ages, to sing in mixed assemblies; there was a mixed multitude that came out of Egypt with the Israelites, in whose presence they sung at the Red Sea, and who very probably joined them in it, since they shared in the common deliverance. It was the resolution and practice of David, to sing the praises of God among the heathen, Psalm xviii. 49. and li. 9. and, indeed, some ends of this ordinance cannot be otherwise answered; which are to declare the Lord's doings, his wonders, and his glory among them, Psalm ix. 11. and xcvi. 3. and this has been an ordinance for conversion; it was of great use in forwarding the reformation from popery, as bishop Burnet,[30] in his history of it, relates; and it has been made very useful to souls under their first awakenings. Austin[31] speaks of it from his own experience; "How much," says he, "have I wept at thy hymns and songs, being exceedingly moved at the voices of thy church sweetly sounding. These voices pierced into my ears; thy truth melted into my heart, and from thence pious affections were raised, and the tears ran, and it was well with me."——3. It is urged, that singing is not proper for persons in any distress, only when in good and comfortable frames; and which is very much grounded on James v. 13. the sense of which is, not that such are the only persons that are to sing psalms, or this the only time of doing it; any more than that

---

[27] Autor. Qu. et. Respons. inter opera Justin. p. 462.
[28] Platina de vitis Pontif. p. 86.
[29] Works. vol. 2. p. 785, 1157. see Targum Jon. in 1 Sam. x. 5. and xix. 20, 23, 24.
[30] Hist. of the Reformation, vol. 2. p. 94.
[31] Confession. l. 9. c. 6.

afflicted persons are the only ones to pray, and the time of affliction the only time of prayer; but as affliction more especially calls for prayer, so a good and joyful frame on account of good things, for singing of psalms. What more distressed condition could a man well be in, than that in which Heman the Ezrahite, was when he penned and sung the lxxxviiith Psalm? as the church sung in the wilderness in the days of her youth, when she came out of Egypt; so it is prophesied that she should hereafter sing there as then; and as the church is now in the wilderness, where she is nourished with the word and ordinances, for a time, and times, and half a time, she has reason to sing on that account, Hos. ii. 14, 15. Rev. xii. 14.

CHAP. VIII.

OF THE CIRCUMSTANCES OF PUBLIC WORSHIP, AS TO PLACE AND TIME.

THE circumstances of *place* and *time* of public worship, deserve consideration; since for public worship there must be some certain *place* to meet and worship in, and some stated *time* to worship at. As to the first of these, it may soon be dispatched; since there does not appear to be any place appointed for it, until the tabernacle was erected in the wilderness. It is probable that there was some certain place where our first parents worshipped, after their expulsion from the garden of Eden; whither Cain and Abel brought their sacrifices, and offered them; but where it was is not easy to say; perhaps the cherubim and flaming sword, at the east of the garden of Eden, were the symbols of the divine presence, since the Lord is frequently represented as dwelling between the cherubim; which may have respect, as to the cherubim in the tabernacle and temple, so to these; and there might be a stream of light, splendour, and glory, an emblem of the Shekinah, or divine Majesty, which had then appeared in the form of a flaming sword; and now near to this, or however in sight of it, might be the place of public worship; and hence when Cain was driven from these parts, he is said to be *hid from the face of God*, and to go out *from the presence of the Lord*, Gen. iii. 24. and iv. 3, 4, 14, 16. As for the patriarchs in succeeding times, before the flood, it does not appear that they had any other places to worship in but their own houses, where families might agree to meet, and worship in them in turn and course. And the patriarchs after the flood, as they were strangers, sojourners, and travellers in the earth; they built altars here and there for their convenience, and where they worshipped. Abraham in his travels came to a place near Bethel, as it was afterwards called, and built an altar, and worshipped; and on his return from Egypt he came to the same place again, and there worshipped as before, Gen. xii. 8. and xiii. 3, 4. Jacob, in his travels, came to a place called Luz, and where he remarkably enjoyed the divine presence, and thought it no other than the house of God, and therefore set up a stone for a pillar, and said it should be the house of God; and called the name of the place Bethel; and which God so honoured as to call himself by the name of the *God of Bethel*; and hither, with his family, he came many years after, and erected an altar unto God, Gen. xxviii. 17—22. and xxxi. 13. and xxxv. 6, 7. There does not seem to be any settled place of worship until the tabernacle was built in the wilderness; and then every man was to bring his offering to the door of the tabernacle of the congregation, and there offer it, before the tabernacle of the Lord, Lev. xvii. 4, 5. and this tabernacle was moveable from place to place; not only while in the wilderness, but when the Israelites were come into the land of Canaan: it was first at Gilgal, then at Shiloh, after that at Nob and Gibeon; hence the Lord says, he had not dwelt in an house, in any fixed place, from the time the Israelites came out of Egypt; as if he had before;[1] but had walked in a tent, in a tabernacle, 2 Sam. vii. 6. It had been said by the Lord, that when the Israelites came into the land that was given them, there would be a place chosen of God to dwell in, and where all offerings were to be brought, and feasts kept, Deut. xii. 10, 11. the name of the place was not mentioned, but it eventually appeared, that the city of Jerusalem, and the temple there, were meant; and the place where the temple was to be built was first discovered by David, and shewn to Solomon; and which was confirmed to him by the Lord himself, to be the place he had chosen for an house of sacrifice, 1 Chron. xxii. 1. 2 Chron. vii. 12. and this continued a place of worship until

---

[1] See my Note on 1 Chron. xvii. 5.

CHAP. VIII. OF THE DAY OF PUBLIC WORSHIP.

destroyed by Nebuchadnezzar; and after the Jews' return from the Babylonish captivity it was rebuilt, and remained to the times of Christ. Indeed, after the captivity, there were synagogues erected in various parts of the land of Judea, which were a sort of chapels of ease, where prayer was made, and Moses and the prophets read and expounded on Sabbath-days; but no sacrifices were offered in them, nor any of the yearly feasts kept there: and whereas there had been, before the times of Christ, there still was a controversy between the Jews and Samaritans, whether the temple at Jerusalem or mount Gerizim, were the place of worship; this was decided by our Lord, who declared that the time was coming, that neither at the one place nor at the other, should God be worshipped; but every where, John iv. 20, 21. as the apostle also says, 1 Tim. ii. 8. and, indeed, since, under the gospel dispensation, as was foretold, the name of the Lord shall be great among the Gentiles, from the rising of the sun to the going down of it; and offerings of prayer and praise should be offered to him in every place, Mal. i. 11. No one place could be fixed on for all the nations of the earth to meet and worship in; and saints are now therefore at liberty to build places of worship for their convenience wherever they please, as the first christians did, and continued to do.

But the circumstance of *time*, or a stated day of worship, requires more particular consideration; it having been a matter of controversy which has exercised the minds of good and learned men, for a century or two past, and not yet decided to the satisfaction of all parties; and in order to obtain what satisfaction we can, it will be proper to enquire,

I. What day has been, or is observed, as a stated time of public worship; with the reasons thereof. And,

First, It has been thought and asserted, that the seventh day from the creation, was enjoined Adam in a state of innocence, as a day of public and religious worship, and so to be observed by his posterity in aftertimes; but if it was enjoined Adam in his state of innocence, it must be either by the law of nature, written on his heart, or by a positive law given him.

1st, It does not seem to be the law of nature written on his heart; for then,——
1. He must be bound to keep a Sabbath before the institution of it; he was created on the sixth day, after the image of God; one part of which was the law of nature, written on his heart; but the institution of the Sabbath-day was not until the seventh day, if it was then; for it is yet a matter of question.——2. There would have been some remains of it in his posterity after the fall; and even among the Gentiles; for these have the *law written in their hearts*, Rom. ii. 14. but now it does not appear that they were ever directed by the law and light of nature to observe, the seventh day of the week as an holy Sabbath; what has been alleged in favour of it will be considered hereafter.——3. Was this the case, it would have been re-inscribed with other laws, in more legible characters on the hearts of God's people in regeneration, according to the promise in the covenant of grace, Heb. viii. 10. and had the law of the seventh-day Sabbath been one of them, it must easily have been discerned by them; and the observance of it would have been out of question. Nor,

2dly, Does it seem to be enjoined Adam, by any positive law; and, indeed, if it had been written on his heart, as a branch of the law of nature, there would have been no need of any such law to have directed and instructed him; and to have a positive law given him, to keep a seventh-day Sabbath, without any positive rules and directions what worship should be observed by him on that day, which do not appear, the law would have been useless; we have no account of any positive law given to Adam in a state of innocence, but that which forbad eating of the tree of knowledge of good and evil; which tree, and its fruit, we know nothing of; and did we, that law would not be binding upon us. The proof of such a law, with respect to the Sabbath, is founded,

1. On Gen. ii. 2, 3. where it is said, that God having ended his work, *rested on the seventh-day, and God blessed the seventh-day and sanctified it*. But,— (1.) No mention is made of a Sabbath, and of the sanctification of that, as in the fourth command, Exod. xx. 11. only of the seventh-day, and not of that as a Sabbath. —(2.) The words are a narrative of what God did himself; but do not contain a precept of what Adam should do; they only declare what God did, that he blessed and sanctified the seventh-day; but do not enjoin Adam to keep it holy, as a Sabbath. —(3.) At most they seem only to design a destination of that day to holy service

hereafter; God *blessed* it, that is, pronounced it an happy day; all his works being finished, and man, an holy creature, the crown and glory of all, made after his image:[2] on a survey of which, God rested, and took delight, pleasure, and refreshment in them, on the seventh-day; which he *sanctified*, not by keeping it holy himself, nor by imparting any holiness to it, which a day is not capable of; but he separated, or set it apart for holy use in after-time, which is a very common sense of this word: so Jeremiah was sanctified before he was born; that is, appointed and ordained to be a holy prophet; which purpose was not carried into execution until some time after; and so God might be said to sanctify or set apart in his mind and purpose, the seventh-day to be an holy Sabbath in future time; though it was not actually executed, as it should seem by what will be hereafter observed, until many hundred years after the creation. Besides,—(4.) The words in Gen. ii. are understood by many learned men proleptically, or by way of anticipation; as other things are in this same chapter; so some places are called by the names they bore in the times of Moses, which they had not from the beginning; see ver. 11—14. or the words may be considered as in a parenthesis; and the rather, since had they been read, or to be read, in common with the preceding, the word *God*, and the phrase *the seventh-day*, would have been omitted; and have been read, *and he blessed and sanctified it*; and the reason for it, which follows, seems manifestly taken from the fourth command, as given on Mount Sinai, Exod. xx. 11. and Moses writing his history of the creation, after this precept was given, took the opportunity of inserting this whole passage, to give the greater sanction to it with the Israelites.—(5.) After all, be it that the text in Genesis enjoins the keeping the seventh-day from the creation, as a Sabbath; which seventh-day now cannot be known by any people or persons whatever; it could never be the same with the Jewish seventh-day Sabbath; for that was to be observed after six days labour of man; *Six days shalt thou labour, &c.* whereas this could be only after the six days labour of God, who rested from his work on the seventh; but it was Adam's first day, and could not with any propriety be called a rest from labour to him, when, as yet, he had not laboured at all: such a Sabbath was not suitable to him in a state of innocence, which supposes imperfection and sin; the creature would not have been in bondage had he not sinned, this was the effect of the fall; Adam, in innocence, had no man-servant, nor maid-servant, nor any cattle in a state of bondage, groaning under burdens, to rest from their labours. This is a law merely calculated for sinful man.

2. The other remaining proof of such a law so early, is taken from Heb. iv. 3, 4. where no mention is made of a seventh-day Sabbath; and in which the apostle takes notice of the several rests which had been under the former dispensation, and shews, that neither of them was the rest promised, and had, under the gospel-dispensation: not the seventh-day rest from the creation, for that was God's rest: not the rest of the Israelites in the land of Canaan, which Joshua gave them; for then David a long time after, would not have spoken of another day of rest, the gospel-dispensation, into which believers now enter. Upon the whole, it must appear at least very dubious and uncertain, that there was any institution of a seventh-day Sabbath from the creation; and especially when it is considered,

Secondly, That there is no proof of the patriarchs, from Adam to the times of Moses, observing such a day. For,

1. We no where read of any law being given them for the observation of the seventh-day Sabbath; Adam and Eve had a law which forbad the eating of the fruit of the tree of knowledge; which Tertullian calls the primordial law; Abel was taught the law of sacrifices; Noah had the laws which forbad eating the blood with the flesh of a beast alive, and the shedding of human blood; and Abraham the law of circumcision; but neither of them had any law, as we know of, which enjoined them to observe the seventh-day Sabbath. The Jews pretend that there were seven laws given to the sons of Noah; but this of keeping the seventh-day Sabbath is not among them.——2. Many of the religious actions of the patriarchs are taken notice of, and commended, both ceremonial and moral; as their offering of sacrifice, calling on the name of the Lord, prayer to God, and meditation on him and his works; their piety, fear of God, and eschewing evil; but not a word of their observance

---

[2] Vid. Heidegger, Hist. Patriarch. Exercit. 3. s. 58. p. 109.

of a seventh-day Sabbath.———3. The sins of men, both before and after the flood, are observed, but Sabbath-breaking does not appear among them. The old world was full of violence, rapine, and oppression; and in the new world, intemperance, incest, idolatry, and other sins, men were chargeable with; but not with this: it does not appear among the sins of Sodom and Gomorrah; nor is it to be found among the abominations for which the old inhabitants of Canaan were cast out of it. But no sooner was the law of the Sabbath given to the Israelites in the wilderness, but we hear of the breach of it, and of a severe punishment for it.———4. It was the general opinion of the ancient fathers of the christian-church, that the patriarchs did not observe a Sabbath, nor were obliged to it; but were righteous men, and saved without it: not Adam, nor Abel, nor Enoch, nor Noah, nor Melchizedek, nor Lot, nor Abraham, nor Job, nor any before Moses; so say Justin Martyr,[3] Irenæus,[4] Tertullian,[5] and Eusebius;[6] by whom are mentioned particularly, all the above persons, as good men, and non-observers of a Sabbath. Some have fancied that they have found instances of a seventh-day Sabbath observed in the time of the patriarchs; as at the offerings of Cain and Abel, which are said to be *in process of time*, or *at the end of days*, Gen. iv. 3. but this phrase seems to design, not the end of a week, or seven days, no number being expressed, but rather the end of a year, days being sometimes put for a year;[7] and so refers to the harvest, at the end of the year, when the fruits of the earth were gathered in; and therefore Cain might think his sacrifice, at that time, would have been the more acceptable. And some conjecture a Sabbath was observed by Noah in the ark, Gen. viii. 10, 12. since he is said to send out the dove again, after seven days; but this number seven has respect, not to the first day of the week, from whence the days were numbered; but to the first sending out of the dove, be it on what day it may. And besides, Noah might have respect to the known course of the moon, which puts on another face every seven days;[8] and which, in its increase and wane, might have an influence upon the water, which he was careful to observe and make trial of this way. Moreover, it is observed, that in Job's time there was a day when the sons of God met together, Job i. 6. and ii. 1. but who these sons of God were, whether angels or men, is not certain; nor where, nor on what day they met; no mention is made of a seventh-day, much less of a Sabbath; nor of a certain rotation of this day every week; nor of the distance between the first and second meeting. Arguments from this, and the above instances, must be very far-fetched, and are very slight and slender grounds to build such an hypothesis upon, as the observation of a seventh-day Sabbath.

Thirdly, There is no mention of a Sabbath before the descent of the manna in the wilderness of Sin: some of the Jewish writers[9] speak of it as given at Marah, a few weeks before, which they suppose is included in the word *statute*, Exod. xv. 25. but this is said without any foundation; but the seventh day from the descent of the manna is expressly called a *Sabbath*, Exod. xvi. 23—26. and is the first we hear of, and which appears to be quite a new thing; for had the Israelites been used to a seventh-day Sabbath, the rulers of the people might easily have conjectured, that the reason of twice as much bread being gathered on the sixth day, was on account of the Sabbath being the day following, as a provision for that, had that been the case, without coming to tell Moses of it, who gave this as a reason of it to them; *To-morrow is*, or rather it should be supplied, *shall be, the rest of the holy Sabbath to the Lord;* for a *to-morrow* cannot be spoken of with propriety in the present tense, *is;* but as future, *shall be;* and therefore on the seventh-day, when the manna ceased, which was a confirmation of it, he says to them, *see,* take notice of it, as something new and wonderful, and a sufficient reason of the institution of the Sabbath, and why that day was given unto them for a Sabbath; and when the fourth command was given, a month after, it is introduced with a *memento,* as the other commands are not; *Remember,* what had been lately enjoined them; and that

---

[3] Dialog. cum Trypho. p. 236, 240, 241, 245, 261, 319.
[4] Adv. Hæres. l. 4. c. 30.
[5] Adv. Judæos, c. 2, 3, 4.
[6] Hist. Eccl. l. 1. c. 2, 4. Demonstr. Evangel. l. 1. c. 6. et Præpar. Evangel. l. 7. c. 6. p. 304.

[7] Vid. Heidegger. Hist. Patriarch. Exercitat. 5. s. 18. p. 178.
[8] Ibid. Exercitat. 18. s. 32. p. 562.
[9] T. Sanhedrin, Fol. 56. 2. Seder Olam Zuta, p. 101. Ed. Meyer. Yalkut, par. 1. fol. 73. 2, 3.

appears to be a new law; for when a man was found guilty of the breach of it, no penalty being as yet declared, the people brought him to Moses, and he was put into the ward, until the mind of God was known concerning it, Numb. xv. 31—36. Moreover, if there had been a Sabbath before the giving of the manna, the Sabbath preceding the seventh-day from the descent of that, must have been the fifteenth of the month, on which day it is certain the Jews had a wearisome journey, by divine appointment, the cloud going before them, Exod. xvi. 1. and was concluded with gathering quails; so that it was not a day of rest to them, nor the rest of the holy Sabbath to the Lord.

Fourthly, The seventh-day Sabbath, as it was declared on the descent of the manna, that it was peculiar to the Jews; *The Lord hath given you the Sabbath;—so the people rested the seventh-day*, Exod. xvi. 29, 30. So it was when it received a further sanction from the fourth precept of the decalogue. For,——1. The whole decalogue, or ten commands of the law of Moses, as such, were given to the Jews only;[10] as a covenant, it was made with the Israelites in the wilderness, and not even with their fathers, which were before them; and in which respect they had the preference to all other nations on earth, as Moses affirms, Deut. v. 2—21. and iv. 6, 7, 8. and as is affirmed by David, Psalm cxlvii. 19, 20. and by the apostle Paul, Rom. ix. 4. and which appears from the preface to the decalogue; *I am the Lord thy God, which brought thee out of the land of Egypt;* which cannot be said of any other nation.——2. The fourth command is particularly and expressly declared as peculiar to them; *My Sabbaths shall ye keep*, saith the Lord; *for it is a sign between me and you*, and not others, Exod. xxxi. 13. that is, of the national covenant between them. The same is repeated, ver. 16, 17. where the children of Israel, as distinct from all other nations to whom it was no sign, are directed to keep the Sabbath. So Nehemiah says, that when God spoke to the Israelites in the wilderness, he made *known to them his holy Sabbath;* which it seems had not been made known unto them before; but now was made known to them, and not to others; and is mentioned along with peculiar precepts, statutes, and laws commanded them, Neh. ix. 14. and the prophet Ezekiel, from the Lord, tells the Jews, that the Lord had *given* to their fathers in the wilderness, his *Sabbaths, to be a sign between him and them;* it is not said he restored them, but *gave* them, denoting a new institution, and as peculiarly belonging to them: and this is the sense of the Jewish nation in general,[11] that the Sabbath only belongs to them, and that the Gentiles are not obliged to keep it, for though a Gentile proselyte or stranger within the gate, for the sake of national decorum, and to avoid offence and scandal, was to do no work on it for an Israelite, yet he might for himself, as the Jews interpret it;[12] but then this supposes, that a stranger not within the gate, was not obliged to observe it. Besides, some of the Jewish writers understand this stranger, or proselyte, of a proselyte of righteousness, who was under equal obligation to the commands of the law, as a Jew.——3. The time and place when and where this precept was given, with the reason of it, shew that it was peculiar to the Jews; it was given them in the wilderness, after they were come out of Egypt; and their deliverance from thence is expressly observed, as the reason why it was commanded them, Deut. v. 15. The Lord's resting on the seventh day from his works of creation, is used as an argument to enforce the keeping of the seventh-day Sabbath, now enjoined; but not as a reason of the institution of it.—— 4. None but Jews were ever charged with the breach of the seventh-day Sabbath; the children of Israel were charged with it in the wilderness, soon after it was enjoined them, Ezek. xx. 20, 21, 23, 24. so in Nehemiah's time, though the Tyrians, who sold fish to the Jews on Sabbath-days, were threatened, and shut out of the city, and forbid to come there with their goods; yet it was the Jews who bought them, who are charged with the profanation of the Sabbath, Neh. xiii. 15—20. and it was the sense of the Jews, that the Gentiles are not to be punished for the breach of it; yea, rather, that they are punishable for keeping it;[13] they having no other laws

---

[10] Vid. Zanchii, Oper. tom. 4. l. 1. c. 11. p. 222, 223.

[11] Zohar in Exod. fol. 26. 4. T. Bab. Sanhedrin, fol. 59. 1. Bartenora in Misn. Sabbat, c. 24. s. 1.

[12] T. Bab. Ceritot, fol. 9. 1. Piske Toscphot Ychamot, art. 84. Maimon. Hilchot Sabbat, c. 20. s. 14.

[13] T. Bab. Betza, fol. 16. 1. et Sanhedrin, fol. 58. 2. et 59. 1. Bemigdbar Rabb. fol. 234. 4. Maimon. Hilchot, Melachim, c. 10. s. 9.

CHAP. VIII. OF THE DAY OF PUBLIC WORSHIP. 969

binding upon them, but the seven laws they speak of, as given to the sons of Noah.——
5. The law of observing the seventh-day Sabbath is not of a moral nature; was it, it would be binding on all mankind, Jews and Gentiles; and could not have been dispensed with, nor abolished, as it is, Matt. xii. 1—12. Col. ii. 16, 17. and if such, as has been observed, it must have been written on the heart of Adam, when created; and would be, not only re-inscribed on the hearts of regenerate men, but even the work of it would appear to be written on the hearts of Gentiles, as their consciences would bear witness; whereas it does not appear. Some, indeed, pretend to say, that the seventh day of the week was reckoned holy with the Gentiles; but of all the instances produced from Clemens and Eusebius, there is but one now extant among the poets, and that is in Hesiod; and the seventh day he speaks of as holy, is not the seventh day of the week, but the seventh day of the month, the birth-day of Apollo, as the poet himself suggests, and the Scholiasts[14] on him; which was the seventh day of the month Thargelion, kept sacred at Athens on that account; hence Apollo was called Ebdomegena.[15] As for the Jews' seventh-day Sabbath, the Heathen writers[16] speak of it as having its origin from Moses, and as peculiar to the Jews,[17] and the day itself was held by them in the utmost contempt; see Lam. i. 7. there is scarce a poet of theirs[18] but has a lash at it, and at the Jews on account of it; and represent them as a parcel of idle people, who keep that day to indulge themselves in sloth; the principal day of the week sacred with the Gentiles, was the first day of the week, dedicated to the sun, and from thence called Sunday: so that if any argument can be drawn from the observation of the heathens, it is in favour of the Christian, and not of the Jewish Sabbath.——6. It is impracticable and impossible, that a seventh-day Sabbath should be kept by all people, in all nations of the world, at the same time exactly and precisely. It was and could only be observed by the Jews themselves, when they were together under a certain meridian; it cannot be kept now by them, as they are scattered about in distant parts of the world, with any precision, at the same time; such an hypothesis proceeds upon a false notion that the earth is plain, and has every where the same horizon, and is not globular, nor having horizons, and meridians, and degrees of longitude different in every place and country; which latter is most certainly true. If the earth is a globe, consisting of two hemispheres, when it is day on one side of the globe, it is night on the other; so that let the sabbath begin at what time you please; if from sun-setting, as the Jews begin theirs, and continue it to sun-setting the next day; when it is sun-setting with us, it is sun-rising with those in the other hemisphere; and so *vice versa*; and if it is begun at midnight, and continued to midnight, as with us; when it is midnight on one side the globe, it will be midday, or noon, on the other: so in each case there must be half a day's difference in the exact time of the Sabbath; and according to the variations in horizons, meridians, and longitudes, will the day differ. If therefore the earth is a globe, as it is certain it is; and as horizons, meridians, and longitudes differ, as they most certainly do, then it is impossible that the same exact precise time should be every where kept; and God has never commanded that which is impossible. Besides, it may be observed, that in Greenland, and other northern countries, for several months together, there is no sun-rising nor sun-setting, and so no days to be distinguished that way, the sun being at such a time always above the horizon; so that a Sabbath-day, consisting of twenty-four hours, or of a day and a night, cannot be observed in such parts of the world; nay, it has been made to appear, that one and the same day, at one and the same place, may be Friday, Saturday, and what is called Sunday. Supposing a Turk, whose Sabbath is Friday, and a Jew, whose Sabbath is Saturday, and a Christian, whose Sabbath is the first day of the week, dwell together; the Turk and the Christian set out on their travels at the same time, leaving the Jew where he was; the Turk by travelling westward loses a day, and the Christian travelling eastward gets one; so that both compassing the world, and meeting together again at the same place, the Jew continuing where he was, the same

---

[14] Proclus et Moschepulus in ibid.
[15] Plutarch. Sympos. l. 8. c. 1.
[16] Justin e Trogo, l. 36. c. 2. Tacit. Hist. l. 5. c. 4.
[17] Cultaque Judæo septima Sacra viro, Ovid. de arte amandi, l. 1.
[18] Juvenal. Satyr. 6. v. 158. Satyr. 14. v. 105, 106. Pers. Satyr. 5. v. 184. Martial. l. 4. ep. 4. vid. Senecam apud Aug. de Civ. Dei, l. 6. c. 11.

day will be Friday to the Turk, a Saturday to the Jew, and Sunday to the Christian; so Dr. Heylin.[19] Those that travel round the world westward, it is observed by others,[20] as this makes their days longer, so they find fewer in compassing the globe, losing one day in tale, though they lose no time; so that if the sabbath of their nation was the seventh, they would find it their sixth on their return: and those that travel eastward, as their days are shorter, are more in number, and gain one in tale; and on their return, would find their eighth, or first day of the week, to be the nation's Sabbath. So there would be three Sabbaths kept in a nation, and all exactly observing time. It may be said, the same objection will lie against the first day as the seventh. It is granted; but then we observe that on another footing, as will be seen presently.

Fifthly, The first day of the week, or Lord's day, is now the day of worship observed by the generality of Christians; upon what account, and by what authority, must be our next enquiry. Not by virtue of any positive precept, or express command of Christ, for which there is none; wherefore some great and good men, as Calvin,[21] Beza,[22] Zanchius,[23] and others, have been of opinion that it was a matter of pure choice, in the first churches, and a branch of their Christian liberty; who were left free, as to choose a place where, so the time when, to worship; and therefore fixed on this day, and substituted it in the room of the Jewish Sabbath, antiquated, as being most proper and suitable, and having the sanction of an apostolic practice; to which I have been inclined to agree; only cannot but be of opinion, that the practice and examples of the apostles of Christ, men inspired by the holy Spirit, who wrote, taught, and practised no other than agreeable to *the commandments of the Lord,* Matt. xxviii. 20. 1 Cor. xiv. 37. carry in them the nature, force, and obligation of a precept. So though there is no express command for infant baptism, yet had it been countenanced, as it has not been, by the like practice and examples of the apostles, we should have judged it our duty to have followed such a practice and such examples; it is upon this footing we observe the first day of the week, as being——

1. The most proper and suitable day for divine worship; as the change of the day of worship was necessary, there being a new dispensation, and new ordinances of divine service; and to testify to the world our faith of Christ's coming, death, and resurrection from the dead; no day was so proper as the first day of the week, which immediately followed upon, and was the next remove from the seventh-day Sabbath, now abrogated; so that the Christian church was never without a day of worship, pointed at so early by the practice of the apostles, who met that very first day of the week on which Christ rose from the dead; and which further shews the propriety and suitableness of this day as a day of rest; Christ had now finished the great work of our redemption and salvation; and so ceased from his work, as God did from his; and it may be further observed, that after our Lord's resurrection from the dead, we never read, throughout the whole New Testament, that ever the Jews' seventh-day Sabbath was kept by any Christian assembly; only the first day of the week. So that,——2. The observation of this day is confirmed by the practice and examples of the disciples of Christ, and of the first churches; for,—(1.) On the very day Christ rose from the dead, which was the first day of the week, the disciples assembled together, and Christ appeared in the midst of them, and by his gracious presence and divine instructions, shewed his approbation of their thus meeting together, and encouraged them to it; and on that day sennight they met again, and Christ again stood in the midst of them; now though there had been a seventh-day preceding this, the disciples did not assemble on that day, but on this, and Christ with them, John xx. 19, 29.—(2.) The apostles met together on the day of Pentecost, which was the first day of the week, as has been proved by many learned writers. Just before our Lord's ascension, he ordered his disciples to wait at Jerusalem for the promise of the Spirit; and though there were two Jewish seventh-day Sabbaths before Pentecost, from the time of his ascension, yet it does not appear that they met together on either of them; but on this day they did; and it looks as if they had an order from Christ to meet on it, and a

---

[19] History of the Sabbath, par. 1. p. 48.
[20] See Dr. Watts's Holiness of Times, &c. p. 55.
[21] Institut. l. 2. c. 8. s. 34.
[22] Confess. Fidei. c. 5. s. 41.
[23] In Precept. 4. tom. 4. p. 670.

CHAP. VIII.   OF THE DAY OF PUBLIC WORSHIP.   971

promise from Christ that they should then have the Spirit descend upon them; and therefore it seems they were waiting for that day, in expectation of having the promise fulfilled on it; and hence it is said, *When the day of Pentecost was fully come, they were all with one accord in one place*, Acts ii. 1. and this day was honoured and confirmed by the miraculous effusion of the Spirit, by preaching the gospel to men of all nations, and by the conversion and baptism of three thousand persons.—(3.) It was on the first day of the week that the disciples at Troas met together to break bread, when Paul preached unto them, Acts xx. 7. Now he had been there seven days before, so that there must have been in that time a seventh-day Sabbath of the Jews; but it does not appear that he and they assembled on that day; but only on the first, and that for religious worship; he, to break bread, to celebrate the Supper of the Lord, and they, to hear him preach.—(4.) The apostle Paul gave orders to the church at Corinth, as he had to the churches of Galatia, to make a collection for the poor saints on the first day of the week, when met together, 1 Cor. xvi. 1, 2. which shews that it was usual to meet on that day; yea, it implies an order, or the renewal and confirmation of an order, to meet on that day, or otherwise how should the collection be made on it; and what day so proper as when the saints meet for divine worship, and their hearts are warmed and refreshed with the word and ordinances. In an ancient copy, mentioned by Beza on the place, after *the first day of the week*, it is added, by way of explanation, the *Lord's day;* and also in others;[24] and so Jerome[25] explains it.—(5.) This is the day John means by the *Lord's day,* when he says, *I was in the Spirit on the Lord's day,* Rev. i. 10. he speaks of it as then a well-known name of it; so called because Christ rose from the dead on it; in commemoration of which it was kept, and in which his gospel was preached and ordinances administered; for it was now upwards of sixty years from the resurrection of Christ, to John's being an exile in Patmos, where he wrote his Revelation; and this day was observed as a day of religious worship in the earliest ages of Christianity. Ignatius,[26] who died but eight or ten years after the apostle John, says, "Let us keep the Lord's day, on which our Life arose." And Justin Martyr,[27] a few years after him, says, on the day commonly called Sunday by the heathens, (meaning the first day of the week) all met together in city and country for divine worship. Dionysius of Corinth, speaks of the Lord's day as an holy day,[28] and Clemens of Alexandria,[29] in the same century, observes, that he that truly keeps the Lord's day, glorifies the resurrection of the Lord. Tertullian,[30] in the beginning of the third century, speaks of the acts of public worship, as *Lord's-day* solemnities. And in the same century Origen[31] and Cyprian[32] make mention of the first day as the *Lord's day,* and the time of worship; and so it has been in all ages to the present time. Now upon the whole, since it does not appear, that a seventh-day Sabbath was enjoined Adam in innocence; nor that the patriarchs ever observed it; and that the first mention of it was at the giving of the *manna;* and that it was ordered to be observed by the Jews, and them only, by the fourth precept of the decalogue, since abrogated; and that the first day of the week, or Lord's day, is substituted in its room, as the day of worship, by the practice and example of the apostles; there surely can remain no scruple about the observance of the latter: but if, after all, the fourth command, with the morality of it, hangs upon the minds of any; be it that that command is still in force, though not granting it, which would bring us back to Judaism, and into a state of bondage; and allow it all the morality that can be ascribed to a day; according to the letter of it, it requires no more nor other than this, a rest on the seventh day, after six days labour; it does not direct to any epocha from whence it is to begin, as from the creation of the world, the seventh day from which the greatest mathematician in the world cannot assure us which it is, nor even the year of the creation; it only directs to, and regards the seventh day from whence a man begins to labour in whatsoever place or country he lives; nor does it direct to any set time or hour when to begin these seven days, or by what

---

[24] Vid. Mill. in loc.
[25] Adv. Vigilantium Oper. tom. 2. fol. 42.
[26] Ad Magnes. p. 35.
[27] Apolog. 2. p. 98, 99.
[28] Apud Euseb. l. 4. c. 23. Irenæus, l. 5. c. 24.
[29] Stromat. l. 7. p. 744.
[30] De Anima, c. 9.
[31] Homil. 5. in Esaiam, fol. 104. 3. et alibi.
[32] Ep. 33. p. 66. et Ep. 58, p. 138.

names to call the days of the week; the rule is only, *Six days shalt thou labour and do all thy work*, or thou mayest if thou wilt, *but the seventh day is the sabbath of the Lord thy God;* and such an account of time as is made in whatsoever place a man lives, is to be taken, and of which every man is capable; it does not require he should be a skilful mathematician; a man that uses a spade, or follows the plough, is capable of counting six days, on which he has wrought, and when he comes to the seventh, he must know it is not his own, but the Lord's; and such an account a man may keep, let him live on what side of the globe he will; in Europe, or in America, north or south; in Great Britain, or in the East and West Indies: nor is the observation of the first day any objection to this rule, since that is after six days labour; the very first day on which Christ rose, kept by his disciples, was after six days labour; for the Jews' sabbath being between that and the six days labour, can be no objection, since that was a day of rest, and not of labour; so that for that time there were two successive days of rest, after the six days of labour; when, upon the next return of the first, which was immediately after, it proceeded regularly, as it does now. In short, the only safe rule to go by is, that of the apostles, be the day what it may; *He that regardeth the day, regardeth it unto the Lord*, Rom. xiv. 16. or he ought so to do. Which leads me to observe,

II. In what manner the Lord's day is to be regarded or observed; not to ourselves, to our own profit and pleasure; but to the Lord, to his service and glory.

1. Not as a Jewish Sabbath; with such strictness and severity as not to kindle a fire, dress any manner of food, and travel no further than what is called a Sabbath-day's journey; though perhaps these were not enjoined with the strictness some have imagined. But,——2. We are not to do our own work; that is, to follow any trade, business, or occupation employed in on other days; otherwise there are works of piety, mercy, and charity to be done; and also of necessity, for the preservation of life, the comfort and health of it, our own or others.——3. It is to be employed more especially in acts of public worship, in assembling together for that purpose, in preaching, and hearing the word preached, in prayer, and singing praises.——4. In private acts of devotion, both before and after public worship; such as has been already observed, when the duty of public hearing the word was considered.——5. The whole of the day should be observed, from morning to evening; the early part should not be indulged in sleep, nor any part spent in doing a man's own business, in casting up his accounts, and setting right his shop-books; nor in carnal pleasures and recreations, in games and sports; nor in walking in the fields; nor in taking needless journeys. But besides public worship, men should attend to reading the scriptures, prayer and meditation, and Christian conferences; and in such pious exercises should they spend the whole day.

A BODY OF PRACTICAL DIVINITY.

BOOK IV.

OF PRIVATE WORSHIP, OR OF VARIOUS DUTIES, PERSONAL, RELATIVE, DOMESTIC, AND CIVIL.

CHAP. I.

OF THE RESPECTIVE DUTIES OF HUSBAND AND WIFE.

HAVING considered Public Worship in all its branches, I now proceed to treat of Private Worship; by which I mean, not merely the private teachings and instructions of a master of a family, to those who are under his care; nor private conferences of the saints, by which they may edify one another; nor private reading of the scriptures, which are to be searched whether the things heard in the ministry of the word are true, and which are to be read in the family for instruction; nor private prayer, in the closet or in the family; nor private singing the praises of God, which may be performed in like manner: which are all branches of private worship, and have been touched on in the preceding Book. But what I mean by private worship, and intend to treat of, are the personal, relative, domestic, and civil duties, incumbent on particular persons, in their different relations to one another; and so every other duty and good work, which all come under the name of *cultus*, or *worship*; being all to be performed with a respect to God, under his authority, according to his will and command, and in obedience to it, and with a view to his glory. In this manner all relative and mutual duties are to be performed; the subjection of wives to their husbands is to be made as *unto the Lord*, the Head of the man, and in obedience to him; and husbands are to love their wives, *as Christ loved the church*, according to his pattern and example, and as influenced by his love, Eph. v. 21, 29. Children are to obey their parents *in the Lord*, as being what he requires, and as encouraged by his promise; and parents, as an act of religion, are to bring up their children *in the nurture and admonition of the Lord*, Eph. vi. 1, 4. Servants are to be obedient to their masters, *as unto the Lord*, as his servants, and *doing the will of God from the heart*, and *with good will doing service as to the Lord, and not to men, fearing God.* And masters are to do their duty to their servants; *Knowing that they also have a master in heaven*, to whom they are accountable, Eph. vi. 5—9. Col. iii. 22, 23, 24. and iv. 1. and subjects are to obey magistrates, as being the *powers ordained of God*, and magistracy an ordinance of God; and magistrates are to protect their subjects, and to be *terrors, not to good works*, but for the encouragement and praise of them, and for the discouragement and punishment of those that are evil, Rom. xiii. 1—4. 1 Pet. ii. 13, 14. God has a concern in all these, and men have a concern with him in them. These I shall briefly treat of in their order; and begin with the respective duties of husband and wife, which are summed up in these two general comprehensive ones; *love* on the one part, and *reverence* on the other, Eph. v. 33. and these arise from a conjugal union and marriage-relation between the said parties; marriage is an union of male and female, of one man and of one woman in lawful wedlock, agreeable to the original creation of man, Gen. i. 27. Mal. ii. 15. and agreeable to the course of Providence, which has been kept to ever since, in all ages and nations; there being continually nearly the same number of males and females born into the world, at most as thirteen to twelve, or fourteen to thirteen; the surplusage on the side of the males, being a provision by the wise Orderer of all things for a supply for war, for the seas, &c. and by this conjugal union, male and female, become one, even one flesh, Gen. ii. 24. Matt. xix. 6. which union is therefore very near and strict, and, indeed, indissoluble but by death, excepting in one case, unfaithfulness in the one to the other, by adultery or fornication, Rom. vii. 2. Matt. v. 32. and this state is to be entered into with mutual consent; indeed with the consent of all parties who have a concern in it; with the consent of parents and guardians, under whose care single persons may be; and especially with their own consent, for none are to be forced into it against their wills; no, not by their superiors; it must be their own voluntary act and deed: and being thus entered into, it is a very honourable state; *Marriage is honourable in all*, Heb. xiii. 4. it being an institution of God, and that of God in paradise; by whom our first parents were directed to it, in a state of purity and innocence; God made the woman for an help-meet, and brought her to the man, proposed her to him, whom he approved and accepted of, and she became his wife, Gen. ii. 18, 22, 23, 24. it was the Lord's act and deed, and to him Christ ascribes the act of marriage, Matt. xix. 6. Christ honoured it by his presence, and at such a solemnity wrought his first miracle, and manifested forth the glory of his Deity, John ii. 1, 2, 11. and what makes this state yet more honourable is, that the marriage of Adam and Eve was a type and emblem of the conjugal union of Christ and the church, Eph. v. 32. Adam was a figure or type of Christ, and, among other things, in his marriage; and Eve, the mother of all living, was a type of the church; Adam was first formed, and then Eve; Christ was before the church, and, indeed, before all things; Eve was formed from Adam, from a rib taken out of his side; the church has her original from Christ, and her subsistence by him; all her grace, blessings, and happiness, are from him; her justification and sanctification are from him, signified by the blood and water which sprung from his pierced side. Eve was brought by the Lord to Adam, not against her will, but with it, and by him presented as a proper match for him, which he approved and accepted of; and the church was brought to Christ, and given to him by his Father, to be his spouse and bride, whom he liked, accepted of, and betrothed to himself; and her consent is obtained by the drawings and influences of his Father's grace: and though this is no direct proof of, yet it has a favourable aspect upon, and may serve to illustrate the *supralapsarian* scheme; that Christ had an interest in his church, and she in him, and was espoused unto him, before she fell in Adam; this marriage transaction between Adam and Eve being before the fall. Moreover, marriage is honourable with respect to the ends of it; which even before the fall, and supposing Adam had stood, hereby he would have had an help-meet; and the first law of creation would have been carried into execution, *increase and multiply;* a godly seed, a legitimate offspring would have sprung from hence; families formed and built up, and the world peopled with inhabitants; and since the fall, the ends and uses of it are to preserve chastity, to prevent incontinence, and to avoid fornication; as well as to answer the other ends: and particularly this state appears honourable when the duties of it are observed by both parties; as,

First, Love on the part of the husband. *Husbands love your wives*, Eph. v. 25. instances of which are in Isaac, Jacob, Elkanah, and others, Gen. xxiv. 67. and xxix. 18, 20. 1 Sam. i. 5. The nature and manner of shewing it, and the reasons of it, might be observed.

1st, The nature of it.———1. It is superior to any shewn to any other creature whatever; as to the neighbour, who, though to be loved by a man as himself, yet a man's wife is himself, and loving her is loving himself, the other part of himself, Eph. v. 28. parents are to be loved, but a wife before them; for a man is to leave father and mother, and to cleave to his wife, Gen. ii. 24. children are to be loved, but the wife before them; as well as the husband by the wife; *Am not I better to thee than ten sons?* 1 Sam. i. 8. and Christ

OF HUSBAND AND WIFE.

is to be loved before any relations, Matt. x. 37. Luke xiv. 26.——2. It should be a love of complacency and delight, taking pleasure and delight in her person, company, and conversation, Prov. v. 18, 19. Eccles. ix. 9. as is the love of Christ to the church, who is his Hephzibah, in whom is all his delight.——3. It should be chaste and single, as the love of Christ is, Cant. vi. 9. and for this reason a man should not have more wives than one, whereby his love would be divided or alienated, and hate the one and love the other, as is commonly the case; and therefore the law provided for the first-born of whichsoever it might be, Deut. xxi. 15, 17. see 1 Cor. vii. 2.——4. It should be mutual; the wife is to love the husband, as the husband the wife, Tit. ii. 4. and generally her love is the most strong and affectionate, 2 Sam. i. 26. and the reason why the husband is more frequently exhorted to it, it may be, is because most wanting in the performance of it.

2*dly*, The manner, or how, and in what way it is to be expressed; not in words only, but in deed and in truth; by real facts, which speak louder than words.

1. In making all proper provision for her temporal good, signified by *nourishing* and *cherishing* her, Eph. v. 29. which include food and raiment, and all the necessaries of life; he is to *provide things honest*, decent, convenient, and suitable to his rank, state, condition, circumstances, and abilities; and he that *provideth not for his own*, especially for his own wife, his own children and family, *is worse than an infidel*, Rom. xii. 17. 1 Tim. v. 3.—— 2. In protecting her from all abuses and injuries: as she is the weaker vessel, she is to be taken under his wing and shelter; he is to be a covering for her, as Abraham was to Sarah; which may be signified by the ceremony used at marriage, or by which that act is expressed, a man's spreading his skirt over the woman, Gen. xx. 16. Ruth iii. 9. he is to expose himself to danger, and even risk his life in her defence, and for her rescue, 1 Sam. xxx. 5, 18.—— 3. In doing every thing that may contribute to her pleasure, peace, comfort, and happiness; *he that is married* is to care *how he may please his wife;* nor does the apostle blame him for it; but rather commends him for it, or recommends it unto him, 1 Cor. vii. 33. *Hatred stirreth up strifes*, contentions, quarrels, the consequence of which is confusion, and every evil work; *but love covereth all sins*, conceals faults, and hides failings and infirmities, Prov. x. 12.——4. In seeking her spiritual welfare; her conversion, if unconverted, and her spiritual peace, comfort, and edification, she being an heir with him of the grace of life; by joining with her in all religious exercises; in family worship, in reading, in prayer, in praise, in Christian conference and conversation; by instructing her in every thing relating to doctrine, duty, and church-discipline; in answer to questions she may and has a right to ask him at home, 1 Cor. xiv. 35. To all which, are opposed hatred and bitterness; *Husbands love your wives, and be not bitter against them;* not giving bitter language, threatening words, sour looks, and especially bitter blows; which is cruel, churlish, barbarous, and brutish, unbecoming the man and the Christian.

3*dly*, The reasons or arguments enforcing this duty of the love of a man to his wife, are such as follow.

1. The nearness between them, she is his own flesh; and *no man ever yet hated his own flesh*, which would be monstrously unnatural; she is *himself*, the other part of *himself*, and to be loved as his own body, which to love is a principle[1] in nature, Eph. v. 28, 29, 33.——2. The help, advantage, and profit he receives by her, she is provided as an help-meet for him, and becomes such to him in the affairs of the family, Gen. ii. 18. she is his companion, and which is used as a reason why he should not deal treacherously with the wife of his youth, Mal. ii. 14. she is his companion in prosperity and adversity; shares with him in his cares and troubles, in his joys and sorrows; sympathizes with him in all conditions, weeps when he weeps, and rejoices when he rejoices; she is a partner with him in the blessings of grace now, and will be a partner with him in eternal glory.——3. The glory and honour she is unto him; *The woman is the glory of the man*, in whom are seen his power and authority, 1 Cor. xi. 7. one who is loving and chaste to him, and is careful of her family affairs, does him honour, and is a credit and crown to him, and makes him respectable among men; his heart safely trusts in her, and through her conduct he is known and respected *in the gates*,

---

[1] Fateor insitam nobis esse corporis nostri charitatem, Seneca Ep. 14.

Prov. xii. 4. and xxxi. 10, 11, 23.——
4. The strongest and most forcible arguments of all, to a good man, is the love of Christ to his church; which is the pattern and exemplar of a man's love to his wife, and most strongly enforces it, Eph. v. 25—28.

Secondly, The duties on the part of the wife, are reverence, subjection, obedience, &c.

1. Reverence. And *let the wife see that she reverence her husband*, Eph. v. 33. which reverence is both internal and external; she ought to think well, and even highly of him, and not despise him in her heart, as Michael, Saul's daughter, did David her husband, 2 Sam. vi. 16. and she should speak of him and to him in a respectful manner, as Sarah did to Abraham, *calling him lord*, 1 Peter iii. 6. Gen. xviii. 12.——2. Subjection and submission to him. *Wives, submit yourselves unto your own husbands*, not to others; *as unto the Lord*, the Lord Christ, the head of every man, and so of the church; *and as the church is subject to Christ, so let the wives be to their own husbands in every thing;* that is, in things relating to family affairs; not in any thing that is contrary to the laws of God and Christ; for God is to be obeyed rather than men, than any man, than husbands themselves, Eph. v. 22, 24. and this subjection and submission is not a servile one; not like that of servants to their masters, or of handmaids to mistresses, and much less like that of slaves to tyrants, or, who have taken them and hold them captives; but as the body, and members of it, are subject to the head, by which they are governed, guided, and directed to what is for their good; and that in a wise, tender, and gentle manner.——3. Obedience. The apostle directs, that wives be *obedient to their own husbands*, Tit. ii. 5. Sarah is an example of this; and an instance we have of her immediate and quick obedience to the orders of Abraham, 1 Pet. iii. 6. Gen. xviii. 6.——4. Assistance and help in family-affairs, agreeable to the original end of her creation; guiding the house with discretion, keeping her children and servants in good order and decorum; abiding at home, and managing all domestic business with wisdom and prudence. 1 Tim. ii. 14. Tit. ii. 5.——
5. Assuming no authority, over her husband, as not in ecclesiastical, so not in domestic matters; seeking to please him in all things, doing nothing without his will and consent, and never contrary to it; not intermeddling with his worldly business and concerns, but leaving them to him. 1 Tim. v. 11, 12. 1 Cor. vii. 34.——
6. Continuance with him in every state and circumstance of life; going with him wherever God in his providence, and his business in life call him; as Sarah with Abraham in the land of promise, in Egypt, and elsewhere; she should do as Ruth proposed to Naomi, Ruth i. 16.

There are reasons why the wife should be found in the performance of these duties. Some,

1. Taken from her creation, time, manner, and end of it. Adam was formed first, and then Eve; and therefore in point of time had the superiority; the man was made not of and for the woman; but the woman was made of and for the man, and to be an help-meet and assistant to him, 1 Tim. ii. 13. 1 Cor. xi. 8, 9. Gen. ii. 18.——
2. From the consideration of the fall, and her concern in it. *Adam was not deceived, but the woman being deceived, was in the transgression*, at least first, and the means of drawing her husband into it; and therefore it is part of the sentence denounced upon her for her transgression, *Thy desire shall be to thy husband, and he shall rule over thee*, 1 Tim. ii. 14. Gen. iii. 16.——3. From the man being the head of the woman; and therefore she should be in subjection to him as such, 1 Cor. xi. 3. Eph. v. 23.
——4. From her being the weaker vessel, and therefore standing in need of his shelter and protection.——5. From her own credit and honour concerned herein; as it would be to her discredit and dishonour to behave irreverently, and to be disobedient; to submit to him, *as is fit in the Lord*, is decent and becoming, Col. iii. 18. and so to be is ornamental to women, and the best ornament they can deck themselves with; *Being in subjection to their own husbands*, 1 Pet. iii. 3, 4, 5.——6. The chief argument of all, is taken from the subjection of the church to Christ, Eph. v. 22, 23, 24. In short, both parties should consult each other's pleasure, peace, comfort, and happiness, and especially the glory of God; that his word, ways, and worship, may not be reproached and evil spoken of, through any conduct of theirs, Tit. ii. 5.

CHAP. II.

OF THE RESPECTIVE DUTIES OF PARENTS AND CHILDREN.

These duties arise from a relation founded in nature. There is a natural instinct[1] in all creatures, even in the brutal creation, and in the more brutish part of that, to love their young, take care of them, provide for them, supply them, protect and defend them; *Even the sea-monsters give suck to their young ones*, Lam. iv. 3. much more such an affection, appears in human and rational beings; *Can a woman forget her sucking child?* &c. Isa. xlix. 15. on the other hand, as they are among the most wicked and abandoned of mankind who are *disobedient to parents;* they are in the same description of them represented as *without natural affection*, Rom. i. 30, 31. 2 Tim. iii. 2, 3. as such must be, as well as guilty of gross ingratitude, *who requite* not *their parents* with filial love and duty for all the care and trouble, pains and expenses, they have been at in bringing them forth, and bringing them up in the world. Their performance of these duties is one part of natural religion. The apostle calls it shewing *piety*,[2] or godliness, 1 Tim. v. 4. The heathens by the light of nature[3] taught these things; Solon,[4] Phocylides,[5] Pythagoras,[6] Isocrates,[7] Plutarch,[8] and others, coupled and ranked them together, and exhorted first to *honour God*, and then to *honour parents;*[9] and indeed, parents in the exercise of their love, power, and care, greatly resemble the divine Being, as the Creator, Sustainer, Protector, and Governor of his creatures; since children receive their being from their parents, under God; who are the instruments of introducing them into the world, and of their sustentation, support, and protection in it; hence Philo[10] observes, that the "fifth command, concerning honouring parents, is placed between the two tables of the law; which seems to be done because the nature of parents is μεθοριον, a middle border, or term between immortal and mortal; being mortal with respect to cognation to men, and other animals, and the corruptible body; immortal, as it resembles in generation God, the parent of all." And children are therefore under great obligation to various duties with respect unto them; with which I shall begin, and the rather, as they stand first in order, in the directions the apostle gives to both parents and children.

First, The duties of children to their parents are included and comprehended in that general exhortation; *Children, obey your parents in the Lord, for this is right*, Eph. vi. 1. The persons of whom this duty is required, are *children;* and the persons to whom it is to be performed, are *parents;* by the former are meant children of each sex, male and female, sons and daughters, being in an equal relation, and in equal obligation to obedience to parents; and of every age, from infancy to manhood; and though the power of parents over children is less when grown up, the duty of observance, gratitude, and filial reverence does not cease; yea, may be the more increased, since it may be then better known; and children of every class, state, and condition of life, though they may be superior to parents in worldly honour, wealth, and riches, are to obey them, as the cases of Joseph and Solomon shew. And though such who are the true and genuine offspring of parents, or who are so in a proper sense, may be chiefly meant, yet in them are included spurious ones, and such who are children by adoption, as Moses and Esther; or by the law of marriage, sons and daughters-in-law, as Moses to Jethro, and Ruth to Naomi, who were all obsequious to those to whom they stood thus related. By *parents* are meant, though chiefly immediate ones, yet include all in the ascending line, as a father's father and mother, a mother's father and mother, or grandfathers and grand-mothers, or if any higher are living they are entitled to obedience; and, indeed, all who stand in the room and stead of parents, as adoptive ones, step-fathers and step-mothers, tutors, guardians, governors, nurses, &c. whilst under

---

[1] Communi autem animantium omnium est conjunctionis appetitus procreandi causa, et cura quædam eorum quæ procreata sunt, Cicero de Officiis, l. 1. c. 4.
[2] Ευσεβειν. Valerius Maximus has a chapter, de Pietate in Parentes, l. 5. c. 4.
[3] Diligere parentes prima naturæ lex, ib. s. 7. et extern. s. 5.
[4] Laert. vit. Solon. p. 46.
[5] Poem Admon. v. 6.
[6] Aurea Carmin. v. 1. 2.
[7] Paræenes. ad Demonic. Orat. 1.
[8] Περι φιλαδελφιας. p. 479. vol. 2.
[9] Πρωτα θεον τιμα, μετεπειτα τε σειο γονηας, Phocyl. Pythag. &c. ut supra.
[10] De Decalogo, 759, 760.

their care, and in a state of minority, obedience is to be yielded to them; but particularly both parents are meant, father and mother, as it is explained in the next verse; *Honour thy Father and Mother;* father is put first, on account of order, of precedence and dignity; sometimes the order is inverted to shew the equal respect that should be had to both, Lev. xix. 3.

The duty enjoined, is *obedience*, which includes love, honour, reverence, gratitude, and subjection.

1. Love; from whence all true obedience to God, to Christ, and to creatures flow; disobedience is owing to a want of love; such who are disobedient to parents, are without natural affections, as before observed: parents are greatly to be loved, but not more than God and Christ; *He that loveth father or mother more than me*, says Christ, *is not worthy of me*, Matt. x. 37. ——2. Honour; obedience is explained by honour, Eph. vi. 1, 2. see Mal. i. 6. which honour lies,—(1.) In thought and estimation; children are to think highly, and to entertain an honourable esteem of their parents; to which is opposed, a *setting light* by them, Deut. xxvii. 16. a mean and contemptible opinion of them leads to disobedience to them, Prov. xxx. 17.—(2.) Is expressed by words; by speaking honourably of them and to them; *I go, Sir*, was language which carried in it honour and respect, though it was not attended with obedience, Matt. xxi. 30. Cursing father or mother with the mouth and lips, is shocking, and was punishable with death by the Levitical law, and followed with the judgments of God, Lev. xx. 9. Prov. xx. 20. and xxx. 17.—(3.) In gesture and behaviour; as by rising up to them, and bowing before them; instances of which are in Joseph and Solomon, Gen. xlvi. 29. and xlviii. 12. 1 Kings ii. 19.——3. Obedience to parents, includes fear and reverence of them, Lev. xix. 3. which is shewn by a patient bearing their reproofs, and by a submission to their corrections, Heb. xii. 2. by an acknowledgment of offences committed, and asking forgiveness of them, Luke xv. 18. by concealing their infirmities, natural and moral, whether through old age or otherwise, an instance of this we have in Shem and Japhet, Gen. ix. 21, 22, 23.——4. Gratitude; a requital of them for all their kindness; by taking care of them when in want and distress, and in old age; so Joseph nourished his father and his family in a time of famine: so Ruth gleaned for Naomi, though only her mother-in-law; and her son Obed was by prophecy to be a nourisher of her in her old age; and David, though in a state of exile himself, provided for his father and his mother, to be with the king of Moab, till he knew how it would be with him, Gen. xlvii. 12. Ruth ii. 18. and iv. 15. 1 Sam. xxii. 3, 4. The Pharisees are charged with a breach of this duty, by a tradition of theirs, which wickedly excused persons from relieving their indigent parents, Matt. xv. 4, 5, 6. The heathens teach better things: Solon[11] pronounces such ignoble and dishonourable, who neglect the care of their parents; in Æneas[12] may be seen a specimen of fillial piety to an aged parent, whom he carried on his back at the destruction of Troy. The storks in the heavens may teach men their duty, who are careful of their dams in old age,[13] which Aristophanes wittily calls an ancient law in the tables of the storks.[14]——5. Subjection and submission to their commands, advice, reproofs, and corrections. The rule is, *Children, obey your parents in all things*, Col. iii. 20. not in things sinful, contrary to the laws of God, and ordinances of Christ; if parents command their children to worship another God, or a graven image; or to do any thing forbidden in the first and second tables of the law; or enjoin them not to profess the name of Christ, nor submit to his ordinances; they are to be rejected, and in a comparative sense, *hated*, Luke xiv. 26. for God is to be obeyed, and not man, not even parents, in such cases; but in things that are lawful and right, agreeable to the will of God, revealed in his word, and even in things indifferent, which are neither forbidden nor commanded, yet if enjoined by parents, are to be observed; an instance of this we have in the Rechabites, and whose filial observance was approved of by the Lord, Jer. xxxv. 6—10, 18, 19. yea, also in things difficult and disagreeable to flesh

---

[11] Laert. vit. Solon. l. 1.
[12] Ergo age, chare pater, cervici imponere nostræ:
   Ipse subibo humeris, nec me labor iste gravabit.
              Virgil. Æneid. l. 2. prope finem.

[13] Plin. Nat. Hist. l. 16. c. 23. Aristot. Hist. Animal. l. 6. c. 13.
[14] Νομος παλαιος, εν τοις των πελαργων κυρϊεσιν, Aves, p. 604.

and blood; as the cases of Isaac in submitting to be sacrificed by his father, and in Jephtha's daughter to be done unto by him according to his vow, shew, Gen. xxii. 9. Judg. xi. 36.

The manner in which this obedience is to be yielded is, *in the Lord*, Eph. vi. 1. which may be considered as a limitation of the above rule; that it must be in things pertaining to the Lord, which are well-pleasing in his sight, which make for his glory, and are done for his sake, according to his command and will, and in obedience to it; and also in imitation of the Lord Christ, who, in his human nature, was subject to his earthly parents, and thereby left an example of filial obedience to tread in his steps, Luke ii. 51. The reason enforcing such obedience is, for it is right; it is agreeable to the law and light of nature, as has been before observed; it is agreeable to reason, and to the law of equity; gratitude demands it, that children who have received so many favours from their parents, should make some suitable returns in a way of filial love, honour, reverence, and obedience; it is agreeable to the law of God; it stands among the precepts of the Decalogue, it is the fifth in order there; but as the apostle says, it is the *first commandment with promise*, with a promise of long life; which was always reckoned a great blessing, which disobedience to parents often deprives of, as in the case of Absalom.

Secondly, There are duties incumbent on parents with respect to their children, which are,

1*st*, Negatively expressed; *Ye Fathers, provoke not your children to wrath*, Eph. vi. 4. which may be done,——1. By words; by laying upon them unjust and unreasonable commands, by frequent, public and severe chidings, by indiscreet and passionate expressions, and by contumelious and reproachful language; such as that of Saul to Jonathan, 1 Sam. xx. 30. ——2. By deeds; as by shewing more love to one than to another; as Jacob did to Joseph, which so incensed his brethren that they hated Joseph, and could not speak peaceably to him, Gen. xxxvii. 8. by not allowing them proper food, and a sufficiency of it, Matt. vii. 9, 10. 1 Tim. v. 8. by not indulging them with innocent recreations, which children should have, Zech. viii. 5. and when at a proper age for marriage, by disposing of them to persons not agreeable to their inclinations;[15] and by restraining them from those that would be, without any just reason; and by squandering away their substance in riotous living, when they should have preserved it, and laid it up for the present use, or future good of their children; and especially by any cruel and inhuman treatment; as that of Saul to Jonathan, when he made an attempt on his life, 1 Sam. xx. 33, 34. Such provocation should be carefully avoided; since it renders all commands, counsel, and corrections ineffectual, alienating the affections of their children from them; the reason to dissuade from it, given by the apostle, is, *lest they be discouraged*, Col. iii. 21. be overwhelmed with grief and sorrow, and thereby their spirits be broken, become pusillanimous, disheartened and dispirited; and despairing of pleasing their parents, and sharing in their affections, become careless of duty, and indolent to business. Parents, no doubt, have a right to rebuke and reprove their children when they do amiss; it was Eli's fault that he was too soft and lenient, and his reproofs too easy, when he should have restrained his sons from acting the vile part; should have frowned upon them, put on stern looks, and laid his commands on them, and severely threatened them and punished them, if refractory, 1 Sam. ii. 23, 24. and iii. 13. And they may use the rod of correction, which they should do betimes, and whilst there is hope; but always with moderation, and in love; and should take some pains with their children to convince them that they do love them; and that it is in love to them, and for their good, that they chastise them. *Fathers* are particularly mentioned, because they are apt to be most severe, and mothers most indulgent.

2*dly*, The duty of parents to children is expressed positively; *But bring them up in the nurture and admonition of the Lord*, Eph. vi. 4. which may relate,

1. To things civil, respecting them, that they should *bring them up*; that is, provide for their sustentation and support, food and raiment suitable and convenient for them, and what is honest in the sight of all men, Rom. xii. 17. 1 Tim. v. 8. take care of their education, suitable to their birth, to their capacity, and to what they are designed for in life; to put them to some trade and business at a proper time; the Jews[16] have a

---

[15] Hostis est uxor, invita quæ ad virum nuptum datur, Plauti Stichus, Act. 1. sc. 2. v. 83.

[16] T. Bab. Kiddushin. fol. 30. 2.

saying "that he that does not teach his son, or cause him to be taught, some trade or business, it is all one as if he taught him to be a thief, to steal privately or rob publicly;" and when of age, to dispose of them in marriage, to take wives for their sons, and to give their daughters to husbands; and to give them portions, and part with some of their substance, to set them up in the world, according to their abilities; for all which purposes, to lay up for their children is their duty, as well as to leave something behind them for their future good.——
2. And this exhortation may have respect to the training of them up in a religious way; in the external ways of God, and paths of godliness, in which they should walk; from whence they will not easily[17] and ordinarily depart, Prov. xxii. 6. It becomes them to set good examples to them, of sobriety, temperance, prudence, &c. and to keep them from the company of such from whom they may learn what is evil; for evil communications corrupt good manners; and whereas the seeds of all sins are in children, which soon appear, they should check them betimes, and nip them in the bud, and expose the sinfulness of those vices they are most inclined unto; as using naughty words, and telling lies, &c. they should frequently pray with and for them, as Abraham for Ishmael; whereby they will be sensible, that they have not only their temporal good, but their spiritual and eternal welfare at heart; and they should bring them under the means of grace, the ministry of the word; and teach them to read the scriptures as soon as may be; and instruct them in the knowledge of divine things as they are able to receive it; which seems to be meant by παιδεια, the *nurture of the Lord*. Though I cannot say I truly approve of the method of education used by some good people; as by teaching them the Creed, a form of belief, saying, I believe so and so, before they have any knowledge of and faith in divine truths; and to babble over the Lord's Prayer, as it is commonly called, and other forms of prayer; which seems to have a tendency to direct them to rest in an outward form, and to trust in an outward shew of righteousness; which they need not be taught to do, it is natural unto them; and whenever they receive the grace of God, all this must be untaught and undone again. It is proper to instruct them in the necessity of faith in God and in Christ, and of the use of prayer; and to lay before them the sinfulness of sin, and shew them what an evil thing it is, and what are the sad effects of it; to teach them their miserable estate by nature, and the way of recovery and salvation by Christ; and to learn them from childhood to read and know the holy scriptures, according to their capacity; and by these to be *admonished* of sin, and of their duty, to fear God, and keep his commandments; which may be meant by the *admonition of the Lord*; and the proper opportunity should be taken to instil these things into their minds, when their minds begin to open, and they are inquisitive into the meaning of things; see Deut. vi. 20. and these several respective duties are to be carefully attended to; since the peace and order of families, the good of the common-wealth, and the prosperity of the church, and increase of the interest of Christ, greatly depend upon them.

CHAP. III.

OF THE RESPECTIVE DUTIES OF MASTERS AND SERVANTS.

These duties arise not from a relation founded in nature, as those of parents and children; but from a relation founded in contract, compact, covenant and agreement. Men are by nature, or as to their original make, alike and equal; there is no difference, of bond and free;[1] God has made of one blood all men, all spring from the same original,[2] whether that be traced up to Noah or to Adam; and, indeed, we hear nothing of a servant before the times of the former; and that threatened as a curse for sin, Gen. ix. 25. for as Austin says,[3] it is sin, and not nature, that deserves this name; it is from the lust of the flesh that wars come, and from these captivity, servitude, and bondage, which is through force, and not will; no man has a legal power to make another man his servant against his will, nor has he any right to his service without his consent: that servitude which arises from contract, compact, and covenant, which

---

[17] Quo semel est imbuta recens, servabit odorem, testa diu, Horat. Epist. l. 1. ep. 2. v. 69.

[1] φυσει δ' ουδεν διαφερειν, aliqui apud Aristot. Politic. l. 1. c. 3.

[2] Vis tu cogitare istum, quem servum tuum vocas, ex iisdem seminibus ortum, eodem frui cœlo, æque spirare, æque vivere, æque mori? Seneca, Ep. 47.

[3] Nomen istud culpa meruit, non natura, August. de Civitate Dei, l. 19. c. 15.

almost only obtains among christians, is of all the most just, lawful, and defensible, because with it best consists the natural liberty of mankind; such as an apprenticeship, which a man enters into of his own will, or with the advice and consent of those under whose care he is; when, by an indenture or covenant, he agrees to serve a master for a certain term of years, on certain conditions, mutually agreed unto; or as when one is hired for certain service, by the year, or by the month, or by the day; of which hired servants the prodigal in the parable speaks; *How many hired servants of my Father*, &c. and were as early as in the times of Job, chap. vii. 1, 2. and it is of the duties of such towards their masters, and of the duties incumbent on masters towards them, that I shall now treat.

First, Of the duties of servants to their masters. These are more largely and frequently spoken of in the epistles of the apostles; because that christian servants were impatient of the yoke of heathen masters, and had it insinuated into them, by some licentious persons and false teachers, that civil servitude was inconsistent with christian liberty; from whence great scandal was like to arise to the name and doctrine of Christ, and the christian religion, which were liable to be blasphemed, and spoken evil of on that account, 1 Cor. vii. 21. 1 Tim. vi. 1. Tit. ii. 10. And it may be proper to consider,

1st, Of whom duty is required, and to whom it is to be performed; *Servants, be obedient to them that are your masters*, Eph. vi. 5. By *servants* are meant such of this character, male and female, men-servants and maid-servants, whose relation to them that are over them, their duty to them, and obligation to it are the same; as also they share alike in privileges and benefits belonging to them, Exod. xx. 10. Job xxxi. 13, 15. and *masters* also include *mistresses*, as well as masters, who are to be submitted to, one as another, Gen. xvi. 8, 9. and those of whatsoever temper and disposition, whether good or ill-natured, kind and gentle, or churlish, morose, and perverse, and froward, 1 Pet. ii. 18. and whether truly gracious and religious, or not; *Masters according to the flesh;* or though carnal, and in a state of nature, and in things belonging to the flesh, outward and temporal things, are to be submitted to, Eph. vi. 5. and especially such who have *believing masters* should not *despise* them, and disobey their commands, *because they are brethren*, in the same spiritual relation, and of the same christian community; but; on the contrary, should rather do them *service*, with all constancy, cheerfulness, and readiness, *because they are faithful*, true believers in Christ, and beloved of God, and of his people; *and partakers of the benefit*, of the same grace, and of the same redemption and salvation by Christ, 1 Tim. vi. 2. and they are *their own masters* they are to be obedient to, and not others, who have no right to their service, Tit. ii. 9.

2*dly*, The duties to be performed by servants to their masters; which are comprehended in these general terms of *subjection* to them, and *obedience* to their lawful commands, Eph. vi. 5. Col. iii. 22. Tit. ii. 9. 1 Pet. ii. 18. and which include *honour*, that is to be given them; for they are to be counted *worthy of all honour*, in mind and thought, and to be expressed by words and gesture. They are to be had in honour and esteem, and to be spoken honourably of, and respectfully to, 1 Tim vi. 1. *Fear*, or reverence, which is to be given to all to whom it is due, to all superiors, and so to masters; *If I be a master, where is my fear*, Mal. i. 6. Strict and close attention to orders given; the words of their mouth are to be hearkened to, and the motions of their hands, pointing and directing to business they are to do, are to be observed, Psalm cxxiii. 2. and a ready and cheerful compliance to execute their commands; *I say to my servant, Do this; and he doth it* immediately, at once, Matt. viii. 9. Seeking to please them in all things, that they may obtain their affection and good will, Tit. ii. 9. Shewing all fidelity in what they are intrusted with; not misspending their time, embezzling their master's goods, and wasting his substance, Tit. ii. 10. Acting the same faithful part as Jacob to Laban, and Joseph to Potiphar, and to the keeper of the prison.

3*dly*, The manner in which this duty of obedience, in its several branches, is to be performed; it must be universal; *in all things*, Col. iii. 22. Tit. ii. 9. not in things sinful; but in all things lawful, which are not contrary to the law of God and gospel of Christ, and to the interest of true religion, and the dictates of conscience; over which masters have no power.[4] Obedience

---

[4] Corpora obnoxia sunt et adscripta dominis; mens quidem sui juris, Seneca de Beneficiis l. 3. c. 20.

should be yielded *with all fear*, 1 Pet. ii. 18. with the fear of masters, of offending them, and incurring their just displeasure; with fear of their frowns, rebukes, and corrections, and especially as fearing God, Col. iii. 22. Servants that fear the Lord will say and act as Nehemiah did; *So did not I, because of the fear of the Lord,* Nehem. v. 15. In *singleness of heart;* with simplicity and sincerity; not with duplicity of mind, dissimulation, fraud, deceit, and lying; as Gehazi behaved to his master Elisha, 2 Kings v. 25, 26. Not *with eye-service;* that is, doing his master's business only whilst under his eye, and in his presence; but in his absence, and while they imagine it will continue, do as the wicked servant in Matt. xxiv. 48, 49. their obedience should be cordial and hearty; what they do, they should do it *heartily as to the Lord, and not to man;* not as pleasing men, but *as the servants of Christ, doing the will of God from the heart, with good-will doing service;* not grudgingly, nor murmuring, nor by force and constraint, but willingly, and of a ready mind, Eph. vi. 5, 6, 7. Col. iii. 23.

4*thly,* The arguments enforcing such obedience are,——1. The authority and command of God; it is by the authority of God that the exhortations to obedience are given; and it is to be yielded in conformity to his will, as if done to him rather than to men.——2. The honour and glory of God, and of Christ, and of his gospel, is concerned herein, that his name and doctrine be not blasphemed, by a contrary behaviour; but that the gospel, and a profession of it, be adorned by a suitable conduct, 1 Tim. vi. 1. Tit. ii. 10.—— 3. The example of Christ must be of great weight with the true lovers of him; who, though equal with God, took on him the form of a servant, and condescended to do the duty of one, was faithful and righteous, always did the things that pleased God, delighted in doing his Father's will and work, and was constant and assiduous in it; in all which he set an example to tread in his steps.——4. The benefit arising to servants from their obedience, in general, what good thing they do, the same they shall receive of the Lord; for God is not unrighteous, to forget their service; but will recompense it either now or hereafter, with a reward of grace, Eph. vi. 8. and particularly with the reward *of the inheritance* which they *know* they shall *receive of the Lord,* Col. iii. 24. by which is meant, the heavenly glory, called an *inheritance,* because their Father's bequest unto them, and a *reward,* not of works, but of grace; and so have the strongest motive and greatest encouragement to obedience that can be had.

Secondly, There are duties incumbent on masters, with respect to their servants; *And ye masters, do the same things unto them,* Eph. vi. 9. not the same duties; but what belong to them, they should do in the same manner, in obedience to the will of God, in the fear of God, and with a view to his glory. And,

1. There are some things they are to do, with respect to the moral, spiritual, and eternal good of their servants.—(1.) They are to set good examples to them, of temperance, sobriety, prudence, virtue, and religion; examples have great force in them; as a man is, so will his servants be, Prov. xxix. 12. David determined to *walk within his house,* before his children and servants, *with a perfect heart,* with all integrity and uprightness, thereby setting an example to them, Psalm ci. 2.—(2.) They are to teach and instruct them in the knowledge of divine things; as Abraham taught his servants, who were trained up in his house, as in civil things, so in matters of religion, Gen. xiv. 14. and xviii. 19. —(3.) They are to pray with them, and for them; for prayer is to be made for all men, as for superiors, for kings, and all in authority; so for inferiors and for servants; which is a part of family worship, Jer. x. 25. Josh. xxiv. 15.—(4.) Should allow time and leisure for religious services, to read and hear the word of God, to pray and praise, and to meditate, according to the provision made for rest and cessation from labour, in the fourth precept of the Decalogue; and they should be put upon as little service as may be on whatsoever day for worship is observed.

2. There are other duties, which relate to their temporal good. As,—(1.) They are to teach them the business they are put apprentices to them for, and learn them the whole mystery of their art, so far as they are capable of receiving it; or otherwise they will not act the faithful part.— (2.) To give them that which is *just and equal,* according to the laws of God and men, of justice and equity, food convenient for them, what is fit to be eaten, and a sufficiency of it; so in the house of the prodigal's father there was bread enough and to spare for the hired servants: raiment

also is to be provided for them,[5] if in the agreement, and what is suitable to their relation and circumstances; and when they are sick they should take care of them, and be concerned for their health, and recovery of it; as the centurion was, who applied to Christ on the behalf of his servant, Matt. viii. 5—10. A contrary behaviour in the Amalekite towards his servant, was barbarous and cruel, 1 Sam. xxx. 13.—(3.) They should pay them their just wages, and that in due time, according as agreed upon; the law of God directs to the payment of them immediately, and not let them abide all night, till the morning, Lev. xix. 13. Deut. xxiv. 15. if they are detained, and they cry unto the Lord, he will avenge them, James v. 4.—(4.) Obedient servants are to be encouraged, and used kindly, and with respect: according to the law of God, enjoined the Jews, when a servant had served out his time, was not only to be let go free, but he was not to be sent away empty; but to be liberally supplied from the flock, from the floor, and from the wine-press, Deut. xv. 12, 13, 14. Disobedient ones are to be corrected; and if they will not be corrected by words, then with stripes; yet to be given with moderation;[6] servants are not to be used in a cruel and inhuman manner, as if they were beasts, and not men. Seneca[7] complains of some masters in his time, who used them worse than beasts, and speaks of them as most proud, most cruel, and most contumelious; see Prov. xxix. 19. Luke xii. 47, 48. the apostle advises, to *forbear threatening*, Eph. vi. 9. that is, not to threaten too much and too often, and with too great severity; nor should they be forward to carry it into execution; and especially when they repent and amend, they should be forgiven.

Now the argument to enforce these duties on masters, is taken from their having a *Master in heaven;* who is no other than Christ, who is a good Master, and where he is his servants shall be; he grants them his presence now, and will enter them into his joy hereafter, Matt. xxiii. 8, 10. and xxv. 21. John xiii. 13, 15. and xii. 26. and who is the Master of masters, as well as of servants, and to whom they are accountable, and with him is no respect of persons, bond or free, Eph. vi. 8, 9. Col. iii. 25. and he is in heaven, from whence he looks down and beholds all that is done on earth, by masters as well as servants, and who is able to plead the cause of the injured, and to avenge them. Happy it is when love and harmony, freedom and familiarity,[8] subsist between masters and servants, so far as is consistent with the relation; an instance of which we have in Boaz, who went to his reapers in the field, and thus saluted them, *The Lord be with you!* To whom they replied, *The Lord bless thee!* Ruth ii. 4. a good master and good servants, mutually happy in each other.

CHAP. IV.

OF THE RESPECTIVE DUTIES OF MAGISTRATES AND SUBJECTS.

The duties of subjection and obedience to magistrates, supreme and subordinate, are frequently inculcated in the sacred writings; and the reason why the apostles so often and so strongly urge them, is because of the scandal to the christian religion, which was like to arise from a contrary behaviour, of which there was danger; since in the first churches were many Jews, who were impatient of the Roman yoke, and christians in general were called Jews by the heathens; and it was enough to fix the charge of sedition on any to say they were Jews, who were troublers of the state, Acts xvi. 20, 21. and of all the Jews the Galileans were reckoned the most turbulent, and factious, and the most averse to payment of taxes to the Roman governors, Acts v. 37. Luke xiii. 1. and Christ and his followers were commonly called Galileans, and so liable to the same imputation; besides, the first christians might not be so willingly subject to heathen magistrates, because they were such, and many of them very wicked men, called, *spiritual wickednesses in high places;* and Nero, the then reigning emperor, when the apostle Paul wrote many of his epistles, was a monster of wickedness; and they might also imagine, that subjection to men was inconsistent with christian liberty. To all which may be added, that there were many false

---

[5] Est aliquid quod Dominus præstare servo debeat, ut cibaria, vestiarium, Seneca, ib. 1. 3. c. 21. necessaria ad victum, c. 22.
[6] Servis imperare moderate, laus est. Seneca de Clementia, 1. 1. c. 18.
[7] Epist. 47.
[8] Vive cum servo clementer, comiter quoque, et in sermonem admitte, et in consilium, et in convictum, ib.

teachers, men of bad principles and practices, who *despised dominion, and spoke evil of dignities;* wherefore the apostles thought it necessary to *put in mind* the saints they wrote to, of their duties of subjection and obedience to civil government; that the gospel, and the religion of Christ, might not be evil spoken of; and for the same reason we who are called Baptists, and by way of reproach Anabaptists, should be careful to observe these duties; since it seems there were some of the same name formerly, in foreign countries, who held, if not misrepresented by many writers, that it was not lawful for a christian man to bear the office of a magistrate; and from thence inferred, that the laws of such were not to be obeyed: and nothing is more common with every puny writer against us, than to upbraid us with the riots and tumults at Munster in Germany; which, though begun by Pædobaptists, yet because some called Anabaptists joined them, men of bad principles and scandalous characters, the whole blame was laid upon them. But be these things as they may, what is all this to us here in England, who disavow and declare against all such principles and practices; as our general behaviour, our writings and public confessions of faith printed at different times, manifestly shew? and yet the calumny is continued; wherefore it becomes us to wipe off the foul aspersion, both by our declared abhorrence of it, and by our conduct and deportment towards our superiors; that those who falsely accuse our good conversation in things civil, may blush, and be ashamed.

Now as the respective duties before treated of, arise from relations of a different nature; those of husbands and wives from a relation founded in marriage; and those of parents and children from a relation founded in nature; and those of masters and servants from a relation founded in contract and compact; so those of magistrates and subjects arise from a relation founded in consent, agreement, and covenant: a coalition of men, and bodies of men, in a political sense, whether it arose from *mutual fear,* as Hobbes[1] says; or rather from a propensity in human nature to society, man being a sociable animal, as Aristotle,[2] and other politicians think;

yet it most certainly was by agreement and consent; and men being thus united together, agreed to choose some from among themselves to preside over them, to keep the better decorum and order among them; with these they entered into covenant, on certain conditions and fundamental laws made; when they agreed, the one to govern according to those laws, and to defend the lives, liberties, and properties of men from lawless persons; and the other swore fidelity to them, and promised a cheerful subjection and obedience to their lawful commands, and to support their government; and this is the original of free and well-regulated states; from whom certain respective duties, both of magistrates and subjects, arise; now to be treated of. And,

First, It will be proper to consider, of whom the duties of subjection and obedience are required, and to whom they are to be yielded.

1*st,* Of whom they are required: of every one that belongs to the commonwealth; *Let every soul be subject to the higher powers,* Rom. xiii. 1. that is, every man; see chap. ii. 9, 10. every man that has a soul, every rational man; and to be subject to and obey civil magistrates, is but his reasonable service; every one of each sex, male and female, men and women; of every age, young and old; and of every state and condition, high and low, rich and poor, bond and free, ecclesiastics not excepted; the papists plead for an exemption of them, but without any reason.

The priests under the law were subject to civil government; as Abiathar to Solomon, 1 Kings ii. 26, 27. and so the ministers of Christ under the gospel; Christ and his apostles paid tribute to Cæsar, and even Peter, whose successor the pope pretends to be, Matt. xvii. 24—27. The apostle Paul appealed to Cæsar, owned his authority, and claimed his protection, Acts xxv. 10, 11. The same doctrine was inculcated by the successors of the apostles in the age following, who professed their subjection to the civil magistrate, and taught it; says Polycarp,[3] we are commanded to honour magistrates, and the powers that are ordained of God; the same doctrine was taught by Ignatius,[4] Irenæus,[5] and Justin;[6] and Pliny the heathen bears witness to the christians of

---

[1] De Cive, c. 1. s. 2.
[2] Politic. l. 1. c. 2.
[3] Apud Euseb. l. 4. c. 15.

[4] Ep. ad. Philadelph.
[5] Adv. Hæres. l. 5. c. 24.
[6] Apolog. 2. p. 64.

OF MAGISTRATES AND SUBJECTS.

the second century, that they did all things in conformity to the civil laws.[7]

2dly, To whom these duties are to be performed. These are the *higher powers*; called *powers* because they are invested with the power of government, and have a right to exercise it; *higher* powers, because they are set in high places, and have a super-eminence over others, Rom. xiii. 1. sometimes they are called *principalities and powers*, Tit. iii. 1. by whom are meant, not angels, to whom men are not put in subjection, on civil accounts; nor ecclesiastical officers, as elders and pastors of churches, whose government is not of a civil, but spiritual nature; they do not bear the temporal sword, nor are they to make any use of that; but civil magistrates, as the words are explained in the same verse, *Obey magistrates;* rulers or governors, and these include supreme and subordinate ones; *Kings, and all that are in authority* under them, and derive their authority from them, for whom prayer is to be made, 1 Tim. ii. 1, 2. *Every ordinance of man*, or every creature of man; that is, every magistrate, who is of man's creating, is to be submitted to; *Whether it be to the king, as supreme, or unto governors, as unto them that are sent* and appointed *by him*, 1 Pet. ii. 13, 14. and as heathen magistrates were to be submitted unto, for such were they designed in the above passages, then certainly christian magistrates; for it is no ways inconsistent with the grace of God, nor for a good man, to be a magistrate; the better man, the better magistrate; such there were under the former dispensation; as Moses, the Judges in Israel, David, Solomon, Jehoshaphat, Hezekiah, Josiah, and others. And under the gospel-dispensation, when the Roman empire became christian, there was a Constantine, the first christian emperor, thought to be a very good man; and there have been such in after-times; though it must be owned they have been rare and few; but there are prophesies of more, and there may be an expectation of more in the latter-day glory; when all kings shall fall down before Christ; when kings shall come to the brightness of Zion, or to the church's rising, and when her gates shall stand open continually for kings to enter in, and become church-members; and when kings shall be nursing-fathers, and queens nursing-mothers: and these are most certainly to be submitted to, and their laws obeyed. I go on,

Secondly, To consider the duties both of magistrates and subjects. And,

1st, Of magistrates; for though the duties of subjection and obedience are incompetent to them; yet there are duties incumbent on them, arising from their relation to their people, and covenant with them. And,

1. They are to make and pass such laws as are for the good of their subjects. The government of the people of Israel was very peculiar; it was a Theocracy; God was their King in a civil sense, and made laws for them, which he delivered to them by the hands of Moses; and their kings had no power to make any new ones; nor did they, not the best and wisest of them, as David, Solomon, &c. but governed according to the laws made to their hands. Our kings have a concern in the making of laws; that is, they have a negative voice, and can put a check upon any laws, and refuse to sign them made by the other branches of the legislature; and it is their duty to refuse to sign such laws as are not salutary to their subjects, or are contrary to the laws of God, and to the fundamental laws of the state.——2. They are to govern according to such righteous and salutary laws, and to execute judgment and justice, as David did, and other good kings do; and then magistrates do their duty, when the king reigns in righteousness, and princes decree judgment, Isa. xxxii. 1.——3. They are to discountenance and suppress impiety and irreligion; and to countenance and encourage religion and virtue; even Aristotle[8] observes in his book of Politics, that the first care of government should be the care of divine things, or what relate to religion. Civil magistrates are appointed for the punishment of evil doers, and for the praise of them that do well; they are to discourage vice, and vicious persons; a king, by his eye, the sternness of his looks, and the frowns of his countenance, should scatter away evil, and evil men; and these being removed from him, his throne will be established in righteousness, Prov. xx. 8. and xxv. 5. Kings are the guardians of the laws of God and man; and christian kings have a peculiar concern with the laws of the two tables, that they are observed, and the violaters of them punished; as sins against the first table, idolatry, worshipping

---

[7] Apud Euseb. l. 3. c. 33.

[8] Πρωτον, την περι το Θειον επιμιλιιαν, ην καλουσιν ιερατειαν, Aristot. Politic. l. 7. c. 8.

of more gods than one, and of graven images, blaspheming the name of God, perjury, and false swearing, and profanation of the day of worship: and those against the second table; as disobedience to parents, murder, adultery, theft, bearing false witness, &c. most of which, under the former dispensation, were capital crimes, and punishable with death; and though the punishment of them, at least not all of them, may not be inflicted with that rigour now as then; yet they are punishable in some way or another; which it is the duty of magistrates to take care of.——4. The principal care and concern of a king is the welfare and safety of his people, that they are secured in their lives, liberties, and property; that they live peaceable and quiet lives, unmolested by any; that they dwell safely, every man under his vine and fig-tree, as Israel did in the times of Solomon; the maxim of the Roman orator is a very good one; *Salus populi suprema lex esto;*[9] Let the safety and welfare of the people be the supreme law of government; the safety of a king and his people is closely connected together, and the one is included in the other: it is an observation of an heathen moralist, that "he is mistaken, who thinks that a king is safe, where there is no safety from him; for," adds he, "security is by compact and covenant, to be established and confirmed through mutual security."[10] Justice, prudence, and clemency, are virtues highly becoming kings.[11]

2*dly*, There are duties to be performed by subjects to magistrates. As,

1. To honour them, and shew reverence to them, Rom. xiii. 7. 1 Pet. ii. 17. Next to the fear of God, is the honour of the king; yea, the fear or reverence of God and the king is joined together, Prov. xxiv. 21. There is a semblance of divine Majesty in a king, which makes him the object of fear and reverence. Kings are called gods, because they are in God's stead, his vicegerents, and personate him; *I said, ye are gods*, Psal. lxxxii. 1, 6.—— 2. As subjects are to think honourably, they are to speak respectfully of rulers; *Thou shalt not revile the gods, nor curse the ruler of thy people;* no, not in thought, nor in the bed-chamber, in the most secret place, since, sooner or later, it may be discovered, and the person be brought to condign punishment, Exod. xxii. 28. Eccles. x. 20. they are reckoned as the vilest and most abandoned among men, and as such described, who *despise government*, and are *not afraid to speak evil of dignities*, 2 Pet. ii. 10. Jude ver. 8. we should speak evil of no man, particularly of magistrates, and more especially of the king, as supreme; not of his person, nor of his administration; there are *arcana imperii*, secrets of government, which we know nothing of, and it is not proper we should; were they to be known in common, the good designs of government would be defeated by the enemy. The springs of action in government we are not acquainted with, and only judge of them by the success of them; which is a fallacious way of judging. A thing may be well planned, and wisely concerted, at the time it was, all circumstances considered, nothing better; and yet by one unforeseen accident or another, the design of it is defeated; and because it met not with success, is condemned as a piece of bad policy.——3. Subjects should speak to a king with great reverence and respect; *Is it fit to say to a king, thou art wicked?* Job xxxiv. 18. it is not decent and becoming; no, not to a wicked king. But if a king does wickedly, must he not be told of it, and reproved for it? He may, but not by every impertinent and impudent fellow; only by persons of eminence, in things sacred and civil, and that in a respectful manner; and perhaps no instance can be given from the word of God, of a king being reproved by any but a prophet, or one sent of God. Herod, a wicked prince, was reproved by John the Baptist, and a reason given for it. David, a good prince, was reproved by Nathan the prophet, sent of God to him; which reproof he delivered in a decent manner, wrapt up in a parable, and he took the proper opportunity to apply it; which had the desired effect. But such language Shimei used to David, was not fit to be used to a king, 2 Sam. xvi. 7.——4. Civil magistrates supreme and subordinate, are to be prayed for, 1 Tim. ii. 1, 2. for their health, happiness, and prosperity, and the peace of their government, and the con-

---

[9] Cicero de Legibus, l. 3. c. 11.
[10] Errat enim siquis existimet tutum esse ibi regem, ubi nihil à rege tutum est. Securitas securitate mutua paciscenda est, Seneca de Clementia, l. 1. c. 19.

[11] Nullum tamen clementia ex omnibus magis quam regem aut principem decet, Seneca de Clementia, l. 1. c. 3.

CHAP. IV.   OF MAGISTRATES AND SUBJECTS.   987

tinuance of it; for in their peace is the peace of subjects, Jer. xxix. 10.——5. They are to be submitted to and obeyed in all things, which are not contrary to the laws of God, and the fundamental laws of the kingdom; for otherwise God is to be obeyed, and not men, Acts iv. 19. and v. 29.——6. They are to be supported in their government, by a payment of all lawful tribute, tax, and custom; *Render to all their dues; tribute to whom tribute is due, custom to whom custom*, Rom. xiii. 7. This is a doctrine taught not only by the apostle, but by Christ himself, and confirmed by his own example and practice, Matt. xxii. 21. and xvii. 27. Government cannot be supported without such methods; and without government there is no safety of a man's life and property; but he must be exposed to a banditti of robbers, plunderers, and levellers, who would strip him at once of all he has: would not any wise man part with some of his substance to secure the rest? without government, as the Roman orator[12] says, "not a family, nor a city, nor a nation, nor all mankind, nor the whole nature of things, nor the world itself, can stand." And government cannot be maintained without defraying the expenses of it, which are many and large, by the payment of tribute and taxes, which ought to be done cheerfully; nor should any illicit methods be taken to defeat the payment of them, which is foolishly called, cheating the king, and that is said to be no sin; whereas men hereby cheat themselves, cheat the public, of which they are a part; some individuals may avail themselves by such unlawful practices, but the public suffers, and so does every honest man; and it is the very means of the multiplicity of taxes complained of; for if a duty is laid on one commodity, and it is defeated by such iniquitous practices, either it must be increased on that commodity, or laid upon another.

Thirdly, There are various reasons to be given, why subjection and obedience should be yielded by subjects to magistrates.

1. Because that magistracy is by the ordination and appointment of God; *The powers that be, are ordained of God;* Rom. xiii. 1. it is he that sets up one and puts down another, Psalm lxxv. 6, 7. Dan. ii. 21. *By me kings reign,* says Wisdom, *and princes decree justice,* Prov. viii. 15. not

that it may be that any particular form of government is of God; there are divers forms; as *monarchy*, which is the government of one man; *aristocracy*, which is the government of the chief and principal persons in a nation; and *democracy*, which lies in the people: which is the best sort of government, I will not take upon me to say; but this I will venture to say, that the worst government is better that none at all; perhaps a mixt government may be best, made up of all three; as ours is. There is an appearance of monarchy in the *king*, of aristocracy in the *nobles*, and of democracy in the *commons*, chosen by the suffrages of the people. Moreover, it is not this or that particular man in government, that is of God; he may assume that to himself which does not belong to him, and so is not of God, but of himself; or he may abuse the power he is possessed of, which, though by divine permission, and may be for a scourge to a people; yet not of God's approbation: it is not therefore this or that form of government, or this or that particular person, but government itself, that is of God; for there is no power but of him; what Adam had over the creatures, the husband has over the wife, parents over their children, and masters over their servants, it is of God; and so is the power magistrates have over subjects, John xix. 11. and therefore are to be obeyed.——2. To resist them, is to resist the ordinance of God, Rom. xiii. 2. Not that magistrates are above the laws; but are to be subject to them, and are liable to the penalty of them, when broken by them; they are under the laws, but over men; so says Cicero;[13] "the laws preside over magistrates, and magistrates over the people; and," adds he, "the magistrate is a speaking law, and the law a mute magistrate." So that these have a close connection with each other; the laws are binding on magistrates, and they are to govern according to them; and when they do that which is wrong, or attempt it, they may be resisted; as Saul, when he would have put his son to death, for the breach of an arbitrary law of his own, and which his son was ignorant of; but the people would not suffer him; and they were in the right: so Uzziah, when he went into the temple to offer incense, which to do was a breach of the law of God, then in being; Azariah, and fourscore priests more, followed

---

[12] Cicero de Legibus, l. 3. c. 9.

[13] De Legibus l. 3. c. 9.

him, and withstood him, and they had the approbation of God; for before the king could get out of the temple, he was smote with a leprosy. But a king, or a civil magistrate, is not to be resisted in the execution of lawful power and authority.
——3. Such who *resist shall receive to themselves damnation,* or *judgment;* either temporal judgment from men or from God; as did Korah, Dathan, and Abiram; or eternal judgment; for for those who despise dominion, and speak evil of dignities, the blackness of darkness is reserved for ever and ever, Jude ver. 7, 8, 11, 13. There are other reasons to be gathered from Rom. xiii. enforcing obedience to civil magistrates; taken from their being the ministers of God for good, for civil good, the protection of men in their lives, liberties, and properties; and for moral good, for the restraint of vice; for if the fence of magistracy was plucked up, vice would issue in like an inundation, and carry all before it; see Judges xxi. 25. and from their being encouragers of good works, and the executors of the wrath of God on evil men; and by good men are to be obeyed, not for wrath's sake, or the fear of punishment, but for conscience sake; and a good conscience cannot be exercised without obedience to them.

CHAP. V.

OF GOOD WORKS IN GENERAL.

GOOD works, or actions, are of various sorts. There are *natural* actions, which respect the animal life; such as eating, drinking, &c. which, when done in moderation, and not to excess, are good, and are necessary for the preservation of health and life. And there are *civil* employments, trades, businesses, and occupations of life, men are called to; and it is good to attend to them; and they are necessary for the support of a man and his family, and that he may do good to others, and are for the credit of religion. These, by some, are thought to be meant by good works, in Tit. iii. 14. There are *relative* duties, or good works to be performed by husbands and wives, parents and children, masters and servants, magistrates and subjects, before treated of. And there are acts of *beneficence* and charity, to fellow-creatures and Christians; which are called *doing good,* and are acceptable and well pleasing to God, Heb. xiii. 16. Gal. vi. 10. There are some good works to be done to men, as men, and are comprehended in that general rule of Christ's, Matt. vii. 12. and others to believers in Christ, who are *by love to serve one another.* Some are of a *positive* kind, in obedience to a positive law of God, the effect of his sovereign will and pleasure; such were the institutions and ordinances of divine service observed under the former dispensation, and Baptism and the Lord's Supper under the present. Others are of a *moral* nature, done in agreement to the moral law, and to the law and light of nature, binding upon all, in all ages. And of good works, some are *materially,* or as to the substance of them, and in appearance good, when they are not *circumstantially* good; or as to the circumstances of them; nor radically, and as to the principle of them: such were the virtues of the heathens Austin calls *splendida peccata,* shining sins; and such the works done by Herod, on hearing John; and by the Pharisees, who were and did things outwardly righteous before men, but at heart wicked; hence it is sometimes said,[1] not *nouns,* but *adverbs,* make good works; it is not barely doing *bonum,* a good thing; but doing that good thing *bene,* well. The circumstances requisite to a good work, are,

1. That it be according to the command and will of God; as every evil work or sin is a transgression of the law of God, and a want of conformity to that; so every good work is in agreement with it, and a conformity to it. By this rule many works are cut off from being good works, done by the Pharisees of old, and by Papists now, though they may have a great shew of religion and holiness, because they are done according to the precepts and traditions of men, and not according to the commands of God.——2. That it spring from love to God, and not influenced by any sinister and selfish motive; *The end of the commandment is charity,* or love; love to God is the root and spring of obedience to it, and is the motive inducing to it, 1 Tim. i. 5. John xiv. 15.——3. It must be done in faith; for what is *not of faith is sin,* and so no good work; without faith it is impossible to please God; herein lay the difference between Abel's work and Cain's; the one was done in faith, the other not, Rom. xiv. 23. Heb. xi. 4, 6.

---

[1] Maccov. Distinct. Theolog. c. 15. s. 10.

―――4. It must be done to the glory of God, 1 Cor. x. 31. The Pharisees prayed, and fasted, and did alms; but all to be seen of men, and to get glory from them, but sought not the glory of God; and so were not good works; good works are *by Jesus Christ, unto the glory and praise of God;* Phil. i. 11. Now concerning these may be observed,

First, The springs and causes of them.

1. The efficient cause is God, who *works* in his people, *both to will and to do;* gives the inclination to a good work, and power to perform it. Every action, as an action, is of God, by whom *we move;* and a good work is not only of God, as an action, but as a good action, who is the fountain of all goodness; the beginning, progress, and perfection of a good work are of God, and so prayed for, Heb. xiii. 21.―――2. The influential cause is the grace of God; it was by that the apostle Paul did works more abundantly than others, and to that he ascribes them; and through that had his conversation in the world, in simplicity and godly sincerity, 1 Cor. xv. 10. 2 Cor. i. 12. The grace of God, both as a principle, and as a doctrine, teaches influentially to deny ungodliness and worldly lusts, and to live soberly, righteously, and godly, Tit. ii. 11, 12.―――3. Good works, that are truly such, are owing to union to Christ; men are *created in Christ Jesus unto good works,* Eph. ii. 10. they are first in Christ as branches in the vine, and then bring forth the fruit of good works; as the branch cannot bring forth fruit of itself, except it is in and abides in the vine, so neither can any, except they are in and abide in Christ, who is the green fir tree, from whom all their fruit is found, John xv. 4. Hos. xiv. 8.―――4. Faith in Christ is productive of them; the heart is purified by faith in the blood of Jesus, which purges the conscience from dead works, whereby men are better fitted to do good works, or to serve the living God; faith without works is dead; and works without faith are dead works: a living faith produces living works; not that the life of faith lies in works; but as Dr. Ames[2] observes, works are second acts, necessarily flowing from the life of faith. Faith, some call it[3] the internal, instrumental cause of works; the external instrumental cause of works is, ―――5. The word of God; as faith comes by hearing it, so the obedience of faith; the word, written and read, preached and heard, is a means of making the man of God, whether in a public or private character, *thoroughly furnished unto all good works,* 2 Tim. iii. 16. see Luke viii. 15.

Secondly, The nature and properties of good works.

1. The best of works, which are done by the best of men, and in the best manner, are but imperfect; there is sin in them all; there are none found perfect in the sight of God, however they may appear before men, Eccles. vii. 20. Rev. iii. 2. knowledge of the will of God, the rule of them is imperfect; and so are faith and love, from whence they spring; and there is indwelling sin, that hinders saints from doing the good they would, and in the manner they are desirous of, and which pollutes their best actions.

2. They are not meritorious of any thing at the hand of God; the requisites of merit are wanting in them.—(1.) To merit, they must be profitable to God; but such they are not; they are no gain to him: men, by their works, give him nothing, nor does he receive any thing from them, and therefore he is under no obligation to them for them, Job xxii. 2. and xxxv. 7. Psalm xvi. 2.—(2.) They are due to God; whereas they should not, if expected to merit by them; but in doing them, men do but what is their duty; for the doing of which they are debtors, and under obligation to perform them. God has a prior right unto them; could these be given him first, a recompense might be expected; but this is not the case, Luke xvii. 10. Rom. viii. 12. and xi. 35, 36.—(3.) They must be done by men in their own strength, and not in the strength and by the assistance of God, of whom it is expected to merit; whereas without the grace and strength of Christ, men can do nothing; but all things through him strengthening them: his strength is made perfect in their weakness, and by his grace they do what they do, and therefore can merit nothing.—(4.) There is no proportion between the works of men, and any mercy and favour of God; they are not *worthy* of the *least* of the temporal mercies they enjoy, and still less of spiritual ones, and especially of eternal life and happiness; between which, and the best works of men, there is no manner of proportion; there is between sin, and the wages of it, death; but none between works of righteousness and eternal life;

[2] Medulla Theolog. l. 2. c. 7. s. 35.

[3] Synops. Purior. Theolog. Disp. 34. s. 9.

that is the free gift of God, Gen. xxxii. 10. Rom. vi. 23. and viii. 18.

Thirdly, The subjects of them, in whom they are found, and by whom performed. Every man is not capable of performing good works; there is an inaptitude, and an impotence to that which is good; men are naturally to every good work reprobate or unfit; to do good they have no knowledge, and have no inclination nor disposition unto it; have neither will nor power; the bias of their minds is another way; they mind the things of the flesh, and their carnal minds are enmity to God, and to all that is good; and hence the truth of that observation, *There is none that doeth good, no not one!* Rom. iii. 12. Such only are capable of doing good works, who, 1. Are made good men; *Make the tree good, and its fruit will be good;* let a man be made a good man, and he will do good works; but it is God that must make him good,[4] none else can; he cannot make himself good; the good work of grace must first be begun in him by the Spirit and grace of God; and then, and not before, will he perform good works; he must be made a new creature in Christ, in order to do good works, Eph. ii. 10.——2. They must first be purified and sanctified: Christ gave himself, his life and blood, for the redemption of his people; *That he might purify unto himself a peculiar people, zealous of good works*, Tit. ii. 14. and a man must be sanctified by the Spirit and grace of God, that he may be *meet for the master's use, and prepared unto every good work*, 2 Tim. ii. 21.——3. They must have the Spirit of Christ, and be strengthened by him, with all might in the inward man, in order to perform them; and for this end is he promised, Ezek. xxxvi. 27.——4. They must have faith in God, and strength from Christ; they that have *believed in God*, in his Son, and in his promises, and in his covenant, ought to be *careful to maintain good works;* as they are the only persons capable of them, since faith is requisite to them; and such are under the greatest obligations to perform them: and strength from Christ is necessary; in whom are both *righteousness* to render them acceptable to God, and *strength* to perform duties incumbent on them, Tit. iii. 8. Isa. xlv. 24. ——5. The apostle says; *Let ours learn to maintain good works*, Tit. iii. 14. Such who are the chosen generation, a peculiar people, the redeemed of the Lord, and who have drank into the same Spirit, have obtained like precious faith, and are heirs together of the grace of life.

Fourthly, The *necessary uses* for which good works are to be performed.

1st, Not to procure salvation, in whole or in part; not to make peace with God, which they cannot effect; nor to make atonement for sin, for which they cannot answer one of a thousand; nor to obtain the pardon of it, which is only by the blood of Christ; nor to justify in the sight of God, for by the deeds of the law no flesh living can be justified, Rom. iii. 20, 28. the best works being impure and imperfect. Salvation in general is denied to be of works; this is the current language of scripture, Eph. ii. 8, 9. 2 Tim. i. 9. Tit. iii. 5. They are not in any rank and class of causes respecting salvation; they are neither efficient, nor moving, nor meritorious, nor adjuvant causes of salvation; nor even conditions of it; they do not go before any part of salvation, but are fruits and effects of it; not of election, which was before the children had done either good or evil; nor of redemption, in consequence of which the redeemed are a peculiar people, zealous of good works; nor of vocation, works before calling are not good works, and those that follow after are fruits and effects of calling grace; *Who hath saved us and called us, not according to our works*, &c. 2 Tim. i. 9. nor do they go before, to make and prepare the way to consummate happiness, but they *follow* after, Rev. xiv. 13. Yet,

2dly, There are uses for which they are necessary. As,——1. With respect to God, they being of his *ordination*, that his people should *walk* in them, and according to his command and will, in obedience to which it is necessary to perform them, Eph. ii. 10. as well as to testify our gratitude for mercies temporal and spiritual we receive from him; and they are to be done with a view to his glory; for hereby is our heavenly Father glorified; and we not only glorify him ourselves, but are the means of others glorifying him also, John xv. 8. Matt. v. 16. 1 Pet. ii. 12.——2. With respect to ourselves; as for the ornament of ourselves, to adorn our profession, and the doctrine of God our Saviour, 1 Tim. ii. 9, 10. Tit. ii. 10. and to testify and shew forth our faith to others, and to make

---

[4] Bonus vir sine Deo nemo est, Seneca, Ep. 41. Nulla sine Deo mens bona est, ibid. Ep. 73.

our calling and election sure; not surer than they are in themselves, nor surer to ourselves, being certified to us by the Spirit and grace of God; but sure to others, by our good works and holy conversation, as fruits of them; which is all the evidence we are capable of giving to the world, or they are capable of receiving from us, James ii. 18. 2 Pet. i. 10.——3. With respect to others, to whom they are good and profitable, and therefore to be done, Tit. iii. 8. both by way of example, and by real benefit received through them, either in a temporal, or in a spiritual way; and because they serve to recommend religion to others; and may be, without the word, a means of winning them to a liking of it; or, however, may serve to stop the mouth of gainsayers, and make them ashamed who falsely accuse the good conversation of the saints; and so prevent any just offence being given to Jew or Gentile, or to the church of God.

CHAP. VI.

A COMPENDIUM OR SUMMARY OF THE DECALOGUE, OR TEN COMMANDS.

THE Commandments of the law are reduced by Christ to two capital ones; Love to God, and Love to the neighbour, Matt. xxii. 36—40. and the apostle Paul says, *All the law is fulfilled in one word, even in this, Thou shalt love thy neighbour as thyself*, Gal. v. 14. he means the commandments of the second table of the law; and, indeed, love, as it includes both branches of it, love to God and to men, briefly comprehends every other command; and therefore with propriety it is said by him, *Love is the fulfilling of the law*, Rom. xiii. 9, 10. and what may serve to epitomise the decalogue, and to sum up the contents of each command, is a rule or two that may be observed; as, that the prohibition of any sin, includes in it a command of the contrary virtue or duty; and so *vice versa;* and that the prohibition of any sin, and the command of any duty, include in them all sins and duties of the same kind and kindred, with all causes, means, and occasions thereof, as may be exemplified in our Lord's exposition of the *sixth* and *seventh* commands, Matt. v. 21, 22, 27, 28. by which it appears, that the law is spiritual, and reaches not only to external actions, done in the body, but to inward thoughts, affections and lusts of the mind.

The preface to the decalogue, contains arguments or motives unto obedience to the commandments in it. As,

1. That it is *the Lord* Jehovah, the author of our beings, the God of our lives and mercies, the sovereign Lord and Governor of the world, who enjoins it; who has a right to command his creatures what he pleases, and it becomes them to obey him.——2. He that enjoins these precepts, is the Lord *thy God;* not only thy Creator, thy Preserver, and Benefactor, but thy covenant-God; as he was peculiarly to the Jews in a national sense, which laid them under great obligation to him; and if he is our God in a special sense, according to the tenor of the covenant of grace, the obligation is still the greater.——3. He is farther described, as he *which have brought thee out of the land of Egypt, out of the house of bondage,* which was only literally true of the people of Israel; which shews that the decalogue, as to the form of it, and as delivered through the hands and ministry of Moses, only concerned that people, and was calculated for their use; though, as to the matter of it, and so far as it is of a moral nature, and agrees with the law and light of nature, it is equally binding on Gentiles; and if the redemption mentioned, is considered as typical of spiritual and eternal redemption by Christ, from the bondage of sin, Satan, and the law, the obligation to serve the Lord, and obey him, is still more strong and forcible; see Tit. ii. 14. 1 Cor. vi. 20. The decalogue itself follows.

I. The *first* command is, *Thou shalt have no other gods before me.* The things required in this precept are,——1. That we should know, own, and acknowledge God, the one, only, true God, and none else, Mark xii. 29. Psalm xlvi. 10. Hos. xiii. 4.——2. That we should worship him, and him only; not any creature with him; nor any more than he; nor indeed, any besides him, Matt. iv. 10. Rom. i. 25.——3. That we should exercise faith and trust in him, hope in him, and love him, John xiv. 1. Jer. xvii. 5. Matt. xxii. 39. The things forbidden by it are,——1. Atheism; denying there is a God, or any of the perfections essential to Deity, as his omniscience, omnipotence, &c. and his providence in, and government of the world, Psalm xiv. 1. Ezek. ix. 9.——2. Polytheism, or the worshipping of many gods, or more than one; as the sun, moon, and stars, the host of heaven, and a multitude of things on earth; either by Jews or Gentiles, Deut. iv. 19. Jer. ii. 28. 1 Cor. viii. 5, 6.——3. Whatever is trusted in, and loved as God, as wealth and riches, which to do is idolatry, Job xxxi. 24. Psalm xlix. 6. Eph. v. 5. or fleshly lusts, as the epicure, whose god is his belly, Phil. iii. 19. or any other lust or idol set up in a man's heart, as self-righteousness, or be it what it may, Ezek. xiv. 4. and xxxvi. 25. The phrase *before me*, is not to be overlooked; which may either point at the omniscience of God, in whose sight such idolatry must be very displeasing; or the placing of any object of worship by him, which is setting up man's post by his, as Manasseh placed a graven image in the temple itself, 2 Kings xxi. 7. or it may be rendered, *Besides me*, and so excludes all other objects of worship, there being no God but him, Isa. xliv. 8. and xlv. 21. I would just propose it, whether the words על פני may not be rendered, *Besides my persons*, besides the Three persons in the Trinity, who are the one God; על frequently signifies *besides*, Gen. xxxi. 50. Lev. xviii. 18. Deut. xix. 9. and פני may be interpreted, *my faces*, or *persons*; see the Body of Doctrinal Divinity, book I. chap. 27.

II. The *second* command is, *Thou shalt not make to thyself any graven image, or any likeness—thou shalt not bow down thyself to them, nor serve them*, &c. which respects the mode of worship. And,——1. Requires, that it should be spiritual, suitable to the nature of God, without any carnal imaginations, and external representations of him, John iv. 23, 24. Phil. iii. 3. and that the parts of divine worship, as prayer, praise, preaching, hearing the word, and administration of ordinances, be observed just as delivered, without any addition to them, corruption and alteration of them. Deut. iv. 2. 1 Cor. xi. 2.——2. It forbids all superstition and will-worship, human traditions. precepts, and ordinances of men; and the introduction of any thing into the worship of God, which he has not commanded, Isa. xxix. 13. Matt. xv. 8. Col. ii. 20—23. and all images, figures, and representations of the divine Being, and of any of the persons in the Godhead; and, indeed, making the likeness of any creature, in heaven, earth, or sea, in order to be worshipped, and used for that purpose, Deut. iv. 15—18. Acts xvii. 29. Rom. 1. 23. and not only images of heathen deities, which were to be broken and burnt; but those of Christ, as a man crucified, of the Virgin Mary, of angels and saints departed, worshipped by Papists, Deut. vii. 5. Rev. ix. 16. Though all pictures, paintings, and sculptures, are not forbidden hereby, only such as are made for, and used in, divine worship; but not which are for ornament, or for the use of history; and to perpetuate to posterity the memory of men, and their actions; otherwise there were images of things, of lions, and oxen, and the cherubim, in the tabernacle and temple, by the express order of God. Exod. xxv. 18. 1 Kings vi. 32. and vii. 29.——3. The motives inducing to obey this command, are taken from God's being a jealous God, who will not give his glory to another, nor his praise to graven images; and from his severe punishment of the breakers of it, and of their posterity, who tread in their steps; and from his mercy shewn to those who, from a principle of love to him, observe it, Isa. xlii. 8. Deut. xxxii. 21, and iv. 23, 24. 1 Kings xix. 18.

III. The *third* command is, *Thou shalt not take the name of the Lord thy God in vain*. Which,——1. Requires an holy and reverend use of the name of God; of his titles, perfections, attributes, word, and works, even in common conversation, and especially in religious worship; expressed by walking in his name, invocation of his name, and giving thanks unto it, Psalm cxi. 9. and lxxxix. 7. Mic. iv. 5. Rom. x. 12. Psalm ciii. 1.——2. It forbids a vain use of the name of God, and of any of his titles, in common conversation, using them in a light way and manner; all profane swearing and cursing by them, Rom. iii. 13. James iii. 9, 10. perjury, or swearing falsely by his name; for though an oath may be taken lawfully, and always by the name of God, and not a creature; yet never to be taken falsely, Deut. vi. 13. Heb. vi. 16. Zech. viii. 17. So likewise blaspheming the name of God, is a breach of this precept, Lev. xxiv. 14. Psalm lxxiv. 10.——3. The argument moving to the observation of it, is taken from the guilt incurred by it, and the punishment inflicted for it; *The Lord will not hold such guiltless*, Zech. v. 4. Mal. iii. 5.

IV. The *fourth* command, respects the time of worship; the keeping a day holy to the Lord; and requires that it should be after six days' labour, Exod. xx. 9. that it should be observed in religious exercises, Isa. lviii. 13. Rom. xiv. 6. and as a rest from bodily labour, from all secular business

CHAP. VI.   A COMPENDIUM OF THE TEN COMMANDS.   993

and worldly employment, excepting works of necessity and mercy; the example urging to it is taken from God's resting from his works of creation, Exod. xxxv. 2, 3. Neh. i. 13. Gen. ii. 1, 2. But this has been treated of in a preceding chapter.

V. The *fifth* command requires honour, reverence, and obedience to be given by inferiors to superiors; as by children to parents, so by scholars to tutors and preceptors, by servants to masters, and by subjects to magistrates; and forbids all disrespect, contempt, irreverence, and disobedience of them; which also has been treated of in some former chapters.

VI. The *sixth* command is, *Thou shalt not kill*. Which,————1. Requires all due care in the use of proper means for the preservation of our lives, and the lives of others; life is and ought to be dear to a man; self-preservation is a first principle in nature; and every lawful method should be used to preserve life; as food, physic, sleep, &c. with all just and lawful defence of it; avoiding every thing that tends to impair health and endanger life, Job ii. 4. 1 Tim. v. 23.————2. It forbids the taking away of life, or murder of every sort, as parricide, fratricide, homicide, and suicide; for this law is *against murderers of fathers, and murderers of mothers, and manslayers*, and destroyers of themselves, 1 Tim. i. 9. no man has a right to take away his own life, nor the life of another; it is contrary to the authority of God the sovereign disposer of life, Deut. xxxii. 39. to the law of nature, Acts xvi. 28. to the goodness of God, who gives it, Job. x. 12. Acts xvii. 28. contrary to the love a man owes to himself, and his neighbour, and is a prejudice to the commonwealth, or public good, thereby deprived of a member, and the king of a subject. Not but that life may be taken away; as in lawful war, which is sometimes *of God, who makes peace and creates evil*, the evil of war; and by the hands of the civil magistrate, who bears the sword of justice, and uses it for the punishment of capital crimes; and it is lawful in self-defence, 1 Chron. v. 22. Isa. xlv. 7. Gen. ix. 6. Rom. xiii. 4. Exod. xxii. 2.————3. All intemperance, immoderate eating and drinking, which tend to destroy life; all sinful anger, undue wrath, inordinate passions, quarrels, blows, contentions, duellings, &c. which often issue in it, are breaches of this law, Prov. xxiii. 1, 2. Matt. v. 21, 22.

VII. The *seventh* command is, *Thou shalt not commit adultery*. Which————1. Requires chastity, and a preservation of it in ourselves and others; in or out of a state of wedlock; and to abstain from all impurity of flesh and spirit; and to make use of all means to preserve it; as lawful marriage, conjugal love, and cohabitation: it requires to keep the body, and members of it, in subjection; to mortify inordinate affection; and to avoid every thing that tends to unchastity; as intemperance, in the case of Lot; sloth and idleness, as in Sodom; immodest apparel and ornament, as in Jezebel; keeping ill company, and frequenting places of diversion, which are nurseries of vice; and also reading impure books.————2. It forbids all the species of uncleanness; not only adultery, but simple fornication, rape, incest, and all unnatural lusts, 1 Cor. vi. 18. 1 Thess. iv. 3. Lev. xviii. 6, 20.————3. All unchaste thoughts and desires, all adulterous looks, obscene words, and filthy actions, rioting and drunkenness, chambering and wantonness, are violations of this command, Matt. v. 27, 28. 2 Pet. ii. 14. Eph. v. 4. Rom. xiii. 14.

VIII. The *eighth* command is, *Thou shalt not steal*. Which,————1. Requires that we should seek to get, preserve, and increase our own wealth, and that of others, in a lawful way; that we should be diligent in our callings, careful to provide for our families; and even things convenient, honest, and reputable in the sight of all; and that we may have somewhat to give to those in need; and that of our own, and not be tempted to steal from others; for God hates robbery for burnt-offering, Prov. xxii. 29. 1 Tim. v. 8. Rom. xii. 17. Eph. iv. 28. Isa. lxi. 8.————2. It requires justice, truth, and faithfulness in all dealings with men; to owe no man any thing, but to give to all their dues; to have and use just weights and measures; to be true to all engagements, promises, and contracts; and to be faithful in whatsoever is committed to our care and trust, Rom. xiii. 7, 8. Lev. xix. 35, 36. and vi. 2—5. Neh. v. 12. ————3. It forbids all unjust ways of increasing our own, and hurting our neighbour's substance, by using false balances, weights, and measures; by over-reaching and circumventing in trade and commerce; by taking away by force or fraud, the goods, properties, and persons of men; by borrowing and not paying again; and by

3 s

oppression, extortion, and unlawful usury; for not all usury is unlawful, only what is exorbitant, and oppressive of the poor; for it is but reasonable, that what one man gains by another man's money, that the other man should have a proportionate share in that gain. Nor was the Israelites borrowing of the Egyptians without payment, any breach of this law, since it was by the order of God, whose all things are; and the words used may be rendered the one *asked*[2] and the other *gave*;[3] and besides, it was but repaying them what was due to them for their past services, Amos viii. 5, 6. 1 Thess. iv. 6. Psalm xxxvii. 21. 1 Cor. vi. 9, 10. Deut. xxiii. 19, 20. Exod. xi. 2. and xii. 35.

IX. The *ninth* command is, *Thou shalt not bear false witness against thy neighbour.* Which,——1. Requires to be careful of our own good name, and that of our neighbour, which is better than precious ointment; and that we should speak every man truth to his neighbour, in private conversation, and especially in public judgment, Eccles. vii. 1. Zech. viii. 16. Eph. iv. 25. ——2. It forbids all lying, which is speaking contrary to a man's mind and conscience, and with a design to deceive; and so condemns all sorts of lies, whether jocose, officious, or more plainly pernicious, and all equivocations, and mental reservations, perjury, and every false oath, bearing a false witness, and subornation of false-witnesses in a court of judicature, Matt. xxvi. 59, 60. Acts vi. 11, 12. against all which God will be a swift witness, Mal. iii. 5. it also forbids all slandering, tale-bearing, raising, receiving, spreading and encouraging an ill report of others, which is contrary to charity, Psalm l. 19, 20. Lev. xix. 16. Jer. xx. 10. 1 Cor. xiii. 7.

X. The *tenth* command is, *Thou shalt not covet, &c.* Which requires,——1. Contentment[4] in every state and condition of life; a lesson the apostle Paul had learnt, and every man should, Phil. iv. 11. Heb. xiii. 5. 1 Tim. vi. 6, 8. as also love, joy, pleasure, and delight in the happiness of others, Psalm xxxv. 27.——2. It forbids all uneasiness and discontent in our present circumstances, and all fretting and envying at the prosperity of others. Psalm xxxvii. 7. and lxxiii. 3. and condemns covetousness as an evil thing, and which is idolatry, and unbecoming saints, Isa. lvii. 17. Col. iii. 8. Eph. v. 3.——3. It mentions the particular objects not to be coveted; not a *neighbour's house*, and take it away by force, as some did, Mic. ii. 2. *nor a neighbour's wife*, as David coveted Bathsheba, 2. Sam. xi. 3. *nor his manservant, nor his maidservant*, which a king would do, take at his will, and put to his work, as Samuel suggested, 1 Sam. viii. 16. *nor his ox nor his ass*, from which evil Samuel exculpated himself, and which was admitted, 1 Sam. xii. 3. *nor any thing that is thy neighbour's*, his gold, silver, apparel, or any goods of his; of which sin the apostle Paul declares himself free, Acts xx. 33.——4. It strikes at the root of all sin, evil concupiscence, internal lust, in-dwelling sin, James i. 13, 14. By this law, lust is known to be sin, and is condemned by it as such, Rom. vii. 7.

From this view of the law, in all its precepts, it appears how large and extensive it is; that David might well say, *Thy commandment is exceeding broad!* Psalm cxix. 96. So that it cannot be perfectly fulfilled by man in this his sinful and fallen state; and therefore he cannot be justified before God by the deeds of it; since it requires a perfect righteousness: and happy for man it is, that there is such a righteousness revealed in the gospel, manifested without the law, though witnessed to by law and prophets, even the righteousness of Christ, consisting of his active and passive obedience; who is *the end*, the fulfilling end, *of the law for righteousness, to every one that believes,* Rom. iii. 20, 21, 22. and x. 4.

---

[2] ושאלו Postulaverunt, Vatablus; Petierunt, Drusius.
[3] וישאלום et dederunt illis, Cartwright.
[4] Of this see Book I. Chap. 12.

THE END OF THE BODY OF PRACTICAL DIVINITY.

A DISSERTATION

CONCERNING

THE BAPTISM OF JEWISH PROSELYTES.

CHAP. I.

OF THE VARIOUS SORTS OF PROSELYTES AMONG THE JEWS.

INTENDING to treat of the admission of proselytes into the Jewish church by baptism, or dipping; it may be proper to consider the different sorts of proselytes among the Jews, and which of them were thus admitted, as is said. The word *proselytes* is originally Greek, and is derived, as Philo[1] observes, απο τȣ προσεληλυθεναι, *from coming to,* that is, from one sect or religion to another, as from heathenism to the Jewish religion; and so Suidas[2] says, proselytes are they οι προσεληλυθοίες, *who come from the gentiles, and live according to the laws of God;* and such an one is called by the Septuagint interpreters of Exod. xii. 19. Isa. xiv. 1. and by the Greek writers following them, γειωξας, which is rightly interpreted by Hesychius, such of another nation who are called proselytes to Israel; and which word comes near to the Hebrew word גר and nearer still to the Chaldee word גיורא used for a proselyte; and is, by Eusebius, interpreted επιμιϰτους,[3] such as were mixed with Israelites.

There are two sorts of proselytes with the Jews, some say three; a proselyte of the gate; a mercenary proselyte; and a proselyte of righteousness; the first and last are most usually observed.

First, One sort was called גר שער *a proselyte of the gate;* and in scripture, *the stranger that is in thy gates,* Deut. xiv. 21. and xxiv. 14. being a sojourner, and permitted to dwell there; hence such an one had also the name of גר תשוב *a proselyte-inhabitant;* see Exod. xii. 15. Lev. xxv. 45, 47. one who was allowed to dwell among the Jews on certain conditions; and is generally distinguished from another sort, called a *proselyte of righteousness,* of whom more hereafter. Though the Jews, not always consistent with themselves, and so not in this matter, sometimes interpret *the stranger in the gate,* of a proselyte inhabitant, or a proselyte by inhabitation, and sometimes of a proselyte of righteousness. So Nachmanides,[4] having explained the stranger in the gate of a proselyte-inhabitant, or one who obliged himself to keep the seven precepts of Noah, according to the usual interpretation of it, observes; "Our doctors interpret it differently, for they say, *thy stranger within thy gate,* simply denotes, a *proselyte of righteousness.*" So that according to them, such a stranger may be taken both for the one and for the other, in different respects; but commonly the proselyte-inhabitant is only understood; who in general was obliged to promise, that he would not be guilty of

---

[1] De Monarchia, l. 1. p. 818.
[2] In voce προσλυτοι.
[3] Eccl. Hist. l. 1. c. 7.

[4] Apud Frischmuth. Dissert. de 7 Noach. Præcept. s. 20, 21.

idolatry, or worship any idol;[5] this he was to promise before three witnesses, for it is asked, "who is Ger Toshab; that is, a proselyte allowed to dwell in Israel; (the answer is) Whoever takes upon him, in the presence of three neighbours, that he will not commit idolatry." It follows, "R. Meir, and the wisemen say, whoever takes upon him the seven precepts which the sons of Noah obliged themselves to observe." Others say, "these do not come into the general rule of such a proselyte. Who then is one? he is a proselyte who eats what dies of itself; (or) who takes upon him to keep all the commandments in the law, except that which forbids the eating of things which die of themselves;"[6] but the usual account of such a proselyte is, that he agrees to observe the seven precepts enjoined the sons of Noah;[7] six of which were given to Adam, the first man, and the seventh was added to them, and given to Noah, and are as follow:[8]

1. Concerning idolatry. By this a son of Noah was forbid to worship the sun, moon, and stars, and images of any sort; nor might he erect a statue, nor plant a grove, nor make any image.——2. Concerning blaspheming the name of God. Such an one might not blaspheme, neither the proper name of God, Jehovah; nor any of his surnames, titles, and epithets. ——3. Concerning shedding blood, or murder. The breach of which command he was guilty of, if he slew one, though an embryo in his mother's womb; and one who pursued another, when he could have escaped from him with the loss of one of his members, &c.——4. Concerning uncleanness, or impure copulations; of which there were six sorts forbidden a son of Noah; as, with an own mother, with a father's wife, (or step mother), with another man's wife, with his sister by the mother's side, with a male, or with mankind, and with a beast.——5. Concerning rapine, or robbery and theft; of which such were guilty, whether they robbed a Gentile or an Israelite, or stole money, or men, or suppressed the wages of an hireling; and the like.——6. Concerning the member of a living creature, taken from it whilst alive, and eating it; this is the command, it is said, which was added to Noah, and his sons, and of which the Jews interpret Gen. ix. 4.——7. Concerning judgments or punishments to be inflicted on those who broke the above laws. This command obliged them to regard the directions, judgment, and sentence of the judges appointed to see the said laws put into execution, and to punish delinquents.

Now such Gentiles, who laid themselves under obligation to observe these commands, had leave to dwell among the Israelites, though not in every one of their cities; not in Jerusalem particularly;[9] wherefore those devout men and proselytes said to dwell in Jerusalem, Acts ii. 5, 10. were not proselytes of the gate, but proselytes of righteousness. Nor are such sort of proselytes now received, only whilst the Jews lived in their own land, and were not under the jurisdiction of another people; or as they express it, while jubilees were in use and observed.[10] This sort of proselytes, though they did not enjoy the privileges the proselytes of righteousness did, yet some they had; they might worship and pray in the court of the Gentiles, though not in the temple; they might offer burnt-offerings, though not other sacrifices; their poor were fed with the poor of Israel, their sick were visited by Israelites, and their dead were buried with them.[11]

Such proselytes as these, as they were not obliged to circumcision, nor to other commands peculiar to the Jews; none but those before observed; so neither were they baptized, or dipped, when made proselytes, which is said of others. Maimonides[12] affirms of such a proselyte, that he is neither circumcised nor dipped. Bishop Kidder[13] is therefore mistaken in saying, that proselytes of the gate were baptized, but not circumcised.

Secondly, There was another sort of proselytes, which are taken notice of, at least, by some as such; who were called שכרים *mercenary* ones, and are reckoned as between proselytes of the gate and Gentiles. In Exod. xii. 44, 45. a mercenary or *hired servant*, is distinguished from a servant bought with money; he being hired only for a certain time, as for six

---

[5] R. Nathan, Sepher Aruch. R. D. Kimchi, Sepher. Shorash. et Elias Levita, Sepher Tishbi in voce גור.
[6] T. Bab. Avodah Zarah, fol. 64, 2.
[7] Philip. Aquinat. Maaric in voce גור.
[8] Maimon. Hilchot Melacim, c. 9. s. 1. &c.
[9] Maimon. Hilchot Beth Habechirah, c.7. s. 14.
[10] T. Bab. Eraoin, fol. 29. 1. Maimon. Obede Cochabim, c. 10. s. 6. Milah, c. 1. s. 6.
[11] Maimon. Melacim, c. 10. s. 12.
[12] Isure Biah, c. 14. s. 7.
[13] Demonstration of the Messiah, part 2. p. 176.

CHAP. I.   OF THE VARIOUS SORTS OF JEWISH PROSELYTES.   997

years; and also from a foreigner, a stranger in the gate, a proselyte of the gate; and both of them are distinguished from the servant bought with money, who was circumcised, and might eat of the passover, when neither of the other might, being both uncircumcised; and therefore R. Levi Barzelonita[14] is thought to be mistaken when he says, " a mercenary is a proselyte, who is circumcised, but not dipped; for so the wise men explain it:" but if a stranger or proselyte of the gate was not circumcised, much less a mercenary, who was far below him; besides, if he was circumcised, he might eat of the passover; which is denied him: and so Ben Melech observes[15] of these two, the foreigner and the hired servant; they are Gentiles, and uncircumcised; and Abendana, in his notes upon him, from the Rabbins, says, the former is a proselyte-inhabitant, or a proselyte of the gate, who takes upon him the seven precepts of the sons of Noah; the latter is a servant whose body is not possessed, that is, is not in the possession of his master, not being bought with his money, is only an hired servant, and so not circumcised. But perhaps Jarchi's note will reconcile this to what Barzelonita says; "Toshab, a foreigner, this is a proselyte-inhabitant; and Shacir, or hired servant, this is a Gentile; but what is the meaning? are they not uncircumcised; (that is, both of them) and it is said, *No uncircumcised person shall eat thereof*: but they are as a circumcised Arabian, and a circumcised Gabnunite, or Gabonite,[16] though circumcised, yet not by Israelites, but by Gentiles, which gave no right to the passover. Hottinger[17] thinks these mercenary-proselytes, and with him Leusden[18] seems to agree, were mechanic strangers, who left their own country, and came among the Jews for the sake of learning some mechanic art; and who,

conforming to certain laws and conditions, prescribed by the Jews, were permitted to sojourn with them until they had learnt the art. There are but few writers who speak of this sort of proselytes. However, it seems agreed on all hands, that whether circumcised or not, they were not baptized, or dipped.

Thirdly, There was another sort of proselyte called גר צדק a *proselyte of righteousness*;[19] see Deut. xvi. 20. a stranger circumcised, and who is so called when he is circumcised; and sometimes גר בן ברית *a proselyte, the son of the covenant*,[20] the same as an Israelite; see Acts iii. 25. This sort of proselytes were the highest, and had in greatest esteem; who not only submitted to circumcision, but embraced all the laws, religion, and worship of the Jews; and were in all respects as they, and enjoyed equally all privileges and immunities, civil and religious, as they did; except being made a king, though one might if his mother was of Israel;[21] and being members of the great Sanhedrim, yet might be of the lesser, provided they were born of an Israelitish woman;[22] nay, even such have been in the great Sanhedrim, as Shemaiah and Abtalion, who were of the posterity of Sennacherib;[23] but their mothers being Israelites, it was lawful for them to judge, that is, in the great Sanhedrim; for one was the prince, and the other the father of that court.[24] So the Jews say,[25] the posterity of Jethro sat in Lishcat Gazith, that is, in the great Sanhedrim, which sat in that room; and for which they quote 1 Chron. ii. 55. yet it has been a question, whether a proselyte should be made a public minister, or president of the congregation, called שליח צבור; but the common opinion was, that he might be one:[26] of this sort of proselytes, of whom they boast, some were persons of note for learning, or wealth, or worldly grandeur;[27] but without sufficient ground.

---

[14] Chinnuch, p. 17.
[15] Miclol Yophi in loc.
[16] Vid. T. Bab. Avodah Zarah, c. 2. fol. 27. 1. et Edzard. not. in ib. p. 292.
[17] Thesaur. Philolog. l. 1. p. 18.
[18] Philolog. Heb. Mixt. Dissert. 21. vid. Carpzov. not. ad Schickard. Jus Regium, p. 323.
[19] Zohar. in Exod. fol. 36. 1. et in num. fol. 69. 4.
[20] R. Levi Ben Gersom, in Exod. xxii. 21. fol. 95. 2.
[21] Maimon. Melacim. c. 1. s. 4.
[22] Ibid. Sanhedrin, c. 2. s. 1. 9.
[23] T. Bab. Sanhedrin, fol. 96. 2.
[24] Juchasin. fol. 17. 2. et 18. 1.

[25] T. Bab. Sanhedrin, fol. 104. 1. et 106. 1. et Sotah, fol. 11. 1.
[26] Vid. Vitringam de Synagoga vet. par. 2. l. 3. c. 6. p. 943.
[27] As Aristotle, Meor Enayim, c. 22. fol. 91. 2. Izates and Monbaz, the sons of queen Helena, both kings, ibid. c. 51. fol. 161. 2. et c. 52. fol. 164. 2. 166, 167. Tzemach David, par. 1. fol. 26. 1. et par. 2. fol. 15. 2. Nebuzaradan, the general of Nebuchadnezzar, T. Bab. Sanhedrin, fol. 96. 2. Antoninus Pius, the Roman Emperor, T. Hieros. Megillah, fol. 72. 1. et 74. 1. Ketiah, a prince in Cæsar's court, Avodah Zarah, fol. 10. 2. Juchasin, fol. 66. 2. Nero, a general of Cæsar's army, from whom sprung R. Meir, T. Bab. Gittin, fol. 56. 1. Juchasin, fol. 41. 1. et 63. 2. Tzemach David.

Some, they own, were not sincere who became proselytes, either through fear, or to gratify some sensual lust, or for some sinister end or another. Some were called *proselytes of lions*,[28] who became so through fear; as the Samaritans, because of the lions sent among them, and that they might be freed from them, embraced the worship of God, though they retained also the worship of their idols. Others were called *proselytes of dreams*; who were directed and encouraged to become proselytes by such who pretended to skill in dreams, as being omens of good things to them. Though some, in the place referred to, instead of חלמות *dreams*, read הלונות *windows*, and render the words *proselytes of windows*, so Alting,[29] meaning the windows of their eyes, who, to gratify the lust of the eyes, became proselytes; as Shechem, being taken with the sight of Dinah, submitted to circumcision for the sake of her; and others were called *proselytes of Mordecai and Esther*, who were like those who became Jews in their times, Esther viii. 17. through fear of the Jews, as there expressed. Others were true and sincere proselytes, who cordially embraced the Jewish religion, and from the heart submitted to the laws and rules of it; these were called ברים גרורים *drawn proselytes*,[30] who were moved of themselves, and of their own good will, without any sinister bias, and out of real love and affection to the Jewish religion, embraced it. Compare the phrase with John vi. 44. And such, they say,[31] all proselytes will be in the time to come, or in the days of the Messiah; and yet sometimes they say, that then none will be received:[32] and when persons propose to be proselytes, the Jews are very careful to ask many questions, in order to try whether they are sincere or no; and such as they take to be sincere they speak very highly of; "Greater," say they,[33] "are the proselytes at this time, than the Israelites when they stood on mount Sinai; because they saw the lightning, heard the thunder, and the sound of the trumpet; but these saw and heard none of these things, and yet have taken upon them the yoke of the kingdom, and are come under the wings of the Shechinah;" though elsewhere, and in common, they speak but slightly of them, and say; "They are as grievous to Israel as a scab in the skin, or, as a razor to it,[34] because they often turn back again, and seduce the Israelites, and carry them off with them; yea, they say they stop the coming of the Messiah."[35] However, they have a saying[36] which shews some regard to them; "A proselyte, even to the tenth generation, do not despise a Syrian, or an heathen before him, he being present, or to his face; because till that time their minds are supposed to incline towards their own people;" and so it is said,[37] the daughter of a proselyte may not be married to a priest, unless her mother is an Israelitess, even unto the tenth generation. And there is another saying[38] of theirs, "Do not trust a proselyte until the twenty-fourth generation, that is, never; not only Priests, Levites, and Israelites, but even Bastards, and the Nethinim, or Gibeonites, were preferred to proselytes."[39] Some of these sayings do not seem so well to agree with the words of Christ, Matt. xxiii. 15. to reconcile which, it is thought,[40] that while the temple was standing, the desire of making proselytes was stronger than after it was destroyed by the Romans; resenting that, they became indifferent about making proselytes, and were unconcerned about the salvation of the Gentiles, and contented themselves with receiving such only who freely came over to them. It never was deemed so honourable to be the descendants of proselytes, as of original Hebrews. Hence the apostle Paul gloried that he was an Hebrew of the Hebrews, both his parents being Hebrews. A Rabbi of note among the Jews, whose parents were both proselytes, or Gentiles, is called not by his proper name, Jochanan, but Ben Bag-Bag; that is, the son of a Gentile man, and the son of a Gentile woman; and for the same reason he is called in a following paragraph, Ben He-He, numerically He being the same with Bag; though it is said, these

---

par. 2. fol. 16. 1, 2. Of the circumcision of these the Jews speak, but say nothing of their baptism.
[28] R. Nehemiah in T. Bab. Yebamot, fol. 24. 2.
[29] Heptas Dissertat. par. 2. Diss. 7. de Proselytis, s. 20.
[30] T. Bab. Avodah Zarah, fol. 3. 2.
[31] Ibid. fol. 34. 1.
[32] Zohar. in Gen. fol. 33. 1. et 40. 2.
[33] Medrash. apud Buxtorf. Lexic. Talmud. Col. 411.
[34] T. Bab. Yebamot, fol. 47. 2. et 109. 2. Kiddushin, fol. 70. 2.
[35] Niddah, fol. 13. 2.
[36] T. Bab. Sanhedrin, fol. 94. 1. Jarchi in Exod. xviii. 9.
[37] Misnah Biccurim, c. 1. s. 5.
[38] Yalkut in Ruth, fol. 163. 4.
[39] T. Hieros. Horaiot, fol. 48. 2.
[40] Vid. Wagenseil. not. in Sotah, p. 754.

abbreviations were used from reverence to him, and a regard for him;[41] and, indeed, the Jews were not to reproach and upbraid proselytes with what they and their ancestors had been, or had done; they were not to say to a proselyte, Remember thy former works; nor were they to say to the sons of proselytes, Remember the works of your fathers;[42] for this is the affliction and oppression of them, as they understand it, they are cautioned against, Exod. xxii. 21. Lev. xix. 33. nay, they were to love them as themselves, because the Lord God loved the stranger, Lev. xix. 34. Deut. x. 18. for of proselytes of righteousness they interpret these passages.[43]

Now it is of this sort of proselytes, proselytes of righteousness, that it is said, they were admitted into covenant, and into the Jewish church, as the Israelites were; the males by circumcision, by טבילת *baptism*, or dipping, and by sacrifice; and the females by baptism, or dipping, and by sacrifice; and it is the baptism or dipping of these proselytes, that will be inquired into, and be the subject of the following Dissertation.

CHAP. II.

THE OCCASION OF THIS DISSERTATION.

SEVERAL learned men, and some of our own nation, whom I shall chiefly take notice of, have asserted, that it was a custom or rite used by the Jews before the times of John the Baptist, Christ, and his apostles, to receive proselytes into their church by baptism, or dipping, as well as by circumcision; and these both adult and infants; and that John and Christ took up the rite of baptizing from thence, and practised, and directed to the practice of it, as they found it; and which, they think, accounts for the silence about infant-baptism in the New Testament, it being no new nor strange practice. The writers among us of most note, who make mention of it are, Broughton, Ainsworth, Selden, Hammond and Lightfoot; men justly esteemed for their learning and knowledge in Jewish affairs. Mr. Hugh Broughton is the first of our nation I have met with who speaks of it. "The Babylonian Talmud, and Rambam (Maimonides)," he says,[1] "record, that in the day of David and Solomon, when many thousands of heathens became proselytes, they were admitted only by baptism, without circumcision. So now, when the New Testament was to be made for the many, that is for all nations, baptism was not strange; neither is John in an astonishment to be; but demanded whether he be Elias or Christ, or that special prophet named in Deuteronomy." A little after he observes, that "Christ from baptism used of them (the Jews) *without commandment, and of small authority*, authorizeth a seal of entering into the rest of Christ, using the Jews' *weakness* as an allurement thither." Where, by the way, he makes this usage to be *without commandment*, that is, of God, and to be but of *small authority*, even from men, and a piece of *weakness* of the Jews, and yet authorized by Christ; which seems incredible. Mr. Henry Ainsworth is the next I shall mention, who takes notice of this custom. His words are,[2] "That we may the better know how they (the Jews) were wont to receive heathens into the church of Israel; I will note it from the Hebrew doctors:" and then gives a large quotation from Maimonides; the substance of which is, that as by three things Israel entered into the covenant, by circumcision, and baptism, and sacrifice; in like manner heathen proselytes were admitted; on which he makes this remark; "Whereupon baptism was nothing strange unto the Jews, when John the Baptist began his ministry, Matt. iii. 5, 6. they made a question of his person that did it, but not of the thing itself, John i. 25." Dr. Hammond, another learned man, speaks of this same custom or rite with the Jews: he says,[3] that "proselytes born of heathen parents, and become proselytes of justice, were admitted by the Jews, not only by circumcision, and (while the temple stood) by sacrifice; but also with the ceremony or solemnity of washing, that is, ablution of the whole body, done solemnly in a river, or other such great place or receptacle of water." So he says, Jethro, Moses's father-in-law, was made a proselyte in this way; and that this ceremony of initiation belonged not only to those, which being of

---

[41] Pirke Abot, c. 5. s. 22, 23. Vid. Fagium et Leusden. in ibid.
[42] Vid. R. David Kimchi, Sepher Shorash. rad. ינה.
[43] R. Levi Ben Gersom, in Lev. xiv. 33, 34.

fol. 163. 3. Ez Hechayim M. S. apud Wagenseil, not. in Sotah, p. 205.
[1] Works, p. 201, 203.
[2] Annotat. on Gen. xvii. 12.
[3] Annotat. in Matt. iii. 1.

years, came over from heathenism to the Jews' religion, but also to their children-infants, if their parents, or the consessus (the sanhedrim) under which they were, did in the behalf of their children desire it ; and on condition that the children, when they came to age, should not renounce the Jewish religion ; nay, he says, the native Jews themselves were thus baptized; for all which he refers to the Talmud, Tr. Repud. by which I suppose he means the tract Gittin, concerning divorces. But I have not met with any thing relating thereunto in that treatise. For the same purposes it is quoted by Dr. Wall, who, I suppose, goes upon the authority of Dr. Hammond, since he acknowledges he was not so well acquainted with the books to be searched for such quotations. Now Dr. Hammond observes, that "having said thus much of the custom among the Jews, it is now most easy to apply it to the practice of John, and after of Christ, *who certainly took this ceremony from them ;*" and further observes, " that by this it appears, how little needful it will be to defend the baptism of christian infants from the law of circumcising the infants among the Jews ; *the foundation being far more fitly laid* in that other of Jewish baptism." Yea, in another of his works, he suggests that this custom is the *true basis of infant baptism*.[4] The very learned Mr. Selden, is more large in his quotations in divers parts of his works,[5] from both Talmuds and other Jewish writers, concerning this rite and custom ; which authorities produced by him, and others, will be given and considered hereafter. At the close of which he makes these remarks ;[6] that the Jewish baptism was as it were a *transition* into christianity, or however, a shadow of a transition, not to be passed over in silence; and that it should be adverted to, that the rite or sacrament of baptism, used at the beginning of christianity, and of the gospel by John, and by the apostles, was not introduced as a *new action*, and as not before heard of, *even as a religious action*, but as well known to the Hebrews, as a rite of initiation, from the use and discipline of their ancestors, and as joined with circumcision. Dr. Lightfoot, who must be allowed to be well versed in Jewish literature, has produced the same authorities Selden has, if not more, in support of the said rite or custom, as in early use with the Jews, and exults and triumphs abundantly over the Antipædobaptists in favour of infant baptism, on account thereof. He asserts, that " baptism had been *in long and common use* among them (the Jews) many generations before John the Baptist came ; they using this for admission of proselytes into the church, and baptizing men, women, and children for that end :—hence a ready reason may be given why there is *so little mention* (no mention at all) of baptizing infants in the New Testament ; and that there is neither *plain precept* nor *example* for it, as some ordinarily plead ; the reason is, because there needed none, baptizing infants having been as *ordinarily used* in the church of the Jews, as ever it hath been in the christian church :—that baptism was no strange thing when John came baptizing ; but the rite was known so well by every one, that nothing was better known what baptism was, and therefore there needed not such punctual and exact *rules* about the manner and object of it, as there had needed, if it had never been seen before :—that Christ took up baptism as it was *in common and known use*, and *in ordinary and familiar practice*, among that nation ; and therefore gave no *rules* for the manner of baptizing, nor for the age and sex of persons to be baptized, which was well enough known already, and needed no *rule* to be prescribed :—observing how very known and frequent the use of baptism was among the Jews, the reason appears very easy, why the Sanhedrim, by their messengers, inquired not of John, concerning the reason of baptism, but concerning the authority of the baptizer ; not what baptism meant ; but whence he had a license so to baptize, John i. 25. Hence also the reason appears why the New Testament does not *prescribe*, by some more *accurate rule*, who the persons are to be baptized :—the whole nation knew well enough that little children used to be baptized ; there was no need for a precept for that, which had ever by common use prevailed."[7] Dr. Wall, upon these authorities, has thought fit to premise an account of this Jewish baptism, to his history of infant-baptism, as serving greatly

---

[4] Six Queries, p. 191, 195.
[5] De Success. ad Leg. Ebr. o. 26. de Jure Natur. et Gent. l. 2. c. 2.
[6] De Synedriis, l. 1. c. 2. p. 27, 31.

[7] Lightfoot's Works, vol. 1. Harmony and Chronicle of the New Testament, p. 9, 10, 17. Harmony of the Four Evangelists, part 1. p. 465, 466. part 2. p. 526, 527. and part 3. p. 583, 584. Vol. 2. Hor. Heb. in Matt. iii. 6.

the cause of it, and as throwing light upon the words of Christ and his apostles, concerning it, and the primitive practice of it; and, animated by such authorities, every puny writer, who does not know his right hand from his left, in this matter, takes it up, and swaggers with it. And, indeed, scarce any will now venture in the defence of infant baptism without it. This is the last refuge and dernier resort of the Pædobaptists; and, indeed, a learned baronet[8] of our nation says, he knows not of any stronger argument in proof of infant baptism, than this is.

Now since so great a stress is laid upon it, and it is made a matter of such great importance, as to be a *transition* into christianity, and to be *closely connected* with christian-baptism; that from whence it is taken, and is the *rule* to direct how to proceed, both with respect to the manner and objects of it; yea, is the *basis and foundation* of infant baptism, and the *strongest argument* in proof of it; and which makes other arguments, heretofore thought of great weight, now *unnecessary:* it is highly proper to inquire what proof can be given of such a rite and custom being in use among the Jews, before the times of John Baptist, Christ, and his apostles; and if so, what force and influence such a custom can, and ought to have, on the faith and practice of christians. The proof of which will next be considered.

CHAP. III.

THE PROOF OF THE BAPTISM OF JEWISH PROSELYTES INQUIRED INTO; WHETHER THERE IS ANY PROOF OF IT BEFORE, AT, OR QUICKLY AFTER THE TIMES OF JOHN AND CHRIST.

THE inquiry to be made is, whether there are writings or records before the times of John, Christ, and his apostles, or at or near those times, or in the third and fourth century from the birth of Christ, or before the Talmuds were written; which make any mention of, or refer to any such rite and custom in use among the Jews, as to admit proselytes to their religion by baptism, or dipping, along with other things. Now upon a search it will be found,

First, That nothing of this kind appears in the writings of the Old Testament, which chiefly concern the Jewish nation. We read of many who either were, or are supposed and said to be made proselytes; as the Shechemites in Jacob's time, the multitude that came out of Egypt with the Israelites,[1] Jethro, Moses's father in law,[2] Shuah,[3] Tamar,[4] Rahab,[5] and Ruth;[6] and many in the times of Mordecai and Esther, who became Jews,[7] Esther viii. 17. but not a word of their being admitted proselytes by baptism. Dr. Lightfoot indeed says,[8] that Jacob admitted the proselytes of Shechem and Syria into his religion by baptism, but offers no proof of it; the Jews[9] pretend that Pharaoh's daughter was a proselytess, and the Babylonian Talmud,[10] quoting the passage in Exod. ii. 5. *And the daughter of Pharaoh came down to wash herself;* R. Jochanan says, she came down to wash herself from the idols of her father's house, and the Gloss on the place is, "to dip on account of proselytism;" but then the Gloss is the work of Jarchi, a writer in the twelfth century; and was it so said in the Talmud itself, it would be no sufficient proof of the fact. Dr. Hammond says, that Jethro was made a proselyte this way; but produces no scripture for it; but refers to the Talmud, Tr. Repud; but there it is not to be found, as before observed: and Schindler[11] asserts the same, as said by the Jews, and seems to refer to the same Tract in general, without directing to any particular place: and from him Hammond seems to have taken it upon trust, and some other writers also, without examination; since no such passage is to be found in that Tract. Pfeiffer,[12] in proof of it, refers to a book called Zennorenna, a commentary on the law, written in Hebrew-German, in the last century, by R. Jacob Ben Isaac, a German Jew.[13] Indeed, in the Talmud,[14] Jethro is said to become a

---

[8] Sir Richard Ellys, Fortuita Sacra, p. 67.
[1] Targum Jon. in Numb. xi. 4.
[2] Ibid. in Exod. xviii. 6, 7.
[3] Ibid. in Gen. xxxviii. 2.
[4] T. Bab. Sotah, fol. 10. 1.
[5] Ibid. Megillah, fol. 14. 2.
[6] Targum in Ruth i. 16.
[7] Targum in Esther.
[8] Chronicle, p. 18.

[9] Targum in 1 Chron. iv. 18.
[10] F. Megillah, fol. 23. 1. Sotah, fol. 12. 1.
[11] Lexic. in voce טבל col. 686. vid. de Dieu, append. ad Matt. xxiii. 15.
[12] Antiqu. Ebr. c. 1. s. 5.
[13] Wolfii Bibliothec. Heb. p. 598.
[14] Zebachim, fol. 16. 1. vid. Shemot Rabba, s. 27. fol. 30. 2, 3.

proselyte, but no mention is made in what manner he was made one; and elsewhere[15] explaining these words, ויחד and *Jethro rejoiced*, says Rab, he made a sharp sword to pass over his flesh; that is, according to the Gloss, he circumcised himself, and became a proselyte; but not a word of his baptism, or dipping; and so the Targum on Exod. xviii. 6, 7. is, " And he said to Moses, I Jethro, thy father-in-law, am come unto thee *to be made a proselyte;* but if thou wilt not receive me for myself, receive me for the sake of thy wife and her two children, who are with her; and Moses went out from under the clouds of glory to meet his father-in-law, and bowing himself, kissed him, and *he made him a proselyte;*" but nothing is said of the manner of doing it. Mr. Broughton also, as before quoted, says, that the Babylonian Talmud, and Rambam record, that in the days of David and Solomon, many thousands of heathens were made proselytes, and admitted by baptism only; but this instance is not to be met with in the Babylonian Talmud; yea, that expressly denies it in two different places;[16] and in which it is asserted, that they did not receive proselytes neither in the days of David, nor in the days of Solomon; Solomon's wife, Pharaoh's daughter, is indeed excepted; because the reason for which they say, proselytes were not then received; namely, because they might be desirous of being made proselytes, that they might be admitted to the king's table, could have no influence on her, since she was the daughter of a mighty king; and yet it is said[17] by some, that though it was Solomon's intention to make her a proselyte, yet he was not able to do it; and she became one of his troublers; and by what is said of her, in 2 Chron. viii. 11. it looks as if she did not become a proselyte; Rambam, or Maimonides, indeed, to reconcile what later writers have said, with those words of the Talmudists, have contrived a distinction between the Sanhedrim and private persons; as if proselytes, though not received in those times by the former, were by the latter. He says,[18] there were many proselytes in those times who were made so before private persons, but not before the Sanhedrim; he owns the Sanhedrim did not receive them, and though they were dipped, yet not by their order, and with their consent; but he produces no passage of scripture to support this private dipping; nor do the scriptures any where speak of such numbers of proselytes in those days, and much less of their baptism; and the strangers, who in the Greek version are called proselytes, whom Solomon numbered and employed at the building of the temple, 2 Chron. ii. 17. at most could only be proselytes at the gate, not of righteousness, and so there can be no pretence for their admission by baptism, or dipping; nor is there any thing of this kind with respect to any persons to be found in the writings of the Old Testament. There is a plain and express law for the admission of proselytes to the Jewish religion, and for what, as a qualification, to partake of the ordinances and privileges of it; particularly to eat of the passover; and that is the circumcision of them, with all their males; and on this condition, and on this only, they and theirs were admitted without any other rite annexed unto it, they were obliged unto; nor does it appear that ever any other was used; no, not this of baptism; there was but one law to the stranger or proselyte, and to the home-born Israelite; see Exod. xii. 48, 49. There were proselytes in the times of Hezekiah, 2 Chron. xxx. 25. who came out of the land of Israel, to eat the passover at Jerusalem, who therefore must be circumcised, according to the said law; but there is no reason to believe they were baptized. There was a law concerning the marriage of a captive-woman taken in war, Deut. xxi. 10—14. previous to which she must become a proselytess; and the law enjoins various particular rites to be observed in order to it, as shaving her head, paring her nails, and putting off the raiment of her captivity; but not a word of her baptism; which one would think could never be omitted, had such a custom prevailed as early as the times of Moses and Jacob, as is pretended. There were divers bathings, baptisms, or dippings, incumbent on the Israelites, and so upon such proselytes who were upon an equal foot with them, and equally under obligation to obey the ceremonial law; which consisted of divers washings, baptisms, or dippings, yet none of them for proselytism; but for

---

[15] T. Bab. Sanhedrin, fol. 94. 1.
[16] T. Bab. Yebamot, fol. 76. 1. Avodah Zara. fol. 3. 2.
[17] Yalkut Chadasha tit. de David, n. 89. Apud Beckii. not. in Targ. 2 Chron. viii. 11.
[18] Issure Biah, c. 13. s. 15.

purification from one uncleanness or another, in a ceremonial sense: these seem to be what a learned writer [19] calls *aquilustria*, lustrations by water; which he thinks it is clear the captive Jews in Babylon observed, from having their solemn meetings by rivers, Ezek. iii. 15. Ezra viii. 15, 21. but it is not so clear they had their abode in such places, whether for a longer or shorter time, on account of them; and it is still less clear what he further says, that these lustrations had a promise of grace annexed to them, were sacraments of the Old Testament, and a type of our baptism. However, though he supposes the returning Jews and proselytes were circumcised, he does not pretend they were baptized; nor does he attempt to prove proselyte baptism from hence. Among the ten families said [20] by the Jews to come out of Babylon, the proselytes are one sort; but they say nothing of their baptism; see Ezra vi. 21. As for those scriptures of the Old Testament the Rabbins make use of to justify this custom of theirs, they will be considered hereafter.

Secondly, Whereas there are several books called Apocrypha, supposed to be written between the writing of the books of the Old Testament and those of the New, and are generally thought to be written by Jews, and to contain things which chiefly have respect to them; and though there is sometimes mention made in them of proselytes to the Jewish religion, yet not a syllable of any such rite or custom, as of baptism or dipping at the admission of them; particularly of Achior the Ammonite, in the times of Judith; upon her cutting off the head of Olophernes it is said, that "he, seeing all that the God of Israel did, strongly believed in God, and circumcised the flesh of his foreskin, and was added to the house of Israel unto this day;" that is, he and his posterity continued in the Jewish religion. Now here is mention made of his being circumcised, previous to his addition, or his being proselyted to the Jewish church; but not a word of baptism, or dipping, in order to it; see Judith xiv. 6.

Thirdly, Mention is made of proselytes in the New Testament, Matt. xxiii. 15.

Acts ii. 10. and vi. 5. and xiii. 43. but nothing is said concerning their admission, and the manner of it. Indeed, in the Ethiopic version of Matt. xxiii. 15. the words are rendered, *They baptize one proselyte;* which seems to have respect to the custom under consideration; but then this is but a translation, and not a just one. The Ethiopic version is not only reckoned not very good, but of no great antiquity. Ernestus Gerhard says [21] of the antiquity of it, he dare not affirm any thing certain. And Ludolph, in his history of Ethiopia, relates,[22] that he could find nothing certain concerning the author and time of this version; but thinks it probable it was made at the time of the conversion of the Habessines, or a little after, but not in the times of the apostles, as some have affirmed; and in the margin, a little after, he observes, that in an Ethiopic martyrology, St. Frumentius, called abbot of Galama, is said to be the author of it; who, according to another place in the said history,[23] seems to have lived in the fourth century, in the times of Athanasius, and is thought to be the first founder of the christian religion in Ethiopia, and the first bishop in it. Scaliger takes the Ethiopic version to be a recent one; and De Dieu,[24] from what the author or authors of the version of the evangelist Matthew, add at the end of it, suspects that they were of the Maronites, who became subject to the pope of Rome, A. D. 1182, and so this version is too late a testimony for the antiquity of such a custom; and the closing the translation of some of the epistles with desiring the prayers of Peter and others, shews what sort of persons they were who translated them, and in what times they lived. The title of the book of the Revelation in this version, is, "The vision of John, which John was bishop of the metropolis of Constantinople, when he suffered persecution;" by which it appears not to be ancient. Hence Dr. Owen [25] calls it a *novel* endeavour of an illiterate person; and the translation of the clause itself in Matt. xxiii. 15. is censured by Ludolphus [26] as ridiculous; the word by which it is rendered being used in the Ethiopic language to convert a man to Christianity, or to make a man a Christian;

---

[19] Eric. Phaletran. de ablatione Sceptr. Jud. c. 9. p. 431.
[20] Misnah, Kiddushin, c. 4. s. 1.
[21] Πεντας Positionum ex Ling. Heb. Chald. Syr. Ar. et Ethiopic Pos. 5.
[22] Hist. Ethiop. l. 3. c. 4.
[23] Ibid. l. 3. c. 2.
[24] In Append. ad Matt. p. 584.
[25] Of the divine Original, &c. of the Scriptures, p. 343. vid. Theologoumen. l. 1. c. 1. p. 4.
[26] Lexic. Ethiop. Col. 414.

which is by it absurdly attributed to the Scribes and Pharisees.

Fourthly, As there are no traces of this custom in the writings before, at, or about the times of John, Christ, and his apostles; so neither are there any in those which were written in any short time after; as, not in Philo the Jew, who lived in the first century; who, though he is said by some to be ignorant of Jewish customs, yet one would think he could not be ignorant of such as were used at the admission of proselytes; since he lived at Alexandria, where it may be supposed many proselytes were, more than in Judea, and of the manner of their admission he could not but have knowledge, both then and in former times; and he makes mention of proselytes, and of them as equally partakers of the same privileges, and to be treated with the same honour and respect as home-born citizens,[27] and as they were admitted by Moses; but is altogether silent about this custom of baptizing, or dipping them; nor is there the least trace or hint of this custom in any Rabbinical books, said by the Jews to be written a little before or after; such as the books of Bahir, Zohar, the Targums of Onkelos on the Pentateuch, and of Jonathan Ben Uzziel on the prophets.

Fifthly, Josephus, the Jewish historian, lived in the same age, a little after Philo, was well versed in the affairs of the Jews, even in their religious rites and ceremonies, having been a priest among them. He not only observes that many of the Gentiles came over to their religion,[28] but even speaks of whole nations who became Jews, and that they were made so by circumcision; as of the Idumæans, whom Hyrcanus conquered, and suffered to remain in their own land, on condition that they would be circumcised, and conform to the laws of the Jews; and who, out of love to their country, did comply with circumcision, and so became Jews,[29] and of the Ituræans, whom Aristobulus fought against, and added part of their country to Judea, and obliged the inhabitants, if they would remain in their country, to be circumcised, and live after the laws of the Jews; and quotes Strabo, who, upon the authority of Timogenes, says, that he enlarged the country of the Jews, and made part of the country of Ituræa theirs, joining them to them by the bond of circumcision.[30] By which accounts it appears, that both these people were made Jews, or were proselyted to them by circumcision; but not a word is said of their baptism, or dipping; which, according to this custom, as is said, must have been of men, women, and children, which, had it been practised, could not have been well omitted by the historian. He also speaks[31] of Helena, queen of Adiabene, and of her son Izates, embracing the Jewish religion; and relates how desirous Izates was of being circumcised, that he might be a perfect Jew, without which he could not: but for a time he was dissuaded from it by his mother, and a Jew merchant, who instructed them; but afterwards, being exhorted to perfect the work by one Eleazer, who was more skilful in Jewish affairs, he submitted to circumcision; but neither Josephus nor Eleazer say a word about his baptism, or dipping; which, yet according to the pretended custom as then prevailing, was necessary, as well as circumcision, to make him a complete proselyte. Nor is any mention made of the baptism or dipping of Helena; which, had it been used at this time, would not have been omitted by the historian; since it was by that only, according to this notion, that females were then made proselytes. He also speaks[32] of another son of Helena, Monbaz, embracing the Jewish religion; but says nothing of his baptism.

Sixthly, It may be inquired, whether or no any mention is made of this custom of receiving proselytes among the Jews by baptism, or dipping, in the Targums, or Chaldee paraphrases. The most ancient ones extant are those of Jonathan Ben Uzziel of the prophets, and of Onkelos of the Pentateuch; the one at the beginning, the other toward the end of the first century; in which nothing is met with concerning the admission of Jewish proselytes by dipping. The other paraphrases are by uncertain authors, and of an uncertain age. The Targum of the Megillot, or five books of Ruth, Ecclesiastes, Canticles, Lamentations,

---

[27] De Vita Mosis, l. 1. p. 625. De Monarchia, l. 1. p. 818. De Legat. ad Caium, p. 1022.
[28] Contra Apion. l. 2. s. 10.
[29] Antiqu. l. 13. c. 9. s. 1. So Josippon Ben Gorion, Hist. Heb. l. 2. c. 9. et. l. 4. c. 4. et. l. 5. c. 23. et. l. 6. c. 13.

[30] Antiqu. ib. c. 11. s. 3. so Josippon, ibid. l. 4. c. 9.
[31] Antiqu. ibid. l. 20. c. 2. s. 1. 5.
[32] Antiqu. c. 3. s. 1. These became proselytes in the times of Claudius Cæsar, Ganz Tzemach David, par. 2. fol. 15. 2. et Juchasin, fol. 141. 1. Of king Izates, see Tacit. Annal. l. 12. c. 13, 14.

and Esther, is written by an unknown author; it is the latest of all the Targums. In that of Esther only the phrase *became Jews*, chap. viii. 12. is rendered *became proselytes*; but nothing is said of their manner of becoming such. In that of Ruth, chap i. 16. the requisites of a proselyte are particularly observed; where Ruth is introduced, saying, that she desired to be *made a proselyte;* when Naomi informs her what commands the Jews were obliged to observe; as to keep the Sabbaths and festivals, and not to walk beyond two thousand cubits (on the Sabbath-day;) not to lodge with Gentiles; to observe the three hundred and thirteen commands; not to worship an idol, &c. to all which Ruth is made to agree; but not a syllable is said about baptism, or dipping; whereas, that, with a sacrifice along with it, before the building of the temple, and while the temple stood, and since, without it, is the only thing, according to this notion, by which females were admitted proselytes. In the Targum of Jonathan of Gen. ix. 27. the sons of Japhet are said to be made proselytes, and to dwell in the school of Shem. In the Jerusalem Targum, and in that of Pseudo-Jonathan, the souls that Abraham and Sarah got in Haran, Gen. xii. 5. are said to be the souls who were made proselytes by them; and in the same Targum of Gen. xxi. 33. at Beersheba, where Abraham planted a grove, he is said to make proselytes, and teach them the way of the world, of the world to come; but nothing more is said of the way and manner in which they were made such. In the Targum of Pseudo-Jonathan of Gen. xxxviii. 2. Judah is said to make the daughter of a Canaanite a proselytess, and then married her; and in the same Targum of Numb. xi. 4. the mixed multitude who came with the Israelites out of Egypt, are interpreted proselytes; and no doubt but many of them were such; and Jarchi thinks the son of the Israelitish woman, whose father was an Egyptian, was a proselyte, since he was among the children of Israel, Lev. xxiv. 10. And Africanus affirms,[33] that the Jews had genealogical tables, in which an account was kept both of original Jews and of proselytes; as of Achior the Ammonite, and Ruth the Moabitess, and those who came out of Egypt mixed with the Israelites; and which continued to the times of Herod, who burnt them, that his family might not be known. But to return to the Targums; in the Pseudo-Jonathan's of Exod. xviii. 6, 7. Jethro is made to say to Moses, as before observed, that he was come to be made a proselyte; and Moses is said to make him one; but in what manner it is not said; and so the rest before mentioned; indeed, the same Targum of Exod. xii. 44. is, "And every stranger who is sold for a servant to an Israelite, bought with money, then thou shalt circumcise him, and thou shalt *dip* him, and so shall he eat of it," the passover. Now in this Targum of Exod. xxvi. 9. not only mention is made of the Misnah, but it abounds with Talmudic fables and traditions, and so must be written after both the Misnah and Talmud; and in the Targum of Numb. xxiv. 19. mention is made of the city of Constantinople, which shews it to be not ancient, and that it is not the work of the true Jonathan. And besides all this, the case of the servant refers not to a proselyte, who became so of choice, but to a bought servant, who, according to the original law in Gen. xvii. 12, 13. was obliged to be circumcised; and so, according to the Rabbinic custom, to be dipped; but then, according to these writers, baptism, or dipping for servitude, was a different thing from baptism, or dipping for proselytism; the one was on a civil, the other on a religious account; the one was repeated when a servant was made a free man, and the other never.[34] The same Pseudo-Jonathan, in his Targum of Deut. xxi. 13. to the conditions required of a beautiful captive, in order to be married to an Israelite, this is added, that she should *dip herself*, and become a proselytess in his house; but the text has nothing of it, nor the Targum of Onkelos; nor is this custom to be met with in the paraphrases of the true Jonathan; only this, which was written after the Talmud, and does not come within the time under consideration.

Seventhly, Nor is there any mention of such a custom in the Jew's Misnah, or Book of Traditions; which is a collection of all the traditions among the Jews, which had been handed down from age to age, and were collected together from all parts, and written in a book of this name, in order to be preserved. This was written by

---

[33] Apud Euseb. Eccl. Hist. l. 1. c. 7.

[34] Vid. Maimon. Issure Biah, c. 13. s. 11, 12. et Schulchan Aruch, par. 2. c. 267. s. 9.

R. Judah Hakkadosh, in the middle of the second century, A. D. 150. or as others in the beginning of the third century, reckoning the date of it one hundred and fifty years from the destruction the temple; which brings it to the year 220. and here, if any where, one might expect to meet with this rite or custom; but no mention is made of it. Dr. Gale [35] seems to allow it upon what Dr. Wall has transcribed from Selden, which he granted without examination. The doctor says,[36] It is not only mentioned in the Gemara, but in the text of the Misnah itself; which, as he suggests, speaks of a child becoming a proselyte by baptism, or dipping; but the passage he has from Selden[37] says no such thing; which runs thus;[38] "A she-stranger, a captive, and a maiden, who are redeemed and become proselytes, and are made free, being *under* (or, as in the following section, *above*) three years and one day old, are allowed the matrimonial dowry;" that is, when they come to age, and are married; but not a word is here of their being made proselytes by baptism, or dipping; indeed, the tradition shews, that minors may be proselyted, and that a man's sons and daughters may become proselytes with him; but there is no need to have recourse to a tradition for this; the law is express, that a stranger who desires to be a proselyte to the Jewish religion, and to eat of the passover, must be circumcised, and all his males, and then he and all his children, males and females, may be admitted to eat of it, Exod. xii. 48, 49. only the circumcision of the males is required, but no baptism, or dipping of any. There is a passage in the Misnah,[39] which perhaps some may think countenances this custom; which is this, "A stranger who is made a proselyte, on the evening of the passover, the house of Shammai say, he *dips* and eats his passover in the evening; but the house of Hillell say, he that separates from uncircumcision, is as he that separates from a grave." Now it should be observed,—— 1. That here is a division about this matter, be it what it may; Shammai, and his party, assert, that a proselyte newly made, might dip and eat his passover that evening; but Hillell, and his party, dissent, for a reason given; and the determination, in all cases, was generally according to Hillell, as it was in this; so we learn from Maimonides.[40]——2. This baptism, or dipping, was not on account of proselytism, but for ceremonial uncleanness; for it goes along with cases of that kind, instanced in before. The canon begins thus, "A mourner (who was unclean according to the ceremonial law) dips and eats his passover in the evening; but eats not of the holy things: he that hears tidings of the death of his (friend or relation), and who gathers to him bones, dips, and eats of the holy things:" and then it follows, "A stranger who is made a proselyte," &c.——3. This rule, according to Shammai, was concerning one already made a proselyte, and therefore the dipping, or baptism, he prescribes to him, in order to his eating the passover that evening, was not to make him a proselyte; but for some other reason. Wherefore,——4. This strongly makes against admission of proselytes by baptism, or dipping, at that time; for if he had been made a proselyte that way, there would have been no reason for a second dipping to qualify him for the passover.——5. The case of such an one, according to Hillell, is, that being just come out of heathenism, he was unclean, as one that touched a dead man, a bone, or a grave; and therefore could not eat of the passover that evening, but must wait seven days, until he was purified according to the law in Numb. xix. 11—19. ——6. After all, the view of Hillell, in putting such a person off from eating the passover the evening he became a proselyte for the reason given, was with respect to the next year, and by way of caution; fearing that should he be then in any uncleanness, which required purification, he would say, Last year I did not dip, or purify myself from any uncleanness, and yet I eat, and now I must dip and eat; not considering that the last year he was an heathen, and uncapable of uncleanness, according to the law, but now he was an Israelite, and capable of it; and so it is explained in the Gemara, [41] and Gloss on it, and by other interpreters.[42] Besides, this baptism, or dipping, was not on account of proselytism, but was common

---

[35] Reflections on Wall's History of Infant Baptism, p. 327.
[36] History, Introduction, p. 49.
[37] De Synedriis, l. 1. c. 3.
[38] Misn. Cetubot. c. 1. s. 2. 4.
[39] Ib. Pesachim, c. 8. s. 8. the same in Misn. Ediot, c. 5. s. 2.
[40] Hilchot Korban Pesach, c. 6.
[41] T. Bab. Pesachim. fol. 92. 1.
[42] Maimon. et Bartenora in Misn. ut supra.

to, and obligatory upon a circumcised Israelite, in order to eat of the passover; as is acknowledged by all. There were several in the times of the Misnic doctors, and before the Misnah was compiled, who were persons of eminence, and said to become proselytes; as Onkelos the Targumist, who, it is said, was made a proselyte in the days of Hillell and Shammai,[43] hence he is called Onkelos the proselyte;[44] some say[45] he was a sister's son of Titus the emperor, and by whom three Roman troops, sent one after another, to take him, were made proselytes also;[46] and Aquila, the author of the Greek version of the Bible, became, as is said,[47] a proselyte in the times of Adrian; and so the emperor Antoninus Pius, and Ketiah, a nobleman in Cæsar's court, as before observed: yea, the famous R. Akiba, a Misnic doctor, was a proselyte;[48] and so was R. Meir.[49] And of the circumcision of most of these we read; but nothing of their baptism; neither in the Misnah, nor any other Jewish writings. Not to take notice of those very early masters of tradition Shemaia and Abtalion, before observed, who were proselytes of righteousness;[50] there were also women of note within this time, who became proselytes; as queen Helena,[51] with her two sons, of whom mention is made in the Misnah;[52] and Beluria, the proselytess, who had a discourse with R. Gamaliel;[53] and the wife of Turnus Rufus, whom R. Akiba married, after she was proselyted.[54] Now though female proselytes were admitted by baptism only, as is pretended, yet nothing is said of the baptism of these women. And as there is no mention of this custom in the Misnah, so neither have I observed any notice taken of it in the Rabbot, which are commentaries on the Pentateuch and five Megillot, before named; and which were written by R. Bar Nachmoni, about A.D. 300, according to Buxtorf;[55] in one of which the text in Gen. xii. 5. is commented on; *And the souls they had gotten in Haran;* which the Targums of Pseudo-Jonathan and Jerusalem, interpret of the souls they proselyted, before observed; and here it is said,[56] "These are the proselytes which they made:—R. Hona said, Abraham proselyted the men, and Sarah proselyted the women;" but not a word is said about the baptism or dipping of either. Yea, Abraham and Sarah are said to be proselytes[57] themselves; but it is not suggested that they were baptized. In these commentaries mention is made of the circumcision of proselytes, particularly of king Monbaz, and his brother, said to be the sons of king Ptolemy;[58] and of Aquila, the Greek translator;[59] but nothing is said of their baptism.

Eighthly, Nor is this rite or custom of receiving Jewish proselytes by baptism, or dipping, once spoken of by any of the christian fathers of the first three or four centuries; which they could not be ignorant of, if from hence christian baptism was taken, and especially such who were Jews, or had any connection with them, or were acquainted with them, and with their affairs, as some of them were. Barnabas was a Jew, and an apostolic man, cotemporary with the apostles; there is an epistle of his still extant, in which he treats chiefly of Jewish rites, and of their being typical of evangelic things, and of their having their fulfilment in them; and yet says not a word of this initiating baptism, which he could not have failed making mention of, had he known any thing of it; yea, he sets himself to find out what was beforehand said concerning the ordinance of baptism; "Let us inquire," says he,[60] "whether the Lord has taken any care to make manifest beforehand any thing concerning the water;" that is, concerning baptism; and then he adds, "Concerning the water, it is written to Israel, how the baptism that leads to the remission of sins, they would not; but appointed for themselves;" meaning their superstitious worship, our Lord inveighs against; but says not a word here, nor elsewhere, of the baptism of proselytes, for which he had a fair opportunity, had he known any thing of it. Justin

---

[43] Meor Enayim, c. 45. Ganz Tzemach David, par. 1. fol. 28. 2.
[44] T. Bab. Bava Bathra, fol. 99. 1. Megillah, fol. 3. 1. et Avodah Zarah, fol. 11. 1.
[45] Juchasin, fol. 52. 2. T. Bab. Gittin, fol. 56. 2.
[46] Avodah Zarah, ut supra.
[47] Shemot Rabba, s. 30. fol. 131. 3.
[48] Zohar in Gen. fol. 28. 4. Tzemach David, ut supra, fol. 28. 1.
[49] Juchasin, fol. 41. 1. Ganz. fol. 29. 1.
[50] Juchasin, fol. 18. 1.
[51] Juchasin, fol. 141. 1.
[52] Yoma, c. 3. s. 10.
[53] Roshashanah, fol. 17. 2.
[54] T. Bab. Nedarim, fol. 50. 2. et Gloss in ibid. Tzemach David, par 1. fol. 28. 1.
[55] Biblioth. Rab. p. 326.
[56] Bereshit Rabba, s. 39. fol. 35. 1.
[57] Bemidbar Rabba, s. 8. fol. 190. 4.
[58] Bereshit Rabba, s. 46. fol. 41. 3.
[59] Shemot Rabba, ut supra.
[60] Barnabæ Epist. c. 9. Ed. Voss.

Martyr, who lived in the second century, was a Samaritan, and had knowledge of Jewish affairs; and had a dispute with Trypho the Jew, the same with Tarphon, a Jewish doctor, frequently mentioned in the Misnah; yet neither he nor Trypho say any thing of this custom. In answer to a question put by Justin, what was necessary to be observed; Trypho replies,[61] "To keep the Sabbath; to be circumcised; to observe the new moons; to be baptized, or dipped, whoever touches any of these things forbidden by Moses;" meaning, that such should be baptized, or dipped, who touched a dead body, or bone, or grave, &c. but not a syllable is here of the baptism, or dipping of proselytes. And Justin himself makes mention of Jewish proselytes, and calls them circumcised proselytes,[62] but not baptized; by which it seems he knew nothing of any such custom, as to baptize them; yea, he does, in effect, deny there was any such custom of baptizing any, that universally obtained among the Jews, since he speaks of a certain sect, whom he will not allow to be truly Jews, called by him Baptists.[63] Whereas, if it was the practice of the whole nation to receive proselytes by baptism, or dipping, a particular sect among them would not be stigmatized by such a name, since they must be all Baptists, both original Jews and proselytes, if they were all admitted into the Jewish church by baptism, as is affirmed. Origen, who lived in the beginning of the third century, in the city of Alexandria, where were great numbers of Jews, with whom he was acquainted, and must know their customs, says of Heracleon, an heretic, he opposes,[64] " That he was not able to shew that ever any prophet baptized;" meaning, a common and ordinary one; and if none of these ever baptized, what foundation could there be for the baptism of proselytes before the times of Christ? Epiphanius, in the fourth century, was born in Palestine, lived some time in Egypt, had great knowledge of the Jews, and of their affairs; but seems to know nothing of this custom, as used neither in former nor in later times: he says,[65] neither had Abraham baptism, nor Isaac, nor Elias, nor Moses, nor any before Noah and Enoch, nor the prophet Isaiah; nor those who were after him: and he speaks of the Samaritans, that when they came over to the Jews, they were circumcised again; and gives an instance in Symmachus, who, when he became a proselyte, was circumcised again. So likewise he speaks of Theodotion being proselyted to Judaism,[66] and of his being circumcised; but not a word of the baptism, or dipping, of either of them. He also speaks of Antipater,[67] the father of Herod the king, that when he became procurator of Judea, he was made a proselyte, and was circumcised, both he and Herod his son; but says nothing of their baptism, or dipping; so Herod is called by the Jews a proselyte;[68] and his reign, and that of his posterity, מלכות הגרים *the reign of the proselytes*,[69] who became so by circumcision, and that only, for ought appears. And of him, as a proselyte, but not of his baptism, speaks Jerom;[70] he lived in the same century, and great part of his time in Judea, was acquainted with several Jews he had for his teachers, and with their traditions, of many of which he makes mention, but never of this of admitting proselytes by baptism, or dipping. He speaks of proselytes, and of their circumcision; and says,[71] that " if strangers received by the law of the Lord, and were circumcised, and were eunuchs, as was he of the queen of Candace, they are not foreign from the salvation of God;" but not a word of their baptism or dipping. The instances given by Dr. Wall,[72] from Tertullian, Cyprian, Gregory Nazianzen, and Basil, only respect either the figurative baptism of the Israelites at the Red Sea; or their baptisms and bathings by immersion, for their purification from ceremonial uncleanness; but not for proselytism. So when the same writer[73] quotes Arrianus, an heathen Stoic philosopher of the second century, as speaking of τυ βιβαμμηνυ, a *baptized Jew*,[74] or one that was dipped; by whom the doctor thinks is meant one made a proselyte by baptism; no other may be designed than either a Jew who bathed his whole body, to purify himself from legal pollutions; or an Hemero-baptist, a sect of the Jews,

---

[61] Dialog. cum Tryph. p. 264.
[62] Dialog, ibid. p. 350, 351.
[63] Ibid. p. 307.
[64] Comment. in Joannem, p. 117.
[65] Contr. Hæres. l. 3. Hær. 70.
[66] De Mensur. et Ponder.
[67] Contr. Hæres. l, 1 Hær. 20.

[68] Juchasin, fol. 18. 1.
[69] Seder Olam Zuta, p. 111. Ed. Meyer.
[70] Comment. in Matt. xxii. fol. 30. 1.
[71] Comment. in Esaiam, c. 56. fol. 96. B
[72] History ut supra, p. 47.
[73] Ibid. p. 45.
[74] Epictet. l. 2. c. 9.

who bathed themselves every day; or rather a christian, as many learned men are of opinion;[75] since it was not unusual with heathen writers to call christians, who were baptized, Jews; because the first christians were Jews, and came from Judea, into other parts of the world, and were reckoned by the heathens a sect of the Jews,[76] and were often confounded with them. Now since it appears there is no mention made of any such rite or custom of admitting Jewish proselytes by baptism, or dipping, to the Jewish religion, in any writings and records before the times of John the Baptist, Christ, and his apostles; nor in any age after them, for the first three or four hundred years; or, however, before the writing of the Talmuds; it may be safely concluded there was no such custom which had obtained in that interval of time. It remains therefore to be considered, what is the true ground and foundation of such a notion, and from whence it sprung, which will be done in the following chapter.

CHAP. IV.

THE PROOF OF THIS CUSTOM IS ONLY FROM THE TALMUDS AND TALMUDICAL WRITERS.

SEEING the rite of receiving proselytes by baptism, or dipping among the Jews, is no where mentioned in any writings before the times of John and Christ, nor in any after, nearer than the third and fourth centuries; it is next to be inquired, when and where we first hear of it; and upon inquiry it will be found, that the first mention of it, for ought as yet appears, is in the Jewish Talmuds. The testimonies from thence concerning it, and the whole evidence, as there given of it, will now be laid before the reader. There are two Talmuds, the one called Jerusalem, the other Babylonian; the one written for the Jews at Jerusalem, and in Judea, after the destruction of the city and temple, and in the Jerusalem-dialect. The other for the use of the Jews in Babylon, and in those parts, and in their style. The former is the most ancient, and therefore I shall begin with it, being finished, as generally supposed, in the year 230; but if the Misnah was not compiled till the year 220, being one hundred and fifty years from the destruction of Jerusalem, there must be a longer space of time than that of ten years between the one and the other. David Nieto, lately belonging to a Jewish synagogue here in London, says,[1] the Jerusalem Talmud was written near a hundred years after the Misnah; but other Jews make it later still, and make a difference of two hundred and thirty-three years between the finishing of the one and the other; the one being finished in 189, and the other in 422,[2] which is much more probable; and so this Talmud was not earlier than the beginning of the fifth century; nay, sometimes they place it in the year 469, the latter end of that century.[3] Scaliger places[4] it in the year 370. Mr. Whiston[5] in 369. And so Elias Levita[6] writes, that R. Jochanan compiled it three hundred years after the destruction of Jerusalem; but Morinus[7] will have it to be after the year 600, which is carrying it down too low. The passages I have met with in it any way relating to the case under consideration; for it will be allowed there are some; and therefore it will be owned that Mr. Rees[8] was mistaken in saying it was not pretended to be found in it. The passages are as follow. In one place[9] a certain Rabbi is represented as saying to another, "Wait, and we will *dip* this proselytess to-morrow. R. Zera asked R. Isaac Bar Nachman, Wherefore? because of the glory of that old man, or because they do not dip a proselyte in the night. He replied to him, Why don't they dip a proselyte in the night? Abda came before

---

[75] Quem locum frustra quidam adducunt, ut probent Judæos ritu baptismi uti solitos fuisse, cum apertissime de christianis loquatur philosophus, Oweni Theologoumen. l. 1. c. 9. p. 109. And with Dr. Owen agrees Dr. Jennings; "It is most likely," says he, "that Arrian meant Christians, in the place alledged; because in his time many persons became proselytes to Christianity but few or none to Judaism.——Besides, if he had spoke of proselytes to Judaism, it is highly probable he would have mentioned their circumcision, for which the heathens derided them, rather than their baptism, which was not so very foreign to some of the heathen rites of purification." Jewish Antiquities vol. 1. c. 3. p. 138.
[76] See Gale's Reflections on Wall's History, Letter 10. p. 355—362.
[1] Metteh Dan, sive Cosri, par. 2. fol. 18. 1.
[2] Vid. Wolfii Præfat. ad Bibliothec, Heb. p. 28.
[3] Fabricii Bibliograph. Antiquar. c. 1. s. 2. p. 3.
[4] De Emend. Temp. l. 7. p. 323.
[5] Chronolog. Tables, Cent. 19.
[6] Præfat. ad Methurgeman, fol. 2.
[7] De Sinceritate Heb. Text. l. 2. Exer. 2. c. 2.
[8] Infant Baptism no Institution of Christ, p. 23.
[9] T. Hieros. Yebmaot, fol. 8. 4.

R. Jose (and said,) What is the meaning then of not dipping a proselyte in the night?" And a little after, in the same column, a saying of R. Hezekiah is reported; "A man finds an infant cast out (an exposed infant,) and he dips it in the name of a servant;" or for a servant, on account of servitude; but then dipping for servitude, and dipping for proselytism, were two different things with the Jews, as before observed; and yet this is the only clause produced by Dr. Lightfoot out of this Talmud, for the above purpose; or by any other that I have seen. However, there are others which speak of the dipping of adult proselytes; which became a matter of controversy. In another treatise, in the same Talmud,[10] mention is made of a proselyte circumcised, but not dipped; (and it is added,) all goes after circumcision; that is, that denominates a proselyte. "R. Joshua says, yea, dipping stays (or retards) it; and Bar Kaphra teaches, that he who is not dipped, this is right (a true proselyte;) for there is no proselyte but dips for accidents;" that is, for accidental and nocturnal pollutions; and it seems such a dipping sufficed for proselytism. Of so little account did these Rabbins make of dipping for proselytism, who first mention it, not only make it insignificant, but as a delay of it, and what was an obstruction and hinderance of it: and further on it is said,[11] " A proselytess less than three years of age and one day, she has not knowledge for dipping (or when she is dipped;) and afterwards returns and is dipped for the name of the holy One of Israel; every one is a proselytess, and she is a proselytess." This looks like Anabaptism, or rebaptization for want of knowledge when first dipped. And a little further still,[12] "A stranger or a proselyte, who has children, and says, I am circumcised, but I am not dipped; he is to be believed, and they dip him on the Sabbath." In another treatise,[13] mention is made of a proselyte who dipped after the illumination of the East, that is, after sunrising. These are all the places I have met with in the Jerusalem-Talmud any way relating to this custom. Dr. Wall[14] refers to two or three other passages in this Talmud, through mistake for the Babylonian-Talmud; in which he may be excused, because, as he himself says, he was not well acquainted with these books; but he cannot be excused of inadvertency in transcribing from his authors, unless they have led him wrong.

The Babylonian-Talmud is next to be considered; from whence testimonies may be brought relating to the custom under consideration. This Talmud was finished, as is usually said, about A.D. 500; according to the account of the Jews it was finished three hundred and sixteen years after the Misnah, and eighty-three after the Jerusalem-Talmud.[15] Though Morinus thinks it did not appear until the seventh or eighth century. According to the Jewish doctors, as related in this Talmud; the Israelites, and the proselytes, were admitted into covenant in the same way and manner; and which they conclude from Numb. xv. 15. *As ye are, so shall the stranger be, before the Lord*: on which they thus descant:[16] "As your fathers entered not into covenant but by circumcision and dipping, and acceptance of blood or sacrifice; so they (the proselytes) enter not into covenant, but by circumcision and dipping, and through acceptance of blood," or sprinkling of blood, as the Gloss is; or by sacrifice, as it is sometimes expressed, which is favourably accepted of God; and without both circumcision and dipping, none were reckoned proper proselytes; this is said two or three times in one leaf;[17] "A man is not a proselyte unless both circumcised and dipped." R. Chiyah Bar Abba went to Gabla, it is said, and he saw the daughters of Israel pregnant by proselytes, who were circumcised but not dipped; he went and told R. Jochanan, who declared their issue bastards, and not children of the law, or legitimate: about this a controversy was raised, related in the same place; "A stranger that is circumcised and not dipped, R. Eliezer says, lo, this is a proselyte; for so we find by our fathers, that they were circumcised, but not dipped; one that is dipped, and not circumcised, R. Joshua says, lo, this is a proselyte; for so we find by our mothers (not maids, or maidservants, as Dr. Lightfoot[18] translates it) that they were dipped and not circumcised." Had the account stopped here, the

---

[10] Kiddushin, fol. 64. 4.
[11] Ibid. fol. 65. 2.
[12] Ibid. fol. 66. 1.
[13] Eruvin, fol. 22. 1.
[14] History of Infant Baptism, Introduct. p. 44.
[15] Vid. Wolfium, ut supra.
[16] T. Bab. Ceritot, fol. 9. 1.
[17] Yebamot, fol. 46. 1, 2. vid. Beracot, fol. 47. 2. Avodah Zarah, fol. 57. 2. et 59. 1.
[18] Works, vol. 1. p. 526. vol. 2. p. 117.

decision must have been against dipping: for it is a rule with the Jews, that when R. Eliezer and R. Joshua dissent, the decision is according to R. Eliezer,[19] whom they often call Eliezer the Great,[20] and say many extravagant things of him; particularly, that if all the wise men of Israel were put into one scale, and Eliezer the son of Hyrcanus, into the other, he would weigh them all down;[21] yet here the wise-men interpose, and say, "He that is dipped and not circumcised, circumcised and not dipped, is no proselyte, until he is both circumcised and dipped; for R. Joshua may learn from the fathers, and R. Eliezer from the mothers." And so in this way they reconciled both; but R. Eliezer continued in the same sentiments, which he afterwards declared for, and affirms, that a proselyte that is circumcised, and not dipped, גר מעליא הוא *he is an honourable proselyte;*[22] so that according to him, dipping was not necessary to one's being a proselyte; and R. Barzelonita[23] says, of a sort of proselyte which have been taken notice of, he is a proselyte who is circumcised and not dipped. So that the Jews are not agreed among themselves about this point. The manner of receiving a proselyte, and dipping him, when circumcised and healed of his wound, and of the dipping of women also, is related in the same treatise of the Babylonian-Talmud;[24] "A stranger, when he comes to be made a proselyte, *at this time,* they say unto him, What dost thou see, to become a proselyte? dost thou not know that the Israelites *at this time* are in distress, and in sorrowful circumstances, driven about and scattered, and are reproached, and chastisements come upon them? If he says, I know this, and I am not worthy (to be joined with them,) they receive him immediately; and make known unto him some of the light, and some of the heavy commands (the particulars of which follow;) if he receives them, they immediately circumcise him; and if there be any thing remains, which hinders circumcision, they return and circumcise him a second time, and when he is healed, they dip him immediately, and two disciples of the wise men stand by him, and make known to him some of the light and some of the heavy commands; then he dips, and goes up, and he is an Israelite. If a woman, the women set her in water up to her neck, and two disciples of the wise men stand by her without, and make known some of the light and some of the heavy commands." Maimonides[25] adds, "After that she *dips* herself before them, and they turn away their faces, and go out, so that they do not see her when *she goes up out of the water.*" Of a woman big with child when she is dipped they have this rule,[26] "A stranger pregnant, who is made a proselytess, her child has no need of dipping, that is, for proselytism, as the Gloss is; because sufficient for it is the dipping of its mother; and a woman that is dipped as unclean according to the doctors, that is sufficient to make her a proselytess." Says R. Chiyah Bar Ame, "I'll dip this heathen woman, in the name or on account of a woman;" that is, as the Gloss is, for the dipping of uncleanness, she being a menstruous woman, and not for the dipping of proselytism. Says R. Joseph, "I'll make it right;" that is, pronounce that she is a perfect proselytess; for though she is not dipped for proselytism, yet being dipped for uncleanness, it serves for proselytism; for a stranger or a heathen is not dipped for uncleanness.[27]

There are various circumstances observed in the same treatise concerning the dipping of proselytes; as the place where they are dipped; "In a place it is said,[28] where a menstruous woman dips, there a proselyte and a freed servant dip;" that is, as the Gloss is, in a quantity of forty seahs of water: the time of its being done is also signified; as that they do not dip in the night; and it is disputed whether it should be done on the Sabbath-day: three witnesses also were required to be present; and where there are three, he (the proselyte) *dips* and goes up, and lo, he is as an Israelite.[29] It is said,[30] "It happened in the house of R. Chiya Bar Rabbi, where were present R. Oschaia Bar Rabbi, and R. Oschaia Bar Chiya, that there came a proselyte before him who was circum-

---

[19] Halicot Olam, p. 201.
[20] T. Bab. Yoma, fol. 54. 1. Megillah, fol. 16. 2. Kiddushin, fol. 39. 1.
[21] Pirke Abot, c. 2. s. 8.
[22] T. Bab. Yebamot, fol. 71, 1.
[23] Chinnuch, p. 17.
[24] T. Bab. Yebamot, fol. 46. 1. 2.
[25] Issure Biah, c. 14. s. 6.
[26] T. Bab. Yebamot, fol. 78. 1.
[27] Ibid. fol. 45. 2. et Gloss in ibid.
[28] T. Bab. Yebamot, fol. 46. 2. et Gloss in ibid.
[29] Ibid.
[30] Ibid.

cised, but not dipped; he said unto him, Wait here till to-morrow, and we will dip thee." Three things are to be learnt from hence.----1. That three persons are required (at the dipping of a proselyte).---- 2. That he is not a proselyte unless he is circumcised and dipped.----3. That they do not dip a proselyte in the night; to which may be added,----4. That they must be three Rabbins who are promoted, that is, are famous and eminent ones, who are witnesses, as it seems these three were.

There is but one instance in this Talmud, that I have met with, of the dipping of a child or a minor, made a proselyte; and a male is so called until he is thirteen years of age and one day; of such an one it is said,[31] "A proselyte, a little one (a minor), they dip him by the decree of the Sanhedrim;" that is, as the Gloss is, one that has no father, and his mother brings him to the Sanhedrim to be made a proselyte, and there are three at his dipping; and they are a father to him, and by their means he is made a proselyte. And in the same place it is observed of a stranger, whose sons and daughters are made proselytes with him, and acquiesce in what their father has done, when they are grown up, they may make it void. There is another instance of the dipping of a minor; but not for proselytism, but for eating the Trumah, or the oblation of the fruits of the earth. So a certain one says,[32] "I remember when I was a child, and was carried on my father's shoulders, that they took me from school, and stripped me of my coat, and dipped me, that I might eat of the Trumah in the evening;" but this was not a proselyte, but an Israelite, the son of a priest, who, it seems, was not qualified to eat of the oblation without dipping. This was one of their divers baptisms, or dippings.

This now is the whole compass of the evidence from the Talmuds for the rite of admitting proselytes among the Jews by baptism, or dipping. I have not omitted any thing relating to it in them that has fallen under my observation. As for the quotations usually made from Maimonides, who lived in the twelfth century, in proof of this custom; whatever may be said for him as an industrious and judicious compiler of things, out of the Talmud, which he has expressed in purer language, and digested in better order; he cannot be thought to be of greater and higher authority than those writings from whence he has derived them; for his work is only a stream from the Talmudic fountain. And as for later writers; as the authors of Lebush, Schulchan Aruch, and others, they derive from him. So that the Talmuds appear to be the spring and source of what is said of this custom, and from whence the proof and evidence of it is to be fetched; but whether the reasonings, decisions, and determinations therein concerning it, can be judged a sufficient proof of it, without better testimonies, especially from the scriptures, deserves consideration.

It must not be concealed, that it is pretended there is proof of it from scripture; which I shall attend unto. The proof of the Jewish fathers entering into covenant by baptism, or dipping, is fetched from Exod. xix. 10. where, two or three days before the giving of the law, the Israelites were ordered to *wash* their clothes; hence it is said in the Talmud,[33] to prove that dipping was used at the entrance of the Israelites into covenant, according to which the baptism, or dipping of proselytes, is said to be; "From whence is it (or a proof of it?) From what is written Exod. xix. 10. where there is an obligation to wash clothes, there is an obligation to dip." And again, chap. xxiv. 8. " Moses *took it* (the blood) *and sprinkled it on the people;* and there is no sprinkling without dipping." And in another place,[34] " Sprinkling of blood (or sacrifice, by which also the Israelites, it is said, were admitted into covenant) of it, it is written, *And he sent young men of the children of Israel, which offered burnt-offerings*, &c. But dipping, from whence is it? From what is written; *And Moses took half of the blood, and sprinkled it on the people;* and there is no sprinkling without dipping." This is the proof, which surely cannot be satisfactory to a judicious mind; dipping is inferred from sprinkling; but though the blood was sprinkled upon the people, they were not dipped into it surely; nor even into water, from what appears; and though dipping and sprinkling are sometimes used together, as in the cleansing of the leper, and in the purification of one unclean, by the touch of an unclean bone, &c. Lev. xiv. 7. Numb. xix. 19. yet the one was not the other. From

---

[31] T. Bab. Cetubot, fol. 11 1.
[32] Cetubot, fol. 26 1.

[33] T. Bab. Ceritot, fol. 9. 1.
[34] T. Bab. Yebamot, fol. 46. 2.

washing of clothes dipping is also inferred, without any reason; for these two, in the above places, and in others, are spoken of as two distinct acts, and are expressed by different words; and yet it is upon this single circumstance the proof depends. Now, as Dr. Owen[35] observes, "This washing of clothes served that single occasion only of shewing reverence of the divine presence, at the peculiar giving of the law; nor did it belong to the stated worship of God; so that the necessity of the baptism of bodies, by a stated and solemn rite for ever, should arise from the single washing of garments, and that depending upon a reason, that would never more recur; of the observation of which no mention is made, nor any trace is extant in the whole Old Testament, and which is not confirmed by any divine command, institution, or direction, seems altogether improbable." And he elsewhere[36] says, "From this latter temporary occasional institution (ceremonial washing at Sinai) such as they (the Jews) had many granted to them, whilst they were in the wilderness, before the giving of the law, the Rabbins have framed a baptism for those who enter into their synagogue; a fancy too greedily embraced by some christian writers, who would have the holy ordinance of the church's baptism to be derived from thence. But this *washing of their clothes*, not of their bodies, was temporary, never repeated; neither is there any thing of any such baptism or washing required in any proselytes either men or women, where the laws of their admission are strictly set down." And it may be farther observed, that the Talmudists give this only as a proof of the admission of Israelites into covenant; whereas, the solemn admission of them into it, even of the whole body of them, men, women, and children, and also of the proselytes who were in their camp, as all the Targums and the Greek version have it, when on the plains of Moab, at Horeb, before their entrance into the land of Canaan, Deut. xxix. 10, 11, 12. was not by *any* of the *three* things they say the admission was, that is, by circumcision, baptism, and sacrifice; of the two latter not the least hint is given, and the former was not practised whilst the Israelites were in the wilderness, not till Joshua had introduced them into the land of Canaan. The Jews seems to be conscious themselves that the baptism or dipping of proselytes, is no command of God; since at the circumcision of them, in the form of blessing they then use, they take no notice of it, which runs thus.[37] "Blessed art thou, O Lord God, the King of the world, who has sanctified us by his precepts, and has *commanded* us *to circumcise proselytes*, and to fetch out of them the blood of the covenant; for if it was not for the blood of the covenant the heaven and earth would not be established; as it is said, *If my covenant with day and night*, &c." Jer. xxxiii. 25.

Dr. Lightfoot[38] carries this custom of admitting proselytes by baptism, or dipping, higher than the Jews themselves do. He ascribes the first institution and use of it to Jacob, when he was going to Bethel to worship, after the murder of the Shechemites, by his sons; when, the doctor says, he chose into his family and church, some Shechemites and other heathens. But some learned men of the Pædobaptist persuasion, have thought the notion is indefensible, and judged it most prudent to leave it to himself to defend it, or whomsoever may choose to undertake it;[39] and he himself was in doubt about the first institution of this sort of baptism; for he afterwards says, "We acknowledge that circumcision was of divine institution; but by whom baptism, that was inseparable from it, was instituted, is doubtful." Certain it is, it has no foundation in what Jacob did, or ordered to be done, when he was about to go to Bethel, and worship there; previous to which he ordered his family to *put away the strange gods* that were among them, which they had brought with them from Shechem; and he likewise ordered them to be *clean*, and *change their garments;* which cleanness, whether to be understood of abstaining from their wives, as some interpret it; or of washing of their bodies, as Aben Ezra, as a purification of them from the pollutions of the slain, as the Targum paraphrases it, and after that Jarchi: and which change of garments, whether understood of the garments of

---

[35] Theologoumen. l. 5. Digress. 1. p. 446.
[36] On Heb. vol. 1 Exercitat. 19. p. 272.
[37] Maimon. Hilchot Milah, c. 3. s. 4.
[38] Chronicle of the Old Testament, p. 18. Harmony of the Evangelists, p. 465. Hor. Heb. in Matt. iii. 6.

[39] Pfeiffer. Antiqu. Ebr. c. 1. s. 5. et addit, uti et ejusdem collationem; quam inter hunc proselytorum baptismum et sacramentum initiationis christianorum instituit cum magno grano salis accipiendam putamus.

idolaters, which the sons of Jacob had taken and put on, when they stripped them; or of their own garments, defiled with the blood of the slain; or of their meaner or more sordid garments, for more pure and splendid ones. All that can be concluded from hence is, and is by the Jews concluded, that when men come before God, they should come with clean bodies, and with clean garments; as an emblem of the more inward purity of their minds, which is necessary to every religious service and act of devotion, such as Jacob and his family were now about to perform, and which the very heathens themselves had a notion of; *Casta placent superis, pura cum veste venito*.[40] But not a word is here of any covenant Jacob and his family entered into, and much less of any proselytes from Shechem and Syria being brought into it with them, by baptism, or dipping, as is pretended.

I have met with another learned man,[41] who carries up this custom higher still; and asserts, that Jacob did not feign out of his own brain this practice of washing the body, and of change of garments; but took it from the history of Adam, and from his example; and he supposes that Adam, at the solemn making the covenant with him, was washed in water, before he put on the garments given him of God; and that as he was the first who sacrificed, he was the first who was baptized by the command of God; and so baptism was the most ancient of all the sacred rites. But let the history of Adam be carefully read over by any man, and he will never find the least hint of this, nor observe the least shadow or appearance of it; but what is it that the imagination of man will not admit and receive, when once a loose is given to it? Pray, who baptized Adam, if he was baptized? Did God baptize him? Or did an angel baptize him? Or did Eve baptize him? Or did he baptize himself?

Since then this rite or custom of admitting into covenant, whether Israelites or proselytes, by baptism or dipping, has no foundation but in the Talmuds; and the proof of it there so miserably supported from scripture, surely it can never be thought that christian baptism was borrowed from thence; or that it is no other which is continued in the christian church, being taken up as it was found by John the Baptist, Christ, and his apostles; the folly and falsehood of which will be evinced in the following chapter.

CHAP. V.

THE REASONS WHY CHRISTIAN BAPTISM IS NOT FOUNDED ON, AND TAKEN FROM, THE PRETENDED JEWISH BAPTISM OF ISRAELITES AND PROSELYTES.

HAVING traced the admission of the Jewish proselytes by baptism, or dipping, to the spring-head of it, the Jewish Talmuds; I shall now proceed to give reasons, why christian baptism cannot be thought to be taken from such a custom; nor that to be a rule according to which it is to be practised.

First, The Talmuds are of too late a date to prove that such a custom obtained before the times of John and Christ, since they were written some centuries after those times, as has been shewn; and besides, there is in them a plain chronological mark, or character, which shews that this custom took place among the Jews since they were driven out of their own land, and scattered among the nations, and suffered reproach and persecution; for among the interrogatories put to persons who came to them to be made proselytes, this question was asked,[1] "What dost thou see to become a proselyte? dost thou not know, or consider, that the Israelites are *now* בזמן הזה *at this time*, in sorrowful circumstances, driven about and scattered, and loaded with reproaches and afflictions? If he says, I know this; and I am not worthy (that is, to be joined to them) they receive him immediately." Many are the surmises and conjectures of learned men concerning the original and rise of this custom. It is scarce worth while, to take notice of the notion of Grotius,[2] that this custom was taken up on account of the flood, and in commemoration of the world's being purified by it: nor of Sir John Marsham's, that it was taken up by the Israelites, in imitation of the Egyptian's manner of initiating persons into the mysteries of their goddess Isis, by washing them; for which he cites Apuleius. A goodly pattern of christian baptism this! it is much it never

---

[40] Tibullus, l. 2. eleg. 1.
[41] Rhenferd. Orat. de Antiqu. Baptism. p. 954. da Calcem Oper. Philolog.

[1] T. Bab. Yebamot. fol. 47. 1.
[2] Annot. in Matt. iii. 6.
[3] Chronic. secul. 9. p. 200.

entered into the thoughts of these learned men, or others, that the Jews took up this rite of dipping their proselytes, as they found it among the Medes and Persians, when they lived in their countries, and so brought it into Judea, some hundreds of years before the coming of Christ, and his forerunner John the Baptist; since of the eighty rites the Persians used in the initiation of men into the mysteries of Mithras, their chief deity, the first and principal was baptism. They *dipped* them in a *bath*, and *signed* them in their *foreheads*, and had a sort of an *Eucharist*, an oblation of bread, as Tertullian has it, and an image of the resurrection (that is, in their baptism;) promising the expiation of sins by the laver; and also had an imitation of martyrdom.[4] Some say,[5] this custom of the Jews was taken up by them out of hatred to the Samaritans, and was added to circumcision, to distinguish them from them: but if so, it is very much that Symmachus the Samaritan, when he came over to the Jews, was not only circumcised again, as he was, but also baptized, or dipped; of which Epiphanius, who gives an account of his becoming a proselyte to them, and of his being circumcised, but not of his being baptized, as before observed. Dr. Owen thinks[6] this custom was taken up by some Antemishnical Rabbins, in imitation of John the Baptist; which is not very probable, though more so than any thing before advanced. To me it seems a clear case, that this custom was framed upon a general notion of the uncleanness of heathens, in their state of heathenism, before their embracing the Jewish religion; and therefore devised this baptism, or dipping, as a symbol of that purity, which was, or ought to be, in them, when they became Jews, of whom they might hope to gain some, they being now dispersed among the nations; and of some they boast, even of some of note: and this was first introduced when they digested the traditions of the elders into a body, or pandect of laws; and were finishing their decisions and determinations upon them, to be observed by their people in future time.

Since I wrote the preceding chapters, I have met with a quotation; for I will not conceal any thing that has occurred to me in reading, relative to this custom of dipping Jewish proselytes; I say, I have met with a quotation by Maimonides,[7] out of a book called Siphri, an ancient commentary on Numbers and Deuteronomy, which has these words: "As the Israelites did not enter into covenant but by three things, by circumcision, dipping, and acceptation of sacrifice; so neither proselytes likewise." Now if this is the ancient book of Siphri, from whence this passage is taken, as may seem, which is a book of an uncertain author and age; and is allowed to be written after the Misnah;[8] yet if it is the same that is referred to in the Babylonian-Talmud,[9] it must be written before that was published, though it might be while it was compiling, and it may be, by some concerned in it; since the rite referred to is expressed in the same words in the one as in the other;[10] and is founded upon and argued from the same passage of scripture, Numb. xv. 15. and seems to be the language and reasoning of the same persons. However, *if* the passage quoted by Maimonides stands in that book, which is a book I never saw, though printed; *if*, I say, these several things can be made plain; it is indeed the earliest testimony we have of this custom; especially if the book was written before the Jerusalem-Talmud, which yet is not certain: but be it as it may, it is a testimony of the same sort of persons, and of no better authority than what has been before produced, and serves to confirm, that this custom is a pure device of the Jewish doctors, and is merely *Rabbinical;* and besides, at most, it can only carry up this custom into the *fifth* century, which is too late for John Baptist and Christ to take up the ordinance from it; and on account of these testimonies not being early enough for such a purpose, the late Dr. Jennings[11] has given up the argument from them, in favour of infant baptism, as insufficient. His words are, "After all, it remains of be proved, not only that christian baptism was instituted in the room of proselyte-baptism; but that the Jews had any such baptism in our Saviour's time: the earliest accounts we have of it, are in the Misnah (but in

---

[4] Witsii Ægyptiaca, l. 2. c. 16. s. 10. vid. Tertullian. de Præscript. Hær. c. 40.
[5] Schickard. et Mayerus, apud Pfeiffer. Antiqu. Ebr. c. 1. s. 5. vid. Selden. de Syned. l. 1. c. 3.
[6] Ut Supra et Theologoumen, p. 447.
[7] Præfat. ad Seder Kodashim.

[8] Mabo. Hagemara ad Calcem Halicot Olam. p. 223.
[9] T. Bab. Kiddushin, fol. 49. 2. Baracct fol. 47. 2.
[10] T. Bab. Ceritot, fol. 9. 1.
[11] Jewish Antiqu. vol. 1. p. 136, 138.

that we have none at all) and Gemara." And again he says, "There wants more evidence of its being as ancient as our Saviour's time, than I apprehend can be produced, to ground an argument upon it, in relation to christian baptism."

Secondly, This custom, though observed as a religious action, yet has scarce any appearance of religion and devotion in it; but looks rather like a civil affair, it being in some cases under the cognizance and by the direction of the Sanhedrim, or court of judicature. There was no divine solemnity in the performance of it. It was not administered in the name of the God of Israel, whom the Jews professed; nor in the name of the Messiah to come, expected by them, as was the baptism of John; nor in the name of the Three divine Persons in the Trinity, which yet the ancient Jews believed. They dipped their proselytes indeed, according to their account, בשם *in the name* of a proselyte, or as one; and a servant, *in the name* of a servant, or on account of servitude; and a free-man, *in the name* of a free-man; but neither of them in the name of any divine Person, or with the invocation of the name of God; so that it had no appearance of a religious solemnity in it. To which may be added, that this custom gave a licence to things the most impure and abominable, things contrary to the light of nature, and not to be named among the Gentiles, and which must make it detestable to all serious persons. According to the Jews, it dissolved all the ties of natural relations, which before subsisted among men; for according to them, "As soon as a man is made a proselyte, a soul flies out of a (celestial) palace, and gets under the wings of the Shechinah, (or divine Majesty) which kisses it, because it is the fruit of the righteous, and sends it into the body of a proselyte, where it abides; and from that time he is called a proselyte of righteousness;[12] so that now he has a new soul, and is a new man, another man than he was before;" not a better man, but, to use our Lord's words, he is made *two-fold more the child of hell*. For, according to them, all his former connections with men are broken, and all obligations to natural relations are dissolved; and he may, without any imputation of crime, be guilty of the most shocking incest, as to marry his own mother or his own sister. But hear their own words, "When a Gentile is made a proselyte, and a servant made free, they are both as *a new-born babe;* and all the relations which they had when a Gentile or a servant, are no more relations to them;" or their kindred and relation by blood is no more; as brother, sister, father, mother, and children, these are no more to be so accounted; insomuch, that, "when one becomes a proselyte, he and they (his quondam kindred) are not guilty, by reason thereof, on account of incest, at all; so that it is according to law (the civil law of the Jews) that a Gentile may marry his own mother, or his sister, by his mother's side (his own sister,) when they become proselytes." But though they allow it to be lawful, they have so much modesty and regard to decency, or rather to their own character, that it is added; "But the wise men forbid this, that they (the proselytes) may not say, we are come from a greater holiness to a lesser one; and what is forbidden to-day is free to-morrow; and so a proselyte who lies with his mother or his sister, and they are in Gentilism, it is no other than if he lay with a stranger."[13] Now can any man, soberly thinking, judge that the New Testament ordinance of baptism was taken up by John and Christ from such a wretched custom, which gave licence to such shocking immorality and uncleanness; or that christian baptism is built on such a basis as this?

Thirdly, To suppose that John took up the practice of baptizing as he found it among the Jews, and from a tradition and custom of theirs, greatly detracts from the character of John, his divine mission, and the credit of baptism, as administered by him; and is contrary to what the scriptures say concerning him. They represent him as the first administrator of baptism, and, for a while, the sole administrator of it; for, for what other reason do they call him the Baptist, and distinguish him by this title, if it was then a common thing, and had been usual in time past, to baptize persons? The scriptures say he was a man sent of God, and sent by him *to baptize with water,* John i. 6, 33. But what need was there of a mission and commission to what was in common use, and had been so time out of mind? The Jews hearing of John's baptizing persons, sent

---

[12] Zohar in Numb. fol. 69. 4. Ed. Sultzbach.
[13] Maimon. Issure Biah, c. 14. s. 11, 12. Schulchan Aruch, par. 2. Yore Dea. Hilchot Gerim, Art. 269. s. 1.

messengers to him, to know who he was that took upon him to baptize; who asked, *Why baptizest thou, if thou art not that Christ, nor Elias, nor that prophet?* As if it was a new thing; and that it was expected he should be some extraordinary person who baptized. But why should such questions be put to him, if this was in common use, and if any ordinary person, however any common doctor or Rabbi, had then, and in former times, been used to baptize persons?[14] The scriptures speak of John's baptism as the *counsel of God:* but according to this notion, it was a device and tradition of men; and had this been the case, the Jews would not have been at a loss, nor under any difficulty, to answer the question Christ put to them, nor indeed, would he ever have put such an one; *The baptism of John, whence was it? from heaven or from men?* for his putting the question thus, supposes the contrary, that it was not from men, but from God, and if it was not of God, but a tradition of men, they could have readily said, *Of men;* without being confuted by him, or exposed to the people; but being thrown into a dilemma, they took the wisest way for themselves, and answered, *We cannot tell.* Dr. Wall[15] says, If John had been baptizing proselytes, and not natural Jews, the Pharisees would not have wondered at it, it being so well known to them; and he suggests, that the wonder was, that natural Jews should be baptized: but why so? for according to this notion, the original natural Jews were received into covenant by baptism; they as the proselytes, and the proselytes as they; the case, according to them was similar. But let us examine this affair, and see how the fact stands. When John first appeared baptizing, the Pharisees and Sadducees, who were natural Jews, came to his baptism, and were not admitted to it, but rejected from it as unfit and improper persons; and others of the same nation and profession, in their turn, *rejected the counsel of God against themselves, not being baptized by John,* Matt. iii. 7. Luke vii. 30. On the other hand, publicans, the Roman tax-gatherers, of whom some indeed were Jews, others heathens, both equally odious, and therefore joined together, these *justified God,* being baptized with the baptism of John; and these *went into the kingdom of God,* into the gospel-state, before the Pharisees, and embraced its doctrines, and submitted to its ordinances, Luke vii. 29. and iii. 12. Matt. xxi. 31. and even soldiers, Roman soldiers, for no other soldiers were then in Judea, were among the multitude who came to be baptized by him, to whom he gave good instructions, but did not refuse to baptize them, Luke iii. 7, 14. and our Lord Jesus Christ, whose forerunner John was, in his ministry and baptism, gave orders to his disciples to baptize indiscriminately, persons of all nations, Jews and Gentiles, who believed in him; and who accordingly did baptize them: so that baptism, in those early times of John, Christ, and his apostles, was not confined to natural Jews; the wonder and the question upon it, as above, were not about the persons baptized, whether Jews or Gentiles, but about baptism itself, and the administrator of it, as being altogether new. The account which Josephus,[16] the Jewish historian, who lived soon after the times of John, gives of him, and his baptism, agrees with the sacred scriptures; and which testimony stands not only in the common editions of that historian, but is preserved by Eusebius,[17] as a choice piece of history; in which, he not only says John was a religious and good man, but, with the scriptures, that he was surnamed the Baptist, to distinguish him from others; and that he ordered the Jews, who lived righteous and godly lives, to come to baptism, and such only did John admit of; and that baptizing was acceptable to God, when used not for removing some sins (by which his baptism is distinguished from Jewish baptisms, which were used to purge from sin in a ceremonial sense) but for the purity of the body, the soul being before purified by righteousness. Also he observes, with the scriptures, that multitudes flocked to him; and that Herod, fearing that by his means his subjects would be drawn into a revolt, put him to death. But why such flockings to him, if baptism had been a common thing? And what had Herod to fear from that? He might reasonably conclude, that if this was no other than what had been usually practised, the people would soon cease from

---

[14] Annon plane innuunt (verba Joan. i. 25.) nullum fuisse baptismi usum, et receptam fuisse opinionem inter ipsos (Judæos), nullum debere esse, usquedum veniret Christus, vel Elias, vel propheta ille? Knatchbul in 1 Pet. iii. 21.

[15] Introduction to his History, p. 64. Ed. 2. 4to.
[16] Antiqu. l. 18. c. 6. s. 2.
[17] Eccl. Hist. l. 1. c. 11.
[18] Ibid. Heb. l. 5. c. 45.

following him. Nay, Josippon Ben Gorion;[18] the Jew's Josephus, the historian whom they value and prefer to the true Josephus, says of John, that עשה טבילה *he made*, instituted, and performed baptism, as if it was a new thing, set on foot by him; and for which later Jews express their resentment at him. One of their virulent writers says,[19] "Who commanded John to institute this baptism? in what law did he find it? neither in the old nor in the new." Now this would not be said by the Jews, if John had taken up his baptism from a custom of theirs; nor would they speak of the ordinance of baptism in such a scandalous and blasphemous manner as they do, and in language too shocking to transcribe.[20]

Fourthly, The Jews will not allow that any proof of baptism can be produced out of the writings of the Old Testament, nor out of their Talmuds. Such passages in the Old Testament which speak of washing, and in which men are exhorted to *wash* and be *clean*, as Isa. i. 16. it is said, are to be understood of men cleansing themselves from their sins, and not of plunging in water; "To plunge a man in water, is no where written; why therefore did Jesus command such baptism," or dipping?[21] and whereas the passage in Ezek. xvi. 9. *Then washed I thee with water*, is by some interpreted of baptism; the Jew observes,[22] the words are not in the future tense; *I will wash thee;* but in the past tense; *I have washed thee;* and so cannot refer to baptism. And whereas the promise in Ezek. xxxvi. 25. *I will sprinkle clean water upon you, and ye shall be clean from all your filthinsss*, &c. is brought by some, I suppose he means some popish writers, as another proof of baptism; the Jew replies,[23] "What sin and uncleanness does baptism take away? and what sin and uncleanness are there in new-born babes? Besides, says he, you do not do so; you do not sprinkle, but you are plunged into water:" which, by the way, shews that sprinkling was not used in baptism when this Jew wrote, which was in the twelfth century, as Wagenseil, the editor of his work, supposes.

The same Jewish writer[24] asks, "If the law of Jesus, and his coming, were known to the prophets, why did they not observe his law; and why did not they *baptize themselves*, according to the law of Jesus?" And he represents[25] David as praying (it must be supposed, under a prophetic spirit) for those who should, in this captivity of the Jews, be forced, against their wills, to baptism, and that they might be delivered from it, Psalm lxix. 1, 15. and cxliv. 7. Nor does this writer take any notice of receiving proselytes by baptism; though he makes mention of receiving men-proselytes,[26] yet by circumcision only; and also of women-proselytes, but not a word of baptism of either; and had he thought the baptism their Talmud speaks of, had any affinity with our baptism, and was the ground of it, he would not have been so gravelled with an objection of the christian, as he was; which is put thus,[27] "We baptize male and female, and hereby receive them into our religion; but you circumcise men only, and not women:" to which he appears to be at an entire loss to answer; whereas he might have readily answered, had the case been as suggested, that we baptize women as well as men, when they are received proselytes, among us. But that the Jews had no notion that Christian baptism was founded upon any prior baptism of proselytes, or others, among them, as related in their Talmud, is manifest from a disputation had between Nachmanides, a famous Jew, and one brother Paul, a christian, in the year 1263.[28] Brother Paul affirmed, that the Talmudists believed in Jesus, that he was the Messiah, and was both God and man: the Jew replied, after observing some other things, "How can brother Paul say so, that they believed in him; for they, and their disciples, died in our religion? and *why were they not baptized*, according to the command of Jesus, as brother Paul was? And I would be glad to hear," says he, "*how he* learned baptism from them (the Talmudists) and *in what place* (of the Talmud?) did not they teach us all our laws which we now observe? and the rites and customs they gathered together for us,

---

[19] Vet. Nizzachon, p. 195. Ed. Wagenseil.
[20] Vet. Nizzachon, p. 62, 64, 70, 74, 77, 150, 191, &c. vid. Maji Synops. Theolog. Jud. loc. 18. s. 2. p. 266. Edzardi not. in Avodah Zarah, c. 2. p. 266. Wagenseil. in Sotah, p. 959.
[21] Nizzachon, p. 53.
[22] Ibid. p. 74.
[23] Nizzachon, p. 192.
[24] Ibid. p. 99.
[25] Ibid. p. 193.
[26] Ibid. p. 242, 243.
[27] Ibid. p. 251.
[28] Apud Wagenseil. Tela Ignea, vol. 2. p. 25, 26.

as they were used when the temple was standing, from the mouths of the prophets, and from the mouth of Moses, our master, on whom be peace ? and if they believed in Jesus, and in his law, they would have done as brother Paul has; does he understand their words better than they themselves?"

Fifthly, To say, as Dr. Lightfoot does, that Christ took baptism into his hands as he found it, that is as practised by the Jews, is greatly to derogate from the character and authority of Christ; it makes him, who came a teacher from God, to teach for doctrines the commandments of men, which he himself condemns. It makes that *all power in heaven and in earth*, said to be given him, in consequence of which he gave his apostles a commission to *teach all nations, baptizing them in the name of the Father, and of the Son, and of the Holy Ghost;* I say, it makes it to dwindle into this only, a power to establish a tradition, and commandment of me long in use before he came. Again, who can believe that Christ, who so severely inveighed against the traditions of the Jews, could ever establish any one of them, and make it an ordinance of his; and particularly, should inveigh against those, respecting the baptisms, or dippings of the Jews then in use among them; and especially without excepting that of their baptism of proselytes from the rest, and without declaring it his will that it should be continued and observed; neither of which he has done.

Sixthly, Such a notion as this, highly reflects dishonour on the ordinance of baptism; that one of the principal ordinances of the New Testament, as that is, should be founded on an human tradition, an invention of men; it must greatly weaken the authority of it, as well as disparage the wisdom of the Lawgiver; and must have a tendency to bring both the author and the ordinance into contempt. Nothing can make an ordinance a christian ordinance, but its being instituted by Christ. If baptism is an institution of men, and received and retained from men, and regulated according to their device, it is no christian ordinance: and, as Witsius says,[29] "Whatever may be said of the antiquity of that rite (proselyte-baptism, which yet with him was dubious and uncertain) there can be no divine institution of it (of baptism) before John the forerunner of Christ, was sent of God to baptize; for to him that was expressly commanded; *The word of God came unto John,"* Luke iii. 2. John i. 33. &c.

Seventhly, If it was the custom of the Jews before the times of John and Christ, to receive young children as proselytes by baptism, or dipping, and this was to be as a rule according to which christian baptism was to be practised; then most surely we should have had some instances of children being baptized by John, or by the apostles of Christ, if "baptizing infants had been as *ordinarily used* in the church of the Jews, as ever it hath been in the christian church," as Dr. Lightfoot says; and yet we have not one instance of this kind; we no where read of any children being brought to John to be baptized, nor of any that were baptized by him; nor of any being brought to the apostles of Christ to be baptized, nor of their being baptized by them; from whence it may be concluded, there was no such custom before their times; or if there was, it never was intended it should be observed by christians in after-times; or otherwise there would have been some precedents of it, directing to and encouraging such a practice; many things would follow on such a supposition, that christian baptism is borrowed from and founded on proselyte-baptism, and the latter the rule directing the practice of the former; for then,

Eighthly, Se-baptizing, or persons baptizing themselves, without making use of an administrator, might be encouraged and established; which is what the Pædobaptists charge, though wrongly, some of the first reformers of the abuses of baptism with; since it is plain, from the quotations before made, that though it is sometimes said, *they*, that is, the doctors or wise men, *baptize*, or *dip*, yet it is also said, both of men and women, that they *dipped themselves;* as of a man הוא טבל *he dipped himself,* and went up from the water; and of a woman, being placed by women in the water, טבלה *she dipped,* that is, herself; and so Leo of Modena says,[30] of a Jew-proselyte, that after he is circumcised, and well of his sore, *he is to wash himself all over in water,* in the presence of three Rabbins, or other persons in authority, and from

---

[29] Oeconom. Foeder. 1. 4. c. 16. s. 8. p. 875. Ed. 3.

[30] History of the Customs of the Jews, par. 5. c. 2.

thenceforth he becomes as a natural Jew; and, indeed, all the Jewish baptisms, or bathings, commanded in the law, were done by persons themselves; see Lev. xiv. 8, 9. Numb. xix. 7, 8. And Dr. Lightfoot[31] thinks that John's baptism was so administered; he supposes, that men, women, and children came unto it; and that they standing in Jordan, were taught by John, that they were baptized into the name of the Messiah, ready to come, and into the profession of the gospel, about faith and repentance; and that *they plunged themselves into the river*, and so came out.

Ninthly, If this Jewish custom is to be regarded as a rule of christian baptism, it will tend to establish the Socinian notion, that only the first converts to christianity in a nation, they and their children are to be baptized, but not their posterity in after ages; for so both Lightfoot and Selden, with others, say, who were sticklers for christian baptism being taken from the custom of baptizing, or dipping Jewish proselytes, and their children; that only the children of proselytes, born before their parents became such, were baptized, or dipped; but not those born afterwards: baptism was never repeated in their posterity; the sons of proselytes, in following generations, were circumcised, but not baptized;[32] and, as Dr. Jennings[33] rightly observes, "it was a maxim with the Rabbins, *Natus baptizati, habetur pro baptizato*." This "restriction of baptism to children born before their parents' proselytism, rests on the same authority as the custom of baptizing any children of proselytes." So that if the one is to be admitted, the other is also; and so the children of christian parents are not to be baptized, only the converts from another religion; and these the first, and their then posterity, but not afterwards.

Tenthly, If this custom, said to be practised before the times of John and Christ, is the rule to direct us in christian baptism, there were several circumstances attending that, which should be observed in christian baptism, to make it regular; it must be done before three witnesses, and these men of eminence; but who, of such a number and character were present at the baptism of the apostle Paul? Acts xxii. 16.

and ix. 18. Nor was it to be performed in the night; what then must be said of the baptism of the jailor, and his family? Acts xvi. 33. nor on a Sabbath-day; nor on a feast-day; yet Lydia, and her household, were baptized on a Sabbath-day, Acts xvi. 13, 15. and the three thousand christian converts were baptized on the day of Pentecost, and which was also the first day of the week, the christian Sabbath, Acts ii. 1, 41. Wherefore, if this Jewish custom was the rule of baptism, and from whence it was taken, and by which it should proceed; (for if in one case, why not in others?) these instances of christian baptism were not rightly performed.

Eleventhly, If the Ethiopian eunuch Philip baptized, was a proselyte, as Grotius and others say, he must be either a proselyte of the gate, a proselyte inhabitant, or a proselyte of righteousness; not the former, for he was no inhabitant in any part of Judea; but most probably he was the latter, since he was a very devout and religious man, had an high opinion of the worship of God among the Jews, and had travelled from a far country to worship at Jerusalem; and so Dr. Jennings[34] justly observes, that "he seems to be rather a proselyte of the covenant, or completely a Jew; not only from his reading the scripture, but because he had taken so long a journey to worship at Jerusalem at the feast of Pentecost, one of the three grand festivals; when all the Jewish males, who were able, were, according to the law, to attend the worship of God at the national altar." He appears to have thoroughly embraced the religion of the Jews, even their whole law, and was conversant with their sacred writings; he was reading in one of their prophets when Philip joined his chariot, and was taken up into it by him: whereas a son of Noah, as the Jews called a proselyte of the gate, might not study in the law, according to their canons,[35] which they say he had nothing to do with; only with the seven precepts of Noah; and, indeed, no Gentile or uncircumcised person.[36] And if the eunuch was a proselyte of righteousness, according to the pretended custom of dipping such, he must have been baptized, or dipped, when he became a proselyte; and since, according to this

---

[31] Hor. Heb. in Matt. iii. 6. vol. 2. p. 122.
[32] See Wall's History of Infant Baptism, Introduct. p. 50, 55.
[33] Jewish Antiquities, ut supra, p. 135. Marg.
[34] Jewish Antiq. p. 159, 160.
[35] Maimon. Melacim. c. 10. s. 9.
[36] T. Bab. Sanhedrin. fol. 59. 1. Shaare Orah, fol. 18. 2.

notion, he must have been baptized with a baptism which John and Christ took up as they found it among the Jews, and which is the basis and foundation of christian baptism, and the rule to direct in the performance of it, it is much he should desire baptism again! and that Philip, who is thought to be a proselyte also, Acts vi. 5. and must know the custom of making proselytes, should administer it to him: and if he had been baptized before, must he not then be an Anabaptist? And so the proselytes in Acts ii. 10. were, as Drusius and others think, proselytes of righteousness, who had embraced the Jewish religion, and were circumcised, and, according to this notion, baptized. Besides, none but proselytes of righteousness might dwell in Jerusalem; as has been observed, chap. 1. And also proselytes of the gate were never called Jews, as these were; only proselytes of righteousness: and if any of these were among the three thousand converted and baptized by the apostles, which is not improbable, must not they be also Anabaptists? The Grecians, or Hellenists, whose widows were neglected in the daily ministration, are thought by Beza, and others, to be widows of Jewish proselytes, and therefore it is highly probable, that their husbands had been members of the christian church at Jerusalem, and so must have been re-baptized; and most certain it is, that Nicholas of Antioch, who was one of the seven appointed to take care of these widows, was a proselyte, and as Grotius truly thinks, a proselyte of righteousness; and so, as he must have been baptized according to this notion, when he became a proselyte, he must have been re-baptized when he became a member of the christian church at Jerusalem, of which he most certainly was, being chosen out of it, and appointed to an office in it, Acts vi. 1, 5.

Twelfthly, It may be observed, in a quotation before made, that if a proselytess big with child was baptized, or dipped, her child needed not baptism, or dipping, the mother's baptism, or dipping, was sufficient for it; but this is not attended to by Pædobaptists; it seems, in the beginning of the fourth century, there were some of the same opinion with the Jews; but a canon in the council of Neocæsarea was made against it; which, as explained, declared that the child of such a person needed baptism, when it came to be capable of choosing for itself;[37] which canon should not have been made, if this Jewish custom is to be regarded as a rule.

Lastly, As an argument *ad hominem*, it may be observed, that if this custom is to be considered as a rule of christian baptism, then sprinkling ought not to be used in it, for the baptism of Jewish proselytes, men, women, and children, was performed by dipping; as all the above quotations shew. To which may be added, that one of their rules respecting proselyte-baptism is, that a proselyte must dip in such a place (or confluence of water) as a menstruous woman dips herself in,[38] or which is sufficient for such an one; and that as the Gloss is, was what held forty seahs of water; and to this agrees the account Maimonides[39] gives of such a confluence of water, that it must be "sufficient for the dipping of the whole body of a man at once; and such the wise men reckon to be a cubit square, and three cubits in depth; and this measure holds forty seahs of water." And he further says,[40] "that, wherever washing of the flesh, and washing of clothes from uncleanness, are mentioned in the law, nothing else is meant but the dipping of the whole body in a confluence of water——and that if he dips his whole body, except the top of his little finger, he is still in his uncleanness:——and that all unclean persons, who are dipped in their clothes, their dipping is right, because the waters come into them (or penetrate through them) and do not divide," or separate between the water and their bodies, so as to hinder its coming to them; so the menstruous woman dipped herself in her clothes; and in like manner the proselyte. Let such observe this, who object to the baptism of persons with their clothes on.

Again, as an argument of the same kind, if baptism was common in all ages, foregoing the times of John, Christ, and his apostles, as is said, then it could not succeed circumcision, since it must be cotemporary with it. Upon the whole, what Dr. Lightfoot,[41] and others after him, have urged in favour of infant-baptism

---

[37] See Stennett against Russen, p. 103, 104.
[38] T. Bab. Yebamot, fol. 47. 2.
[39] Hilchot Mikvaot, c. 4. s. 1. T. Bab. Eruvim fol. 14. 2.
[40] Mikvaot, c. 1. s. 2, 7.
[41] Hor. Heb. in Matt. iii. 6. vol. 2. p. 119.

from hence, is quite impertinent; that "there was need of a plain and open prohibition, that infants and little children should not be baptized, if our Saviour would not have had them baptized, for since it was most common in all ages foregoing, that little children should be baptized, if Christ had been minded to have had that custom abolished, he would have openly forbidden it; therefore his silence, and the silence of the scripture in this matter, confirms Pædobaptism, and continues it unto all ages." But first, it does not appear that any such custom was ever practised before the times of John, Christ, and his apostles, as to admit into the Jewish church by baptism, proselytes, whether adult or minors. No testimony has been, and I believe none can be given of it. And, as some very learned men have truly observed,[42] and as Dr. Owen[43] affirms, there are not the least footsteps of any such usage among the Jews, until after the days of John the Baptist, in imitation of whom, he thinks, it was taken up by some Ante-Mishnical Rabbins; and, as he elsewhere says,[44] "The institution of the rite of baptism is no where mentioned in the Old Testament; no example is extant; nor during the Jewish church, was it ever used in the admission of proselytes; no mention of it is to be met with in Philo, Josephus, nor in Jesus the son of Syrach; nor in the evangelic history." What testimony has been given of this custom, falls greatly short of proving it; wherefore Christ could have no concern about abolishing a custom which had not obtained in his time; nor was there any room nor reason for it, since it had never been practised, for ought appears: his silence about what never existed, can give no existence to it, nor to that which is founded on it, Pædobaptism; and which is neither warranted and confirmed by any such custom, nor by the word of God, in which there is an high silence about both. This custom of baptizing little children was so far from being common in all ages foregoing the times of John, Christ, and his apostles, that not a single instance can be given of any one that ever was baptized; if there can, let it be produced; if not, what comes of all this bluster and harangue? With much more propriety and strength of reasoning might it be retorted; that since it is plain the children of the Jews, both male and female, did eat of the passover, which was not an human custom and tradition, but an ordinance of God, common in all ages foregoing the times of John, &c. and since, according to the hypothesis of the Pædobaptists, the Lord's supper came in the room of the passover; for which there is much more reason in analogy, than for baptism coming in the room of circumcision; it should seem, if our Saviour would not have had children eat of the Lord's supper, as they did of the passover, he would have openly forbidden it. A plain and open prohibition of this was more needful than a prohibition of the baptism of infants, if not his will, had there been such a custom before prevailing, as there was not; since that could only be a custom and tradition of men; and it was enough that Christ inveighed against those of the Jews in general, which obtained before, and in his time; and against their baptisms and dippings in particular. And after all, it is amazing that christian baptism should be founded upon a tradition, of which there is no evidence but from the Rabbins, and that very intricate, perplexed, and contradictory, and not as in being in the times referred to; upon a tradition of a set of men blinded and besotted, and enemies to christianity, its doctrines and ordinances; and who at other times, reckoned by these very men, who so warmly urge this custom of theirs, the most stupid, sottish, and despicable, of all men upon the face of the earth! If this is the basis of infant-baptism, it is built upon the sand, and will, ere long, fall, and be no more.

I conclude this Dissertation in the words of Dr. Owen,[45] "That the opinion of some learned men concerning transferring the rite of Jewish baptism, by the Lord Jesus, which, indeed, did not then exist, for the use of his disciples, is destitute of all probability." And after all, perhaps, the Pædobaptists will find their account better in consulting the baptism of the ancient heathens, and its rites, than that of the

---

[42] Proselytorum baptismum ante Johannem extitisse nullo testimonio certe constat, Fabricii Bibliograph. Antiqu. c. 11. p. 392. ita Deylingius in ibid. p. 386.
[43] On Heb. vol. 1. Exercitat. 19. p. 272.
[44] Theologoumen. l. 5. Digress. 1. p. 447.

[45] Omni ideo probabilitate caret sententia ista doctorom quorundam virorum de translatione ritus baptismatis Judaici, qui revera eo tempore nullus erat, in usum discipulorum suorum per Dominum Jesum facienda, Theologoum. ibid.

Jews; said[46] to be in use before the times of Moses, and in ages since, and that among all nations; and being more ancient than christian baptism, a learned writer referred to, says, it is as a sort of preamble to it. And from whom the Pædobaptists may be supplied with materials for their purpose.

[46] Sperlingius de baptismo veterum Ethnicorum, p. 116, 117, 120, 129, 210.

FINIS.

APPENDIX 1

MEMOIR OF JOHN GILL

A BRIEF

MEMOIR

OF

THE LIFE, LABOURS, AND CHARACTER

OF THE

REVEREND AND LEARNED

JOHN GILL, D.D.

THERE is in the human mind a natural anxiety to trace the source of its enjoyments; hence it is we are generally concerned to know the name, and something of the character of the Preacher, or Author, from whom we have received either pleasure or instruction. Perhaps too, on the subject of Theology, we are apt to attach too much importance to the instrument, and too little to that sacred Agent by whom he was fitted for his work, and who also renders his labours profitable to us. Here however we feel pleasure in saying, we cannot contemplate the life and character of JOHN GILL, without pronouncing him one of the greatest and best of men. He was born at Kettering, in Northamptonshire, Nov. 23, 1697, of amiable and pious parents, Edward Gill, and Elizabeth his wife, whose maiden name was Walker. By an indulgent providence they were equally saved from the trials of poverty, and the snares of affluence, and spent their days pleasantly and profitably, in the pious circle where a covenant God assigned their lot.

The father, Mr. Edward Gill, first became a member of the dissenting congregation in that town, then consisting of Presbyterians, Independents, and Baptists. Besides their pastor, they had a teaching elder of the Baptist denomination, Mr. William Wallis, who was the administrator of Baptism by immersion, to such persons among them as desired it. At length the Baptists, having been rendered uncomfortable in their communion, by some particular persons, they were obliged to separate, with Mr. Wallis their teacher, and soon formed themselves into a distinct church, of the *Particular Baptist* denomination. Of this number was Mr. Edward Gill, who was in due time chosen to the office of Deacon among them, and to the last obtained a good report, for his grace, his piety, and holy conversation.

His young Son, with the dawn of reason, discovered a fine capacity for instruction; and being soon out of the reach of common teachers, was very early sent to the grammar school in his native town, which he attended with uncommon diligence, and unwearied application; quickly surpassing those of his own age, and others who were far his seniors. Here he continued till he was about *eleven* years old, by which time he had mastered the principal Latin Classics, and made such a proficiency in the Greek, as obtained for him marks of distinction from several of the neighbouring Clergy, who condescended occasionally to examine and encourage his progress, when they met him at a bookseller's shop on market-days, when only it was open. This shop he so regularly attended, for the sake of consulting different Authors, that it became an usual asseveration with the people in the neighbourhood, when they desired to express a certainty,—" It is as sure, as that JOHN GILL is in the bookseller's shop." And as the same studious disposition attended him through life, so did nearly the same remark; those who knew him usually employing this mode of affirmation,—" As surely as DR. GILL is in his study."

But he was obliged to leave the grammar school, thus *early*, because the *Master* of it insisted that all the children (those of *Dissenters*, as well as others) should learn the *Church* Catechism, and go with him to the *Parish* Church, &c. As his *parents* could not violate their consciences, they were *obliged* to take him from school at a time when he was making a rapid progress in human literature. Still he kept on studying, and improving his mind, in the Latin and Greek, which he had acquired; and also learned Hebrew, without any living assistance, by the help of Buxtorf's grammar and lexicon; and soon was able to read with great ease and pleasure.

About twelve years of age, his mind was seriously impressed with divine things, especially after hearing Mr. Wallis preach a sermon on Gen. iii. 9. *And the Lord God called unto Adam and said unto him, where art thou?* These interrogations sounded in his ears, and pierced his very soul; " Sinner where art thou? what a wretched condition art thou in! what will be thy state eternally? art thou able to endure everlasting burnings?"

He now began to see and feel, the depravity of his nature, the exceeding sinfulness of sin; his need of salvation, and a better righteousness than his own, even the righteousness of Christ, in order to escape the damnation of hell, and obtain the kingdom of God. It does not however appear, that this distress of soul was of long continuance; God was soon graciously pleased to reveal his Son in him, and afford him joy, and peace in believing. Soon after this event, Mr. Wallis died, but young GILL to whom the Lord had blessed his labours, survived him many years, and still lives in his valuable writings, to edify and bless the church of God. On the 1st of November, 1716, Mr. GILL was publicly baptized in a river, by Mr. Thomas Wallis, who succeeded Mr. W. Wallis in the pastoral office. Mr. GILL used to remark, " that many spectators beheld the solemn scene, which was truly imposing." The following Lord's day, Nov. 4th, he was received a member of the church, and sat down at the Lord's table. The same evening, at a meeting for prayer in a private house, he read and expounded the 53rd chapter of Isaiah; and the friends present estimated the services, as a favourable specimen of the ministerial talents, which the great Head of the church had conferred upon him, and encouraged him to proceed in the exercise of his gifts. Accordingly, the next Lord's day evening, in the same place, he delivered a discourse upon 1 Cor. ii. 2. *For I determined not to know anything among you, save Jesus Christ and him crucified.**
This, his first discourse, was heard with great pleasure; and the godly people who heard

---

* It is not a little singular, that one person who heard him deliver his *first* sermon at Kettering; nearly *fifty five years after*, heard him also deliver his *last*, in Carter Lane, London.

it, said they had a charming season. Soon after this, at the instance of some of his London friends, who had conversed with him at Kettering, he removed to Higham-Ferrers, about seven miles from Kettering; his own design was, to pursue his studies under the Rev. John Davis of that place, with whom he was to board; the design of his friends was, that he might preach occasionally in the adjacent villages, and thus be useful to the young interest at Higham-Ferrers. Here he continued the year following, and contracted an acquaintance with a young lady, who was a member of the newly gathered church, whom he married in 1718. His marriage with this excellent woman, he always considered the principal object for which God sent him to that place, for she proved herself a careful, discreet, and affectionate wife; and was continued to him upwards of forty-six years. His sermon on her death, has been esteemed one of the best of his funeral discourses. It is founded upon Heb. xi. 16. *But now they desire a better country, that is, an heavenly, &c.* By this amiable woman, he had many children, all of whom died in their infancy, except three :—Elizabeth, who departed this life, May 30, 1738, in the *thirteenth* year of her age. The funeral sermon which her father preached for her, was published, and contains a pleasing account of her dying experience. Mary, was a member of her father's church, who married Mr. George Keith, bookseller in Gracechurch Street. John, was a goldsmith, and lived many years in the same street. These children were a great happiness to their parents. During Mr. GILL's stay at Higham-Ferrers, he frequently preached to the church at Kettering, and as their pastor needed assistance, he wholly removed thither soon after his marriage. Here his ministry from the first had been blessed, not only to the conversion, but to the comfort of many, who long continued to adorn their profession, and will, we doubt not, be the crown of his rejoicing, when the Master comes. Yet here his stay was short, for early in the year 1719, the church meeting at Fair Street, Horselydown, Southwark, London, having by death lost their pastor, Mr. Benjamin Stinton, (son-in-law of the famous Benjamin Keach, and his successor in the pastoral office,) invited Mr. GILL to come up and preach to them, which he did in the months of April and May, and then returned into the country. About two months after, the church requested him to return, which he did, and preached to them till the beginning of September. On Thursday evening, September 10th, the question was put to the church, whether they should on the next Lord's day evening proceed to the election of Mr. GILL to the Pastoral office. The question was carried in the affirmative by the whole, except 12 or 13 persons. On the following Lord's day evening, the same question passed in the affirmative, by *a large majority.*

Mr. GILL accepted the call; but owing to trouble arising out of his election, he was not ordained till March 22nd, 1720. Here we have the gratification of shewing the order of our Ordination services, one hundred and thirty-nine years ago. "The early part of the meeting being intended chiefly for the members, and serious hearers; they spent some time in prayer among themselves, and when they had sung a hymn, paused. This was felt to be a pleasant preparation for the more public work before them. Accordingly, as soon as the pastors of the churches who had been invited to be present on the occasion, came in; the Rev. John Skepp, author of that valuable book, entitled "Divine Energy," proposed several questions to the church; which were answered by Mr. Thomas Crosby, a deacon, afterwards author of the 'History of the Baptists;' who stated, in the course of what he said, that on the day which had been previously appointed by the church, to proceed to the election of a pastor, Mr. GILL was chosen by *a great majority*. The Rev. Messrs. Matthews and Ridgeway now prayed, when the Rev. Mr. Noble desired the members of the church to recognize their choice of Mr. GILL to the pastoral office. He then requested Mr. GILL to confirm his acceptance of the call, which he did, with a full and solemn declaration. The Rev. Mr. Curtis, and the aged and Rev. Mark Key, of Devonshire Square, were appointed to take the lead in the distinctive part of Ordination; and the excellent man was ordained by the laying on of hands. Three brethren were also ordained and set apart to the office of deacons, Mr. GILL joining with the other elders in the imposition of hands. Mr. Noble then went into the pulpit and delivered an exhortation to the pastor and deacons, from Acts xx. 23. *Take heed therefore unto yourselves, &c.* The church records say, ' The sermons were suitable to the occasion, and excellent.' Mr. GILL then went up and called upon the Lord ; they then sung the 133rd psalm, (Patrick's version) and Mr. GILL dismissed the assembly, with one of the apostolical benedictions."

Thus we have traced the life of Mr. GILL, up to his public settlement in the pastoral office, over one of the oldest churches of our denomination in the Metropolis ; we now see him standing in the place of the justly celebrated Benjamin Keach, who was a frequent sufferer for his principles, by fines, imprisonments, and pillory ; henceforward, it will be our business to trace his career through the several departments of public life, in which he stood prominent.

First, we shall view him as a man of letters. Here he shone as a star of no ordinary lustre, of which it might be sufficient to note, the many and learned works which he has left behind are the best proof. Among these; his dissertation concerning the " Antiquity of the Hebrew language, letters, vowel-points, and accents." This masterly effort of profound research, would have shewn our author to be a prodigy of reading and literature, had he never published a syllable upon any other subject. Scholars of the first class have expressed themselves astonished at the erudition every where so conspicuous in this book. We have before noticed his very early acquiring a knowledge of the Latin, Greek, and Hebrew languages. To these he afterwards added the Arabic, Syriac, Chaldaic, Persiac, and other oriental languages, together with an extensive acquaintance with the languages of modern Europe ; the knowledge of which induced that sensible and learned man, the Rev. Augustus Toplady, to say of him, " If any one man can be said to have trodden the whole circle of human learning, it was Dr. GILL." As it relates to the extent of his reading, let the following statement which was forced from him in self-vindication in the year 1736, when he was forty-two years of age, testify.—That he had read the Classics and Virgil at nine years of age.—That he had read Logic, Rhetoric, Ethics, Physics, and Metaphysics. The Ethnic Philosophers, Platonists and Stoics. The Greek and Roman Historians, Herodotus, Pausanias, Livy, Sallust, &c. The Greek and Latin Fathers of the christian Church, and church history. —That he had also read the Jewish-Targums, the Misnah, the two Talmuds, Babylonian, and Jerusalem ; the Rabbot, Midrashim, Zohar, with other writings of the Jews, ancient and modern.

One thing however we desire the reader to keep in mind, lest he should charge the good man with egotism ; he had been called a *botcher in Divinity*, by one who was considered far his inferior, and who represented him as one out of only *two* or *three* who had even the smatterings of learning.

He then added, " I am not now too old to learn, and through divine goodness do not want industry, diligence and application." Of this last sentence he gave full proof, for after he had penned the above section, he published his Exposition of the whole Bible; his Body of Divinity; with many other of his excellent works.

If any thing more is needed upon this head, we would refer to his deep acquaintance with *Rabbinical* literature, of which he has made such copious use in his Exposition; his dissertation upon the vowel-points, and Jewish Proselyte Baptism. Entirely on these grounds, Mr. Gill was in the year 1748 presented with a Diploma from the Marischal College, Aberdeen, creating him D. D. which was sent him gratuitously. The following is a short extract from that document.—" Whereas we have discovered, that the Rev. John Gill, A. M. Pastor of a church in London, has made a very distinguished progress in sacred literature, the oriental languages, and Jewish Antiquities; and is endowed with those manners which become a pious and upright man: Know ye, that we have created and constituted him Doctor of Sacred Divinity, and we do hereby earnestly recommend him to the cultivators of science and virtue, wherever they be."

When his friends complimented him upon the honour which had been conferred upon him, the good man jocosely and quaintly replied, " I neither *sought* it, nor *thought* it, nor *bought* it."

We now take a view of Dr. GILL in the character of a Preacher of the Gospel. Here he sustained no ordinary reputation. In his early days, few persons were more animated, or preached with greater fluency and ease to themselves, or profit to their hearers, than he did. He came at times into the pulpit, evidently from the mount of secret communion with God; his face shining with a heavenly lustre, his heart warm with the fire of love, and really in the fulness of the gospel of Christ; enriched, and generally enriching. He usually wrote a very short outline of his sermon, which served to impress the substance of it upon his memory, and rendered his subject familiar to him while preaching; but he never resorted to the servile method of delivering his sermons, *memoriter*, as it is called. Of him it cannot be said—

> " He toil'd and stow'd his lumber in his brain,
> He toil'd, and then he dragg'd it out again."

His heart was full, and out of the abundance of his heart, his mouth freely spake.

When the fervour of youth had abated, his public services sustained great reputation by his expressive language, his perspicuous method, his accurate delivery, but above all by the solidity, fulness, and preciousness of the matter, with which they were fraught. Whatever was his subject, the leading doctrines of Salvation ran through it from beginning to end; so that his hearers could always perceive he was encircled in everlasting love, resting upon the atonement of Jesus, and animated by the Holy Ghost. If any one man who has ever appeared in the character of a minister of Christ, deserved to be called a clear, faithful, discriminating, and consistent preacher, Dr. GILL was that man.

Hence it was, that in the year 1729, many members of other churches, being anxious to hear him, united themselves into a society, and invited him to undertake a lecture on a

Wednesday evening, in "Great East Cheap;"* to this he assented, and commenced by preaching on Psalm lxxi. 16. *I will go in the strength of the Lord God, I will make mention of thy righteousness, even of thine only.* He tells his hearers, he selected these words, partly to shew he did not undertake the lecture in his own strength, but in the strength of Christ; and partly to shew that his resolutions were to preach the great and glorious doctrine of a sinner's justification before God, by the righteousness of Christ imputed to him; which he considered to be the centre arch of that bridge, by which the believer passes out of time into a blissful eternity.

This lecture, which he preached more than 26 years, was productive, not only of many of his excellent sermons, but also of whole treatises,—on the Trinity, Justification, Cause of God and Truth, and also many of his Commentaries.

This service, however, he declined in 1756, and upon March 24th, preached his farewell sermon from Acts xxvi. 22, 23. *Having therefore obtained help of God, I continue until this day,* &c. Here he tells his audience, "I have nothing to complain of, the lecture was never in better circumstances than it is now; but I find my natural strength will not admit me to preach so frequently, being now in the *fortieth* year of my ministry, so that it is time for me to have done with extra service. But a more principal reason is, that I may have a little more time to attend to, and finish, an arduous work upon my hands, 'An Exposition of the whole Old Testament;' and I have no other way of easing myself, but by dropping this lecture. These, and these only, are my reasons for so doing."†

Another proof of Dr. GILL's popularity as a preacher, is, that he was so frequently employed in preaching ordination and funeral sermons, together with other public services, amongst the Dissenters generally, and his own denomination in particular.

Again, we contemplate Dr. GILL as the *consistent and unflinching advocate of Evangelical Truth.* In this department, he shone as a star of the very first magnitude. This trait in his character, shines throughout all his voluminous writings, and imparts to them an excellency seldom to be met with in other Authors. Hence his "Cause of God and Truth," in 4 vols. 8vo. published in 1735, and three following years, occasioned by the reprinting of Dr. Whitby's book upon the *five points*,‡ which was boasted of as unanswerable, insomuch, that the Arminians used to say, "Why not answer Dr. Whitby?" To this book, GILL did reply, and to his reply no answer has ever been given, nor *can* be, while the word of God continues the standard of faith; and reason exists, to judge between truth and error. But why do we select this work, apart from others, seeing all his writings are not only illustrative of the great doctrines and precepts of the gospel, but most of them were published in direct defence of the truths which they illustrate. It is also worthy of observation, that GILL's controversial works, were generally, if not exclusively, on the *defensive* side of the question. His own retired, quiet, and peace-

---

* This meeting-house has since been pulled down.

† Farewell Sermon at Great East-Cheap Lecture.

‡ The *five points.*—It may not be amiss to enumerate those five points, which were originally disputed between the Arminians and Calvinists. 1. Election. 2. Particular redemption. 3. Original sin. 4. Efficacious grace. 5. Final perseverance. These were the five *main* points, but there were many others.

able disposition, would never have allowed him to become an aggressive polemic; but whenever he perceived the honour of his master assailed, or any branch of divine truth reviled, his soul was always roused into thought, his tongue was prepared to speak, and his hand ready to seize his pen, regardless of what men might say, or even timid friends suggest. Hence when Dr. Abraham Taylor attacked the doctrines of Eternal union and justification, in a sermon which Dr. GILL heard, and which was read to several ministers for their approbation, before being sent to the Press; the Doctor went prepared to offer his reasons, in a kind manner, why those passages should be left out; but to his great pleasure he found the sentences *were* omitted, therefore of course he said nothing, hoping Dr. Taylor had altered his mind respecting them. But when the sermon issued from the press, with those objectionable sentences in it, our friend felt it his duty publicly to remonstrate with Dr. Taylor; he therefore wrote and printed a letter, entitled " The doctrine of God's everlasting love to his elect, and their eternal union with Christ; together with some other truths stated and defended, in a letter to Dr. Abraham Taylor." This letter has by some been thought to be the *very best* production of his pen; every sentence being replete with precious truth, so encouraging to the timid, so establishing to the wavering, and so rich with the unction of the Holy Ghost. When the Doctor was preparing this publication for the press, some of his people waited upon him, and dissuaded him from going on; urging among other things, that he would lose the esteem, and of course the subscriptions of some wealthy persons, who were Taylor's friends. To this he in a moment replied,—" Dont tell me of losing, I value nothing in comparison of gospel truths. I am not afraid to be poor. I have chosen to suffer reproach, the loss of good name and reputation, to forego popularity, wealth, and friends; yea, to be traduced as an antinomian, rather than to *drop or conceal one branch of truth respecting Christ and free grace.*"

At the commencement of his spiritual campaign, he buckled on his Armour, and never unloosed it but to put on his Shroud. Hence we find him vindicating the divine authority of Solomon's Song; in a series of 122 discourses; forming a folio volume. Concerning which, that excellent judge of men and books, the Rev. James Hervey, has passed the following encomium :*—" It has such a copious view of sanctified invention running through it, and is interspersed with such a variety of delicate and brilliant images, as cannot but highly entertain a curious mind. It presents us also with such rich and charming displays of the glory of Christ's person, the freeness of his grace to sinners, and the tenderness of his love to the church, as cannot but administer the most exquisite delight to the believing soul. Considered in *both* these views, I think the work resembles the Paradisaical garden described by MILTON the poet, in which

> Blossoms, and fruits, at once of golden
> Hue appeared, with gay enamell'd colors mixed."

The Messiahship of Christ also, from the prophecies of the Old Testament; the doctrine of the Trinity; the whole Calvinistic scheme of Truths, in his defence of the Cause of God and Truth; shewing those doctrines to be based upon the scriptures, in harmony with reason; and in agreement with the christian writers of the first four centuries.

* Theron and Aspasio, letter 9th.

Also, his EXPOSITION OF THE BIBLE, in nine vols. folio. This is a most wonderful production, in every view we can take of it; as a work of labour it is Herculean; and as the production of *one* man, certainly is a prodigy. It must not be lost sight of, that in Dr. GILL's Exposition, you have *every verse included.* It is not a running paraphrase of a section, nor a brief comment upon a paragraph, in which you frequently discover the ingenuity of the author by his getting over a difficult verse, with a short maxim or pretty saying, shewing how expert he is in leaving a perplexity behind: but he *meets* the difficulty, examines it on every side; and, if he does not remove it, he generally *illuminates* the subject for us. We see that he has laboured his point, and seldom rise from the perusal of his criticisms, without deriving some benefit from his labours.

" In short," says Dr. Rippon, " his Exposition is of unquestionable celebrity, in the republic of letters, as well for its unparalleled learning, as for its profound research: and has obtained the affluence of fame among all the evangelical denominations, at home and abroad. It yields to no theological publication whatever, in decision of character, and in a manly avowal of the grand fundamental doctrines of the gospel, considered in their native dignity and in their practical influence. It is also the only Exposition of the Old and New Testament, which the Baptists can, at present, claim as their own, either in Great Britain, or in America." That great man, John Ryland, Senr., has recorded the following commendation :—" Dr. Gill's Exposition of the Old and New Testament, is an *ocean of sound* divinity. The remarkable excellences of this great work, are, *a consistency with his truly evangelical principles throughout the whole.* Not to mention the vast treasures of learning in the Jewish Targums and Talmuds, which that man possessed *above all* the divines of our age."

But perhaps, amidst all the ten thousand folio pages of Dr. GILL, the Work which crowns the whole is, his BODY OF DIVINITY. This was his last work, and contains the substance of what he delivered to his people through the space of five or six years. Here you see his whole heart, in stating, illustrating, and defending the truth as it is in Jesus. Here you perceive his system ; the harmony of one truth with another, and each and all with the sacred oracles of God. We cannot but congratulate the student in divinity, and the christian world at large, upon the reprinting of the present edition of this matchless work ; so admirably calculated to assist the humble enquirer after truth, and counteract that spurious calvinism so rife in the present day. Indeed we venture to assert, respecting the leading Doctrinal sentiments of Dr. GILL ; that they are in harmony with the *Scriptures*, and with *themselves.*

GILL was neither an antinomian, nor an arminian. Not an antinomian, for he maintained the law as the rule of the believer's conduct ; not an arminian, for no man more fully defended the five calvinistic points, than himself. Yea, so uniformly consistent was his creed considered, that his name, in connection with Theology, indicated harmonious truth. Hence the following lines from the pen of that admirer of consistent divinity, the late Mr. Thos. Gurney, short-hand writer, at the conclusion of his poem called the " Mongrel Calvinist."*

" Whenever I hear, if I might have my will;
I'd have it all of a piece, either *Whitby* or *Gill.*"

* Lately reprinted, sold by Highams, Chiswell Street.

Ryland says, "Dr. GILL is the only systematic writer in our language who has treated wisely on the divine perfections. His discourses are clear, judicious, and very correct."* Indeed, so highly was his judgment appreciated, that the elegant and ingenious James Hervey, whose name has already been mentioned, desired he would "run over Theron and Aspasio, with his pen in his hand, and minute down whatever he saw unevangelical in doctrine, inconclusive in argument, obscure, ambiguous, or improper in expression." In this letter Mr. Hervey says, "I owe you thanks for your sermons on the ransom, on faith, and on good Mr. Seward's death; they are all sweet to my taste, and I trust have been a blessing to my soul." Concluding as follows—" Your affectionate though very weak brother in Christ. James Hervey."

We now return to trace the character of Dr. GILL, as the uniform Dissenter, and consistent Baptist. We have shewn at the beginning of this memoir, that his parents were Baptists, and that early in life he was himself baptized, and cast in his lot with that body of christians; and we feel pleasure in recording the fact, that from these principles he never swerved in the slightest degree.

Directly upon the subject of *Dissent* he wrote but little, but his Tract called, " The Dissenters reasons for separating from the Church of England," is clear, and concise; and shews in every line the hand of a master; it were devoutly to be wished this little book could be put into the hand of every man, woman, and child, in the kingdom.

Our author was first called into the field of controversy upon the baptismal question in the year 1726, in reply to a dialogue, written by a Mr. Maurice, at Rowel, Northamptonshire. The baptists in those parts, especially at Kettering, about two miles off, considered themselves struck at by this pamphlet, and therefore sent it up to him, and requested he would reply to it; he accordingly soon gratified them by publishing a piece called " *The ancient mode of baptism by immersion.*" To this Mr. Maurice replied in 1727. This GILL answered in the same year, in a tract which he designated " A defence of the ancient mode," &c.

Mr. Maurice sent several of his pamphlets into North America, and the baptists there, hearing of Mr. GILL's answer, wrote for some of them, and the remaining part of the impression was sent over, at the expense of the baptist fund.

On account of this controversy, GILL received from Tilbury Fort, in Essex, a very spirited anonymous letter; animating him to continue in it, and not to be intimidated by his puny adversary; concluding with the following lines :—

> Stennett,† at first, his furious foe did meet,
> Cleanly compell'd him to a swift retreat :
> Next powerful *Gale*,‡ by mighty blast made fall,
> The church's Dagon, the gigantic *Wall :* §
> May you with like success be victor still,
> And give your rude antagonist his fill,
> To see that *Gale* is yet alive in *Gill*.

---

* Contemplations, vol. 2. 412.

† Mr. Joseph Stennett, a very learned baptist minister, who died July 11th, 1713. He wrote a triumphant reply to David Russen's book, entitled "Fundamentals without a foundation, or a true picture of the anabaptists."

‡ Dr. Gale, a learned general baptist; author of " Reflections on Dr. Wall's history of Infant Baptism."

§ Dr. Wall, who wrote the history of Infant Baptism: but it is not a little singular, that he advocated *immersion* as the mode. See Ivimey, p. 563. vol. 1.

Our author having once commenced writing on the subject of Baptism, and being determined in the strength of the Lord to contend for the whole range of truth *ritually*, as well as *doctrinally*, found plenty of work cut out for him, nor did he flinch from the performance of it; but whenever the authority of the Redeemer was impugned, he was always found at his post, and his numerous pieces upon the subject, all clearly shew, how well he was qualified for the part he took in the controversy. One, out of the nine or ten Tracts upon this point, has so singular a title, and so fully justifies the startling designation which he has given it, that it deserves more than barely to be mentioned:

In the preface to one of his books, the Doctor used the following language,—"The pædobaptists are ever restless and uneasy, endeavouring to support, if possible, their unscriptural practice of Infant Baptism; though it is no other than a pillar of Popery; that by which Antichrist has spread his baneful influence over many nations; is the basis of national churches, and worldly establishments; that which unites the church and the world, and keeps them together; nor can there be a full separation of the one from the other, nor a thorough reformation in religion, until it is wholly removed. And though it has so long and so largely obtained, and still does obtain, I believe with a firm and unshaken faith, that the time is hastening on, when Infant Baptism will be no more practised in the world; when churches will be formed on the same plan they were in the times of the apostles; when gospel-doctrine and discipline, will be restored to their primitive lustre and purity; when the ordinances of Baptism and the Lord's Supper will be administered as they were first delivered, clear of all present corruption and superstition; all which will be accomplished when the Lord shall be king over all the earth, and there shall be one Lord, and his name one."

When this paragraph appeared in print, he was called upon, either to expunge, or prove it; he chose the *latter;* and wrote a book entitled, "Infant Baptism, a part and pillar of Popery." It is an easy task to make assertions, though much more difficult to prove them; but whoever has read with an unbiassed mind, the nineteen quarto pages referred to, must feel convinced that not only did the good Dr. justify his assertion, but triumphantly established his premises; by shewing that "Infant Baptism is in reality a *part and pillar* of Popery."

We cannot, however, in justice to DR. GILL, close our remarks upon this part of his memoir, without noticing the fact of his having razed one of the foundations upon which Infant Baptism is built, completely to the ground: (viz.) "Jewish Proselyte Baptism." It had been asserted by some pædobaptists of literary eminence;—"That it was a custom among the Jews before the time of Christ, to receive proselytes into their church by baptism, as well as by circumcision; and these both adults and infants; that John and Christ took up the ordinance of baptism from them, practised it, and directed to the continued use of it; and that this circumstance accounts for the silence about Infant Baptism in the New Testament:" it being as they say, no new practice. Dr. Hammond had said, "*this* was the basis of Infant Baptism;" and Sir Richard Ellys had declared, "he knew not of *any stronger argument in favour of Infant Baptism, than this*." Assertions like these, determined GILL to examine the point fully and carefully for himself. Therefore he waded through all the labyrinths of rabbinical literature; and arrived at the perfect satisfaction, that not a single instance can be given, from any rabbinical work *before* the time of Christ, of any one proselyte being baptized. Such being the case, he triumphantly concludes; "If this is the basis of Infant Baptism, it is built upon the sand; and will ere long fall, and be no more."

One thing more deserves to be mentioned, before we quit this view of the Doctor's character. That he uniformly advocated and practised, what is now sinking into disrepute; (viz.) Baptism upon a profession of faith, as a pre-requisite to the Lord's table.

Our lot is cast in an age remarkable for accommodation: if simple truth offends, the parties must be accommodated, by softening down, or explaining away, that part of it which appears most objectionable; and if the baptism of believers in order to church-fellowship, be considered too troublesome, the door must be thrown open wide enough to receive those who cannot see baptism to be an act of personal religion, enjoined upon every follower of the Lamb, by him who said, *Go teach all nations, baptizing them in the name of the Father, and of the Son, and of the Holy Ghost.* Now upon this subject no less than others, was our good Doctor at a point.

To justify these remarks, we subjoin the two following quotations. The first is an article which he drew up himself, and inserted in the Church book with his own hand.—" We believe that baptism and the Lord's supper are ordinances of Christ, to be continued until his second coming; and that the former is absolutely requisite to the latter: that is to say, that those only are to be admitted into the communion of the church, and to participate of all ordinances in it, who, upon a profession of their faith, have been baptized by immersion, in the name of the Father, and of the Son, and of the Holy Ghost."

The other extract is from a Sermon entitled, "The Scriptures, the only guide in matters of religion."—

Speaking of Baptism he says,—" This is a way of duty, but not of life and salvation; it is a command of Christ to be obeyed by all believers in him, but not to be trusted in and depended on; it is ESSENTIAL TO CHURCH COMMUNION, but not to salvation. It is indeed no indifferent thing whether it is performed or no; this ought not to be said or thought, of any ordinance of Christ; or whether in this or the other manner, or administered to this or the other subject. It ought to be done as Christ has directed it should; but when it is best done, it is no saving ordinance: this, I the rather mention, to remove from us a wicked and foolish imputation, that we make an idol of this ordinance, and place our confidence and dependence on it, and put it in the room of the Saviour. I call it wicked, because false; and foolish, because contrary to an avowed and well-known principle on which we proceed; namely, that faith in Christ alone for salvation, is a pre-requisite to baptism. Can any man in his senses think that we depend on this ordinance for salvation, when we require that a person should believe in Christ, and profess that he believes in Christ alone for salvation, before he is baptized; or otherwise we judge he is not a fit subject? But, on the other hand, those that insinuate such a notion as this, would do well to consider, if their own conduct does not bespeak something of this kind; or otherwise, what means the stir and bustle that is made when a child is ill, and not yet sprinkled, &c. What means such language as this, 'Run, fetch the minister to baptize the child, the child is dying!' Does it not look as if this was thought to be a saving business, or as if a child could not be saved unless it is sprinkled; and which, when done, they are quite easy and satisfied about its state."[a]

[a] Scriptures the only guide in matters of religion, vol. 2. p. 493. 4to.

The above quotation exhibits, what we conceive to be, a just and scriptural view of the importance of believer's baptism; shewing the position it occupies in relation to the church of Christ, and its binding obligation upon all believers; not in order to secure their salvation, but as an act of *personal religion*, and *spiritual worship*, arising out of their relationship to him who *loved them and gave himself for them*. They are therefore baptized, because, when he condescended to set them the example in Jordan, he said, *Thus it becometh us to fulfil all righteousness*.

We now return to review our author as a christian Pastor. Here we are supplied with very scanty materials; but these were in his day sufficient to weave for him a wreath of honour, which will not soon fade away. In his heart he was sympathetic; in his prayers for his people he was copious, pointed, and ardent; and in his carriage conciliating and kind, especially when he saw weakness blended with christian sincerity. An anecdote illustrative of this part of his character is recorded, and deserves a place here. A godly woman visited him one day in great trouble about the singing; for the clerk in about *three years*, had introduced *two new* tunes. With this improvement, the young people were pleased, but the good woman was distressed. After patiently listening to her doleful tale, the Doctor asked her, whether she understood singing? No, she said. What! cannot you sing? "No, she was no singer, nor her aged father before her; and though they had had about a hundred years between them to learn the Old Hundredth tune, they could not sing either that, or any other tune." The Doctor did not wound her feelings by telling her, that people who did not understand singing were the last who should complain; but kindly said, "Sister, what tunes should you like us to sing?" "Why, sir," she replied, "I should very much like *David's tunes!*" "Well, (said he) if you will get David's tunes for us, we can then try to sing them."

In fine, he was not only respected, but beloved by his members generally, for his prayers and preaching, as well as for his amiable and upright conduct in the church. Dr. Rippon says of those that survived him, "They gladly made him the subject of their conversation, and were always happy to hear any one speak of him, with his merited respect."

His ministerial and pastoral labours, by the blessing of God, were much owned for the awakening, conversion, comfort, edification and establishment of many. Several persons, who had been converted under his ministry, were afterwards called to the important work themselves. The Rev. Messrs. John Brine, William Anderson, and James Fall: these *three* he thought of with pleasure and gratitude. *Mr. Brine* is a well-known writer of the superior cast, belonging to the *old* school; he was for many years Pastor of the Baptist Church in Currier's Hall, Cripplegate. And *Mr. Anderson*, who settled at Grafton Street, Soho; as well as *Mr, Fall*, who was pastor of the Baptist Church at Watford, maintained respectable characters; they died before Dr. GILL, and for each of them he printed a funeral sermon, from which they appear in an honourable light.

It ought also to be recorded, that a Son of the last mentioned minister, became a member of Dr. GILL's church; was called to the work of the ministry, and upon the death of Mr. Wilson, of Prescott Street, preached on probation to that church for nearly eleven months; at the expiration of which period, he was chosen by a small majority, to the pastoral office. Unhappily, however, the deacons, trustees, and principal part of the influence, being on the side of the minority, Mr. Fall's friends were obliged to withdraw, in order to retain the minister of their choice. This painful event, led to the erection of the chapel in *Little Alie Street*, which was opened for public worship, June 26th, 1754. There the ministry of Mr. Fall was much blessed, till death terminated his labours, Oct. 1756. Thus we see the separation which the enemy of souls intended for evil, has been overruled for great good; for the all-wise head of the church, has, till this day, not only maintained the existence of the church in Little Alie Street, but abundantly blessed the gospel there, to the ingathering of the scattered objects of redeeming love to the friend of sinners.

It remains now for us to take one more glance at our worthy author, and divine; in that most of all important character; the humble, holy, and happy christian.

Of his conversion to God in early life, we have already given some account; it might therefore be sufficient to add, *that* character he sustained, holily, and unblamably, throughout a long life. He walked with God, until the time came that he was not, for God took him. Respecting his health, the Lord was very merciful to him, being seldom interrupted in his work by affliction. In his sight also, he was much favoured, for although it was what is usually termed a short sight, yet it was so strong, that he could, till within a few weeks of his death, read the smallest print without glasses, *which he never used.* His last labours among his people, were the sermons which he preached from Luke i. 77, 78. *To give knowledge of salvation unto his people by the remission of their sins, through the tender mercy of our God; whereby the day-spring from on high hath visited us.* This was the last text he ever preached from.

His health had for some time been on the decline, and he thought his work was done. Still, he more than once expressed a desire to finish the song of Zacharias, proceed as far as good old Simeon, and then "depart in peace." But this desire his heavenly Father did not see fit to grant. The decay of nature however was very gradual, attended with much pain, and loss of appetite. This visitation of his gracious God, he was enabled to bear with patient composure, and sweet resignation, never uttering a single complaint; and although he was unable to preach, he employed himself in his study till within two or three weeks of his decease; and while so employed, was seized for death: yet his faith was unshaken, and his hope firm to the last. Writing to his nephew, Mr. John Gill, of St. Albans,* he thus expresses himself:—
"I depend wholly, and alone, upon the free, sovereign, eternal, unchangeable love of God; the firm and everlasting covenant of grace, and my interest in the Persons of the Trinity, for my whole salvation; and not upon any righteousness of my own; or on anything in me, or done by me under the influences of the Holy Spirit." And then, as confirming what he had written, added, "Not upon any services of mine, which I have been assisted to perform for the good of the church, but, upon my interest in the Persons of the Trinity, the free grace of God, and the blessings of grace streaming to me through the blood and righteousness of Christ, as the ground of my hope. These are no new things to me, but what I have long been acquainted with; what I can live and die by. I apprehend I shall not be here long, but this you may tell to any of my friends."

* This worthy minister departed this life March 8th, 1809, aged 79 years.

He expressed himself in a similar manner to other friends; to one he said, "I have nothing to make me uneasy;" adding, in honour of the glorious Redeemer, the following lines of the pious Watts.

> He rais'd me from the deeps of sin,
> The gates of gaping hell;
> And fix'd my standing more secure,
> Than 'twas before I fell.

This holy calmness, and heavenly peace of mind, never left him. That Jesus, whom he had extolled as a Lawgiver, a King, and a Saviour, continued precious to him; and that Holy Spirit, whose distinct personality, office-character, and agency, he had uniformly advocated, lifted up a standard against the enemy, and imparted to his soul, "while stretched for the flight, and ready to be gone," those sacred prelibations of glory which enabled him joyfully to exclaim with his dying breath, " O my Father, my Father!" which were the last words he was heard to utter.

Thus honourably, peaceably, and happily, terminated the mortal career of the *great John Gill*, on the 14th of October, 1771, aged seventy-three years, ten months, and ten days.

His mortal remains were interred in Bunhill Fields, whither they were followed by a vast train of mourning coaches, and weeping friends. His friend and admirer, the Rev. Augustus Toplady, earnestly desired he might officiate at his grave. This affectionate respect was suitably acknowledged; but, as he finished his course most intimately united to his own denomination, without even the semblance of a dereliction either of principle or practice, the church very courteously declined the offer; and chose the Rev. Benjamin Wallin, M. A. of Maze Pond, to perform that last token of respect. Dr. Samuel Stennett preached his funeral sermon; besides which, the number of others which were preached all through Great Britain, and in various parts of America, when the providence became known, exceeded, probably, all that had ever been known before or since, respecting an individual; proclaiming, as with the voice of unusual lamentation, "A GREAT MAN IS FALLEN IN ISRAEL."

> Great GILL to dust! how dreadful is the sound!
> How vast the stroke is, and how wide the wound!
> The muse that mourns a nation's fall,
> Should wait at Gill's sad funeral.
> Should mingle Majesty and groans,
> Such as she sings to sinking thrones;
> And, in deep sounding numbers, tell
> How Sion trembled, when this Pillar fell.

His *Tomb*, according to the division of the ground in Bunhill-fields, is situated 19 east and west, and 65 and 66 north and south. The following is a *translation* of the Latin inscription upon the Stone, which was drawn up by his friend, the Rev. Dr. Stennett.*

In this Sepulchre
Are deposited the remains
Of JOHN GILL,
Professor of sacred Theology;
A man of unblemished reputation,
A sincere disciple of Jesus,
An excellent preacher of the gospel,
A courageous defender of the Christian faith:
Who,
Adorned with piety, learning, and skill,
Was unwearied in works of prodigious labour,
For more than fifty years.
To obey the commands of his great Master,
To advance the interests of the church,
To promote the salvation of men,
Impelled with unabated ardour,
He put forth all his strength.
He placidly fell asleep in Christ,
The fourteenth day of October,
In the year of our Lord, 1771,
In the seventy-fourth year of his age.

Had the whole works of this pre-eminently great man, been published in uniform *folio,* they would have amounted to the amazing aggregate, of MORE THAN TEN THOUSAND PAGES. All written with his own hand, and all corrected, as they passed through the press, by himself alone. They comprise,

1. An EXPOSITION of the OLD and NEW TESTAMENT, in nine vols. folio. This matchless work was republished by Matthews and Leigh, in 1810, in nine vols. quarto; it is now getting scarce.

2. DISCOURSES upon the BOOK of CANTICLES, folio. This work has been several times reprinted; but is now scarce.

3. The CAUSE OF GOD AND TRUTH. Originally published in four vols. octavo. This also has passed through several editions; the last of which has just issued from the press, in one vol. octavo, it is beautiful, and cheap.

4. SERMONS and TRACTS, published at different times. These were principally republished after the Doctor's death, by his son-in-law, Mr. Keith of Gracechurch Street, in three beautiful quarto vols. These are now scarce, and fetch a high price.

5. A BODY of DOCTRINAL and PRACTICAL DIVINITY. This was first given to the public in three vols. quarto, in the years 1769, and 1770; was reprinted in 1795, in three vols.

---

* Ivimey's History of the Baptists, vol. 3. p. 453.

royal octavo; but the paper was bad, and the whole of the getting up was unworthy the character of such a valuable and standard work. In 1815 another edition was published, in one vol. quarto; this was neat and handsome; but, before the commencement of the present reprint, was very scarce. Besides, it wanted a *portrait* of the author, and a *memoir* of his life, which had never before accompanied this work.

In addition to all the above works, Dr. GILL republished Dr. CRISP's *Sermons*, in 2 vols. octavo, with *explanatory notes* on such passages in them as had been considered *exceptionable*. To which he prefixed, brief memoirs of Crisp. He also wrote a recommendatory preface to SKEPP's most excellent posthumous work on DIVINE ENERGY.

It is a subject much to be lamented, that a complete and uniform edition of GILL's WORKS, has never been presented to the public. It was, we believe, once attempted by Keith; but he finished his course, before he had completed his design; leaving only the Exposition from the 132nd Psalm, to the end of the Prophets, incomplete. Had the life of Mr. Keith been spared a little longer, we should then have had the whole of Dr. GILL's works, in *twenty-two* vols. 4to. in a style of perfection seldom excelled. Surely while the press is teeming with the frothy and flimsy productions of the present day; and the Arminian and Semi-Arminian books of the past century; it is rather a reflection upon the zeal of the friends of TRUTH, that sixty-seven years should have been suffered to run out, without an uniform edition of Dr. GILL's writings.

> "So heav'n-taught GILL! shone thy transparent breast
> With light divine! imbib'd from the sole fount
> Of evangelic and celestial Truth.
> Deep did'st thou dig in *Revelation's* mine
> For soul-adorning truths! which far excel
> The glowing rubies of the Persian court;
> And shine transparent through thy golden page.
> Close was thy converse, intimate and sweet,
> For half a Century, with the men of God,
> Apostles, prophets, patriarchs, priests, and kings;
> Who, from the mouth of *Inspiration*, wrote
> The *Sacred Volume!* Thy *industrious* pen
> With arduous toil, and skill profound *explain'd*.
> The awful wonders of the mystic *cross*,
> And the vast joys of the *celestial* world,
> Were thy exalted and thy darling theme.
> Thy nervous pen describ'd th' *eternal hills*,
> Where the clear stream of full salvation *springs*;
> And how that stream of full salvation *flows*
> In vast meanders down to earth and time.
> Thy radiant page *harmonious* Truth displays;
> Deep penetration, and seraphic love.
> Nor will it cease to shine, from age to age,
> Till, the bright dawn of everlasting Day!"
>
> B. FRANCIS.

We close this imperfect Memoir, with the following brilliant sketch, written by that *elegant* and *extraordinary* man, the REV. AUGUSTUS MONTAGUE TOPLADY.

"Such were the indefatigable labours, such the exemplary life, and such the comfortable death, of this great and eminent person. If any one man can be supposed to have trod the *whole circle* of human learning, it was DR. GILL." His attainments, both in abstruse and polite literature, were, what is very uncommon, equally extensive and profound. Providence had, to this end, endued him with a firmness of constitution, and an unremitting vigour of mind, which rarely fall to the lot of the sedentary and learned. It would, perhaps, try the constitutions of half the *literati* in *England*, only to *read*, with care and attention, the whole of what he wrote.

The Doctor considered not any subject superficially, or by halves. As deeply as human sagacity, enlightened by grace, could penetrate, he went to the bottom of every thing he engaged in. With a solidity of judgment, and with an acuteness of discernment, peculiar to few, he exhausted as it were, the very soul and substance of most arguments he undertook. His *style* too, resembles himself; it is manly, nervous, plain; conscious, if I may so speak, of the unutterable dignity, value, and importance of the freight it conveys; it drives, directly and perspicuously, to the point in view, regardless of affected cadence, and superior to the little niceties of professed refinement.

Perhaps no man, since the days of St. Austin, has written so largely in defence of the *system of Grace*; and certainly, no man has treated that momentous subject, in all its branches, more closely, judiciously, and successfully. What was said of *Edward* the Black Prince, that he *never fought a battle, which he did not win;* what has been remarked of the Duke of *Marlborough*, that he *never undertook a siege, which he did not carry;* may be justly accommodated to our great Philosopher and Divine: who, *so far as the distinguishing* DOCTRINES *of the gospel are concerned*, never besieged an *Error*, which he did not force from its strong holds; nor ever encountered an Adversary, whom *he* did not baffle and subdue.

His learning and labours, if exceedable, were exceeded only by the invariable sanctity of his life and conversation. From his childhood to his entrance on the ministry, and from his entrance on the ministry, to the moment of his dissolution, not one of his most inveterate opposers, was ever able to charge him with the least shadow of immorality. HIMSELF, no less than his writings, DEMONSTRATED, THAT THE DOCTRINE OF GRACE DOES NOT LEAD TO LICENTIOUSNESS. Those who had the honour and happiness of being admitted into the number of his friends, can go still *further* in their testimony. They know that his moral demeanour was more than blameless; it was from first to last consistently *exemplary*. And, indeed, an *undeviating consistency*, both in his views of evangelical *truths*, and in his *obedience* as a servant of God, was one of those qualities, by which his cast of character was eminently marked. He was, in *every* respect, *a burning and a shining light;—Burning*, with love to God, to Truth, and to Souls; —*Shining*, "as an ensample to Believers, in word, in faith, in purity:" a pattern of good works, and a model of all holy conversation and godliness.

The Doctor has been accused of *Bigotry*, by some who were unacquainted with his real temper and character. Bigotry may be defined, *such a* BLIND *and* FURIOUS *attachment to any particular principle, or set of principles, as disposes us to* WISH ILL *to those persons who differ from us in judgment.* Simple bigotry, therefore, is, *the spirit of persecution without the power;* and *persecution* is no other than *bigotry armed with force, and carrying its malevolence into act.* Hence it appears, that to be *clearly convinced* of certain propositions, as true; and to be *steadfast* in adhering to them, upon that conviction; nay, to *assent* and *defend* those propositions, to the utmost extent of argument; can no more be called *bigotry*, than the shining of the Sun can be termed ostentation. If in any parts of his Controversial Writings, the Doctor has been warmed into some little neglects of ceremony towards his assailants; it is to be ascribed, not to *Bigotry*, (for he possessed a very large share of benevolence and candour,) but to that complexional sensibility, inseparable, perhaps, from human nature in its present state; and from which, it is certain the apostles themeslves were not exempt.

His Doctrinal and Practical Writings will live, and be admired, and be a standing blessing to posterity, when their opposers are forgotten, or only remembered by the refutations he has given them. While true Religion, and sound Learning, have a single friend remaining in the British Empire, the *Works* and Name of GILL will be *precious* and revered.

May the readers of this inadequate sketch, together with him, who (though of a very different denomination from the Doctor,) pays this last and unexaggerated tribute of justice to the honoured memory of so excellent a person, participate on earth, and everlastingly celebrate in heaven, that SOVEREIGN GRACE, which its departed Champion so largely *experienced*,—to which he was so distinguished an *ornament*,—and of which he was so able a *defender!*"

>If, from *good works*, could rise our last relief,
>Who *more* could boast than this renowned Chief?
>But, these afforded not the least delight;
>They vanish'd, like a vapour, out of sight.—
>Not on his *character*, which stood renown'd,
>Not on his *labours*, which Jehovah crown'd,
>He placed the *least* dependance; from his soul
>He did most steadily *renounce the whole:*
>And, for *salvation*, fix'd on the rich *blood*
>And *righteousness*, of his incarnate God.
>*There* were his hopes, his rest, his joy, his crown;
>And, at *His* feet, he laid his *labours* down.
>Clear was his prospect of the *promised land,*
>Where in full view he saw his Saviour stand;
>He on his everlasting *love* rely'd,
>*Sunk in his arms*, and, IN FULL GLORY died.

APPENDIX 2

PUBLISHER'S FOREWORD TO OUR 1984 EDITION

PUBLISHER'S FOREWORD

This edition of Dr. John Gill's "**Complete Body of Doctrinal & Practical Divinity**" is the first volume to be published of a projected open-end set of Baptist publications entitled: "THE BAPTIST FAITH SERIES". This set will represent an exposition and defense of the "Historically Distinctive" doctrines and practices of the Strict Baptists. The publishers are unashamedly Strict Old School Baptists. We do not, however, believe that there is any power or soul-saving virtue in that name. That title is no magic amulet to be worn to ward off evil spirits nor does it insure salvation or infallibility. But, that name is a name of distinction, or so it ought to be. The name "Baptist" has been Historically and Scripturally identified with certain particular doctrines and practices. Baptists believe that an acceptance of their "Historically Distinctive" doctrines and practices is absolutely necessary to a **consistent** recognition of the Kingship of Christ as the only Head and Lawgiver of the New Testament Church. The reason the Baptist people have been willing to suffer (and die if necessary) for their distinctive beliefs is because they are convinced that loyalty to the Supremacy of Christ demands it. If we Baptists have no distinctively Scriptural beliefs and practices that are worthy of proclamation and perpetuation, then in all due honor to God and honesty to the souls of men, let us denounce our name, disband our assemblies, affiliate with the most consistently Scriptural religious organization we can find and quit adding to the "Babel and Confusion of Sectarianism", because we have no justification for our existence. If, on the other hand, we have Scriptural, Theological and Historical precedents for our beliefs and practices, let us defend them at all cost and forsake them at no cost. Some justification for this projected work, (if any be called for), is found in the five following considerations:

I. CLARITY & HONESTY DEMAND THIS RE-PUBLICATION WORK-... Strict Baptists agree, generally, with those Independent and Protestant groups that preach the Sovereignty of God and the Doctrines of Discriminating Grace, but there are some other areas of definite disagreement. These differences are no minor differences for they deal with such vital issues as the Decrees, the Covenant of Grace, the time of Justification, the utility of the Gospel, the origin, nature, government and officers of the New Testament Church, and the subjects, mode and purpose of Baptism, to name just a few disagreements. It would not be honoring to Christ, nor honest with men's souls, to cover-up or stand silent about these vitally important and extremely divisive issues. Lev. 10:9-11 states: "...it shall be a statute forever...that ye may put difference between holy and unholy, unclean and clean". Ezek. 44:23 says "...they shall teach my people the difference between the holy and profane, and cause them to discern between the unclean and the clean.", (see Isa. 40:1-6; 57:14; 62:10). These verses teach us that the servant of God is to remove obstacles that impede the saints' progress. They are to make the issues plain for the people to see. In fact, condemnation is pronounced upon those who confuse or refuse to expose the Spiritual issues and make it difficult for God's people to discern truth from error. (Isa. 5:20) "Woe unto them that call evil good and good evil; that put darkness for light and light for darkness; that put bitter for sweet, and sweet for bitter." The same condemnation was pronounced by Christ in Matt. 18:6 and Mark 9:42.

For the sake of Clarity, the Strict Baptists view the current religious scene the same way they always have, as aptly described in Song of Solomon 6:8,9, "There are threescore queens, and fourscore concubines and virgins without number, (said the Lord Jesus Christ), but my dove, my undefiled is but one." Isaiah the prophet gave further light on the religious scene of the last days in Isa. 4:1, "In that day seven women shall take hold of one man, saying, we will eat our own bread, (i.e., we will live by our own doctrine) and we will wear our own apparel, (i.e., we will be covered by a robe of our own creating), only let us be called by thy name, (i.e., recognized as belonging to Christ), to take away our reproach." The religious assemblies of all denominations claim to be the true New Testament Church. The Catholics claim this. The Episcopalians claim this, as do Presbyterians, the various Reformed groups, the Pentacostals, the Methodists and the various Arminian and Calvinistic Baptists. All the various groups make their claims and counter-claims to being the true New Testament Church, as the verses just quoted, (Song of Sol. 6:8,9; Isa. 4:1) may be used to exemplify. But, with different doctrines, different practices, different gospels, different Gods, different Christs, different origins and founders, different officers, different governments, different goals and purposes, it ought to be apparent to every thinking mind that they cannot **all** be right. Surely, ". . .an enemy hath done this.", (Matt. 13:24-30). They can **all** be wrong, but they cannot **all** be right, and only a false and spurious charity and liberality would even attempt to think them so! (Isa. 8:20).

It is a well-known and much-attested fact, that Strict Old School Baptists make the claim of being of New Testament Church origin and New Testament Church order. Their claim is based upon their concept of salvation and of baptism. Simply stated we believe that:

1. Any religious assembly that preaches a false gospel and/or practices a false baptism cannot be recognized as a true New Testament Church of gospel order. All such assemblies who fundamentally, characteristically and permanently preach a false gospel come under the indictment of Gal. 1:6-9.
2. Salvation and a profession of faith are undeniably prerequisite to baptism. Salvation is not by means of baptism. True believing disciples are the only proper subjects for baptism. Immersion is the only proper mode of baptism.
3. Scriptural baptism is absolutely necessary to church constitution, organization and existence, so much so, that where there is no Scriptural baptism there is no Scriptural church. No baptism, no church.
4. There is an intimate and inevitable connection between the true doctrine of salvation and the proper administration of baptism. Scriptural baptism is the representation of and the identification with the Scriptural plan of salvation.
5. According to the commands of Christ, the practice of the early churches of the New Testament, the Epistles of Paul, and the Confessions of Faith of all evangelical religious denominations. . . .baptism as an ordinance, was delivered to the New Testament Church to be administered by it according to Christ's commands until He returns.
6. All the aspects of baptism, (the mode, subject, purpose and administrator) are irrevocably fixed and prescribed by Christ's example and commands. These are to remain permanent and unchanged. A consistent recognition of Christ's Kingship over the soul demands that these things be so, (Mal. 1:6; Luke 6:46), for Christ only has the authority to make, give or alter the doctrines and practices of the New Testament Church.

7. Only churches of New Testament origin and New Testament order can give Scriptural baptism. Therefore, any religious society that preaches a false gospel cannot give Scriptural baptism.

What are the **ramifications** of these concepts? Consider:

1. Strict Baptists have always believed that Catholicism is a false religion that preaches a false gospel, described no doubt in Rev. 17:1-18:24. Catholic assemblies cannot, therefore, give Scriptural baptism. Many others have taken this same position as to the invalidity of Catholic baptism. The Presbyterians, for example, took the same position at the Presbyterian General Assembly (Old School), May, 1845. This is recorded in **"The Collected Writings of J.H. Thornwell"** Vol. 3, pp. 277-413, Banner of Truth Edition, 1974. We state again, Catholic baptism is unscriptural, invalid, null and void.
2. Any person with Catholic baptism has no baptism. Any denomination founded upon Catholic baptism has no baptism and therefore no church validity. The reason? . . .Number 3 above: "No baptism, no church." (See R. L. Dabney's **"Lectures in Systematic Theology"**, lecture 64, pp. 774-775, for the same conclusion, i.e., "No baptism means no church").

These concepts are the reasons for the "historic" Baptist practice of baptizing all those who came over to them from any religious society that is not of "like faith and order". This is why Baptists will not accept Protestant rantism. All Protestant denominations are founded upon Catholic and infant rantism.

Dr. John Gill, the author of the following book, was a consistent Strict Baptist. He was not a Puritan from the Episcopalians, not a Presbyterian, not a Congregationalist, not a Protestant. He was a Strict and Particular Baptist. In fact, he was not just "a Baptist," but one of their main spokesmen for over half a century. According to Dr. Richard B. Cook, pastor of the Second Baptist Church, Wilmington, Delaware, "Dr. John Gill and Rev. John Brine were for nearly half a century the chief men in the Baptist denomination", **"The Story of the Baptists in All Ages and Countries"**, 1884, Chpt. 17, p. 189. Dr. Henry C. Vedder, professor of Church History, Crozer Theological Seminary, quoted that: "Dr. John Gill was the ablest and most learned of the Baptists of his time", **"A Short History of the Baptists"**, 1907, Chpt. 16, p. 240. Dr. William Cathcart, pastor of the Second Baptist Church, Philadelphia, Penn., for 28 years, said: ". . .for 51 years Dr. John Gill was a power in London and a religious authority all over Great Britain and America- . . .his 'Body of Divinity', published in 1769, is a work without which no Theological library is complete", **"The Baptist Encyclopedia"**, 1881, pp. 452-454. The first Baptist association in America, the old Philadelphia Baptist Association, Philadelphia, Penn., esteemed Dr. Gill so highly as a sound exponent of Baptist Theology, that in their official minutes, October, 1807, they recommended that each member church of the association "subscribe for a copy of Dr. Gill's incomparable 'Exposition of the Old & New Testaments' for the use of their minister and urged all sister associations to aid in the accomplishment of this desirable object," **"The Minutes of the Philadelphia Association"**, Oct., 1807; American Baptist Publication Society, 1851, p. 439. Certainly we can say then, that Dr.

John Gill was considered to be a theologically sound Baptist by the Baptists on both sides of the Atlantic. He was esteemed to be one of the leading spokesmen, (if not "the leading spokesman"), of Baptist principles from 1726 to as late as 1807.

Clarity & Honesty demand now that we consider some of the practical conclusions of the above-mentioned facts and concepts:

1. If Dr. John Gill's theology was held in such high regard among the English and American Baptists from 1726 to as late as 1807, why is it not so today? Obviously, the majority of English and American Baptists and the Philadelphia Association were, what is "contemptuously" called today, "Gillite" Baptists, as late as 1807. What does this say for the modern Reformed or Arminian Baptists (?) who repudiate John Gill's Supralapsarian and High-Church Theology? If those who were Strict Baptists then believed like John Gill, ought not those who are really Strict Baptists believe the same today? This conclusion is inevitable, unless you take the position that the majority of Baptists then were unscriptural in their theology or that what was true then is not true now, i.e., the mutability of Divine truth. The modern Reformed, Arminian and Universal-Church Baptists (?), like the American Baptist Churches of United States, the Southern Baptist Convention and the American Baptist Association, are faced with a dilemma: (1) they must either confess that their forefathers, (the Strict and Particular Baptists of England, Scotland, Ireland, Wales and early America, the Philadelphia Baptist Association and all her sister associations), believed and preached a "false gospel" in their advocating Dr. John Gill's theology or (2) they must confess that today, they themselves preach a "new gospel" and have departed from "the faith once delivered", in repudiating Dr. John Gill's theology. Have the modern "New School" Baptists forsaken the "Old Paths"? We think so.
2. The modern Calvinistic Protestants and Independents who have "rejoiced in Dr. Gill's light for a season" must also face some pertinent questions: How can they **consistently** accept Gill's Soteriology without seriously considering his Ecclesiology? How will they answer Dr. Gill's refutation of the Protestant view of the Covenant of Grace in, **"The Divine Right of Infant-Baptism Examined and Disproved"**, 1749 or his **"Infant-Baptism a Part and Pillar of Popery,"** 1766?
3. The practical ramifications of whole-heartedly accepting Dr. Gill's principles are earth-shaking for both the modern Baptists and Protestants. No doubt, some among both groups will voice the same opinion about John Gill - "Bury the dead out of my sight". We believe, that as far as the opponents of the writings of the Strict Baptists are concerned, a conscientious effort has been made to do just that. But we also believe that there are some, (Rom. 11:5), among both groups who esteem God's Word "more than their necessary food". It is for these we are concerned.

Therefore, Clarity and Honesty about these vital and divisive issues demand that the publications which best explain those "Historically Distinctive" doctrines and practices of the Strict Baptists be made available once again to the public.

II. HISTORY DEMANDS THIS RE-PUBLICATION WORK.... "A people not conscious of their own past are adrift without purpose." This can be amplified by saying: "A people not conscious of their own past have no purpose for the present and therefore no plans for the future!" This idea relates to us the importance of knowing our history.

As far as I can judge by the light of Scripture and personal observation, there has never been a time when, generally speaking, the Baptist people were, on the one hand, more doctrinally uncertain and on the other hand, more dogmatically unscriptural than they are today. There exists among most "contemporary" Baptist people basically 3 attitudes towards their own history and doctrines: (1) apathy (2) ignorance and confusion and (3) arrogance. How has this situation come about? (Isa. 9:16) ". . .the leaders of this people cause them to err." There has been a failure on the part of leaders to speak-up and speak-out against sin. Either intentionally or ignorantly, spiritual leaders have been hesitant and lazy about properly labeling truth and error in the light of God's Word. This cowardly "soft-peddling" with sins and doctrinal defections has helped create a situation of doctrinal and theological fogs and ethical and moral twilights. It has desensitized consciences, darkened hearts and disconcerted minds to the extent that unbelief and rebellion, humanism and pragmatism have become the prevailing methodology of most Baptist Congregations. The unregenerate, in wholesale numbers, have entered our pews and our pulpits thereby subverting the spiritual nature of Christ's Kingdom and its spiritual work.

Now, a sanctified knowledge of Baptist history will go a long way in preventing and correcting this deplorable situation. Consider:

1. A knowledge of history is **commanded,** "Remember the days of old, consider the years of many generations: ask thy father and he will shew thee; thy elders and they will teach thee", (Deut. 32:7-9). . . .
2. A knowledge of history is **comforting;** David said, "I remembered Thy judgments of old, O Lord: and have comforted myself.", (Psalms 119:52).
3. A knowledge of history is **conducive** to growth in the knowledge of God Himself, so much so, that we can say that our knowledge of God is going to be hindered by our lack of knowledge about history, "The Lord is known by the judgment which he executeth: the wicked is snared in the work of his own hands.", (Psalms 9:16).
4. A knowledge of history is **convicting;** David said unto the Levites: "Sanctify yourselves. . .that ye may bring up the ark of the Lord God. . .for because ye did it not at the first, the Lord God made a breach upon us, for that we sought Him not after the due order.", (I Chron. 15:12,13). "Ask for the Old Paths where is the good way, and walk therein and ye shall find rest for your souls. But they said, we will not walk therein," (Jer. 6:16). . .(I Cor. 14:40). A study of Baptist history will make it very plain what Baptist forefathers believed and practiced. From this we can observe how far "contemporary" Baptists have departed from the "Old Paths". Surely, it is convicting. . . .in the light of the history of our Baptist forefathers, to consider Isaac Watts' words:

"Must I be carried to the skies
On flow'ry beds of ease,
While others fought to win the prize,
and sailed thro' bloody seas?"

All this leads us to see that where there is an absence of knowledge about Baptist history generally, and the "Historically Distinctive" Baptist doctrines and practices specifically, there is sure to follow:

1. a **loss** of identity
2. a **lack** of purpose and mission
3. a **looseness** and **laxity** in doctrine and practice.

There is a certain sacredness, a certain self-examination, a certain sense of responsibility that goes along with the study of history. Therefore, the solemnity, utility, and responsibility of the knowledge of Baptist history demand that those publications which best explain the history and the "Historically Distinctive" Strict Baptist doctrines and practices be made available once again to the public.

III. DUTY DEMANDS THIS RE-PUBLICATION WORK.... There is an inseparable connection between doctrine and duty. When the great fundamental doctrines of the Gospel are held in contempt and disregard, practical godliness will be at a low ebb. When the full moon of Gospel truth is brilliantly apparent, then the high tide of Gospel godliness will also be. Our convictions mold our conversation, (Prov. 23:7). The relationship between sound doctrine and godly deportment is like that which exists between a tree and the fruit it bears. It is out of the tree of sound doctrine that the fruit of godliness develops. The tree of sound doctrine is like its counterpart, the tree of the regenerated soul. . . .**both** are "of the Lord's planting", (Deut. 32:2; Psa. 1:1-3; 104:16; 92:12-14; Isa. 61:1-3; Jer. 17:7-8) and **both** inevitably have "their fruit", (Psa. 1:3; Matt. 3:10; 7:18-20; 12:33; Luke 6:43-45; John 15:1-16; I Tim. 6:3-5). Every system of false doctrine is like every unregenerate soul, it **cannot** "bring forth good fruit", (Matt. 7:18-20; Luke 6:43-45; Rom. 8:8); in the end, it **shall** be "rooted up", (Prov. 2:22; Matt. 15:13; John 15:2).

I Tim. 6:3 speaks of the "doctrine which is according to godliness." This verse defines the nature and purpose of true doctrine, which is the bringing about of a right temper of mind and a godly deportment of life; it is pure and purifying. There is no doctrine revealed in Scripture for a merely speculative, intellectual consideration, but all is to exert a potent influence upon conduct. Those who have doctrine without practice are "vainly puffed up" in their fleshly minds, (Col. 2:18). Observe in I Tim. 1:9-10 all those despicable characters listed. They are said to be among the things "which are contrary to sound doctrine," i.e., they are contrary to the conduct which sound doctrine produces.

Most "Contemporary" Baptists have not learned this concept. They have not realized the necessity for instruction "in the way of God more perfectly", (Acts 18:26). If we ever hope to see practical godliness and Christ-honoring holiness in our life and in the lives of the saints, there must be exposure to sound doctrines of discriminating grace, baptism and the true New Testament Church, and all practical duties as well, (John 17:17). Dr. John Gill believed and taught this concept of sound doctrine. Contrary to accusation, Dr. Gill was not an Antinomian, as a consideration of his printed works will prove:
1738 - "The Doctrine of Grace Cleared From the Charge of Licentiousness."

1739 - "The Law Established by the Gospel."
1739 - "The Necessity of Good Works unto Salvation."
1754 - "Neglect of Fervent Prayer Complained of."
1761 - "The Law in the Hand of Christ."
1770 - "A Body of Practical Divinity". . . As clear proof Dr. Gill was no Antinomian, listen to his own words: "I abhor the thoughts of setting the law of God aside as the rule of walk and conversation; and constantly affirm (according to Scripture) that all who believe in Christ for righteousness should be careful to maintain good works for necessary uses." **Remarks on Mr. Samuel Chandler's Sermon, Relating to the Moral Nature and Fitness of Things,** published in 1738.

It is with full purpose in mind that we re-publish the Old Strict Baptist works. We wish to promote holy living and separation from the world by exposing our readers to the sound doctrine of our forefathers. We wish to "stop the mouths of the gainsayers" who repeatedly charge Strict Baptist with Antinomianism. We hope to lay "the axe to the root of the trees", (Matt. 3:10) by revealing the cause for the lack of good works among "Modern" Baptists of all factions, i.e., there is a lack of sound doctrine.

Therefore, the obligation, purpose and means of Christian Duty and the over-all lack of "good works" among professing saints, demand that those publications which are best suited to promote holiness be made available once again to the public.

IV. POSTERITY DEMANDS THIS RE-PUBLICATION WORK. . . . .Surely, there are many who read this and many more who ought to, who have little children, sons and daughters, in their homes. Surely, common **sympathy** and parental **charity** towards our children, demand that we make every effort to acquaint them with "the Faith of their Fathers." Christian **duty** (Deut. 4:1-13; 6:5-7; 31:9-13; Psa. 48:12-14; 79:13; 145:4; Prov. 22:6; Eph. 6:4; 2 Tim. 2:2), demands this effort towards our posterity. A faithful **conformity** to the example of our fathers (Prov. 17:6; Psa. 44:1-8; Psa. 78:1-9) demands that we make it possible for this generation and the next to see what their forefathers believed. Practical **sagacity** and obvious **necessity** combine together to obligate us to make this effort. We can look ahead and see that the future existence, prosperity and peace of our Baptist Zion demand that we instruct our children in the "Historically Distinctive" doctrines and practices of our faith. If they are not "rooted and grounded" in the faith and "established in grace," they will be easily "tossed to and fro, and carried about by every wind of doctrine, by the sleight of men and cunning craftiness, whereby they lie in wait to deceive;", (Eph. 4:14, 15).

As every generation must be **evangelized,** (Matt. 28:18-20; Mk. 16:15,16; Lk. 24:44-48; John 20:21; Acts 1:4-8), so every generation must be **educated,** (Matt. 28:20; Lev. 10:1-11; Deut. 4:1-13; 6:5-7; Psa. 48:12-14; 79:13; 145:4; Eph. 6:4; 2 Tim. 2:3).

An acquaintance with the author of the following book will go a long way toward accomplishing this goal. A knowledge of the writings of Dr. John Gill will certainly strengthen the foundations of our future Baptist Zion. Therefore, Posterity, from which ever point of view you consider it, demands that the publications, (explaining our

"Historically Distinctive" doctrines and practices), which are best adapted to the sound instruction of our children, be made available once again.

V. LOYALTY DEMANDS THIS RE-PUBLICATION WORK. . . . "the Love of Christ constraineth us," (2 Cor. 5:9-16). We have saved this reason for the last, not because it is least important, but because it is most important; not to gloss over, or cancel out anything we have already said, but to state the compelling reason for all. We have found in Christ the pre-eminent object of glory, honor, virtue, goodness, love and truth. If we know our own hearts, we love Him above all things. We have read in His own Word that our love for Him should be manifested in:

1. faithful service to Christ's **Commands,** (John 14:15, 23; 15:14; I John 2:3)
2. faithful service to Christ's **Children,** (John 21:15-17); and
3. faithful service in Christ's **Church,** (Eph. 5:25; I Cor. 11:22)

The glory and honor of God is the ultimate purpose and goal for all things, (I Cor. 6:20; I Cor. 10:31; Psa. 22:23; Matt. 5:16; John 15:8; Rom. 15:6; Eph. 3:21). The Lord Jesus Christ is to be honored as his Father is honored, (John 5:23). Therefore, we believe that loyalty to Him "Whom our soul loveth", (Song of Sol. 3:1-4), demands that we make every effort to make His glory known. We believe that the "Historically Distinctive" doctrines and practices of the Strict Baptists are those doctrines which most glorify Christ as "King of the Saints". Therefore, loyalty and love combine together to demand that those publications which exalt Christ in fact, as well as name, as the only Head and Lawgiver of the New Testament Church be made available once again to the public.

IN CONCLUSION, we want our readers to be mindful of two things:

1. We would not leave you with the impression that we worship Dr. Gill. We do not think him infallible. In fact, we at this point in time feel like we cannot agree completely with Dr. Gill's statements in three areas:
    a. in his **Practical Divinity,** book three, Chpt. 1, pp. 896-915, his introductory remarks about baptism are confusing. If that were all he had ever said relative to this subject, it would have been, and no doubt is, a stumbling block. But, for those who have trouble with this particular passage we suggest they reserve their final opinion about Dr. Gill's views of baptism until they have read his 12 other works on this subject, which, D.V., we intend to re-publish in the not too distant future.
    b. in his **Practical Divinity,** book two, Chpt. 6, pp. 886-895, on Church discipline. . . . we feel that his interpretation of some of the key passages on this subject are unsound and not in line with the majority of scholarly opinion.
    c. in his **Doctrinal Divinity,** book seven, Chpt. 8, pp. 643-667, on the Millennium . . . . we wish we had more of his opinion on this subject before we make a final statement, but we are decidedly Amillennial.
    Other than these few items we esteem this work the clearest setting forth of Strict Baptist views available today.
2. We do not court controversy, (2 Cor. 4:13), but neither are we intimidated by it. If our views can be shown to be erroneous, let them be. Our instructors have only done us a

great favor thereby. We will be wiser after we are instructed in "the way of God more perfectly." If we know our own minds, we seek the prosperity and unanimity of all who believe the truth. But if our views cannot be refuted, then let them be accepted. The writings of the following author, are no exception to that statement. He will be more easily denounced than disproved.

The Baptist Standard Bearer
(Psa. 60:4,5; Isa. 59:19; 62:10-12)

Stonehaven
Paris, Arkansas
October 20, 1984

A TABLE OF TEXTS OF SCRIPTURE

EXPLAINED OR ILLUSTRATED

IN THIS BODY OF DIVINITY.

INTRODUCTION.

GENESIS.

Ch. Ver.	Page.
IV. 1, 25	xxxiii

ACTS.

Ch. Ver.	Page.
XVII. 2, 3	xxvii
XX. 21	xxvi

ROMANS.

Ch. Ver.	Page.
VI. 17	xxv
XII. 6	xxvi

2 TIMOTHY.

Ch. Ver.	Page.
I. 13	xxvi

HEBREWS.

Ch. Ver.	Page.
VI. 1, 2	xxiv

1 PETER.

Ch. Ver.	Page.
III. 21	xxxiv

GENESIS.

Ch. Ver.	Page.
I. 1	26, 131
I. 26	132, 269, 274
II. 2, 3	965
II. 8	309
II. 17	312
II. 19	311
III. 15	348
III. 21, 24	348
III. 22	133
IV. 3	967
IV. 25	349
VIII. 10, 11	967
VIII. 21	333
IX. 26, 27	351
XI. 7	133
XII. 7, 8	27
XIV. 18	27
XV. 2	28
XV. 6	351
XVI. 7	134
XVII. 1	27
XVIII. 2	134
XXII. 11	134
XXII. 18	435
XXXIII. 9, 11	790
XLIII. 9	240
XLVIII. 15, 16	134, 699

EXODUS.

Ch. Ver.	Page.
III. 2	134
III. 13, 14	29
VI. 3	28
XX. 2	991
XXXIII. 14, 15	131

LEVITICUS.

Ch. Ver.	Page.
X. 2	813

DEUTERONOMY.

Ch. Ver.	Page.
IV. 37	131
VI. 4	131
XVIII. 15, 18	424

1 SAMUEL.

Ch. Ver.	Page.
I. 3, 11	27
II. 3	59
III. 18	814

2 SAMUEL.

Ch. Ver.	Page.
XXIII. 2, 3	137
XXIII. 5	250

JOB.

Ch. Ver.	Page.
I. 6	967
X. 21	593
XIV. 10	593
XVII. 9	559
XIX. 25	605
XIX. 26, 27	610
XXXIII. 23	431
XXXVIII. 7	156, 262

PSALMS.

Ch. Ver.	Page.
I. 5	608
II. 7	154, 410
V. 5	100
XVI. 2, 3	120
XVI. 4	431
XVI. 10	406
XIX. 7	18
XXII. 15	407
XXXII. 1	494
XXXII. 2	494
XXXIII. 6	137
XXXIV. 10	117
XXXVII. 29	640
XLV.	646
XLVI. 10	812
XLVII. 5	415
L. 3	630
LI. 9	494
LI. 5	333
LXVIII. 4	29
LXVIII. 18	416
LXIX. 9	828
LXXII. 15	699
LXXII. 17	151
LXXVIII. 39	592
XCIV. 14	560
XCVI.	646
XCVII. 3, 4, 5	630
CII. 26	634
CX. 1	416
CXXV. 1, 2	560
CXXXIX. 7—10	43
CXXXIX. 16	221
CXLV. 9	191
CXLVI. 4	593
CXLVII. 5	41

PROVERBS.

Ch. Ver.	Page.
VIII. 22	155
VIII. 30	252
XVI. 4	196
XVI. 33	299
XIX. 2	705
XXII. 2	295

ECCLESIASTES.

Ch. Ver.	Page.
III. 19, 20	593
IV. 2	594
VII. 1	608
VII. 29	276
IX. 5	600
XII. 1	270

ISAIAH.

Ch. Ver.	Page.
VI. 2, 3	104
VI. 8	133
XI. 10	407
XXIV.	630
XXIV. 23	646
XXVI. 14	608
XXVI. 19	411, 606
XXVIII. 29	30
XXX. 26	647
XXX. 33	679
XLI. 21, 22, 23	134
XLII. 1	253
XLII. 6	226
XLIII. 13	49
XLIV. 22	494
XLV. 7	300
XLVIII. 16	138, 210

INDEX.

Ch. Ver.	Page.
XLIX. 5, 6	220, 252
LIII. 8	154
LIII. 9	407
LV. 3	411
LVII. 1, 2	594
LX. 21	640
LXIII. 7, 14	137
LXV. 17	636
LXVI. 15, 16	630

JEREMIAH.

Ch. Ver.	Page.
XX. 7	111
XXIII. 5, 6	647
XXXI. 15	593, 610
XXXII. 38	117
XXXII. 40	560

EZEKIEL.

Ch. Ver.	Page.
XVIII. 2, 3, 4	329
XVIII. 4	592
XVIII. 24	568
XXI. 27	648
XXXIX. 12	624
XLI. 18	307
XLVIII. 35	648

DANIEL.

Ch. Ver.	Page.
II. 44	648
IV. 17	132
VII.	648
VII. 8, 20, 26	450
VII. 13, 14	416
VII. 14	616, 652
IX. 27	361
XII. 1, 3	617
XII. 2	606, 608
XII. 11, 12	624

HOSEA.

Ch. Ver.	Page.
XIII. 14	415
VI. 7	312

JOEL.

Ch. Ver.	Page.
III. 2, 12	676

AMOS.

Ch. Ver.	Page.
III. 6	300

MICAH.

Ch. Ver.	Page.
II. 13	416
IV. 7, 8	652
V. 2	154
VI. 9	814

NAHUM.

Ch. Ver.	Page.
I. 3, 4, 5	631

ZEPHANIAH.

Ch. Ver.	Page.
I. 2, 3, 18	631

HAGGAI.

Ch. Ver.	Page.
II. 4, 5	138, 217
II. 6	362

ZECHARIAH.

Ch. Ver.	Page.
I. 11, 12, 13	433
III. 1, 4	433
VI. 13	211
XI. 4, 7	222

Ch. Ver.	Page.
XIV. 4, 5	617
XIV. 6, 7	448
XIV. 9	448, 648

MALACHI.

Ch. Ver.	Page.
I. 6	132
II. 5	216
III. 6	35, 564
IV. 1, 3	617
IV. 1, 2, 3	631

MATTHEW.

Ch. Ver.	Page.
III. 16, 17	139, 169
IV. 1, &c.	392
IV. 10	697
VI. 9	104
VI. 10	649
XIII. 4—8	935
XIII. 20, 21	570
XVIII. 15, 16, 17	892
XVIII. 17	888
XIX. 14	900
XIX. 17	92
XIX. 28	653
XX. 21, 22	649
XXIV. 3	617
XXV.	618
XXV. 10	780
XXVIII. 19	140, 901, 914

MARK.

Ch. Ver.	Page.
VI. 3	391
XII. 28, 30	126

LUKE.

Ch. Ver.	Page.
I. 32, 33	650
I. 32, 35	139, 150
II. 10, 11	467
IX. 26	621
XII. 50	912
XVI. 22, 23	595
XIX. 12	618
XX. 36	653
XXII. 29, 30	650
XXIII. 42, 43	595

JOHN.

Ch. Ver.	Page.
I. 7	468
I. 14	379, 389
I. 12, 13	202
I. 29	472
III. 13	387
III. 14, 15	356
III. 16	472
III. 36	98
IV. 22, 24	31
IV. 42	472
V. 17	172
V. 28, 29	611
VI. 32	355
VI. 38	384
IX. 2, 3	330
X. 28	561
X. 36	152
XI. 51, 52	202
XII. 32	468
XIV. 2, 3	619
XIV. 16	139
XIV. 23	134
XV. 2, 6	570

Ch. Ver.	Page.
XVII. 3	126
XVII. 4, 5	210
XVII. 12	568
XX. 23	315

ACTS.

Ch. Ver.	Page.
I. 6	650
I. 11	619
II. 37, 38	376
II. 37, 38, 41	900
III. 19, 21	619
VI. 3	884
XIII. 48	178
XIV. 23	867
XV. 10	901
XVI. 14, 15	902
XVI. 33	913
XVII. 25	121
XIX. 37	852
XXII. 16	913

ROMANS.

Ch. Ver.	Page.
III. 4	110
III. 25	489
III. 30	129
V. 5	760
V. 14	316
V. 18	469
V. 19	324
VIII. 5, 6	838
VIII. 29	189
VIII. 30	208
IX. 29	186
IX. 11, 13	101
XI. 17, 22	571
XI. 16	906
XI. 33	65
XIII. 1	984
XIII. 7	986
XIV. 15	474
XV. 5	89

1 CORINTHIANS.

Ch. Ver.	Page.
V. 3, 5	889
V. 7	355
VI. 11	209
VII. 14	907
VIII. 6	130
VIII. 12	474
IX. 27	571
X. 1, 2	912
X. 3, 4	355
X. 12	576
XI. 18, 20	22, 915
XIII.	771
XV. 24, 28	148
XV. 37, 38	610
XV. 42, 44	610
XV. 53, 54	610
XV. 47	384
XVI. 1, 2	971
XVI. 15	902

2 CORINTHIANS.

Ch. Ver.	Page.
I. 21, 22	140
V. 1, 8	595
V. 14, 15	470
V. 19	211, 473
XIII. 14	140

INDEX.

GALATIANS.

Ch. Ver.	Page
I. 15	297
IV. 4	396
IV. 6	139, 202
IV. 8	30
V. 4	572

EPHESIANS.

Ch. Ver.	Page
I. 4	180, 181, 186
I. 6	205
I. 7, 8	68
II. 2	308
II. 3	98
II. 4, 5	85
II. 18	698
IV. 11	863
V. 21, 29	973
V. 33	976
VI. 1	979
VI. 4	979
VI. 5	981
VI. 9	982

PHILIPPIANS.

Ch. Ver.	Page
I. 21, 23	596
II. 6	30
II. 7, 8	395
II. 7	396
III. 10	415
IV. 11	788

COLOSSIANS.

Ch. Ver.	Page
I. 15, 16, 17	166
III. 20	978
III. 22, 23, 24	981

1 THESSALONIANS.

Ch. Ver.	Page
IV. 3	187
IV. 16	609
V. 8	762
V. 12, 13	877

2 THESSALONIANS.

Ch. Ver.	Page
II. 3, 8	450
II. 13	185, 187
II. 16	760

1 TIMOTHY.

Ch. Ver.	Page
I. 16	90
I. 19	572
II. 1	944
II. 4	470
II. 5	130, 387
III. 1, 4, 5	864
III. 8—12	884
IV. 8	704
IV. 10	471
V. 21	192
VI. 15, 16	52, 123

2 TIMOTHY.

Ch. Ver.	Page
I. 9	297
II. 13	55
III. 16, 17	19, 20
IV. 1	651

TITUS.

Ch. Ver.	Page
II. 11, 12	471
III. 1	985
III. 10	889

HEBREWS.

Ch. Ver.	Page
I. 2	160
I. 3	146
II. 5	651
II. 9	471
II. 10	476
III. 12	576
IV. 3, 4	966
IV. 8	356
IV. 14	153
V. 8	153, 234
VI. 19	761
VI. 4, 5, 6	573
VII. 22	237
VIII. 7, 8	363
VIII. 13	364
IX. 10	361
IX. 15	363
X. 26	574
X. 38	575
XI. 4	349, 432
XII. 1	818
XII. 23	853
XIII. 5	787
XIII. 7, 17, 18	878

JAMES.

Ch. Ver.	Page
I. 4	818
III. 17	833

1 PETER.

Ch. Ver.	Page
I. 1, 2	188
I. 3	761
I. 5	564
III. 20, 21	914

2 PETER.

Ch. Ver.	Page
I. 4	30, 274
II. 1	474
II. 20, 22	575
III. 9	472
III. 10, 12	625
III. 13	636
III. 17	576

1 JOHN.

Ch. Ver.	Page
I. 7	153
II. 2	473
III. 3	761
IV. 8, 16	78, 80
V. 7, 8	128, 135

2 JOHN

Ver.	Page
3	112
8	576

JUDE.

Ver.	Page
4	194, 197
14, 15	616
21	576

REVELATION.

Ch. Ver.	Page
I. 10	971
III. 14	165
IV. 11	119, 251
VII. 9	640
XI. 19	450
XII. 4	308
XIV. 13	596
XX. 1, 2, 3	620
XX. 4	653
XX. 5	659
XX. 12	674
XXI. 1, 2, &c.	641

THE BAPTIST STANDARD BEARER, INC.
A non-profit, tax-exempt corporation
committed to the Publication & Preservation
of The Baptist Heritage.

SAMPLE TITLES FOR PUBLICATIONS AVAILABLE IN OUR VARIOUS SERIES:

THE BAPTIST *COMMENTARY* SERIES
Sample of authors/works in or near republication:
John Gill - *Exposition of the Old & New Testaments (9 & 18 Vol. Sets)*
(*Volumes from the 18 vol. set can be purchased individually*)

THE BAPTIST *FAITH* SERIES:
Sample of authors/works in or near republication:
Abraham Booth - *The Reign of Grace*
Abraham Booth - *Paedobaptism Examined (3 Vols.)*
John Gill - *A Complete Body of Doctrinal Divinity*

THE BAPTIST *HISTORY* SERIES:
Sample of authors/works in or near republication:
Thomas Armitage - *A History of the Baptists (2 Vols.)*
Isaac Backus - *History of the New England Baptists (2 Vols.)*
William Cathcart - *The Baptist Encyclopaedia (3 Vols.)*
J. M. Cramp - *Baptist History*

THE BAPTIST *DISTINCTIVES* SERIES:
Sample of authors/works in or near republication:
Alexander Carson - *Ecclesiastical Polity of the New Testament Churches*
E.C. Dargan - *Ecclesiology: A Study of the Churches*
J. M. Frost - *Paedobaptism: Is It From Heaven?*
R. B. C. Howell - *The Evils of Infant Baptism*

THE *DISSENT & NONCONFORMITY* SERIES:
Sample of authors/works in or near republication:
Champlin Burrage - *The Early English Dissenters (2 Vols.)*
Franklin H. Littell - *The Anabaptist View of the Church*
Albert H. Newman - *History of Anti-Paedobaptism*
Walter Wilson - *History & Antiquities of the Dissenting Churches (4 Vols.)*

For a complete list of current authors/titles, visit our internet site at
www.standardbearer.com or write us at:

The Baptist Standard Bearer, Inc.
No. 1 Iron Oaks Drive • Paris, Arkansas 72855

Telephone: (501) 963-3831   Fax: (501) 963-8083
E-mail: baptist@arkansas.net
Internet: http://www.standardbearer.com

Specialists in Baptist Reprints and Rare Books

Thou hast given a *standard* to them that fear thee; that it may be displayed because of the truth. -- *Psalm 60:4*

www.ingramcontent.com/pod-product-compliance
Lightning Source LLC
Chambersburg PA
CBHW021830220426
43663CB00005B/187